The Origins of Nazi Genocide

ADOLF HITLER

Reichsleiter B o u h l e r   und

Dr. med. B r a n d t

sind unter Verantwortung beauftragt, die Befug -

nisse namentlich zu bestimmender Ärzte so zu er -

weitern, dass nach menschlichem Ermessen unheilbar

Kranken bei kritischster Beurteilung ihres Krank -

heitszustandes der Gnadentod gewährt werden kann.

Adolf Hitler's authorization for the euthanasia killing operation,
signed in October 1939 but dated 1 September 1939.

The Origins of
Nazi Genocide

FROM EUTHANASIA TO THE FINAL SOLUTION

Henry Friedlander

The University of North Carolina Press   *Chapel Hill & London*

Publication of this book has
been supported by a generous
grant from the Lucius N. Littauer
Foundation.

The paper in this book meets
the guidelines for permanence
and durability of the Committee
on Production Guidelines for
Book Longevity of the Council
on Library Resources.

Library of Congress Cataloging-in-Publication Data
Friedlander, Henry, 1930–
    The origins of Nazi genocide : from euthanasia to the
final solution / by Henry Friedlander.
    p. cm.
    Includes bibliographical references and index.
    ISBN 0-8078-2208-6 (cloth: alk. paper)
    ISBN 0-8078-4675-9 (pbk.: alk. paper)
    1. Germany — Politics and government — 1933–1945.
2. National socialism — Moral and ethical aspects.
3. Euthanasia — Political aspects — Germany — History — 20th
century.   4. Medical ethics — Germany — History — 20th
century.   5. Genocide — Germany — History — 20th century.
6. Holocaust, Jewish (1939–1945)   7. World War, 1939–1945 —
Gypsies.   8. Handicapped — Germany — History — 20th century.
9. World War, 1939–1945 — Atrocities.   I. Title.
DD256.5.F739 1995
943.086 — dc20   94-40941
                         CIP

01   00   99   98   97   7   6   5   4   3

IN MEMORIAM

Ruth Friedländer née Löwenthal

Brandenburg 1902, Birkenau 1944

CONTENTS

TABLES

Every book has its history, and this one is no exception. I examined the euthanasia killings for the first time during my investigation of postwar German trials of Nazi criminals. In the immediate postwar years, during the late 1940s, the Allies did not permit German courts to judge German crimes against Allied nationals. Early German trials therefore dealt only with crimes committed against German nationals, and, with only one exception, these did not involve systematic mass murder. The euthanasia killings were that exception.

After presenting my findings on the early postwar euthanasia trials at the 1981 annual meeting of the American Historical Association in Los Angeles, I decided to use postwar trial records to construct a history of the Nazi euthanasia program. Although one of the first American war crimes trials in postwar Germany concerned Hadamar, the notorious euthanasia hospital, and the first Nuremberg successor trial, known as the Medical Trial, also dealt in part with the crime of euthanasia, the mass murder of hospital patients had never been adequately treated in histories of the Nazi period. I became convinced that these murders deserve study as a prologue to Nazi genocide.

I soon discovered that a massive documentary record substantiated the nature of these crimes. In addition to the Allied, German, and Austrian trials of the late 1940s, the German judiciary had conducted numerous detailed investigations and long trials during the 1960s and 1970s. I followed the paper trail, which led me to numerous offices of German state attorneys and through archives in the United States, Germany, and Austria.

As I read through the evidence, I realized that the traditional description of the victims of euthanasia as "mental patients [*Geisteskranke*]" was inaccurate. Of course, I had always known that the use of the term "euthanasia" by the Nazi killers was a euphemism to camouflage their murder of human beings they had designated as "life unworthy of life"; that their aim was not to shorten the lives of persons with painful terminal diseases but to kill human beings they considered inferior, who could otherwise have lived for many years. Although the victims were institutionalized in state hospitals and nursing homes, only some suffered from mental illness. Many were hospitalized only because they were retarded, blind, deaf, or epileptic or because they had a physical deformity. They were handicapped patients, persons who in the United States today are covered by the Act for Disabled Americans. Nor were these patients murdered to free hospital space or to save money; the killers were motivated by an ideological obsession to create a homogeneous and robust nation based on race. They wanted to purge the handicapped from the national gene pool.

In 1985, after I had finished about half of my research, the German journalist Ernst Klee published his valuable, detailed account of the so-called euthanasia program, and his book was soon followed in Germany by many regional and local accounts of the euthanasia killings. These German works acknowledged the criminality of the killings that had been mislabeled euthanasia. They analyzed them as one aspect of Nazi medical crimes. This led to a scholarly discussion about the evolution of German medicine and science, producing in Germany, Britain, and the United States numerous interesting academic works on race hygiene, physicians, and public health in modern Germany.

My interest was different. It was not my aim to write about German medicine; I wanted to understand the crimes of the Nazi regime. By the mid-1980s, my reading of the documents had convinced me that the euthanasia program had been intimately connected to Nazi genocide. I realized that the ideology, the decision-making process, the personnel, and the killing technique tied euthanasia to the "final solution." But I still thought of euthanasia as only a prologue to genocide. In 1984, the geneticist Benno Müller-Hill published an analysis of the involvement of scientists in Nazi crimes, and his arguments forced me to reevaluate my interpretation. I began to see that euthanasia was not simply a prologue but the first chapter of Nazi genocide.

I know, of course, that the term "genocide" was coined to refer to the murder of national or ethnic groups. Nazi genocide, however, was not directed at national groups but at groups of human beings who supposedly shared racial characteristics. Heredity determined the selection of the victims. I was thus forced to define Nazi genocide—what is now commonly called the Holocaust—as the mass murder of human beings because they belonged to a biologically defined group.

Since the publication in the mid-1950s of Gerald Reitlinger's work on the so-called final solution, historians have categorized the Nazis' murder of the European Jews as totally different from their murder of other groups. Reitlinger's work showed that while the Nazis persecuted, incarcerated, and often killed men and women for their politics, nationality, religion, and behavior, they applied against the Jews a consistent and inclusive policy of extermination. In their drive against the Jews, they even killed infants and the very old, a policy they did not follow in their treatment of such enemies, for example, as communists, Poles, Jehovah's Witnesses, and homosexuals.

My research convinced me that this definition of Nazi genocide had to be slightly revised because Jews were not the only biologically selected target. Alongside Jews, the Nazis murdered the European Gypsies. Defined as a "dark-skinned" racial group, Gypsy men, women, and children could not escape their fate as victims of Nazi genocide. Biology also determined the fate of the handicapped, who, just as Jews and Gypsies, could not change their condition to escape death. The Nazis killed handicapped infants in hospital wards as well as elderly men and women in nursing homes. I realized that the Nazi regime systematically murdered only three groups of human beings: the handicapped, Jews, and Gypsies.

This book is an attempt to explain how Nazi genocide developed. From the first, the regime excluded members of the three targeted groups from the national community. During the 1930s, the regime consistently escalated persecution, embracing ever more radical exclusionary policies, including compulsory sterilization for the handicapped, incarceration for Gypsies, and forced emigration for Jews. Eventually, the regime decided to implement a program of mass murder to eradicate these three targeted groups.

The chronology of Nazi mass murder unambiguously shows that the killing of the handicapped preceded the systematic murder of Jews and Gypsies. The record shows that Hitler made the decision and that government and party bureaucrats implemented it in January 1940. They devised a method to select the victims, created killing centers using gas, a unique German invention, and developed a technique that processed human beings on an assembly line through these centers.

The Chancellery of the Führer, with help from the Reich Ministry of Interior, directed this euthanasia program, working through a front organization known as T4 after its Berlin headquarters at Tiergarten Straße number 4. But all attempts at maintaining secrecy failed to prevent knowledge about the murders from becoming widespread, forcing Hitler in August 1941 to order the closing of killing centers on German soil. But the killings continued in other institutions and by other means.

As soon as conditions permitted, with the invasion of the Soviet Union in June 1941, the killings were extended to include Jews and Gypsies. Hitler commissioned Heinrich Himmler's SS and police to implement this final solution. After experimenting with mass shootings, which proved too public, too inefficient, and too demanding for the killers, Himmler's minions borrowed the tested T4 killing technique of gassing. They created killing centers and staffed them with experienced T4 killers. In any event, the T4 killings had shown that ordinary men and women were willing to become professional killers.

The euthanasia killing program occupies the largest portion of this book, partly because it is not as familiar as is the final solution and partly because it served as the model for all Nazi killing operations. In the remainder of the book, I have attempted to show the connection between the euthanasia killings and the final solution. I have provided a relatively detailed account of the murder of the Gypsies because their annihilation has until now received little attention. I have not covered the murder of the Jews, which has been the subject of much scrutiny and is relatively well known, in great detail but have discussed their persecution to make comparisons, show analogies, and point to connections. I have discussed the murder of handicapped Jews in detail, however, because their fate has not previously been recorded.

I have examined the ideological setting for genocide in the first chapter, attempting to show how belief in the inequality of man produced theories that pointed to the inferiority, degeneracy, and criminality of the handicapped and of members of different races. Antisemitism was one aspect of that ideology of inequality, but because its history is well known, I have not focused on the Judeophobia of the Nazi leaders. Nazi ideology was pervasive, and the T4 killers shared the common ideological outlook on race. Since their adherence to Nazi ideology is a given, I have concentrated on their party involvement, which reflected their commitment to that ideology, as well as on their non-ideological motives for becoming killers.

Nazi genocide, the mass murder of entire biologically determined groups of human beings, cost the lives of millions of men, women, and children in the short period of four years and four months. The figure of 6 million dead is certainly not excessive if we are to account for all the Jews, Gypsies, and handicapped murdered by the Nazis.

Bethesda, Maryland
September 1993

ABBREVIATIONS

The following abbreviations are used in the text. For abbreviations used in the notes, see pp. 303–4.

Central Accounting Office	Zentralverrechnungsstelle Heil- und Pflegeanstalten (Central Accounting Office for State Hospitals and Nursing Homes)
DFG	Deutsche Forschungsgemeinschaft (German Research Foundation)
DGT	Deutscher Gemeindetag (German Association of Cities)
ERO	Eugenics Record Office
Foundation	Gemeinnützige Stiftung für Anstaltspflege (Charitable Foundation for Institutional Care)
Gekrat	Gemeinnützige Kranken-Transport G.m.b.H. (Charitable Foundation for the Transport of Patients, Inc.)
Gestapo	Geheime Staatspolizei (secret state police)
HSSPF	Höherer SS- und Polizeiführer (higher SS and police leader)
KdF	Kanzlei des Führers (Chancellery of the Führer)
KL	Konzentrationslager (concentration camp)
Kripo	Kriminalpolizei (detective forces)
KTI	Kriminaltechnisches Institut (Technical Institute for the Detection of Crime)
KWI	Kaiser Wilhelm Institute
NSDAP	Nationalsozialistische Deutsche Arbeiter Partei (National Socialist German Workers Party [Nazi party])
NSDStB	Nationalsozialistischer Deutscher Studentenbund (National Socialist German Student Union)
RAG	Reichsarbeitsgemeinschaft Heil- und Pflegeanstalten (Reich Cooperative for State Hospitals and Nursing Homes)
Reich Committee	Reichsausschuß zur wissenschaftlichen Erfassung von erb- und anlagebedingten schweren Leiden (Reich

Committee for the Scientific Registration of Severe Hereditary Ailments)

RFSS	Reichsführer SS (Reich leader SS)
RJM	Reichsjustizministerium (Reich Ministry of Justice)
RKPA	Reichskriminalpolizeiamt (Central Office of the Reich Detective Forces)
RMdI	Reichsministerium des Innern (Reich Ministry of Interior)
RSHA	Reichssicherheitshauptamt (Central Office for Reich Security)
RuSHA	Rasse- und Siedlungshauptamt (Central Office for Race and Settlement)
SA	Sturmabteilung (brown-shirt storm troopers)
SD	Sicherheitsdienst (security service of the SS)
Sipo	Sicherheitspolizei (security police [Gestapo and Kripo])
SS	Schutzstaffel (black-shirt storm troopers)
SSPF	SS- und Polizeiführer (SS and police leader)
T4	Popular name for the euthanasia program after the address of its Berlin headquarters at Tiergarten Straße number 4
WVHA	Wirtschaftsverwaltungshauptamt (Central Office for Economy and Administration)

NOTE ON LANGUAGE

Those who write about Nazi Germany and the Holocaust face delicate problems concerning how they use language. They must avoid the language usage employed by the perpetrators but often have no choice but to use terms coined by the Nazis because these terms have become common. But there must be no confusion about the meaning of such terms.

The term "euthanasia" poses such a problem. In common usage, the term means the act of painlessly putting to death a person suffering from a terminal and incurable disease. This is not its meaning in this book. The Nazis used the term "euthanasia," and also "mercy death," as a euphemism to disguise their murder of the handicapped. They killed them for racial and eugenic reasons, not to ease the suffering of the individual. Their killing operation was a secret government program and not an act of individual mercy. It was not applied against persons suffering from common physical diseases like cancer but only against those considered "life unworthy of life." The Nazis' victims did not suffer from diseases that were terminal or from disabilities that were necessarily incurable. And their deaths were certainly not painless.

When used in this book, the term "euthanasia" thus refers to the Nazi killing operation, which had nothing to do with the common meaning of the word. To make this clear, many authors enclose the word in quotation marks or always place "so-called" before it. But such usage, which could also be applied to "final solution" and other phrases, burdens the reader by making the text less readable. For the same reasons, I have not capitalized "final solution" or "euthanasia." In my discussion of euthanasia and the final solution, I have attempted to make the meaning of these terms perfectly clear without excessive use of quotation marks, "so-called," or capitalization. The reader will know that they refer to a government enterprise of outright murder.

The killing operation of Nazi Germany was directed against three biologically defined groups. The Nazis carefully defined, excluded, and tried to murder all members of these groups, in the process imposing on them a common identity that disregarded existing differences. Although we must realize that these persecuted groups were not homogeneous, it is impossible to discuss the victims without using a common term to describe them. But we must be aware that every group has the right of collective self-definition. I have identified the members of one persecuted group as "Jews," but I also know that it included persons who considered themselves Christians and others who preferred to be known as "Hebrews" or "persons of the Mosaic faith." I have identified another persecuted group as "Gypsies," a term usually used by outsiders, although I know that members of this group call themselves "Roma and Sinti." I have identified members of the third persecuted group as the "handicapped." This term, sometimes used interchangeably with the term "disabled," has become common, but it was not used during the Nazi period. At that time, members of this diverse group were labeled as "idiots," "crazies," and "cripples." Such defamatory terms are of course neither appropriate nor accurate. I have used "handicapped" to describe members of this group, because they suffered some disability that stigmatized them in the eyes of their persecutors as "life unworthy of life." I hope that the reader will understand that my use of such identifying terms is only an attempt to describe very diverse groups whose members became victims of racial hatred.

Clarity concerning the true meaning of terms used by the Nazis is especially important because such terms do reverberate today in discussions of national policy. Partisans have pointed to Nazi policies and terminology in current debates about abortion and assisted suicide. But such usage is fraught with danger; it is easy to misunderstand or misapply these Nazi terms. Whatever one's position on either abortion or assisted suicide, comparisons with Nazi killing operations do not illuminate today's discussion. It seems to me, however, that one general lesson can be applied. Government programs launched by the Nazi regime to exclude and kill clearly show that there are private spheres of human life where no state interest is sufficiently compelling to justify intervention. Only the individual directly affected, and possibly his or her closest relatives, should make such intimate decisions. True, individuals might err, but even mistakes by millions of private citizens about their bodies or their lives are far less open to abuse than are judgments legislated by the state and imposed by its agents.

The translation of German terms, titles, and institutional names presents different difficulties. I have tried to find common English equivalents for these terms, but this has not always been possible. One particular frequently used term has been especially difficult to translate and can serve as an example of the kind of compromises the translator must make. The difficult term is "Heil- und Pflegeanstalt," the German name for institutions holding handicapped patients. At the beginning of this century, "Heil- und Pflegeanstalt" replaced older pejorative names, such as "insane asylum [Irrenanstalt]." A literal translation would be "healing and nursing institution," but such a translation would be both awkward and meaningless, while "asylum" is pejorative and "sanatorium" not applicable. I decided to use "state hospital and nursing home." I chose "state hospital" because in the United States this designation has come to mean, at least in popular discourse, a hospital for institutionalized patients. I realized, however, that I would have to drop the word "state" when referring to a private hospital. I chose "nursing home" because it is a term very familiar to Americans, although it is usually not associated with state hospitals for institutionalized patients. Nevertheless, the combination "state hospital and nursing home" appears to me the best translation of the German "Heil- und Pflegeanstalt."

The Origins of Nazi Genocide

Chapter 1 **The Setting**

Nazi genocide did not take place in a vacuum. Genocide was only the most radical method of excluding groups of human beings from the German national community. The policy of exclusion followed and drew upon more than fifty years of scientific opposition to the equality of man. Since the turn of the century, the German elite—that is, the members of the educated professional classes—had increasingly accepted an ideology of human inequality. Geneticists, anthropologists, and psychiatrists advanced a theory of human heredity that merged with the racist doctrine of ultra-nationalists to form a political ideology based on race.[1] The Nazi movement both absorbed and advanced this ideology. After their assumption of power in 1933, the Nazis created the political framework that made it possible to translate this ideology of inequality into a policy of exclusion. At the same time, the German bureaucratic, professional, and scientific elite provided the legitimacy the regime needed for the smooth implementation of this policy.[2]

The growing importance of the biological sciences in the nineteenth century, following the discoveries of Charles Darwin, led most scientists to advance theories of human inequality as matters of scientific fact.[3] In the middle of the century, a widely accepted theory maintained that there was a causal relationship between the size of the human brain and human intelligence.[4] In 1861 the anthropologist Paul Broca thus asserted that "there is a remarkable relationship between the development of intelligence and the volume of the brain," and he argued that studies based on this premise showed that "in general, the brain is larger in mature adults than in the elderly, in men than in women, in eminent men than in men of mediocre talent, in superior races than in inferior races." [5]

Belief in inequality coexisted with the principles of equality proclaimed by American and French revolutionaries. Scientists, themselves products of their times, constructed "rank-order or value-judgment hierarchies" that placed human beings on a single scale of intelligence, thus incorporating popular prejudices into their theories. As proof they offered meaningless, but carefully compiled, correlations between the size of the brain and presumed intelligence. But such scientific data, "no matter how numerically sophisticated, have recorded little more than social prejudice." [6] Popular prejudice accepted that males were more intelligent than females, and in 1879 Gustave Le Bon, the founder of social psychology, concurred: "In the most intelligent races, as among the Parisians, there are a large number of women whose brains are closer in size to those of gorillas than to the most developed male brains. This inferiority is so obvious that no one can contest it for a moment; only its degree is worth discussion."[7]

Popular prejudice also accepted as self-evident the superiority of the white race over all others, placing blacks at the bottom of a ranking order of races. In 1864 the German anatomist Carl Vogt reflected this prejudice by stating that "the grown-up Negro partakes, as regards his intellectual faculties, of the nature of the child, the female, and the senile white."[8] Finally, the prejudices of the scientists themselves led them to conclude that the wealthy and the educated inherited greater intelligence than the lower socioeconomic classes. The American paleontologist E. D. Cope thus "identified four groups of lower human forms," including—along with women, nonwhites, and Jews— all "lower classes within superior races."[9]

In this way, the biological sciences of the nineteenth century simply recorded traditional prejudices. Without any evidence, scientists concluded that human differences were hereditary and unalterable, and in doing so, they "precluded redemption" because they imposed "the additional burden of intrinsic inferiority upon despised groups."[10] Science thus showed "the tenacity of unconscious bias and the surprising malleability of 'objective,' quantitative data in the interest of a preconceived idea."[11]

Darwinian evolution provided a biological basis for judging the human condition, but during most of the century, there existed two possible theories to explain heredity. The theory advanced by Jean-Baptiste Lamarck at the beginning of the century argued that acquired characteristics could be inherited and that environment could therefore influence group standing. This optimistic theory provided for the improvement of status for groups and individuals through social change. But at the end of the century, theories based on the work of Gregor Mendel gained ascendancy, maintaining that heredity followed a rigid pattern uninfluenced by environment. This pessimistic theory condemned selected groups and individuals to permanent inferiority.[12] The German zoologist August Weismann advanced a Mendelian theory of an "independent, immutable germ plasm" to explain heredity, leading his followers to search for "single genes" that built "even the most complex" body parts and to argue that the social environment "was impotent to alter the human condition."[13] But as we know today, "virtually every major feature of our body is built by the interaction of many genes with each other and with an external environment."[14]

At the end of the nineteenth century, scientists turned from weighing human brains to measuring human skulls and other body parts. Previously, they had ranked human groups by intelligence and argued that inferior humans lacked culture; now they would also claim that such humans were immoral, depraved, and criminal. Anthropometric techniques served to bolster

THE ORIGINS OF NAZI GENOCIDE

a new theory based on evolution. The German zoologist Ernst Haeckel suggested that human beings go through the chronological stages of evolution as they advance from embryo to adult. This "recapitulation" could be used to discover an individual's standing on the scale of evolution, and measurements would reveal at what stage the individual's maturation had been arrested.[15] Using anthropometric techniques, the Italian physician Cesare Lombroso, father of criminal anthropology, argued that recapitulation explained human criminality: "Criminals are apes in our midst, marked by the anatomical stigmata of atavism."[16]

The work of Lombroso and his followers provided society with a biological basis for judging criminality. One of his followers explained that "a study of the anthropological factors of crime provides the guardians and administrators of the law with new and more certain methods in the detection of the guilty."[17] The conclusions presented by Lombroso and his followers, then considered members of a "positive school of criminology," also led to a re-examination of how police and courts should deal with criminals. Lombroso argued that some criminals were "born for evil" and could not change, and he concluded that since "atavism shows us the inefficacy of punishment for born criminals," we are compelled "to eliminate them completely, even by death."[18]

Lombroso not only attributed atavistic criminality to individuals from the lower classes who committed crimes but also depicted entire groups as criminal. The handicapped were one such group. He thus defined "epilepsy as a mark of criminality," asserting "that almost every 'born criminal' suffers from epilepsy to some degree."[19] The Gypsies were another group Lombroso characterized as criminal: "They are vain, like all delinquents, but they have no fear or shame. Everything they earn they spend for drink and ornaments. They may be seen barefooted, but with bright-colored or lace-bedecked clothing; without stockings, but with yellow shoes. They have the improvidence of the savage and that of the criminal as well."[20]

As we shall see, the Nazi killers used the language of Lombroso to target the same victim groups, including Gypsies and the handicapped. Thus members of the judiciary considered the killing of convicted criminals if their "physical shape no longer deserved to be called human."[21]

Still, while the use of measurements to analyze human traits continued to influence the biological and social sciences through much of the twentieth century, the belief that such measurements revealed intelligence slowly lost status. However, early in the century scientists discovered new ways to measure human intelligence. The French psychologist Alfred Binet discovered that intelligence tests produced better results than craniometry and developed the method that was eventually capable of producing an intelligence quotient — the so-called IQ — for each human being. Binet did not consider the IQ number an exact analogue of human intelligence, but his American followers —

Henry H. Goddard, Robert M. Yerkes, and Lewis M. Terman—reified IQ numbers; they regarded the IQ as a measure of an "entity called intelligence," assuming that it represented inherited, innate qualities and thus imposed immutable limits on personal development.[22] Later, two psychologists at London University—Charles Spearman and Sir Cyril Burt—used factor analysis, a sophisticated "mathematical technique," to bolster the belief that knowledge and skills revealed by tests disclose a hereditary quality known as intelligence.[23] One critic pointed out the fallacy of such belief in reification: "To the statistician's dictum that whatever exists can be measured, the factorist has added the assumption that whatever can be 'measured' must exist. But the relation may not be reversible, and the assumption may be false."[24]

The American psychologists classified persons on the basis of IQ tests, labeling those judged feebleminded in descending order as morons, imbeciles, or idiots.[25] Considering mental disabilities as innate and immutable qualities running in families by the laws of Mendelian heredity, they interpreted their findings, as had earlier scientists, to "prove" the validity of popular prejudices. But unlike their predecessors, they proposed to change the human population through the manipulation of heredity. The psychologists therefore joined like-minded scientists from the biological sciences in the growing eugenics movement.

The term "eugenics" was coined in 1881 by the British naturalist and mathematician Francis Galton and described by the leading American eugenicist, Charles B. Davenport, as "the science of the improvement of the human race by better breeding."[26] Eugenics developed within the larger movement of Social Darwinism, which applied Darwin's "struggle for survival" to human affairs. In the United States, Social Darwinism was used to justify unbridled economic competition and the "survival of the fittest" as a law of nature. Eugenics provided a biological basis for these ideas. Recruited from the biological and social sciences, or what today may be called the life sciences, eugenicists firmly believed that just as the Mendelian laws governed the hereditary transmission of human traits like color blindness or a particular blood group, these laws also determined the inheritance of social traits. Davenport thus believed that a single Mendelian gene for thalassophilia (love of the sea) explained why "naval careers ran in families" and that "nomadism, the impulse to wander, was obviously hereditary because such racial groups as Comanches, Gypsies, and Huns were all nomadic."[27]

Although various local eugenic societies and research groups existed in the United States, the most important center for eugenic research and dissemination of findings was the Eugenics Record Office (ERO) at Cold Spring Harbor in Long Island, New York, founded by Davenport, directed by Harry Hamilton Laughlin, and financed with Carnegie, Harriman, and Rockefeller money. The eugenics movement in general and the ERO specifically represented the special interests of the new class of professional managers and their financial benefactors. These professionals—biologists, geneticists, engineers, social workers, psychologists, and sociologists—wanted to introduce rational social planning into human affairs and believed that biological manipulation would achieve their ends.[28]

The eugenics movement in the United States and elsewhere pursued two connected policies. First, it sponsored research to investigate the transmission of social traits, especially undesirable ones, and undertook to classify individuals, groups, and nations on a scale of human worth. Second, it proposed biological solutions to social problems and lobbied for their implementation.

Eugenic research involved the construction of family trees and pedigree charts on the basis of questionnaires and fieldwork. In the United States, for example, the ERO investigated the "racial origin of inventiveness, hereditary lineage of aviators, [and] alien crime" and studied hereditary patterns in selected large families and entire small towns.[29] In Britain, Sir Cyril Burt sought to establish the preeminence of heredity by testing large numbers of "identical twins raised apart," a favorite method of eugenic research.[30] American psychologists collected similar data by administering intelligence tests to large groups. During World War I, the Harvard psychologist Robert M. Yerkes persuaded the U.S. Army to allow his team to administer the first mass-produced tests to 1.75 million soldiers in 1917.[31] The later evaluation of these test results yielded conclusions that matched those of the ERO eugenicists. Although many of the tests were given to recent immigrants unfamiliar with the English language and American culture, the psychologists concluded that the results revealed not cultural differences but hereditary intelligence.[32] These mass tests served as a model for others; for example, one of Yerkes's followers, the Princeton psychologist Carl C. Brigham, later served as secretary of the College Entrance Examination Board and developed the Scholastic Aptitude Test.[33]

Eugenic research, both anthropological fieldwork and psychological testing, was designed to isolate and record individuals with inferior intelligence and other social disabilities. Eugenicists claimed that their research on individuals and families proved the inferiority of entire groups. Using mass testing, the psychologists classified the American population by IQ on a ranking scale, predictably placing the wealthy and professionals at the top of the scale as the most intelligent. The psychologist Henry H. Goddard, director of research at the Vineland Training School for Feeble-Minded Girls and Boys in New Jersey, who had introduced the Binet scale to the United States and had coined the term "moron," believed that "democracy means that the people rule by selecting the wisest, most intelligent and most human to tell them what to do to be happy."[34] But apart from several investigations of the intelligent—for example, the "project to record the IQ of past geniuses"—eugenicists concentrated their research on the lower classes.[35] They used their findings to "prove" that class differences reflected intelligence. Stanford psychologist Lewis M. Terman, creator of the Stanford-Binet test, argued that "class boundaries had been set by innate intelligence"; his analysis of test scores led him to jump to the conclusion that "the children of successful and cultured parents test higher than children from wretched and ignorant homes for the simple reason that their heredity is better."[36]

Eugenicists focused attention on the feebleminded—labeled as idiots, imbeciles, or morons—and argued that their findings proved the existence of a relationship between low intelligence and both immorality and crime. They saw the cause of the social problems of their time, such as alcoholism and prostitution, as inherited feeblemindedness and viewed the manifestations of poverty, such as intermittent unemployment and chronic illness, as a hereditary degeneracy.[37] Terman thus concluded: "Not all criminals are feebleminded, but all feeble-minded persons are at least potential criminals. That every feeble-minded woman is a potential prostitute would hardly be disputed by anyone."[38] Considering the acceptance of the connection between low intelligence and degenerate behavior, it is hardly surprising that Goddard, one of the scientists whose works were published by the ERO, commented, "How can there be such a thing as social equality with this wide range of mental capacity?"[39]

The eugenicists ascribed degeneracy not only to class but also to race and ethnic group. Yerkes concluded that the U.S. Army test scores proved that the "darker peoples of southern Europe and the Slavs of eastern Europe are less intelligent than the fair peoples of western and northern Europe" and that the "Negro lies at the bottom of the scale" of intelligence.[40] Convinced of the inferiority and even criminality of other races, the eugenicists wanted to maintain the purity of the American pioneer stock and opposed marriages between people of different races. The ERO director, Harry Hamilton Laughlin, "compared human racial crossing with mongrelization in the animal world" and argued that "immigrants from southern and eastern Europe, especially Jews, were racially so different from, and genetically so inferior to, the current American population that any racial mixture would be deleterious."[41]

Confronted with low test scores of Jewish immigrants examined at Ellis Island and in the U.S. Army on the one hand and the achievements of Jewish intellectuals on the other, Princeton psychologist Brigham theorized that "the able Jew is popularly recognized not only because of his ability, but because he is able and a Jew," concluding that "our figures, then, would rather tend to disprove the popular belief that the Jew is highly intelligent."[42]

Viewed from our vantage point, eugenic research during the first half of the twentieth century was seriously flawed. The data collected by the ERO was highly subjective.[43] The methodology that governed psychological mass

6   THE ORIGINS OF NAZI GENOCIDE

testing was still rudimentary.[44] Later investigators found that Sir Cyril Burt had falsified his data on twin research.[45] It is not correct, however, to label the scientific research of eugenicists as pseudoscientific. Fabricated results are not unknown in today's respectable sciences, and at the start, many new scientific fields use faulty methodology. By the scientific standards of the time, eugenic research was on the cutting edge of science. Its practitioners were respected scholars from various scientific disciplines who occupied important positions in major universities and published their results in major scholarly journals. Their research tools were the most advanced available at the time, and they prided themselves on applying them meticulously. Their failing was not methodological error but their inability to recognize the ways in which their own prejudices corrupted their premises and tainted their conclusions. In their time, the results obtained by eugenicists were generally accepted by the scientific community, and only advances in neurosurgery and the discovery of DNA after World War II provided the tools to prove that their research conclusions had been faulty. Even the eugenic research conducted in Germany—as well as other places—which violated all ethical standards in its use of unprincipled methods, did not violate the canon of science.[46]

The research results of the eugenicists were accepted not only by fellow scientists but also by national policy makers. Pointing to their findings as proof of human inequality, eugenicists in Britain and the United States campaigned for changes in public policy to halt the degeneration of society. In Britain, this led to the introduction of the eleven-plus examinations, designed to exclude the unfit from higher education.[47] In the United States, eugenicists labeled groups from southern and eastern Europe as inferior and campaigned to restrict the immigration of members of those ethnic groups. Their research and lobbying assured passage of the 1924 Johnson Act (Immigration Restriction Act), which imposed quotas that severely limited immigration from countries whose inhabitants were identified as unfit.[48]

Individuals from inferior races and ethnic groups could be prohibited from entering the country, but other solutions had to be found to deal with feebleminded individuals who already resided in the United States. Goddard advocated "colonization," a term he used to disguise incarceration in closed institutions, and Terman proposed "permanent custodial care."[49] But this was not a permanent solution to the problem of the unfit. The favorite solution proposed by the eugenicists was sterilization. Eugenicists viewed individuals with mental disabilities as a burden to society and a threat to civilization. In 1910 Charles Davenport thus advocated sterilization "to dry up the springs that feed the torrent of defective and degenerate protoplasm."[50] Similarly, in 1914 Goddard, who regarded handicapped individuals as immoral beings totally unable to control their sexual urges, stated a position that reflected universal eugenic opinion: "If both parents are feeble-minded all the children will be feeble-minded. It is obvious that such matings should not be allowed. It is perfectly clear that no feeble-minded person should ever be allowed to marry or to become a parent. It is obvious that if this rule is to be carried out the intelligent part of society must enforce it." [51]

The political campaign of the eugenics movement in favor of sterilization was relatively successful. In 1907 Indiana enacted the first sterilization law, and by the middle of the 1930s, more than half of the states had passed laws that authorized the sterilization of "inmates of mental institutions, persons convicted more than once of sex crimes, those deemed to be feeble-minded by IQ tests, 'moral degenerate persons,' and epileptics." [52] In 1927, one such law, a Virginia statute, which authorized directors of state institutions to order the compulsory sterilization of handicapped patients diagnosed as suffering from "an hereditary form of insanity or imbecility," reached the Supreme Court. [53] The case involved an order for the compulsory sterilization of a woman diagnosed as feebleminded, whose mother had been classified the same way, and whose child had also been stigmatized as retarded. In his prescient plea to the Court, I. P. Whitehead, attorney for plaintiff Carrie Bell, warned the justices that if the state can impose a procedure that "violates her constitutional right of bodily integrity," the results would be ominous:

> If this Act be a valid enactment, then the limits of the power of the State (which in the end is nothing more than the faction in control of the government) to rid itself of those citizens deemed undesirable according to its standards, by means of surgical sterilization, have not been set. We will have "established in the State the science of medicine and a corresponding system of judicature." A reign of doctors will be inaugurated and in the name of science new classes will be added, even races may be brought within the scope of such regulation, and the worst forms of tyranny practiced. [54]

Oliver Wendell Holmes, speaking for the eight-man majority of the Court (Louis Brandeis, William Howard Taft, Harlan Fiske Stone, Willis Van Devanter, James C. McReynolds, George Sutherland, and Edward T. Sanford), pushed aside such arguments. His justification for upholding the Virginia law presaged the arguments used later to justify eugenic killings in Nazi Germany:

> We have seen more than once that the public welfare may call upon the best citizens for their lives. It would be strange if it could not call upon those who already sap the strength of the State for these lesser sacrifices, often not felt to be such by those concerned, in order to prevent our being swamped with incompetence. It is better for all the world, if instead of waiting to execute degenerate offspring for crime, or to let them starve for their imbecility, society can prevent those who are manifestly unfit from

THE ORIGINS OF NAZI GENOCIDE

continuing their kind. The principle that sustains compulsory vaccination is broad enough to cover cutting the Fallopian tubes. Three generations of imbeciles are enough.[55]

In the United States, eugenics eventually lost scientific acceptance and public support. New scientific discoveries led to the rejection of eugenic research results. Moreover, events in Nazi Germany during the 1930s, and the close cooperation between American and German eugenicists, seriously damaged the standing of the American eugenics movement, and the revelation of Nazi crimes in the 1940s discredited eugenic theories.[56]

The development of eugenics in Germany resembled developments in the United States, but there were differences. In Germany, university scientists enjoyed far greater status than they did in the United States, and they played a more active role in the eugenics movement. Most scientists in the eugenics movement were physicians, medical education being the preferred career path for research in biology and anthropology at the turn of the century. In the United States, psychologists played an active role in the movement, but their counterparts in Germany were academic psychiatrists, trained in medicine and biology, who staffed state hospitals and university clinics.[57] The psychiatrists shared the analysis about degeneration among the lower classes advanced by their colleagues from the fields of biology, genetics, and anthropology but also transformed the term "degeneracy" into a "diagnostic concept," applying it to such conditions as alcoholism, homosexuality, and hysteria.[58]

Until World War I, German eugenics paralleled the eugenics movement in the United States. German scientists did not differ from their European and American colleagues in using studies of the brain to determine intelligence, and they accepted the value judgments common to all scientists. Ernst Haeckel popularized Darwin's theory of evolution in Germany, and, as elsewhere, Social Darwinism was widely accepted. Based on Weismann's "independent, immutable germ plasm," German scientists accepted the idea that heredity alone determined natural selection.[59] Similar to their colleagues in the United States, the German eugenicists studied family genealogies and problems of degeneration, dividing populations into superior (*hochwertig*) and inferior (*minderwertig*) individuals; they hoped to safeguard the nation's "genetic heritage [*Erbgut*]" and viewed degeneration (*Entartung*) as a threat.[60]

Although the German eugenics movement, led until the Weimar years by Alfred Ploetz and Wilhelm Schallmayer, did not differ radically from the American movement, it was more centralized. Unlike in the United States, where federalism and political heterogeneity encouraged diversity even within a single movement, in Germany one society, the German Society for Race Hygiene (Deutsche Gesellschaft für Rassenhygiene), eventually represented all eugenicists, while one journal, the *Archiv für Rassen- und Gesell-schafts-Biologie*, founded by Ploetz in 1904, remained the primary scientific publication of German eugenics.[61]

Until the defeat of Germany in World War I, the Germans focused on positive eugenics.[62] Of course, they shared the anxieties of their American colleagues about the degeneration of the lower classes and opposed social legislation enacted to aid the poor, arguing that this "social net" prevented the operation of natural selection.[63] They also shared the concerns of most fellow Germans that the "yellow peril" or the "Slavic threat" could lead to the "Slavization of Germany."[64] However, they did not believe that they could win support for sterilization and therefore concentrated on positive measures, especially attempts to increase the birth rate of "superior" populations.[65]

During the period of the Empire and the Weimar Republic, support for eugenics came from all political parties—conservative, liberal, even socialist. The Social Democrat Alfred Grotjahn, who occupied the chair for social hygiene at the University of Berlin during the Weimar Republic, was a leading eugenicist who advocated colonization and sterilization of the unfit.[66] Eugenic thinking influenced policy toward public health on the left as well as on the right. Thus Karl Kautsky, the leading theoretician of German Social Democracy, opposed leaving abortion decisions to individual women as "unsocialist," and the Vienna physicians allied with Austrian Social Democracy proposed that such decisions be made only by physicians and only on "medical, social, and eugenic" grounds.[67] Of course, many on the left tended to favor a Lamarckian approach to eugenics to provide room for environmental influences on heredity, while those on the right, as well as some on the left, adhered to a strictly Mendelian approach.[68]

Whereas in the United States race and ethnicity were politically important, before World War I German eugenics focused on class and therefore race did not at first occupy a central role.[69] Nevertheless, two diverging approaches appeared at the beginning: the Nordic and the anti-Nordic. Alfred Ploetz, one of the founders of German eugenics, subscribed to the belief in the superior qualities of the Nordic or Germanic peoples, while Wilhelm Schallmayer, the other founder, did not share this enthusiasm for the so-called Aryan race. This division was perpetuated in the next generation of eugenicists, in which Fritz Lenz, Ernst Rüdin, Eugen Fischer, and Hans F. K. Günther supported the theory of Aryan supremacy, while Hermann Muckermann, Arthur Ostermann, and Alfred Grotjahn opposed it.[70] The Aryan supremacists did not, however, at first embrace racial antisemitism. This attitude changed in the Weimar Republic, as exemplified by Ploetz, and was abandoned completely after the Nazi assumption of power.[71]

The struggle over what to call eugenics in Germany reflected the movement's diverging trends. The anti-Nordic faction at first favored the term "hereditary hygiene [*Erbhygiene*]," and Grotjahn proposed the variation "reproductive hygiene [*Fortpflanzungshygiene*]," but later "*Eugenik*" became the faction's preferred designation. The Aryan supremacists chose Ploetz's term "race hygiene [*Rassenhygiene*]." At first, it was not clear whether the name implied the entire human race or the individual races making up humanity, but in the end, race hygiene referred to the study of the "races," with "a consequent hierarchy of racial worth."[72] During the Weimar period, both designations — *Rassenhygiene* and *Eugenik* — were used in the name of the eugenics society.[73] After the Nazi assumption of power, when the society embraced racial antisemitism and expelled Jewish members, race hygiene was the only term used, and thereafter it became the appropriate term to designate eugenics in Germany.[74]

The early moderation on questions of race did not apply, however, to people with different skin colors, because the German eugenicists believed as strongly as their American colleagues in "the racial and cultural superiority of Caucasians."[75] Although the German population did not include non-Caucasians, Germans did confront other races in their African colonies. In German Southwest Africa, today Namibia, the colonial administration repressed the native population and, when the Hereros and Hottentots revolted in 1904, waged a three-year war of annihilation against them.[76] Although German law permitted marriages between Germans and Africans, German colonial governors prohibited intermarriages.[77] These colonies also served as a favorite laboratory for German race hygienists to conduct anthropological research.

The Freiburg anthropologist Eugen Fischer conducted his research in Southwest Africa in 1908, one year after the defeat of the Hereros and the Hottentots. He studied — that is, measured and observed — the Rehoboth Basters, offspring of "legally recognized and religiously consecrated unions between Dutch men and Hottentot women," who spoke Dutch and had Dutch names.[78] In 1913 Fischer published his results in *Die Rohoboter Bastards und das Bastardisierungsproblem beim Menschen* (The Rehoboth Bastards and the problem of miscegenation among humans). This study not only established his reputation but also influenced all subsequent German racial legislation, including the Nuremberg racial laws.[79] In his study, Fischer concluded: "We still do not know a great deal about the mingling of the races [*Rassenmischung*]. But we certainly do know this: Without exception, every European nation [*Volk*] that has accepted the blood of inferior races — and only romantics can deny that Negroes, Hottentots, and many others are inferior — has paid for its acceptance of inferior elements with spiritual and cultural degeneration."[80] Thereupon Fischer proposed the following: "Consequently, one should grant them the amount of protection that an inferior race confronting us requires to survive, no more and no less and only for so long as they are of use to us — otherwise free competition, that is, in my opinion, destruction."[81] Fischer not only rejected marriages between whites and blacks but also objected to "colored, Jewish, and Gypsy hybrids," the so-called *Mischlinge*.[82]

Race hygiene changed during the Weimar Republic. The experiences of war and defeat, as well as the political, social, and economic turmoil of the postwar years, radicalized the professional classes. Rejecting Weimar democracy, large numbers of the professional classes embraced the racial ideology of radical Germanic nationalism. They sympathized with the movements that called for a strong leader to command a community based on racial purity and strength, a conception called *völkisch*. Adherents of the *völkisch* ideology occupied positions on all levels of German society.[83] These trends created a split between the Berlin and Munich chapters of the German Society for Race Hygiene. The Munich chapter embraced the Nordic ideology, while the Berlin chapter rejected Aryan supremacy.[84]

Fritz Lenz, after Ploetz the most prominent advocate of the Nordic ideology, led the Munich chapter and served as coeditor of the *Archiv*. In 1923 the University of Munich appointed Lenz to the first German chair in race hygiene, and after Hitler assumed power, Lenz occupied the race hygiene chair in Berlin.[85] In 1931, two years before Hitler's assumption of power, Lenz provided the Nazi leader with the following testimonial: "Hitler is the first politician with truly wide influence who has recognized that the central mission of all politics is race hygiene and who will actively support this mission."[86] Eugen Fischer and Ernst Rüdin were closely associated with Lenz in the leadership of the Nordic wing of the society, while two younger race hygiene scientists, Otmar Freiherr von Verschuer and Hans F. K. Günther, played leading roles among the next generation of Nordic supremacists.

Eugen Fischer emerged, after the publication of his Southwest African research, as the leading scientific expert on race mingling, a firm proponent of Nordic supremacy, and a major patron of eugenic research. In 1927 he became director of the newly created Kaiser Wilhelm Institute for Anthropology in Berlin-Dahlem and at the same time professor of anthropology at the University of Berlin.[87] Ernst Rüdin, a Swiss national, was one of the founding members of the Society for Race Hygiene and a leading member of its Nordic wing. In 1931 he became director of the Kaiser Wilhelm Institute for Psychiatry in Munich, and in 1933 he was appointed by the Nazi regime to head the Society for Race Hygiene.[88] Otmar Freiherr von Verschuer, a physician specializing in genetics and internal medicine, was known for his eugenic research on twins. A proponent of Aryan supremacy, Verschuer served as a department head in Fischer's institute, left Berlin in 1935 to head the Frankfurt Institute for Hereditary Biology and Race Hygiene, and returned to Berlin as Fischer's successor in 1942.[89] Hans F. K. Günther, who was appointed in 1930 to the university chair in racial anthropology at Jena by Wilhelm Frick and later occupied the chair at Freiburg, became a Nazi party member in 1932 and was thus perhaps the only leading race hygiene figure to join the party prior to Hitler's assumption of power (Rüdin joined in 1937 and both Fischer and Verschuer joined in 1940).[90]

The years of the Weimar Republic witnessed a growing interest in race hygiene. The Munich chair occupied by Lenz in 1923 was only the beginning; by 1932 more than forty courses on race hygiene were offered at German universities, and in the Nazi period, chairs were established at almost every university.[91] In 1921 the Munich publisher Julius Friedrich Lehmann issued the work that would become the classic text of the science of race, the *Grundriß der menschlichen Erblehre und Rassenhygiene* (Outline of human genetics and racial hygiene). The two-volume work had three authors—Erwin Baur, Eugen Fischer, and Fritz Lenz—and was thus commonly known as Baur-Fischer-Lenz.[92] Baur, who died in 1933, was a highly respected botanist and headed the Kaiser Wilhelm Institute for Plant Cultivation and Genetic Research.[93] The *Grundriß* deeply influenced the development and application of the science of race. Lehmann, the publisher, gave a copy of the 1923 second edition to the imprisoned Adolf Hitler, who read it and used its ideas in *Mein Kampf*, and later the authors of the official commentaries on the Nazi racial laws quoted the work as their scientific basis.[94]

A number of research centers with a focus on eugenics were also established during the Weimar years, and they advanced the growth of the field of race hygiene in Germany, serving as models for the vast number of similar institutes established during the Nazi period.[95] Two of these institutes were of special importance, both founded under the umbrella of the prestigious Kaiser Wilhelm Society, sponsor of major scientific research. The German Research Institute for Psychiatry in Munich, established in 1918 with funds from the Rockefeller Foundation, became associated with the society in 1924 as the Kaiser Wilhelm Institute for Genealogy and Demography of the German Research Institute for Psychiatry (Kaiser Wilhelm Institut für Genealogie und Demographie der Deutschen Forschungsanstalt für Psychiatrie), and, as we have seen, was headed by Ernst Rüdin after 1931.[96] The Kaiser Wilhelm Institute for Anthropology, Human Heredity, and Eugenics (Kaiser Wilhelm Institut für Anthropologie, menschliche Erblehre und Eugenik) opened in 1927 in the Berlin suburb of Dahlem. Headed by Eugen Fischer, the board of directors (Kuratorium) included Alfred Grotjahn and Erwin Baur. The institute had three departments: racial anthropology headed by Fischer, human heredity headed by Verschuer, and eugenics headed by Hermann Muckermann. After Muckermann was fired in 1933, Lenz assumed direction of the third department, and after Verschuer left to head his own institute in Frankfurt in 1935, Fischer and Lenz became joint heads of the second department. Other departments—tuberculosis research (Karl Diehl), race science (Wolfgang Abel), experimental genetic pathology (Hans Nachtsheim), and embryology (Wouter Ströer) — were later also established.[97]

Although the leaders of the Nordic supremacy wing of the race hygiene movement stressed the superiority of the "Aryan race," they "found [Hitler's] maniacal anti-Semitism too extreme."[98] They did, however, sympathize with the antisemitic movement as represented, for example, by the Gobineau Society, and they applauded the Nazi program without joining the party. Their contact with the publisher Lehmann placed them among the circle that included leading Nazis, and, as we have seen, they praised Hitler and his commitment to race hygiene.[99] But before the victory of the Nazis altered the rules of the game for academics, they did not consider Jews inferior or demand their exclusion. They only argued that Jews were different and that racial mingling of Jews and Aryans was undesirable.[100] One observer has speculated that their public positions remained moderate because they "valued and feared" their successful Jewish colleagues.[101] But privately they sometimes went further. In 1924 Verschuer told students that "the German, *völkisch* struggle is primarily directed against the Jews, because alien Jewish penetration [*jüdische Überfremdung*] is a special threat to the German race."[102]

The attitude exhibited by scientists toward the disabled "degenerates" among the lower classes could not, however, be described as moderate. As early as 1920, two eminent scholars proposed the most radical solution to the problem posed by institutionalized handicapped patients in Germany. In that year, Karl Binding and Alfred Hoche published a polemical work entitled *Die Freigabe der Vernichtung lebensunwerten Lebens* (Authorization for the destruction of life unworthy of life). Karl Binding, a widely published legal scholar who died just before the book appeared, argued that the law should permit the killing of "incurable feebleminded" individuals.[103] Alfred Hoche, a psychiatrist and specialist in neuropathology, analyzed Binding's arguments from a "medical perspective."[104] Both men lived in Freiburg, a city that was also the center of the Nordic wing of the race hygiene movement. Hoche was a professor at Freiburg University, and Binding, who had taught at Leipzig, had retired in Freiburg. Both Binding and Hoche were right-wing nationalists who rejected individual rights and championed the rights of the national community.[105]

Binding argued that suicide, which he labeled a "human right," should not be unlawful.[106] He also maintained that euthanasia, that is, assisted suicide, should not be penalized, referring to the desire for assisted suicide of many critically ill individuals dying a painful death. As an example, he pointed to terminal cancer patients who receive from their physicians a "deadly injection of morphine" and die "without pain, perhaps also faster, but possibly only after a somewhat longer time."[107]

The discussion of suicide and terminal cancer patients was ancillary to

Binding's main concern. His polemic focused on the fate of individuals considered "unworthy of life [*lebensunwert*]," which could mean both individuals whose lives were no longer worth living because of pain and incapacity and individuals who were considered so inferior that their lives could be labeled unworthy. He used the argument that the terminally ill deserved the right to a relatively painless death to justify the murder of those considered inferior. Binding and all subsequent proponents of his argument consciously confused the discussion by pointing to the suicide rights of terminal cancer patients facing a certain and painful death when in reality they wanted to "destroy" the "unworthy life" of healthy but "degenerate" individuals.

Binding's definition of unworthy life was not very precise, but he did make it clear that he referred to inferiors who should be killed even if they could live painlessly for many years. He added a new criteria when he asserted that whether a life was worth living was determined not only by its worth to the individual but also by its worth to society.[108] Emphasizing in a footnote that millions had given their lives for their fatherland during the world war, Binding made the following point to underline his argument: "If one thinks of a battlefield covered with thousands of dead youth ... and contrasts this with our institutions for the feebleminded [*Idioteninstitute*] with their solicitude for their living patients—then one would be deeply shocked by the glaring disjunction between the sacrifice of the most valuable possession of humanity on one side and on the other the greatest care of beings who are not only worthless but even manifest negative value."[109] Binding's comparison of the death of worthy individuals in the service of their nation and the survival of pampered inferiors was a staple of eugenic argumentation and, as we have seen, mirrored the argument in favor of sterilization advanced by Oliver Wendell Holmes.

Describing the individuals whose lives were unworthy of life as suffering from "incurable feeblemindedness," Binding argued that their lives were "without purpose" and imposed a "terribly difficult burden" on both relatives and society. Although they had no value, the care of such individuals, Binding argued, occupied an entire profession of healthy individuals, which was a total misappropriation of valuable human resources.[110] Alfred Hoche fully supported his coauthor's argument. Hoche offered a variety of definitions of unworthy life, such as, for example, incurable mental retardation or incurable feeblemindedness, but he did not hesitate to use the popular term "*Ballastexistenzen*," that is, beings who are nothing but ballast that can be jettisoned.[111] He also advanced a utilitarian argument, bemoaning the loss of "national resources" for "nonproductive purposes," concluding that "it is a distressing idea that entire generations of nurses shall vegetate next to such empty human shells [*leeren Menschenhülsen*], many of whom will live to be seventy years or even older."[112]

Hoche did not accept the traditional obligation of physicians to do no harm. Dismissing the Hippocratic oath as a "physician's oath of ancient times," he argued that physicians always balance benefits against risks and thus protect "higher values." He did not expect opposition from the medical profession, pointing out that young physicians no longer follow absolute ethical rules but orient themselves according to the teachings of their professors and the opinions of their peers.[113]

In two areas of special concern to physicians, Hoche added to the arguments advanced by Binding. First, he insisted that physicians must be protected against prosecution for euthanasia, because even relatives who ask for the death of patients sometimes change their minds.[114] Second, he argued that the killing of defective patients would expand research opportunities, particularly brain research.[115]

In conclusion, Binding discussed the procedures necessary to implement the destruction of unworthy life. The handicapped patient, the physician, or the patient's relatives could apply for euthanasia, but Binding reserved the right to authorize the killing to the state, which would appoint an "authorization committee" composed of one jurist and two physicians to make an "objective expert evaluation."[116] Binding added a number of further requirements: the decision had to rest on advanced scientific knowledge, the means to accomplish the killing had to be appropriate and "absolutely painless," and only an expert (*Sachverständiger*) could actually kill.[117] Binding acknowledged the possibility of error (*Irrtumsrisiko*), except perhaps with "idiots," but he argued that "humanity loses due to error so many members, that one more or less really does not make a difference."[118]

The Binding-Hoche polemic was followed by other publications favoring euthanasia for those deemed unworthy of life, and, although the idea was never officially accepted during the Weimar Republic, it was widely discussed in German medical circles.[119] In the United States and Great Britain, where public discussion of euthanasia centered on mercy killing for terminal patients and not the killing of unworthy life, the Binding-Hoche polemic made no impression.[120] In Germany, however, it was very influential; eventually the Nazi killers would adopt many of its arguments and later use them as justification. Although the German race hygienists did not originally advocate eugenic euthanasia, they did accept it as "the logical outgrowth of the cost-benefit analysis at the heart of race hygiene."[121]

We might ask why American eugenics withered and died while German race hygiene succeeded in imposing on society its radical vision of a biological-social utopia. The answer is politics. The political climate of the Weimar Republic, especially the ideology of the right-wing *völkisch* movements, provided a hospitable milieu where race hygiene could prosper. But most important, in January 1933 the National Socialist German Workers Party (Nationalsozialistische Deutsche Arbeiter Partei, or NSDAP) captured the German government. This assumption of power by the Nazis, the most radical *völkisch* movement, made the implementation of the race hygiene utopia possible. The Nazis had pledged to preserve the "purity of German blood," that is, they were determined to cleanse the German gene pool.[122] To accomplish that end, the Nazi regime introduced radical social engineering designed to create a society racially homogeneous, physically hardy, and mentally healthy.[123]

A policy of exclusion stood at the center of the Nazi utopia. Killing operations were only the most radical, final stage of exclusion. As we shall see, Adolf Hitler, who was totally committed to the politics of exclusion, ordered the killings once domestic and foreign restraints were removed. The party leaders, the uniformed party formations, and the civil service promptly implemented his orders. And the professional classes, protected by Hitler's authorization, readily cooperated in the killings.

Exclusion institutionalized human inequality. It was applied to entire groups of human beings who simply did not fit into this utopian community, including all those long designated as degenerate (*entartet*) by the teachings of race scientists. First, exclusion was applied to the handicapped, that is, the physically malformed, mentally disturbed, and intellectually retarded. In 1932 the prominent Social Democratic physician Julius Moses predicted that the medical profession under the Nazis would "destroy and exterminate" incurable patients because they were "unproductive" and "unworthy."[124] And as race scientists had always considered criminality an outgrowth of degeneration, exclusion of the handicapped was also designed to apply to individuals considered antisocial or criminal—prostitutes, beggars, vagabonds, habitual criminals—and was later extended to include anyone whose behavior was "alien to the community [*gemeinschaftsfremd*]." The adjective "antisocial" is translated in German as *asozial*; race scientists transformed this adjective into the noun *Asozial* in order to label and stigmatize individuals and groups. One official definition of members of the *Asozialen* group described them as "human beings with a hereditary and irreversible mental attitude, who, due to this nature, incline toward alcoholism and immorality, have repeatedly come into conflict with government agencies and the courts, and thus appear unrestrained and a threat to humanity."[125]

Second, exclusion was applied to racially alien peoples whose physical and intellectual penetration of the so-called Aryan race was also viewed as degeneration. All non-Caucasian races were to be excluded, but the policy primarily concerned two ethnic groups residing in Germany and designated as alien (*artfremde*) races: Jews and Gypsies.[126] Although they may have emphasized different dangers posed by specific groups, the Nazis thus applied exclusion to exactly the same groups that had been targeted by the Aryan supremacist wing of the race hygiene movement. During the 1930s, exclusion became official German government policy.

Exclusion was applied differently to each group. The exclusion of the handicapped, who were for the most part already institutionalized, did not pose a serious administrative problem. In the Weimar Republic, psychiatrists and others in the race hygiene movement had argued that cost containment must apply to institutions caring for the handicapped, and in 1932 Prussia reduced support for so-called defectives. During the 1930s, conditions imposed on the institutionalized handicapped deteriorated precipitously because physicians considered it "obvious" that incurable patients should receive less food than those able to return to work.[127] During the war, conditions became even worse when institutions for the disabled, the senile, alcoholics, and others were denied the additional food regular hospitals received.[128] Antisocial individuals were committed to concentration camps as early as 1933 and were sent to the camps in growing numbers after 1937.[129] During the war, psychiatrists even sought to transfer troublesome handicapped patients from state hospitals to concentration camps.[130] Also, in 1932 the Weimar bureaucracy drafted a voluntary sterilization law for the handicapped, which the Nazi regime implemented in 1933 as a compulsory law.[131]

The method of exclusion applied to those considered aliens on the basis of race depended on the size and importance of the group. For example, the small number of German blacks—children of black French soldiers and German women—were sterilized during the 1930s to prevent future black offspring. This sterilization, illegal even under German law in the Nazi era, was validated by scientific recommendations from Eugen Fischer, Fritz Lenz, Hans F. K. Günther, Alfred Ploetz, and others.[132] Against the larger group of German Gypsies—Roma and Sinti—the regime simply intensified existing discriminatory laws traditionally enforced by the police. In 1936 German scientists embarked on a massive effort to register and classify all Gypsies, while the police severely limited their mobility and incarcerated large numbers in special Gypsy camps.[133]

These simple methods of exclusion could not be imposed as easily on Jews, members of the largest and most visible minority considered alien on the basis of race. Although Hitler and the Nazi movement were fixated on the threat supposedly presented by "international Jewry," they found it difficult to reverse immediately the legal, social, and economic integration of Jews into German society. The process of exclusion required a number of years and involved both domestic and foreign policy considerations. Racial laws and regulations, as well as general harassment, slowly excluded Jews from active participation in the life of the nation. But during the 1930s, the party and state bureaucracy considered the emigration of Jews from Germany as the most promising and the most feasible form of total exclusion.[134]

The Nazi regime issued numerous laws and regulations during the 1930s to implement its eugenic and racial program, and, as we shall see, the practitioners of race hygiene—anthropologists, geneticists, psychiatrists, and physicians—were involved in drafting and applying them. Of course, their role had changed. They profited from being governed by a regime that favored race hygiene, but they also had to accommodate themselves to the regime's political needs. They continued to consider the Nazis "vulgar and ordinary" and Nazi antisemitism somewhat extreme, but they accepted, even applauded, Nazi policies because they reflected an ideology they as individuals and as scientists had long supported.[135] But even though they may have tried to maintain a certain scientific detachment, their assistants and students enthusiastically embraced all aspects of Nazi ideology.[136]

At times, however, Nazi ideology made life inconvenient for the race scientists. Fritz Lenz discovered the futility of objecting to one of Heinrich Himmler's pet projects. At a committee meeting attended by Himmler, Lenz opposed equality for illegitimate children because he believed it would have a negative impact on the quality of the transmitted germ plasm. Himmler disagreed. The powerful Reich leader SS argued that illegitimacy was not a disgrace in the "real world" and that equality was needed to assure a high birthrate and to prevent the spread of homosexuality and abortion.[137]

German science was rapidly synchronized (*gleichgeschaltet*) with Nazi ideology after 1933, especially after scientists opposed to the new regime, as well as those with the wrong ethnic background, were fired. There was no effective resistance. Still, not all science was dominated by Nazi ideology in disregard of the German scientific tradition. For example, the attempt to establish an Aryan physics failed as older traditions reasserted themselves.[138]

Such restraints did not apply in the biological sciences concerned with questions of race and heredity. There Nazi ideology and German scientific tradition complemented each other. Without hesitation, the race scientists fired their Jewish colleagues. Eugen Fischer dismissed Jewish faculty as Rektor of the University of Berlin. This housecleaning also took place in the Kaiser Wilhelm Society, where Richard Goldschmidt, for example, was forced to retire as director of the Kaiser Wilhelm Institute for Biology. Two leading members of the anti-Nordic wing of race hygiene, Hermann Muckermann and Arthur Ostermann, were also forced to resign. The German Society for Race Hygiene, synchronized under the command of Ernst Rüdin, adopted new bylaws, restricting membership to "Germans of Aryan ancestry."[139] While the dismissal of scientists devastated physics, surprisingly only a few of the prestigious and influential chairs in psychiatry changed occupants after 1933. Only three vacancies occurred, and the regime had to wait for normal retirements to make new appointments in psychiatry.[140]

The scientists of race hygiene thus rapidly adjusted to the new political realities, adopting the language and tenor of the new regime. Neither the scientists nor the Nazi leadership saw a distinction between racial and eugenic policies. They joined hands in their common struggle against "degeneration." Newly empowered party and government officials—for example, Arthur Gütt of the Reich Ministry of Interior and Walter Gross of the Nazi party's Office for Race and Politics—admired the work and supported the goals of the scientists.[141] In turn, leading scientists—for example, Rüdin, Verschuer, and Theodor Mollison of Munich—adopted the harsh position on race espoused by the Nazi movement.[142] Spreading the gospel of race hygiene, the scientists offered courses on race and eugenics to public health officers, SS physicians, teachers, nurses, and civil servants.[143] Profiting from the increased demand for genealogies created by the new race laws, they provided anthropological, racial evaluations of individuals—both living and dead—to prove or disprove Aryan descent.[144] They fully supported the regime's policy of exclusion, designed to improve the racial stock of the German nation. In the language used by both the Nazis and the scientists, this policy was called "*Aufartung durch Ausmerzung*," which can be translated as "improvement through exclusion." But this translation does not fully transmit the perversion and brutality of the phrase. A better translation is "physical regeneration through eradication," that is, the Nazi regime and its scientists wanted to improve the stock of the German *Volk* through the eradication of its inferior members and of the racial aliens dwelling among them.[145]

The policy of exclusion required precise definitions of groups and individuals, which only race science could provide. However arbitrary, the "criteria for selection" had to be scientific, and the cooperation of the scientists was an important prerequisite for the successful implementation of the policy of exclusion. Scientific exactitude provided *Rechtssicherheit*, that is, legal reassurance for the masses that the law would protect their own security.[146]

Exclusion not only stripped individuals of rights and standing but also barred them from receiving the state's assistance. Of course, the removal of the safety net for inferiors had always been one of the central themes of eugenics, both in Germany and elsewhere, and opposition to public welfare expenditures had become even more vocal during the depression.[147] It is thus not surprising that the Nazi regime manipulated public welfare to exclude Jews and Gypsies.

The German public welfare system was both expensive and tightly regulated, and the regime could thus use its control of both administration and finances to bar undesirables from receiving public welfare. The Reich authorities responsible for the regulations governing welfare used them to exclude undesirable groups. Obviously, local governments responsible for paying the mandated welfare costs attempted to relieve their burden by excluding as many undesirables as possible from the welfare rolls. The Reich complied by forcing Jewish welfare agencies to assume all responsibility for Jewish welfare recipients. The Reich also decreed that Gypsies were to receive the same treatment as Jews, but because Gypsies did not possess their own welfare agencies, their level of welfare was left to the discretion of local welfare offices; however, Gypsies were to receive less aid than Aryans.[148]

As the Nazi regime moved toward war, Hitler authorized state and party planners to proceed from the exclusionary policies of emigration, incarceration, and sterilization to the most radical exclusionary solution of killings. The first group targeted were the handicapped. They were excluded by being institutionalized, but this was not enough. Hostile to their existence, institutions reduced services and sought to cut the costs of caring for mental and disabled patients. Excluded, incarcerated, sterilized, and neglected, the handicapped were viewed as expendable, and thus a logical progression led to the killing of the handicapped in the so-called euthanasia program.[149] The other group of undesirables—the *Asozialen*—were treated similarly: those committed to institutions by the courts were among the first killed; others were later selected for killing when euthanasia was applied within the concentration camps.[150]

In 1940 and early 1941, when the radical killing solution was already being applied to the handicapped, the policy toward Jews did not yet include killings. At that time, limited emigration, ghettoization, and schemes calling for the establishment of Jewish reservations remained the only exclusionary policy options for Jews. But when international conditions and the progress of the war made a more radical solution possible, the killings were expanded to include Jews.[151]

The much smaller group of Gypsies was also not at first a target of the killing solution. Gypsies were initially subjected to persecution by the police, who incarcerated them as criminals and *Asoziale* by virtue of social stereotype. Then they were studied and sterilized by anthropologists and psychiatrists, in a close collaboration between the police and health authorities. Eventually, after they had been classified by the race scientists as racially inferior, they were killed alongside Jews.[152]

The killing operations that commenced with the start of World War II were the result of old beliefs and recent policies. Although the Nazi policies of exclusion, including compulsory sterilization, provided a crucial stepping-stone toward the implementation of the killings, old beliefs that predated Hitler's assumption of power were equally essential. As we have seen, as early as 1920 Binding and Hoche had called for the "destruction of life unworthy of life," euphemistically called euthanasia. The Nazi regime merely put their proposal into practice.

The euthanasia killings—that is, the "systematic and secret execution" of the handicapped[153]—were Nazi Germany's first organized mass murder, in which the killers developed their killing technique. They created the method for selecting the victims. They invented techniques to gas people and burn their bodies. They employed subterfuge to hide the killings, and they did not hesitate to pillage the corpses.

The euthanasia killings proved to be the opening act of Nazi genocide. The mass murder of the handicapped preceded that of Jews and Gypsies; the final solution followed euthanasia. In euthanasia, the perpetrators recognized their limitations and, to avoid popular disapproval, transferred the killings from the Reich to the East. No substantive difference existed, however, between the killing operations directed against the handicapped, Jews, and Gypsies. The killing technique that had been developed and tested in euthanasia was used again and again. The killers who learned their trade in the euthanasia killing centers of Brandenburg, Grafeneck, Hartheim, Sonnenstein, Bernburg, and Hadamar also staffed the killing centers at Belzec, Sobibor, and Treblinka. The instigators had learned that individuals selected at random would carry out terrible crimes "without scruples."[154]

Chapter 2   Excluding the Handicapped

Hitler's appointment as German chancellor on 30 January 1933 and the Nazi consolidation of power shortly thereafter made possible the implementation of the eugenic and racial policies long advocated by the Nazi movement.[1] For implementation, the regime needed the willing collaboration of the civil service as well as the participation of the professional classes, including racial scientists, physicians, jurists, and statisticians. It readily received the needed support.[2] While the regime created concentration camps and mobilized the SA, SS, and police against its political enemies, it issued laws and activated the civil service to exclude its biological enemies. At first, the regime used violence to intimidate its enemies, but public violence disrupted order, threatened to alienate conservative opinion, and damaged the image of Germany abroad. Although the threat of violence never disappeared, its use was restricted and formalized. The regime accomplished its ends by legal and formal exclusion. After the Nazi assumption of power, the German government rapidly enacted legislation to exclude all outsiders; laws, decrees, and regulations were issued in rapid succession. Newly enacted laws clearly isolated, excluded, and penalized the handicapped, Jews, and Gypsies.

Against the handicapped, the regime enacted into law the program long advocated by race scientists to control a population considered degenerate and inferior. The so-called sterilization law, promulgated in July 1933, served throughout the Nazi period as the model for all eugenic legislation.[3] It introduced compulsory sterilization for persons suffering from a variety of mental and physical disorders and in the process defined the groups to be excluded from the national community. This legislation was followed in October 1935 by the Marriage Health Law, which mandated screening the entire population to prevent marriages of persons considered carriers of hereditary degeneracy, particularly those covered by the sterilization law.[4] Numerous ordinances defining and enlarging these two laws followed.[5] As race hygiene had always linked the handicapped to criminal and antisocial behavior, the bureaucrats drafting this legislation believed that their eugenic laws should also cover "inherited criminal traits."[6] To accomplish this, the regime enacted in November 1933 the Law against Dangerous Habitual Criminals and the Law on Measures of Security and Reform.[7] The new provisions—articles 20a and 42a–m of the penal code—gave the courts substantial new powers to confine and punish persons considered habitual criminals. In addition to the penalties already provided by the penal code, the courts were authorized to commit the *Aso-*

zialen to state hospitals, to impose protective custody or longer prison terms on habitual criminals, to mandate castration for sexual offenders, and to prohibit defendants from practicing their professions or occupations.[8]

Against Jews, the regime promulgated a large number of laws and amplified them with innumerable ordinances. A listing of these laws and decrees, with brief summaries, occupies a book of over 400 pages.[9] The first major legislation directed against Jews was the Law for the Restoration of the Professional Civil Service, enacted in April 1933. Breaching civil service law to permit the regime to fire political opponents from the civil service, the law also included provisions for the removal of so-called non-Aryan, mostly Jewish, civil servants.[10] A vast number of regulations followed on both the national and local levels to drive Jews from all positions in government, education, the media, and the arts. After 1937 laws and regulations also began to curb the economic activities of Jews, to limit their participation in the social and cultural life of the nation, and to restrict their freedom of movement.[11]

The centerpiece of the anti-Jewish legislation was enacted in September 1935 as the Reich Citizenship Law and the Law for the Protection of German Blood and German Honor, together known as the Nuremberg racial laws.[12] The drafters of these laws rejected the use of the terms "Aryan" and "non-Aryan," probably because they were imprecise, although these terms continued to be used in numerous other regulations; instead, the laws defined so-called Aryans as persons with "German or related blood."[13] The Blood Protection Law (Blutschutzgesetz) excluded Jews from the German national family by prohibiting marriages, and also sexual relations outside marriage, between Jews and citizens with German or related blood. It also prohibited Jews from employing as domestics females with German or related blood unless they were over forty-five years old. Finally, it excluded Jews from the national community by prohibiting them from displaying the Reich flag or the national colors. The Reich Citizenship Law was an afterthought ordered by Hitler and drafted by the bureaucracy in a few hours. The law did not alter the status of Jews as citizens (*Staatsangehörige*), conceding citizenship (*Staatsangehörigkeit*) to all German nationals, including Jews, and thus retaining for Jews the rights and protections traditional citizenship conferred. Instead, the law stigmatized Jews as citizens of lesser worth by creating the elevated position of Reich citizen (*Reichsbürger*), which only those with German or related blood could hold. Reich citizens were to be the sole bearers of political rights, but those rights were not defined and, considering the centralization of dictatorial political power, were basically meaningless. In fact, the Reich citizenship warrants were never issued.[14]

Although the Nuremberg racial laws were primarily directed against Jews as the minority considered most dangerous to German society and the German gene pool, the provisions of the laws were also applied to other minorities. The Reich minister of interior, Wilhelm Frick, who administered the laws, defined "alien blood" as follows: "No Jew can become a Reich citizen, because German blood [*Deutschblütigkeit*] is a prerequisite in the Reich citizenship code. But the same also applies to members of other races whose blood is not related to German blood, as, for example, Gypsies and Negroes."[15] However, European minorities residing in Germany, such as Danes and Poles, could be Reich citizens.[16] The Blood Protection Law mentioned only Jews, but article 6 of the law's First Decree made it possible to add other groups.[17] It prohibited marriage if offspring from such a union would endanger the purity of German blood. The official commentators saw article 6 as the means of excluding "other racially alien blood," particularly that of "Negroes and Gypsies."[18]

An exact definition of who belonged to the excluded groups was essential for the administration of the eugenic and racial laws. But while the eugenic legislation included a precise definition in the law itself, the racial laws did not, leaving precise definition to the implementation decrees and regulations. The First Decree to the Reich Citizenship Law thus defined the meaning of the term "Jew," including the various levels of German-Jewish hybrids (*Mischlinge*).[19] The scientists provided the definitions. The civil servants drafting the laws and compiling the commentaries based their definitions on the writings of the race scientists; they quoted Eugen Fischer and Hans F. K. Günther and sat on committees with Fischer, Fritz Lenz, Ernst Rüdin, and Otmar von Verschuer.[20]

Against Gypsies, the authorities increased the powers of repression traditionally imposed by the police.[21] In 1936 Reich Leader SS Heinrich Himmler, in his capacity as chief of the German police in the Reich Ministry of Interior (Reichsministerium des Innern, or RMdI), issued detailed regulations concerning ways in which the police should restrict the freedom of Gypsies to travel and trade, and in 1937 the ministry authorized the police to use preventive arrests to incarcerate Gypsies.[22] Although these regulations, which increased in number in the late 1930s and early 1940s, categorized Gypsies as antisocial elements that had to be contained by the police, their persecution was based on race. Gypsies as a group were defined as criminal and antisocial, obviously a categorization based on race or ethnicity, and thus individual Gypsies, as members of that racially defined group, were automatically classified as antisocial criminals.[23] The provisions of the Nuremberg racial laws were applied to them as much as to Jews. Thus the RMdI, charged with the enforcement of the racial laws, decided that "in Europe only Jews and Gypsies are considered alien races."[24] And the same government and party officials — for example, Arthur Gütt and Walter Gross — played crucial roles in the formulation of both the eugenic legislation and the Nuremberg racial laws.[25]

The sterilization law, issued on 14 July 1933 with the cumbersome name of

Law for the Prevention of Offspring with Hereditary Diseases (Gesetz zur Ver-hütung erbkranken Nachwuchses), opened the attack upon the handicapped and served as the cornerstone of the regime's eugenic and racial legislation.[26] The civil service had moved rapidly, and the first eugenic law had been approved by Hitler and his cabinet less than six months after his accession to power. As we have seen, the preparatory work had been completed prior to 1933. Attempts to alter the penal code and introduce special legislation during the Weimar Republic had led in 1932 to a serious proposal for sterilization legislation in the state of Prussia. This Prussian proposal included all the ingredients of the later Nazi law; the main difference was that it required the consent of the individuals concerned. The Nazi law went beyond the Prussian proposal by introducing compulsion.[27]

The sterilization law was designed to deal with hereditary diseases (*Erb-krankheiten*) and persons carrying such diseases (*Erbkranke*).[28] The opening of the law proclaimed its content: "Any person suffering from a hereditary disease can be sterilized if medical knowledge indicates that his offspring will suffer from severe hereditary physical or mental damage." The law defined a person "suffering from a hereditary disease," and thus a candidate for sterilization, as anyone afflicted with one of the following:[29]

1. congenital feeblemindedness [*Schwachsinn*],
2. schizophrenia,
3. *folie circulaire* (manic-depressive psychosis),
4. hereditary epilepsy,
5. hereditary St. Vitus's dance (Huntington's chorea),
6. hereditary blindness,
7. hereditary deafness,
8. severe hereditary physical deformity, or
9. severe alcoholism on a discretionary basis.

The law created a legal structure for enforcement. The handicapped could apply for sterilization, but application could also be made by physicians of the public health service or, for patients and prisoners, by directors of hospitals, homes, and prisons. Newly created hereditary health courts (Erb-gesundheitsgerichte) were attached to the lowest courts of general jurisdiction (Amtsgerichte) to decide all cases in camera; three members — a judge of the Amtsgericht as chair, a physician of the public health service, and another physician with expert knowledge about the laws of heredity — would make up this court. The law also created appellate courts of hereditary health, attached to the regional circuit courts (Oberlandesgerichte), again composed of two physicians — one in the public health service — and chaired by a judge of the circuit court. The decision of the appellate courts was final.[30]

The law included provisions for compulsory sterilization. Once the courts

TABLE 2.1. Sterilization Applications and Decisions, 1934–1936

Year	Applications	Positive decisions	Percent	Negative decisions	Percent
1934	84,604	62,463	92.8	4,874	7.2
1935	88,193	71,760	88.9	8,976	11.1
1936	86,254	64,646	84.8	11,619	15.2

Source: BAK, R18/5585: "Übersicht über die Durchführung des Gesetzes zur Verhütung erbkranken Nachwuchses."

had decided in favor of sterilization, surgical intervention could be carried out "even against the will" of the individual. If needed, the police were empowered to use force to ensure compliance.[31]

Passed by the cabinet on the same day it approved the Concordat with the Vatican, 14 July 1933, the law was not published until 25 July to assure that it would not hinder the agreement with Rome.[32] It took effect on the first day of 1934. The impact was immediate; large numbers of German nationals, both men and women, were sterilized against their will because the physicians and administrators of the health care system judged them to be suffering from hereditary diseases.

The number of denunciations was enormous in the beginning: 388,400 during 1934–35. Of these, 35 percent were reported by directors of institutions, 21 percent by physicians of the public health service, and 20 percent by other physicians; only 20 percent came from other sources. As many heads of institutions were also physicians, almost 75 percent of all denunciations came from the medical profession.[33] And because two out of three members of each hereditary court were physicians (and only one out of three was a trained judge), the selection of sterilization victims was a medical procedure disguised as a legal proceeding.

Not all denunciations led to immediate decisions by the hereditary health courts; of the 388,400 denunciations during 1934–35, only 259,051 came before the courts during the three years following the implementation of the law. Further, the courts were overloaded, and not all cases considered were decided. In 1934 the courts considered 84,604 cases but ruled on only 67,337; in 1935 they considered 88,193 cases and decided only 80,736; and in 1936 they considered 86,254 cases and settled only 76,265. The courts thus had a backlog of 34,713 active cases at the end of the first three years of sterilization. (See table 2.1.)

Of the cases settled, however, the overwhelming majority resulted in sterilization. In 1934 the courts imposed sterilization in 62,463 cases, rejecting

TABLE 2.2. Sterilization Surgeries, 1934–1936

Year	Positive decisions	Surgeries performed
1934	62,463	32,268
1935	71,760	73,174
1936	64,646	63,547

Source: BAK, R18/5585: "Übersicht über die Durchführung des Gesetzes zur Verhütung erbkranken Nachwuchses."

TABLE 2.3. Deaths from Sterilization Surgery for Men and Women, 1934–1936

Year	Men sterilized	Women sterilized	Deaths from surgery	Deaths of men	Deaths of women
1934	16,238	16,030	102	21	81
1935	37,834	35,340	208	35	173
1936	32,887	30,624	127	14	113

Source: BAK, R18/5585: "Übersicht über die Durchführung des Gesetzes zur Verhütung erbkranken Nachwuchses."

sterilization in only 4,874. The figures rose for 1935: 71,760 sterilizations and 8,976 rejections. In 1936 sterilizations sank slightly to 64,646 and rejections rose slightly to 11,619. But the percentages of settled cases resulting in sterilization remained high: 92.8 percent in 1934, 88.9 percent in 1935, and 84.8 percent in 1936.[34]

The medical profession's capacity to perform surgical sterilization in 1934 was not equal to the ability of the courts to mandate this procedure. Only about half of the imposed sterilizations were actually performed that year. Although this capacity increased in 1935 and 1936, the system did not catch up. The figures for 1937, available only for the first half of the year, show 28,430 operations, which does not alter that picture. (See table 2.2.)

The number of men and women sterilized was more or less equal, with the number of men slightly higher. But the number of deaths resulting from surgery was far higher for women than for men, reflecting the greater difficulty of this operation when performed on women. (See table 2.3.)

For the year 1934, a breakdown by diagnosis of victims undergoing mandatory sterilizations is available.[35] The largest number — 52.9 percent of all those sterilized — were diagnosed as suffering from feeblemindedness; schizophrenics were the second largest category with 25.4 percent, and epileptics the

THE ORIGINS OF NAZI GENOCIDE

TABLE 2.4. Sterilizations Classified by Disease, 1934

Diagnosis	Sterilizations (percent)	Men sterilized (percent)	Women sterilized (percent)
Congenital feeblemindedness	17,070 (52.9%)	7,901 (48.7%)	9,169 (57.3%)
Schizophrenia	8,194 (25.4%)	4,261 (26.2%)	3,933 (24.5%)
Hereditary epilepsy	4,520 (14.0%)	2,539 (15.6%)	1,981 (12.4%)
Manic-depressive psychosis	1,017 (3.2%)	384 (2.4%)	633 (3.9%)
Severe alcoholism	775 (2.4%)	755 (4.6%)	20 (0.1%)
Hereditary deafness	337 (1.0%)	190 (1.2%)	147 (0.9%)
Hereditary blindness	201 (0.6%)	126 (0.8%)	75 (0.5%)
Severe malformations	94 (0.3%)	45 (0.3%)	49 (0.3%)
St. Vitus's Dance (Huntington's chorea)	60 (0.2%)	37 (0.2%)	23 (0.1%)

Source: BAK, R18/5585: "Übersicht über die Durchführung des Gesetzes zur Verhütung erbkranken Nachwuchses."

third largest with 14 percent. The percentages of all other diagnoses were much smaller. Although roughly the same number of men and women were sterilized, their distribution among diagnoses differed slightly. Among those diagnosed as feebleminded, the largest category, women outnumbered men 9,169 to 7,901; among alcoholics, men outnumbered women 755 to 20. (See table 2.4.)

Despite the fact that these surviving statistics cover only the early years of the law's application, they indicate a trend. Of course, the reservoir of persons most available for sterilization—patients suffering from mental illness (schizophrenics and manic-depressives), St. Vitus's dance, epilepsy, and severe malformations—was not unlimited. Other categories, however, provided a pool of candidates that could be expanded. The numbers involved fluctuated depending on the flexibility of the application of definitions. This was certainly true for blindness and deafness; the category of those diagnosed with malformations could be expanded indefinitely if harelips, clubfeet, and similar defects were—as a matter of course—considered sufficient cause for sterilization. Further, the definitions for the category of feeblemindedness, which in 1933–36 already provided the largest number of persons for sterilization, were largely determined by social criteria and therefore lacked scientific precision and could be applied to an ever increasing number of persons. The group deemed alcoholics, providing a small but substantial number for sterilization during 1933–34, had no doubt been selected on the basis of social and economic position and obviously had not been exhausted by the end of the 1930s.

Although exact figures on the number of persons sterilized after 1936 are not available, it is generally agreed that at least 300,000 persons were sterilized during the years preceding World War II. During the war, when euthanasia largely replaced sterilization as a means to control so-called inferiors (*Minderwertige*), sterilization was devalued; still, an estimated additional 75,000 persons were probably sterilized after 1939, including those in areas recently incorporated into the German Reich: Austria, Sudetenland, Danzig, and Memel.[36] Although the sterilization law was not implemented in the Protectorate of Bohemia and Moravia, German citizens residing in the Protectorate were transferred to the incorporated Sudetenland for the sterilization operation.[37] The conservative figure of about 375,000 persons sterilized is still very high, representing about 0.5 percent of the German population.[38]

The sterilization law was only the first shot in the eugenic war launched by the Nazi regime against the handicapped. It was soon followed by numerous regulations and amendments.[39] The regulations defined terms, specified the selection of judges, assigned hospitals for the surgery, and regulated financial obligations. Of special interest is a regulation issued jointly by the Reich Ministries of Interior and Justice on 5 December 1933 permitting persons to postpone sterilization by committing themselves to an institution; however, they could not be released from the institution until they had been sterilized.[40]

Even more important were the amendments to the law. The first, issued on 26 June 1935, attempted to close the loophole involving pregnancies that commenced prior to sterilization. In September 1934, the Reich physician leader, Gerhard Wagner, had issued a circular advising physicians that the Führer would grant them amnesty for any abortions performed to prevent births of children with hereditary taints; this would apply not only if the mother was diseased but also if the mother was healthy but the father suffered from a hereditary disease.[41] The amendment, which required the consent of the pregnant woman, regularized the procedure authorized by the earlier circular. Further, sterilization and abortion could henceforth be performed simultaneously. Thus the law requiring sterilization for the so-called unfit had been expanded into a law also permitting abortion for the proscribed group. At the same time, the amendment restated the prohibition under heavy penalties of sterilization and abortion for persons judged healthy.[42]

Initially, the methods of sterilization were vasectomies for men and tubal ligations for women.[43] But the second amendment to the law, issued on 4 February 1936, provided that under certain conditions the Reich Ministries of

Interior and Justice could prescribe a nonsurgical method, and the regulation of 25 February 1936 permitted the use of X-rays for the sterilization of women.[44]

Castration had been authorized in November 1933 as a preventive punishment for sex offenders; unlike the prevention of procreation in sterilization, it involved the prevention of sexual intercourse.[45] The amendment of 26 June 1936, which also dealt with abortion, reiterated this authorization to castrate sex offenders; it also granted permission to castrate homosexuals, but, as with pregnant women, only with their consent.[46] During the first ten years, 2,300 castrations were performed.[47]

The next logical step in erecting a legal structure designed to exclude those judged biologically deficient was the passage of a law regulating marriages. The Nuremberg Blutschutzgesetz, prohibiting marriages and any sexual contact between Jews and Germans, was enacted in the middle of September 1935. One month later, on 18 October, the German government enacted a similar law directed against the handicapped: the Law for the Protection of the Hereditary Health of the German Nation.[48]

This so-called Marriage Health Law (Ehegesundheitsgesetz) prohibited a marriage if either party met certain conditions, that is, if either suffered from a mental derangement that appeared to make the marriage undesirable for the national community (Volksgemeinschaft), had a hereditary disease specified in the sterilization law, or was placed under legal guardianship. In addition, marriage was also prohibited if either partner suffered from a contagious illness; tuberculosis and venereal disease were specified in particular.[49] Before marriage, a couple had to prove that no impediment existed under this law by securing a Marriage Fitness Certificate from the public health office. The first regulation under the law, issued on 29 November 1935, defined the procedure.[50] These prohibitions did not apply if one of the parties was sterile or had been sterilized or if the male, but not the female, was not a German national. And the law applied, as did the Blutschutzgesetz, even to marriages contracted by German nationals outside the borders of the German Reich.

Feeblemindedness had been the favorite target of eugenicists on both sides of the Atlantic, and, as we have seen, this category also accounted for the largest number of persons affected by the German eugenic legislation. This category was most flexible; inclusion was determined more by social than by medical criteria. Just as the IQ number had been used to define the feebleminded in the United States at the beginning of the century, the diagnosis for hereditary feeblemindedness under the German sterilization law was based almost exclusively on a specially constructed intelligence test.[51] The test measured learning far more than innate ability; the section on "acquired knowledge," for example, shows this clearly:

Acquired Knowledge
Hometown?
Located in which province?
Capital of Germany?
Capital of France?
Who was Luther?
Who was Bismarck?
What form of government do we now have?
Who discovered America?
When is Christmas?
What is the meaning of Christmas? . . .
How many days of the week? —
Forwards and backwards?
How many months? —
Forwards and backwards?

These tests were administered orally, and the subjective judgment of the examiner usually determined the results. This subjectivity is demonstrated by the evaluations the examiner was asked to make at the end of the test:

> *Conduct during Interview*: Bearing, eyes, mimicry, voice, pronunciation, word syntax, rapidity of answers, responsiveness, participation in the conversation.

The test and diagnosis of Erwin Ammann, a twenty-one-year-old male institutionalized in the Tyrol, serves as a good example of this subjectivity. His answers were for the most part correct. For example, in the section on acquired knowledge, he knew his hometown and its province, and he could rapidly name the days of the week and the months of the year forwards and backwards. He identified the capital of Germany as Berlin and of France as Paris; he named Columbus as the discoverer of America. He identified Luther as "the founder of Protestantism" and Bismarck as "a Reich chancellor, ca. 1870, 1880." He knew the date and meaning of Christmas and also of Easter. His answer to the question about the current form of government was "national socialism, he [*sic*] founded the Third Reich." But his knowledge was given lesser weight than the examiner's subjective evaluation. Although the examiner noted that Ammann's "school knowledge is surprisingly good" and that he generally gave "surprisingly prompt answers," he concluded that Ammann displayed a "feebleminded appearance and behavior." The diagnosis remained feeblemindedness; the decision ordered sterilization.[52]

The determination of the medical profession and the public health bureaucracy to diagnose feeblemindedness and prescribe sterilization is best revealed in the rare cases in which the hereditary courts rejected an application for sterilization. For example, the public health physician in the city of Gera rendered a diagnosis of feeblemindedness and applied for sterilization in the case of Herbert Büchner, a twenty-five-year-old male factory worker. The physician claimed that the intelligence test revealed slow mental processes and a weakness in writing and arithmetic. But the hereditary health court in Gera ruled against the public health officer. The court found that the individual had held a steady job for ten years and carefully managed his money; he was aware of the coronation festivities in England, understood about banks, and recognized the function of the Nazi Labor Front. Finally, he made a good impression on the court.[53] Undaunted, the Gera public health physician appealed this decision to the appellate court of hereditary health in Jena. This court sent someone to observe Büchner at work, who reported that he was quite skilled at handling his machines. Büchner's personality and character made a good impression on the court, and it rejected sterilization.[54]

The public health service and the medical profession thus clamored for sterilization even when the hereditary health courts, not usually known for their leniency, turned down their applications. And as we have seen, those considered for sterilization were not only institutionalized patients with significant mental disorders but also persons able to live and work without serious difficulties. This enthusiasm for sterilization waned, however, when the disabled individual belonged to the same professional class as the examiners. The case of a physician with a harelip and a cleft palate provides a good example. Although under the guidelines of the law both conditions were sufficient cause for sterilization, in an official memo, a functionary called this "nonsense." After all, this physician, a longtime party member who had even sat on a hereditary health court, had four children "who have proved themselves" and was "an esteemed physician, a good National Socialist, and a splendid human being."[55] His status as a professional and as a party member thus made him an unacceptable candidate for sterilization.

Of course, not all party members were automatically excluded from sterilization. Party member Johannes Schmidt, who had joined the Hitler Youth in 1930 at the age of sixteen, was sterilized against his will. Schmidt was a postal worker who had obtained his job through party and SA connections. In 1938 he was institutionalized for schizophrenia. In October 1938 the hereditary health court ordered his sterilization, and in November the appeals court upheld this decision. Schmidt fled, was apprehended by the police, and was sterilized in December. He was then discharged from the state hospital, returned to his job at the post office, and continued as a party member.[56]

Patients confined in closed institutions — state hospitals and nursing homes, the so-called Heil- und Pflegeanstalten — were obvious targets for the application of eugenic legislation.[57] They were the largest group of persons judged to be suffering from one of the proscribed hereditary diseases; more than half of all patients in these institutions were diagnosed as suffering from a hereditary disease. These patients thus became the primary victims of compulsory sterilization; in the same way, they later became the principal victims of euthanasia. Some statistics documenting the widespread practice of sterilization in state hospitals have survived; these figures also provide some indication of the size of the pool from which the victims of euthanasia were later selected.

In 1935 the German Association of Cities (Deutscher Gemeindetag, or DGT) solicited information on the application of the sterilization law in state hospitals and nursing homes. The RMdI realized the importance of this enterprise and lent its support to the collection of data. In a circular of 8 January 1936, the ministry requested that all Prussian provinces and non-Prussian states cooperate.[58] The ministry demanded absolute confidentiality; if the statistics should become public, they might serve as the object of criticism in the foreign press.[59] The ministry's long-range objective was the construction of genealogical charts (*Sippentafeln*), which, compiled by public health offices in collaboration with state hospitals, would ensure the registration of the largest possible group of persons subject to the eugenic legislation.[60]

The surviving statistics are not totally reliable but provide a rough picture. Responses from the non-Prussian states did not survive, therefore we have data only from the Prussian provinces. The figures were collected only on specified dates, so patients admitted, discharged, or deceased between those dates were not fully counted. Some institutions did not report, and one province provided only partial figures. Different criteria were employed in various provinces; some included private hospitals and others only public institutions. The DGT did not have the staff to compile summaries with a great deal of sophistication; frequently, discrepancies occurred between the summaries and the raw data.[61]

The DGT's summary shows 82,993 patients in public, and some private, institutions in Prussia on the last day of 1935. Of these, 47,278 were diagnosed as suffering from hereditary diseases. This figure is too low, however, because it does not include patients from Lower Silesia or Berlin. If Berlin's figures, supplied by the city but not included in the summary, are added, the number rises to 52,744. (See tables 2.5 and 2.6.)

Over a reporting period of two years, the figures show that the legal process leading to sterilization was relatively slow. First, the hereditary health court had to render a decision; second, the appellate court of hereditary health had to review that decision. Only after all reviews were completed did the decision become legally binding (*rechtskräftig*). In East Prussia, for example, out of 1,305 decisions on the first level, only 1,265 had become legally binding. Thus only 16,627 legally binding decisions (not including Lower Silesia) on sterilization had been rendered in Prussia. But almost all decisions prescribed steril-

TABLE 2.5. Sterilization in State Hospitals and Nursing Homes by Prussian Province, 1934–1935

Prussian province	Patients	Erbkranke patients	Court decisions	Legally binding decisions	Legally binding positive decisions	Legally binding negative decisions	Surgeries performed	Sterilized and released
East Prussia	4,697	3,524	1,305	1,265	1,249	16	1,217	857
Brandenburg	12,627	10,929	1,896	1,813	1,781	38	1,639	744
Pomerania	4,371	3,555	1,222	1,121	1,118	35	1,065	639
Border region, Posen– West Prussia	770	595	147	141	138	3	125	88
Lower Silesia	8,936	—	—	—	—	—	804	—
Upper Silesia	2,293	1,880	904	892	867	25	759	656
Saxony	6,854	5,480	1,336	1,301	1,083	51	1,182	565
Schleswig- Holstein	3,580	2,850	602	570	564	6	520	353
Hanover	4,760	—	1,413	1,413	1,383	30	1,299	696
Westphalia	9,105	7,127	1,463	1,398	1,341	57	1,219	877
Hessen-Kassel	2,274	1,859	419	396	385	11	346	244
Hessen-Nassau	2,799	2,201	683	652	612	50	557	406
Rhine Province	10,290	7,138	3,513	3,428	3,221	212	2,787	1,180
Hohenzollern	201	140	49	49	42	7	36	33
Berlin	9,436	—	—	2,188	2,077	111	1,835	867

Source: BAK, R36/1373: DGT, "Ergebnis der Rundfrage III 5696/35, Durchführung des Gesetzes zur Verhütung des erbkranken Nachwuchses in den Provinzial-Heilanstalten," 31 Dec. 1935.

TABLE 2.6. Sterilization in State Hospitals and Nursing Homes in the City of Berlin, 1934–1935

Institution	Patients	Erbkranke patients	Legally binding court decisions	Legally binding positive decisions	Legally binding negative decisions	Surgeries performed	Sterilized and released
Wittenau	2,653	1,498	—	831	46	715	349 [47]
Herzberge	1,818	1,059	351	341	22	295	116 [34]
Buch	2,720	1,833	549	528	13	465	178 [33]
Wuhlgarten	1,334	1,076	511	447	27	446	136 [18]
Total	8,525	5,466	1,411	2,147	108	1,921	779 [132]

Source: BAK, R36/1373: DGT Rundfrage, Der Oberbürgermeister, Berlin, 8 Jan. 1936 (statistics as of 31 Dec. 1935).
Note: In last column, the figures in brackets are additional patients released for family care.

TABLE 2.7. Sterilization in State Hospitals and Nursing Homes in the Prussian Province of Brandenburg, 1934–1939

Institution	Patients	Erbkranke patients	Court decisions	Legally binding decisions	Legally binding positive decisions	Legally binding negative decisions	Surgeries performed	Sterilized and released
Eberswalde	1,629	1,264	456	452	428	24	385	299
Sorau	1,122	1,058	506	480	463	17	435	265
Landsberg	1,894	1,478	366	353	340	13	330	273
Neuruppin	2,437	1,968	365	365	350	15	347	184
Görden	2,097	1,445	451	427	416	11	415	281
Teupitz	1,527	1,219	328	321	294	27	279	184
Lübben	1,337	1,189	169	167	167	—	164	64
Wittstock	267	216	100	100	100	—	97	33
Total	12,428	9,958	3,454	3,321	3,236	96	3,104	1,835

Source: BAK, R36/1373: DGT Rundfrage, Der Oberpräsident der Provinz Brandenburg (Verwaltung des Provinzialverbandes), Potsdam, 16 May 1940.

Note: These figures do not include 105 patients from institutions not run by the province (nicht provinzialeigenen Anstalten).

ization; only a minute number of cases resulted in a legally binding decision against sterilization. However, implementation was swift. Unlike the population at large, the patients in closed institutions were sterilized rapidly because hospital staff and facilities could be utilized immediately. And the figures also show that about half of all sterilized patients were released after surgery.

Surviving statistics from the end of the 1930s show that the picture had not changed. For example, the Prussian province of Brandenburg, the central area surrounding Berlin, reported on the last day of 1939 that most of its institutionalized patients were still suffering from a hereditary disease. The number of sterilization decisions had risen but still constituted only a third of all those eligible. The ratio between decisions for and against sterilization had remained the same, most decisions were still implemented immediately, and the number of those released after sterilization had remained about the same. (See table 2.7.) By late 1939, the next phase of eugenic selection—euthanasia—had already commenced; the period of sterilization was ending, the period of the killings had begun.

From 1934 to 1939, state and party fought for control of the institutional implementation of the eugenic laws.[62] The Nazi party, intent upon seizing power from the civil service, couched its attack on the state monopoly in populist terms. In 1937 the Reich physician leader, Gerhard Wagner, representing the party, put his objections before Hitler.[63] On the one hand, the

THE ORIGINS OF NAZI GENOCIDE

party wanted to politicize procedures; it objected to the legal formalism employed by the hereditary health courts and was opposed to many of the physicians and jurists involved in the courts because they were not party members. On the other hand, it attacked the enthusiasm for sterilization exhibited by the civil service; far too many persons were sterilized even when there was no proof that their impairments were in fact hereditary. Although also pointing to abuses involving decisions about other hereditary diseases, from schizophrenia to epilepsy, the party objected most to the way feeblemindedness was diagnosed; it rejected exclusive reliance on intelligence tests.

The civil service fought back. The RMdI prepared a detailed refutation of Wagner's charges.[64] While the party appeared as the champion of the masses, defending the average German against a formalistic and uncaring state bureaucracy, the civil service utilized science and impartiality as a defense. Again and again, the civil service stressed the scientific basis for the eugenic laws; it argued that empirical studies, especially those involving twins, justified the contested decisions of the hereditary health courts. Further, it asserted that only formal court proceedings assured impartiality and that the involvement of party offices would damage the image of scientific impartiality in eugenic proceedings. Admitting that inexperience and human weakness might have resulted in some erroneous decisions, it proposed the creation of a national appeals court for hereditary health to assure uniformity in eugenic court decisions.

Only a decision by the Führer could settle this conflict between party and state. At a meeting between Wagner and Hitler on 14 June 1937, the Führer agreed that procedures should be improved, but he refused to grant Wagner power over the implementation of eugenic legislation. Instead, Hitler demanded cooperation between state and party. He charged State Secretary Hans Heinrich Lammers, chief of the Reich Chancellery, with the task of negotiating an agreement between the two contending parties.[65]

The negotiations between party and state dragged on for over a year.[66] During this time, even the introduction of the sterilization and hereditary marriage laws into newly incorporated Austria was suspended.[67] The final agreement was not reached until late 1939. By that time, Wagner had died and his successor as Reich physician leader, Leonardo Conti, issued the necessary regulations.[68] The civil service continued to be in charge of implementing the eugenic legislation, but the party had gained a veto. Before the public health service could initiate an application for sterilization, it had to obtain agreement from the Nazi party regional leader, the Gauleiter.

The conflict between state and party had not, however, been completely resolved. The civil service had maintained its preeminence; the party had been co-opted by the bureaucracy. Conti, a longtime member of the party and the SS, not only had succeeded Wagner as Reich physician leader and

Reich health leader but also had been appointed state secretary for health in the RMdI.[69] Although the agreement had not settled the power struggle between state and party, it had assured that eugenic laws would be implemented without disruption. In the next phase—the euthanasia killing program—the power struggle would reopen without, however, disrupting the smooth operation of the killings.

THE ORIGINS OF NAZI GENOCIDE

Chapter 3   Killing Handicapped Children

The attack on handicapped patients in state hospitals and nursing homes had opened in 1933 with sterilization and a reduced standard of care. But this was only the beginning. In 1935 Adolf Hitler had told Gerhard Wagner, the Reich physician leader, that once war began he would implement euthanasia.[1] He kept his word. When war started on 1 September 1939, the machinery to kill the handicapped was in place and the killings began. And just as the sterilization legislation enacted against the handicapped was followed by that enacted against Jews and Gypsies, the murder of the handicapped would be followed by the murder of Jews and Gypsies.

First came the murder of handicapped children. In 1938 the newly born infant of a family named Knauer served as the pretext for Hitler to set in motion the program of euthanasia he had intended to institute. The Knauer baby, sex unknown, was apparently born with severe handicaps. The exact nature of its affliction cannot be reconstructed with certainty, but testimony does seem to agree that it was born with a leg and part of an arm missing. Some evidence suggests that it was also blind, and the physicians also diagnosed it as an "idiot." But its blindness was not noted by all observers, and the diagnosis "idiot" was not definite. In addition, the baby apparently suffered from convulsions.[2]

The child's father consulted Werner Catel, the director of the Leipzig University Children's Clinic, and asked him to admit the infant. Catel, who admitted the child to the hospital, later claimed that the father requested that he kill the child and that he refused because this was against the law.[3] Shortly thereafter, the Knauer family appealed to Hitler to grant permission to have the infant killed. Such appeals reached Hitler through his private chancellery, where similar appeals had already been collected. This Chancellery of the Führer (Kanzlei des Führers, or KdF), headed by Philipp Bouhler, prepared the information for Hitler, who decided to act in the Knauer case. He instructed his escorting physician (*Begleitarzt*), Karl Brandt, to visit the Knauer infant, consult with the Leipzig physicians, and kill the child if his diagnosis agreed with the conditions outlined in the appeal.[4] In Leipzig, Brandt consulted with the attending physicians, confirmed the diagnosis, and authorized euthanasia; the baby was killed.[5]

After the killing of the Knauer infant, Hitler authorized Brandt and Bouhler to institute a program of killing children suffering from physical or mental defects. Hitler thus appointed Brandt and Bouhler as his plenipotentiaries for this so-called children's euthanasia program.[6] Like most Nazi leaders, they were relatively young men: Brandt was thirty-five and Bouhler was thirty-nine years old. Brandt, who had been placed in charge of the Knauer decision, was an obvious choice; Bouhler was not. Bouhler was no doubt chosen because Hitler wanted to place the KdF in charge of the enterprise. Some agency had to organize and direct the killing operation, and the KdF, which had already become involved through the Knauer case, was a perfect choice. If direction had been handed to a government department, for example, the RMdI, the circle of the initiated would have grown and the killings would not have remained secret. The cooperation of too many government offices and too many civil servants would have been required. Further, charging the government with the execution of this task would have required official written orders that Hitler was unwilling to issue. If direction had been handed to a visible office of the Nazi party, for example, the Nazi Party Chancellery or the party's Schutzstaffel, the SS, such open involvement of local party leaders and offices would have made orderly and secret implementation difficult. Further, Hitler was not willing to risk public disapproval directed at the party before ascertaining the level of public support.[7]

The KdF as an implementing office had none of these drawbacks. It was not a government agency. Although it was a party agency—its full name was Chancellery of the Führer of the Nazi Party—it was totally independent of the Munich party headquarters, the Nazi Party Chancellery headed by Martin Bormann.[8] The KdF served as Hitler's private chancellery, alongside but separate from Hitler's Presidential Chancellery, headed by Otto Meissner, and his Reich Chancellery, headed by Hans Heinrich Lammers. Hidden from public view and relatively small, the KdF could direct the killings without involving too many people and without becoming too visible.

The KdF, located in Berlin on Lützow Ufer, and later at Voss Straße number 8, was divided into five central offices. (See table 3.1.) The first of these handled Hitler's private affairs and was headed by Martin's brother Albert Bormann. The second dealt with matters concerning government and party and was headed by Viktor Brack. This central office also dealt with clemency petitions, including those requesting mercy killing; it was through this office that the Knauer petition had reached Hitler. The third central office handled pardons for party members sentenced by party courts, the fourth covered social and economic affairs, and the fifth dealt with internal administrative and personnel matters. Bouhler assigned the job of organizing the killings to Central Office II and thus appointed the thirty-four-year-old Brack as the day-to-day manager of the euthanasia killing program.

In the KdF's Central Office II, Viktor Brack had created four offices. (See table 3.2.) Office IIa was occupied by Brack's deputy Werner Blankenburg; offices IIc and IId dealt with the affairs of the armed forces, the police and SS,

THE ORIGINS OF NAZI GENOCIDE

TABLE 3.1. Organization of the Chancellery of the Führer

Office	Jurisdiction	Chief
Chancellery of the Führer (Kanzlei des Führers, or KdF)		Reichsleiter Philipp Bouhler
Central Office I (Hauptamt I)	Personal Affairs (Privatkanzlei)	Oberdienstleiter Albert Bormann
Central Office II (Hauptamt II)	State and Party Affairs (Angelegenheiten betr. Staat und Partei)	Oberdienstleiter Viktor Brack
Central Office III (Hauptamt III)	Pardon Office for Party Affairs (Gnadenamt für Parteiangelegenheiten)	Oberdienstleiter Hubert Berkenkamp After 1941: Kurt Giese
Central Office IV (Hauptamt IV)	Social and Economic Affairs (Sozial- und Wirtschaftsangelegenheiten)	Hauptamtsleiter Heinrich Cnyrim
Central Office V (Hauptamt V)	Internal Affairs and Personnel Matters (Internes und Personal)	Oberdienstleiter Herbert Jaensch

Sources: GStA Frankfurt, Anklage Werner Heyde, Gerhard Bohne und Hans Hefelmann, Ks 2/63 (GStA), Js 17/59 (GStA), 22 May 1962, pp. 45–46; StA Hamburg, Anklage Friedrich Lensch und Kurt Struve, 147 Js 58/67, 24 Apr. 1973, pp. 95–96.

and the Nazi party. Office IIb, which dealt with the Reich government, except the armed forces and police, was also responsible for clemency petitions. Brack assigned to this office the task of coordinating children's euthanasia. Hans Hefelmann headed it, and Richard von Hegener served as his deputy.

Hefelmann was born in Dresden in October 1906 and was thus only thirty-two years old when he assumed a central place in the Nazi regime's first massive killing operation. Son of a textile manufacturer, Hefelmann received his doctorate in agriculture in 1932. He had joined the Nazi party in February 1931, and after a short stint in private business, he joined the staff of the economics department at Nazi headquarters, switching to the KdF in January 1936. Appointed head of Office IIb in 1937, he directed this department and also children's euthanasia until his call-up by the army in 1943.[9] In 1942 Bouhler recommended Hefelmann for a war decoration; like many others involved in killing operations, Hefelmann was decorated for his service behind the lines. Although he employed the language used to hide the killings, Bouhler obviously referred to children's euthanasia in justifying the award of the War Service Cross Second Class: "In addition to his especially important con-

TABLE 3.2. Organization of KdF Central Office II

Office	Jurisdiction	Chief
Central Office II	State and Party Affairs	Oberdienstleiter Viktor Brack
Office IIa	Deputy of chief of Central Office II	Oberreichsleiter Werner Blankenburg
Office IIb	Matters concerning the Reich Ministries; also clemency petitions (*Gnadengesuche*)	Amtsleiter Dr. Hans Hefelmann Deputy: Richard von Hegener
Office IIc	Matters concerning the armed forces, the police, the SS security service, and churches	Amtsleiter Reinhold Vorberg
Office IId	Matters concerning the Nazi party	Amtsleiter Buchholz After 1942: Dr. Brümmel

Sources: GStA Frankfurt, Anklage Werner Heyde, Gerhard Bohne und Hans Hefelmann, Ks 2/63 (GStA), Js 17/59 (GStA), 22 May 1962, pp. 45–46; StA Hamburg, Anklage Friedrich Lensch und Kurt Struve, 147 Js 58/67, 24 Apr. 1973, pp. 96–98.

tributions relating to matters of public health handled by Central Office II, party comrade Dr. Hefelmann provided the intellectual basis for the implementation of a special task important to the war effort and assigned by the Führer. He directs a separate department with independent responsibility for this special task."[10]

Von Hegener, the son of an army officer, was born in September 1905 in East Prussia and was thus only one year older than Hefelmann. After graduation from secondary school in 1923, he entered the business world; he worked for the Dresdner Bank from 1923 to 1929, for a trucking firm until 1931, and thereafter as a statistician for the Association of German Iron and Steel Producers. He had joined the Nazi party in 1931 and had been active in local party affairs. In 1937 he joined the staff of the KdF and eventually served as Hefelmann's deputy in Office IIb and in the children's euthanasia program. His work was appreciated; on the same date and for the same reasons, Bouhler recommended him for the same decoration as Hefelmann.[11]

Between February and May 1939, the men charged with the direction of children's euthanasia met and worked out the methods for implementation.[12] At first, Brack and Hefelmann of the KdF met privately with Herbert Linden from the RMdI. Linden represented Department IV, whose collaboration was essential for the successful implementation of the euthanasia killing operation. (See table 3.3.)

TABLE 3.3. The Reich Ministry of Interior
and Its Health Department, 1933–1939

Office	Chief
Reich minister	Wilhelm Frick
State secretary	Hans Pfundtner
State secretary	Wilhelm Stuckart
Department IV: National Health (Volksgesundheit)	Ministerialdirigent Dr. Arthur Gütt
Section (Referat) for state hospitals and nursing homes	Ministerialrat Dr. Herbert Linden

Sources: BAK, R18/3356, R18/3672, R18/5583.

In the RMdI, Department IV dealt with public health and had thus enforced the racial and eugenic legislation, including the sterilization law. It
supervised the health authorities in the federal states (*Länder*) and the Prussian provinces; the state hospitals and nursing homes (Heil- und Pflegeanstalten); and the local public health officers (Amtsärzte).[13] Until his retirement on disability late in 1939, Ministerialdirigent Arthur Gütt headed the
department. Born in 1891, Gütt had received his medical license in 1918. He
joined the Nazi party in September 1932 and the SS in July 1933, rising to the
rank of SS brigadier general in 1938.[14] He demonstrated his special interest in
race and eugenics by becoming the senior coauthor of two of the semiofficial
commentaries on the laws of heredity and the Nuremberg racial laws.[15]

Much less information is available on Herbert Linden. His rank was Ministerialrat (ministerial councillor), one level below the Ministerialdirigent. He
served as section chief (Referent) in Gütt's department and was apparently responsible for state hospitals and nursing homes as well as the implementation
of the sterilization and marriage laws. More important, he was also one of
Gütt's coauthors for the commentary on the race and marriage laws.[16] Linden
was born in Konstanz, Baden, in September 1899 and received his medical
license in 1925. We do not know when he entered government service, but he
apparently spent most of his career as a civil servant; his surviving membership record in the Association of Physicians does not show that he had ever
had a private medical practice and does not indicate that he ever qualified for
a medical specialty.[17] He joined the Nazi party early, on 23 November 1925,
but apparently did not occupy a party post or join either the SA or the SS.[18]
At the end of the war, Linden escaped arrest and interrogation; on 27 April

1945, he committed suicide.[19] Linden thus remains the most obscure of the key persons responsible for the euthanasia killings.

After Brack, Hefelmann, and Linden had agreed on ways to proceed, they enlarged their planning group by including a select number of physicians: Karl Brandt, Werner Catel, Hans Heinze, Hellmuth Unger, and Ernst Wentzler.[20] Except for Brandt, who was born in January 1904, these physicians were in their forties. Brandt, who had joined the Nazi party in 1932 and the SS in 1934, was an obvious choice; he had handled the Knauer case and had been appointed one of the two plenipotentiaries for euthanasia by Hitler. Catel, who had joined the Nazi party only in May 1937, was another obvious choice because the Knauer baby had been killed in his clinic. Heinze, a specialist in psychiatry and neurology who headed the state hospital at Brandenburg-Görden, had joined the Nazi party in May 1933; he was added to the group on the recommendation of Linden. Unger was an ophthalmologist who had applied for party membership but had not yet been accepted. His novel *Sendung und Gewissen* had advocated euthanasia; it was later adapted for the 1941 euthanasia propaganda film *Ich klage an* (I accuse). Von Hegener's sister had recommended Unger to Hefelmann. Wentzler, who had joined the Nazi party in 1934, was a successful Berlin pediatrician; he had been recommended to the KdF by Leonardo Conti, the Reich physician leader.[21]

From the beginning, the planning and implementation of euthanasia was classified "top secret [*geheime Reichssache*]," and the role of the KdF had to remain hidden. The planners thus fabricated a fictitious organization to camouflage the KdF's direction of children's euthanasia. They chose the imaginative title Reich Committee for the Scientific Registration of Severe Hereditary Ailments (Reichsausschuß zur wissenschaftlichen Erfassung von erb- und anlagebedingten schweren Leiden). This fictitious agency, called the Reich Committee for short, existed only on paper; its mailing address was a post office box. It served only as a cover for the activities of the KdF. Hefelmann and von Hegener headed it but obviously never used their own names, signing documents as "Dr. Klein"; as we shall see, all officials of the KdF used code names when dealing with the euthanasia operation. For the uninitiated, the Reich Committee served to hide the killing operation; its convoluted name perfectly fit its purported role as a scientific research institute.[22]

This small group of physicians and managers worked out the euthanasia system during their meetings in the spring of 1939. They decided that the process of selection would be based on registration forms, the Meldebogen. They further agreed that the data thus collected would be evaluated by experts, the *Gutachter*, who would decide whether the child under review should be killed.[23] By the summer of 1939, the group had completed the planning, and the project could move toward implementation. The first killings took place in about October 1939.[24]

THE ORIGINS OF NAZI GENOCIDE

Neither the KdF nor the Reich Committee could initiate and impleme.
the killing project. For this, the planners needed the RMdI because only a
ministry could enforce compliance. On 18 August 1939, the RMdI therefore
circulated a decree entitled "Requirement to Report Deformed etc. Newborn"
(Meldepflicht für mißgestaltete usw. Neugeborene).[25] It was marked "strictly
confidential" and was not published in the official ministry gazette; prepared
by Department IV, it was signed by State Secretary Wilhelm Stuckart in the
name of Reich Minister Wilhelm Frick.[26]

The decree ordered midwifes and physicians to report all infants born with
specified medical conditions:

1. idiocy as well as mongolism (especially cases also involving blindness
   and deafness),
2. microcephaly (abnormally small head size),
3. severe or progressive hydrocephalus,
4. all deformities, especially missing limbs, severely defective closure of
   the head and the vertebral column, etc., and
5. paralysis, including Little's disease (spastic diplegia).

In addition to newborns, physicians were required to report all children below
age three with such conditions.

A sample reporting form was attached to the decree.[27] The form required
the following information, in addition to the name, age, and sex of the child:
a detailed description of the illness; an explanation of how the ability of the
child to function is disrupted by the illness; details about hospital stay and
name of hospital; projected life expectancy; and chances for improvement.
The form occupied only one side of one page; not much room was provided
for detailed descriptions. Midwifes and physicians were instructed to submit
their reports to the local public health officer, who was to verify the information and then transmit the report to the Reich Committee at Post Office Box
101, Berlin W 9.

The opening sentence of the circulated decree created the desired impression that the ministry's objective was a scientific investigation that would aid
children with serious medical conditions: "Early registration of the appropriate cases involving hereditary deformations and mental retardation is essential for the clarification of scientific questions." Although the failure of the
RMdI to publish this decree and the use of a private research institute with
a post office box address might have alerted the suspicious, the decree appears to have been widely accepted as a simple request for information for a
statistical survey. At no time did the decree reveal the actual reasons for this
requirement to report handicapped children.

The original form used to report the children proved insufficient. On
7 June 1940, the RMdI therefore circulated a decree announcing the introduc-

w form.[28] The new form required far more details. While the old
only for the name, age, and sex of the child, the new form also re-
hild's address and religion. The questions concerning the child's
dition were more detailed but not substantially different. Most
he new form demanded information about the child's birth and
the medical histories of parents, siblings, and other relatives.[29]

The RMdI had set in motion the program that would lead to the killing
of handicapped children. But the ministry was only the "mail carrier"; the
Reich Committee administered the program.[30] The Reich Committee had two
functions, one considered administrative and the other medical. Administration was centered in the KdF's Office IIb, where Hefelmann and von Hegener
directed the enterprise. The medical direction of the Reich Committee rested
with the expert evaluators.[31]

The forms reporting the children were completed by midwifes and physicians, who turned them over to the local public health offices; to avoid confusion, the health offices on the state and provincial levels kept records and
oversaw the transmittal of the forms to the Reich Committee.[32] Hefelmann
and von Hegener retrieved the forms from the Reich Committee's post office
box; at the KdF they logged and sorted them. These two functionaries, who
had no training in medicine whatever, decided which reported cases merited
the special attention of the medical experts and forwarded the selected forms
to them for their decision.[33]

The three experts were Werner Catel, Hans Heinze, and Ernst Wentzler,
all members of the planning committee and committed proponents of euthanasia.[34] They based their decisions to kill or not to kill solely on the reporting
forms; they never saw the children and did not even consult existing medical
case histories. The experts recorded their votes next to their names on stationery that read "Reich Committee" but was prepared by the KdF for each
child under review. There was no room for lengthy comments. A simple plus
sign (+) indicated inclusion in the program and thus the killing of the child;
a simple minus sign (–) indicated exclusion, meaning the child could continue to live. If the expert was undecided, he recorded "observation," which
postponed the decision. Because the KdF did not possess a copying machine,
multiple copies of the reporting forms could not be sent to the evaluators.[35]
Thus, Catel, Heinze, and Wentzler did not vote separately; the same sheet to
record votes, and the same reporting form, was passed from one to the other,
so that they knew each other's votes.[36]

For the killing of the children—known as "Reich Committee children
[Reichsausschußkinder]" once they became enmeshed in the operation—the
Reich Committee created so-called children's wards for expert care (Kinder-
fachabteilungen) at state hospitals and clinics. (See table 3.4.) The first of these
was rapidly established under the direction of Hans Heinze at his institution

THE ORIGINS OF NAZI GENOCIDE

TABLE 3.4. The Reich Committee's Euthanasia Wards for Children

Institution	Physician
Ansbach (Bavaria)	Dr. Irene Asam-Bruckmüller
Berlin: Dr. Wentzler's Children's Clinic	Dr. Ernst Wentzler
Berlin: Municipal Clinic	Dr. Ernst Hefter
Brandenburg-Görden	Prof. Dr. Hans Heinze
Eglfing-Haar in suburban Munich	Dr. Hermann Pfannmüller
Eichberg near Eltville (Hessen)	Dr. Friedrich Mennecke
	Dr. Walter Eugen Schmidt
Hamburg-Langenhorn	Dr. Friedrich Knigge
Hamburg-Rothenburgsort	Dr. Wilhelm Bayer
Kalmenhof near Idstein in the Taunus (Hessen)	Dr. Wilhelm Grossmann
	Dr. Mathilde Weber
	Dr. Hermann Wesse
Kaufbeuren (Bavaria)	Dr. Valentin Faltlhauser
Leipzig: University Children's Clinic	Prof. Dr. Werner Catel
Leipzig-Dösen	Dr. Mittag
Lüneburg	Dr. Baumert
Meseritz-Obrawalde (Pomerania)	Dr. Hilde Wernicke
Niedermarsberg near Kassel	Dr. Theo Steinmeyer
Sachsenberg near Schwerin	Dr. Alfred Leu
Stadtroda (Thuringia)	Prof. Dr. Gerhard Kloos
Stuttgart: Municipal Children's Home	Dr. Müller-Bruckmüller
Uchtspringe (Prussian province of Saxony)	Dr. Hildegard Wesse
Vienna: Am Spiegelgrund	Dr. Erwin Jekelius
	Dr. Ernst Illing
Waldniel near Andernach in the Rhineland	Dr. Georg Renno
	Dr. Hermann Wesse
Wiesloch near Heidelberg	Dr. Josef Artur Schreck

Sources: GStA Frankfurt, Anklage Werner Heyde, Gerhard Bohne und Hans Hefelmann, Ks 2/63 (GStA), Js 17/59 (GStA), 22 May 1962, pp. 147ff.; StA Hamburg, Anklage Friedrich Lensch und Kurt Struve, 147 Js 58/67, 24 Apr. 1973, pp. 157ff.; Nuremberg Doc. PS-3865.

in Brandenburg-Görden; the others took time to create because the KdF had to recruit institutional directors willing to house the wards as well as physicians willing to do the killing.

On 1 July 1940, the RMdI circulated a decree announcing the creation (which had actually taken place sometime earlier) of the Reich Committee's first children's ward at Brandenburg-Görden near Berlin. Continuing to hide the real intent of the program, it informed public health offices that "under expert medical supervision the psychiatric children's ward at Görden near Brandenburg on the Havel will provide all available therapeutic interventions made possible by recent scientific discoveries."[37]

The same disinformation was included in all other decrees circulated by the RMdI. On 18 June 1940, for example, the ministry asked that the welfare system underwrite the costs for needy families. Again pointing to advanced scientific therapies designed to "save the children from permanent invalidism," the ministry advised welfare agencies that the money would be well spent because even if the child's condition improved in only a few cases, future savings in welfare would recoup expenditures.[38]

However, the actual cost of the so-called treatment could not be disclosed to parents or welfare agencies because it would have revealed too much; the parents expected the treatment to last for years or decades and thus cost a great deal, and the authorities, who knew that the treatment would be concluded rapidly, could not enlighten them. In the beginning, even reporting physicians did not realize the truth. A public health officer interested in arranging the transfer of several children to the newly opened institution in Görden complained that Görden did not reply to his inquiries about cost.[39] The Reich Committee did have funds to pay for all expenses when there was no alternative, but it tried, whenever possible, to induce parents or welfare agencies to pay for the secret killings.[40]

The killing system depended on the cooperation of bureaucrats, physicians, and parents. The RMdI facilitated the collaboration of the civil service, including the public health service. The KdF recruited the physicians, nurses, and staff needed for the actual killings. And the bureaucrats and physicians worked to make the parents acquiesce.

As the system of reporting and evaluating disabled children commenced, the need to establish and staff additional killing wards became urgent; Görden's children's ward alone could not handle all expected victims. The KdF recruited the physicians needed for the actual killings, who then became associates of the Reich Committee. Hefelmann, von Hegener, and Linden selected them directly or through the health authorities in the federal states and Prussian provinces.[41] Most of the selected physicians cooperated with the killing operation; a few refused and were excused from participation.[42]

As we shall see, the killing of handicapped adults would soon exceed the killing of the children, involving far larger numbers of killers and victims. Several physicians—for example, the directors of the Görden, Eichberg, and Eglfing-Haar state hospitals—would play a large role in the killing of both children and adults, and it is often no longer possible to reconstruct exactly how the involvement of such physicians in the children's killing program evolved into their participation in adult euthanasia.[43] Eventually, at least twenty-two killing wards for children were established by the Reich Committee.[44] Little is known about some wards except that they existed; others have become infamous through postwar revelations in judicial proceedings.

THE ORIGINS OF NAZI GENOCIDE

Görden was a natural choice as the first killing ward for children. A large hospital complex, it served as a public institution for the Prussian province of Brandenburg. It was located near the city of Brandenburg and its adult euthanasia killing center, which, as we shall see, was established even before Görden opened its children's ward. Görden was not far from Berlin, and rapid communication with the KdF would thus pose no problem. Further, Görden was headed by Hans Heinze, who served as one of the three evaluators for children's euthanasia.[45]

The Görden ward and the methods introduced there by Heinze served as the model for other children's wards; Görden became a training center for physicians assigned to direct the killing of children. For example, Hermann Wesse was trained in Görden in May 1941 before he assumed command of the children's ward in the Rhineland institution Waldniel near Andernach and again in January and February 1942 before he was shifted successively to the killing wards in Uchtspringe and in Kalmenhof near Idstein.[46] In addition, unlike almost all other children's wards, Görden had ample research facilities where Heinze and his students performed medical experiments on the children before and after they were killed.[47] In addition, Görden used the nearby euthanasia killing center at Brandenburg to assure the rapid killing of groups of children.[48]

At least two other killing wards for children were established in 1940. One was set up in the massive state institution Am Steinhof in Vienna. In July 1940, the children's pedagogical sanatorium Am Spiegelgrund opened with 640 beds in buildings located within the confines of Am Steinhof. It served as the children's killing ward for Austria.[49] The first medical director was Erwin Jekelius, and the second director, who assumed the post in July 1942 after Jekelius was drafted, was Ernst Illing.[50] Illing had served at Görden as an assistant to Heinze; there, he had learned his trade and performed his first killings.[51] The transfer was negotiated between Heinze and the Vienna public health service, and all parties knew that Illing's assignment in Vienna included the implementation of children's euthanasia "without attracting public notice."[52]

Another children's killing ward was established in 1940 in the federal state of Bavaria in the large public institution Eglfing-Haar near Munich. This hospital complex treated both adults and children; the killing ward for children was located apart from the regular children's pavilions.[53] Eglfing-Haar was headed by Hermann Pfannmüller, an early participant in adult and children's euthanasia.[54] Pfannmüller, who had received his medical license in 1913 and his specialty certification in psychiatry in 1918, had served in various state institutions—often specializing in the treatment of alcoholics—before his appointment as director of Eglfing-Haar.[55] Pfannmüller was an old Nazi party member; he had joined in 1922 but as a civil servant had been forced to resign shortly thereafter and had not been able to rejoin until May 1933. Pfannmüller participated in the enforcement of the racial and eugenic legislation, heading in 1935 the Augsburg office for racial heredity; he was also an early advocate of euthanasia.[56] In Eglfing-Haar, he rapidly introduced a system that subjected his patients to a rigorous regimen; he also conducted tours through his institution to educate the public about the biological deficiency of his charges.

We have unusually graphic testimony about these Pfannmüller tours and the treatment of patients at Eglfing-Haar even before euthanasia had officially commenced. Ludwig Lehner, a Bavarian schoolteacher, testified in 1946 in London, where he was then held as a German POW, about his experiences on one of these Pfannmüller tours. Lehner, an opponent of the Nazi regime, took this tour in the "fall of 1939," shortly after his release from Dachau. Although he was drafted in 1940 and spent the war years as a German soldier, Lehner vividly remembered his tour through Eglfing-Haar and described to his British captors what he remembered:

> During my tour, I was eyewitness to the following events: After visiting a few other wards, the institution's director himself, as far as I remember he was called Pfannmüller, led us into a children's ward. This hall impressed me as clean and well-kept. About 15 to 25 cribs contained that number of children, aged approximately one to five years. In this ward Pfannmüller explicated his opinions in particular detail. I remember pretty accurately the sense of his speech, because it was, either due to cynicism or clumsiness, surprisingly frank: "For me as a National Socialist, these creatures (meaning these children) obviously represent only a burden for our healthy national body [*Volkskörper*]. We do not kill (he might also have used a euphemism instead of the word 'kill') with poison, injections, etc., because that would only provide new slanderous campaign material for the foreign press and certain gentlemen in Switzerland. No, our method is, as you can see, much simpler and far more natural." As he spoke these words, [Pfannmüller] and a nurse from the ward pulled a child from its crib. Displaying the child like a dead rabbit, he pontificated with the air of a connoisseur and a cynical smirk something like this: "With this one, for example, it will still take two to three days." I can still clearly visualize the spectacle of this fat and smirking man with the whimpering skeleton in his fleshy hand, surrounded by other starving children. Furthermore, the murderer then pointed out that they did not suddenly withdraw food, but instead slowly reduced rations.[57]

As a witness before the U.S. Military Tribunal, Pfannmüller responded to this accusation: "If he says I tore a poor child out of its bed with my fat hands, I would say in my life I never had fat hands. I certainly never grinned at such a thing. I never laughed."[58] In fact, Pfannmüller pointed to the killing

THE ORIGINS OF NAZI GENOCIDE

of children in Eglfing-Haar with pride, telling a postwar German court that "putting the children to sleep was the cleanest form of euthanasia."[59]

Most children's wards were established by the Reich Committee after 1940. Eichberg near Eltville, a state institution in the Wiesbaden district of the Prussian province of Hessen-Nassau, was one of the most prominent. Its director, Friedrich Mennecke, had already been recruited to participate in adult euthanasia when Hefelmann and von Hegener visited Eichberg in 1941, instructing him to open a killing ward for children. They had already obtained permission from the bureaucrat overseeing all institutions in the district, Fritz Bernotat, a committed Nazi and enthusiastic proponent of the killings.[60] After the war, Mennecke could no longer remember exactly when the Eichberg children's ward opened but assumed that it was in April 1941.[61]

Although Mennecke served as director of Eichberg and supervised the children's ward, the daily operation of the killing ward was assigned to his deputy, Walter Eugen Schmidt. Mennecke completed the Reich Committee paperwork and ordered the killings; Schmidt supervised and sometimes even carried out the killings. When Mennecke was drafted in 1942, Schmidt became acting director of the institution and sole chief of the children's killing ward.[62] Still, even when Mennecke was absent, Schmidt kept him informed about Eichberg in letters that were filled with local gossip, including news about each killing.[63]

A second children's ward was established in Hessen-Nassau, providing that relatively small province with an unusually large number of killing wards. The second ward was established in late 1941 or early 1942 in Kalmenhof near Idstein in the Taunus. Kalmenhof-Idstein was a pedagogical sanatorium established in the nineteenth century as a private foundation. After the Nazi assumption of power, it was unable to retain its independence, and eventually Fritz Bernotat became chairman of the foundation that owned the Kalmenhof institution. After the war had started and several physicians had been drafted, Mathilde Weber, who had come to Idstein after receiving her medical license in 1938, became Kalmenhof's chief medical officer and as such also directed the children's ward.[64] In 1944 Weber stepped down to undergo treatment for tuberculosis; she was replaced by the experienced Hermann Wesse, who had been trained at Görden and had already served in the killing wards at Waldniel and Uchtspringe.[65]

In Bavaria, which was already served by Eglfing-Haar, an additional children's killing ward was opened in the Swabian institution Kaufbeuren. This public institution and its Irsee affiliate had been headed since 1929 by the physician Valentin Faltlhauser. Although he did not join the Nazi party until late 1935, Faltlhauser supported both adult and children's euthanasia.[66] In his capacity as director of Kaufbeuren-Irsee, he also directed its children's killing ward; there, he continued to kill children even after the war had ended.

American soldiers arresting Faltlhauser discovered that the last child victim had died on 29 May 1945, twenty-one days after Germany's unconditional surrender.[67]

Eventually, the Reich Committee established children's killing wards throughout Germany, although many were relatively small. Most of them were undoubtedly established by the Reich Committee in consultation with local officials. Thus in the federal state of Württemberg Hefelmann and von Hegener worked with the two physicians directing the health care system in the Württemberg Ministry of Interior: Eugen Stähle and his subordinate in charge of mental institutions and psychiatric services (*Irrenwesen*), Otto Mauthe.[68] Stähle and Mauthe cooperated with the Reich Committee from the beginning and readily agreed to transfer children from Württemberg institutions to children's killing wards outside their state. When the Reich Committee wanted to establish a children's killing ward in Württemberg, it naturally turned to Stähle and Mauthe. The Württemberg officials recommended the Municipal Children's Home in Stuttgart, and during late 1942 discussions between the Reich Committee and the municipal health authorities in Stuttgart led to an agreement to establish a children's killing ward.[69]

The same cooperation with local officials took place in other federal states. For example, in the state of Baden, Ludwig Sprauer, who headed the health department in the Baden Ministry of Interior, arranged for the establishment of a children's killing ward in Wiesloch. But unlike Württemberg, where Hefelmann and von Hegener settled matters directly, in Baden, Linden of the RMdI requested Sprauer's cooperation. The children's killing ward at Wiesloch, established early in 1941, was supervised by Josef Artur Schreck, the institution's deputy director. After killing three children, Schreck declined to perform further killings, stating that "a hospital is not the appropriate place" for such killings; he did, however, continue to supervise the killing ward, while a Dr. Kühnke, a young physician from Eglfing-Haar, performed the actual killings during occasional visits to Wiesloch.[70]

This cooperation between the Reich Committee and the local authorities also worked in the Prussian provinces. When the committee wanted to establish a children's ward in the Rhineland province, Hefelmann and von Hegener made an unsuccessful attempt to persuade the director of the Andernach state hospital to open a children's ward at his institution;[71] they therefore approached the official in the provincial administration responsible for state hospitals, the psychiatry professor Walter Creutz. In May 1941, Hefelmann and von Hegener visited Creutz in Düsseldorf, and together they planned a children's killing ward with a 200-bed capacity, located in a separate building on the grounds of the public institution Waldniel near Andernach. Staffing proved more difficult, however. Creutz was unable or unwilling to provide a physician employed by the Rhineland province to head the ward, and the

THE ORIGINS OF NAZI GENOCIDE

Reich Committee had to import Georg Renno, a thirty-three-year-old physician who had joined the Nazi party in 1930 and the SS in 1931.[72] As we shall see, Renno had already served in the killing operation against adults before he went to Waldniel and would do so again after leaving Waldniel.[73] When Renno left early in 1942, the Reich Committee again helped the local officials by providing Hermann Wesse as a replacement. Wesse was five years younger than Renno and had not joined the Nazi party until April 1933.[74] In December 1941, Wesse met Hefelmann, von Hegener, and Renno in the waiting room of the Düsseldorf railroad station and agreed to accept the appointment to head the Waldniel killing ward. Creutz did not object but did express concern about Wesse's lack of medical experience, as if medical knowledge was a prerequisite for killing children. Wesse was consequently assigned for training in Görden and in the Bonn psychiatric clinic before assuming command in Waldniel.[75]

Sometimes the choice of institution and physician was more informal. For example, the appointment of Alfred Leu as director of the children's ward in Sachsenberg near Schwerin in the federal state of Mecklenburg reflected an informal selection process. Leu was one of several senior physicians in Sachsenberg; his appointment to head the killing ward seems to have been due to his close contacts in the provincial Nazi party leadership.[76] Bypassing local officials, Hefelmann and von Hegener invited Leu to visit them in their offices at the KdF and asked him to undertake the job. He accepted. Later he would claim that he did not actually kill any children; he only supervised the ward, while the nursing staff did the actual killings.[77]

Sachsenberg was not the only children's ward established through personal contacts. Two of the expert evaluators—Catel and Wentzler—eventually opened killing wards in their own institutions: Catel at his Leipzig University Children's Clinic and Wentzler at his private children's clinic in Berlin. Also, as we have seen, the first killing ward had opened in Görden under the direction of Heinze, the third evaluator. The evaluators also recommended to the KdF likely physicians for the job of killing children. Wentzler recommended the Hamburg physician Wilhelm Bayer, who had headed the 450-bed children's hospital Hamburg-Rothenburgsort since 1934; Wentzler and Bayer had both been fellow assistants at the Charité in Berlin. Bayer accepted, and Hamburg-Rothenburgsort became another host for a children's killing ward.[78]

The child-killing policy was initiated and directed by the bureaucrats of the KdF, but its implementation was left to specialists, the physicians in the children's wards. The KdF bureaucrats did not care how the children were killed; they depended on the expert knowledge of the physicians they had selected. These physicians had to find the best method. Thus Bayer was told at a meeting at the KdF offices that the means were left to the discretion of the physicians.[79]

One possible killing method was starvation. We know that this method was sometimes applied; rations had been consistently cut and approached starvation levels, and late in the war, starvation and "starvation pavilions" were common in many institutions. However, starvation was not the method generally adopted in the killing wards for children.[80]

The favored method was the use of medication. Although the decision about which medication to use was left to each practitioner, physicians exchanged information on medications when they visited each other or met in Berlin.[81] Pfannmüller, for example, visited Am Steinhof in Vienna and noticed that those doing the killing were using morphine-scopolamine; he, however, preferred the barbiturates luminal (a sedative) and veronal (sleeping tablets).[82] Bayer was told in Berlin that bromide, morphine, veronal, and luminal were effective.[83] Of these, luminal became the preferred method for most physicians, with morphine-scopolamine as the second choice, usually for those resistant to luminal or veronal.[84]

The physicians could also choose how they or their nurses administered the medicine. Usually the deadly medication was given in tablet form, sometimes in liquid form; on rare occasions, when the patient could not or would not swallow, it was given as an injection. The tablets were usually dissolved in a liquid such as tea so that the child would ingest the medicine with regular food.[85]

The advantage of this method for a secret killing operation was obvious. These medicines were regularly administered in all medical facilities; they became lethal only in increased dosages.[86] The children were therefore killed not as a result of the ingestion of alien poisons but through an overdose of a common medicine. Further, overdoses of barbiturates and similar forms of medication did not result in immediate death. Instead, they led to medical complications, especially pneumonia, that eventually — usually in two or three days — resulted in death. The physicians could then report a "natural death."[87] Pfannmüller, who after the war denied all evidence that he had starved his patients, also testified to this fiction before the U.S. Military Tribunal: "I must emphasize this is not a matter of poisoning. The child simply dies of a certain congestion in the lungs, it does not die of poisoning."[88]

However, one problem remained: How could the hospitals obtain the large amounts of medication the killings required and still keep their activities secret? The physicians could not solve this problem; it had to be solved by the bureaucrats in the KdF. But neither the KdF nor the Reich Committee it had created as a front could legitimately purchase large amounts of medication. The KdF had to find another agency to act as intermediary.

The KdF officials turned for help to the SS and police empire headed by Heinrich Himmler, the Reich leader SS and chief of the German police. They received the needed cooperation from the Kripo (the detective forces [Kriminalpolizei]), which, together with the Gestapo (the secret state police

THE ORIGINS OF NAZI GENOCIDE

TABLE 3.5. Chain of Command for the Technical Institute for the Detection of Crime

Office	Chief
Reich leader SS and chief of the German police (RFSS u. ChdDtPol)	Heinrich Himmler
Chief of the security police (Sipo) and the SS security service (SD)	Reinhard Heydrich (succeeded in Jan. 1943 by Ernst Kaltenbrunner)
Central Office of the Reich Detective Forces (Reichskriminalpolizeiamt, or RKPA)	Arthur Nebe (succeeded in 1944 by Friedrich Panzinger) Deputy: Paul Werner
Group D: Technical Institute for the Detection of Crime (Kriminaltechnisches Institut, or KTI)	SS Standartenführer and Kriminaldirektor Dr. Walter Heess
Section for Chemistry (Referat Chemie)	SS Hauptsturmführer Dr. Albert Widmann

Sources: BAK, R58; ZStL, Bd. 141; Staatsarchiv Potsdam (today Bundesarchiv-Potsdam), Dokumentationszentrale Freienwalderstraße; StA Stuttgart, Anklage Albert Widmann und August Becker, (19) 13 Js 328/60, 29 Aug. 1962. See also Henry Friedlander, "The SS and Police," in *Genocide: Critical Issues of the Holocaust*, edited by Alex Grobman, Daniel Landes, and Sybil Milton (New York: Rossel Books and Simon Wiesenthal Center, 1983), pp. 150–54.

[Geheime Staatspolizei]), constituted the security police (Sicherheitspolizei, or Sipo). The Sipo in turn combined in 1939 with the SS security service (Sicherheitsdienst, or SD) to form the Central Office for Reich Security (Reichssicherheitshauptamt, or RSHA). The RSHA, headed by Reinhard Heydrich, thus combined in one structure two government agencies, the detective forces (Kripo) and the political police (Gestapo), with the intelligence organization (SD) of a political party formation.[89] The Central Office of the Reich Detective Forces (Reichskriminalpolizeiamt, or RKPA), designated Office V of the RSHA, was headed by Arthur Nebe, who, together with his deputy Paul Werner, reached an agreement with the KdF concerning the collaboration of the Kripo in the euthanasia killings. Henceforth, the Kripo would provide the medication that would be used by physicians in the killing wards as a poison to kill handicapped children and later also handicapped adults. Nebe gave the job of obtaining the poison to the RKPA's Technical Institute for the Detection of Crime (Kriminaltechnisches Institut, or KTI).[90] (See table 3.5.)

Although located within the RKPA, the KTI, headed by the engineer Walter Heess, served as a technical support group for the entire Sipo. Its duties involved the investigation of documentary forgery and arson and the examination of firearms and other evidence that required analysis in a police laboratory. The task of obtaining poison fell to the section for chemical analysis (Referat Chemie) within the KTI; its chief was Albert Widmann, an SS officer with a doctorate in chemical engineering.[91]

Widmann apparently received his orders to cooperate with the KdF directly from Nebe, and a lasting collaboration developed between the KTI's chemistry section and the KdF. Widmann's office served as cover (*Deckadresse*) for the KdF, and von Hegener served as the contact. Starting in 1940, the KTI's chemistry section produced poison for the KdF, especially suppositories with overdoses of morphine-scopolamine, and sent them to the KdF for distribution; ampoules were sometimes even kept in the safe of the KdF offices.[92] Later in the war, after the expansion of the SS fighting units made supplies more available to the KTI as a part of the SS and police empire, Widmann's office obtained a large variety of poisons (including luminal and morphine) from the medical service of the Waffen SS. The KTI then transmitted the medicines to the KdF (often in person to von Hegener), and the KdF thereafter sent them via the Reich Committee to the wards; often, however, the KTI delivered medicines directly to various institutions.[93]

In order to kill the children, the Reich Committee had to transfer them to the killing wards. This required an extensive operation involving large numbers of offices. The process was initiated when a physician or midwife filled out a report about the child, transmitted via the local health authorities. Based on this report, the experts made their decision. If they decided that the child should be included in their operation, the Reich Committee, that is, Hefelmann or von Hegener at the KdF, initiated the next step.

The Reich Committee would not deal directly with the children's relatives or their physicians. It had no official status and no coercive powers; further, direct contact had to be avoided to prevent exposure of the involvement of the KdF. The committee therefore turned to the health authorities in the federal states and the Prussian provinces; these agencies arranged the transfer of the children.[94] In Württemberg, Stähle of the Württemberg Ministry of Interior and the local public health offices arranged the transfer of at least 93 children into out-of-state killing wards.[95] Similarly, the Hamburg authorities transferred 24 children on 8 August 1943 from the Hamburg institution Langenhorn to the Hessen-Nassau killing ward at Eichberg. All 24 children died in Eichberg within two months: 4 in August, 13 in September, and 7 in October 1943.[96]

If a child was already in an institution, especially one that had a children's killing ward, transfer posed no problem.[97] But most newborn infants and young children reported to the Reich Committee were at home or in local hospitals; in these cases, the parents had to be persuaded to permit the transfer. The health authorities in the federal states and Prussian provinces usually gave this job to the local public health officers.[98]

THE ORIGINS OF NAZI GENOCIDE

Once the child was transferred, the experts of the Reich Committee could proceed in one of two ways. One option was to order the killing of the child as soon as it arrived at the killing ward.[99] Another option, often employed, was to request that the ward's physician observe the child and report on its progress; only after the physician issued a negative report was the order to kill given.[100] This period of so-called observation was supposedly designed to prevent mistakes. However, the physicians in the killing wards did not usually give favorable reports; neither the Reich Committee nor the physicians in the killing wards wanted to release the Reich Committee children once they had been admitted.[101]

The actual order to kill a child was issued by the Reich Committee.[102] An official-looking document printed on the stationery of the fictitious Reich Committee but signed by an official of the KdF, this killing order was euphemistically called an "authorization" to "treat" the child. The term "authorization [*Ermächtigung*]" was used because the myth of euthanasia as ordered by Hitler was based on the deception that in implementing the program the state only facilitated and authorized an action a physician wished to take for humane reasons but which the archaic penal code prohibited. The term "treatment [*Behandlung*]" was used simply because words such as "to kill" were considered too revealing even for secret documents.[103] After the war, Schmidt of the Eichberg killing ward would testify that "Berlin sent us so-called 'authorizing documents' and these children, after a little while, would arrive too"; he added: "The children were assisted in dying." [104]

Although most Reich Committee children were obviously not suffering painful or terminal diseases, the killers defended their actions on the grounds that their afflictions were disabling and incurable. The disabilities that had to be reported were indeed serious physical ailments. They included neurological disorders and physical deformities considered incurable and hereditary by the standards of medical knowledge at that time.[105] But even this criterion for killing—that a disease should be incurable though not necessarily terminal—remained only theory. After the children's euthanasia program had started, the Reich Committee and its physicians did not follow their own rules or observe sufficient restraint in making decisions concerning whether to include children in the program.

First, diagnosis for inclusion was often imprecise and too narrow. Physicians disagreed about the chances for improvement, and the expert evaluators, dependent on descriptions provided by these physicians, often accepted the least favorable prognosis. The physicians in the killing wards often found conditions incurable even if the family physicians, who knew the children best, had not considered them serious.[106]

Second, the physicians involved in the program assumed that the disabilities listed as warranting inclusion would prevent the infant from ever functioning independently in the adult world. But even the chief physician of adult euthanasia found the procedures for making such a determination faulty; pointing to the case of the blind and deaf Helen Keller, he argued that infancy was much too early to reach a definitive conclusion about a child's future abilities.[107] Likewise, the expert Wentzler had at the beginning objected to the inclusion of mongoloid children, claiming that they have a special appreciation for music and love of life.[108]

Third, the category "idiocy as well as mongolism" was sufficiently vague to permit the inclusion of retarded children on the basis of their intelligence and behavior. In fact, judgments were made about these children on the basis of a simplistic, and fallible, evaluation of their intelligence and education.[109] Often social values, including those focusing on the child's behavior, influenced the decision to kill, just as they had affected the decision to sterilize.[110]

The physicians in the killing wards were as essential to the decision-making process as the three expert evaluators because they saw the children and reported on them. Often they were young and inexperienced, unqualified to make such judgments. Although they received some special training, many did not even have a license as a specialist.[111]

If we examine the killing ward physicians we have discussed most frequently so far—Heinze, Illing, Jekelius, Mennecke, Pfannmüller, Renno, Schmidt, and Wesse—we find that four had been certified in a specialty (psychiatry or neurology or both): Pfannmüller in 1918, Heinze in 1928, Illing in 1937, and Jekelius in 1938. The other four were never certified, however.[112] They did try to obtain certification during the war—for example, in 1940 Mennecke applied to the medical board and at the same time approached the KdF and the RMdI for help—but their efforts were unsuccessful.[113] These physicians simply did not have the training or experience to make the decisions that those in charge of killing wards were expected to make. Even Heidelberg professor Carl Schneider, himself deeply involved with the program, commented that their "training was limited and their diagnoses not always accurate."[114]

Nevertheless, these physicians were ambitious, anxious to fulfill their quotas, and they complained if not enough children were sent to them.[115] The Reich Committee rewarded good work; a productive killing ward staff received a financial bonus.[116]

The Reich Committee children were killed because they did not fit into the projected future German society. In addition, however, the physicians were eager to use their deaths to advance science and their own training; as we shall see, the euthanasia killings also served as a laboratory for the "advancement of science."[117] Because the killing wards did not have the equipment, and the physicians there did not have the training, scientific investigations were conducted elsewhere. Numerous scientific institutes profited from the killings, but two were closely associated with the program of children's euthanasia:

THE ORIGINS OF NAZI GENOCIDE

the Clinic for Psychiatry and Neurology of Heidelberg University, directed by Carl Schneider, and the research station at the Görden institution, directed by Heinze. These and other research centers studied selected Reich Committee children before they were killed and performed autopsies on them afterward; they also removed organs from the killed children, especially brains, for scientific study.[118] The young physicians in the killing wards could also profit by taking courses at the research centers, using the proceeds of their handiwork to earn advanced degrees.[119]

From the moment the reporting forms were filed, through a variety of inevitable steps—observation, evaluation, killing, dissection—the children became the wards of the Reich Committee. To gain control over the children, the committee and its physicians used lies and threats to obtain the cooperation of parents. Except in cases where the children were already institutionalized, the program could only work if parents surrendered their children to the killing wards. Usually this posed no problem; the authorities simply deceived the parents, telling them that their children could be cured in the wards. As we have seen, the circular of the RMdI to public health offices promised advanced scientific therapies, and this deception usually convinced parents to commit their children. Some parents, however, objected. They did not wish to part with their children, suspected a false diagnosis because their own physicians had reached a more positive prognosis, or feared the worst after hearing rumors about euthanasia killings. Against these parents, the Reich Committee applied pressure.

On 20 September 1941, the RMdI circulated a decree to administrations in the federal states and Prussian provinces, as well as to all public health offices, attempting to refute the objections raised to the commitment of children.[120] Pointing again to the great therapeutic benefits the Reich Committee was offering, it explained in detail how institutionalization of disabled children would free the family to care for healthy siblings. It accused both relatives and family physicians of misjudging the gravity of such disabilities, especially in the case of mongoloid children, whose "happy disposition or love of music" is misinterpreted as cause for optimism. It deflected some parents' objection that the Reich Committee's wards were located in state hospitals by stating that they were really "open wards for expert care of children and youth."

The decree encouraged public health offices and physicians to persuade parents by using arguments provided by the ministry, but it also indicated that force might be used.[121] At the end of the decree, the ministry pointed out that refusal to commit the child, once all the facts had been explained, would be harmful to the family and to the remaining healthy children. In such cases, the public health authorities "might have to investigate whether such refusal is a transgression against the right to custody."

The threat of denying parents' custodial rights usually worked.[122] Even greater pressure could be applied against mothers when fathers were absent as soldiers during the war. In such cases, the Reich Committee, pointing to an agreement between the labor and interior ministries, requested the local labor office to assign the recalcitrant mother to contractual labor; at that point, the mother had little choice but to commit the child.[123] Obviously, such coercive measures were effective only against working-class mothers, unable to finance child care, especially after subsidies for children were denied those not certified to be a "useful, racial compatriot [*brauchbarer Volksgenosse*]."[124]

Similar tactics were employed against parents who attempted to remove their children from the killing wards. In theory, removal of a child was an option, just as commitment was supposedly voluntary; in fact, it was virtually impossible. The physicians in the killing wards did everything in their power to prevent parents from removing their children.[125] Some parents petitioned the institution, some denounced it to the courts, and some used subterfuge to get their children back.[126] Few succeeded.

After the war, the managers and physicians involved in children's euthanasia did not want to admit that they had killed the children without the permission of their parents, but they could not completely hide this reality. They pointed to parents and relatives, who no doubt existed, who were happy to permit the authorities to free them from the burden of a disabled child; often these relatives came from the ranks of the Nazi party and its SS and SA formations.[127]

For the most part, however, few parents consented to the killing of their children. Furthermore, the physicians regularly interpreted consent in a bizarre manner. Although parents were never told that their child would be killed, it was often the practice to prepare them by telling them a false story about an operation with great risks, possibly including death, that might cure their child. If the parents agreed to this operation, the physicians interpreted this as consent to apply euthanasia.[128] The myth of parental agreement did not die easy and was advanced in a variety of arguments. Pfannmüller of Eglfing-Haar produced the strangest argument during his cross-examination by the U.S. prosecutor at Nuremberg:

Q: When you decided that children should be subjected to euthanasia to relieve them from their suffering, did you then notify the parents or guardian of the children concerned?
A: Yes, they were told ahead of time by my departmental physician.
Q: They were told before you applied the euthanasia?
A: Oh, yes. We told the relatives that it would be expedient to visit the child because the child was sick and the relatives did come. In the beginning of Luminal treatment the child wakes up from time to time until the final cumulative effect of Luminal sets in.

THE ORIGINS OF NAZI GENOCIDE

Q: Did you instruct the parents and guardian that you were going to administer Luminal treatment to the child?

A: No, no, that was a top secret matter.[129]

The killing of the children came first. It commenced the euthanasia killing program. The children were considered especially crucial because they represented posterity; elimination of those considered diseased and deformed was essential if the eugenic and racial purification program was to succeed. However, soon the project to kill handicapped children was overshadowed by that for the killing of handicapped adults. But when Hitler ordered an end to the first phase of adult euthanasia in August 1941, the children were not included in this so-called stop order, and children's euthanasia continued until the end of the war.[130] By that time, the scope of children's euthanasia had been expanded. At first, it included only infants and small children, none above the age of three. But later older children were also included, and eventually even teens were killed in the children's wards.[131] Hitler, who reserved for himself the authority to resolve problems, made the decision to include the older children.[132] It is important to remember that not all the children killed were suffering from incurable diseases or permanently disabling deformities; many were institutionalized for less severe disabilities or simply because they were slow learners with behavior problems.

Because many records of the killings have not survived, it is impossible to calculate the number of children killed in the children's wards during World War II. The best estimate is a total of at least 5,000 murdered children.[133]

Chapter 4 Killing Handicapped Adults

Children were only the first victims. Even before the killing of children began, the killing operation expanded to adults. Although the murder of handicapped adults was both unnecessary and senseless because they were already sterilized and thus unable to produce descendants, for the killers a logical progression led from exclusion to extermination.[1] First, the regime had implemented compulsory sterilization to inhibit the birth of potentially unfit infants. Second, it had introduced euthanasia for children to eliminate any such infant not prevented by the sterilization program. Third, having assured the future, it proposed to cleanse the present and erase the past by launching euthanasia for adults. The American postwar indictment in the Nuremberg Medical Case concisely described this so-called euthanasia program: "This program involved the systematic and secret execution of the aged, insane, incurably ill, or deformed children and other persons by gas, lethal injections, and diverse other means in nursing homes, hospitals, and asylums."[2]

The move to rid Germany of institutionalized handicapped adults might have been expected. As we have seen, the funds spent for the upkeep of institutionalized patients had already been reduced drastically, and it had become customary to refer to them as "life unworthy of life."[3] Hitler, who had told Gerhard Wagner in 1935 that he would institute compulsory euthanasia once war came, had not been alone in this desire. At a 1938 meeting of government officials responsible for the administration of mental institutions, for example, one speaker concluded that "a solution for the field of mental health would simply require that one eliminates those people."[4] Fritz Bernotat, the Nazi radical who administered state hospitals in Hessen-Nassau, was later more explicit when he told a meeting of institutional directors who were complaining about overcrowding: "If you have too many patients in your institution, just beat them to death, and then you will have space."[5]

In the summer of 1939 Hitler initiated the policy of killing handicapped adults. This killing operation would involve far larger numbers of victims than the relatively limited operation against children. Hitler turned first to the government agency normally responsible for public health. The Führer sent for Leonardo Conti, who would soon succeed the deceased Wagner as Reich physician leader. Unlike Wagner, who had held only a Nazi party office, Conti also occupied the newly created position of state secretary for health in the RMdI.[6]

Hitler met with Conti, Hans Heinrich Lammers, the chief of the Reich Chancellery with the title of Reich minister, and Martin Bormann, the chief of the Nazi Party Chancellery.[7] At the meeting, Hitler told them "that he considered it appropriate that life unfit for living of severely insane patients should be ended by intervention that would result in death." Like numerous others who advocated the killing of the handicapped, Hitler used as an example the hypothetical case of patients so incapacitated that they could not keep themselves clean and "took their own excrement as food" — an example used extensively by the killers at their postwar trials, although none of the murdered patients probably exhibited this aberrational behavior.[8] As an additional argument to convince the bureaucrats, Hitler added that killing adult patients would also produce "a certain saving in hospitals, physicians, and nursing personnel."

Conti accepted the assignment, but he did not remain in charge long; within a few weeks, Hitler replaced him.[9] Apparently, a power struggle developed within the Nazi leadership over control of adult euthanasia. Philipp Bouhler, in charge of children's euthanasia, convinced Hitler that the KdF should undertake the killing of handicapped adults as well. Bouhler was probably urged to embark on this jurisdictional struggle by Viktor Brack and the KdF staff. In addition, Bouhler feared that the appointment of Conti, who headed the party office for national health in the Nazi Party Chancellery, would ensure Martin Bormann's control over the euthanasia operation; in his intrigue against Bormann and Conti, Bouhler apparently allied himself with Hermann Göring, Heinrich Himmler, and Wilhelm Frick.[10]

Hitler granted Bouhler's request and informed Karl Brandt of his decision. Brandt and Bouhler, already in charge of children's euthanasia and now also appointed plenipotentiaries for the killing of handicapped adults, accepted the new commission and began to confer on how to implement it.[11] No doubt, considerations of secrecy also prompted Hitler to substitute Brandt and Bouhler for Conti. As in children's euthanasia, administrative direction by the KdF ensured that neither the party, through its visible SS formations, nor the state, subject to budgetary controls, would be openly involved. And once again, Hitler "desired a non-bureaucratic solution."[12]

When did Hitler make these decisions and appointments? It is impossible to fix the time with absolute certainty. At Nuremberg, both Brandt and Lammers placed Hitler's appointment of Conti in the early period of the war, September or early October 1939, and the change to Brandt and Bouhler several weeks later.[13] But Brack at Nuremberg, and other witnesses interrogated by German prosecutors years later, placed these events several months earlier.[14] Evidence does support the earlier date; thus it seems likely that the KdF called its first planning session for adult euthanasia before the start of the war.[15] We can assume that Hitler met with Conti no later than July 1939 and that he gave the final assignment to Brandt and Bouhler no later than August.

Considering that the chronology of Nazi mass murder unambiguously shows that the murder of the handicapped preceded the murder of Jews and Gypsies, we should first ask why Hitler and his circle decided to kill the handicapped. Of course, we know that the "destruction" of human beings designated as "life unworthy of life" had long been part of Nazi ideology. But were they also pursuing some "rational" goal? At the time, the Nazis themselves, and later also historians and others, pointed to the need to free hospital space as a cause for the killings. But the conservation of resources could not on its own have been a "rational" reason for the killings, although the Nazi leaders might have considered it a useful side effect. The effort expended was totally out of proportion to the economic benefits expected. Moreover, economic benefits could not balance the potential danger to the regime from negative Allied and German public opinion. Unlike the process of making ordinary economic and military decisions, the decision-making process for killing operations did not include, as far as we can tell, analyses that balanced dangers against benefits. Hitler thus made his decision because he intuitively felt that he could do it, make it stick, and get away with it. This may not be surprising, but it is startling that the entire party, government, military, and professional elite accepted such a radical, irrational decision.

Bouhler charged Brack and his KdF Central Office II, which already ran children's euthanasia, with the administrative details. The RMdI, in particular Department IV, responsible for national health, was to serve in a supportive role.[16] State Secretary Conti attended some meetings and signed the necessary circulars, but he did not involve himself in daily administrative chores. Instead, Herbert Linden, already active in children's euthanasia, represented the RMdI in the inner circle of the KdF killing operation; in this, he had the full support of his chief, Fritz Cropp, who had succeeded Arthur Gütt as director of Department IV.[17] Linden became the civil servant responsible for euthanasia, an activity that was for Linden simply a continuation of his prewar work as the RMdI Department IV specialist responsible for state institutions. As he expanded his specialty to include euthanasia, he advanced in the ministry. He was promoted to the high rank of Ministerialdirigent, headed a newly created subdepartment for heredity and race, and eventually became Reich plenipotentiary for state hospitals and nursing homes.[18] (See table 4.1.)

Bouhler's first steps toward the implementation of adult euthanasia involved, as in children's euthanasia, the collection of expert advisers who would plan procedures. First, he mobilized the KdF bureaucrats from Brack's department. Second, he enlisted Linden from the RMdI. Third, he authorized the recruitment of physicians. Apart from those physicians already involved in planning children's euthanasia, whose specialty was pediatrics, however,

TABLE 4.1. The Reich Ministry of Interior and Its Health Department, 1939–1945

Office	Chief
Reich minister	Wilhelm Frick
Senior state secretary	Hans Pfundtner
State secretary for defense and administration	Wilhelm Stuckart
State secretary for health affairs	Dr. Leonardo Conti
Department IV: National Health (Volksgesundheit)	Ministerialdirigent Dr. Fritz Cropp
Subdepartment for Heredity and Race (Unterabteilung Erb- und Rassenpflege)	Ministerialdirigent Dr. Herbert Linden
Reich plenipotentiary for state hospitals and nursing homes (Reichsbeauftragter für die Heil- und Pflegeanstalten)	Ministerialdirigent Dr. Herbert Linden

Sources: BAK, R18/3356, R18/3672, R18/5583.

the KdF did not know any suitable physicians, especially psychiatrists. Bouhler knew only one name, that of Professor Werner Heyde.

Heyde was to become the key psychiatrist for adult euthanasia. Bouhler knew his name because Heyde had been involved years earlier in the conflict between the Nazi party regional leader (Gauleiter) of the Saarland-Palatinate, Josef Bürckel, and the SS commander Theodor Eicke. But Bouhler did not know how to reach Heyde and thus assigned Brack the task of finding him, something that Brack could accomplish only by seeking Himmler's aid.[19] Heyde was well known to Reich Leader SS Himmler, who helped locate and recruit him.

Heyde's career had advanced rapidly with the aid of the SS. Born in 1902, he had received his medical license in 1926 and his specialty certification in psychiatry and neurology in 1929.[20] Heyde served as a physician in the psychiatric clinic of the University of Würzburg and, after obtaining his license (*Habilitation*) to teach at universities in 1932, was promoted to tenured assistant at the clinic and untenured lecturer at the university.[21] In 1933 fate intervened to advance Heyde's career. In March Josef Bürckel arranged to have Theodor Eicke committed for mental observation, and Eicke was sent to the Würzburg clinic, where he met Heyde.[22] The young psychiatrist and the SS officer, who apparently shared a proclivity toward homosexuality, became friends, and Heyde sent an appeal on behalf of Eicke directly to Himmler.[23] This led to Eicke's release and to his appointment as commandant of the Dachau concentration camp. After he had proven his value by reorganizing

Dachau, and also by assassinating SA chief Ernst Röhm, Eicke was promoted to inspector of all concentration camps and commander of the SS death head units, a job he retained until he advanced to the command of a Waffen SS division at the start of the war.[24]

Eicke in turn advanced Heyde's career. Although he had served during the immediate post–World War I years with the counterrevolutionary Free Corps at home and in the Baltic, Heyde had joined no political party before he met Eicke.[25] But in May 1933 he joined the Nazi party, and in June 1936 he entered the SS as a captain.[26]

Thereafter, Heyde advanced rapidly. In 1934 he became senior physician (*Oberarzt*) at the Würzburg clinic, in part because his Jewish predecessor was forced to leave.[27] At the same time, he delivered lectures on hereditary diseases, provided court testimony as an expert witness, served on the local sterilization court, and was chief of the Würzburg Nazi party race office.[28] Further, through Eicke's intervention, Heyde became an adviser in psychiatry to the Gestapo; he was also appointed to Eicke's concentration camp administration to investigate hereditary diseases among the camp prisoners.[29] Finally, these political connections led to his appointment to the chair of psychiatry at Würzburg.

All other physicians invited to collaborate in the planning of adult euthanasia were recommended to the KdF by Linden and by Ernst Robert Grawitz, the SS Reich physician.[30] The list of medical planning advisers, about ten to fifteen physicians, included, in addition to Heyde and Linden, the physicians Ernst Wentzler and Hellmuth Unger, already involved in children's euthanasia. Further, the KdF invited the psychiatry professors Max de Crinis from Berlin, Carl Schneider from Heidelberg, and Berthold Kihn from Jena and the directors of large public institutions Valentin Faltlhauser from Kaufbeuren, Hans Heinze from Görden, Paul Nitsche from Sonnenstein, Hermann Pfannmüller from Eglfing-Haar, and Bender from the Buch state hospital in Berlin.[31]

The KdF invited these medical advisers to a meeting, probably set for early August 1939, chaired by Bouhler. Conti, who thereafter took no active part, also attended.[32] At this meeting, Bouhler outlined the proposed undertaking, discussed the legal basis, and asked for cooperation. Although it was made perfectly clear that no one would be coerced, all attending physicians pledged their support.[33] The KdF followed up this introductory meeting with smaller planning sessions involving fewer persons. From these sessions emerged the scheme on how to proceed with the killings and how to obscure KdF participation.[34]

Brandt, Bouhler, and their associates faced one problem: they had to convince the cooperating professionals, especially physicians, that they would not be prosecuted for killing patients. Killing a human being, except enemy

THE ORIGINS OF NAZI GENOCIDE

soldiers in battle or criminals legally convicted by a court, continued to be a crime in Nazi Germany; the pre-Nazi penal code was never abolished, and its articles 211 and 212 prohibiting the intentional killing of a human being remained in full force and effect.[35] In the earliest discussions about adult euthanasia, Lammers suggested the promulgation of a law authorizing the killings, but Hitler absolutely refused to consider such a law during wartime.[36] In the same way, later attempts by the euthanasia physicians to draft such a law failed because Hitler continued to oppose the enactment, and thus publication, of a law authorizing the killings.[37]

One of the professed benefits of centrally directed euthanasia killings was decriminalization, that is, the removal of the threat of prosecution from physicians who killed their patients.[38] Hitler's refusal to promulgate a law prevented public decriminalization. Although almost everyone accepted the principle that the Führer's word was law, the KdF functionaries had difficulty convincing physicians and civil servants that they would not be criminally liable for murder in the absence of a duly enacted law clearly authorizing the killing of handicapped patients. To convince their collaborators, and possibly to cover themselves as well, they decided to ask Hitler for written orders.

In October 1939, Hitler signed a document, more an authorization than an order, that had been prepared by the KdF.[39] But to emphasize that war would not only alter the international status of the Reich but also herald "domestic purification," he predated it to 1 September 1939, the day World War II began.[40] Prepared on Hitler's personal stationery, as if mass murder was his "private affair," but never promulgated or published in any legal gazette, this authorization did not actually have the force of law.[41] It was to serve, however, as the legal basis for the killing operation, and it was used to convince physicians to collaborate in the killings.[42]

Typed on white stationery, with the German eagle and swastika as well as the name "Adolf Hitler" printed on the top left, the authorization read as follows:

Berlin, 1 Sept. 1939
Reich Leader Bouhler and Dr. med. Brandt are charged with the responsibility of enlarging the competence of certain physicians, designated by name, so that patients who, on the basis of human judgment, are considered incurable, can be granted mercy death after a discerning diagnosis.
(signed) A. Hitler

The original was kept in a safe at the KdF; copies were shown to various prospective collaborators. One copy was later sent to the Reich minister of justice, Franz Gürtner. The original and all but one copy were destroyed when the war ended. The photocopy sent to Gürtner survived, with a handwritten notation:

Transmitted to me by Bouhler on 27.8.40
(signed) Dr. Gürtner.[43]

The most important and urgent job facing Viktor Brack, the KdF official appointed to run adult euthanasia, was the creation of an organization that could, like the Reich Committee in children's euthanasia, serve as a front to hide the fact that the killings were a KdF operation. As in the case of the children, the adult program was directed by the KdF; but unlike children's euthanasia, the adult project was too large for the KdF staff to operate. Additional staff had to be recruited, and the Voss Straße offices of the KdF could not accommodate them. The office in charge of adult euthanasia first moved into the Columbus House on the Potsdamer Platz, an office complex located at Berlin's busiest intersection. Soon it had to expand, and the central office moved into a confiscated Jewish villa at number 4 on Tiergarten Straße; because of this Tiergarten Straße number 4 address, adult euthanasia was soon known as Operation T4, or simply as T4.[44]

Brandt and Bouhler were Hitler's appointed plenipotentiaries for euthanasia; they wrote guidelines, discussed problems, and, keeping Hitler informed, received his policy orders.[45] But Brandt, who was one of a number of young professionals who became attached to Hitler in the early 1930s and would later in the war rise to the position of plenipotentiary for medicine and health, did not take an active part in the daily management of euthanasia; he never even visited the offices of T4.[46] Bouhler was a longtime Nazi party activist who headed Hitler's personal chancellery.[47] Responsible for the program's administration, he was exclusively accountable for implementation.[48] But even Bouhler did not involve himself in day-to-day operations; he left that to Brack.

Viktor Brack, the manager of euthanasia for children and adults, was born the son of a physician in Haaren near Aachen in November 1904. After completing his secondary education in 1923, he studied agriculture at the Technical University in Munich, receiving his diploma in 1928. Thereafter, he ran the estate attached to his father's sanatorium and was also a test driver for BMW. He joined the Nazi party and the SS in December 1929, although he later claimed to have been active in the party since 1924 without officially joining. In 1930 and 1931 Brack frequently served as Himmler's driver; he knew the Himmler family because his father had delivered one of the SS leader's children. In 1932 he became Bouhler's adjutant, and in 1934 his chief of staff. When Bouhler and the KdF moved from Munich to Berlin, Brack assumed direction of Central Office II.[49]

Appointed to direct the implementation of the euthanasia killing program, Brack zealously executed his new duties, testifying after the war that "we welcomed it, because it was based on the ethical principle of sympathy and had

THE ORIGINS OF NAZI GENOCIDE

humane considerations in its favor. ... I admit that there were imperfections in its execution, but that does not change the decency of the original idea, as Bouhler and Brandt and I myself understood it." [50]

Brack, who used the pseudonym "Jennerwein" [51] when dealing with euthanasia matters, relied on his deputy, Werner Blankenburg, the chief of Office IIa, who used the pseudonym "Brenner," [52] to oversee many of the details of the T4 operation. After Brack left the KdF for the front as a major (Sturmbannführer) of the Waffen SS in 1942, Blankenburg succeeded him as day-to-day manager of T4. [53] Blankenburg was born in 1905, joined the Nazi party and the SA storm troopers in 1929, and worked as a sales representative in business before joining the KdF. [54]

Officials from the KdF's Central Office II, headed by Brack and Blankenburg, occupied key positions in the euthanasia operation. We have already discussed Hefelmann's and von Hegener's direction of children's euthanasia; these two also participated in the operation against handicapped adults, attending meetings and visiting institutions. Although in theory the work of the Reich Committee against the children was separate from Operation T4, in fact children's euthanasia was considered part of the T4 effort. In many ways—for example, in the involvement of the offices of the KdF and in the assignment of physicians—the two killing operations complemented each other.

Reinhold Vorberg was another official from Brack's KdF office who occupied a key position in T4. Born in 1904, Vorberg completed training in business, visited Spain and Southwest Africa during the 1920s, established a costume jewelry business in 1932, and, after it failed in 1935, joined the KdF, probably through the intervention of his cousin Viktor Brack. [55] Like most KdF functionaries, Vorberg had joined the Nazi party early, becoming a member in 1929. [56]

Viktor Brack created the administrative structure for adult euthanasia. [57] (See table 4.2.) He did not, however, have enough KdF personnel to staff T4 and therefore had to hire people for these jobs. He recruited them through a network of personal contacts and party connections. No one was forced to participate; all joined voluntarily. [58] Although Brack and Blankenburg oversaw the operation from their offices at the KdF on Voss Straße, the various administrative offices of T4 were located on Tiergarten Straße and in the Columbus House. Brack and Blankenburg obviously retained ultimate control over the T4 operation, but for the day-to-day administration they appointed a business manager (Geschäftsführer), who headed the T4 Central Office (Zentraldienststelle). Gerhard Bohne served as the first manager; he departed in the summer of 1940. Dietrich Allers, who exercised substantial influence, subsequently served as manager until the end of the war.

Bohne joined T4 early and was responsible for the creation of its administrative structure. Born in 1902 the son of a railroad inspector, Bohne studied

TABLE 4.2. Organization of T4

Office	Chief
KdF Central Office II	Viktor Brack Deputy: Werner Blankenburg
T4 Central Office (Zentraldienststelle)	Manager (Geschäftsführer) Dr. Gerhard Bohne Summer 1940: Dietrich Allers
T4 Medical Office (Medizinische Abteilung)	Prof. Dr. Werner Heyde Dec. 1941: Prof. Dr. Paul Nitsche
T4 Administrative Office (Büroabteilung)	Dr. Gerhard Bohne Summer 1940: Friedrich Tillmann

T4 Central Finance Office
(Hauptwirtschafts-
abteilung)
	Willy Schneider
	  Mar. 1941: Fritz Schmiedel
	  Jan. 1942: Friedrich Robert Lorent

T4 Transport Office (Transportabteilung)	Reinhold Vorberg Deputy: Gerhard Siebert
T4 Personnel Office (Personalabteilung)	Friedrich Haus Arnold Oels
T4 Inspector's Office (Inspektionsabteilung)	Adolf Gustav Kaufmann

Source: GStA Frankfurt, Anklage Reinhold Vorberg und Dietrich Allers, Js 20/61 (GStA), 15 Feb. 1966, pp. 36–46.

law at the University of Cologne, passed his law examinations in 1924, and earned his doctorate in jurisprudence in 1928. For several years, he worked in the civil service but left in 1930 to practice law in Berlin. He returned to the civil service in 1935 and thereafter served as an administrative judge for one of the government's economic agencies. Bohne had joined the Nazi party in 1930; at the same time he had joined the SA, but he switched to the SS in 1935.[59]

Bohne left T4 in the summer of 1940, charging Brack and his associates, as well as many of the T4 physicians, with corruption and disreputable behavior.[60] Dietrich Allers, his successor, was born in 1910 the son of a state attorney and joined the Nazi party in 1932 and the SA in 1934.[61] Like Bohne, he studied law. He passed his first law examination in 1933 and his advanced second examination in 1937. After brief employment in the judicial system, he changed to the Prussian administrative service. Allers had risen to the civil service rank of Regierungsrat when he replaced Bohne as T4 manager.[62]

As business managers of the T4 Zentraldienststelle, Bohne and later Allers administered several offices, each responsible for one aspect of adult euthanasia. The T4 Medical Office (Medizinische Abteilung) was headed by Werner

Heyde until his departure from active administration in December 1941; he probably had to step down because of accusations that he was a homosexual.[63] Heyde was succeeded by his deputy, Paul Nitsche, longtime director, with the title of professor, of the Sonnenstein state hospital in Saxony. Born in 1876, Nitsche had received his medical license in 1901 and was thus a senior psychiatrist whose professional life predated the Nazi period and who had been known as an advocate of progressive therapies for mental patients. Although he had joined the Nazi party relatively late, in May 1933, he was a committed supporter of eugenics and euthanasia and had participated in early killing experiments.[64]

The medical office was responsible for the evaluation of patients and their selection for euthanasia. It commissioned and directed the expert medical evaluators, supervised the collection of data on patients, appointed and instructed the physicians and nurses assigned to the killing centers, and oversaw the T4 registrar, who kept the records on all evaluated patients.[65]

The T4 Administrative Office (Büroabteilung) was directed by the business manager, Gerhard Bohne. After his departure, however, the next manager, Dietrich Allers, supervised but did not directly administer the office, leaving this responsibility to Friedrich Tillmann. The office coordinated the efforts to hide the killings, which involved misleading relatives and various agencies involved in committing patients and paying for their care. The clerical work involved — such as writing death notices, returning personal belongings, and arranging burial details — was handled by the administrative offices attached to the killing centers and only coordinated at headquarters. However, as we shall see, a subsection of this office, located in the Columbus House in Berlin, managed the centralized disinformation to hide the killings of Jewish patients. Finally, the department ran the courier service that assured rapid mail delivery between the T4 Central Office and the killing centers.[66]

The T4 Central Finance Office (Hauptwirtschaftsabteilung) was first directed by Willy Schneider, then Fritz Schmiedel, but its final and most influential chief was Friedrich Robert Lorent. Born in 1905, Lorent left school for vocational training first in agriculture and then in business. After joining the Nazi party in 1930 and the SA in 1932, he occupied various full-time offices in the party and in the SA as a business administrator. After further training as a bookkeeper, he held the job of accountant for one of the Nazi party agencies and at the beginning of the war for German agencies in occupied Poland. Brack, who had known Lorent as a fellow party bureaucrat during the 1930s, hired him to head the central finance office.[67]

The central finance office administered the properties and disbursed the budget of T4. At Nuremberg, Brack claimed to have had little knowledge of T4 finances, arguing that only Bouhler handled such matters; he stated that he thought the Ministry of Finance somehow provided the needed funds. He did admit, however, that discussions were held with the treasurer of the Nazi party.[68] In fact, the budget of T4 came from the Nazi party; this obviated the need for a public accounting that receiving official monies from government sources would have necessitated.[69] In addition, T4 also derived substantial profit from defrauding the patients, their relatives, insurance companies, and government welfare agencies.[70]

The central finance office managed the motor pool, the photocopy facilities, and the financial audit. It also ordered and paid for poisons, including gas, needed to kill the patients. Finally, later it also financed the salaries and met other needs of T4 personnel transferred for duty to the killing centers in the East.[71] For this purpose, Lorent even visited the killing centers of Operation Reinhard: Belzec, Sobibor, and Treblinka.[72]

The T4 Transport Office (Transportabteilung) was headed by KdF official Reinhold Vorberg, who took the pseudonym "Hintertal,"[73] and his deputy Gerhard Siebert, who was a relative of Vorberg. This office arranged for the transfer of patients to the killing centers. It also took care of the correspondence with relatives and institutions concerning the transfer and, until Allers placed this function under his own direct control, collected the fees charged for transportation and other transfer costs.[74]

The T4 Personnel Office (Personalabteilung), headed by Friedrich Haus and Arnold Oels, hired the staffs needed to run T4 both at headquarters and at the killing centers. This office also administered the obligatory secrecy oath.[75]

Finally, the T4 Inspector's Office (Inspektionsabteilung) was headed by Adolf Gustav Kaufmann. Born in 1902 in the Polish part of the Austrian Empire, he served during World War I as a fifteen-year-old in the Austrian army and then took vocational training as a mechanic. He joined the illegal precursor of the Austrian Nazi party and SA as early as 1923 and thereafter worked full-time for the SA in Austria. After the German incorporation of Austria, he accepted an appointment of the Nazi party in Germany, serving as party inspector in Pomerania. In 1940 his personal friend Brack recruited him for work with T4.[76]

As head of the inspector's office, Kaufmann reported directly to Brack. His duties involved the maintenance of good relations concerning euthanasia between the KdF and local government and party offices. Kaufmann selected the institutions that were to serve as killing centers, rebuilt and furnished them so they could fulfill their functions, looked after the welfare of the personnel employed there, and periodically inspected the killing centers to assure smooth functioning. Finally, Kaufmann also oversaw the establishment and operation of the vacation home T4 established for its personnel in Weißenbach at the Attersee in the Austrian Salzkammergut vacation area.[77]

T4 and its various offices rationalized the operations of adult euthanasia. But although it could also serve as a front to obscure the involvement of the

KdF, T4 itself was nevertheless to remain secret. The KdF therefore created front organizations (*Tarnorganisationen*) to hide the existence of this central killing agency. Like the Reich Committee in children's euthanasia, these fronts were simply names on stationery designed to protect the identity of the various T4 offices and ultimately the KdF. The KdF and T4 had contact with the public only through one of these front organizations. In adult euthanasia, four such fronts existed: the Reich Cooperative for State Hospitals and Nursing Homes, the Charitable Foundation for Institutional Care, the Charitable Foundation for the Transport of Patients, Inc., and the Central Accounting Office for State Hospitals and Nursing Homes.[78] (See table 4.3.)

The Reich Cooperative for State Hospitals and Nursing Homes (Reichsarbeitsgemeinschaft Heil- und Pflegeanstalten), known for short as the RAG, served as a front for the T4 Medical Office. It corresponded with government agencies, public health officers, institutions, and sometimes the relatives of patients concerning the registration, evaluation, and selection of patients for adult euthanasia. In the beginning, T4 business manager Gerhard Bohne served as head of the RAG, but after his departure, the chief physician of T4 directed the front, first Werner Heyde and then Paul Nitsche. The address of the RAG was Post Office Box 262, Berlin W 9, and sometimes Potsdamer Platz 1, the address of the Columbus House.[79]

The Charitable Foundation for Institutional Care (Gemeinnützige Stiftung für Anstaltspflege), known for short as the Foundation (Stiftung), was headed by the T4 business manager, first Bohne and then Allers. It represented T4 in all official dealings with other government and party agencies involving the hiring, payment, fringe benefits, and other concerns of the T4 personnel. It also represented T4 in other matters concerning the collection and payment of money; it received the party subventions and paid the bills. The Foundation used the Columbus House address.[80]

The Charitable Foundation for the Transport of Patients, Inc. (Gemeinnützige Kranken-Transport G.m.b.H.), known for short as Gekrat, served as the front for the T4 Transport Office and was headed by Reinhold Vorberg. It transported the patients to the killing centers. It handled the transport lists, ran the notorious gray buses, collected the fees, and notified institutions, other agencies, and sometimes relatives. It used the Potsdamer Platz 1 address.[81] Gekrat was the only T4 front that was incorporated, and it was registered as such in Berlin-Charlottenburg.[82]

The Central Accounting Office for State Hospitals and Nursing Homes (Zentralverrechnungsstelle Heil- und Pflegeanstalten) corresponded with relatives and others paying for the care of patients. Often T4 continued to collect per diem payments for patients who had already been killed. In this way, the T4 organization collected additional money to finance its operation. Dietrich Allers headed the Central Accounting Office, and Hans-Joachim Becker

TABLE 4.3. The T4 Fronts (*Tarnorganisationen*)

Organization	Chief	Function
Reich Cooperative for State Hospitals and Nursing Homes (Reichsarbeitsgemeinschaft Heil- und Pflegeanstalten, or RAG)	Dr. Gerhard Bohne Summer 1940: Dr. Werner Heyde Dec. 1941: Dr. Paul Nitsche	Correspondence with institutions about the registration and transfer of patients
Charitable Foundation for Institutional Care (Gemeinnützige Stiftung für Anstaltspflege, or Stiftung)	Dr. Gerhard Bohne Summer 1940: Dietrich Allers	Correspondence with and about T4 personnel; legal entity empowered to sign all contracts
Charitable Foundation for the Transport of Patients, Inc. (Gemeinnützige Kranken-Transport, G.m.b.H, or Gekrat)	Reinhold Vorberg	Subcontractor for the physical movement of patients to killing centers
Central Accounting Office for State Hospitals and Nursing Homes (Zentralverrechnungsstelle Heil- und Pflegeanstalten)	Dietrich Allers Hans-Joachim Becker	Collection of payments for patients already killed
Reich Committee for the Scientific Registration of Severe Hereditary Ailments (Reichsausschuß zur wissenschaftlichen Erfassung von erb- und anlagebedingten schweren Leiden)	Hans Hefelmann Richard von Hegener	Responsible for children's euthanasia

Source: GStA Frankfurt, Anklage Reinhold Vorberg und Dietrich Allers, Js 20/61 (GStA), 15 Feb. 1966, pp. 47–51.

served as his deputy.[83] Born in 1909, Becker was trained in business. After several years of doing office work at a local factory, he found employment with the finance office of local government. He did not join the Nazi party until 1937.[84] He was hired by T4 through the intervention of his cousin, the wife of Herbert Linden. Becker managed the day-to-day affairs of the Central Accounting Office and later testified that he collected for T4 6 million to 8 million RM per year, in one year even collecting 10 million RM; among his colleagues, he was known as "Million Mark Becker [*Millionen-Becker*]."[85]

The procedures developed for adult euthanasia during the planning sessions resembled those established earlier for children's euthanasia: data about patients was to be collected through registration forms, patients were to be evaluated and their fate determined by medical experts, and patients were to be transferred to special institutions to be killed.[86]

The process that would lead to the killing of adult patients started with a decree circulated by the RMdI on 21 September 1939, just one month and three days after another RMdI decree had initiated the killing of children. This September decree, signed by Leonardo Conti and circulated by the RMdI to all government administrations in the federal states and Prussian provinces, was entitled "The Registration of State Hospitals and Nursing Homes [Erfassung der Heil- und Pflegeanstalten]."[87]

The RMdI requested that local governments provide by 15 October 1939 a complete listing of all institutions in their geographic area holding "mental patients, epileptics, and the feebleminded." The listing was to include public, charitable, religious, and private institutions, and it was to specify the institution's name, address, affiliation, and patient capacity. Pointing out that state hospitals were not the only institutions holding such patients, the RMdI required that all institutions with such patients, for example, old-age homes and sanatoriums, must be listed. However, places that accommodated these patients only for short periods for observation and diagnosis, such as university clinics, did not have to be included. Finally, the RMdI informed local governments that this information was needed because it was preparing questionnaires for these institutions; the ministry planned to deal with the institutions directly but would require support from local governments if questionnaires were not returned on time.

The lists of institutions arrived at the RMdI in the middle of October. For example, the government of the city-state of Hamburg mailed its response on 14 October.[88] It listed ten institutions with a total capacity of 6,329 patients.[89]

After the RMdI received the replies from local governments, Linden's department usually approached the individual institutions directly, but sometimes via local governments, asking them to comply with the requirements of "registering state hospitals for economic planning [planwirtschaftliche Erfassung]."[90] But since all institutions could not be reviewed at one time, questionnaires were mailed to groups of institutions at different times. Thus those in Württemberg apparently received questionnaires in October 1939, while others, for example, those in Bonn and Hamburg, were sent questionnaires much later.[91]

Each institution received a one-page questionnaire, known as Meldebogen 2, requesting specific information about the institution itself: size of property and number of buildings, number of staff, number of patients, number of patients committed for criminal offenses, number of Jewish patients, and exact location with distance to transportation networks.[92] This questionnaire was designed to help T4 decide how to utilize the institution concerned in the killing operation; from it, the T4 managers could learn the number of patients involved, the legal status of the patient population, and the difficulties transportation might pose.

Each institution also received a supply of one-page registration forms, known as Meldebogen 1; each form was designed to provide specific information on one patient. It had to be completed by a physician and asked for the following information: name, date of birth, citizenship, race, length of time in institution, names of nearest relatives and whether they visited on a regular basis, name and address of guardian and of those responsible for payments, and whether the patient was committed as criminally insane. Further, a very small space was provided for diagnosis and an equally small space for the type of work the patient could and did do.[93]

After a period of practical experience with these registration forms, the ministry issued a slightly revised one-page form. Added questions concerned the marital status and religion of the patient, original date of illness, whether the patient was previously in other institutions, whether the patient was a twin, and whether any blood relatives were insane. Further, the revised form asked for more detailed information about diagnosis, symptoms, and therapy; it also demanded more information about the kind of work the patient did and whether discharge from the institution was imminent.[94]

The registration forms for patients were accompanied by a one-page instruction sheet (Merkblatt) specifying who had to be reported:

1. patients institutionalized for five or more years;
2. patients with the following conditions if they were also unable to do work in the institution or could do only routine labor:
   a. schizophrenia;
   b. epilepsy;
   c. senile diseases;
   d. therapy-resistant (progressive) paralysis and other forms of syphilis;
   e. encephalitis;
   f. Huntington's disease and other terminal neurological diseases;
   g. every type of feeblemindedness;
3. patients committed as criminally insane;
4. patients without German citizenship; and
5. patients not of "Germanic or related blood."

For patients falling under categories 4 and 5 of the instructions, that is, foreigners and "non-Aryans," the physicians had to provide information about citizenship and race. A footnote explained the racial categories that should be listed: "Jew, Jewish hybrid [*Mischling*] of the first or second degree, Negro, Negro hybrid, Gypsy, Gypsy hybrid, etc."[95]

THE ORIGINS OF NAZI GENOCIDE

A supplementary page of instructions was later added. It requested that diagnosis be as specific as possible and asked for information about the trauma that had caused the condition, giving as examples wounds suffered in battle and accidents occurring at work. It also urged physicians to be specific about the kind of work patients were able to do.[96]

The questions had a purpose. The institution's size and its proximity to transportation determined the logistics of moving patients to the killing centers, and the amount and type of work patients could do influenced the decision on inclusion in the killing operation. At least in the beginning, however, the physicians completing the forms did not know the purpose of the questions. Often they assumed that patients able to do work might be removed from the institution and sent elsewhere to perform war-related labor, and to retain them, they listed their good workers as unable to work.[97] But most important, the space provided on the forms for diagnosis and prognosis was totally insufficient; without actual medical histories, such short statements were misleading and certainly useless for making careful decisions about the life and death of patients.[98]

As in children's euthanasia, the completed forms were submitted to so-called medical experts (*Gutachter*) for evaluation. But whereas only three specialists decided the fate of the children, the far larger number of adult patients required a much larger group of experts. In fact, the T4 Medical Office, known to the institutions as the RAG, constructed two layers of experts. The forms were first submitted to junior medical experts (*Untergutachter*) and then reviewed by senior medical experts (*Obergutachter*).[99]

The junior experts were recruited through a network of personal contacts and recommendations.[100] Of course, the KdF did not simply accept any name offered. The physician recommended had to be known as dependable, and when not enough information was available, the KdF requested confidential information from local Nazi party offices concerning the ideological reliability of the physician.[101] Apparently this system worked well. Very few physicians who were recommended and who received a positive evaluation from a local Nazi party office refused in the end to participate in the killing of handicapped patients.[102]

Selected physicians were usually invited as a group to a meeting in Berlin at which senior officials of T4, both bureaucrats and physicians, informed them about the proposed killing operation.[103] They were then given the option to refuse participation; no one was forced to remain. But after they agreed to participate, stringent requirements for secrecy were imposed. After the war, participants differed about procedural details. Some remembered taking specific individual secrecy oaths; others remembered merely shaking hands as a group. Some said they had received written appointments as experts; others claimed never to have received anything in writing.[104]

To gain respectability, T4 tried in August 1940 to recruit established professors and institutional directors as experts. They were invited to Berlin to meet with Heyde and Nitsche as well as senior KdF functionaries.[105] Almost all those invited agreed to serve as experts; only two institutional directors quietly left the meeting and thereafter declined to cooperate.[106] In addition, Gottfried Ewald, who occupied the chair in psychiatry at Göttingen and headed Göttingen University Clinic as well as the local state hospital, told the meeting that he would not participate.[107] Ewald's sympathies during the 1920s had been right wing and *völkisch*, and he had been a member of one of the radical Free Corps organizations and the SA reserve but never the Nazi party. Party evaluations of Ewald were always positive, despite the fact that his attempt to join the Nazi party in 1938 was rejected without prejudice on formal grounds.[108] While Ewald accepted killings in the event that the nation faced "extreme conditions" (for example, failing food supplies during war) or if the state could point to a "compelling interest" (as with sterilization of the unfit), he rejected the 1940 killings for pragmatic reasons; he thought them unnecessary and potentially divisive. He explained his position in writing to several senior officials, including his former student Leonardo Conti, who answered that he recognized the validity of some of Ewald's arguments but was nevertheless of a different opinion.[109] Ewald did not serve as expert; on the other hand, he did not prevent the evacuation of his own handicapped patients.[110]

At his postwar trial, Friedrich Mennecke described one of the T4 recruitment sessions for experts. His particular group session took place at the Columbus House in February 1940 and was attended by about eight to ten physicians. Brack explained the proposed euthanasia operation and, presenting Hitler's authorization as an official law, assured the physicians that the killing of "life unworthy of life" was perfectly legal. He further explained the methods of evaluation through registration forms, and he urged the physicians to evaluate patients in such a way that more rather than fewer patients would be selected for killing. Finally, Brack asked those attending whether they would be willing to serve as junior medical experts. All agreed.[111] Mennecke described his decision to participate: "The remainder of the physicians who were assembled there besides me were all elderly gentlemen. Among them were some big personalities, as I was to discover later. Since these gentlemen also gave their consent unconditionally, I also favored this position, and I volunteered as a consultant." [112]

Two surviving lists of men who served as T4 medical experts at various times show about forty physicians, including nine university professors of medicine.[113] All but two of these were junior experts, who made life-and-death decisions in the first round of evaluation. In the second round, senior medical experts were to review their decisions.[114] Their review supposedly guaranteed that the medical evaluation was correct.[115] It not only served as a

THE ORIGINS OF NAZI GENOCIDE

cover to make the process seem scientific but also assured young physicians that their inexperience would not lead to incorrect evaluations. Mennecke later described the attitudes of these junior physicians: "I saw at least an extensive safety vent. I know that a university professor is not infallible and even in the medical field, but in general these gentlemen have great experience and one can have a certain amount of confidence in their work. To that extent the activity of the top experts over us as experts gave me certain inner confidence that in the case of an unconscious mistake on my part, the top expert would still be able to correct it." [116] In fact, this was not true. Apparently, only three physicians served as senior medical experts: Heyde, Nitsche, and Linden.[117] Obviously, these men, who were busy directing their offices, could not carefully review the work of numerous junior experts.

Psychiatrists directed the killing of adult patients. However, among the physicians serving T4 at the central office, at the killing centers and wards, and as medical experts, there were a number of younger physicians who had not even received their certification in psychiatry at the time they first participated in the killings.[118]

It must also be noted that the field of psychiatry in Germany at that time was not the same as psychiatry in the United States today. Most German psychiatrists rejected the work of Sigmund Freud and the discipline of psychoanalysis. Moreover, even non-Freudian psychotherapy, which included physicians among its professionals and which did survive in Nazi Germany, had not established itself in the university medical faculties, the public health bureaucracy, and mental institutions. Psychotherapists were not appointed as university professors of medicine, heads of research centers, chiefs of the public health service, and directors of state hospitals.[119]

Psychiatry was controlled by physicians trained to view the causes and cures of mental disorders solely from a biological and chemical perspective. Certified in one or both of the two interacting fields of psychiatry and neurology, these medical practitioners feared the interference of psychotherapists, viewing psychotherapy as a field without scientific and ideological merit. One leading professor of psychiatry involved in the killing operations of T4 exemplified this hostile attitude: "Furthermore, modern psychotherapy continues to be penetrated, even after the revolution [*Umbruch*], by Jewish patterns of thought through the influence of Freud and Adler. Psychotherapy is substantially individualistic and its psycho-babble [*Psychagogik*] is definitely not based on biology." [120] While physicians practicing psychotherapy were denounced as potential competitors, psychologists without medical training were rejected with contempt. An attempt to admit them into courses in psychiatry was rejected because of the likelihood that professors of psychiatry "would refuse to present cases to psychologists, who are not physicians, or to test psychologists in medicine." [121]

The impressive medical edifice constructed by T4 to safeguard against unprofessional evaluations was a facade. In fact, these evaluations, which determined whether a patient would be killed and which were supposedly based only on medical criteria, were made by these medical experts in a hasty and unprofessional manner. We have already seen that senior experts did not have time to review all cases and that decisions over life and death were in practice left to the junior experts. These experts examined neither the patients nor their medical records; they made their fateful decisions entirely on the basis of the skimpy details on the registration forms.[122] Furthermore, the junior experts did not even analyze the meager information provided by the reporting forms.

For example, Hermann Pfannmüller, who did his evaluations in the spare time left to him after performing his duties as director of the large Eglfing-Haar state hospital, processed the forms with unbelievable speed. He regularly received stacks of reporting forms—usually 200 to 300 at a time—from the RAG and shortly thereafter returned them to Berlin with his evaluations. At Nuremberg, the American prosecutor confronted Pfannmüller with evidence that he evaluated 2,058 patients between 12 November and 1 December 1940, which meant that he made 121 decisions a day about the life and death of patients or one decision every five minutes in a ten-hour day. Pfannmüller, who described himself as "a medical expert just as any medical expert appearing in a case before a court," could only reply that "here I am a doctor confronted with a lawyer and our points of view are completely divergent."[123] And Pfannmüller was not the only expert who rapidly evaluated thousands of patients.[124]

Like Pfannmüller, most experts did not see themselves as killers. They looked upon their participation in the killing process as a normal medical practice, as the supervision of a new type of therapy. Mennecke no doubt spoke for them all when he stated: "It was not my duty to shorten the lives of the insane persons, it was my duty to act as a medical expert."[125]

The criteria used to select patients for killing were equally arbitrary. As we have seen, institutions had to report *all* patients who had been institutionalized for five or more years. In addition, even patients institutionalized for less than five years had to be reported if they had been committed by the courts, did not belong to the so-called Aryan race, or suffered from any of a number of listed diseases. Therefore all but the most transient patients were reported, providing the T4 physicians with a very large pool of potential victims.

Although it was—and still is—popular to describe these patients as suffering from mental disorders, many among them were not mental patients. As with the children, the pool of adult patients included many suffering from physical disabilities; the criteria for inclusion in the pool were virtually the same as those imposed earlier for eugenic reasons in sterilization. The basic motive for the euthanasia killings was the same as the motive for sterilization: "the eugenic call for a rejuvenation of the race." [126] Thus the victims included, for example, the blind, the deaf and mute, the epileptic, and the feebleminded, who could hardly be considered mental patients. [127] Further, the killers always rationalized that these patients were like animals who neither recognized nor cared for their environment; in fact, however, the majority of patients killed were "orderly and conscious" and were "worthy persons." [128]

In addition, one important criterion for inclusion was not medical; it was utilitarian and based on a patient's level of productivity. [129] The patients, denounced as "life unworthy of life [*lebensunwertes Leben*]," were considered "burdensome lives [*Ballastexistenzen*]" and "useless eaters [*unnütze Esser*]." Patients were thus judged not only by their medical condition but also by their ability to work. Postponing the "selection" of productive patients, the T4 medical experts applied a criterion later copied by SS physicians "selecting" at the Auschwitz railroad siding, and did so in an equally haphazard manner.

Two brief documents showing the criteria used in selecting victims have survived. They summarized decisions made in 1941 by Bouhler and Brandt, the two plenipotentiaries for euthanasia. These decisions also probably involved Hitler because they were based in part on discussions at his retreat in Berchtesgaden. [130]

The plenipotentiaries were not called upon to make decisions involving mental patients, no doubt because questions concerning these patients were not controversial and had already been settled. [131] The determination whether to kill senile patients, however, required further definition. Excluding "patients with psychoses who have grown old" because they would be killed without question, the plenipotentiaries urged the experts to use "a great deal of discretion" in their evaluations of cases involving senile patients. This ruling of 1941 shows that persons institutionalized as senile had already been included in the killing operation, but killing them was still considered somewhat controversial. [132] In the future, such cases were decided by political and not medical authorities. The plenipotentiaries decreed that in cases involving senile patients, "Jennerwein," that is, Brack, would decide. Viktor Brack, the party hack, was thus empowered to make decisions supposedly reserved for the medical experts, although after the war, when asked why patients who were not terminal were included in the euthanasia program, Brack replied: "Well, I really cannot judge that. Please ask a physician." [133]

The status of veterans was another controversial issue confronting the plenipotentiaries. Fearful that killing veterans might weaken the fighting spirit of the troops if rumors spread that wounded soldiers would be killed, the plenipotentiaries exempted veterans of World War I. But unwilling to exclude too many, they imposed restrictions: only veterans who had received medals, had been wounded, or had performed with special valor at the front were to be excluded from the killings.[134] In fact, this policy was not consistently enforced; some veterans were exempted at the last moment inside the killing centers, while others, even those with medals, were transferred and killed.[135]

The most important criterion for deciding whether patients should be killed was economic. As we have seen, the guidelines from the beginning included as potential victims all patients unable to work or those able to do only routine work. Because judgments about whether work was "routine" could differ (the T4 managers applied a far more stringent standard than did most state hospitals),[136] the plenipotentiaries in their guidelines redefined routine work in purely utilitarian terms as "nonproductive" work, thus exempting from the killing operation only those patients considered to have economic value. This motive was only thinly disguised when Brandt later argued that the criterion of work had medical relevance because if patients could work they were not very sick.[137]

These utilitarian guidelines dominated the medical evaluations from the beginning. They appeared in the instructions to the registration forms, and they were also stressed during the orientation sessions for medical experts.[138] In addition, local public health offices fully collaborated with this utilitarian approach; they divided their institutionalized patients, for purposes of reporting, into three groups:

1. incurable but still able to work (meaning *productive* work);
2. able to do work as part of treatment; and
3. incurable and no longer able to do work.[139]

Such considerations also certainly influenced the diagnostic findings of the medical experts. Asked whether pragmatic concerns determined the fate of patients who were considered "useless eaters," one of these experts later explained: "Yes; that was pointed out too. It was pointed out that, during the war, in numerous cases, healthy people had to give up their lives and these severely ill people continued to live and would continue to live unless this action started, and that, in addition, the nursing situation and the nourishment situation would justify the elimination of these people."[140]

The true criteria were clearly revealed when the T4 physicians visited local institutions to supervise the selection of patients on the spot. They visited institutions that had failed to complete and submit registration forms for their patients and that needed additional personnel to speed the processing; they also personally selected victims when they believed that an institution had falsified the forms by listing too many patients as "good workers." When the

THE ORIGINS OF NAZI GENOCIDE

T4 physicians, either singly or as members of a panel, reviewed a local institution's reporting of patients, their criteria for selection were extremely harsh. They selected large numbers of patients, and their overriding criterion was the ability to do productive work.[141]

The procedures used to process the registration forms and complete the selections were relatively simple. The completed registration forms were returned by the local institutions to the RMdI, and Linden transmitted them to the headquarters of T4. There they were sorted and cataloged by the registrar attached to the T4 Medical Office, known to outsiders as the RAG. Stacks of photocopied forms were then sent to the junior medical experts, who recorded their votes with a plus sign "+" in red for death or a minus sign "–" in blue for life, and sometimes a question mark indicating borderline cases.[142] Each form was reviewed by three junior experts, but unanimity was not required; the vote of one expert in favor of life would not save the patient from inclusion in the killing operation.[143] After the junior experts had returned the forms, they were submitted to one of the three senior experts. The senior expert, who was not bound by the consensus of the junior experts, briefly reviewed the form. The plus or minus sign recorded by the senior experts represented the final decision concerning the life or death of handicapped patients.[144]

Once the patients had been selected, T4 activated the mechanism that would kill them; no patients would henceforth be permitted to escape, and institutions were required to report all deaths and all transfers to the RAG.[145] The names of the selected patients were sent to the T4 Transport Office, which then compiled transport lists.[146] This office—through its front organization, known as Gekrat—managed the necessary logistics. Schedules had to be arranged to assure that the killing centers would have neither too many nor too few victims at any one time; only a consistent and constant flow of patients could guarantee a cost- and labor-effective killing operation. Gekrat therefore insisted that institutions have the correct number of patients ready for transfer at the expected time.

The institutions holding the selected patients, known in the language of T4 as the "surrendering institution [*Abgabeanstalt*]," received notification a few days before the transfer. This notification originated with the RAG but was officially transmitted by Linden's department in the RMdI to the interior ministries in the federal states or comparable authorities in the Prussian provinces. The local authorities then notified the institutions that on a particular date Gekrat would pick up a certain number of patients.[147] At the same time, the institutions were told how they were to prepare the patients for transfer. All personnel reports and medical records had to accompany the patients; their personal belongings, money, and valuables must be ready and must be recorded on specially provided forms. Patients were to have pieces of tape with their names attached to their backs between the shoulder blades; sedatives were to be administered to disturbed patients.[148]

Gekrat transported the handicapped patients. Shortly before pickup, it sent the transport list to the surrendering institution, and about a day before pickup, the Gekrat functionary in charge of the transport, the Transportleiter, arrived to discuss arrangements.[149] The transport lists supposedly represented the end result of a careful system of medical selections, but directors of institutions, who discovered the names of those selected only when they received the lists, often found that patients with good records as workers, who were thus needed by their institutions, had been included. At that point, they negotiated with the Gekrat functionaries and were sometimes able to have these desirable patients struck from the lists. However, the numbers had to be correct, so other patients, in violation of the medical evaluation scheme, were substituted, revealing that the true object of the killings was the reduction of the number of institutionalized handicapped patients.[150] On the designated day, Gekrat arrived to move the patients in large gray buses; the surrendering institution was given a receipt from Gekrat for the patients handed over for transfer.[151] The patients, who usually suspected their fate, often had to be coerced before they entered the notorious vehicles.[152]

The handicapped patients were killed without the agreement of the patients themselves. They were also transferred and killed without permission from those responsible for them: their relatives and legal guardians. Likewise, the killers did not inform the judicial offices that may have committed them or the *Kostenträger*, that is, the welfare or insurance agencies paying for their care.

Obviously, the patients themselves were never asked if they wished to die. Although most patients killed in this euthanasia program were fully able to know and object to their fate, the killers argued "that the insane person himself is in no position to judge his situation." [153]

The killings labeled by the government and the collaborating health professionals as euthanasia affected not only the patients but also their relatives and guardians. Since the killings were to be kept secret, the transfers to the killing centers had to take place without the approval and knowledge of relatives and guardians. They were disguised as relocation due to the war emergency; even the surrendering institutions did not at first know the purpose of these transfers. Relatives were informed only after the fact. The killers believed themselves justified in their failure to consult relatives, revealing at the same time much of their true motives: "In the case of the insane the consent of the relatives was not obtained. . . . First of all, the question of secrecy was important. But more important from the medical point of view was the fact that the layman is not able to judge the condition of his sick relative. . . .

THE ORIGINS OF NAZI GENOCIDE

He can be deceived by uncritical pity.... Another decisive point was that one cannot expect a relative to decide about the life or death of someone else. It was the opinion that the doctor, with the support of the state, has to take the responsibility."[154]

This is how the deception worked. At the time of notification about the forthcoming transfer, the surrendering institutions were ordered not to inform relatives or guardians prior to the transfer; further, they were not permitted to notify the agencies paying for the patients' care about the forthcoming relocation.[155] Only after the transfer — actually only after the patients had been killed — did the paperwork begin.

First, the surrendering institution sent a form letter notifying the relatives that on the orders of the Reich defense commissar the patient had been transferred to another institution by Gekrat and that the receiving institution would contact them in due time. It also asked relatives to wait for notification and not to inquire further.[156] Shortly thereafter, the killing center, masquerading as the receiving institution, informed relatives that the patient had arrived. But it also notified the relatives that visits were prohibited at that time, promising to inform them if there was any change in the patient's condition and requesting that they abstain from further inquiries.[157] Thereafter, relatives were notified that the patient had died, that due to the danger of epidemics the body had already been cremated, and that the urn with the patient's ashes could be obtained.[158]

As we shall see, in August 1941 Hitler issued his "stop" order to Brandt, who transmitted it to Bouhler, thus ending the first phase of the adult killings.[159] The number of victims of this first phase has been calculated as at least 70,000 human beings.[160]

Chapter 5 The Killing Centers

The T4 physicians used medication to kill handicapped children, but to kill the far larger number of handicapped adults, they had to devise a different method. For those patients, the T4 technicians established killing centers, thus creating the unprecedented institution that would symbolize Nazi Germany and the early twentieth century.[1]

At Nuremberg, Karl Brandt described to his interrogator how the killers decided on this method for murder. At first, the physicians wanted to use injections of narcotics (in Brandt's words "Barbitur-Acid"), but this method would be too cumbersome; death would take time and was thus not considered "humane." Other physicians suggested the use of the gas carbon monoxide (in Brandt's words "coal-oxide"). Brandt claimed that he opposed this suggestion at first but changed his mind when he remembered that he had once passed out "painlessly" after inhaling fumes from a malfunctioning stove.[2] Such recollections of a personal experience with gas, through a malfunctioning stove or a running automobile engine, were later mentioned by a number of persons involved with the development, at that time or later, of the killing method using gas.[3] In addition, this method was generally known because the police were familiar with cases of suicide or accidental death through the inhalation of gas; for example, in Berlin such a case had been investigated in depth just before euthanasia gassing commenced.[4]

Brandt discussed the various killing methods with the Führer, and when Hitler supposedly asked him "which is the more humane way," Brandt recommended the use of gas. Thereupon they agreed on this agent for the mass killings.[5] After giving this account, Karl Brandt proudly told his American interrogator: "This is just one case where in medical history major jumps are being made."[6] This bizarre comment was not an isolated statement but only an extreme example of the fascination with technology exhibited by the managers of killing operations. Thus, when the engineer Walter Heess, who headed the KTI, was asked how one could justify using gas to kill human beings, he replied: "What are you talking about; after all, it works."[7]

Although they did not disagree about the outcome, participants remembered the scenario leading to the final decision differently. Albert Widmann, the KTI chemist, told investigators after the war that Leonardo Conti in the RMdI vetoed the use of injections and suggested the use of gas. Widmann thereafter discussed the technical details with Viktor Brack, and they tried to determine the best way to administer the gas. Widmann claimed that he

86

suggested releasing gas into the hospital dormitories while the patients slept.[8] But such a method was not practical; therefore, the idea of bringing the gas to the patients was abandoned in favor of bringing the patients to the gas.

The technology for gassing people had to be invented. Here theory was not enough; a demonstration was needed to confirm the feasibility of the operation, test methods, and teach techniques. The managers of T4 chose Brandenburg on the Havel as the site for the testing, probably because it was a short train ride from Berlin. The old jail building at number 90-C on Neuendorfer Straße in the city of Brandenburg, empty since 1932, when the jail was moved to a new penitentiary in Brandenburg-Görden, served as the first killing center.[9] Workmen borrowed from the SS central construction office built the necessary facilities, including a gas chamber. "The gas chamber was constructed to resemble showers. Three by five meters large [about 10 by 17 feet] and 3 meters high [about 10 feet], it was paneled with ceramic tiles. Benches for the patients lined the walls. About 10 centimeters [about 4 inches] above the floor, a pipe with a circumference of about one inch ran along the wall; in this pipe there were small holes through which the gas could enter the chamber. ... The door to the chamber was constructed like a metal air raid shelter door, with a rectangular window for viewing."[10] Once finished, this Brandenburg gas chamber served as the setting for the two day–long gassing demonstration. The date is not certain; witnesses after the war could not remember the exact date. However, all agreed that it was winter, either December 1939 or January 1940.[11]

We cannot be absolutely certain who attended the gassing demonstration at Brandenburg in the winter of 1939–40, but we do have testimony that the following persons were present. Hitler's two plenipotentiaries for euthanasia, Karl Brandt and Philipp Bouhler, and Leonardo Conti, the state secretary for health in the RMdI, were the highest-ranking functionaries attending. Also in attendance were Herbert Linden from the RMdI and the KdF bureaucrats responsible for the implementation of euthanasia: Viktor Brack, Werner Blankenburg, Hans Hefelmann, Reinhold Vorberg, Richard von Hegener, and Gerhard Bohne. Further, the T4 physicians Werner Heyde, Paul Nitsche, Irmfried Eberl, Horst Schumann, and Ernst Baumhard participated in the demonstration, as well as the KTI chemists Albert Widmann and August Becker. Finally, the Stuttgart police officer Christian Wirth, who, as we shall see, was to play an important role in Nazi killing operations, was also present during this first demonstration of systematic mass murder.[12]

A number of handicapped patients had been collected to serve as experimental subjects; where they were transferred from is unknown. Several were selected for killing with injections, a method tested by Paul Nitsche at Leipzig-Dösen early in 1940.[13] Their killing was to serve as a comparison to illustrate the efficiency of gassing; a few days earlier, Karl Brandt had traveled to Brandenburg to discuss with persons already assembled there the respective virtues of the two killing methods.[14]

The two senior physicians attending the Brandenburg experiment, Brandt and Conti, administered the deadly injections, thus proving for all present that even senior officials were prepared to involve themselves in this killing operation; in the same way, high SS officers would later prove their solidarity with the SS rank and file by performing or supervising killings in the East. The method of killing by injection proved slow and unreliable, and the victims were later also gassed.

Thereafter, eight patients, all men, were selected for the gassing demonstration. They undressed and entered the chamber, supposedly suspecting nothing. The gas was stored in a small room next to the chamber and was administered by the chemist Widmann, who also instructed the physicians Eberl and Baumhard as well as fellow chemist Becker on how to measure the strength and duration for the best results. The assembled dignitaries watched the procedure and the deaths through the viewing window.[15]

The T4 managers of mass murder eventually established six killing centers. (See table 5.1.) Two were replacement institutions for the first two when they were phased out, however, so only four operated at any one time. Brandenburg and Grafeneck were the first to be established; both opened at approximately the same time, first Brandenburg, then Grafeneck, in about January 1940. As we shall see, they were shut down for a number of reasons; Brandenburg closed in September and Grafeneck in December 1940. In the spring and early summer of 1940, two further killing centers were opened to handle the growing number of victims: Hartheim in May and Sonnenstein in June. In September 1940, Bernburg replaced Brandenburg, and in December, Hadamar replaced Grafeneck.[16] Each killing center was assigned a code that was to be used in all phone conversations and written communications with the T4 central offices: "A" was assigned to Grafeneck, "B" to Brandenburg, "C" to Hartheim, "D" to Sonnenstein, "Be" to Bernburg, and "E" to Hadamar.[17] Although there were differences between the various killing centers, the killing process was the same in all of them, and the facilities were therefore roughly similar. Viktor Brack described at Nuremberg the simple design of the actual gas chambers in all killing centers: "No special gas chambers were built. A room suitable in the planning of the hospital was used, a room attached to the reception ward. . . . That was made into a gas chamber. It was sealed, it was given special doors and windows, and then a few meters of gas pipe was laid, some kind of pipe with holes in it. Outside of this room there was a bottle, a compressed bottle, with the necessary apparatus, necessary instruments, a pressure gauge, etc."[18]

The old prison in Brandenburg on the Havel was history's first operational killing center.[19] The Brandenburg facility was probably chosen by T4 for its

THE ORIGINS OF NAZI GENOCIDE

TABLE 5.1. The Euthanasia Killing Centers

Center (code letter)	Dates	Physician
Grafeneck in Württemberg (A)	Jan. to Dec. 1940	Dr. Horst Schumann Dr. Ernst Baumhard Dr. Günther Hennecke
Brandenburg on the Havel near Berlin (B)	Winter 1939–40 to Sept. 1940	Dr. Irmfried Eberl Dr. Heinrich Bunke Dr. Aquilin Ullrich
Hartheim near Linz (C)	May 1940 to Dec. 1944	Dr. Rudolf Lonauer Dr. Georg Renno
Sonnenstein in Pirna in Saxony (D)	June 1940 to 1943	Dr. Horst Schumann Dr. Kurt Borm Dr. Klaus Endruweit Dr. Kurt Schmalenbach Dr. Ewald Worthmann
Bernburg on the Saale in the Prussian province of Saxony (Be)	Sept. 1940 to 1943	Dr. Irmfried Eberl Dr. Heinrich Bunke Dr. Kurt Borm
Hadamar in Hessen (E)	Dec. 1940 to Aug. 1941[a]	Dr. Ernst Baumhard Dr. Günther Hennecke Dr. Friedrich Berner Dr. Hans-Bodo Gorgaß

Sources: ZStL, Heidelberg Docs. 127,890–93; GStA Frankfurt, Anklage Reinhold Vorberg und Dietrich Allers, Js 20/61 (GStA), 15 Feb. 1966, pp. 55–58; GStA Frankfurt, Anklage Werner Heyde, Gerhard Bohne und Hans Hefelmann, Ks 2/63 (GStA), Js 17/59 (GStA), 22 May 1962, pp. 261–87; AMM, B/15/8, 13; Ernst Klee, ed., *Dokumente zur "Euthanasie"* (Frankfurt: Fischer Taschenbuch Verlag, 1985), pp. 17–26.

[a] After gassing ended, served as institution of "wild" euthanasia.

convenient location.[20] Its first director was Adolf Gustav Kaufmann, chief of the T4 Inspector's Office, who supervised the work needed to transform the prison into a killing center. As soon as remodeling was finished, Kaufmann turned over the installation to Irmfried Eberl, the physician-in-charge.[21]

The actual killing facility was located on the ground floor; a number of rooms were used for receiving and collecting the arriving patients, undressing them, and presenting them to the physicians. The gas chamber and the crematorium were on the same floor. The Brandenburg gas chamber was disguised as a shower room, but at first no showerheads were installed and patients were therefore told that they were entering an "inhalation room" for therapeutic reasons. Only later were showerheads added. A small adjacent room served as storage for the carbon monoxide tanks, and from there, the physicians could

operate the valve that allowed the gas to enter the chamber.[22] The crematorium was located next to the gas chamber and consisted of two mobile ovens
attached to the chimney of the building and heated with oil. But the chimney
was too low for this task, and flames often escaped from the top. In addition,
an unpleasant smell of burning flesh engulfed the city. In about July 1940, the
crematorium was moved due to these problems. The mobile ovens were set up
in an isolated house surrounded by a high wooden fence and located about
three miles from town, and the corpses were driven there in a post office van at
night.[23] Attached to the building housing the killing facilities was the former
jail, three floors high, which was remodeled for offices and staff quarters.[24]

The Brandenburg killing center used the name Brandenburg State Hospital
and Nursing Home (Heil- und Pflegeanstalt Brandenburg), although it had
never been a health care institution. All other killing centers also used this
designation, but unlike Brandenburg, they had all previously been hospitals.
For example, Grafeneck, which opened shortly after Brandenburg as the second killing center, had previously been a hospital for the handicapped. Early
in October 1939, Linden visited Eugen Stähle, the official in the Württemberg
Ministry of Interior responsible for health care, and asked his cooperation in
finding a relatively small institution "to implement euthanasia"; Stähle offered
Grafeneck.[25] Thereafter, Linden and Brack inspected Grafeneck and, finding
it acceptable, decided to confiscate it.[26] On 12 October, Stähle informed the
county administrator (Landrat) of the Münsingen district, where Grafeneck
was located, that the institution would have to be evacuated within two days.[27]
On 12 December, the new institution at Grafeneck was granted the right to
have its own registry for vital statistics, removing it from the supervision
of the registry to which it had previously belonged. It could now officially
record births, deaths, and changes of residence without outside interference;
the right to record marriages, however, not a job deemed necessary for its
mission, was withheld.[28] Brack and an advance team arrived in Grafeneck
on 17 October, but the entire staff, including the physician-in-charge, Horst
Schumann (later succeeded by Ernst Baumhard), did not assemble at the killing center until the middle of January 1940, when the necessary remodeling
had been completed; shortly thereafter, Grafeneck received its first victims.[29]

The Grafeneck hospital for the handicapped, a Württemberg institution
owned and operated prior to its seizure by a Protestant nursing order, the
Samaritan Foundation, was housed in a castle sufficiently isolated to make it
an ideal killing center. The offices and the quarters for the personnel were
located in the main building. The actual killing facilities were situated about
1,000 feet behind the castle. There a wooden barrack served as the reception
center for arriving patients. Next to it, an old coach house was converted
to accommodate the gas chamber; it was disguised as a shower room with
showerheads and wooden benches. At first, the chamber had the capacity to

THE ORIGINS OF NAZI GENOCIDE

gas forty to fifty persons at one time; later it was enlarged to hold seventy-five persons. A small room adjacent to the chamber contained, as in Brandenburg, the valves to activate the gassing process. Further, a small window permitted the physician to observe the chamber while he turned the valve. The crematorium nearby contained two mobile ovens, using oil as fuel. Finally, there was a garage for three buses to transport patients. This killing facility at the back of the property was surrounded by a picket fence about ten to twelve feet high, and an additional fifteen-foot-high screen hid the gas chamber and crematorium.[30]

A third killing center was constructed in Austria. There T4 selected Hartheim castle in the village of Alkoven, not far from Linz and close to the Mauthausen concentration camp. Hartheim castle, dating from the ninth century, had served as a mental hospital since the end of the nineteenth century. In 1939, after the incorporation of Austria, the institution was confiscated. Soon thereafter, the remodeling needed to transform Hartheim into a killing center started under the supervision of Kaufmann and lasted through the first four months of 1940. T4 appointed Rudolf Lonauer as physician-in-charge; and in the spring of 1940, Kaufmann, and also Brack, arrived in Linz to hire the staff for the killing center. In May 1940, Hartheim received its first victims.[31]

Offices and staff quarters were located on the upper floors of Hartheim castle, while the killing installation occupied the ground floor, which surrounded an inner courtyard. A high fence at the west gate, through which the buses entered, blocked the view for outsiders, and a fence inside the courtyard hid the crematorium from arriving patients. Various rooms for receiving, examining, and undressing patients lined the courtyard. The gas chamber, located on the east side of the courtyard, was disguised as a shower room and had a capacity of up to 150 persons; as usual, the gassing process was activated from an adjacent room. At least two crematoria, one located in a room on the east side of the courtyard and one in the courtyard itself, were available for burning the corpses. The heavy smoke from the crematoria could be observed at some distance, and the smell of burning flesh pervaded the region; during the night, the staff carted the ashes to the Danube River and dumped them there.[32]

The fourth killing center opened in June 1940 in the Sonnenstein institution, located in the city of Pirna near Dresden. The Sonnenstein state hospital had been headed by the respected longtime director Paul Nitsche, Heyde's successor as medical chief of T4, who left in May 1939 to head the Leipzig-Dösen clinic, where he carried out experimental euthanasia killings with barbiturates.[33] Early in 1940, Kaufmann visited Sonnenstein, a former castle located on a hill, and T4 thereafter confiscated a portion of the institution.[34]

The Sonnenstein killing center differed from most others because it did not occupy the entire hospital, which made total secrecy impossible. A portion of the institution, located behind the main buildings and not included as part of the killing center, had been used earlier to house ethnic German refugees from Bessarabia. Another portion of the institution, also in the rear of the property, was retained as a regular mental hospital after confiscation and assumed the name Mariaheim. The killing center, which appropriated the Sonnenstein name, was thus located only in buildings 1–3 at the front of the property. Building 3 served as a reception area for the arriving victims, and buildings 1–2 provided office space and staff quarters. Building 2 contained the actual killing facility, including the gas chamber and a crematorium with two stationary ovens located in the basement.[35] The physician-in-charge, Horst Schumann, who transferred from Grafeneck, arrived late in April or early in May to supervise the final remodeling, and the killing started in June 1940.[36]

The fifth and sixth killing centers — Bernburg and Hadamar — were designed to replace Brandenburg and Grafeneck. Bernburg replaced Brandenburg in September 1940, and the Brandenburg staff, including physician-in-charge Irmfried Eberl, moved as a group to the new killing center. Located in the city of Bernburg on the Saale River not far from Dessau, the institution had served prior to 1940 as the Bernburg State Hospital and Nursing Home under the direction of Dr. Willi Enke. In the fall of 1940, Kaufmann visited Bernburg, confiscated a portion of the institution for T4, supervised remodeling, and arranged the transfer of staff from Brandenburg. Like Sonnenstein but unlike most other killing centers, the old Bernburg institution continued its operations, sharing property and buildings with the killing center. The old institution evacuated its patients from several buildings, and there T4 constructed the killing center, which assumed the name of the old institution. The old institution, which soon named itself the Anhalt Psychiatric Clinic in Bernburg, was called "Department Dr. Enke" by the staff, while the killing center was referred to as "Department Dr. Eberl."[37]

Most of the space at the Bernburg killing center accommodated offices and staff quarters. On the ground floor of the building formerly housing male patients, several rooms served to receive arriving patients, while the killing installation was located in the basement of the same building. The gas chamber, about ten by fifteen feet large, was disguised as a shower room and contained the usual pipes with small holes to facilitate the administration of gas from an adjacent room. A mirror installed inside the chamber permitted the physician to view the patients through a window in the door. The crematorium contained two stationary ovens, fueled with coal and attached to an existing chimney. Next to the building, a garage had been constructed for buses to transport patients.[38]

Hadamar replaced Grafeneck in December 1940, thus becoming the sixth and last killing center.[39] Located on a hill, the Mönchsberg, overlooking the town of Hadamar in Hessen, north of Wiesbaden, it was originally a state hospital and nursing home that opened in the nineteenth century. In 1939 the patients were moved and the institution was transformed into a military hospital. In 1940 Kaufmann, together with Fritz Bernotat, the administrator of state hospitals in Hessen-Nassau who strongly supported euthanasia, inspected the site, and thereafter T4 signed a contract with Bernotat to occupy and use the Hadamar hospital. Kaufmann supervised the remodeling and arranged the transfer of the Grafeneck staff, including the physician-in-charge, Ernst Baumhard. Staff and offices occupied several buildings, and one building served as the killing facility. Rooms to receive arriving patients were located on the first floor, and the gas chamber and crematorium were placed in the basement. As usual, the gas chamber was disguised as a shower room, and the gas entered from an adjacent room through pipes with holes. The crematorium had two stationary ovens attached to a chimney. Signs on the road leading to Hadamar warned that the danger of epidemics prohibited entry, but the chimney's smoke and the smell made local inhabitants aware of the nature of the operation.[40]

Each killing center was more or less responsible for killing handicapped patients from institutions in a limited geographic region. The territory assigned to the Brandenburg killing center included the Prussian provinces of Brandenburg, Saxony, and Schleswig-Holstein; the states of Brunswick, Mecklenburg, Anhalt, and Hamburg; and the city of Berlin. Later the replacement center of Bernburg assumed this territory. The Grafeneck killing center covered south Germany, that is, the states of Bavaria, Württemberg, and Baden, as well as some north German institutions. Later the replacement center of Hadamar assumed this territory, in addition to the state of Hessen and the Prussian province of Hanover. The Hartheim killing center was responsible for institutions in Austria but also some institutions in south Germany and Saxony. The Sonnenstein killing center covered the states of Saxony and Thuringia and the Prussian province of Silesia but also some institutions in south Germany.[41]

The creation of the gas chamber was a unique invention of Nazi Germany, but the method developed to lure the victims to the chambers, to kill them on an assembly line, and to process their corpses was an even more important creation. If we were to apply the computer language of today, we would call the gas chambers the "killing hardware" and the method of application the "killing software." Hardware and software together comprised the killing technique, institutionalized in the killing center, that Nazi Germany bequeathed to the world.

From the moment they arrived at the killing center, patients were inexorably moved through a process designed to make their murder smooth and efficient. Contrary to the official arguments advanced by the T4 bureaucracy and the medical establishment that these patients were incapable of perceiving reality, the evidence shows that they were sufficiently aware of their surroundings to exhibit great fear concerning their fate. Thus "wild scenes" took place when patients were collected from their home institutions, and force had to be applied to get them into the notorious Gekrat buses.[42] The Gekrat staff had to restrain patients or administer sedatives to prevent resistance.[43] Once the patients arrived at the killing center, force could be applied and sedatives could be administered, but the preferred method involved the use of guile to trick the patients into cooperating.

The subterfuge developed by the killing center staffs to deceive the patients was the appearance of normality. Every procedure was designed to conceal the function of the killing center and to simulate a normal hospital.[44] Although the order might differ slightly from place to place, the procedures were generally the same at all killing centers. Patients arrived in Gekrat buses, and in Hartheim and Bernburg, they sometimes also arrived by train. Often buses stationed at the killing centers were used to pick up and transport them; in Hadamar local "death buses" collected patients from transfer institutions, and in Hartheim these local buses picked up patients from the railroad station at Linz.[45]

At the killing center, the arriving patients were met by the staff and led to the reception room by a male or female nurse, who might have accompanied them on their trip; clerical workers also often performed this function. At the reception area, the patients were told to undress. Usually a transport was composed of either males or females; if it contained both, however, separate facilities for undressing were provided. The patients' clothing and other belongings were sorted, labeled, and given a number; patients believed that this was done so that all items could eventually be returned to the rightful owner, but obviously it served the purpose of efficient disposal after death. Thereafter, the patients were measured and weighed.[46]

After the reception process, the naked patients were taken one at a time into the examination room, where a physician briefly examined each patient. This was not a regular medical examination, however; the physicians serving in the killing centers did not have the experience, training, or qualifications to make psychiatric evaluations. Together with the office staff present in the examination room, the physician established the identity of the patient on the basis of his or her medical records, and with "relative speed," he "gained a general impression from those people."[47]

After the war, T4 managers, supervisors, and physicians argued that this superficial examination served as the final safeguard against possible errors made during the medical evaluation process. In fact, the young physicians at the killing centers had the authority to reprieve patients only if the records were incomplete or the patient was a foreigner or a war veteran.[48] However,

　　　　　THE ORIGINS OF NAZI GENOCIDE

this procedure did pacify the patients; the checking of medical records by a physician in a white coat provided the deceptive appearance of normality.[49] The physician, however, used the period of observation to gain ideas about the fraudulent cause of death he would later have to certify. Viewing the naked patient, he could get hints on an appropriate cause of death, and looking for scars, he could guard against mistakes such as listing appendicitis as a cause when the patient's appendix had been removed years earlier.[50]

At this point, another mark was made on the naked bodies of the patients; those possessing gold teeth or gold bridges were identified with a cross on their backs or their shoulders. This mark later served to identify corpses with valuable dental work.[51]

After examination by the physician, the patients were each assigned a number, which was stamped onto their bodies or attached with adhesive tape and was about 1½ inches high; then they entered an adjacent room to be photographed "sitting, from the front, from the side, and standing." These final pictures, identified by the stamped or attached numbers, were designed to complete the record and to show the physical inferiority of the murdered patients "for scientific reasons"; they were eventually collected and cataloged at T4 headquarters in Berlin.[52] In several killing centers, T4 also produced propaganda films to show the "deterioration" of the handicapped.[53] At Eglfing-Haar and other local hospitals, handicapped patients slated to be transferred — especially "interesting cases" — were also photographed for "science" and "propaganda" before departure.[54]

After all examinations and other formalities were completed, the patients, still naked, were assembled so that they could be led into the gas chamber.[55] These chambers, as we have seen, were disguised to look like shower rooms with tiled floors, wooden benches along the walls, and showerheads along the ceiling.[56] The patients were already prepared for the showers because while they were undressing the nurses had told them that they would be bathed.[57] The exact procedure differed from place to place, depending in part on the location of the gas chamber. In Brandenburg, Grafeneck, and Hartheim, the gas chambers were located on the ground floor and patients moved from the reception and examination rooms directly to the chambers. In Bernburg and Hadamar, the gas chambers were located in the basement and patients had to descend steps from the examination room to reach the chamber after the completion of formalities. In Sonnenstein, both examination room and gas chamber were in the basement. Thus, for example, in Hartheim, patients were led from the photo room back to the examination room and from there through a steel door into the gas chamber.[58] In Bernburg, however, patients were assembled in a waiting room and led from there in a group down the stairs to the gas chamber in the basement.[59]

The reception process preceding the actual killings, which gave the appearance of serving medical purposes, lulled the patients into believing they were following a normal hospital admission routine. Thus most patients accepted the nurses' explanation that they were going to the showers; in Brandenburg, where they were told they were to inhale a therapeutic substance, cooperation required a great deal of credulity. Still, "in general most patients were unsuspecting" when they entered the gas chamber.[60] Many, however, suspected the truth. Suspicious patients were given sedatives before they were led into the chamber.[61] When recalcitrant patients refused to enter the chamber, the killing center staff applied force.[62] In general, though, they preferred to use subterfuge. Thus when a suspicious group of patients, mostly persons who had been sentenced by the courts for treatment in state hospitals, refused to enter the gas chamber in Brandenburg, the local supervisor, Christian Wirth, coaxed them into the room by telling them that they had to enter it to receive clothing.[63] The staff was nevertheless always prepared to use stronger measures. For example, in Hartheim, the same Wirth simply shot four female patients suspected of suffering from typhus to prevent the spread of the disease to the staff during the usual killing process.[64]

Once all patients had entered the gas chamber, the staff closed the steel door and made sure that the door and the ventilation shafts were hermetically sealed. The physician in the adjacent room then opened the valve of the compressed gas canister — obtained by the killing centers through T4's August Becker from BASF, the I.G. Farben factory at Ludwigshafen — and the lethal gas entered the chamber.[65]

In theory, only physicians were supposed to administer the gas because it was considered a medical procedure, and Hitler had only authorized selected physicians, "designated by name," to "[grant] mercy death."[66] Some physicians scrupulously carried out these instructions; Irmfried Eberl, for example, permitted only physicians to administer the gas.[67] In fact, however, the gas was not always administered by physicians; often they delegated this job and only supervised its execution. In Hartheim, for example, the gas was administered by Valasta, the senior stoker (*Oberbrenner*).[68] The Hartheim physicians supervised the gassing but were not always present, believing the job did not require special talents. Georg Renno told his postwar interrogators: "I did not study medicine to operate a gas valve [*Gashahn*]."[69]

The number of patients gassed at any one time differed somewhat from transport to transport and from center to center. At least in the beginning, twenty to fifty patients were usually killed at one time.[70] Later the capacity of some chambers was increased to hold about seventy-five patients. But sometimes far larger numbers were killed at one time. Thus a Hartheim staff member reported: "Once 150 persons were gassed at one time. The gas chamber was so full that the people in it could scarcely fall down, and the corpses were therefore so jammed together that we could pry them apart only with great difficulty."[71]

Using a pressure gauge, the physician (or another staff member) measured the amount of gas released; usually the gas valve was opened for about ten minutes. After about five minutes, all patients were unconscious, and in about ten minutes, they were all dead.[72] The staff then waited for one to two hours before ventilating the chamber.[73] Observers differed on the effects of the gas. Although at Brandenburg one observer reported that "I myself was once a witness of how rapidly gas caused death. It is my opinion that they did not feel any pain,"[74] the comments of an observer at Hadamar were probably more accurate:

Did I ever watch a gassing? Dear God, unfortunately, yes. And it was all due to my curiosity. . . . Downstairs on the left was a short pathway, and there I looked through the window. . . . In the chamber there were patients, naked people, some semi-collapsed, others with their mouths terribly wide open, their chests heaving. I saw that, I have never seen anything more gruesome. I turned away, went up the steps, upstairs was a toilet. I vomited everything I had eaten. This pursued me days on end. . . . Looking into the chamber, I could not imagine that this was completely without pain. Of course, I am a layman and this is just my opinion. A few were lying on the ground. The spines of all the naked people protruded. Some sat on the bench with their mouth wide open, their eyes wide open, and breathing with difficulty.[75]

After the ventilation of the gas chamber through the use of fans had been completed, the physicians pronounced death and the bodies were removed.[76] They were dragged, not carried, from the chamber by staff members charged with the task of burning them; these staff members were known as stokers (*Heizer* or *Brenner*) or decontaminators (*Desinfekteure*). They had to disentangle the corpses and drag them from the gas chamber to the room, usually known as the death room, where they were piled up prior to cremation. In some places, this was an otherwise empty room; in other places, the autopsy room served this purpose.[77]

At this point, prior to cremation, the staff proceeded to loot and mutilate the corpses to enrich the killing program. Specially selected corpses, usually identified by the physicians prior to the gassing, underwent autopsies. This served two purposes: it provided young killing center physicians with training and academic credit toward their specialization, and it recovered organs, especially brains, for scientific study at medical institutes.[78]

Furthermore, as we have seen, all patients with dental work containing gold had been identified with a cross on their backs. The corpses with such crosses were collected after death, and the stokers broke out all gold teeth.[79]

These gold teeth were delivered to the killing center office, where a secretary collected them in a paper carton; when enough gold had been accumulated, it was sent by special courier to the T4 Central Office in Berlin.[80] This gold, together with that later collected by similar means elsewhere, eventually found its way into the coffers of the German Reich, but T4 no doubt received, as did other agencies involved in this type of pillage, an equivalent credit to its budget.[81]

The stokers placed the corpses on a metal pallet, which they pushed onto a clay grill in the crematorium oven, or, as one of them later described it, "on a pan ... as in a baking oven."[82] Although they usually cremated two to eight bodies at one time, far more time was required to burn the bodies than to kill the patients; the disposal of corpses proved technically far more difficult than the murder of people. The stokers worked in shifts, and frequently they had to work through the night to cremate the murdered patients from one transport.[83] Often the backlog was so great that some of the bodies had begun to decompose before the stokers reached them.[84] And sometimes fires broke out. The chimneys were not designed for such heavy use of the ovens, and they caught fire. In Hartheim, a chimney fire interrupted the killing operation for several weeks.[85] As previously mentioned, in Brandenburg, flames shot out of the chimney and the crematorium had to be moved out of town.[86] In Sonnenstein, flames escaping from the chimney forced the killing center to consult an expert from the KTI; he concluded that the chimney had not been built correctly and that the center had burned too many corpses at one time.[87]

The killing center thus "processed" living human beings into ashes in less than twenty-four hours; in the language of T4, this was called "disinfection [Desinfektion]."[88] After cremation, the stokers used a mill (Knochenmühle) to grind into a powder the human bones not totally pulverized by the fire. Ashes were placed into urns for burial, about three kilos (about seven pounds) for every human being. The relatives of the murdered patients could obtain such an urn, but they were not told that the ashes did not belong to the person whose name was stamped on the urn; the stokers simply took ashes from a "large pile" to fill the urns.[89]

The actual murder of handicapped patients and the disposal of their bodies did not encompass the entire killing process. Besides the physical killings, the process required bureaucratic complicity. The subterfuge that deceived the victims had to be accompanied by paperwork that misled their relatives and guardians. This was the job of the killing center office staffs.

Competition soon developed between two authorities with jurisdiction in two separate but overlapping segments of the killing process. The physicians had always argued that the killings were a medical procedure and that physicians should therefore oversee the killing centers and the killing process. But as we have seen, many crucial decisions in the euthanasia killing program

THE ORIGINS OF NAZI GENOCIDE

for children and adults were made by KdF functionaries without any medical qualifications. In the same way, the nonmedical personnel in the killing centers often exercised jurisdiction in areas theoretically reserved for physicians. As one participant later described it, the KdF tended to support the non-medical personnel in jurisdictional quarrels, and the authority traditionally granted to physicians could not be maintained in the T4 program.[90]

The T4 Medical Office in Berlin selected and directed the physicians in the killing centers, while the T4 Administrative Office coordinated the work of the killing center office staffs. The administrative office appointed a supervisor, usually called office chief (*Büroleiter*), for each killing center, who exercised authority over all nonmedical activities. Although the physician-in-charge was officially designated head of the center, in fact the supervisor often had as much and sometimes even more influence. In part, this depended on the people involved; a strong personality could dominate a center. Irmfried Eberl thus dominated the Brandenburg and Bernburg killing centers when he served there as physician-in-charge, while Christian Wirth certainly had a decisive position of power wherever he served as supervisor.

The physician-in-charge absolutely controlled three areas. He was in charge of the actual gassing of the patients. He was also responsible for maintaining all medical records, including the determination of the cause of death. Finally, he officially represented the killing center, masquerading as a hospital, to the outside world. The supervisor, in turn, controlled security and documentation; he was responsible for the smooth operation of the killing process and the meticulous completion of all documents. He served as the custodian of the official record.

To maintain secrecy and to shield the center from outside interference, state and provincial governments removed the killing centers from the police and record-keeping authority of local government. Copying a system long used in the concentration camps, every killing center was thus constituted for purposes of security and documentation as a separate administrative unit. Each killing center had its own police office (Ortspolizeibehörde) and its own registry of vital statistics (Standesamt). The supervisor, or sometimes one of his deputies, headed these units. He directed the office staff and all other personnel except physicians; in this capacity, he was involved in hiring and he usually administered the oath of secrecy to the staff.[91]

The supervisor served as the police officer responsible for the killing center; in fact, most supervisors were police officers on loan to T4. For example, Christian Wirth, who served as a supervisor and troubleshooter in several killing centers, was a Kripo police officer from Stuttgart. Police captain Fritz Hirsche was a supervisor in Brandenburg and Bernburg, Kripo officer Jacob Wöger in Grafeneck, and police lieutenant Fritz Tauscher in Sonnenstein. Kripo officer Hermann Holzschuh was Wöger's assistant in Grafeneck and

Hirsche's assistant in Bernburg, and Austrian police officers Franz Reichleitner and Franz Stangl served as Wirth's assistants in Hartheim.[92]

The killing operations of T4 showed how precise and scrupulous Nazi functionaries and German bureaucrats were in keeping records about mass murder. But these records were secret and could not be shared with other agencies. For this reason, all paperwork sent from and to Berlin was carried by special couriers and all urgent problems were settled in daily telephone conversations.[93] Of course, some paperwork had to be released to other agencies and relatives of patients, but much of that documentation was fraudulent. Still, originals or copies of all paperwork generated by the killing program were retained, including record books and lists for internal T4 use, correspondence with outsiders, and the medical records of the killed patients.[94] To organize the paperwork, each killing center kept a death book (Sterbebuch), sometimes known as the book of patients (Krankenbuch).[95]

These records were retained even after killing centers closed. When Grafeneck was shut down, its records were transferred to Hadamar, and there they were put in order in a special "department Grafeneck."[96] Eventually, all such records were shipped to T4 headquarters in Berlin, and there they were again checked for accuracy.[97] Later in the war, when Berlin was heavily bombed, records were transferred for safekeeping to Hartheim and to Hadamar; at the end of the war, most were destroyed.[98] Some records, however, survived. First, the correspondence between the killing centers and various ministries, local governments, and patients' relatives survived in the hands of outsiders. Second, some correspondence and reports from the office of the T4 medical director, Paul Nitsche, were discovered by the Allies at the vacation resort maintained for T4 personnel in Weißenbach at the Attersee in Austria. Third, statistical reports on the number of patients killed were recovered by American soldiers from a safe at Hartheim.[99] Finally, some unofficial records survived; Irmfried Eberl, the physician-in-charge, recorded in his pocket diary the transports he gassed at Brandenburg during 1940, thus providing us with dates, surrendering institutions, and gender composition.[100]

The staffs of the killing centers were theoretically divided into three groups.[101] First, male and female nurses were charged with accompanying patients on their journey to the center and, after arrival, guiding them through the registration process. Second, clerks and secretaries were hired to handle the registration of patients and the paperwork that followed their murder. Third, laborers assigned to do the work required to gas patients and burn their bodies but also to keep the center in order, perform various tasks for the staff, and serve as guards. This third group was composed largely of unskilled workers, many of them storm troopers, but also included craftsmen such as carpenters, mechanics, plumbers, drivers, and photographers.[102] In practice, however, the division of labor did not work perfectly. Clerks and secretaries sometimes had to undress patients, and nurses sometimes had to do paperwork; and sometimes both nurses and office workers had to clean and cook.[103] On rare occasions, nurses might even have to remove bodies from the gas chamber, a job usually reserved for unskilled laborers.[104]

Every killing center had a personnel office, which reported the size of the work force to T4 in Berlin every day.[105] Although personnel strength differed from time to time and from place to place, the number of persons required to operate a killing center was always relatively small. At one point during the period of construction, about 130 to 140 people were apparently employed at Hadamar, but only 42 seem to have worked at Bernburg during gassing operations, and in both Hartheim and Bernburg at least 20 clerks and secretaries were solely occupied with office work.[106]

The paperwork started as soon as the patient arrived at the killing center. As we have seen, the surrendering institution notified the relatives or guardian that the patient had been transferred, without, however, providing the name or address of the receiving killing center.[107] The institutions surrendering the patients did, however, send along their medical records and various forms providing vital statistics, addresses of relatives, and a list of personal property.[108] In the examination room, the physicians reviewed these records while viewing the naked patients. While the physicians were examining the patients to determine what cause of death they might later assign and whether the patient might belong to an excluded category, the supervisor and his staff, who were also present in the examination room, reviewed these records to see that they were complete.[109]

The cause of death officially assigned to the murdered patients played a central role in the effort to hide the killings. Thousands of patients could not simply disappear; eventually their relatives or guardians had to be informed. But since they could not be told the truth, a fraudulent cause of death had to be certified. This cause of death appeared on death certificates, in letters to relatives or guardians, and in official documents. It was the job of the physicians at the killing centers to assign this cause of death. As we have seen, each killing center was constituted as its own registry of vital statistics so that these fraudulent causes would not be open to public scrutiny at the regular local registry.[110]

To be credible, the cause of death had to be natural and plausible, and errors had to be avoided. The physicians examined the naked patients in part to decide on a fake cause that would be believable. Still, a few causes predominated. One former clerk listed the most common causes for her postwar interrogators as "heart attack, circulatory collapse, pneumonia, stroke, etc."[111] To aid the physicians, who were mostly inexperienced young practitioners, the T4 Medical Office supplied them with lists of possible causes and a description of their symptoms; T4 also collected and compiled the causes used by the killing centers.[112] To coordinate efforts to arrive at acceptable natural causes, the medical directors of the various killing centers considered holding a conference, and at least one physician attended two meetings of killing center supervisors at Sonnenstein, where errors in assigning causes of death were discussed.[113]

Tuberculosis was a popular cause of death assigned by the killing center physicians. Rudolf Lonauer and Georg Renno, the physician-in-charge and his assistant at Hartheim, were particularly fond of this cause. A surviving letter to Lonauer from Irmfried Eberl, the physician-in-charge at Brandenburg and Bernburg, provides evidence of how seriously the T4 physicians treated the assignment of the cause of death.[114]

On Lonauer's instructions, Renno had written to Eberl defending the use of tuberculosis as a cause of death. Eberl's reply rejected Renno's arguments, pointing out that tuberculosis as a cause did not satisfy the need for secrecy and plausibility. Eberl listed the following criteria that he felt should determine whether an illness could serve as a plausible cause of death in the T4 program:

1. The illness must usually cause death within a short span of time (at most, fourteen days), unless the medical records show that the condition has been present for some time and thus could cause death due to a sudden deterioration.

2. The illness must not have appeared previously, except in cases such as tuberculosis where symptoms have already been observed.

3. Treatment of the illness must not require measures prescribed by law, such as, for example, filing reports to the health office, or by regulations applying in epidemics like quarantine of the institution or similar actions.

Eberl then pointed out that tuberculosis did not meet these criteria. Although this disease can exist undetected for a long time before sudden deterioration, it is nevertheless accompanied by symptoms such as coughing, loss of weight, fatigue, and pain. Of these, he argued, only pain is sufficiently subjective to be overlooked; the other three symptoms would have been detected in institutionalized patients. Thus relatives suspicious about the certification of tuberculosis as the cause of death would approach the surrendering institution, and physicians there, "who are after all no fools," would obviously know whether the patient had exhibited symptoms indicating tuberculosis.

The death certificate was an official document, and the physician assigning the cause of death acted as an agent of the state. The assignment of fraudulent causes was therefore a crime. For this reason, the physicians did not use their own names when signing the death certificates but instead employed pseudonyms. (See table 5.2.) In addition, several young physicians who had not yet earned their doctorates used the title "doctor" with their pseudo-

TABLE 5.2. The Euthanasia Killing Center Physicians and Their Pseudonyms

Physician	Killing center	Pseudonym
Ernst Baumhard	Grafeneck and Hadamar	Dr. Jäger
Friedrich Berner	Hadamar	Dr. Barth
Kurt Borm	Sonnenstein and Bernburg	Dr. Storm
Heinrich Bunke	Brandenburg and Bernburg	Dr. Rieper Dr. Keller
Irmfried Eberl	Brandenburg and Bernburg	Dr. Schneider Dr. Meyer (?)
Klaus Endruweit	Sonnenstein	Dr. Bader
Hans-Bodo Gorgaß	Hadamar	Dr. Kramer
Günther Hennecke	Grafeneck and Hadamar	Dr. Ott (?)
Rudolf Lonauer	Hartheim	Not known
Georg Renno	Hartheim	Not known
Kurt Schmalenbach	Sonnenstein	Dr. Blume (?)
Horst Schumann	Grafeneck and Sonnenstein	Dr. Keim
Aquilin Ullrich	Brandenburg	Dr. Schmitt
Ewald Worthmann	Sonnenstein	Not known

Sources: GStA Frankfurt, Anklage Werner Heyde, Gerhard Bohne und Hans Hefelmann, Ks 2/63 (GStA), Js 17/59 (GStA), 22 May 1962, p. 409; HHStA, 461/32061/7; Ernst Klee, ed., *Dokumente zur "Euthanasie"* (Frankfurt: Fischer Taschenbuch Verlag, 1985), pp. 17–26.

nyms. Physicians who transferred from one killing center to another used two pseudonyms so that outsiders would not guess the existence of a centrally directed killing program.[115] The physicians were not the only ones to hide behind pseudonyms; supervisors also used false names when, as registrars, they certified the date and cause of death.[116]

After the patients had been killed, the killing center office staff wrote and mailed the letters that made it appear that the patients had died from natural causes. First, they notified the relatives or guardian that the patient had arrived; this was the first information relatives received concerning the final destination of the transfers. Obviously, the killing center could not permit visits from relatives, and the notifications thus requested "timely written notice" from relatives if they planned to visit the patient.[117]

Since the patients were usually killed as soon as they arrived, they were already dead when the notification of their safe arrival was mailed. Thus this notice, and all notices that followed, contained false dates. Thereafter, the killing center office staff waited a reasonable amount of time—about ten days—before sending the notification that the patient had died. The relatives would have assumed after receiving the first notice that the patient was in good health. They had been notified of a safe arrival without any indication of problems, and the surrendering institution in its notification of the transfer had not mentioned any deterioration in the condition of the patient; in fact, relatives assumed that physically ill patients would not be transferred, and the transfer itself therefore indicated relatively good health. Notification of death immediately after arrival would thus have aroused suspicion; as we shall see, even the short delay in notification did not diminish disbelief.

Thus about ten days after the patient had arrived and had been killed, the office staff mailed the so-called condolence letter (*Trostbrief*). It was a form letter typed in the "department for condolence letters [*Trostbriefabteilung*]" of the killing center; the format of the letters, composed and distributed by the T4 Administrative Office, differed from center to center and from time to time in style but not in substance.[118]

The opening paragraph of the condolence letter informed relatives of the death of the patient. A letter from Grafeneck opened as follows: "We are truly sorry to inform you that your daughter Franziska Schmidt, who was moved to our institution on 26 July 1940 as a result of measures taken by the Reich commissioner for defense, suddenly and unexpectedly died here on 5 August 1940 due to encephalitis."[119] Occasionally, a stock phrase was added to imply routine medical procedures. For example, in a letter from Brandenburg, the opening paragraph ended with the following: "In spite of all medical efforts, we were unable to save your husband"; and a letter from Hartheim ended: "Medical intervention was unfortunately not possible."[120]

The second paragraph of the condolence letter was designed to mollify the relatives. It advanced the arguments already made popular by official propaganda in favor of euthanasia. The Brandenburg letter mentioned above contained the following paragraph: "But as the nature and the severity of your husband's illness did not encourage hope for improvement, and thus there was no longer any expectation that he could ever be released from an institution, one can understand his death as deliverance [*Erlösung*], as it delivered him from his suffering and spared him from institutionalization for life. May this thought be solace to you."[121] Most letters did not include such an elaborate explanation but simply stated, for example: "We offer our heartfelt condolence for your loss, and beg you to find comfort in the thought that your son was released from a severe and incurable disease."[122] Another version read as follows: "He died quietly and without pain. Considering his serious and incurable illness, death meant relief for him."[123] Yet another version put it this way: "Considering her severe and incurable illness, life was agony for the deceased. You must therefore understand her death as deliverance."[124]

The third paragraph concerned the disposition of the body. Normally an institution would be expected to ship the body of the deceased to the relatives for burial. But it was impossible to return the bodies of the victims to their families because the relatives and their private physicians could then have discovered the real cause of death. The killing centers therefore informed the relatives that the legal requirement to combat epidemics (*aus seuchenpolizei-lichen Gründen*) had necessitated cremation.[125] Usually this was stated in only one sentence: "On orders of the police we had to cremate the body immediately to prevent the spread of infectious diseases, which during the war pose a great threat for the home front."[126] Sometimes the letter mentioned a specific threat to the institution: "Because at the present time there is the danger of an epidemic in this institution, the police ordered the immediate cremation of the body."[127] And sometimes the rationalization for cremation was more elaborate:

> Our institution served only as transfer station for patients to be transferred to other institutions in this region, and they were here only for the purpose of discovering carriers of infectious diseases; as is well known, such carriers are constantly found among such patients. To prevent such infectious diseases and their transmittal, the local police office in Bernburg-Gröna therefore imposed, in agreement with all other interested offices, far-reaching preventive measures, and ordered the immediate cremation of the deceased and the disinfection of his possessions under § 22 of the Decree to Combat Infectious Diseases. In these cases agreement of relatives etc. is not required.[128]

The remainder of the condolence letter involved bureaucratic details. It offered to transmit an urn with the ashes of the deceased, requesting that relatives respond within fourteen days and that they submit a certificate from a cemetery administration that burial arrangements had been made. If the relatives did not reply, the urn was interred in a mass grave at the killing center, and if they requested "just any cemetery," it was sent for burial to a large city picked at random.[129] As we have seen, however, these urns did not contain the correct ashes.[130] Further, the letter informed relatives that valuables and mementos would be forwarded but that clothing would be turned over to the Nazi party welfare organization because it had been damaged during disinfection.[131] In fact, however, the killing centers often stole these possessions; for example, staff members received clothing for their contributions to the killing process.[132] Finally, the letter again discouraged visits; to avoid infection, it explained, all inquiries must be made in writing.[133] Enclosed with the letter were two copies of the death certificate; they were signed, often with a pseudonym, by the killing center's registrar of vital statistics.[134]

As discussed above, the reported cause of death was fraudulent. Furthermore, the date of death was also falsified. Since the patient was already dead when the relatives were first informed of his or her safe arrival, death had to be postdated, and dates had to be changed so that patients who were members of the same family, or were from the same village, would not appear to have died at the same time. This deception yielded a profit on the side. Since those responsible for the patients' upkeep—relatives, welfare agencies, pension plans, insurance companies—paid the institution until the day of death, postdating death brought T4 a substantial sum of money; the haggling over payments due continued long after the patients had been murdered.[135]

Cause and date of death were not the only fraudulent data supplied by the killing centers; the recorded place of death was sometimes also false. To prevent suspicion, the killing centers avoided sending similar death notices to large numbers of persons in one village, town, or region. Each killing center office therefore established a distribution department (*Absteckabteilung*) where, for every patient killed, staff members stuck a colored pin on a large wall map, showing his or her home residence. If too many pins accumulated in one place, both date and place of death were altered. Thus it would not appear that too many patients had died at the same time in the same institution.[136]

The killing centers played a shell game to hide the true place of death. They exchanged name lists so that death notices could be mailed from a center other than the one where the patients had actually been killed.[137] In such cases, the letter from the killing center announcing the safe arrival of the patient was later followed by a letter of condolence from a different center. Although the patients were already dead, these letters claimed that they had been transferred once again and that they had died after this final transfer. For example, Brandenburg notified relatives that a patient had died there, although she had arrived and had been killed at Sonnenstein one week earlier; in another example, a patient arrived in Hadamar and was killed there, but one week later the relatives received notification from Bernburg that he had died there.[138]

The killing centers had reason to worry about the reaction of relatives, and they therefore did everything to pacify them. In addition, they monitored their response. One Hartheim clerk who was charged with keeping such records testified after the war that "some cursed, some expressed gratitude, and most simply did not reply."[139]

The fear that knowledge about the killing centers would cause unrest among the local population led to the closing of Brandenburg and Grafeneck. However, they were replaced by Bernburg and Hadamar, so the decision to shut them down was only a tactical maneuver that did nothing to abrogate the killing program. Although Brandenburg was probably closed due to the fact that the town noticed the crematorium and its smell, which first led the center to move it out of town, other considerations might have played a role

　　　　　THE ORIGINS OF NAZI GENOCIDE

in terminating the killings in Brandenburg. But the evidence clearly shows that Grafeneck was closed at the end of 1940 in response to local hostility.[140]

Rumors about what was taking place at Grafeneck spread during the second half of 1940.[141] In August the Stuttgart attorney general reported that "mysterious events in certain mental hospitals have produced great excitement among wide circles of the population," and in November the presiding judge of the Stuttgart circuit court reported that "slowly serious unrest is spreading among the population" and that "knowledge about these things is spreading. ... Children bring such news from school and from the street."[142] And in late July, a private informant reported that "for several weeks already, gossip circulates in the villages around Grafeneck that things cannot be okay at the castle"; patients arrive, "but they are never seen again, nor can they be visited," and "equally suspicious is the frequently visible smoke."[143]

On 25 November 1940, Else von Löwis of Menar, a member of a Swabian aristocratic family, wrote a letter to the wife of Walter Buch, the presiding judge of the Nazi party court. Von Löwis, an old friend of the Buchs, was an ardent Nazi and a leader of the party's women's movement. In her letter, she expressed the hope that the Buchs would transmit to Hitler her concern that the killing of patients was taxing the loyalty of the population toward the Nazi movement: "Surely you know about the measures currently used by us to dispose of incurable mental patients. Still, you may not fully realize how it is accomplished and the vast scope of the undertaking, nor the terrible impression it leaves with the population! Here in Württemberg the tragedy takes place in Grafeneck on the Swabian Jura, and this place has thus acquired an ominous reputation." Von Löwis argued that a euthanasia law modeled on the sterilization law would be accepted by the population but that the present illegal system was not acceptable. The power over life and death must be legally regulated, otherwise "everything would be totally vulnerable to dangerous passions and to crime." In this instance, the events in Grafeneck and elsewhere were widely known and had become a "public secret," producing a "terrible feeling of insecurity"; people were asking, "What can one still believe? Where will this lead us and what will be its limits?" At this time, the people still believed that "the Führer obviously does not know about this," but the party could lose this trust if it continued to mislead the populace.[144]

On 7 December 1940, Walter Buch transmitted this letter to Heinrich Himmler. In his cover letter to the Reich leader SS, Buch vouched for von Löwis, pointing out, however, that men must carry out essential national tasks that should be kept from women. Still, if the happenings in Grafeneck could not remain hidden and caused such unrest, a different approach must be found.[145] On 19 December, Himmler replied to Buch: "Many thanks for your letter of 7 December 1940. I can inform you in confidence that the events that take place there are authorized by the Führer and are carried out by a panel of physicians. . . . The SS only assists with trucks, cars, and the like. I agree with you on one point. The process must be faulty if the matter has become as public as it appears. . . . I will immediately contact the office that has jurisdiction to point out these errors, and advise them to deactivate Grafeneck."[146] Himmler did exactly that. On the same day, the Reich leader SS wrote to Viktor Brack, advising the manager of T4 at the KdF, who was also a colonel in the SS, to close Grafeneck: "As I have heard, there is great excitement in the Swabian Jura due to the institution Grafeneck. The populace recognizes the gray automobile of the SS, and thinks it knows what is happening under the constant smoke of the crematorium. What takes place there is a secret, and yet is no longer a secret. Thus the worst public mood has taken hold there, and in my opinion there remains only one option: discontinue the operation of the institution in this locality."[147]

Brandenburg and Grafeneck were closed, but the killings continued without interruption. Nevertheless, the public response that led to the closings did force T4 to reevaluate its procedures, which resulted in the creation of transit institutions (*Zwischenanstalten*). Beginning in the fall of 1940, patients were collected in these institutions, whose own patients had been killed to make room, and after two or three weeks were transferred from there as a group to the killing center.[148] Thus patients left the surrendering institution to go to the transit institution and then traveled from there to the killing center.[149] This "constant movement" assured greater secrecy about the final destination.[150] It added an extra layer of disinformation given to the relatives, who received notice of the patient's arrival and then departure from the transit institution, thus confusing the issue and making complaints less effective. Again, the relatives were not permitted to visit during this hiatus.[151]

The transit institutions were undoubtedly designed to confuse the public and ensure secrecy.[152] After the war, however, the T4 managers and physicians rationalized that these institutions served as an additional layer of protection against errors in the selection process because the physicians at the transfer institutions could review the decision to kill.[153] In fact, this did not happen. The transferred patients were new to the institution and were therefore never treated as regular patients; the bond between staff and patients necessary for a sympathetic evaluation never developed, and the transit institution thus did not care to fight to retain these patients.[154] In any case, after some transit institutions did attempt to reclaim patients they found useful as workers, T4 demanded that all exemptions stop; only T4 and not the transit institutions had the power to reclaim patients.[155] At the time, Vorberg argued that the transit institutions were established not to save patients but to improve "transfer technology [*aus transporttechnischen Gründen*]."[156] The ultimate destination of all selected patients remained the killing center.

Transit institutions were established in the various regions of Germany;

THE ORIGINS OF NAZI GENOCIDE

TABLE 5.3. The Euthanasia Killing Centers: Number of Victims, 1940–1941

Center (code letter)	Victims in 1940	Victims in 1941	Total
Grafeneck (A)	9,839	Closed	9,839
Brandenburg (B)	9,772	Closed	9,772
Hartheim (C)	9,670	8,599	18,269
Sonnenstein (D)	5,943	7,777	13,720
Bernburg (Be)	Not yet open	8,601	8,601
Hadamar (E)	Not yet open	10,072	10,072
Total	35,224	35,049	70,273

Source: NARA, RG 338, Microfilm Publication T-1021, roll 18, frame 98, "Hartheim Statistics."

each served as a collection point for a specific killing center, and each killing center received patients from several of these institutions. After Grafeneck closed, the Weinsberg institution thus served as a transfer point for Württemberg patients sent to Hadamar, and the Eichberg institution, already used as a killing ward for children, also became a transfer institution for Hadamar.[157]

An unusual relationship existed between the Hartheim killing center and the Niedernhart transfer institution near Linz. The two institutions worked in tandem, a "linkage [that] did not exist elsewhere."[158] In 1938, after the incorporation of Austria, Rudolf Lonauer had been appointed director of Niedernhart, and he retained this job when he became physician-in-charge at Hartheim.[159] Unlike all other transfer institutions, Niedernhart did not have a separate identity but served exclusively as the anteroom for the Hartheim killing center. The Hartheim physicians Lonauer and Renno inspected the patients that arrived in Linz from various institutions in Austria and Germany, unless they had already selected them at originating Austrian institutions. They picked some for immediate gassing at Hartheim and others for temporary placement into transfer ward 8 at Niedernhart. Those least able to function, as well as those considered "disorderly," went directly to Hartheim. However, when "the crematorium at Hartheim was working above capacity," an entire transport would first go to Niedernhart.[160]

The smooth operation of the killing process depended, at least in part, on the staff who ran the killing centers. As we shall see, these men and women were recruited almost at random, and they gained experience on the job. But the killing of human beings on an assembly line led to the total brutalization of the staff. The behavior of Christian Wirth, the supervisor at Hartheim and other centers, who was commonly regarded as a "beast," was symptomatic of the behavior of many staff members.[161] It was common for staff members to receive special liquor rations, and many of them were drunk much of the time.[162] Along with heavy drinking, staff members engaged in indiscriminate sexual relations: "In Hartheim almost all employees were intimate with each other."[163]

Hadamar can serve as a good example of the brutalization and licentiousness rampant among the staffs of the killing centers. The staff at Hadamar arranged for a celebration when the number of patients killed there reached 10,000. On the orders of the physicians, the entire staff assembled at the basement crematorium to participate in the burning of the ten thousandth victim. A naked corpse lay on a stretcher, covered with flowers. The supervisor Bünger made a speech, and a staff member dressed up as a cleric performed a ceremony. Every staff member received a bottle of beer.[164]

In August 1941, Hitler ordered a stop to the gassings at the killing centers and thus, as we shall see, ended the first phase of the euthanasia killings. Since the records of T4 were destroyed before the end of the war, the number of patients killed in the killing centers during 1940 and 1941 can only be approximated.

A statistician employed by T4 compiled a summary of the numbers of patients killed. In his report, found after the war at Hartheim, he provided monthly figures for each killing center, arriving at a total of 70,273 persons "disinfected." Of these, 35,224 were killed in 1940 and 35,049 in 1941. With 18,269 persons gassed, Hartheim killed the largest number of victims, followed by Sonnenstein with 13,720. But if we combine the 9,839 persons killed at Grafeneck with the 10,072 gassed at the successor institution of Hadamar, we get the even larger total of 19,911. Likewise, combining the 9,772 victims at Brandenburg with the 8,601 at the successor institution of Bernburg creates another large total of 18,373.[165] (See table 5.3.)

Postwar German prosecutors believed, however, that these figures were too small. Basing their calculations on all available documents and interrogations, they argued that T4 probably distributed the number of patients equally between the killing centers. They counted about 20,000 victims each for Hartheim and Sonnenstein, and also 20,000 each for Brandenburg combined with Bernburg and for Grafeneck combined with Hadamar. This provided a total of 80,000 patients killed, although they believed it probable that the actual figure was even higher.[166]

The bizarre T4 statistics found at Hartheim also provided an exact account of future expenditures saved by killing the handicapped. The T4 statistician figured that 70,273 "disinfections" saved the German Reich 885,439,980 RM over a period of ten years.[167] Computing future savings of food, he argued, for example, that 70,273 murdered patients saved Germany 13,492,440 kilograms of meat and wurst[168]—a macabre utilitarianism designed to rationalize the eugenic and racial ideology that created the killing centers.

Chapter 6 Toward the Killing Pause

On 24 August 1941, Hitler ordered an end to the first phase of adult euthanasia. He gave this order to Karl Brandt, who transmitted it to the KdF.[1] Popular history and special pleading have credited opposition by the churches with this abrogation of the killing operation. But Hitler was probably pushed to issue his so-called stop order primarily by widespread public knowledge about the killings and far less by church opposition, an opposition that merely reflected general popular disquiet about the way euthanasia was implemented.[2] The Protestant (Lutheran) and (Roman) Catholic churches were, in any event, ambivalent toward Nazi health care policies, including sterilization and euthanasia, and their resistance could have been overcome.[3] In the same way, opposition from the judiciary, which also reflected popular disquiet, had been quietly settled before the stop order.

Public knowledge and popular disquiet were thus the principal reasons for Hitler's decision. In 1940 public knowledge and discontent had led Himmler to suggest the closing of Grafeneck; the same reasons led Hitler to issue his order in August 1941. By the summer of 1941, the secret of the euthanasia killings had become public knowledge and was even known in neutral countries as well as in the nations fighting against Germany.[4] In any case, Hitler's stop order was only a tactical retreat. Children's euthanasia, for example, continued without interruption.[5] And as we shall see, the stop order did not end adult euthanasia; in the second phase, it resumed with great intensity but out of public view. Further, we shall see that some of the killing centers subsequently murdered other victims and that the T4 killing personnel moved to the East for larger tasks.

As killing operations expanded to include Jews and Gypsies, the experiences of euthanasia forced the killers to change their procedures. They transferred the killing arena to the East. To limit opposition from close relatives, an opposition that had vexed the killing operation against the handicapped, they deported not individual Jews and Gypsies but entire nuclear families, did not deport Jews living in mixed marriages unless the non-Jewish relatives had died, and even in Auschwitz usually sent healthy young mothers to the gas chamber with their young children while those without children were often selected for labor. At the same time, jurisdictional disputes were revived. In 1939 the KdF had persuaded Hitler to entrust it with the first killing operation, and Leonardo Conti at the RMdI and Reinhard Heydrich at the RSHA supplied only support services.[6] But for the larger killing tasks of 1941, Hitler transferred authority to Reich Leader SS Heinrich Himmler.

The fear that public knowledge about the killings would spark popular unrest had been the reason for classifying euthanasia top secret and for Hitler's consistent refusal to promulgate a euthanasia law.[7] But all attempts at secrecy failed for a number of reasons.

First, the massive killing operation involving large numbers of the handicapped at one time and in one place posed insurmountable security problems. The sudden deaths of large numbers of handicapped patients could not be explained, and their deaths shortly after their secret transfer obviously aroused suspicion. In addition, these deaths occurred in a few isolated institutions, and all attempts on paper to juggle the dates and places of death did not mislead the public. Finally, the assembly line killings in centers located inside the German Reich could not remain hidden. The local population watched the disappearance of large numbers of the handicapped behind the walls of the killing centers, saw the smoke from the crematoria, and smelled the burning flesh; in the countryside, the villages, and the small towns, rumors about the killings spread rapidly.

Second, the policy of exclusion had not been as acceptable for the handicapped as it had been for Jews and Gypsies. Although the regime increased the physical isolation of institutionalized handicapped patients, stigmatized them as "life unworthy of life," and victimized them through forced sterilization, the bond between many patients and their relatives had not been severed. Thus the attack on the handicapped did not strike at an isolated ethnic minority but instead at a group of fellow citizen still connected to family and neighbors.

Third, the attempt to hide the involvement of the Nazi leadership with the killing operation by creating various front organizations did not deceive everyone. Although the state through its health offices and state hospitals appeared before the public as the agent of the transfer of patients, popular opinion blamed the Nazi movement.[8] Nazi propaganda against the handicapped, labeling them as "burdensome lives" and "useless eaters," had revealed the complicity of the movement; the public suspected that the party stood behind the killings and believed, for example, that Gekrat transportation involved "the gray buses of the SS."[9]

From the beginning, Hitler feared that opposition from the churches might make it politically too costly to implement the euthanasia killings and had therefore waited until war was imminent to issue his orders.[10] As it turned out, Hitler had been correct in his assessment that during the war church opposition would be muted. The churches did not prevent the successful mass murder of more than 70,000 handicapped patients during 1940 and 1941 and did not stop the murder of an even larger number of patients from 1942 to 1945.

THE ORIGINS OF NAZI GENOCIDE

The Protestant church in Germany had long supported positive eugenics involving the expansion of healthy and desirable population groups and did not totally reject negative eugenic measures such as sterilization. Although it had opposed coerced sterilization, once the sterilization law had been passed, it did support nonvoluntary sterilization with some hesitation and a few limitations. The Catholic church was on record in opposition to negative eugenics and particularly sterilization, and both the Vatican and the German bishops denounced the sterilization law. But they compromised their position and offered only verbal opposition because they did not want to endanger the Concordat and because they wanted to protect Catholic institutions and Catholic jobs.[11] In general, hospitals and homes administered by the churches were loyal to the state and to the regime; for example, we shall later see how they discriminated against Jewish patients. But when sterilization changed into euthanasia, that is, when exclusion through killing replaced exclusion through surgical birth control, the churches were forced into opposition. However, even then the response was not as effective as might have been expected.

Church protest developed only after the full extent of the killings had become apparent by the late summer of 1940. At that time, some member hospitals of the Protestant Home Mission (Innere Mission) and the Catholic Charity Association (Caritasverband) attempted to prevent, or at least delay, the registration and transfer of their patients, but the bureaucrats of T4 and their local allies were easily able to overcome this resistance.[12] Some hospital directors appealed to the government and also notified their superiors in the church.[13] Reports from their hospitals mobilized the church leaders, who then attempted to influence the authorities. This happened first in Württemberg.

Due to the large number of intermarriages among the rural population of this south German federal state, Württemberg had a large number of institutionalized handicapped patients. This probably explains why Grafeneck was chosen as one of the first killing centers and why Württemberg was the first region where T4 implemented the transfers. On 19 July 1940, about six months after the start of the killings, Theophil Wurm, the Protestant bishop of Württemberg, wrote a letter of protest to Reich Minister Wilhelm Frick at the RMdI, with a copy to Reich Minister Franz Gürtner at the Reich Ministry of Justice (Reichsjustizministerium, or RJM), appealing for an end to the killings; when he did not receive an answer, he wrote to Frick again on 5 September asking, "Does the Führer know, does he approve?"[14]

At approximately the same time, Pastor Paul Gerhard Braune, director of the Hoffnungstaler hospitals and vice president of the central committee of the Home Mission, and Pastor Friedrich von Bodelschwingh, director of the famous Bethel hospital complex, approached various influential officials considered sympathetic to their viewpoint to request their support for efforts to end or at least limit the euthanasia killings.[15] They spoke to persons they knew at the Reich Chancellery, military intelligence (the *Abwehr*), and various ministries. They also approached Hermann Göring through his cousin, the psychotherapist Matthias Heinrich Göring, and also through Hermann's wife Erna, whose brother was a patient at Bethel, but they accomplished nothing.

Although many of those approached no doubt already knew about the killings, they professed astonishment and shock and urged the pastors to present all the facts in a thorough report. After a meeting with Gürtner at the RJM, also attended by the surgeon Ferdinand Sauerbruch, who headed the Reich Research Council, Braune decided to submit a detailed report; only Braune signed it because he did not want Bodelschwingh to risk repercussions. On 9 July 1940, he sent his "Memorandum for Adolf Hitler" to Hans Heinrich Lammers at the Reich Chancellery; apparently, it did reach the Führer.[16]

Soon thereafter, Braune was arrested by the Gestapo, which claimed, however, that the arrest was unrelated to the report; after a short incarceration under relatively good conditions, he was released but had to promise not to sabotage measures of the state. Contacts with prominent circles had led to Braune's release, but neither Braune nor Bodelschwingh could persuade the regime to stop its killing program.[17]

The Catholic church also objected to the euthanasia killings, and it did so with the backing of the Vatican. As in the case of the Protestant churches, however, more than six months passed before Catholic church leaders lodged a formal complaint with the government. On 11 August 1940, Cardinal Adolf Bertram, archbishop of Breslau, wrote in his capacity as chairman of the Fulda Conference of Bishops to Lammers at the Reich Chancellery; pointing to popular disquiet triggered by the news that handicapped patients were being killed, he reiterated the objections raised by the church against euthanasia proposals during the 1930s.[18] Thereafter, the Fulda Conference apparently attempted to negotiate with those responsible for the killings; in November, the executive of the Fulda Conference, Bishop Heinrich Wienken, discussed with Herbert Linden and Viktor Brack ways to permit priests to administer the sacraments to euthanasia victims.[19] But these attempts at Catholic accommodation failed when the Vatican rejected compromise.[20]

As in the Protestant church, individual Catholic bishops also approached the government. On 6 November 1940, Cardinal Michael Faulhaber, archbishop of Munich, wrote to Franz Gürtner at the RJM, protesting the euthanasia killings. Although his argument followed the line advanced by the Fulda Conference, his language was less compromising, and he quoted the biblical commandment, "Thou shall not kill." In addition, he pointed out that the killings were undermining the trust of the nation in government and health care agencies.[21] Faulhaber's letter to the RJM, which transmitted a copy to the

KdF, caused a certain amount of concern in official circles, especially after a translation appeared in Sweden.[22] Nevertheless, the killings continued.

Six months later, in June 1941, the Fulda Conference of Bishops acted again. It sent a memorandum to the Reich minister of church affairs, Hanns Kerrl; it also issued a pastoral letter, read from the pulpits of all Catholic churches on 6 July 1941, warning that "never, under any circumstances, except in war and justified self-defense, is it permissible to kill an innocent human being."[23]

Following the intervention of the Fulda Conference, several bishops appealed to the RJM. On 13 August 1941, Antonius Hilfrich, the bishop of Limburg, whose diocese included the killing center at Hadamar, pointed out that the killing of handicapped patients contravened not only the biblical commandment but also prohibitions in the German penal code and that public sentiment had reached the point where people were saying that "Germany cannot win the war if there is still a just God."[24] On 28 August, four days after Hitler issued his stop order but before it was widely known, Wilhelm Berning, the bishop of Osnabrück, writing in the name of the bishops of Cologne and Paderborn, appealed to the RJM and also pointed to prohibitions against killing in the German penal code.[25]

The protest of Count Clemens August von Galen, the bishop of Münster, had the greatest public impact. On 3 August 1941, von Galen preached a sermon in Münster, which was also read from the pulpits of his diocese.[26] Combining his attack on euthanasia with one on the persecution of the church, he reported that he had already protested the killings as a violation of the murder statute of the penal code but that the removal of handicapped patients had continued and transfers had now reached Westphalia. He denounced the killings, which, he had been told, "are openly talked about in the Reich Ministry of Interior and in the office of Reich Physician Leader Dr. Conti." He closed his sermon with this warning: "My brothers in Christ, I hope there is still time, but time is running out."

Although there was some pressure to arrest, even execute, von Galen, Hitler refused to sanction any move against the bishop because he feared the impact on Catholic opinion during wartime if this conservative bishop became an anti-Nazi martyr.[27] In fact, as the treatment of Pastor Braune has also shown, virtually no church leader suffered serious consequences for opposition to the euthanasia killings.[28] One exception was Bernhard Lichtenberg, the provost of St. Hedwig's Cathedral in Berlin. On 26 August 1941, he wrote to Leonardo Conti, with copies to the Reich Chancellery, various ministries, and the Gestapo, supporting von Galen's sermon; as a German, he demanded that Conti render an account "for the crimes, committed upon your orders or with your compliance, which invite that the Lord who rules over life and death will impose retribution upon the German people."[29] Lichtenberg was arrested in October 1941, tried and sentenced to two years in prison, and thereafter committed to a concentration camp; he died on his way to Dachau in November 1943.[30] But his protest against euthanasia alone did not cause his arrest; he was arrested, sentenced, and killed for also protesting the persecution of the Jews.[31]

The objections raised by the churches came from outside the government bureaucracy, and although at first they were voiced only in private communications, they did eventually reach a relatively large public audience. Still, the protest of the churches lagged behind public outrage and did not become public until the secret killings had become widely known inside Germany and across its borders. In contrast, the objections raised by the judiciary came from inside the bureaucracy and therefore posed potential dangers for the killing program different from those posed by the churches.[32] Although the judiciary was also motivated by public complaints, civil service traditions made it unlikely that the judiciary would issue public declarations; on the other hand, it could investigate complaints and bring charges against the perpetrators. Whereas the organizers of the killings could disregard the protest of the churches, they had to neutralize the judiciary if they hoped to continue the killing program. In fact, Hitler had specifically assigned management of the killing operation to the KdF to avoid the publicity and the obstruction that involvement of the civil service would invite.

The euthanasia killings were a secret enterprise ordered and authorized by the Führer; they were planned, disguised, and implemented by the state. Although the realities of Nazi Germany made it appear that Hitler's private authorization had legalized these killings, they clearly violated the provisions of the penal code still in force; in fact, the managers of the euthanasia killings knew that during the 1930s the commission charged with the revision of the penal code had refused to legalize euthanasia.[33] The regime could thus guarantee only that those involved in the killings would not be prosecuted.[34]

Since the Führer adamantly refused to sanction a public law on euthanasia, the putative legal basis for the killings—Hitler's private authorization—had to remain hidden from public view.[35] In fact, the reason for secrecy was the fear that the public would not approve of such killings even if they were legal. To the public, and to the judiciary, these killings were homicides, prohibited by article 211 (murder) and article 212 (manslaughter) of the penal code. And since article 139 of the penal code required all private persons knowing of a crime to warn the intended victim or to report it to the authorities, numerous relatives of killed patients, as well as other concerned persons, could and did officially bring charges against physicians and hospitals. This placed state attorneys and the courts in a difficult position, especially since article 152 of the code of criminal procedure did not leave prosecution to the discretion of state attorneys but required them to initiate proceedings if they knew that a crime had been committed.[36]

The judiciary, which had not even been informed about the T4 operation, discovered its existence either through reports from the public or through routine judicial inquiries.[37] These inquiries often concerned either persons who were wards of the courts and thus remained, even after commitment, the responsibility of judges acting as guardians (Vormundschaftsrichter) or persons who had died while committed and therefore concerned the probate courts (Nachlaßgerichte). However, most often such inquiries concerned persons committed to state hospitals under article 42b of the penal code, which proscribed commitment if the perpetrator of a crime suffered from diminished capacity to comprehend or be responsible for his acts (*Zurechnungsunfähigkeit*). Such persons remained, even after commitment, under the jurisdiction of the local offices of the state attorneys (Staatsanwaltschaften), but because they were considered criminally insane regardless of the nature of their crime or the condition of their commitment, T4 always selected them to be killed.[38]

The first hard news reached the judiciary in February 1940, immediately after the killing operation had started, as local state attorneys inquired about the whereabouts of their charges, who had been committed but were needed for ongoing proceedings. When a local state attorney (Staatsanwalt) discovered that the patients under his charge had been transferred without his knowledge or permission, and when he subsequently either could not discover their locations or received notice that they had died, he reported his problem to the attorney general (Generalstaatsanwalt) in his district and asked for instructions. The attorneys general soon found that they too could not uncover the truth, and they, in turn, reported their misgivings to the RJM.[39] (See table 6.1.)

Starting in February 1940 and continuing through 1941, local state attorneys searched unsuccessfully for persons committed to state hospitals.[40] They needed some as witnesses and others as defendants to stand trial. They also searched for some because the courts had vacated their commitment under article 42f of the penal code, which covered the duration of court-mandated commitment and the conditions for release.[41] The hospitals would tell the state attorneys only that these patients had been transferred, adding that they should approach Gekrat for information.[42] But when they tried to telephone Gekrat in Berlin, they were unable to reach this organization and eventually discovered that it did not exist; one state attorney consulted the Office for Emergency Services of the City of Berlin only to be told that no such organization existed.[43]

When the state attorneys wrote to the post office box that served as the ad-

TABLE 6.1. Chain of Command for the German Judiciary

Ministry	Minister	State secretary (StS)	Department
Reich Ministry of Justice (Reichsjustiz-ministerium, or RJM)	Franz Gürtner (to Jan. 1941)	Franz Schlegelberger (acting minister after Jan. 1941) Roland Freisler	Department III: Penal Law, Ministerialdirektor Wilhelm Crohne

Court	Chief	Prosecution	Chief
Circuit Court (Oberlandes-gericht, or OLG)	Circuit Court President (Oberlandes-gerichtspräsident, or OLGPräs)	State Attorney's Office at the Circuit Court (Staatsanwaltschaft [StA] bei dem Oberlandesgericht)	Attorney general (Generalstaats-anwalt, or GStA)
District Court (Landgericht, or LG)	District Court President (Land-gerichtspräsident, or LGPräs)	State Attorney's Office at the District Court (Staatsanwaltschaft [StA] bei dem Landgericht)	Senior state attorney in charge (Leitender Oberstaatsanwalt, or Ltd. OStA)
Magistrate Court (Amtsgericht, or AG)	Magistrate Court President or Director (Amts-gerichtspräsident [or] direktor, or AGPräs)	State Attorney's Office at the District Court (Staatsanwaltschaft [StA] bei dem Landgericht)	Senior state attorney in charge (Leitender Oberstaatsanwalt, or Ltd. OStA)

Sources: Lothar Gruchmann, *Justiz im Dritten Reich, 1933–1940: Anpassung und Unterwerfung in der Ära Gürtner* (Munich: R. Oldenbourg Verlag, 1988), pp. 1149–1214; Adalbert Rückerl, *NS-Verbrechen vor Gericht* (Heidelberg: C. F. Müller Juristischer Verlag, 1982); Henry Friedlander, "The Judiciary and Nazi Crimes in Postwar Germany," *Simon Wiesenthal Center Annual* 1 (1984): 27–44.
Note: The Supreme Court (Reichsgericht) and the People's Court (Volksgerichtshof), which were not directly involved in the discussions of the euthanasia killings, are not included in this table.

dress for Gekrat, they usually received an answer not from Gekrat but from one of the killing centers. The attorney general in Dresden received, in reply to his inquiry to Gekrat, a letter from the Brandenburg killing center, signed with the fictitious name of Dr. Meyer. In this communication, the killing center, masquerading as "Brandenburg State Nursing Home" on its letterhead, informed the attorney general that the patient in question had died from a heart attack.[44]

Sometimes the hospitals referred the state attorneys to the local ministries of interior or simply forwarded their requests to the ministries.[45] One hospital told the senior state attorney (Oberstaatsanwalt) in Heidelberg that "the transfer is top secret" and that only the Baden Ministry of Interior could answer questions.[46] In response, the attorney general in Karlsruhe could only request of the ministry that it henceforth notify state attorneys of the new location of transferred patients.[47]

At the same time that the attorneys general reported the disappearance of prisoners committed to hospitals, courts concerned about the disappearance of their wards also turned to the RJM. The first complaint from a judge about his missing wards came from a Vormundschaftsrichter in the city of Brandenburg. On 8 July 1940, Lothar Kreyssig, a judge in charge of guardianships on the lowest court of general jurisdiction, the Amtsgericht, wrote to Franz Gürtner, the Reich minister of justice. He reported that numerous wards of his court had died suddenly after transfer to certain institutions, that he had concluded that they were killed there as part of an ongoing program, and that as a Christian he must object. Moreover, he stated that these killings violated existing law and that as legal guardian he must act to protect his wards. Before doing so, however, he considered it his duty "to obtain information and advice from my superiors."[48] Kreyssig was not the only Vormundschaftsrichter to report on the disappearance of his wards; many such complaints from other judges were passed to the RJM through the chain of command.[49]

Most of the news about the killings that reached the judiciary and the RJM came in the form of public complaints. Relatives of patients already killed as well as those who feared for the lives of patients turned to the state attorneys and the RJM, demanding investigations and prosecutions. Numerous anonymous letters reached the RJM. Some were appeals to the minister to save the lives of patients.[50] For example, a senior civil servant from Ulm who refused to give his name sent a handwritten letter to the Reich minister of justice, and at the same time also to Hitler, threatening that if his son, a patient in an institution in Württemberg, was murdered, he would demand prosecution and also publish the news in the foreign press.[51]

At the same time, the attorneys general and the presiding judges of the circuit courts (Oberlandesgerichtspräsidenten) reported to the RJM that rumors about the killings were circulating widely.[52] The Stuttgart attorney general as well as the presiding judge of the Stuttgart circuit court reported on the unrest caused by rumors about Grafeneck, including stories that the "mass murder" involved not only mental patients but also soldiers wounded in the war. The large numbers of death notices that had arrived at the probate court in Stuttgart from the special registry offices of vital statistics established at Grafeneck and other killing centers seemed to substantiate these rumors.[53] The Stuttgart attorney general inquired whether he should ask the Gestapo to investigate.[54]

The presiding judge of the circuit court in Frankfurt reported similar rumors about the killings at Hadamar.[55] The attorney general in Graz reported that the killings had been discussed at a meeting of attorneys general from the Eastern March (Austria); he argued that "*secret* killings, which do not and *cannot* remain secret, undermine trust in the law," and he appealed to Franz Gürtner to save the "honor of the judiciary."[56]

This highly critical public discussion about the killings posed an additional problem for the judiciary. Normally, such talk was punishable under the stringent laws against malicious (*heimtückisch*) attacks against government and party. But proceedings against those making the complaints could not be initiated because the secret killings would then have to be revealed in open court.[57] Further, in a number of cases, relatives of patients killed in the T4 program filed charges that forced the state attorneys to open murder investigations against unknown persons.[58]

The RJM moved slowly. Until the early summer of 1940, it simply collected information; all documentation about the killings was collected in the office of State Secretary Roland Freisler, and the RJM requested that the attorneys general collect but not act on all such information.[59] Gürtner was not yet prepared to act. As we have seen, early in July 1940, Gürtner received additional information about the killings from Protestant leaders. Although he undoubtedly feigned surprise during his private meeting with Pastor Paul Gerhard Braune, there is no reason to doubt Braune's account that Gürtner was shocked by the revelations.[60] Late in July, the accumulating materials and the growing number of inquiries forced Gürtner to act.

The judiciary was united in the belief that the T4 killings were undermining public confidence and were placing the judiciary in an impossible position. Judges, state attorneys, and ministerial bureaucrats therefore demanded either an end to the killings or the promulgation of a law to regularize them. On this, there appears to have been no difference of opinion between Nazi ideologues, such as State Secretary Roland Freisler, later the notorious presiding judge of the People's Court, and conservatives who had held office prior to Hitler's appointment as chancellor, such as Reich Minister Franz Gürtner and Franz Schlegelberger, the senior state secretary.[61]

Gürtner turned for information to Lammers at the Reich Chancellery, meeting with him on 23 July 1940. Lammers, who had been privy to most of the decisions concerning euthanasia, informed Gürtner that the Führer had refused to issue a law. On 24 July, Gürtner wrote to Lammers and, referring to their conversation of the preceding day, pointed out that since Hitler refused to issue a law, the killings would have to be stopped. Attached to the letter were copies of a number of reports on the killings that had reached the RJM from the judiciary and the public.[62]

Lammers did not, however, intend to act on behalf of the RJM and therefore referred Gürtner to Philipp Bouhler. On 27 July 1940, Schlegelberger sent Bouhler copies of Gürtner's letter to Lammers and the attached reports.[63] But the RJM failed even in attempts to convince the KdF to issue written guidelines that would at least standardize the killings, and Bouhler informed Gürtner on 5 September 1940 that "based on the authorization of the Führer and as the only one responsible for the implementation of the requisite measures, I have issued directives that seemed necessary to me. Any additional written regulations for implementation are no longer required."[64]

Undaunted by such rebuffs, the RJM continued during the fall of 1940 to forward reports about the killings to Lammers.[65] Lammers, however, simply transmitted these reports to Leonardo Conti at the RMdI.[66] But the RJM had already approached the RMdI, requesting that the courts be informed if their committed wards were to be transferred.[67] Conti replied that the RMdI was responsible only for distributing the questionnaires and for ordering that patients be turned over to "offices authorized to implement these measures," referring the RJM to Bouhler's letter.[68]

Finally, on 27 August 1940, Bouhler sent Gürtner a copy of Hitler's euthanasia authorization.[69] Although Gürtner realized that even in Nazi Germany this authorization was not a proper substitute for a law, he decided that the RJM could not oppose the will of the Führer, the "supreme source of the law."[70] The ministry thereupon moved to prevent the judiciary from interfering with the T4 program. Attorneys general were called to Berlin, where they received instructions from Freisler on how to deal with problems posed by the killing operation.[71] In the same way, the ministry permitted ongoing investigations to lapse.[72]

The treatment of Lothar Kreyssig is revealing. As we have seen, this judge from Brandenburg had informed the RJM early in July 1940 that wards of his court had been killed, had raised moral and legal objections to these killings, and had asked for instructions. Kreyssig met twice with Freisler, who apparently provided details about the T4 program. Kreyssig thereupon filed a murder complaint with the state attorney in Potsdam.[73] When nothing changed, Kreyssig in August 1940 informed the various hospitals where his wards were committed that under existing laws he could not permit their transfer without his prior approval.[74] Three days later, he informed the ministry of his actions.[75] Thereupon Kreyssig was again called to Berlin; this time, he was received by Gürtner. The minister told him about Hitler's authorization, and when Kreyssig still refused to abandon his obstruction, Gürtner ordered his early retirement.[76]

Franz Gürtner died on 29 January 1941. It is not clear how far he would have carried his collaboration with the T4 program, but there is no reason to suppose he would have acted differently than did Schlegelberger, who succeeded him as acting minister.

Schlegelberger decided that close cooperation with the KdF would be the best protection against errors that would expose the T4 program and embarrass the judiciary. The RJM therefore exchanged information about complaints with the KdF, transmitting copies of the confidential reports from the attorneys general and the presiding judges of the circuit courts, miscellaneous correspondence about particular cases, and letters from private sources.[77] The KdF in turn transmitted to the RJM copies of the forms used in the T4 operation.[78] Both the RJM and the KdF did this to prevent blunders that might jeopardize the T4 operation. The RJM stressed that T4 must promptly notify the judiciary once the patients had been killed, so that they could coordinate their response and thus disguise the killing.[79] The KdF requested all data available at the RJM so that it could check whether poor management by T4 personnel had been responsible for leaks.[80] In addition to an exchange of materials, Wilhelm Crohne, chief of the RJM department dealing with penal law, met with representatives of the KdF to discuss and iron out special problems.[81]

The cooperation of the judiciary with the managers of the T4 killing operation reached its zenith in April 1941. At a private meeting, Schlegelberger and Bouhler decided that they must take additional steps aimed at damage control to pacify the judiciary and protect the T4 program.[82] Schlegelberger therefore called a meeting in Berlin to be attended by all attorneys general; all presiding judges of the circuit courts; Freisler and senior RJM officials; the presiding judges of the Supreme Court (Reichsgericht), the Supreme Probate Court, the People's Court, and the Patent Court; and the Reich attorneys at the Supreme Court.[83] At that meeting, which took place on 23 and 24 April 1941, the leaders of the German judiciary received detailed information about the T4 killing program and instructions on how to respond officially.

By special invitation, Viktor Brack and Werner Heyde addressed the meeting. Brack explained the legal basis for the killing operation and passed the Hitler authorization around the room for inspection. He further explained the organization of T4 and the methods of concealment. Heyde lectured on the methods used to select the patients for the killings. None of those present raised any objections.[84]

The instructions issued to the assembled leaders of the judiciary involved the ways in which they were to deal with the killings. Upon arrival, each attorney general and presiding judge had received a memo from Schlegelberger: "I request that you reserve for yourselves all decisions in each individual case that might involve the destruction of life unworthy of life in your district."[85] It was made clear to the attorneys general and the presiding judges that they were not to act on such cases but were simply to forward them to the RJM.[86] In addition, they were to notify some of their subordinates about the T4 operation in confidence; thus presiding judges of the district courts (Landgerichte), but not those of the magistrate courts (Amtsgerichte), were

THE ORIGINS OF NAZI GENOCIDE

to be informed.[87] The judiciary followed these instructions, and the damage was contained.

Thereafter, the support of the judiciary for the killing operation increased substantially; the RJM moved from passive cooperation to active collaboration. At a meeting of physicians involved in the killings, representatives of the RJM joined those from the KdF and the RMdI to coordinate the use of transfer institutions in the T4 program.[88] Eventually, after Georg Thierack had replaced Schlegelberger as minister, the RJM simply turned over to the police all patients committed under article 42b of the penal code.[89]

Church leaders and members of the judiciary were not the only professionals involved in one form or another with the T4 killing program. Scientists also played a crucial role. Among those scientists involved in the T4 operation were holders of university chairs, that is, full professors, the so-called *Ordinarien* so powerful at German universities; directors of government research institutes, who often also held chairs at universities or headed university hospitals; heads of large state hospitals, some of whom also had the title of professor; and researchers with government grants.

As we have seen, even before 1933 leading scientists advocated radical measures in the field of racial science. Prominent eugenicists—anthropologists, geneticists, psychiatrists—influenced both Nazi ideologues and a generation of scientists and physicians. (See table 6.2.) Two books were especially influential. One was the 1920 polemic by Karl Binding and Alfred Hoche, which guided, inspired, and justified the euthanasia killers. The other was the 1921 textbook on racial science by Erwin Baur, Eugen Fischer, and Fritz Lenz, which influenced Adolf Hitler when he read it in 1923 or 1924. The text went through numerous editions and title changes but continued to inspire scientists throughout the Nazi period and beyond.[90]

The participation of German scientists in the Nazi killing operations was no aberration. German psychiatrists, anthropologists, and physicians held views concerning race and heredity that mirrored those of the Nazi party and the state bureaucracy. A leading postwar German geneticist has described it best:

The ideology of the Nazis can be explained simply. They claimed that the differences among human beings are based on biology. Their blood, that is to say their genes, turns Jews into Jews, Gypsies into Gypsies, antisocial individuals into antisocials, and mental patients into mental patients. All these, as well as others, are inferior, and thus the inferior cannot receive rights equal to the superior. It is possible that the inferior will produce more children than the superior, and therefore the inferior must be excluded, sterilized, extirpated, and eliminated, that is killed, otherwise we will be responsible for the destruction of civilization [*Kultur*]. ... Com-

TABLE 6.2. German Scientists Involved in Nazi Crimes:
The Intellectual Mentors

Erwin Baur (1875–1933)	Chair in botany, Berlin Agricultural College, and KWI Breeding Research	Advocate of racial research
Eugen Fischer (1874–1967)	Chair in anthropology, Berlin, and KWI Anthropology	Advocate of racial research
Hans F. K. Günther (1891–1968)	Chair in anthropology, Jena, Berlin, Freiburg	Advocate of racial research
Alfred Hoche (1865–1943)	Chair in psychiatry, Freiburg	Advocate of euthanasia
Fritz Lenz (1897–1976)	Chair in racial hygiene, Munich, and section chief, KWI Anthropology	Advocate of racial research
Theodor Mollison (1874–1952)	Chair in anthropology, Munich	Advocate of racial research
Ernst Rüdin (1874–1952)	Director, KWI Psychiatry, Munich	Advocate of racial research and euthanasia

Sources: Max Weinreich, *Hitler's Professors: The Part of Scholarship in Germany's Crimes against the Jewish People* (New York: Yivo, 1946); Benno Müller-Hill, *Tödliche Wissenschaft: Die Aussonderung von Juden, Zigeunern und Geisteskranken, 1933–1945* (Reinbek bei Hamburg: Rowohlt Taschenbuch Verlag, 1984); Christian Pross and Götz Aly, eds., *Der Wert des Menschen: Medizin in Deutschland, 1918–1945* (Berlin: Edition Hentrich, 1989).

paring the ideological, scientific, and bureaucratic efforts of psychiatrists and anthropologists (eugenicists, race hygienists, ethnologists, behavioral scientists), we are at first surprised to discover that they had similar goals and held similar positions. The anthropologists strove to identify and exclude inferior non-Germans (Jews, Gypsies, Slavs, Negroes); the psychiatrists labored to identify and exclude inferior Germans (schizophrenics, epileptics, imbeciles, psychopaths). However ... this division of labor was never strictly observed.[91]

Academics in medicine and psychiatry had from the beginning participated in the planning and implementation of the euthanasia killing program. For example, Werner Catel, who served as senior expert for children's euthanasia, occupied the chair in pediatrics at Leipzig, and Werner Heyde, who headed the medical department of T4, held the chair in psychiatry at Würzburg.[92] Further, physicians occupied the key party and state posts responsible for the imposition of coercive eugenic and racial measures. (See table 6.3.)

TABLE 6.3. German Scientists Involved in Nazi Crimes:
The Scientific Administrators

Karl Brandt	Traveling physician to the Führer; general commissar for health and sanitation	Plenipotentiary for euthanasia
Leonardo Conti	RMdI state secretary; Reich physician leader	Support services for euthanasia
Fritz Cropp	RMdI department head	Support services for euthanasia
Walter Gross	Chief, Racial-Political Office of Nazi party	Advocate of racial science
Arthur Gütt	RMdI department head	Advocate of racial science
Herbert Linden	RMdI section head	Administrator and expert for euthanasia
Gerhard Wagner	Reich physician leader	Advocate of racial science and euthanasia

Sources: BDC dossiers; ZStL, Heidelberg Docs. 125,709-27; Benno Müller-Hill, *Tödliche Wissenschaft: Die Aussonderung von Juden, Zigeunern und Geisteskranken, 1933-1945* (Reinbek bei Hamburg: Rowohlt Taschenbuch Verlag, 1984); Achim Thom and Genadij Ivanovic Caregorodcev, eds., *Medizin unterm Hakenkreuz* (Berlin: VEB Verlag Volk und Gesundheit, 1989).

Moreover, the medical establishment had earlier supported forced sterilization almost without dissent. Even after he had retired in 1938 from the prestigious chair in psychiatry in Berlin, the respected Karl Bonhoeffer, for example, objected to remarriage for a woman whose schizophrenia he classified as hereditary, even though she had been sterilized six years earlier.[93] Paul Nitsche's comments concerning the role played by psychiatry, which could also apply to anthropology and genetics, make scientific participation abundantly clear: "As a rule, outsiders have not been able to appreciate how especially psychiatry rendered a fundamental service when its scientific findings revealed the gravity of the danger posed by degeneration [*Entartung*]; in this way psychiatry encouraged us to perceive the danger and the need for a defense, and thus it provided the basis for effective countermeasures."[94]

German science rapidly accommodated itself to the new ideologies of race and eugenics. The enthusiastic participation of the scientific and medical establishment in the sterilization program was an indication of the fact that its ideology meshed with that of the Nazi movement. The use of the science of racial hygiene in the formulation of the regime's eugenic and racial policies is exemplified by the expert opinions rendered by anthropologists on matters of Aryan parentage, the investigation by anthropologists and psychiatrists of Gypsy heredity, and the courses in racial hygiene arranged by prominent scientists for SS physicians.[95] Moreover, throughout Germany, directors of state hospitals established research departments for the study of heredity. In addition, a number of scientists established central research institutes; one example was the Institute for the Psychiatric and Neurological Study of Heredity in the Rhineland Province (Rheinisches Provinzialinstitut für psychiatrisch-neurologische Erbforschung), opened in Bonn in 1935 by Kurt Pohlisch and Friedrich Panse.[96] But the political agenda of racial hygiene and the attempts to establish laws of heredity through anthropological investigations involving primarily statistical analyses show that from the vantage point of post-DNA genetics these ideological efforts lacked a true scientific basis.[97] The attempts to classify humanity on the basis of racial characteristics derived from measurements or an evaluation of photographs were simply "scientific fraud."[98]

As the so-called science of racial hygiene assumed official status, adherence to it became a prerequisite for advancement. Loyalty to ideology determined access to research grants and job opportunities. A good example is the career of Konrad Lorenz. This young Austrian researcher, who studied animals to discover how heredity and environment determine behavior, had neither a tenured university appointment nor government research funds but had attracted the attention of the German scientific establishment. However, German scientific institutions, for example, the prestigious and influential Kaiser Wilhelm Society, were by statute prohibited from giving grants to foreigners working in their native countries.[99] The German scientists therefore recommended Lorenz to the official German Research Foundation, the Deutsche Forschungsgemeinschaft (DFG), which could give such grants, and in May 1937, almost a year before the incorporation of Austria, the thirty-four-year-old Lorenz applied to the DFG for a research grant.[100] Although his application was rejected because there was some doubt about his ideological reliability and Aryan ancestry, Lorenz was encouraged to reapply.[101]

In December 1937, the DFG received an application for Lorenz, submitted in his name by the director of the Kaiser Wilhelm Institute for Biology.[102] In support, several confidential letters from Viennese academics considered politically reliable were appended. Professor Fritz Knoll certified that the family tree of Lorenz did not contain any Jewish ancestors and pointed out that Lorenz could not obtain Austrian money because in Austria "the ruling circles have for ideological reasons devalued biology, especially the aspect Lorenz has explored in such an excellent manner."[103] Dr. A. Pichler, a university lecturer, also certified the non-Jewish ancestry of Lorenz, adding that recently "Dr. Lorenz indicated to me several times his growing interest in national socialism and spoke about its ideology in a positive way."[104] Professor Otto Antonius certified that Lorenz "never concealed his admiration for

THE ORIGINS OF NAZI GENOCIDE

the new conditions in Germany and for the achievements in all fields."[105] Professor Ferdinand Hochstetter wrote that "the character and national outlook of Lorenz are above reproach" and that Lorenz agreed "that the fate of Germans in Austria is inextricably tied to that of Germans in the Reich."[106]

In January 1938, Lorenz submitted as part of his application his personnel questionnaire, attaching to it proof of his own and his wife's Aryan ancestry.[107] He received his grant, and shortly thereafter, when Germany incorporated Austria, his scientific career prospered. In 1938 he joined the Nazi party, and in 1940 he accepted a tenured professorship in psychology at Königsberg.[108] Lorenz, a post–World War II Nobel laureate, did not find it difficult to succeed under the Nazi regime; both his science and his personal outlook were eminently compatible with the regime's racial ideology.[109]

When the radical solution of euthanasia replaced the slower method of mass sterilization, science stood ready to lead and profit from this program. (See table 6.4.) From the beginning, researchers participated in the killings.[110] As we have seen, senior psychiatrists directed the T4 Medical Office and served as experts evaluating handicapped patients. As we have also seen, the young physicians recruited to run the killing centers were inexperienced and lacked advanced training, and T4 provided research opportunities for them. Thus Heinrich Bunke, who received his medical license in September 1939 and later served as physician at Brandenburg and Bernburg, gave the following explanation after the war for accepting the invitation to join T4: "It provided the opportunity to collaborate with experienced professors, to do scientific work, and to complete my education [Ausbildung]."[111] Autopsies at the killing centers provided training for these young physicians. But these autopsies also did something else—they yielded human organs for scientific research.

When the euthanasia program began, scientists associated with T4 decided that researchers should capitalize on the opportunities afforded by the killing program.[112] Two research institutes took the lead in exploiting the euthanasia killings: the Clinic for Psychiatry and Neurology of Heidelberg University, directed by Professor Carl Schneider, and the observation ward and research station at the state hospital in Brandenburg-Görden, headed by Hans Heinze. Both men conducted research on the victims of euthanasia and also trained young physicians assigned to T4.

The Görden research station of Hans Heinze employed a number of physicians in training. For example, Ernst Illing worked as a researcher at Görden before he was posted to Vienna to head the children's ward at Am Spiegelgrund.[113] He had received his license to practice medicine in 1930 and had specialized in psychiatry and neurology in 1937, but he did not complete until 1942 the Habilitation that was the prerequisite for university teaching.[114]

The Heidelberg clinic of Carl Schneider invited physicians for brief periods of training. For example, Friedrich Mennecke, who had received his license

TABLE 6.4. German Scientists Involved in Nazi Crimes: The Medical Experts

Werner Catel	Chair in pediatrics, Leipzig	Medical expert for children's euthanasia
Max de Crinis	Chair in psychiatry, Cologne, Berlin	Medical expert for adult euthanasia
Julius Hallervorden	Director, KWI Brain Research	Brain research on euthanasia victims
Hans Heinze	Chief, Brandenburg-Görden hospital	Director, T4 research center
Werner Heyde	Chair in psychiatry, Würzburg	T4 medical director
Berthold Kihn	Chair in psychiatry, Jena	Medical expert for adult euthanasia
Friedrich Mauz	Chair in psychiatry, Königsberg	Medical expert for adult euthanasia
Hans Nachtsheim	Chief, KWI Hereditary Pathology	Experimental research on epileptic children
Paul Nitsche	Chief, Sonnenstein hospital	T4 medical director
Friedrich Panse	Professor of psychiatry, Bonn	Medical expert for adult euthanasia
Kurt Pohlisch	Chair in psychiatry, Bonn	Medical expert for adult euthanasia
Robert Ritter	Chief, racial research, Reich Health Office and RKPA Berlin	Anthropological research on Gypsies
Carl Schneider	Chair in psychiatry, Heidelberg	Director, T4 research center
Otmar von Verschuer	Chair in anthropology, Frankfurt, and KWI Anthropology	Advocate of racial research
Werner Villinger	Chair in psychiatry, Breslau	Medical expert for adult euthanasia
Viktor von Weizsäcker	Chair in psychiatry-neurology, Breslau	Brain research on euthanasia victims
Konrad Zucker	Professor of psychiatry, Heidelberg	Brain research on euthanasia victims

Sources: BDC dossiers; BAK, R73/14005, 15341–42; ZStL, Heidelberg Docs. 125,709–27, 127,890–93; Benno Müller-Hill, *Tödliche Wissenschaft: Die Aussonderung von Juden, Zigeunern und Geisteskranken, 1933–1945* (Reinbek bei Hamburg: Rowohlt Taschenbuch Verlag, 1984); Achim Thom and Genadij Ivanovic Caregorodcev, eds., *Medizin unterm Hakenkreuz* (Berlin: VEB Verlag Volk und Gesundheit, 1989).

to practice medicine in 1935 and served as director of the Eichberg hospital and its children's ward without additional certification in a specialty, received training at the Heidelberg clinic, with T4 paying his expenses and those of his wife, who worked as his laboratory assistant.[115]

The training these young physicians received — at Görden, Heidelberg, the children's wards, and the killing centers — involved the exploitation of euthanasia victims for medical research. At the killing centers, the young physicians performed autopsies and harvested organs.[116] The brain was in greatest demand. Julius Hallervorden, the director of the Kaiser Wilhelm Institute for Brain Research, who collaborated with the Görden research station, and Professor Carl Schneider, who launched ambitious research projects at his Heidelberg clinic, were most prominent in this final violation of the victims.[117]

Of course, Hallervorden and Schneider were not the only scientists to desecrate euthanasia victims for research. For example, organs taken from children killed in the Lubliniec hospital in Upper Silesia were sent for research use to the Neurological Research Institute of the chair in neurology at Breslau University held by Viktor von Weizsäcker.[118] Similarly, physicians in Vienna's Am Spiegelgrund did autopsies of their more interesting victims; two of these "researchers" — Heinrich Gross and Barbara Uiberrak — published as late as 1955 "discoveries" based on the medical history and dissected brain of a Hamburg girl murdered eleven years earlier.[119]

Research on the brains removed from subjects did not take place at Görden. The brains were transferred to Julius Hallervorden, whose institute was located in Buch, the same Berlin suburb that housed the large Prussian state hospital. Hallervorden bargained with both the Brandenburg killing center and the Görden research station to obtain brains from euthanasia victims. On 5 October 1940, Irmfried Eberl, the medical director of the Brandenburg killing center, and Hans Heinze, the chief of the Görden research station, met with Hallervorden at Buch.[120] Thereafter, Hallervorden obtained the brains of persons killed at the Brandenburg killing center and even visited Brandenburg to do some of the autopsies. After Brandenburg closed, Eberl and his assistant, Heinrich Bunke, performed the same services for Hallervorden at the Bernburg killing center. Hallervorden eventually collected at least 697 brains.[121]

For the most effective use of this kind of research, it was necessary to have as much data as possible on the brain donors prior to death. The T4 program therefore initiated a project late in 1941 to make brain research more effective. Using the usual euphemism of "decontamination" for killing, the T4 medical director, Professor Paul Nitsche, proposed in two memoranda that "still-available cases of hereditary retardation and epilepsy be studied prior to decontamination."[122] For this project, Nitsche needed a research institute, and on 19 September 1941, he visited Görden and met with Hans Heinze, who volunteered to make Görden available for research on victims.[123]

The Görden observation ward and research station for both men and women acquired through T4 the services of three physicians, Drs. Schmorl, Schumacher, and Asmussen; fourteen nurses; three student nurses; and two secretaries loaned to Görden by the Bernburg and Sonnenstein killing centers. During the first nine months of 1942, for example, fifty-six male and forty-one female patients suffering from retardation, epilepsy, or brain injuries were delivered to Görden as subjects for research. The subjects were observed and tested at Görden; eventually they were killed and their brains were removed and studied, with particular attention to a comparison between the anatomical findings and the data collected earlier.[124] Although the number of physicians and nurses fluctuated thereafter, a growing number of patients suffering from a variety of hereditary ailments were subjected to observation, testing, killing, and removal of organs.[125]

An even more ambitious project to subject euthanasia victims to dubious medical research was launched by Carl Schneider at the Clinic for Psychiatry and Neurology of Heidelberg University. Schneider was considered T4's senior researcher, and his clinic was thought to be the leading research center associated with the euthanasia killing program. Thus Schneider influenced developments at Görden. Heinze consulted with Schneider, and the three junior Görden physicians visited Heidelberg.[126] Further, Görden sent the brains of killed retarded persons (*Gehirnen von Idioten*) to Heidelberg.[127] Moreover, Schneider even proposed that after the war Heinze and his research station should relocate to Heidelberg.[128]

Supported by a research grant from T4 and the RMdI, Schneider also established special wards where subjects could be observed and tested.[129] Furthermore, he obtained, in addition to his chief physician, Konrad Zucker, the temporary services of Drs. Deussen, Rauch, Schmieder, Schmorl, Suckow, and Wendt.[130] Because his Heidelberg clinic facilities were insufficient, he negotiated with several institutions for space to establish such wards. One research station was created at the Baden state hospital at Wiesloch. After discussions in May 1942 among Schneider, Paul Nitsche, Ludwig Sprauer of the Baden Ministry of Interior, and the director of Wiesloch, a Dr. Möckel, the Heidelberg clinic entered into an agreement with Wiesloch to establish an observation and research station for men and women.[131] But the Wiesloch facilities proved unsatisfactory, and within a year, the research station was closed.[132]

Another research station was established at the Eichberg hospital, which already had a children's killing ward. In May 1942, discussions led to an agreement that Eichberg would host one ward each for males and females to "observe, test, and treat" subjects. The agreement involved Carl Schneider, Paul Nitsche from T4, Herbert Linden from the RMdI, Fritz Bernotat representing institutions in Hessen-Nassau, and the director of Eichberg, Friedrich Mennecke. Unlike Wiesloch, the Eichberg research station was designed not only to observe and test subjects but also to experiment with the use of insulin in shock therapy.[133]

Eichberg's ability to provide brains for research at Heidelberg was of special importance. The Reich Committee transferred children from various hospitals, some as far away as Hamburg-Langenhorn, to the Eichberg hospital. There they were observed, killed, and dissected, and their brains were sent to Heidelberg.[134] Eichberg continued as a research station even after Wiesloch had closed, despite the fact that its facilities were also unsatisfactory.[135] At any rate, Schneider continued his research at the Heidelberg clinic.[136]

Carl Schneider, collecting subjects from various institutions for transfer to Wiesloch, Eichberg, or Heidelberg, concentrated his research on the mentally retarded.[137] Late in 1942, he urgently requested from T4 a list of *Idiotenanstalten*, that is, institutions that held retarded patients.[138] In the summer of 1943, he urged Paul Nitsche to transfer every month ten to twelve retarded patients (*Idioten*) to Heidelberg.[139] Wherever he traveled, Schneider looked for suitable research subjects. After one trip, he informed Nitsche: "We have found many wonderful idiots [*schöne Idioten*] in Hirth's Alsatian institution in Strasbourg. Transfer requests will follow."[140]

But as the war progressed, research conditions deteriorated. Physicians were called to the front, assistants could not be obtained, equipment was in short supply, and the number of subjects declined; in August 1944, Schneider complained that Eichberg was delivering only one to two retarded subjects a month.[141] In the last year of the war, Schneider's research was frustrated because autopsies were not performed on the Reich Committee children killed at Eichberg, leaving him without essential material.[142]

After the Nazi assumption of power in 1933, German scientists, freed from the constraints of laws protecting the rights of patients, could pursue the most unscrupulous methods of research and treatment. The terrible experiments carried out in the concentration camps were symptomatic of this amoral attitude of the German scientific community. Using prisoners who had not volunteered, physicians performed experiments without regard to the welfare of their human subjects. Indeed, at times researchers even designed "terminal experiments," that is, experiments constructed in such a way that the death of the subjects was both expected and predetermined.[143]

The medical experiments on camp prisoners fall into two distinct categories.[144] One type of experiment was designed to aid Germany's war effort and was conducted in the camps under the direction of the medical services of the German armed forces. For example, the German air force conducted high altitude experiments at the Dachau concentration camp to duplicate in low pressure chambers conditions encountered by pilots.[145] Another air force experiment at Dachau attempted to duplicate extreme hypothermia.[146] The air force and the navy also experimented at Dachau with ways to enable humans to consume sea water.[147] The Waffen SS tested vaccines against typhus, yellow fever, smallpox, cholera, and diphtheria at the Buchenwald and Natzweiler concentration camps and against epidemic jaundice at Sachsenhausen and Natzweiler.[148] The Waffen SS also conducted experiments at the women's concentration camp of Ravensbrück on how to treat combat wounds. Deliberately inflicted wounds were treated with the antibiotic sulfonamide to test its efficacy, while other experiments tested methods of bone, muscle, and nerve regeneration as well as bone transplants.[149] Another Waffen SS experiment, conducted at Sachsenhausen and Natzweiler, tested ways to counteract mustard and phosgene gases.[150]

In addition, individual physicians undertook private research in the camps to advance their own reputations. Johann Paul Kremer, a professor of medicine at the University of Münster who served as a substitute SS physician at Auschwitz in late 1942, is an excellent example of physicians who availed themselves of the research opportunities the concentration camps provided. Interested in the effect of hunger on humans, he had selected prisoners killed so that he could remove their livers, spleens, and pancreases for study.[151]

Although the goals of these experiments were viable, the use of coerced human beings was not. Moreover, terminal experiments on human subjects are never justified. Furthermore, aside from the question of the morality of viewing human beings as abused laboratory rats, the methods of some researchers were both flawed and fraudulent. A good example of a medical fraud who performed such experiments was Sigmund Rascher, an air force physician who transferred to the SS and whose scientific and personal misconduct eventually led to his execution.[152]

A second category of experiments was designed to advance the ideological goals of the Nazi regime. (See table 6.5.) The sterilization experiments are the best example. As we have seen, sterilization as negative population control had been used by the regime throughout the 1930s against those considered diseased. During the war, the number of people considered unworthy of procreation—Jews, Gypsies, Slavs—increased enormously. The traditional method of sterilization was too expensive and too time-consuming to use against large populations. Reich Leader SS Himmler, therefore, commissioned research projects designed to perfect a method by which large numbers of persons could be sterilized rapidly and if possible without their knowledge.

Professor Carl Clauberg, a specialist in obstetrics and gynecology with an international reputation, convinced Himmler that large numbers of women could be sterilized by injecting chemicals into the uterus. He believed that one physician and ten assistants could sterilize up to 1,000 women a day. And

THE ORIGINS OF NAZI GENOCIDE

TABLE 6.5. German Scientists Involved in Nazi Crimes: Selected Researchers

Carl Clauberg	Professor of gynecology, Königsberg	Sterilization experiments at Auschwitz
Irmfried Eberl	Director, Brandenburg and Bernburg	T4 physician and commandant at Treblinka
Sophie Ehrhardt	Associate of Ritter at Reich Health Office	Anthropological research on Jews and Gypsies
Günther Hillmann	Butenandt's assistant, KWI Biochemistry	Tested Mengele's blood samples
August Hirt	Chair in anthropology, Strasbourg	Anatomical research on concentration camp prisoners
Eva Justin	Assistant of Ritter at RKPA	Anthropological research on Gypsies
Johann Paul Kremer	Professor of anatomy, Münster	Medical experiments at Auschwitz
Rudolf Lonauer	Director, Hartheim	T4 physician
Josef Mengele	Assistant of Verschuer at KWI	Medical experiments at Auschwitz
Horst Schumann	Director, Grafeneck and Sonnenstein	T4 physician; Auschwitz experiments

Sources: BDC dossiers; BAK, R73/14005, 15341–42; Alexander Mitscherlich and Fred Mielke, eds., *Medizin ohne Menschlichkeit: Dokumente des Nürnberger Ärzteprozesses* (Frankfurt: Fischer Taschenbuch Verlag, 1960); Benno Müller-Hill, *Tödliche Wissenschaft: Die Aussonderung von Juden, Zigeunern und Geisteskranken, 1933–1945* (Reinbek bei Hamburg: Rowohlt Taschenbuch Verlag, 1984); Achim Thom and Genadij Ivanovic Caregorodcev, eds., *Medizin unterm Hakenkreuz* (Berlin: VEB Verlag Volk und Gesundheit, 1989).

since these injections would be part of a "routine" physical examination, he did not believe the women would notice.[153]

Viktor Brack brought another sterilization researcher to Himmler's attention. Horst Schumann, a young physician who had served as medical director at the Grafeneck and Sonnenstein killing centers but had never been certified in any specialty, proposed to use X-rays to sterilize large numbers of men. The idea was simple: the men would briefly stop at a counter where a hidden X-ray machine would sterilize them without their knowledge.[154] Both Clauberg and Schumann carried out experiments that killed or maimed human subjects at Auschwitz and Ravensbrück, but neither ever perfected the sterilization methods they touted.[155]

An equally bizarre research project was proposed by August Hirt, a professor of anatomy at the University of Strasbourg. He sought to collect the skulls of "Jewish-Bolshevik Commissars" to advance anthropological knowledge and secured Himmler's authorization to obtain the required Jewish concentration camp prisoners from Auschwitz. They were transferred to the Natzweiler concentration camp, killed in its gas chamber, and then shipped to the anatomical institute at Strasbourg so that Hirt could create his collection of skeletons.[156]

As euthanasia yielded first place in mass murder to the final solution, science prepared to profit from the escalated killing program. While physicians like Carl Clauberg, Horst Schumann, and August Hirt conducted medical experiments of special interest to Reich Leader SS Himmler, scientists like Robert Ritter, Eva Justin, Sophie Ehrhardt, and Adolf Würth, as we shall see, combed the camps for anthropological subjects. The Auschwitz experiments of Josef Mengele remain, however, the most egregious example of the collaboration of unscrupulous researchers with equally unscrupulous senior scientists and prestigious scientific institutions.[157]

Born in the Swabian section of Bavaria in 1911 into an upper middle-class family, Mengele eventually earned two doctorates.[158] The first doctorate was in physical anthropology at Munich under Theodor Mollison in 1935 and the second was in medicine at Frankfurt under Otmar Freiherr von Verschuer in 1938. He received his license to practice medicine in late 1937 but apparently did not pursue certification in a specialty. Instead, he opted for research. His two dissertation supervisors were eugenicists, and his dissertations in anthropology at Munich and in medicine at Frankfurt both dealt with research in racial hygiene. After finishing his second doctorate, Mengele continued his research in Verschuer's Frankfurt Institute for Hereditary Biology and Race Hygiene. As principal investigator, Verschuer supervised the research of numerous assistants under a variety of DFG research grants.[159] His 1938 report to the DFG on this sponsored research, focusing on the genetic study of twins and families, lists the work and publications of his assistant Mengele.[160]

Although Mengele did not join the Nazi party until 1938, he belonged to the brown-shirt storm troopers, the SA, during 1933–34 and in 1938 joined the SS. As an SS member, he was drafted during the war into the Waffen SS instead of the Wehrmacht, advancing by 1943 to the rank of captain (Hauptsturmführer). He served as an SS physician on the Eastern front until he was wounded and therefore posted to the concentration camp death head units in the rear. He functioned during 1943–44 as one of the SS physicians at the Auschwitz-Birkenau extermination camp.

In his new post, Mengele performed the usual duties of a concentration camp SS physician as well as the special Auschwitz assignment of directing selections for the gas chamber. In addition, Auschwitz opened up unlimited opportunities for an ambitious researcher. Research subjects were available

THE ORIGINS OF NAZI GENOCIDE

in large numbers, and the restraints of medical ethics did not apply. Further, Mengele could compel highly skilled inmate physicians to design and conduct research, perform tests and autopsies, and produce research papers, without the need to share credit with them.[161] It is therefore not surprising that Mengele used Auschwitz as a research laboratory.

Otmar von Verschuer, Mengele's mentor who was himself a protégé of Eugen Fischer, had left Frankfurt for Berlin in 1942 to succeed Fischer as director of the Kaiser Wilhelm Institute for Anthropology. Mengele worked at the institute during SS assignments to Berlin and thus continued to contribute to Verschuer's research projects. When Mengele went to Auschwitz, Verschuer realized the potential of this posting, and as principal investigator, he carried Mengele's Auschwitz experiments on his DFG grants. In his progress report to the DFG, Verschuer told the foundation about this new research arrangement: "My assistant Dr. Dr. Mengele is another contributor who has joined this research project. He was posted to the Auschwitz concentration camp as an SS captain and camp physician. With approval of the Reich leader SS, he has conducted anthropological research on various racial groups in the camp, and has transmitted blood samples to my laboratory for testing."[162]

Mengele mailed the results of his research on Jewish and Gypsy twins to the Kaiser Wilhelm Institute. There scientists analyzed the samples of blood obtained before death and the organs obtained after dissection. Mengele's investigation of eye color was only one bizarre example of such criminal experiments. He collected pairs of eyes if one of the pair had a different color, hoping that he could discover ways to change eye color. At one time, Mengele killed an entire Gypsy family to send their eyes for analysis to research assistant Karin Magnussen at the Kaiser Wilhelm Institute.[163] In this manner, so-called scientific research accompanied the killing operations until the total defeat of Nazi Germany.

Chapter 7

The Expanded Killing Program

Hitler's stop order did not end the killings; they soon continued in German hospitals by other means. At the same time, however, the killings expanded to include inmates of the concentration camps. The involvement of the SS should come as no surprise. Although the KdF had directed the killings in Germany, and the role of the SS had been minimal, Himmler's men did not restrain themselves on the borders of the Reich and in the newly occupied Polish territories, killing the handicapped even before the euthanasia murders had started inside Germany.

The first handicapped victims were executed. They were handicapped patients from various state hospitals and nursing homes in Pomerania, the Prussian province bordering on Poland in the north.[1] As the war started, Reich Leader SS Heinrich Himmler and Franz Schwede-Coburg, who served in Pomerania as both Gauleiter and Oberpräsident (provincial governor), reached an agreement, which provided for the transfer to the SS of a number of Pomeranian state hospitals. The patients of these hospitals were evacuated. While some were transferred to other institutions, those judged incurable and those without concerned relatives were simply killed.

These early euthanasia killings took place without the cover of medical evaluation, the subterfuge of condolence letters, or the use of sophisticated technology. Instead, they employed the primitive method of mass execution. These killings of the handicapped happened at the same time that the RMdI mailed the first questionnaires to hospitals in Württemberg and before the first experimental gassing occurred at Brandenburg. They showed that once the decision was made to kill the handicapped, only pragmatic concerns would limit the means. In the Reich, public opinion imposed restraints that required subterfuge, but in wartime such limitations did not apply in the East.

The job of killing the Pomeranian patients was given to the SS in neighboring Danzig–West Prussia, a newly created German province encompassing the former Free City of Danzig and the area of West Prussia seized from Poland. Specifically, the task was assigned to SS Major (Sturmbannführer) Kurt Eimann, commander of an auxiliary police unit formed in the summer of 1939 from about 2,000 members of the Danzig City SS Regiment and known as the Eimann Battalion (Sturmbann).

The handicapped patients from Pomerania arrived by train at the town of Neustadt in West Prussia and were killed in a forest nearby. Polish political prisoners from the SS prison camp Stutthof near Danzig dug large pits to serve as mass graves.[2] The patients were transported by truck from the railroad station to the place of execution. Patients were escorted singly to the pit by two SS men; when they faced the pit, a third SS man, who had walked behind, administered the so-called *Genickschuß* by shooting them in the base of the skull. The patient then fell into the pit. When the grave was full, the Stutthof prisoners filled it in.

The first transport from Pomerania arrived at Neustadt in late October 1939, and the handicapped patients were immediately taken to the forest and shot. The first victim was a female patient approximately fifty years old, and the first shot was fired by Eimann himself: "In front of the pit [Eimann] shot the woman through the base of the skull. The woman, who had walked in front of him without suspecting anything, was instantaneously killed and fell into the pit."[3]

The killings continued through November 1939, including the patients from the Konradstein hospital in Danzig; the total number shot was about 3,500. After the patients from the last transport had been killed, the Eimann Battalion eliminated all witnesses by killing the Stutthof prisoners.

The killed Pomeranian patients were German nationals, but the killings soon expanded to include non-Germans. Inside the Reich, euthanasia did not, for the most part, include non-Germans.[4] But the questionnaires in Germany did call for information about the nationality of patients, and Polish patients were deported to occupied Poland.[5] There they shared the fate of all Polish handicapped patients. To kill handicapped patients in occupied Poland, primitive methods similar to those used by the Eimann Battalion were employed between 1939 and 1941.[6] For example, at the psychiatric hospital in Chelm near Lublin, members of the German security police shot all 420 patients on 12 January 1940.[7]

The mass killing of handicapped patients proceeded even more systematically in the Polish territories annexed by Germany. On 7 December 1939, for example, the evacuation and killing of the 1,172 patients in the psychiatric hospital in Tiegenhof (Dziekanka in Polish) near Gnesen in the province of Posen (Poznan in Polish) began.[8] This province, German prior to 1918, and the city and district of Lodz (renamed Litzmannstadt), part of Congress Poland prior to 1918, were incorporated into Germany as the Wartheland, with the city of Posen as capital. Hitler appointed Arthur Greiser as governor and party leader of the Wartheland, and Himmler appointed Wilhelm Koppe as his representative. (See table 7.1.)

The German authorities in the Wartheland emptied the state hospitals by killing the patients. For this purpose, Higher SS and Police Leader (Höherer SS- und Polizeiführer [HSSPF]) Koppe and Ernst Damzog, the inspector of the Sipo and SD, created the Lange Commando. SS Captain (Hauptsturmführer) Herbert Lange, who had served with the Aachen, Stettin, and Trier

TABLE 7.1. Chain of Command for SS and Police in the Occupied Territories

Office	Function	Chain of command
Reich leader SS and chief of the German police (RFSS)		To report to Hitler
Chief (CdS) of the security police (Sipo) and the SS security service (SD)	Head of Central Office for Reich Security (RSHA), including the Sipo (Gestapo and Kripo) and SD (foreign and domestic)	To report to RFSS
Chief (CdO) of the order police (Orpo)	Head of Central Office of the Order Police (HAOrpo)	To report to RFSS
Higher SS and police leader (HSSPF)	Representative of RFSS and in command of SS, police, and Waffen SS in an occupied region	To report to RFSS; to coordinate with RSHA, HAOrpo, and Waffen SS
Befehlshaber of the Sipo and SD (BdS) (in Reich held title of inspector [IdS])	Representative of RSHA and in command of the Sipo and SD in an occupied region	To report to RSHA and HSSPF
Befehlshaber of the order police (BdO) (in Reich held title of inspector [IdO])	Representative of HAOrpo and in command of Orpo (Schupo and Gendarmerie) in an occupied region	To report to HAOrpo and HSSPF
SS and police leader (SSPF)	Representative of RFSS and in command of SS, police, and Waffen SS in an occupied district	To report to RFSS and HSSPF; to coordinate with BdS, BdO, RSHA, HAOrpo, and Waffen SS
Kommandeur of the Sipo and SD (KdS)	Representative of BdS and in command of the Sipo and SD in an occupied district	To report to BdS, SSPF, and RSHA
Kommandeur of the order police (KdO)	Representative of BdO and in command of Orpo in an occupied district	To report to BdO, SSPF, and HAOrpo

Sources: BAK, R58. See also Henry Friedlander, "The SS and Police," in *Genocide: Critical Issues of the Holocaust*, edited by Alex Grobman, Daniel Landes, and Sybil Milton (New York: Rossel Books and Simon Wiesenthal Center, 1983), pp. 150–54.

Gestapo, was a thirty-year-old commissar of detectives (Kriminalkommissar) who entered Poland with Einsatzgruppe Naumann in September 1939. After the incorporation of the Wartheland, he was assigned to the Posen Gestapo and, for a time, headed the guards assigned to Greiser.[9] Early in 1940 Lange assumed command of a special unit (Sonderkommando) composed of members of the Sipo from Posen and Lodz.[10] Their first task was the killing of handicapped patients in the Wartheland.

The Lange Commando killed patients in numerous Wartheland hospitals, but we know the most about its work in the hospitals in Wartha near Lodz in March and in Tiegenhof near Gnesen in late 1940.[11] Unlike the Eimann Battalion, the Lange Commando did not shoot its victims; it used gas. For this purpose, a kind of mobile gas chamber had been invented. We do not know the inventor, but the KTI was probably involved. The Lange Commando used trucks, usually described by witnesses as resembling moving vans. At least some of them had "Kaisers Kaffee Geschäft" (Kaiser Coffee Company) painted on the side. These early gas vans differed from those developed late in 1941 by the Sipo to cut costs through the use of exhaust gas. Like the gas chambers in the euthanasia killing centers, these early vans in the Wartheland used carbon monoxide tanks; the driver opened the valve on the container, and the pure carbon monoxide gas entered the van's enclosed cab through a rubber hose. The Lange Commando arrived at the hospitals, collected the patients, loaded them into the vans, and gassed them while driving away.[12] After killing handicapped patients in 1940, the commando possibly also killed Jews in the small villages of the Wartheland with these early gas vans.[13] And as we shall see, late in 1941 the commando headed by Herbert Lange, and after April 1942 by Hans Bothmann, constructed and operated the first killing center of the final solution at Chelmno (renamed Kulmhof) in the Wartheland.

The best-known killing spree conducted by Herbert Lange and his commando against handicapped patients took place in an East Prussian camp at Soldau in May and June 1940. The inspector of the Sipo and SD in Königsberg, Dr. Otto Rasch, established the Soldau camp late in 1939 as a place where Polish political prisoners could be secretly executed.[14] Alongside Polish prisoners, the camp commandant, SS Captain (Hauptsturmführer) Hans Krause, also shot handicapped patients sent to Soldau.[15] But when the East Prussian state hospitals were vacated in May 1940, as had occurred earlier in Pomerania, the Soldau camp personnel was apparently unable to execute such large numbers, and the Lange Commando was dispatched to Soldau to kill these German patients.[16]

The onetime operation of the Lange Commando outside the Wartheland was due to a chance encounter, although Viktor Brack was apparently also involved.[17] When the Königsberg HSSPF Wilhelm Rediess visited Posen, HSSPF Koppe told him how Lange and his commando had used gas vans to kill large numbers of patients in the Wartheland. As he had made a deal with Erich Koch, the East Prussian provincial governor and Nazi party leader, to kill the East Prussian patients in return for the use by the SS of a vacated hospital, Rediess asked Koppe to loan him the Lange Commando and its gas van.

Koppe agreed, and after Reich Leader SS Himmler had given his permission, the inspectors of the Sipo and SD in Posen and Königsberg, Ernst Damzog and Otto Rasch, made all specific arrangements.[18]

The Lange Commando and its gas van were in Soldau from 21 May until 8 June 1940, a total of nineteen days, during which time it gassed 1,558 East Prussian patients who had been selected for killing according to the guidelines used to choose the victims in Pomerania. The Lange Commando loaded forty patients into its gas van on each trip, killed the victims during the trip, disposed of their bodies in the surrounding countryside, and returned with the empty van about three hours later.[19]

A sequel to this episode illuminates the attitude that characterized these euthanasia killing operations in the East. When Koppe loaned the Lange Commando to Rediess, he had in turn demanded payment to the Wartheland SS of 10 RM for each patient killed, but Rediess did not pay. After waiting for payment, Koppe requested in October the 15,580 RM owed, minus 2,000 RM advanced by Rasch to Lange at Soldau. In a letter to Königsberg, Koppe reviewed the agreement, pointing out that his Lange Commando had killed 1,558 patients; following the language regulations for such correspondence, he described the killings as "evacuations."[20] But by October 1940, Rediess had been posted to Oslo, and Koppe had to write to Jakob Sporrenberg, Rediess's successor in Königsberg.[21] Sporrenberg did not want to pay and simply forwarded Koppe's letter to Rediess in Oslo.

In November Rediess replied in a letter and a telegram to Karl Wolff, the chief of Himmler's personal staff, requesting a decision by the Reich leader SS. Rediess acknowledged that he had requested the services of the Lange Commando and that this commando had killed 1,558 patients at Soldau, adding that it had even expanded its services to include also "250–300 Polish crazies [*Irre*]" from the Polish territories incorporated into East Prussia, for which Koppe had not required payment. But Rediess argued that he had never taken Koppe's demands seriously because the killing operation had been for the benefit of the German Reich and not the East Prussian SS. Further, Gauleiter Koch had not paid the SS but had instead provided it with an East Prussian hospital.[22] Himmler did not issue a ruling, and in February 1941, Koppe also turned to Wolff. He reiterated his demand for payment and pointed out that at the time Koch had agreed to pay for the cost of killing the patients, and thus Rediess must have received the money.[23] The surviving documents do not reveal the outcome of this intramural squabble over money.

The killing of the handicapped in occupied Poland during 1939–41 was only the prelude to the massive killing operations that commenced with the invasion of the Soviet Union on 22 June 1941. During the summer and fall of 1941, the Nazi regime launched the so-called final solution against Jews and Gypsies. Alongside Jews and Gypsies, who were slated for extermination because they were born into the two targeted ethnic groups, the handicapped, victims of mass murder since the winter of 1939–40, were the third group of human beings condemned to death on the basis of their biology.[24]

The task of performing these killings was assigned to the Einsatzgruppen of the Sipo and SD. These Einsatzgruppen, subdivided into Einsatzkommandos, employed—on a much larger scale—the method of mass execution tested by the Eimann Battalion on Pomeranian patients. The Einsatzkommandos arrived at cities, towns, and villages to round up their victims, transported them to isolated areas, shot them individually or in small groups, and buried them in mass graves.[25]

Although the Einsatzgruppen focused primarily on the killing of Jews and Gypsies, as well as Soviet POWs, they did not overlook the handicapped.[26] Whenever it seemed convenient or when the Germans required hospital space, the handicapped were included in the killing operations.[27] Obviously, the handicapped had been classified as expendable, as had Jews and Gypsies. Soviet civilian Vladimir Romanenko, who had been arrested as a spy, serves as a good example. Although the Germans cleared him of the charge of espionage, they executed him because he was handicapped. Sonderkommando 11a explained this decision as follows: "As the Romanenko case involved a retarded person, who admitted that he had already been committed to a mental hospital three times, he was executed on 9 September 1941 for reasons of hereditary health."[28]

Events in Minsk and Mogilev provide another example of the fact that the handicapped were considered expendable. In the fall of 1941, Arthur Nebe, the chief of the Reich Office of the Detective Forces (Office V in the RSHA) and at that time also chief of Einsatzgruppe B, ordered Albert Widmann of the KTI to visit him in Smolensk to perform a special task. Widmann and his assistant, Hans Schmidt, traveled to Bielorussia, bringing along a large amount of dynamite. The task Nebe asked them to perform had been requested by Heinrich Himmler, and it involved experiments in killing groups of human beings rapidly, cheaply, and expeditiously.[29] The Russian civilians selected as subjects in this bizarre experiment were the handicapped, taken from state hospitals in Minsk and Mogilev. They seemed the logical victims since Nebe had told his deputy Paul Werner that "he could not ask his troops to shoot these incurably insane people."[30]

The first experiment took place in Minsk, where handicapped patients were locked into a pillbox that was then dynamited. The results were macabre. The pillbox and the victims were totally destroyed; parts of bodies were strewn over a relatively large area, and the killers had to collect limbs from the surrounding trees. Nebe and Widmann had to conclude that the use of dynamite as a killing method was not efficient. The second experiment took place the next day in Mogilev. There handicapped patients were locked into a sealed room, and exhaust gas first from a car and then from a truck was fed into the room through hoses. This method did prove efficient and later served as the model for the method used in the killing centers of the final solution.[31]

A third example is provided by the postwar Allied interrogation of Dr. Wilhelm Gustav Schueppe. From the fall of Kiev in September 1941 until March 1942, Schueppe was assigned by the representative of Leonardo Conti, the Reich physician leader, to the Kiev Pathological Institute, heading, first as deputy and then as chief, a commando of about twenty persons, including about ten physicians, supplemented by members of the SD dressed as medics. There Schueppe participated in a special operation (*Sonderaktion*) he described as the "destruction of life unworthy of life." This included the handicapped as well as members of inferior races, that is, Jews, Gypsies, and Turkmen.[32] At the institute, these persons were killed with injections. Schueppe defined the handicapped as those suffering from particular ailments, including the diseases enumerated in both the sterilization law and the RMdI questionnaires that initiated the euthanasia program. Schueppe estimated that during his service at the institute more than 100,000 victims were killed in Kiev.[33]

The euthanasia program not only followed German arms to the East but also spawned expansion at home. In 1940 German concentration camps were growing in number and size, but they did not yet possess the facilities to kill large numbers of prisoners at one time. Methods used to kill individual prisoners during the prewar years—such as forced labor, harsh living conditions, beatings, and executions—were too slow to reduce the growing camp population.[34] The SS therefore turned to the KdF to determine how to utilize T4's killing capabilities. Early in 1941, Reich Leader SS Himmler conferred with KdF chief Philipp Bouhler concerning "whether and how the personnel and the facilities of T4 can be utilized for the concentration camps."[35] Soon thereafter, in the spring of 1941, a new killing operation commenced, aimed at prisoners in the German concentration camps.

The killing of selected concentration camp prisoners in the gas chambers of the T4 killing centers was designated "Special Treatment 14f13."[36] "Special treatment [*Sonderbehandlung*]" was the term prescribed for killing in the language regulations used by the SS and the police.[37] The code 14f13 was the file number used by the Inspectorate of the Concentration Camps for the killing of prisoners in T4 centers. At the Inspectorate, the category 14f included all files involving the death of prisoners. Thus, for example, 14f7 files concerned death through natural causes, 14f8 applied to suicides, and 14f14 involved executions.[38]

Collaboration between the Inspectorate of the Concentration Camps and the T4 administrators did not require meticulous interdepartmental negotiations. As we have seen, Himmler's SS and police had provided some support services for T4 killing operations, and this collaborative effort had been ar-

TABLE 7.2. The Concentration Camps Administered by
the Inspectorate in 1941

Camp	Opening date	Location
Dachau	Mar. 1933	Town of Dachau near Munich
Sachsenhausen (Oranienburg)	Aug. 1936	Town of Oranienburg near Berlin
Buchenwald	July 1937	City of Weimar
Flossenbürg	May 1938	Near city of Hof in Bavaria
Mauthausen	Aug. 1938	Near city of Linz in Upper Austria
Neuengamme	Dec. 1938	City of Hamburg
Ravensbrück	May 1939	Town of Fürstenberg north of Berlin
Wewelsburg (Niederhagen)	Jan. 1940	Near town of Paderborn in Westphalia
Auschwitz	May 1940	Town of Oswiecim in Upper Silesia near Cracow
Gross-Rosen	Aug. 1940	Town of Rogoznica in Lower Silesia
Natzweiler	July 1941	Near Strasbourg in Alsace

Source: International Tracing Service, *Vorläufiges Verzeichnis der Konzentrationslager und deren Außenkommandos sowie anderer Haftstätten unter dem Reichsführer-SS in Deutschland und deutsch besetzten Gebieten, 1933–1945* (Arolsen, 1969).

ranged smoothly by Viktor Brack, an active member of the SS who had a close, long-standing relationship with Himmler. In addition, Werner Heyde, the medical chief of T4, had in 1933 befriended Theodor Eicke, who had headed the concentration camps before the war. Due to this friendship, Heyde had joined the SS and had been appointed psychiatric adviser to the Gestapo and to the Inspectorate of the Concentration Camps. Further, in another collaborative SS-T4 effort, designed to circumvent the requirements of the sterilization law, the Inspectorate had authorized the sterilization of concentration camp prisoners as long as T4's Reich Committee sanctioned the procedure.[39] Thus, once Himmler and Bouhler had reached an agreement on the killing of concentration camp prisoners, Brack simply coordinated the joint killing operation.[40]

The T4 killing operation designated 14f13 involved selected prisoners from all camps administered by the Inspectorate of the Concentration Camps, except Natzweiler, which was established too late to be included. (See table 7.2.) This SS-T4 collaboration encompassed both the process of selecting the victims and the actual killing operation.

The selection process involved a two-tier approach. SS camp physicians preselected a pool of potential victims, and T4 physicians then picked the actual victims from this pool.[41] The exact criteria used by the SS camp physicians to select prisoners are not known. Officially, the Inspectorate apparently directed SS camp physicians to select those suffering from incurable physical diseases who were permanently unable to do physical labor. In a circular sent to all concentration camps, the Inspectorate officially advised camp physicians that the process of selection should be based on those questions "underlined in red" in the questionnaire (Meldebogen) required for each selected prisoner.[42] These questionnaires were the same as those used by T4 for handicapped patients, but since most of the questions did not apply, only those underlined needed to be answered. In addition to personal data, the reason for arrest, and the date of incarceration, SS camp physicians had to provide details about physical ailments but not about the disabilities that had been used to evaluate the handicapped.[43]

Unofficially, the Inspectorate applied other criteria, which were not transmitted in writing. Camp personnel either had to report to the Inspectorate for oral instructions, or senior SS functionaries visited the camps to deliver instructions personally.[44] The unofficial instructions covered racial and eugenic criteria for selection. For example, the Inspectorate ordered that at the Buchenwald concentration camp the selection for 14f13 was to include the handicapped and Jews.[45] In addition, the SS camp physicians were apparently also instructed to include a large proportion of prisoners with criminal or antisocial records, since prior criminal charges and current behavior had to be listed in the questionnaire.[46] In reality, however, the major criterion for selection was the prisoner's ability to do physical labor, but even there, the SS physicians picked their victims in the arbitrary manner common in the concentration camps.[47] Eventually, even the Inspectorate found that the selection process lacked precision.[48]

In the camps, the SS spread the rumor that sick and weak prisoners could report for transfer to a sanatorium; in Mauthausen the official announcement mentioned "camp sanatorium Dachau." Among prisoners, 14f13 was therefore commonly known as "Operation Invalids." [49]

Panels of physicians from T4 visited the concentration camps to make the final selection of victims. The use of T4 physicians to comb through institutions to select victims was nothing new. The rapid completion of questionnaires had been an essential precondition for the smooth execution of the adult euthanasia killing operation, and the operation could not have functioned well if hospital physicians completing questionnaires used optimistic diagnoses to defer patients. To prevent delays and fulfill quotas, T4 had therefore dispatched teams of physicians to hospitals and nursing homes to complete or review questionnaires.[50] A notorious example was the February 1941 visit of a panel of T4 physicians, headed by Karl Brandt and Werner Heyde, to the famous Bethel institution to expedite the registration and murder of its patients.[51]

The same review system was used in Operation 14f13 in the concentration camps. But although the reason for sending such panels to public and private hospitals is clear, the reason for using them in 14f13 is not, and we do not know what guidelines, if any, the T4 physicians were instructed to follow.[52] In the operation designed to kill the handicapped, the T4 managers dispatched their own physicians because they did not trust hospital physicians to apply T4 selection criteria with sufficient severity. But this hardly applied to Operation 14f13 because SS camp physicians could be trusted to select with utmost rigor. Viktor Brack's postwar argument that a "humane" Himmler did not trust SS camp physicians to make proper selections and thus wanted impartial outsiders to be involved is obviously not credible.[53]

In the only postwar study of Operation 14f13, the author argues that T4 physicians provided medical cover to convince the staffs of the killing centers, some of whom did the actual killing of the prisoners, that concentration camp prisoners were as "unworthy of life" as handicapped patients.[54] But even if those staffs needed to be convinced, and the evidence does not indicate that they did, that task could have been accomplished easily without the special effort and expense needed to dispatch T4 physicians to the concentration camps. It seems far more reasonable that interagency competition led to the use of T4 physicians. Hitler had granted sole commission to the KdF to institute the euthanasia killings, and the KdF had already frustrated an earlier attempt by Leonardo Conti and the RMdI to wrest that assignment from its grasp. When Bouhler placed the services of T4 at the disposal of the SS, he would thus have been unwilling simply to surrender T4 facilities for use by the Reich leader SS and, to preserve the KdF's monopoly, would probably have insisted on a selection process involving T4 personnel. The T4 managers were not really concerned about the substance of the process but insisted that the formalities of established procedures be observed, including the participation of T4 physicians and the use of T4 questionnaires.[55]

T4 assigned at least twelve physicians to visit the concentration camps: Hans-Bodo Gorgaß, Otto Hebold, Werner Heyde, Rudolf Lonauer, Friedrich Mennecke, Robert Müller, Paul Nitsche, Viktor Ratka, Kurt Schmalenbach, Horst Schumann, Theodor Steinmeyer, and Gerhard Wischer.[56] They were experienced T4 collaborators who had functioned as expert evaluators in the euthanasia program. Heyde and Nitsche headed T4's medical department, while Lonauer and Schumann directed T4 killing centers. Several worked for the T4 Central Office (Hebold, Müller, Ratka, Schmalenbach, and Wischer), and three assisted in T4 killing centers (Gorgaß, Schmalenbach, and Steinmeyer). Mennecke headed the Eichberg hospital and its children's ward, and Ratka the Tiegenhof killing hospital in the East.[57]

These T4 emissaries visited the camps either singly, in teams of two, or as panels of several physicians.[58] We know a great deal about their work habits from postwar interrogations of SS and T4 physicians as well as from testimonies of concentration camp prisoners.[59] The most detailed evidence, however, was provided by the physician Friedrich Mennecke. Throughout his professional career, Mennecke wrote innumerable, extremely detailed letters to his wife Eva, whom he addressed as "mommy [*Mutti*]," and his letters from various concentration camps remain a revealing and essential source in furthering our understanding of how Operation 14f13 functioned.[60]

Mennecke's first letter, written in Oranienburg and dated 4 April 1941, is the earliest source to mention a T4 camp visit.[61] As far as we can determine, his visit to the Sachsenhausen concentration camp on the outskirts of Oranienburg in early April marked the start of 14f13, although the process obviously commenced earlier. Thus arrangements for T4 questionnaires, T4 visits, and preselection by SS camp physicians must have preceded that date, and it is at least possible that other T4 physicians visited other camps even earlier.

At Sachsenhausen, Friedrich Mennecke and Theodor Steinmeyer together selected prisoners, and they were later joined by Otto Hebold. Mennecke described his "work" in Sachsenhausen as "very, very, interesting."[62] He stayed at the Eilers Hotel in Oranienburg and described in great detail his "big and pleasant room," his Sunday excursion trip, his meals in the SS officers' mess, and his late-afternoon coffee and Kuchen; Steinmeyer, however, commuted each day from Berlin on the Metro (S-Bahn).[63] In four days at Sachsenhausen, Mennecke completed questionnaires for about 135 prisoners; together, the three T4 physicians managed to "process" between 350 and 400 prisoners.[64]

The job of the T4 physicians was primarily to ensure that the T4 questionnaires were properly completed. The questionnaires had been transmitted to the camps prior to their arrival, and the SS had already filled in the obligatory information: name, date and place of birth, last residence, family status, citizenship, religion, race, and date of arrest. The T4 physicians thus only needed to check the completed information, enter the diagnosis, and make the final decision.[65] Thereafter, the questionnaires were delivered to T4 headquarters in Berlin.[66]

The collaboration between T4 and the SS camp physicians was close and cordial. They were, after all, both participating in a joint killing operation, and unlike civilian physicians, who distanced themselves from visiting T4 physicians during hospital evaluations, the SS camp physicians enthusiastically supported the work of the T4 visitors. Also, T4 and camp physicians were ideologically compatible. All T4 physicians were members of the Nazi party, three were SS officers (Heyde, Lonauer, and Mennecke), and one held officer rank in the brown-shirt SA (Ratka).[67]

The preselected prisoners filed past tables manned by T4 physicians, who, if they decided to select a prisoner, placed a cross (+) in a box at the bottom of the questionnaire.[68] They made no attempt to perform a physical examination, and the speed with which they surveyed large numbers of prisoners—in

Buchenwald, two of them "processed" 873 prisoners in five days—precluded any serious medical evaluation.[69] The T4 physicians merely verified the information on the questionnaires. Friedrich Mennecke, who selected victims as a T4 physician in the concentration camps of Auschwitz, Buchenwald, Dachau, Gross-Rosen, Neuengamme, Ravensbrück, Sachsenhausen, and Wewelsburg, thus wrote his wife that the "examination" of a prisoner involved only "the presentation of the individual whose file served to corroborate the answers on the questionnaire" and later told his postwar interrogators that "this did not involve medical evaluations, because in the concentration camps I only had the assignment to fill out questionnaires."[70]

The T4 physicians did have to provide a diagnosis, unless it had already been supplied by the SS camp physicians, but they made no attempt to ascertain whether it was accurate. The sample questionnaire thus suggested stomach cancer as a common diagnosis, although this was obvious fiction. The T4 physicians also had to evaluate the conduct of the prisoner in the camp and his or her prior police record, and they based their evaluations on information supplied by the SS camp administration. Since there was not enough room on the T4 questionnaire, they summarized this information on the reverse side.[71]

Friedrich Mennecke described his work at the Ravensbrück concentration camp in one of his numerous letters to his wife: "The work moves swiftly [flutscht], because the answers to questions on top have already been typed on the form and I only have to record the diagnosis, chief symptoms, etc. I would prefer not to describe the composition of the patients in a letter, more about that later in person. [SS First Lieutenant (Obersturmführer)] Dr. Sonntag [the camp physician] sits next to me and supplies information about their behavior in the camp, an SS sergeant [Scharführer] brings in the patients —everything moves without a hitch [klappt tadellos]."[72] In fact, prisoners' record and conduct determined evaluation as much as their physical condition because these medical practitioners of racial hygiene firmly believed that good behavior reflected genetic health while poor behavior reflected genetic disease. Alternately, this meant that those judged inferior could not but behave poorly.

This focus on behavior applied especially to prisoners designated as racial aliens. It is therefore not surprising that the T4 physicians judged Jewish prisoners with greater severity. For Jews, they did not even bother to enact the pretense of a physical examination. In one of his letters, Friedrich Mennecke described the procedure: "As a second allotment there then followed altogether 1,200 Jews, who did not first have to be 'examined,' but where it is sufficient to extract from the files the reasons for their arrest (often very extensive!) and to record them on the questionnaires."[73] In these cases, Mennecke simply recorded his reading of the individual's record as his "medical" diagnosis. Five surviving diagnostic statements concerning Jewish prisoners exemplify the attitude of the T4 physicians toward those considered to be members of an alien race:

1. *Isidor Israel G.* [Born] 25 April 1902 [in] Kolomza. Construction worker. Stateless, anti-German Jewish agitator [*Hetzjude*]. In the camp lazy and insolent.
2. *Hans R.* Jew from the Protectorate, anti-German behavior! Crime of miscegenation. In the camp lazy, insolent. Multiple camp punishments: tied to stake.
3. *Ottilie Sara S.* [Born] 6 December 1879. Single. Clerk. Czech Jewess. Marxist functionary. Vile Germanophobe. Relations to English Embassy.
4. *Anna Sara S.* [Born] 26 November 1906 [in] Gotha. Polish citizen. Jewess. Deportation prisoner [*Abschiebungshäftling*], who returned illegally from abroad. Suffers from venereal disease (clap).
5. *Anna Sara B.* [Born] 7 December 1892 [in] Poland. Single. Business woman in Rumburg, Sudetenland. Expulsion prisoner [*Ausweisungshäftling*]. Attitude hostile to the state.[74]

Although after the war the T4 physicians denied all knowledge of the purposes of 14f13, at the time, they enjoyed their junkets to the concentration camps, often in the company of their wives and even their children. For example, on a visit to Dachau, a panel of six physicians—Lonauer, Mennecke, Nitsche, Ratka, Steinmeyer, and Wischer—raved about their Munich city tour, their evening of dinner and the cinema, and their excursion to the beach at Starnberger Lake.[75]

Two T4 physicians certainly knew the purpose of Operation 14f13. Rudolf Lonauer and Horst Schumann headed T4 killing centers and had thus participated in the entire killing process from selection to cremation.[76] After the mass murder by gas of institutionalized handicapped patients ended late in August 1941, gassing operations at the T4 killing centers involved only concentration camp prisoners.[77] The killing technique employed against prisoners did not essentially differ from that applied earlier against patients. Only the paperwork differed because prisoners were not registered at the killing centers and thus did not generate any work for the office staff.[78] Instead, all paperwork was handled in the concentration camps, and if necessary, the camps informed agencies and relatives of the deaths of prisoners.[79]

Before August 1941, the victims of Operation 14f13 were gassed in the facilities otherwise occupied with the killing of the handicapped, specifically at Hartheim and Sonnenstein.[80] After late August 1941, when Hitler ordered a stop to the murder of the handicapped by gas, only concentration camp prisoners were gassed in T4 killing centers. Four centers were still operational:

Bernburg, Hadamar, Hartheim, and Sonnenstein. But Hadamar was never used for this purpose, and its gassing facilities were demolished in the summer of 1942.[81] Bernburg and Sonnenstein, however, remained functional until 1943 for the killings of 14f13, while Hartheim continued to gas concentration camp prisoners until the end of 1944.

There is no evidence that the staffs of the killing centers cared whether their victims were handicapped patients or concentration camp prisoners. Staff members noted only superficial differences between the handicapped and prisoners, commenting only on the different types of paperwork each group generated. Further, in postwar interrogations, staff members remembered that rather than the solid gray uniforms worn in ordinary jails, the victims of 14f13 wore "zebra uniforms [*gestreifte Kleider*]" that distinguished concentration camp prisoners.[82]

Documents from the Gross-Rosen concentration camp show how the system worked. On 19 and 20 January 1942, Friedrich Mennecke selected about 214 prisoners at Gross-Rosen and sent their questionnaires to T4 headquarters in Berlin, which then transmitted the list of selected prisoners to the Bernburg killing center. On 3 March, Bernburg requested that Gross-Rosen transfer the 214 prisoners, and on 6 March, Gross-Rosen replied that the 125 prisoners who remained would be transferred on 23 March.[83] The difference in number resulted from the deaths since January of thirty-six prisoners and the reclassification of fifty-one prisoners, including forty-two Jews, because they were indeed able to work.[84]

By March 1942, the Inspectorate of the Concentration Camps had become concerned that the camps were not fully exploiting prisoner labor and admonished camp administrations that the selection process for 14f13 must include only prisoners unable to work.[85] About one year later, as the SS need for concentration camp labor increased and the size of the Auschwitz gassing facilities surpassed that of the T4 facilities, Heinrich Himmler ordered the cessation of 14f13 by restricting selection to prisoners with mental, not physical, disorders, a group obviously too small to require T4 intervention.[86] Thereafter, the gassing installations were dismantled at the Bernburg and Sonnenstein killing centers. As we shall see, when 14f13 ended in 1943, both T4 and the SS had already embarked on a far more ambitious killing operation in the East.

Only Hartheim, located near the Mauthausen concentration camp, remained operational. Hartheim's physicians, Rudolf Lonauer and Georg Renno, both SS officers, had cordial relations with the Mauthausen commandant, Franz Ziereis, and his staff, attending social evenings with their SS colleagues at the camp's officers' mess.[87] Close cooperation between Mauthausen and Hartheim continued even after 14f13 ended. In 1944 approximately 3,000 prisoners from Mauthausen and Gusen, Mauthausen's largest subsidiary camp, were gassed at Hartheim. These late killings, however, did not follow the earlier procedures. The SS selected prisoners without question-naires or visiting physicians. It delivered the victims to Hartheim to be gassed as a kind of professional courtesy to a neighboring institution.[88] Finally, in December 1944, as Germany faced certain defeat, the gassing facilities at Hartheim were demolished; Mauthausen prisoners were ordered to do the job.[89]

From 10,000 to 20,000 persons were killed in Operation 14f13. The number was probably closer to 20,000; those from Mauthausen and Gusen alone num-bered almost 5,500.[90] Although these numbers might be considered relatively modest — especially if we consider the millions murdered by the Nazis — the SS-T4 collaboration in 14f13 was significant because it formed yet another link between euthanasia and the final solution.

Chapter 8   The Continued Killing Program

Hitler's stop order of August 1941 did not end the destruction of those considered "unworthy of life." The belief that his stop order ended the killings is based on a postwar myth. The stop order applied only to the killing centers; mass murder of the handicapped continued by other means. Moreover, the stop order did not apply to children's euthanasia, which had never utilized gas chambers. As with the children, after the stop order physicians and nurses killed handicapped adults with tablets, injections, and starvation. In fact, more victims of euthanasia perished after the stop order was issued than before.

The stop order had not reversed the decision to kill the handicapped. As we have seen, the long-range goal of ridding Germany of the disabled involved at first compulsory sterilization and then mass murder. Killing handicapped newborns was the highest priority; euthanasia organizers considered it crucial to prevent a new generation of disabled persons. Children's euthanasia was therefore initiated first and continued unabated even after the stop order.[1] Furthermore, the killing of handicapped adults was just a radicalized substitution for sterilization, consuming at least 70,000 victims before Hitler issued his stop order. And Hitler issued this order only because popular knowledge of the killings and subsequent disquiet posed problems for the regime.

Some historians have argued that the stop order was issued in part because the first sweep had killed enough patients to make hospital space available for other purposes.[2] But contrary to official claims, emptied hospitals were often not confiscated for military use; they were simply turned over to Nazi party organizations. The savings from killing about 70,000 handicapped wards of the state were not sufficient to have served as motivation for the murders.[3]

The first killing sweep had cleared out most patients from some regions but had left those in other regions virtually untouched. In the same way, in their first sweep through the occupied Soviet Union during the summer of 1941, the SS killing squads left alive large pockets of Jews and Gypsies to use as forced labor in camps and ghettos until it was convenient to kill them. Similarly, the killing frenzy in the Polish killing centers during 1942 and 1943 left alive some Jews and Gypsies for exploitation as concentration camp labor. The first sweep of euthanasia thus resembled the first sweep of the final solution, and the exploitation and killing of the handicapped after the stop order resembled the unsystematic and arbitrary method of destruction practiced in the concentration camps toward the end of the war.[4]

Although the euthanasia killings resumed slowly after the stop order, the paperwork essential for the selection of victims continued unabated. The RMdI continued to distribute questionnaires every six months to collect information on all institutionalized patients, and Herbert Linden transmitted the completed questionnaires to the KdF. T4 could thus continue to "register and evaluate" patients, providing work for office staffs and medical experts, who still made life-and-death decisions.[5]

The victims of children's euthanasia had never been killed in gas chambers but instead had been killed by specially selected physicians in hospital wards through the use of regular medication or starvation. This method not only continued after the stop order but was expanded through the inclusion of older children and teens.[6] Similarly, so-called research on handicapped children and their subsequent killing also continued.[7] After the stop order ended the use of gas for handicapped victims, T4 applied the lessons of children's euthanasia to the killing of disabled adults. Physicians in designated institutions were empowered to kill selected patients through medication or starvation; the killers designated this decentralized method as "wild" euthanasia.[8]

As we have seen, in three of the four functioning killing centers, the gas chambers remained operational for the 14f13 killing operation after the stop order. Hadamar, the fourth killing center, was not needed for this purpose, and after a short interval, the basement "gas chamber and crematorium were dismantled and some of the personnel was transferred," so that after August 1942 Hadamar appeared to have returned to normal. But this appearance was deceptive because Hadamar remained a "wild" euthanasia killing hospital, where thousands were killed through the administration of an "overdose of narcotics or sedatives."[9]

Hadamar was not the only killing hospital during the period of "wild" euthanasia. Hospitals with children's killing wards, such as Eichberg, Kalmenhof, and Eglfing-Haar, which had also functioned as transfer institutions, were obvious places for killing adults after the stop order.[10] Two institutions, Meseritz-Obrawalde in Pomerania and Tiegenhof (Dziekanka) in the Wartheland, whose location at the eastern border of the German Reich served to hide mass death from the German population, were converted into killing hospitals.[11] Finally, a vast number of hospitals, unable after 1941 to utilize the killing centers, simply murdered their handicapped patients.[12]

The fate of institutionalized handicapped patients in the city-state of Hamburg can serve as an example of how the euthanasia killings took place after the stop order.[13] In addition to the infants killed in children's wards at the Langenhorn state hospital and the Rothenburgsort children's hospital in Hamburg, established respectively in December 1940 and early 1941, about fifty adults from Hamburg became victims of euthanasia prior to the stop order. They had been picked up by Gekrat from Langenhorn in July 1941,

THE ORIGINS OF NAZI GENOCIDE

deposited at the Königslutter transfer institution, moved by Gekrat from there to Bernburg, and gassed at that killing center on 24 August, the day Hitler issued the stop order.[14] Two further transports from Langenhorn arrived in Königslutter in late July and early August. But those 106 handicapped patients — 30 women and 76 men — arrived too late to be gassed in Bernburg because the stop order intervened. They were not returned to Hamburg but remained at Königslutter; 81 of those 106 patients were killed in Königslutter during the next three years.[15]

Most of the handicapped of Hamburg had been registered too late to be killed in the gas chambers of the killing centers but were killed during the period of "wild" euthanasia. Those later killings did not take place in Hamburg; instead, victims were transferred to institutions with killing capabilities outside Hamburg. Thus handicapped patients were dispatched to Uchtspringe, Königslutter, Scheuern, Mainkofen, and Am Steinhof in Vienna. They never returned.[16] But five other institutions received most of the Hamburg victims: Eichberg, Hadamar, Kalmenhof, Meseritz-Obrawalde, and Tiegenhof.

On 7 August 1943, the T4 transport organization Gekrat transferred 208 handicapped patients from Hamburg to Eichberg and Kalmenhof. Of these, 79 came from the Langenhorn state hospital and 129 from the Alsterdorfer Institutions of the Protestant Home Mission; 82 were children. Only an eleven-year-old survived.[17] Similarly, weekly transports of handicapped female patients left Langenhorn for Hadamar between 22 June and 7 August 1943. Of the 347 women, 307 were killed.[18] In November 1941, Gekrat transferred 203 handicapped patients — 102 men and 101 women — from Langenhorn and the Alsterdorfer Institutions to Tiegenhof. Of these, 173 were killed: 12 in 1941, 124 in 1942, 24 in 1943, and 13 in 1944.[19] Similarly, few of the 407 handicapped patients — 213 men, 189 women, and 5 children — transferred from Hamburg to Meseritz-Obrawalde in 1943 and early 1944 survived the war.[20]

Of course, handicapped patients from Hamburg were not the only victims killed after the stop order. And Eichberg, Hadamar, Kalmenhof, Meseritz-Obrawalde, and Tiegenhof were only a few of the many places where the handicapped were killed in the "wild" euthanasia period. And although it appears that the T4 Central Office directed and managed the process of the annihilation of the handicapped from registration to death, the killing operations of "wild" euthanasia were actually decentralized and chaotic.

Although the RMdI and the KdF continued to distribute and evaluate questionnaires and to generate the transfer lists used by Gekrat to relocate patients, the T4 Central Office no longer managed patients' so-called treatment at the receiving institutions.[21] At the killing centers, the handicapped victims had been killed as soon as they arrived, and the killing method had been managed and coordinated by the T4 Central Office. Such micromanagement was no longer possible after the stop order. The relatively large number of receiving institutions made coordination difficult. Further, these institutions continued to operate as normal hospitals, so the killings had to be fitted into the regular institutional schedule. Moreover, when medication replaced gas as the killing method, the need to hide the murders forced the killers to space the deaths of their victims over weeks or months.[22]

The medical professionals involved with the T4 killing operation had urged from the beginning that the killing process be defined in law and be uniform in practice. During 1940, the KdF proposed a euthanasia law and circulated a draft to a selected group of physicians, psychiatrists, public health officials, and academic eugenicists.[23] The experts submitted their opinions to the KdF in writing. One such written reply—from Irmfried Eberl, physician-in-charge at the Brandenburg and Bernburg killing centers—has survived.[24] The Sipo joined the discussion and attempted to broaden the list of victims to include antisocial elements—the so-called *Asozialen*, also designated "aliens to the community *[Gemeinschaftsfremde]*"—but the physicians blocked this expansion.[25]

Experts met to hammer out the precise language of the proposed law as well as the provisions covered in needed implementation decrees. A surviving protocol of one such meeting, which also included Reinhard Heydrich, provides a fascinating view of medical and academic professionals as killers. As a group, they favored precise definitions and central direction; they viewed the killings as medical procedures governed by professional criteria.[26]

As we know, Hitler refused to sanction such a law.[27] Unlike the experts directly involved, who later claimed that only the need to impede "Allied atrocity propaganda" had precluded publication of the law, postwar historians have argued that Hitler refused to sanction a law because he did not believe that the German people would accept it.[28] This is probably true, but an additional reason might have been Hitler's unwillingness to limit his options by defining his victims; similarly, in the occupied East, Heinrich Himmler opposed "decrees that define the concept 'Jew' " because "we just tie our own hands with such foolish commitments *[törichten Festlegungen]*."[29]

Without a euthanasia law, the medical killers could only bemoan the absence of "central control," complain about the "insanity" of "wild euthanasia procedures," and worry about preserving the "reputation of the field of psychiatry."[30] They did, however, continue to provide direction for the euthanasia killings. First, they agonized about the status of psychiatry, projecting for their profession a future in which all patients not killed could be cured. Second, they investigated all institutions to discover patients who should be killed and to decide what uses each institution should serve. Third, they consulted and conspired to reinstitute a centrally directed euthanasia killing operation. Fourth, they processed the paperwork generated by children's

THE ORIGINS OF NAZI GENOCIDE

euthanasia, "wild" euthanasia, and euthanasia-related research. Fifth, they recruited, supplied, and counseled the killers at the local hospitals.

The surviving correspondence of Paul Nitsche, who succeeded Werner Heyde as T4's medical chief, provides insight into the attitudes and concerns of the T4 medical staff and their friends.[31] The senior members of the T4 medical circle shared professional interests and belonged to the same professional organizations; they contributed to the same journals, served as referees for those journals, contributed to *Festschriften* for each other, and reviewed each other's books.[32] They also served as a network for friends and students seeking jobs in universities and institutions.[33]

The T4 medical men exerted influence not only through their university and institutional positions but also through their professional organizations. The most important of these was the Association of German Neurologists and Psychiatrists (Gesellschaft deutscher Neurologen und Psychiater). Founded in 1935, the association was chaired by Ernst Rüdin, the influential director of the Kaiser Wilhelm Institute's German Research Institute for Psychiatry in Munich, and Paul Nitsche served as its executive secretary (Geschäftsführer) until 1939.[34] The executive committee (Vorstand) and advisory council (Beirat) of the association included, among others, leading psychiatrists and neurologists involved in T4 operations: Walter Creutz, Max de Crinis, Werner Heyde, Paul Nitsche, Kurt Pohlisch, Ernst Rüdin, Carl Schneider, and Viktor von Weizsäcker.[35] The association served as a reservoir of talent and ideas for the euthanasia killing program; T4 provided financial subsidies for the association, which in turn pledged "to do everything to advance the work that is also of interest to party and state."[36]

The leading psychiatrists in the association, who also belonged to the inner circle of the T4 program, were determined to exercise control over all aspects of the field of mental health. They thus sought to dominate the Association for Child Psychiatry and Therapeutic Education (Gesellschaft für Kinderpsychiatrie und Heilpädagogik), created in 1940 to advance the claims of psychiatrists in the field of psychotherapy. The surviving correspondence about the move to control this association also reveals the rivalries, based on competing personal ambitions, among the circle of T4 psychiatrists. While Paul Nitsche, Herbert Linden, Ernst Rüdin, and the KdF supported Hans Heinze as chairman of the Association for Child Psychiatry and Therapeutic Education, Hans Reiter, the president of the Reich Health Office, opposed Heinze and supported instead the Breslau professor Werner Villinger, who had also served as a T4 medical expert.[37]

Although psychiatrists maintained their dominance in universities, hospitals, and professional associations, they feared competition from psychotherapists, accusing them of undervaluing biological causes, overvaluing individualism, and remaining under the influence of Freud's and Adler's Jewish ideas.[38] Unable, however, to exclude psychotherapists, who were led and protected by Hermann Göring's cousin Matthias Heinrich Göring, psychiatrists proposed a merger but failed to accomplish this.[39]

Psychiatrists feared that the future status of their profession was uncertain. Determined to continue euthanasia, that is, killing handicapped patients, they faced a time when they would have no patients at all. Moreover, as killing evolved into psychiatry's primary function, the status of the profession declined as relatives of potential patients began to shun psychiatric institutions, medical students tended to avoid psychiatry as a field of specialization, and junior psychiatrists became demoralized.[40] The leadership was therefore determined to "raise the human and scientific status of psychiatrists."[41]

Twenty years earlier, psychiatrists had experienced similar damage to their reputation due to their brutal treatment of soldiers considered malingerers during World War I. They had eventually introduced progressive therapies that elevated their professional status. Most prominent was a technique that assigned work to patients. This occupational therapy (*Arbeitstherapie*) proved successful and popular, although it tended to reinforce authoritarian hospital structures by imposing forced labor on institutionalized patients and limiting their freedom of movement.[42]

Similarly, as the euthanasia killing operation emptied state hospitals, the T4 psychiatrists embraced new therapies, which had, in their opinion, already brought "noticeable successes."[43] These therapies focused on shock treatments, which had been used in World War I to force shell-shocked soldiers to return to the front.[44] By 1940 psychiatrists had developed various so-called active therapies in which shock was induced either by an electric current or the administration of medication.[45] But psychiatrists did not find it easy to obtain the needed equipment and drugs during the war. The equipment required for electroshock therapy, produced by Siemens, could be obtained by clinics and hospitals only through the efforts of Herbert Linden at the RMdI and Richard von Hegener at the KdF.[46] The drug required for insulin-shock therapy was severely rationed during the war, and for shock treatments, psychiatrists could obtain insulin — essential for the survival of diabetics — only through Herbert Linden's intervention.[47]

Scientific research and new therapies were designed to remove from psychiatry the odium of euthanasia, although all three activities — research, therapies, and killings — occurred simultaneously. To emphasize their commitment to research and new cures, hospital directors rushed to change the names of their medical complexes from "institution" to "clinic," although Herbert Linden of the RMdI believed that the German word *Anstalt* was far superior to the foreign word *Klinik*.[48] Moreover, leading T4 physicians meeting at the KdF in early 1942 planned a research clinic for children where new therapies would be evolved and tested; however, children who did not measure up would be sent to the Eichberg children's killing ward. The Eichberg director applauded this collaboration as "the project of the future."[49] Others wanted to combine research, therapy, and killing in one institution. For example, one of the younger T4 physicians, Robert Müller, proposed the following: "Thus, for the future: No more nursing homes [Pflegeanstalten] for substandard cases; instead only hospitals [Heilanstalten] with the most active therapy and scientific research and—with facilities for euthanasia."[50]

These plans for the future of psychiatry required coordination. To accomplish this task, the RMdI created the office of the Reich plenipotentiary for state hospitals and nursing homes (Reichsbeauftragter für die Heil- und Pflegeanstalten) and in October 1941 appointed Herbert Linden as Reich plenipotentiary.[51] Thereafter, the close cooperation between Linden and the KdF, which had existed since the inception of the euthanasia killing program, continued, but with Linden as the driving force.

Karl Brandt also played an important role during the last three years of the war. Appointed plenipotentiary for medicine and health (Bevollmächtigter für das Sanitäts- und Gesundheitswesen) by Hitler in July 1942, and granted additional powers by the Führer in September 1943, Brandt advanced to a position of central medical authority. Outmaneuvering Leonardo Conti in the intraparty power struggle, Brandt established his authority, especially concerning the allocation of hospital beds and other medical resources.[52] The T4 managers turned therefore to Brandt as a matter of course to gain his support in their efforts to regularize the "wild" euthanasia killings.[53]

In support of the efforts of Brandt and Conti to allocate hospital beds for casualties in the air war, T4 prepared statistical summaries of the number of handicapped patients and the number of beds occupied or available in public and private institutions.[54] Its experts argued that even if the euthanasia program continued, the increased number of beds thus freed would soon decline because "euthanasia cannot influence the number of new admissions."[55] These T4 experts visited institutions in every German state and Prussian province to investigate their status, reporting to the central office on the number of available beds, the number of patients still subject to euthanasia, and the possible future uses of those institutions.[56] Throughout, the T4 experts demanded above all that the remaining handicapped patients should be able to do productive work.[57]

The T4 planning commissions, including both T4 physicians and a business manager who worked for Plenipotentiary Linden, visited all institutions, including small homes for the aged, the poor, and the homeless.[58] Because they obviously resembled the earlier commissions that had selected patients in hospitals (and concentration camps) for killing, they tried to reassure suspicious local officials that their visits were for long-range planning only.[59] The planning commission members reported the obvious finding that many state hospitals had been allocated for other purposes because the euthanasia killing operation had reduced the number of handicapped patients.[60] They found that this was the case especially in the province of Pomerania, where "arbitrary and wild" killings by the Eimann Battalion had produced "reductions" without proper planning.[61] The T4 experts argued that even after the killings, and even if the killings continued henceforth, it would be necessary to retain for the handicapped 2,000 hospital beds per every 1 million people.[62]

Although the T4 experts refused to make concessions to accommodate local differences in their centralization efforts, they had to accept political realities in the newly annexed areas of the German Reich. They complained that in the Protectorate of Bohemia and Moravia handicapped patients had remained in Czech hospitals administered by Czech physicians and had been neither sterilized nor killed, adding that in Prague there was even a ward for handicapped Jewish patients with a Jewish physician. German patients had been concentrated in two hospitals—one in Bohemia and one in Moravia— and had from there been transferred to the Sudetenland for sterilization and killing; the similar removal of 700 ethnic Germans from the independent puppet state of Slovakia led to rumors that they had been "turned into soap [*zu Seife verkocht*]."[63] In the annexed western Polish territories known as the Wartheland, however, we have seen that German administrators seized control of the hospitals and killed the Polish patients. The T4 experts could therefore report that the number of handicapped patients had been substantially reduced in the Wartheland, also adding that the "Israelite Mental Institution" in the Lodz ghetto had been cleared on 1 September 1942.[64]

At every inspected institution, the T4 experts also discussed the euthanasia killing operation with the staff, reporting on the "attitude"—"positive" or "negative"—toward euthanasia of directors and physicians.[65] Rarely did the T4 experts meet the kind of opposition they encountered in a Württemberg institution for deaf-mute children. The warden, a Swiss national named Heinrich Hermann, opposed the transfer of his charges, using the word "killed [*getötet*]" while discussing their fate with the visiting T4 representatives. Unused to such blunt language, the T4 experts, who consistently used euphemisms to describe the killings, reported on this dispute with Hermann in detail, demanding that "such foreign national" be removed from such a sensitive position.[66]

These efforts by T4 did not, however, solve the problem of decentralized killings outside its control. The demands of the war and the reduced role of the T4 Central Office forced financial retrenchment that included reorganization and staff reduction.[67] Attempts to gain backing for greater centralization from Plenipotentiary Karl Brandt produced an order in August 1943 that T4 could authorize selected institutional directors to use drugs to kill handicapped patients.[68] Although this order provided T4 managers with greater authority to continue their work, Paul Nitsche soon thereafter complained that he still had no control over when the designated institutional directors would receive the required drugs.[69] In the end, T4 received drugs for the killings of "wild" euthanasia only through the intermittent efforts of the Waffen SS and the KTI.[70]

Although its control over the localized euthanasia killings lacked the precision of the earlier killing-center phase, the T4 Central Office did continue to recruit and direct. T4 agents discussed euthanasia with physicians at the institutions they inspected and thus facilitated contacts between the central office and the killers in the field.[71] T4 collaborators who served as institutional directors informed the central office when they selected patients for killings. For example, Valentin Faltlhauser, the physician in charge of the Kaufbeuren hospital, submitted a list of 421 patients selected for killing, asking that the central office validate his admittedly Spartan criteria.[72] T4 also expanded the pool of potential victims; persons suffering from senility and other diseases of old age were included as T4 combed through old-age homes and poorhouses, T4 physicians classified so-called antisocial elements as mentally diseased, and T4 arranged for the transfer of some patients to concentration camps.[73]

As we have seen, the "wild" euthanasia killings took place in various institutions as part of the normal hospital routine. Although the killings were known to both staff and patients, they could be hidden from outside observers. T4 realized that a major benefit of "wild" euthanasia was the cover that hospital routine provided for the killings. In one T4 planning report, this method was championed as the best way to organize the killings: "With few exceptions, the death of the person undergoing euthanasia will thus hardly differ from a natural death. That is the goal we must reach."[74]

The T4 killings thus took place in numerous hospitals throughout the Greater German Reich, but only a small number of hospitals specialized in killing the handicapped. These hospitals became slaughterhouses where, under the guise of normal hospital operations, conditions resembled those in the Nazi concentration camps. One former inmate of the Eichberg hospital, who was transferred from there to several concentration camps, testified after the war that her experiences at Eichberg had been as terrible as her experiences in the camps.[75] Yet Eichberg, where 2,722 adult patients died between 1941 and 1945, functioned as only a "minor" killing center of "wild" euthanasia.[76]

Many other hospitals resembled Eichberg in the brutal treatment of their handicapped patients. The activities of the Austrian physician Emil Gelny can serve as an example. Born in 1890 and licensed to practice medicine in 1915, Gelny joined the Nazi party in 1932 and served as major in the brown-shirt SA at the time of the Anschluß.[77] On 1 October 1943, Gelny was appointed director of the Gugging state hospital in Lower Austria, although he had spent his entire medical career as a general practitioner and only qualified in psychiatry in August 1943. Gelny owed his appointment to an old party comrade, Josef Mayer, who headed the internal administration under Hugo Jury, the governor of Lower Austria. Gelny's appointment was designed to speed the killings of "wild" euthanasia, and he immediately instituted a reign of terror at the Gugging institution. One year later, in November 1944, his assignment was enlarged to include the Maur-Öhling state hospital. Gelny not only used the traditional killing method of administering medication but also introduced a killing innovation symbolizing T4's dual goal of therapy and killing. Using the electric chair as his model, Gelny killed handicapped patients with electroshock treatments.[78] He implemented these killings without central direction, as he had no contact with T4 prior to February 1944; only then did the central office recognize his value and co-opt him into T4's medical inner circle.[79]

The Meseritz-Obrawalde hospital in the Prussian province of Pomerania, officially designated as the Provincial Mental Institution Obrawalde near Meseritz (Provinzial-Irrenanstalt Obrawalde bei Meseritz), was probably the most notorious killing hospital of "wild" euthanasia.[80] During the period preceding the so-called euthanasia stop, large numbers of patients had been transferred from Meseritz-Obrawalde "to the East" and had, like patients from other Pomeranian institutions, simply disappeared. In November 1941, Gauleiter Franz Schwede-Coburg appointed Walter Grabowski administrator of Meseritz-Obrawalde, and he thereafter organized the killings. Handicapped patients arrived in transports from at least twenty-six German cities, usually in the middle of the night. The staff selected for killing those patients unable to work, but the process was arbitrary and those selected included "patients who caused extra work for the nurses, those who were deaf-mute, ill, obstructive, or undisciplined, and anyone else who was simply annoying" as well as patients "who had fled and were recaptured, and those engaging in undesirable sexual liaisons."[81]

The selected handicapped victims were taken to so-called killing rooms where physicians and nurses killed them using orally administered drug overdoses or lethal injections. Most of the naked corpses were buried in mass graves, but some were cremated in Frankfurt on the Oder. Construction of an institutional crematorium to handle the large number of corpses was begun, but the project was not yet completed when Soviet troops liberated the hospital on 29 January 1945. Meseritz-Obrawalde had 900 patients in 1939, but during the war the institution was filled to capacity with 2,000 patients. The exact number of patients killed will never be known since only a portion of the institutional records survived, but even the most conservative estimate of

6,991 patients killed exceeds more than three times the hospital's maximum occupancy.[82] A less conservative but probably more accurate estimate by the postwar German judiciary placed the number of handicapped patients killed at Meseritz-Obrawalde at more than 10,000.[83]

Hadamar was the only institution utilized as a killing center both during the first killing phase using gas and, after the stop order, during the phase of "wild" euthanasia using medication. Under the control of Fritz Bernotat, the administrative chief of all institutions in Hessen-Nassau, Hadamar served, alongside the other two provincial institutions, Eichberg and Kalmenhof-Idstein, as a notorious killing center. Not only did Hadamar receive and kill handicapped patients from various German cities, including Hamburg, but it was also chosen to serve as a killing center for other targeted groups.[84] As we shall see, Bernotat established at Hadamar a special killing ward for so-called Jewish hybrid children (*Mischlingskinder*), that is, healthy children with partly Jewish ancestry.[85] But Hadamar achieved the greatest notoriety as a killing center for forced laborers from eastern Europe.

By 1944 the German Reich contained vast numbers of so-called *Ostarbeiter* (Eastern workers) — men, women, and children imported for forced labor from Poland and the occupied territories of the Soviet Union. Those unable to work because they suffered from infectious diseases — mostly tuberculosis — had to be released from their forced labor assignments.[86] But due to the advance of the Red Army, it was no longer feasible to return them to their homeland, and thus they became a burden on the German economy. Unwilling to place these forced laborers into overcrowded German hospitals, the managers of the health care system decided, instead, to kill the tubercular *Ostarbeiter*. The job was given to the T4 organization.

On 6 September 1944, the RMdI instructed all local governments that *Ostarbeiter* unable to work due to "mental illness" must be collected in designated regional hospitals.[87] Although these workers were suffering from a physical disease, the RMdI described their ailment as "mental," a label that had been used throughout against the handicapped. The eleven designated state hospitals included several infamous killing institutions: Tiegenhof for East and West Prussia and the Wartheland; Kaufbeuren for Bavaria; Maur-Öhling for Austria; and Hadamar for Hessen. The T4 Central Office arranged the transports and managed the finances of this final killing operation.[88] In Hadamar the *Ostarbeiter* were killed by injections shortly after they were admitted to the institution. As soon as they arrived, the janitor telephoned Alfons Klein, the administrative director, to inform him that "the Russians are here." After they had been killed by the male and female nurses, the medical director, Adolf Wahlmann, viewed the corpses and prepared the fraudulent death certificates.[89]

In one of the first postwar American war crimes trials, held in Wiesbaden in October 1945, the trial judge advocate, Colonel Leon Jaworski, prosecuted the Hadamar killers before a U.S. Military Commission for the murder of the tubercular *Ostarbeiter*.[90] Although the killers admitted that their eastern European victims had not been handicapped but had suffered from a physical illness, they considered the killing of the *Ostarbeiter* during 1944 and 1945 simply a continuation of "wild" euthanasia initiated in 1942. Repeating the usual rationalizations about euthanasia, Wahlmann revealed his belief that this continuation was self-evident during his examination by the court:

Q: Who determined the method of putting away, as you have described it, the Russians and Poles?

A: The method?

Q: Yes.

A: That is a certainty; that is a certainty in euthanasia.

Q: Who decided these injections were the proper method?

A: The method of the injection is a completely painless method, and "euthanasia," the term comes from the Greek "eu" which means beautiful.

Q: Yes. I am not interested in where the term came from. I want to know who determined that was the proper method to use, who made that decision.

A: We did it since the year 1942. Whether I ordered it at that time or whether it was generally done at that time I don't know now.[91]

The Bavarian state hospital at Kaufbeuren best illustrates the matter-of-fact brutality that pervaded the institutions implementing "wild" euthanasia. Headed by Valentin Faltlhauser, Kaufbeuren and its branch at Irsee served as a transfer institution prior to the stop order and thereafter as a center for "wild" euthanasia.[92] It also housed a children's killing ward.[93] Late in April 1945, American troops occupied Kaufbeuren but, placing the state hospital "off limits," did not interfere with its operation. For two months, the institution was able to function without change "less than half a mile from the Military Government, C.I.C., and M.P. Headquarters in this idyllic Swabian town." Only on 2 July, after rumors had reached military offices in Munich, did American soldiers enter the hospital and discover "a wholesale extermination plant." The American investigators were shocked by the sight that confronted them: "Scabies, lice, and other vermin were encountered throughout, linens were dirty and quarantine measures non-existent upon investigators' arrival."[94]

Kaufbeuren had continued to function as a killing center even after the end of the war. On 29 May 1945, "fully thirty-three days after American troops had occupied Kaufbeuren," the staff killed a child in the children's ward for the last time, and at 1:10 P.M. (13:10 German time), Faltlhauser recorded the death of the child from "typhus."[95] Twenty-one days after Germany's unconditional surrender, Richard Jenne, just four years old, became the last victim of the euthanasia killers.[96]

Chapter 9   The Handicapped Victims

The victims of Nazi mass murder are now but grisly statistics. It is difficult to see individual faces behind the vastness of the number 6 million. The men, women, and children murdered in the so-called euthanasia program are among the most invisible of the 6 million. Many of the survivors were kept institutionalized even after liberation. In fact, we have seen that in at least one institution the killings continued even after the war until discovered by the Allies. Only a few handicapped survivors appeared as witnesses at war crimes trials, although they had much to tell; most had been sterilized against their will and all had lived through years of fear and abuse. Stigmatized as "cripples," "psychotics," or "psychopaths," they did not publicly discuss their terrible experiences. We have no memoirs from the survivors of the euthanasia program. A narrative of their experiences can be reconstructed only from surviving documents and postwar trial records. Only recently have some case histories of those who perished and some oral histories and private letters of their relatives been published.[1]

Surviving photographs are of no help. Staged Nazi propaganda pictures simply depicted individual members of inferior groups as proof of their supposed degeneration; this applies to the handicapped as well as Jews, Gypsies, and blacks.[2] Only a few surviving family photographs give us a glimpse of the shadowy victims.[3]

Even surviving documents often provide only a tantalizing impression but few if any details about the lives, suffering, and deaths of individual victims. About some victims we know almost nothing, although documents concerning them have survived. For example, we know nothing about Otto Martin, born in 1889, who possibly survived. His killers could not find him. Gekrat wrote twice to the Thuringian Ministry of Interior, asking for Martin's location. He had been placed on the list for transfer but was misplaced afterward; possibly he and his records had been moved to another institution. We have no idea whether he escaped his killers.[4]

We also know nothing specific about Alma Wäldchen, born in 1891, except that she was killed in 1940. Surviving documents that mention her name concern the state insurance company responsible for her disability pension (*Invalidenrente*). The company knew only that Wäldchen had been transferred and asked the Thuringian Ministry of Interior to release her current address. The T4 Central Accounting Office for State Hospitals and Nursing Homes finally informed the ministry of her death.[5]

About some victims we know only what someone else remembered about them. For example, one eyewitness recounted in 1947 that "one day in 1943 or early 1944 a Spaniard named Angel Rodriguez" arrived at the Linz hospital Niedernhart, which served as the anteroom for Hartheim. The witness, a senior male nurse who "did not know why [Rodriguez] had been committed," testified that the Spaniard "did not suspect anything" and "was mentally fully normal." Three weeks after admission, Rodriguez was transferred to the killing ward at Niedernhart, probably on orders of the physician Rudolf Lonauer, and "next day they brought the dead Spaniard to the morgue." The witness reported that "two days after the murder of the Spaniard we received an order to transfer him to the Mauthausen concentration camp, but it was already too late."[6] We can only guess at the circumstances surrounding the death of this victim. We can assume that he was one of thousands of Spanish Republicans arrested in France for deportation to Mauthausen.[7] We can only wonder what accident sent him to Niedernhart and why he was killed there before he could be redirected to the nearby concentration camp. We know nothing about him, except that his name was Angel Rodriguez.

We do know that Rodriguez was not the only single, non-German individual killed in a euthanasia hospital, but we know even less about those other victims. For example, in 1943 the T4 business manager, Dietrich Allers, wrote Rudolf Lonauer, the physician-in-charge at the Hartheim killing center, that Herbert Linden of the RMdI wanted to transfer a "mentally ill" Russian named Boris Mirkolo to Hartheim and that Lonauer "should have no difficulty understanding the purpose." The Hartheim administrator, who picked up Mirkolo in Graz, later testified that he did not believe Mirkolo, who spoke German, was mentally ill. At Hartheim he was shot and then, because he was not yet dead, dragged into the gas chamber and gassed.[8]

Another witness's account is equally fragmentary. In the records of the postwar Eichberg trial, there is an unsigned letter to the state attorney from a former inmate of the Eichberg hospital. The letter writer had been incarcerated at Eichberg as a welfare ward (*Fürsorgezögling*) during 1942. We do not know why she was committed. Walter Schmidt, the Eichberg physician, accused the nineteen-year-old girl of being pregnant, and when she denied it, he responded, "When I tell you that you are pregnant, you are pregnant." She escaped but was returned to Eichberg. There she was threatened, beaten, and tortured until she admitted to having had an abortion. Although she could produce a statement from a gynecologist that she had never been pregnant, she was convicted and sentenced to four months in jail and, on the recommendation of Schmidt, subsequently remanded to the concentration camps. In her letter, she described the tortures and murders she observed at Eichberg and, even after surviving Auschwitz and Ravensbrück, concluded: "On the Eichberg I experienced the most painful period of my young life."[9] Seriously ill with tuberculosis upon liberation from the camps, she did not receive any restitution or support because she had been convicted and incarcerated as a "criminal." We do not know her name, the exact circumstances of her original commitment, or her eventual fate.

The transfer of persons from the state hospitals run by psychiatrists to the concentration camps run by the SS was not unusual and had become a matter of policy during the latter part of the war. Friedrich Mennecke, for example, reported after one of his concentration camp trips that "he had seen former patients" in Auschwitz.[10] In fact, conditions in the hospital system of euthanasia had begun to resemble those in the concentration camp system. The killing centers of euthanasia served, as we shall see, as models for the extermination camps of the final solution. The system of "selection" practiced to pick handicapped victims was not very different from that later practiced in the extermination camps. The method of transporting handicapped patients was not very different from that used to send deportees to those camps. For example, many patients from Hamburg arrived dead at Meseritz-Obrawalde after traveling in unheated trains in the middle of winter.[11] Testifying after the war to the Polish commission investigating the crimes committed at Meseritz-Obrawalde, former patients told of terrible conditions that included features also common to concentration camp life, such as roll call (*Appell*), forced labor, selections, and the use of inmate trustees similar to the inmate functionaries in the camps.[12]

Just as members of the SS were masters over the life and death of concentration camp inmates, physicians and nurses exercised arbitrary power over their charges. Of course, their power was sometimes limited. As we have seen, parents had to agree before their children could be assigned to the children's killing wards, and agreement was obtained by a mixture of subterfuge and coercion. But these tactics were not always successful. When parents insisted on taking a child out of the killing ward, physicians could harass them but could not always stop them. Physicians insisted that parents removing their children sign release papers, acknowledging that they acted against medical advice and that they assumed full responsibility for any possible fatal result. In one file at Eglfing-Haar, the physician noted that "against medical advice, the child had to be given to the unreasonable father." In another file he wrote: "The parents, who are obviously infatuated [*vergafft*] with their idiot child, can take it home on their own responsibility at any time, but only against medical advice."[13] When victims escaped his clutches, the killer expressed his indignation through entries in the medical files that reflected not only the arrogance of the physician but also the frustration of the bureaucrat whose authority had been challenged.

As in the concentration camps, the deaths continued until the last moment. At the postwar trial of Hermann Pfannmüller, the medical director at

Eglfing-Haar, Johann Lavenberger testified about the death of his stepson, Karl Memmel. The boy had always complained about the Eglfing starvation diet to his visiting parents. The stepfather brought food, and the nurses assured him that the boy would receive it. When he received notification of Karl's death, he and his wife traveled to Eglfing. At first, their demand to see the body was refused, but they persisted and eventually were allowed to see Karl. Having found his body emaciated, Lavenberger told the court that "he can only have starved to death," a plausible conclusion for a patient at Eglfing-Haar, known for its infamous "starvation houses [*Hungerhäuser*]." The stepfather had last talked to Karl on the Sunday before his death, which was "the Sunday before the Americans arrived." [14]

Karl Memmel's death at Eglfing-Haar at the last moment was not an anomaly. Pfannmüller's successor, appointed after the German surrender, wrote about the killing of two Silesian refugee girls—Ruth and Marie—on 30 April and 1 May, only days before the surrender and after Hitler had already committed suicide. He concluded that both girls "had been protected and carried along during the long flight from the Russians, only to be intentionally killed in a German hospital." [15]

The case of the fifteen-year-old Karl-Heinz Zey reveals how the hospitals of euthanasia could serve as surrogates for the concentration camps. The events that eventually led to the death of Karl-Heinz were set in motion in August 1944, when the local labor office requested that the state attorney in Limburg in the Wiesbaden district commit the teenager to a youth camp for education through labor (*Jugendarbeitserziehungslager*). The labor office made this appeal because the boy, characterized as dissolute, had consistently absented himself from his assigned factory job and had thus violated the law governing breaches of labor contracts during wartime. As part of the legal proceedings, his village school provided an evaluation: he was a troublesome student who "performed poorly in almost all subjects," which was due not to a lack of "hereditary abilities" but to "laziness" because he did pass in reading, writing, composition, drawing, and music. Further, the school pointed out that the boy's paternal uncle had been the "terror and scandal" of the village and that two children of his maternal aunt should have been assigned to special education (*Hilfsschule*) or even an institution. In addition, the mother had not supervised her boy sufficiently because she went out in the evenings to enjoy herself. An evaluation from the village policeman added that Karl-Heinz was suspected of having had "immoral conversations" with younger children, basing this on a local woman's claim that he had taught her son "dirty words." The court assigned Karl-Heinz to a youth labor camp.

After only six days in the labor camp, Karl-Heinz Zey was transferred to the Kalmenhof-Idstein state hospital. He escaped three times, complaining of mistreatment and beatings, but was returned by the police each time. Ten days after he was returned to Kalmenhof-Idstein for the last time, his mother received a telegram that Karl-Heinz had "suddenly died." When his mother, Maria Zey, telephoned to obtain details, the institution informed her that the boy had been ill for some time, that he had died from poor blood circulation (*Kreislaufschwäche*), and that a return of the body for a local funeral was not permitted. Suspicious about the cause of death, the parents traveled to Kalmenhof-Idstein and there successfully argued for their right to their child's body. In a postwar letter to the authorities, the mother described what she and witnesses observed after they opened the coffin, concluding that "it is obvious that the boy had been beaten to death." At the postwar Kalmenhof trial, the mother read the note she had found in her son's clothing: "They have left and locked me up. Dear mommy, I will not stay with these people for even eight days. I will go my own way, I will not stay here. Come and get me." [16]

Many other examples demonstrate the cruel, callous, and uncaring treatment of institutionalized patients. A pregnant woman patient was transferred for gassing from the Eichberg hospital to the killing center but was returned that evening, probably because she was pregnant. Friedrich Mennecke, however, ordered her sent back the next day with another transport. This time she did not return.[17]

A male patient named Hofmann had been committed to Eichberg for political reasons; he had been accused of stabbing an SA storm trooper. Another political inmate at Eichberg testified in court after the war that Walter Schmidt punished Hofmann numerous times because he considered him "rabid and abusive." In early 1944, Hofmann got sick. His fellow patient told the court that neither the ward physician nor the nurses paid any attention to Hofmann: "The man moaned day and night, and not a soul helped him." Many days later, Schmidt passed by and asked, "Well, how are you doing?" Hofmann could hardly talk but answered, "Herr Medizinalrat, please have me taken to Wiesbaden. I am so sick." Schmidt simply answered, "No." About half an hour later, a male nurse appeared and gave Hofmann a shot; within ten minutes he was dead.[18]

Survival often depended on successful escapes from these hospitals. Three brief surviving documents clearly show this. On 31 October 1944, the Wiesbaden police informed Karl Krämer, then thirty-one years old, that the public health physician had determined that his illness made his institutionalization necessary. The police therefore issued an order for Krämer's commitment to a state hospital, adding that the "public interest demands immediate execution of the order." After the war had ended, on 23 May 1945, Eichberg issued Krämer a document attesting that he was at the hospital from 31 October 1944 until 10 February 1945, at which time he escaped, and that now — "subsequent to his escape" — the hospital could certify his release. On 15 June 1945, the Wiesbaden police rescinded the commitment order.[19]

THE ORIGINS OF NAZI GENOCIDE

Arbitrary decisions or pure accident often determined who would die and who would survive. One patient died to conceal an error. In one institution, there had been two patients named Keller, one of whom was transferred to a killing center. By mistake, the medical records of both patients were sent along, and thus relatives of both patients received death notices. To hide the error, the second Keller, who had never been on any list for transfer, was picked up by car, taken to the killing center, and gassed.[20]

Salvation could come just as unexpectedly. At one institution, a patient had been selected, and the Gekrat buses had already arrived to load him and the other patients for their trip to the killing center. But a secretary to the director liked him and intervened. She had discovered that he was a veteran, had called other hospitals where he had been treated to get a positive evaluation, and was able to reclaim him before he entered the bus. She told a postwar trial: "He is still alive today." [21]

Arbitrary decisions also played a role in the fates of two Reich Committee children assigned to the children's killing wards because they had physical defects. One child whose legs and lower body were paralyzed was killed. Surgical neurological intervention could have cured this condition, but the so-called specialists at the children's ward failed to recognize this possibility. Another child with a similar condition was saved because a referral to the surgeons at the university clinic prevented an uninformed decision.[22]

Terror stalked the halls of the euthanasia hospitals not only because patients feared being selected for killing at any time or because some of the staff beat and maltreated them but also because some medical procedures imposed unusual pain. At the Gugging and Mauer-Öhling Austrian state hospitals, physician Emil Gelny, who was not a psychiatrist, employed a machine designed to give electroshock treatments and thus inflict torture. Electroconvulsive therapy, common in psychiatric hospitals during that period, was an even more painful procedure before the postwar introduction of anesthesia and muscle relaxants. Gelny used these machines, with minor adjustments, to kill patients. After two trial executions by Erwin Jekelius at the Am Steinhof hospital in Vienna, Gelny installed these machines at Gugging and Mauer-Öhling and used them to kill hundreds of handicapped patients.[23]

In the children's killing wards, the "treatment" of disabled children involved spinal taps, among other procedures. At Eichberg, Walter Schmidt, who had learned the procedure from Professor Carl Schneider at Heidelberg, replaced spinal fluid with air to enable clear X-rays of the brain. A physician who was also an Eichberg patient testified at Schmidt's postwar trial that Schmidt was not an expert at carrying out this painful procedure and that he removed far more fluid than necessary.[24] At any rate, these painful diagnostic procedures were not designed to aid the children, who had already been condemned to death.[25]

The proponents of euthanasia maintained—both at the time and after the war—that only brain-dead patients (*geistig Tote*) were included in the killing program. Citing the 1920 work by Binding and Hoche, they argued that those sent to the gas chambers no longer possessed a desire to live.[26] The postwar courts, however, found that this was not true. Expert witnesses concluded that during the war 6 to 7 percent of institutionalized handicapped patients at most were brain-dead, and one court concluded that only 1 percent had lacked the "natural desire to live."[27]

Overwhelming anecdotal evidence supports these conclusions. Observers reported that the arrival of the Gekrat buses created a "sinister mood [*Unheimlichkeitsstimmung*]" in the hospitals, and even those classified as "intellectually débile" knew something terrible was happening and felt "raw fear."[28] The authorities were obviously aware that the condemned patients suspected their fate since they administered tranquilizers to assure their acquiescence.[29] In any case, many handicapped patients were not mentally deficient but only suffered from a physical deformity; their disfigurement (*Schönheitsfehler*) condemned them.[30] Obviously, they knew their fate. One patient suffering from a hipbone deformity later described his feelings: "From one transport to the other, I was always afraid that I would be taken along."[31] One of the Kalmenhof-Idstein nurses later reported the following about her ten-year-old charges: "Everyone talked about it, even the children talked about it. They were all afraid to go to the hospital. They were fearful that they would not come back. It was a general rumor. The children played a coffin game. We were astonished that the children understood."[32]

They certainly understood. One female patient asked on the way to the Gekrat buses: "Is it my fault that I am born this way, and that they do this to me?"[33] One Eglfing-Haar patient wrote the following letter in June 1941: "Dear mother! I want to write these final lines to you, because I must leave here and do not know the destination. It is difficult for me. I thank you all wholeheartedly and say farewell, if not in this world then *hopefully* in heaven! With heartfelt greeting, your grateful son."[34] A patient named Lohne reported to a postwar court that a fellow patient at Kalmenhof, Margarethe Schmidt, told him the following as she lay dying in the institution's air raid shelter, where she had been deposited by her killers: " 'Lohne,' she told me, 'that's how they did me in. Be careful!' That is true, absolutely. That's what she said."[35]

At the Eichberg hospital, it took four injections over several days to kill one patient, certainly an indication that he did possess a "natural desire to live." The male nurse administering one of the injections commented: "I'll be damned, but that fellow has a tenacious hold on life."[36]

Hundreds of handicapped patients proved their "natural desire to live," and retained their dignity, by raising their voices to shame and denounce their killers. Getting on a Gekrat bus, one male patient donned his Iron Cross and one female patient, a Catholic nun, told those around her: "All of us, who have been condemned to death, are now getting on the bus."[37] At one hospital, a female patient asked a visiting panel of T4 physicians: "Well, are you again looking for new victims, you mass murderers?"[38] Another female patient shouted from the Gekrat bus that was taking her to the killing center: "Yes, we shall die, but that Hitler will go to hell."[39] At times, these inmates of state hospitals understood reality in wartime Germany better than the mass of the German population. At the Zwiefalten hospital in Württemberg, for example, one female patient was considered demented because, talking to herself at night, she repeated over and over, "This Hitler, who wants to murder and rape me."[40]

The T4 killers maintained not only that their victims had been brain-dead but also that the relatives approved of the killings. To gain such approval, T4 produced a great deal of propaganda and, when public opinion turned against them, collaborated in the production of the successful 1942 propaganda entertainment film *Ich klage an*.[41] This film and other forms of propaganda in favor of euthanasia—focusing on "mercy deaths" that actually had no relation to the killing program—undoubtedly had some impact, although they did not reverse popular opposition.[42] This lack of support applied especially to the procedure of mass transfer of adult patients to the killing centers. For example, Eglfing-Haar did not receive a single letter from relatives approving of the secret transfers.[43]

Nevertheless, it is true that there were those who, for a variety of reasons, wanted their handicapped relatives "released from their suffering." In Hamburg, the father of a handicapped female infant named Jutta asked physicians at the Alsterdorfer institution to arrange her death, apparently to relieve the anxiety of her mother. After a nurse told him that he should have his daughter transferred, he insisted that she be moved from the Alsterdorfer hospital, where there was no children's killing ward and where he believed that her life was being artificially prolonged, to the Langenhorn state hospital. Even there, the physician of the children's killing ward was hesitant to administer a fatal treatment for Jutta, but the father persisted and the child was killed.[44]

Those requesting the killing of their children were motivated by many interconnected factors. These motives involved the difficulty and expense of caring for a handicapped child, the demands placed on the time and emotions of at least one of the parents (usually the mother), and concern for the development of "healthy" siblings. Such basically materialistic motives, which concerned the welfare of the family and not the child, were mingled with popular National Socialist and race hygiene arguments.[45] Such mixed motives were displayed by the Tyrolian father of a handicapped child named Paul, who considered it his "greatest duty" to "maintain the purity of his family tree" and who was also determined to relieve the anxiety of his wife.

On 9 May 1942, Paul was transferred — at his father's request — from the Bethel hospital to the Eglfing-Haar children's ward. Six months later, on 10 November, the boy, then almost five years old, died on schedule.[46]

Of course, the T4 physicians could not openly admit killing patients even when relatives requested it. Although staff members undoubtedly used camouflaged comments and a revealing tone of voice — as did Jutta's nurse — to provide sufficient information for relatives, officially the fiction of a natural death had to be maintained. For example, three-year-old Rosemarie's father, a corporal (Unterscharführer) in the Waffen SS, demanded that his brain-damaged daughter be killed. The attending physician rejected this demand for "euthanasia," but one month later, Rosemarie died from an unlikely ailment.[47]

Parents who wanted their handicapped children to be "released from suffering" did not always know exactly which agency was in charge and therefore used various connections to accomplish their ends. Gauleiter Erich Koch wrote SS chief Heinrich Himmler about Charlotte Poeck and her four-year-old son Rüdiger, whose condition was considered "incurable." Koch informed the Reich leader SS that "Mrs. Poeck would be grateful if the child could be brought to one of your 'clinics,' and if it could be released from its suffering."[48]

At times, approving relatives threw the T4 bureaucracy into consternation. Marie Kehr of Nuremberg wrote to the Sonnenstein killing center about the death of her two sisters. She suspected that their simultaneous deaths at Sonnenstein were not a coincidence and wanted to know whether the killing of her sisters was legal: "I can only find peace if I could be certain that a law of the Reich enables the release of human beings from their incurable ailments." The Sonnenstein director, Horst Schumann, was not certain how to respond and wrote for advice to Werner Heyde, who then consulted with others. One month later, Herbert Linden of the RMdI wrote to the Nuremberg Nazi party regional office about this case, asking that they verbally answer Marie Kehr's question, but only "if K. is politically unobjectionable and has no church ties." Ten days later, the Nuremberg office wrote Linden that Kehr and her brother-in-law had been informed.[49]

Still, crass demands from relatives that their kin be killed were rare. The request of a woman that her schizophrenic husband at the Zwiefalten hospital be killed because she wanted to remarry without a divorce is unusual.[50] One researcher very familiar with the surviving euthanasia records has concluded that individuals requesting the killing of their relatives were a small minority, one that could be found in any society.[51] Family ties are simply stronger than ideology. Similarly, postwar courts found only very few instances in which non-Jewish Germans divorced their Jewish spouses to encourage their deportation.[52]

Handicapped institutionalized patients were categorized not only on the

172   THE ORIGINS OF NAZI GENOCIDE

basis of the kind of ailments they suffered or the kind of work they could perform, both important criteria for selection by the T4 bureaucracy, but also on the basis of other, nonmedical criteria. One such category included individuals committed to the state hospitals by the courts. As we have seen, these patients posed a technical problem because the judiciary wanted to decide their fate, and T4 had to negotiate on the highest level to pacify the judicial system. But the quarrel was over bureaucratic prerogatives and not the personal fate of individuals. Persons committed by the courts were considered a double threat because they were labeled as both insane and criminal. Of course, this was not always true. Their transgressions were often minor, or even political, and the judgment of diminished capacity by the courts was often legal and not medical. These considerations did not matter to the T4 bureaucrats. The T4 physicians usually selected for killing most persons committed under article 42 of the penal code.[53]

The shoemaker Willy Erler—thirty-five years old and blind—was committed in July 1939 and in February 1940 was transferred by Gekrat, presumably to a killing center. The Waldheim hospital labeled him a "dangerous habitual criminal" but certified that he was "not mentally ill."[54] Dr. Hermann Wirsting, a fifty-seven-year-old dentist with a drug-dependency problem, was committed to the same hospital, arriving on 15 April 1940; the next day, Gekrat transferred him to his death.[55] In October 1937, a court committed the twenty-five-year-old deaf-mute cigarmaker Erich Strelow to the same hospital. In February 1940, the hospital notified the state attorney that there was no further need for his institutionalization, suggesting that he should be admitted to an institution for deaf-mutes. The court thereupon revoked the commitment order, but Strelow had already been murdered in the Brandenburg killing center.[56]

The attorney general of Naumburg on the Saale River discovered that six of his charges, committed because of diminished capacity after their conviction for relatively minor offenses, had all died in Brandenburg on the same day. These persons included, for example, Ernst Schmiedel, a manual worker born in 1897, who had been sentenced to one year and four months on moral charges involving homosexual conduct.[57]

Assistant judge Fritz Freudenberger was convicted in 1937 for a political crime, but a "compassionate court-appointed expert" was able to convince the court to commit him to the Eichberg hospital instead of imposing a stiff sentence. However, this commitment proved to be a death sentence, because in 1941 Freudenberger was transferred to a killing center.[58]

Two other patients committed by the courts were somewhat luckier; they escaped the killing centers but ended up in the concentration camps. The thirty-year-old male patient S. had been convicted of exposing himself to women and children when under the influence of alcohol. He was committed to the Wittenauer hospital complex in Berlin, where physicians diagnosed chronic alcoholism and certified that he was not feebleminded. He was discharged in January 1942 but was immediately rearrested by the police, who had been notified by the hospital of his impending release, and was sent to a concentration camp.[59]

A male patient at Eglfing-Haar, thirty-six years old, had also been committed for exhibitionism. His diagnosis was "psychopathology" and "traumatic brain weakness." On the T4 questionnaire, the physician had listed the patient's entire criminal record, including minor thefts, panhandling, and, in his youth, truancy from school. Surprisingly, T4 did not select him, probably because when he was committed in August 1941, the first phase of euthanasia had just ended. In 1943 Eglfing-Haar reported the patient again, commenting on the questionnaire, "Case already reported in 1941! Belongs in a concentration camp." [60]

Veterans of World War I formed a second group of patients who received special consideration. Veterans were to be exempted, especially if they had been awarded medals, had been wounded, or had performed with special valor at the front. In fact, however, this exemption was not applied with any consistency. Status as a veteran could not always prevent exclusion or even killing. One case of exclusion illustrates this clearly. In February 1942, the Vienna public health department committed the veteran Ludwig Kuntschik to the alcoholics ward (*Trinkerheilstätte*) of the Am Steinhof state hospital despite his protest and without examination by physicians. Upon appeal by his attorney, Alfred Hardix, the magistrate court ordered his discharge after two months of incarceration. Hardix thereupon asked for an administrative hearing against the responsible public health officer. The public health office defended the officer's actions by describing Kuntschik as a "notorious alcoholic" as well as a "known communist," who would have been sent to a camp for *Asoziale* if he had not been a veteran who had lost both legs in World War I.[61]

This case illustrates the fact that status as a disabled veteran did not always prevent exclusion; another case shows that such status did not always prevent murder. The fifty-eight-year-old Karl Rueff, a lieutenant in the reserves who had been awarded an Iron Cross First Class, was institutionalized in south Germany due to a head wound he had suffered in World War I. His father, a retired consul general, and his sister, the medical chief of a psychiatric clinic, visited him often. His disability pension paid for his institutional care, and he was relatively healthy, suffering only from occasional epileptic seizures. Nevertheless, in 1940 he was transferred to Grafeneck and killed.[62]

A third group of handicapped patients who required special attention consisted of members of the Nazi party and those with party connections. Nazi party membership and connections obviously played a role in influencing the

THE ORIGINS OF NAZI GENOCIDE

life-and-death decisions rendered on individuals. Those who made the decisions were governed, at least in part, by opportunistic self-interest even as they professed their commitment to ideological or scientific purity. But the two groups involved in decision making—the political leaders of the Nazi movement on one side and the scientists and physicians on the other—did not always have the same concerns.

The scientists and physicians who implemented exclusion through sterilization, institutionalization, and later killings approached their task in what they considered an objective, scientific way. Of course, often their scientific judgment was merely a disguise for arbitrary and utilitarian decisions. Still, unless their concern for personal advancement interfered, their actions were largely determined by their professional convictions. On the other hand, although they absorbed, championed, and used the supposed findings of the scientists, the Nazi political leaders were sufficiently pragmatic to reject dogmatic scientific positions if they compromised their political and ideological aims. As we have seen, this difference led to conflict between Himmler and Fritz Lenz and between Gerhard Wagner and the RMdI bureaucracy. Further, opportunistic reasons obviously prevented the application of the scientific criteria of exclusion to persons occupying high party offices. The scientific rules of exclusion thus did not apply to Joseph Goebbels's physical deformity or Robert Ley's alcoholism. These differences between political and scientific purity did not, however, prevent the Nazi leadership from utilizing scientists or encouraging them to serve the Nazi cause. Similarly, although Hitler detested lawyers and legalisms, he used willing lawyers and bureaucrats to implement the policy of repression as well as the final solution.

The guardians of race hygiene tended to be tolerant when exclusion threatened someone in their own professional or social class. As we have seen, they proposed exemption for a colleague with a harelip and a cleft palate because he was "an esteemed physician, a good National Socialist, and a splendid human being." [63] We have also seen that party membership alone, without status or connections, did not necessarily help. Membership in the party and the SA did not prevent the exclusion through sterilization of the simple worker Johannes Schmidt.[64] However, membership in the party, especially holding local party office, did gain for the member some consideration. One local Nazi party leader (Ortsgruppenleiter) who suffered occasional epileptic attacks and was sentenced by the hereditary health court, was able to obtain a second, positive opinion from Paul Nitsche.[65] At any rate, when personal relationships were involved, even convinced Nazis, including SS officers, attempted to intervene to save handicapped relatives.[66]

Still, preferential treatment for party members was not automatic. As with war veterans, handicapped party members were killed alongside everyone else unless chance or someone influential intervened. Dr. Friedrich Froboeß, committed to the Waldheim hospital in January 1940, was transferred and killed in February although he was an "old party member."[67]

Sometimes connections having nothing to do with politics led to a patient's exemption, such as "professional courtesy." Gretel Weckmann, a senior nurse at the Frankfurt City Hospital who was active in nursing affairs, was warned by Eichberg nurses to remove her sister after she was placed on the list of transfers to Hadamar. Weckmann took her home, and the sister, who had been at the institution for eleven years, survived the war.[68]

Apparently, the essential factor was connections, not Nazi party membership. Membership did not play any role in the release of Anna Gasse, a child in the Eichberg children's ward. Someone had intervened in her behalf with Karl Brandt, one of the two plenipotentiaries for euthanasia, and the Reich Committee asked Walter Schmidt for a "detailed report" on the patient, advising him at the same time that for the "reputation of the institution" it might be best to discharge her.[69]

Of course, connections could also work against the handicapped patient. Albert Geis, a party member employed at the Bernburg killing center, approached the center's physician-in-charge, Irmfried Eberl, concerning his handicapped niece, Karen Dreer. Without his sister's knowledge, Geis asked that his niece be included in the killing operation of children's euthanasia, and Eberl forwarded the request to Paul Nitsche.[70]

The surviving documents of the case of Ernst Knoll, a retired army captain employed by the Junker aircraft works, illustrate the importance of connections, although the case did not involve the killing operation directly. The state attorney in Hildesheim, who initiated proceedings against Knoll for making false accusations, had to consider whether a defense of diminished capacity was appropriate. He commissioned an expert opinion from the psychiatrist W. Jacobi of Osnabrück, whose conclusions were not favorable to Knoll. This was apparently a sensitive case because the files were forwarded to the RKPA, Office V of the RSHA. At some point, the KdF became involved in settling the question of diminished capacity. Reinhold Vorberg approached Paul Nitsche, who arranged for Knoll to be transferred for observation to a hospital directed by a T4 collaborator. After Hans Heinze at Görden declined for technical reasons, Knoll was committed to the Pfafferode hospital in Mühlhausen in Thuringia, headed by Theo Steinmeyer. Vorberg had initiated the affair in September 1943, but because the files were misplaced, nothing had yet been resolved by late February 1944, except that Steinmeyer had concluded on the basis of personal contact with Knoll that he ought to be released. The surviving letters do not reveal the details of the Knoll case, except that he was described by the KdF as someone "who had gained merit for serving the national interest and also the party." This case expended con-

THE ORIGINS OF NAZI GENOCIDE

siderable T4 resources for at least six months, whereas it often took only five minutes for T4 bureaucrats and physicians to decide the fate of individuals without connections.[71]

Relatives of handicapped victims always posed a serious threat to the euthanasia killing program. Since only a minority of relatives supported the killings, and most of them did not approve of the way they were carried out, the T4 managers had to develop strategies to deceive the majority that opposed the program. These strategies included transfers without prior notification, the establishment of transfer institutions, and the dispatch of documents with totally fraudulent and deceptive information. But this paper trail, including notices of transfers, condolence letters, and death certificates, in turn engendered the suspicion and hostility that forced Hitler to issue his stop order. The intervention of relatives generated a record that provides us with a great deal of information about the killing program as well as individual victims and their families.

We have already discussed the scheme used by T4 to deceive relatives through the use of letters filled with lies, but we have not yet examined the impact of those communications on the relatives. The letters received by Adolf Wächtler in Dresden provide a good example. On 2 August 1940, Wächtler was notified by Sonnenstein that his daughter, Anna Frieda Lohse née Wächtler, had been transferred to that institution on orders of the Reich defense commissar. Undoubtedly killed there at the time of arrival, she was probably already dead when this letter was written, but her father did not know that. On 4 August, probably the day he received the Sonnenstein letter, Wächtler wrote to inquire about her. Sonnenstein responded on 7 August that his daughter had been transferred to another institution on 5 August but that the name of that institution was not available. On 13 August, the Brandenburg killing center wrote to Wächtler that his daughter had been "transferred to our institution" but that "it is our sad duty to notify you today of the unfortunate news that your daughter died here from pneumonia and cardiac insufficiency on 12 August 1940."[72]

For about two weeks, Adolf Wächtler had worried and inquired about his daughter, who was most likely already dead. Finally informed of her death, he probably blamed the institutions involved, even if he had no suspicions about the killings. After all, he had reason to suspect that the pneumonia was the result of the rapid transfer from institution to institution and was undoubtedly angry that he had not been informed in time.

As we know, this kind of shell game about the place and date of death was common. The Hadamar killing center informed Daniel Riedesel on 10 February 1941 that his wife Martha had arrived, and the death notice came from Bernburg on 19 February.[73] The span of time covered by these letters was usually about two weeks. For example, the Kalmenhof hospital notified police sergeant (Gendarmeriehauptwachtmeister) Hugo Seidler on 30 April 1941 that his son Heinz had been transferred by Gekrat. Hadamar in turn informed him on 5 May that Heinz had arrived and then wrote again on 15 May that his son had died that day.[74] Sometimes, however, the sequence of letters did not reflect the time that had supposedly elapsed. The Eichberg hospital notified the parent of Cäcilie Bauer that she had been transferred on 21 February 1941, but this letter was dated 10 March 1941. On the same day, a Hadamar letter notified Professor Bauer that her daughter had died on 9 March.[75]

During the period of "wild" euthanasia, letters to relatives from hospitals were neither timed as precisely nor written as carefully as the letters that had been sent by the killing centers. They were, of course, equally fraudulent, but because they did not usually follow immediately after transfer, they tended to be more convincing. Nevertheless, they often included comments that must have made relatives suspicious. The Austrian institution at Gugging informed Maria Wegscheider on 12 April 1943 that her daughter had "suddenly" died on 7 April. Although she was "up and around," she "suddenly felt sick and immediately lost consciousness, and died shortly thereafter without suffering." The diagnosis provided was "cardiac insufficiency," which did at least sound plausible. But attempting to be more convincing, the hospital explained that "cardiac insufficiency is common with mental patients," adding that an earlier mild case of typhus, "not noticed at the time," had helped damage the heart.[76] Although typhus was not uncommon during wartime, the mother might well have wondered how such an epidemic disease could have gone unnoticed.

Often other evidence made relatives suspicious. Usually this involved earlier reports that the patient's condition was satisfactory. For example, the Eichberg hospital wrote to Anna Krämer on 7 February 1941 about her son Ludwig, informing her that his mental condition had not improved but that his "physical condition is satisfactory." On 23 February, Hadamar wrote that he had arrived there, and on 4 March, that he had died of an acute infection.[77]

The impact of these announcements on the relatives was devastating. In 1971 there appeared in a Hamburg newspaper a letter from a woman whose child was murdered in Eichberg in 1944. In it, she made the following statement: "I have brought seven children into the world, including two who were premature, but all are healthy and normal. Still, to this day I have not been able to get over the death of this one child of mine, although I am now seventy-two years old."[78] One young woman, whose aunt had been killed at Grafeneck, wrote this on the notification form: "One cannot even visit Ida's grave, and as far as the ashes they send you are concerned, one does not know, after all, whether they belonged to Ida."[79]

In 1944 another woman whose daughter had died at Meseritz-Obrawalde wrote to the home institution: "How can one still have the courage to trust a physician?"[80] Yet another woman wrote to the institution to inquire about

THE ORIGINS OF NAZI GENOCIDE

her transferred relative: "To this day all our inquiries have yielded no answer and no sign of life from my sister Luise. Thus we must assume that she is no longer among the living. After all, a human being cannot disappear without a trace and no one wants to know the destination."[81]

Tormented relatives vented their anger at the authorities, although most hesitated to go as far as one father, who sent the following telegram to the Linz state attorney: "Please seize body and medical files of Walter Buddrich from Soltau who died Hartheim state hospital on 16 June 1941 because this involves bodily injury resulting in death. Evidence follows by express mail."[82]

The correspondence between Eichberg physician Walter Schmidt and retired philologist F. H. concerning his son Hans, born in Stuttgart in 1909, illustrates the conflict between the medical authorities and parents of victims. It also reveals that the T4 physicians simply failed to understand how their code words would enrage relatives.

On 6 January 1944, the unsuspecting father inquired about Hans's condition, asking whether "schizophrenia has been diagnosed" and whether he had deteriorated so far that "recovery seems impossible." On 14 January, Schmidt answered that Hans's condition "has not yet improved," that he had "no inclination" for "regular work," and that he had "stopped working, because he claims he does not belong here and indicates that he wants to escape." Having emphasized the son's poor behavior without actually answering the father's question, Schmidt concluded that Hans "needs further institutional care," foolishly adding that "physically his condition is good," although he had probably already decided to kill the patient.

Following T4 language rules, on 5 April 1944 Eichberg informed F. H. that "a gentle death has delivered [Hans] from his incurable affliction." This phrase, which did not explain the unexpected death, led the father to write to the Eichberg hospital on 22 April. F. H. indicated that the family had been "deeply shocked" by the news but had also been surprised because they had been told nothing about an "incurable affliction." The father demanded exact information, especially since Schmidt's last letter, which had given no indication of a physical illness, did not agree with the report from his children, who attended their brother's funeral at Eichberg and who told him that Hans had reportedly been confined to his bed for two months. F. H. concluded: "It was unsurpassed thoughtlessness vis-à-vis parents to hide our son's true condition and thus intentionally prevent a timely farewell visit."

Schmidt replied on 28 April. First, he denied that the parents had not been informed, pointing out that they had been told that their son's "condition had not improved," although mental illness obviously did not cause death. Second, he finally provided information about the cause of death and the failure to notify the family in time for a final visit. On 17 March, Hans fell ill with fever and headaches, "probably from influenza, which was making the rounds." His condition got worse, but due to "terror air raids" on Frankfurt, the hospital was overcrowded and "we thus had unfortunately no time to notify you." Third, he tried once more to use the prescribed euthanasia language, concluding: "In your pain over the loss of your son, let the idea give you solace that death saved him from a long period of institutionalization, which his type of affliction (schizophrenia) always requires."

Not pacified, F. H. replied on 10 May. He informed Eichberg that at Hans's funeral his "horrified" siblings had noticed that their brother was "emaciated" and looked like a "skeleton," no doubt due to the "Eichberg diet." The father continued by commenting that now Hans obviously "no longer needs institutional treatment," asking: "What have you done to our strong, physically well developed son with your institutional treatment?" The father also asked how Schmidt could have told him in January that Hans was physically in good condition when such a statement was clearly "contrary to the truth." The father concluded: "This affair appears to be rather murky."

In his reply of 16 May, Schmidt counterattacked: "Over the years we have repeatedly been exposed to the ingratitude of relatives of patients suffering from a *hereditary* mental disease" (emphasis in original). He repeated that the hospital had informed F. H. about his son's condition, adding that because F. H. was retired, he apparently did not seem to grasp the "immense burden placed on the institution and the demands made on institutional physicians." Schmidt reiterated that circumstances created by the war explained why the family was not informed in detail about the approaching end of "his son's affliction," which, after all, constituted, he once again admonished, "release [*Erlösung*] for the patient himself." Rejecting as unfounded rumors any information Hans's siblings might have received from other patients at the funeral, Schmidt advised F. H. not to depend on "testimony from mentally ill individuals" but instead trust the "statements made by reliable physicians." Schmidt resented the comment "rather murky" but added as a veiled threat that "considering the hereditary nature of your son's ailment, we will not blame you." Finally, Schmidt mentioned that prior to his death, the father had "barely bothered himself" about his son, while the hospital did everything possible for him, including the administration of insulin-shock and electroshock treatments. Further, his son had been given plenty of opportunities to do outside work and thus get additional food and fresh air but had rejected this offer due to his "pathological motives."

In his brief answer, F. H. denied Schmidt's charge that he had neglected his son and rejected the implication that he himself was mentally ill. Schmidt replied on 12 June 1944. This time the killer assumed the mantle of a public official and arrogantly threatened his victim's father: "The content and tone of your letter ... force me to consider psychiatric measures against you.

I am compelled to inform you, that should you continue to harass us with further communications, I shall be forced to have you examined by a public health physician. After all, you are dealing with a government office [*öffentliche Dienststelle*], which you simply cannot insult at your pleasure."[83]

The arrogance exhibited by Schmidt toward F. H. was not unusual. Mistreatment of patients, insensitivity toward relatives, and autocratic conduct were commonplace. Another example of such behavior is the conflict between Schmidt and Johann Risch, the father of another Eichberg patient. Schmidt refused the father's request that his son receive a furlough to visit the family. The son escaped but was returned to Eichberg. As punishment, he was locked in the basement, dressed only in shirt and shorts, and placed on reduced rations. The father was not permitted to visit him. When the father appeared at Eichberg, Schmidt would not talk to him and simply walked away. On 29 February 1944, Johann Risch protested in a letter to Schmidt, warning that he would "complain to the state attorney about your behavior toward me and the conditions in your institution."[84]

Walter Schmidt was not the only T4 functionary to issue threats to silence relatives. When the wife of the patient Georg S. wrote to Hadamar in October 1944 objecting to her husband's transfer to that hospital because of her suspicion that he would be killed there, the hospital administrator Alfons Klein, not himself a physician, answered with a threat: "I herewith acknowledge receipt of your letter of 4 October. I am sorry, but I must take legal actions against you for your comment that Hadamar is the final stop for your husband. You will then have the opportunity to reveal who has passed on such defamatory information. You must know that this is a state hospital and as such we cannot submit to such slander."[85] The wife replied, "Go ahead, take me to court." She was right to call Klein's bluff because the regime had no intention of making the killings public by initiating legal actions.

Another case also illustrates how T4 physicians confronted by relatives blustered and lied. This case involved the teenage son of Elisabeth Rettig. After running away from home, he was caught by the police and committed for observation at the Kalmenhof-Idstein state hospital. He escaped but was caught and returned. About a week later, his mother was notified that he had died. Other Kalmenhof teenage inmates told her that two days before his death he had been at work until he was taken to the feared hospital ward, from which he did not reappear. In fact, this was not an unusual "treatment" for inmates who escaped. At the postwar Kalmenhof trial, the mother testified about her conversation with the physician Hermann Wesse: "He said: Your son was sick. I said: No, he was not sick. He: All the same, he was sick. I said: That is impossible. I have thoroughly healthy children, who have never been sick except for mumps, measles, and once in a while he wet his bed. Yes, he said, in any case he was sick, he had intestinal flu with fever [*fieberhafte Darmgrippe*]. I said: No, that is not true. He: I had to give him two injections, I was not able to give him an antidote, I had to watch as he died." [86]

Relatives of patients did not believe the protestations of physicians, who in turn complained that relatives were totally unreasonable. Gerhard Kloos, medical director of the Thuringian State Hospital at Stadtroda and its children's ward, complained in a letter to the Thuringian Ministry of Interior in Weimar about the behavior of the mother of his patient Ilse Wiefel. Kloos diagnosed Ilse as suffering from a "schizophrenic psychosis" and then cataloged her various violent episodes, especially her attacks on nurses. Kloos then described the behavior of the mother, who insisted on seeing her daughter after visiting hours, as "brazen and arrogant." Most important, he objected that the mother had gone over his head to government agencies and resented her explanation that "in her opinion, that was the only way to get her daughter released from this hospital." Kloos concluded: "Although I made the greatest effort, I was not able to educate Mrs. Wiefel about the facts or to convince her that her opinions are in error." [87]

Handicapped patients survived the euthanasia killings mostly by chance. Survival depended on many factors totally outside the control of the victims. For example, much depended on the whims of physicians and nurses; T4 experts evaluating the cases, hospital directors and their attitudes toward individual patients, physicians at the ward level who made arbitrary choices, and nurses who could intervene for particular patients could determine a patient's fate. The date the patient was transferred also played a role. Those selected before the stop order had much less chance of survival than those selected later; once processed at the killing center, no one could escape the gas chambers, while survival was still possible after selection at the hospitals of "wild" euthanasia. In this respect, the killing centers and hospitals of euthanasia did not differ substantially from the extermination and concentration camps of the final solution; there, too, virtually no one survived camps that served only as killing centers, while there was a slight chance for survival at the camps that combined killing and slave labor.[88]

Obviously, outside intervention could improve the chances for survival, and the efforts of relatives was usually the only intercession that could possibly succeed. Once news of the killings had spread, many persons attempted to free their relatives, but success usually depended on timing and local conditions.

A Viennese mother, Anny Wödl, whose six-year-old handicapped son had been institutionalized in the Gugging hospital, made a heroic but unsuccessful effort to save her boy. She approached various officials and even traveled to Berlin to talk to Herbert Linden but discovered that these men firmly believed in the killing program and would not yield to a mother without

THE ORIGINS OF NAZI GENOCIDE

connections.[89] Another mother, Katharina Budin, had better luck. Her three-year-old daughter had been institutionalized at the Viennese Am Steinhof hospital. The child was "mentally and physically normal" but had been committed because the unmarried mother was considered an unfit parent. The mother persisted in her efforts to remove her child and was successful: "I had to fight very hard to get my child out of there."[90] Wödl and Budin seem to have been equally persistent. The dissimilarity in their children's condition might have made the difference, but probably it was pure chance that saved one and not the other.

The seventy-year-old Dr. Leopold Widerhofer was able to save his daughter from the Am Steinhof hospital in Vienna. Gerta Widerhofer had been admitted to the hospital in 1938 suffering from schizophrenia. In August 1940, Widerhofer heard about the transfers and, hoping to rescue Gerta, approached Erwin Jekelius, then head of the Vienna health office and later chief of the Am Spiegelgrund children's ward. During a heated one-hour conversation, Widerhofer was unable to persuade Jekelius, who told the insistent father several times, "Your daughter must die." Still, Widerhofer, who served as head (*Gymnasial-Direktor*) of one of Vienna's academic secondary schools, was able to persuade two junior physicians to move his daughter to other wards during the transfer period, and she survived the war.[91]

Irmgard Hörnecke was not able to save her mother, Johanna Karoline Schmidt, a patient at the Kalmenhof-Idstein hospital. Although the daughter appealed to the Reich minister of interior, the provincial governor, the Nazi party Gauleiter, and the hospital physicians, her mother was transferred to Hadamar and killed.[92]

Anna Mader, the mother of the Eglfing-Haar patient Maria Mader, was probably equally unsuccessful. She wanted to take her daughter home and therefore appealed to the director Hermann Pfannmüller in person, threatening to commit suicide if Maria was transferred. Since Maria was already on the transfer list for Hartheim, Pfannmüller refused to remove her, and she was transferred by Gekrat on 29 April 1941. He did, however, inform the Niedernhart transit institution that its physicians should decide about the mother's request.[93] The records do not reveal the outcome, but it is unlikely that the Hartheim physicians Lonauer and Renno, who also directed Niedernhart, permitted the exemption of Maria Mader.

At times, parents — even those with connections — could not act fast enough to save their children. An employee of the Leipzig state attorney's office attempted to remove her son from the Waldheim hospital, but he was rapidly transferred to Hartheim and killed. She was devastated and outraged and made her attitude very clear at her office by accusing the state attorney of concealing from her the fact that her son had been murdered, thus disconcerting the attorney general in Dresden and the RJM in Berlin.[94]

The parents of Heinz S. were also too late. Born in 1922, the boy was partially paralyzed as a result of meningitis at the age of two years. Apart from his physical disability, the boy was mentally normal and had successfully attended public school. After graduation, his parents wanted to place him in an institution for the physically disabled but were unable to afford an exclusive private sanatorium. He thus became a private patient at the Kalmenhof-Idstein state hospital. Admitted in May 1939, he did well at the hospital and even spent two weeks at home during the 1940 Christmas holidays. On 29 April 1941, Heinz telephoned his mother and begged her to take him home "because he is to be transferred and that means his death." The mother telephoned Kalmenhof and was assured that her son would not be transferred without her knowledge. The next morning, the father traveled to the hospital but discovered that Heinz had been transferred to Hadamar; the death notice arrived on 15 May.[95]

A general practitioner from Stuttgart was also too late to save his daughter, who had been hospitalized as an epileptic. Although her correspondence was censored, she was able to smuggle out some letters and thus keep her family informed. In 1940 she wrote that she was "constantly afraid that she would be picked up and killed." The father petitioned the Stuttgart health department and the authorities in Berlin but was unable to prevent his daughter's transfer. She smuggled out a farewell letter, but by the time the family received it, she had already been transferred. Although the condolence letter came from Brandenburg, she was killed in Grafeneck. Soon thereafter, Berlin issued an exemption for the daughter.[96]

Although the killing technique applied to the victims of euthanasia was relatively uniform, the circumstances of the murdered victims were, as we have seen, as diverse as that of any group of human beings. The victims, ranging in age from infancy to old age, came from various backgrounds, suffered — or did not suffer — from various ailments, and had different institutional experiences. A few examples illustrate this diversity.

At Eglfing-Haar, a patient named Thoma, an engineer, was healthy enough to have lengthy conversations with his nurses. One of them later recalled that "he did not work, just always did drawings for himself." Scheduled for transfer, he promised to write to his nurses to let them know where the transport had gone. Together with other patients, he left by rail for Linz and was murdered at Hartheim.[97] The forty-three-year-old pharmacist Wilhelm Ballast, a sales representative for a drug company, had been committed in 1941 to the Eichberg state hospital for drug addiction. At the institution, the medical director, Walter Schmidt, valued his services as a professional pharmacist and even maintained friendly personal relations with this educated and intelligent person. But since Ballast was able to obtain drugs, his addiction continued, and he eventually contracted tuberculosis. Postwar investigators concluded

THE ORIGINS OF NAZI GENOCIDE

that Schmidt killed him with an injection because "his drug addiction had become inconvenient, and his behavior had become tiresome."[98]

Erna Metzger was "feebleminded" but physically healthy. She was committed in May 1943 to a local institution because her mother had died and her father, who lived elsewhere, did not want the responsibility of raising her. In November 1943, the child was transferred to the Eichberg state hospital, where ten-year-old Erna was killed on 1 September 1944.[99] In another case, four-month-old Siegfried was killed because he had been born with no arms. The consulting Munich physician recommended death because he wanted to save him from "the terrible fate of a life without pleasure," and in November 1940, Siegfried was admitted to the children's ward at Eglfing-Haar.[100]

In 1943 Maria Tillian from Spittal in Carinthia entered a local old-age home (*Siechenhaus*) because at her advanced age she was unable to receive the necessary home care. In 1944 she was transferred to the old-age ward at the Klagenfurt state hospital. A neighbor testified after the war that he found her locked up during his last visit to her at Klagenfurt. She told him that they punished her with reduced food rations and physical beatings. She died in November 1944.[101]

Paula B. was born in 1892, had a normal childhood, graduated from school, and was trained as a typist. Serving in Ghent as a nurse during the last year of World War I, she suffered a nervous breakdown and began having seizures, eventually receiving a pension as a war invalid. She married in 1920 and in 1926 gave birth to a healthy girl named Margot. Suffering from epileptic seizures, Paula was institutionalized in the 1930s. Although events after birth had caused her condition, and her daughter did not inherit it, the physicians simply followed the guidelines and classified her as suffering from a hereditary disease. The hospital's application for her sterilization was rejected only because she was too old to have children, but her husband's application for a divorce was supported by the physicians and easily granted. Her daughter visited her for the last time during Easter 1941. She asked her daughter to tell her former husband to try to get her out: "There are things going on here, which I cannot explain to you, because you are still too young." In May 1941, she was killed at Hadamar.[102]

The diverse victims were also of various nationalities. Frieda Nardoni, an Italian citizen, had been a supporter of Marshal Pietro Badoglio, and as such SS troops kidnapped and beat her and kept her in a camp in Bavaria for seven months. In June 1942, she was transferred to work at the Hadamar state hospital. During the day, she worked in the city, and during evening hours, she, as well as other non-German inmates, was forced to help the nurses kill patients. The women had to hold the patients while the nurses administered tablets or injections; she described after the war how the patients had screamed, "I don't want to die, I'm not sick." These foreign women lived with the constant fear that they would also be killed. Nardoni was raped by one of the male nurses, who told her, "It's either this or an injection."[103]

Regardless of background, ailment, age, or nationality, the victims died at the hands of killers certified as physicians and nurses. They died in hospitals that were built to aid and cure but had been perverted into places to kill. At the Hadamar trial of October 1945, one of the first American war crimes trials, Colonel Leon Jaworski, the trial judge advocate, described the murder of patients by their physicians as follows: "Oh, what a vicious falsehood, what a terrible thing, what an evil and wicked thing to do to a person who is already suffering and already carrying burdens, to build up the false hope that sunshine was to enter their hearts. They told them they would be given medication that would help them. Oh, yes, they were given medications, medications of poison that gripped their heart and closed their eyelids still; that is the sort of medication they were given."[104]

Chapter 10 Managers and Supervisors

The Nazi killers are usually called perpetrators, in German, *Täter*, a term commonly applied to criminals by police and courts. Unlike biographies of the victims, those of the perpetrators are not difficult for the historian to reconstruct. The victims, reduced to numbers, emerge as individuals only in memoirs, oral histories, and fiction, and even those few sources rarely deal with handicapped victims. In contrast, documentation about the perpetrators is plentiful because they left a paper trail that survived the war, including orders, letters, and personnel records. Further, except for those who committed suicide as the war ended, they also provided detailed accounts of their lives and deeds as defendants and witnesses in court proceedings. In addition, the literature about individual perpetrators and the group of perpetrators is large and growing ever larger as historians, psychologists, and journalists examine their motives.[1]

The perpetrators were dull and uninteresting men and women. Although they were competent at their jobs, most lacked imagination, had pedestrian minds, and led conventional lives. This fact emerges from their postwar testimonies and even more clearly from the few surviving personal letters. Their writings were bureaucratic, their speeches were cliché-ridden, and their postwar testimonies were evasive, insensitive, and self-pitying. Thus when suspicion that the secret diary of the Führer of all the perpetrators had been discovered led to an international media bidding war for the diary in 1984, the fact that media conglomerates and prominent historians accepted as Hitler's writing the dull musings of an unimaginative forger strongly supports Hannah Arendt's conclusions about the "banality" of the evildoer.[2]

Before turning to the perpetrators, we must briefly digress to examine the role German society played in the killings. First, we must ask whether popular opinion could have influenced the regime's activities. Although the argument, which was popular in the immediate postwar years, that the population could not oppose the all-powerful totalitarian state has lost a great deal of support, it is still widely believed that individual Germans were unable to register disapproval or openly oppose any of the regime's actions. But such arguments overlook the fact that the regime needed popular support to wage total war and thus could not afford to alienate large numbers of its citizens. To gain support, or at least obtain acquiescence, the regime had to enact its draconian, exclusionary policies into law, so that the mass of the population — those not excluded — could continue to believe that the legal system would protect their own security.[3] This need to provide legal cover for arbitrary actions also helps to explain why the bureaucrats who administered exclusionary policies generated such an avalanche of directives and announcements couched in legal language and filled with euphemisms.

The fiction of legal security, what the Germans called *Rechtssicherheit*, could not be maintained for the killing operations. In the case of the euthanasia killing program, bureaucrats and physicians did propose legislation to provide legal security for their operation, but Hitler absolutely forbade it as an unrealistic solution during wartime. Killing operations thus required secrecy. Officially, the structure of legal security remained; in secret, however, the killers disregarded the established law. In the killing of the handicapped, secrecy did impose limitations. The handicapped could be killed only if they were institutionalized, and although the killers often lured or forced handicapped individuals into institutions, they could not initiate wholesale roundups during wartime without alienating the populace. Secrecy also forced the killers to resort to subterfuge, and this inevitably led to embarrassing slipups. The killings soon became a public secret, which the authorities could not admit. As we have seen, opposition to the killing program was based, at least in part, on its illegality and secrecy. The killers, who had assumed that the program would be welcomed by the majority of the population, were surprised by the strength of public opposition. At first, they believed that they needed only better communications and thus launched a propaganda drive to make the killings acceptable. But propaganda, even the popular entertainment film sponsored by T4, could not replace legal security, and the regime had to retreat. Although opposition did not stop the killings, it first forced the closing of Grafeneck and Brandenburg and eventually the "stop" of gassing. Of course, decentralized "wild" euthanasia then replaced the centralized euthanasia of the killing centers, permitting the regime to hide the deaths as a by-product of an escalating total war.

Second, we must ask why the euthanasia killing program faced popular opposition while other killing operations, which were equally unlawful, did not. This contrast in public response has led some to maintain that there was a fundamental difference between euthanasia and the final solution. One historian has thus argued that the German public considered the murder of handicapped Germans an unacceptable "breach" of "moral law" whereas it did not consider the murder of Jews such a transgression.[4] But this answer disregards a much simpler explanation. As we have seen, relatives of the handicapped victims led the opposition against the killings, supported at times by others—in villages and small towns but usually not in cities—who saw the victims and their relatives as valued neighbors. In one south German village, peasant women refused to sell cherries to nurses from the local state hospital, telling them: "You don't get cherries here, just move on. We will not sell you anything, because you treat our neighbors in such a terrible way, simply transporting them away and shooting them."[5]

Such solidarity did not generally apply to Jews. But it did apply whenever Jews were related to non-Jewish Germans, either as so-called hybrids (*Mischlinge*) or as partners in so-called mixed marriages (*Mischehen*). Thus when the SS arrested Jewish spouses in mixed marriages during the Berlin factory roundups (*Fabrikaktion*) in February 1943, their German non-Jewish wives staged public demonstrations in the center of the city, forcing the regime to release their husbands.[6] Close relations with potential victims, not ideology, thus determined whether a sense of "moral law" led to opposition.

Those who have studied Nazi crimes and Nazi criminals have always asked two fundamental questions: who committed these crimes and why did they commit them? We must now ask these questions of the euthanasia killers.

The chief perpetrators—Hitler and his intimate circle—are well known, and much has been written about them. Apart from Hitler himself, whose orders initiated the killings and whose authorization protected the killers, most members of this inner circle did not actively participate in this first killing operation. Only three senior members of the Nazi elite were directly involved: Karl Brandt, Philipp Bouhler, and Leonardo Conti.

Brandt was Hitler's attending physician, whose responsibility was primarily the care of Hitler and his staff when away from home; his official title was *Begleitarzt*. Although Brandt occupied a key role as the physician charged by Hitler with supervision over euthanasia, his function was more that of the health administrator than of the physician. Eventually, he advanced as Conti's competitor to a central place in the wartime administration of public health and carried out his duties as plenipotentiary for euthanasia only in passing. His background and attitude were very similar to those of Albert Speer. The two men were close friends, both were technocrats, and Brandt considered the killing of the handicapped only a minor aspect of his larger task concerning public health in the same way that Speer viewed the use of concentration camp labor as only a means to achieve the goal of producing armaments.[7]

As Reich leader (Reichsleiter) of the Nazi party and chief of the KdF, Bouhler belonged to the regime's ruling elite, although he did not have the power and influence of a Bormann or a Himmler. But just as with Brandt, his duties as plenipotentiary for euthanasia occupied only a small portion of his general responsibilities. He assigned the job of implementation to Viktor Brack and the KdF staff and, together with Brandt, concentrated on setting policy. Of course, both Brandt and Bouhler became involved whenever T4 faced problems, as, for example, in its dealings with the Bethel institution.[8] Obviously, Bouhler played a more active role when T4 had to deal with other party agencies and government offices, and he also obtained the money to finance the killing operation.[9] And as we shall see, Bouhler negotiated with Himmler the transfer of T4 personnel to the killing centers in the East.[10]

As the Nazi party's Reich physician leader and, even more important, as state secretary for health in the RMdI, Leonardo Conti was obviously involved with the euthanasia killing program. But after Hitler transferred to Bouhler the commission to supervise euthanasia he had first given to Conti, the government agencies headed by Conti served only an auxiliary function.[11] Although Conti was undoubtedly informed about the operation and signed most of the crucial circulars that started the killing program, he left the daily operation of the killing support services to Fritz Cropp and, especially, Herbert Linden.

The chief perpetrators left the implementation of mass murder to a group of managers. These T4 managers were innovators who operated history's first technological killing operation. Their project involved the murder of the handicapped, but the euthanasia program was not the only killing operation involving the KdF and T4. As we shall discuss later in greater detail, the KdF was from the beginning also involved in the implementation of the final solution, the mass murder of the European Jews and Gypsies.[12] After the stop order, the KdF in 1942 dispatched selected members of the T4 staff to Lublin to serve under SS and Police Leader (SSPF) Odilo Globocnik in Operation Reinhard, named for the assassinated Heydrich. There they ran the killing centers of Belzec, Sobibor, and Treblinka. After the completion of Operation Reinhard in 1943, the KdF posted its men as a group to Trieste to serve again under Globocnik, newly appointed HSSPF in Dalmatia, as Special Commando Adriatic Coastline. There the T4 contingent not only provided security, fought partisans, and deported Jews but also created a concentration camp and killing center in the Risiera di San Sabba, a former rice factory in the San Sabba district of the city of Trieste.[13]

The men charged with directing the day-to-day killing operation of T4 were mid-level bureaucrats.[14] As we have seen from the biographies discussed in earlier chapters, the careers of these managers were lackluster until the Nazi revolution lifted them from obscurity. Not counting the physicians, an extraordinarily small number of men managed T4: Viktor Brack, Werner Blankenburg, Dietrich Allers, Hans-Joachim Becker, Gerhard Bohne, Friedrich Haus, Hans Hefelmann, Richard von Hegener, Adolf Gustav Kaufmann, Friedrich Robert Lorent, Arnold Oels, Fritz Schmiedel, Willy Schneider, Gerhard Siebert, Friedrich Tillmann, and Reinhold Vorberg.[15] Five of them—Brack, Blankenburg, Hefelmann, von Hegener, and Vorberg—were officials of the KdF before the killings; the others came on board to help run the killing operation. But even this number is deceptive. The five KdF officials also had duties in their jobs at the chancellery and thus could not devote their

THE ORIGINS OF NAZI GENOCIDE

full-time efforts to T4; they did, however, receive additional, tax-free compensation every month for their extra work.[16] The others, full-time T4 managers, were not all working at the same time. Allers joined to replace the departing Bohne, Oels replaced Haus, Schneider was replaced by Schmiedel, who was in turn replaced by Lorent.[17]

Except possibly for Schmiedel, whose birth date is not available, all were born between 1900 and 1910. They were unexceptional for men of their age group. All came from a relatively similar milieu. They were raised in modest circumstances, and most were members of the pre–World War I lower middle class. Brack's father was a physician, Allers's was an attorney, and von Hegener's was a military officer and member of the minor nobility. The fathers of the others, as far as can be determined, were small businessmen, and Tillmann's was a craftsman. Five attended institutions of higher education: Bohne and Allers became lawyers (Bohne with a doctorate); Hefelmann earned a doctorate in agriculture; Brack received a certificate in economics; and Schmiedel was certified in engineering. The others attended secondary school, with or without graduation diplomas, and thereafter received on-the-job training in business, except Kaufmann, who was trained as a mechanic. None was well established when the Nazis came to power in 1933.

Although the professional careers of the T4 managers were ordinary, their past politics proved an advantage under the Nazi regime. Almost all had joined the Nazi movement in their early or middle twenties, prior to Hitler's assumption of power, and we can therefore assume that they had embraced Nazi ideology, including its racial and eugenic component. Obviously, the date they joined the party depended in part on their date of birth. Brack had joined in 1929 at age twenty-five, Blankenburg in 1929 at twenty-four, Allers in 1932 at twenty-two, Bohne in 1930 at twenty-eight, Haus in 1930 at twenty-one, Hefelmann in 1931 at twenty-five, von Hegener in 1931 at twenty-six, Kaufmann in 1923 at twenty-one, Lorent in 1930 at twenty-five, Oels in 1933 at twenty-five, Siebert in 1931 at twenty-six, Tillmann in 1923 at twenty, and Vorberg in 1929 at twenty-five. In addition, these men had also been active in the party's paramilitary formations. Allers, Blankenburg, Haus, Kaufmann, and Lorent had joined the SA; Brack had joined the SS; Bohne had joined both the SA and SS; and Oels was a member of the SA who volunteered for service in the Waffen SS.

Brack and Bohne had been active in Nazi and right-wing politics for several years before they had actually joined the party. Kaufmann had joined in Austria and had been active there during the party's illegal period. Becker had not joined until 1937 but was only twenty-eight years old at that time. For Schneider and Schmiedel, we do not have the date they first joined, but both appear to have been active in Nazi politics. In 1936 Schneider, then thirty-six years old, was a staff member of the Nazi party's central office in Munich.

TABLE 10.1. German Civil Service Ranks

German rank	English translation
Regierungsrat	Government councillor
Oberregierungsrat	Senior government councillor
Regierungsdirektor	Government director
Ministerialrat	Ministerial councillor
Ministerialdirigent	Ministerial section head
Ministerialdirektor	Ministerial director
Staatssekretär	State secretary

Source: Henry Friedlander and Sybil Milton, eds., *Bundesarchiv of the Federal Republic of Germany, Koblenz and Freiburg*, Archives of the Holocaust Series, vol. 20 (New York: Garland Publishing, 1993), p. xvii.

Schmiedel was sufficiently involved in the Nazi movement to be taken into the Waffen SS, and not the Wehrmacht, during World War II.

Still, these young men only held auxiliary, not leading, party positions. Brack, the leader of the group, had the most impressive party career, first as Himmler's driver and then as Bouhler's chief of staff. Several were staff members for central agencies of the party: Haus in the SS central office, Hefelmann in the economics department of Nazi party headquarters, and Schneider in the party treasurer's office. Kaufmann was a party inspector in Pomerania, Lorent was an accountant for a party agency, and von Hegener, then employed as a statistician in private industry, was active in local party affairs. Several had used their party connections to rise in local government: Allers served in the Prussian administration as government councillor (Regierungsrat), Bohne was an administrative judge, and Tillmann served in the welfare department of the Cologne district as senior government councillor (Oberregierungsrat). Both Blankenburg and Vorberg held no party posts, moving directly from private business onto the staff of the KdF. (See table 10.1.)

For these young men, jobs at the KdF provided access to influence, power, and future advancement. These jobs spelled success. In addition, they brought personal benefits. Kaufmann, drafted into the navy, wanted a safe rear-area job (*Druckposten*) so he could visit his sick wife.[18] Becker, who was released from military duty due to poor health, did not like his wartime civilian assignment in Danzig and wanted to use his connections to get a better job.[19] Allers had been drafted as a noncommissioned officer and apparently did not like this low status; stationed in Poland, he obtained his appointment at T4 through his mother's intervention with Blankenburg.[20] Lorent, who wanted to leave his assigned post in occupied Poland, visited the KdF to obtain another job.[21] Oels was unemployed after his discharge from the Waffen SS following the French campaign.[22]

We may ask how these men were selected. Obviously, it was not an open competition. Instead, a variety of factors determined recruitment, including party credentials, availability, friendships, nepotism, and required skills. Brack advanced from driving Himmler to serving as Bouhler's adjutant, and when Bouhler established the KdF, he made Brack his deputy. Hefelmann and Blankenburg were recruited to the staff and later advanced to senior positions. Von Hegener was a brother-in-law of Hans Reiter, president of the Reich Health Office. Vorberg was Brack's cousin. These men were already in place when the KdF assumed responsibility for the killing operation, and they simply took on the extra duties as part of their regular jobs. The others were recruited directly into T4. Bohne and Allers, the two business managers of T4, came with legal experience. Becker, who had served in the finance division of the Kassel government, was recruited to run the finance office of T4; he was a cousin of Herbert Linden's wife. Kaufmann, Lorent, Haus, Schneider, and Schmiedel were friends or acquaintances of Brack. Linden had met and recruited Tillmann. Oels's Viennese girlfriend worked at Hadamar and told him to apply at T4. Siebert was a cousin of Brack and Vorberg.

These men had therefore been selected for their loyalty to the party and to the men who recruited them. There is no evidence, however, that those who recruited them were looking for killers. Of course, the men also qualified because they possessed certain skills. But the expertise required involved technical knowledge such as, for example, legal, office management, or accounting experience. It did not involve proficiency in killing people. Nevertheless, a willingness to collaborate in a killing enterprise was a job requirement. Since the men newly hired by T4 were either relatives or friends of the KdF managers, and since they also had solid party credentials, we can assume that their collaboration was never in question. We know of no instance in which a manager recruited by the KdF refused to join.

Some managers left after a short period with T4, but there is no evidence that they did so because they morally objected to their assignment. Instead, they simply moved on to other jobs. Brack did tell his postwar interrogators that he applied and transferred to front duty with the Waffen SS in the late summer of 1942 because he objected to the killing program against the Jews but not the handicapped; the evidence, however, does not confirm this supposed motive.[23] The departure of Gerhard Bohne in the summer of 1940 was caused by his opposition to the way the euthanasia killings were implemented, but not on moral grounds. Bohne criticized the personal behavior of T4 personnel, whom he accused of sexual licentiousness, misuse of resources, and arrogant conduct involving local staff and visiting dignitaries at the killing centers. His aim was to improve efficiency, not to stop the killings. Bohne simply argued that "loose morals soon lead to a general decline of government service."[24]

The T4 managers can be classified as bureaucratic killers, in German, *Schreibtischtäter*, which is usually translated as "desk murderers." Historians have argued that the job of these bureaucrats "frequently consisted of tiny steps in the overall killing process" and that they "performed them in a routine manner, never seeing the victims their actions affected."[25] But this analysis implies greater distance from the killing fields than was actually true. It might apply to bureaucrats who never left their offices and never saw a victim or a killing but not to the T4 managers. As we have seen, the experimental gassing at Brandenburg was attended by the T4 managers Brack, Blankenburg, Bohne, Hefelmann, von Hegener, and Vorberg, as well as by their bosses Brandt, Bouhler, and Conti, who directed policy. But this was certainly not the only time the T4 managers observed the killings.

Adolf Gustav Kaufmann, who headed the inspector's office, not only set up five of the six killing centers—installing gas chambers and crematoria, establishing office procedures, and hiring nonmedical staff—but also later continuously inspected all centers to assure the smooth operation of the killing process.[26] Still, after the war, Kaufmann testified: "I never looked at an actual gassing. I did not even ask permission to watch, because I did not want to see those things."[27] This self-serving statement was designed to limit his legal liability, but it could not have been true since anyone inspecting one of the euthanasia killing centers, smaller in size than those later established in the East, could not have escaped the reality of the killings. Also, this familiarity with the victims and the killing scene applied not only to all T4 managers but also to various visiting dignitaries. Georg Renno, the Hartheim physician, testified that Hartheim was "visited" by Reich Minister Wilhelm Frick, State Secretary Leonardo Conti, Plenipotentiary Fritz Sauckel, and Gauleiter August Eigruber.[28]

During the early period of gassings, Gekrat was directed by Reinhold Vorberg from headquarters located at the Grafeneck killing center. Vorberg not only resided at Grafeneck but also inspected the transport departments at various other killing centers. Vorberg, who together with Blankenburg later visited the killing centers in the East, often confronted his victims when he personally directed Gekrat transports.[29] Dietrich Allers, the T4 business manager who married a secretary who had worked at T4 headquarters and at Hartheim, visited the T4 killing centers numerous times, as well as the extermination camps in the East, and in the spring of 1944 assumed command of the Trieste special unit (Sonderkommando).[30] Friedrich Tillmann, who headed the T4 Administrative Office, chaired the meeting of local T4 office managers at various killing centers once a month and on one occasion used this opportunity also to "watch a gassing."[31] In 1944, when several

T4 offices, including the Central Accounting Office, headed by Hans-Joachim Becker, moved to Hartheim, Becker was appointed chief of the newly created Hartheim Agency and in addition served as office manager of the killing center.[32] Friedrich Robert Lorent, who headed the T4 Central Finance Office, visited various killing centers and was present in Hartheim during the processing of one concentration camp transport, claiming after the war that he had been unable to watch the gassing. This did not prevent him, however, from stopping at Hartheim many times, watching at least one gassing, and even visiting the extermination camps in the East.[33]

In addition, the paperwork processed by the bureaucratic killers was not as innocuous as is often assumed. For example, it involved, as we have seen, the supply of gas and poisons, and the bureaucrats writing requisition orders and telephoning about deliveries could not hide from themselves the reason the killing centers and hospitals needed these supplies.[34]

These managers thus knew what they were doing and had witnessed the final result of their actions. Why did they agree to manage mass murder? Historians have offered the following commonsense explanations, which they have applied to the managers as well as to the rank and file who did the actual killings: authoritarianism, careerism, duress, and peer pressure.[35]

Peer pressure, which might have explained the actions of the rank and file, does not seem to have played a major role in the managers' decisions to collaborate. Group cohesion did not matter as much to individual managers as it did to the rank and file in the field. Office rivalries, competition for influence, and personal ambition inhibited the pressure exercised by fellow managers. As we have seen, several managers left for more congenial positions, and Gerhard Bohne did not hesitate to castigate his fellow managers. We must, however, offer one caveat. Many of the T4 managers were tied to each other because they were relatives or old friends. Pressure exercised by this kind of relationship, however, is unusual and does not correspond to the customary meaning of peer pressure.

T4 managers did not act under duress.[36] Of course, after the war, many perpetrators argued that they participated in killing operations only because they feared that refusal would lead to their execution or incarceration. But even if we accept that this could have happened to perpetrators—and it did not—it certainly did not apply to the T4 managers.[37] They needed no coercion to comply. They were recruited unofficially and were never ordered to participate. Furthermore, they were free to leave for other jobs or for the front, as the departure of several managers illustrates. No duress was involved in their initial participation or in their continuation.

The authoritarian structure of the German state and the Nazi party does in part explain the participation of the T4 managers. This structure was not based on democratic consensus but on the leadership principle, which required those below to carry out orders from above. This applied especially to orders from the Führer himself. Although they did not deal with their Führer in person, the T4 managers operated only two levels below Hitler, who had commissioned Bouhler, who had, in turn, passed on the order to Brack and his associates. However, Bouhler had to maneuver to get this commission, which had at one point been given to Conti, and it was thus not merely a direct order to be obeyed but a plum to be sought. The T4 managers wanted this commission, and the fact that their Führer had ordered the task to be performed did not compel anyone to collaborate. Because they did not object to the killings for personal or moral reasons, the T4 managers automatically carried out their Führer's order. They also used that order to persuade others to join and to justify their own participation.

Career considerations undoubtedly were the most important reason the T4 managers agreed to direct the killings. A job at the KdF placed these men close to the center of power. This applied not only to the five members of the KdF staff but also to those at T4 because the secrecy surrounding T4 forced them to use the authority of the KdF when dealing with outsiders. Of course, the prestige of the job rested as much on the perception as on the reality of its importance. Often those dealing with the T4 managers mistakenly thought they worked for the Reich Chancellery (Reichskanzlei), the official and traditional center of government authority. All of this meant that these young men had reached positions commonly considered important and influential. In addition, these jobs involved an assignment that was secret, sensitive, and significant. They operated at the center of events.

These jobs also involved other benefits. First, they provided a secure berth on the home front without the stigma of civilian work and even with the opportunity for obtaining medals. Second, they provided material benefits, including monetary allowances, travel, and expense accounts. Third, they brought power over others, the right to command, and the ability to make life-and-death decisions. The managers exercised this power and appeared to others to be arrogant men of influence.

One motivation—ideology—is missing from this analysis. Some historians have argued that Nazi ideology was a crucial motivation that led the perpetrators to comply with murderous orders.[38] This argument is usually advanced in analyses of the murder of Jews, focusing on the antisemitism of the perpetrators, but it applies also to the T4 killers, who obviously shared the hostility exhibited by the Nazi movement toward Jews. They also exhibited hostility toward the handicapped, as well as adhering to most other components of Nazi ideology. After all, they were Nazis.

What did it mean to be a Nazi? Membership in the party or its formations obviously signified that someone was a Nazi, especially if he or she had joined prior to 1933. But what did this tell us about the person's ideological commitment? In general, we can assume that such persons embraced the basic creed of the Nazi movement, including its leadership principle, its anti-democratic and antiparliamentarian posture, and its devotion to the *völkisch* community. But the Nazis shared this outlook with many other Germans, and it alone did not set them apart. In the same way, the belief of the Nazi movement in inequality among humans—leading to its racial and eugenic program—which provided the ideological underpinning for exclusion and genocide, was shared by many Germans who had not joined the party before it came to power. Except for political opponents incarcerated in the concentration camps and their sympathizers, most Germans accepted Nazi ideology at least in part. The Nazis differed, however, from the majority of Germans in the depth of their commitment and the degree of their radicalism.

The resolve to impose the will and ideology of the movement and the willingness to apply the most radical methods distinguished those usually described as "fanatic Nazis" from the mass of the German population. Often surface appearances led to such a description, for example, wearing party insignia or insisting on the Hitler salute.[39] The label usually applied to the local Nazi bosses, who were often primitive bullies spouting party slogans to intimidate and terrorize. Fritz Bernotat, the administrator of state hospitals in Hessen-Nassau, has always been portrayed as such. A Nazi party and SS member of long-standing, he terrorized the hospital staffs and imposed the most radical form of euthanasia on his domain.[40] But not all fanatic Nazis resembled Bernotat. Some were educated and polite, but they were nevertheless just as deadly. In fact, most bureaucratic killers—including Brandt, Bouhler, Brack, and even Heydrich—did not resemble Bernotat. The T4 managers belonged to this circle of committed Nazis, and their belief in racial purity undoubtedly made it easy for them to accept their T4 assignment.

Personal considerations and ideological commitment thus led the T4 managers to organize the murder of the handicapped. Without any qualifications in medicine, they made the basic decisions about the life and death of institutionalized handicapped patients. Postwar German prosecutors summarized as follows the motives they believed had led these managers to commit mass murder:

They readily joined because of their Nazi convictions, illustrated by their early memberships and their leading positions in the Nazi party and its formations, their "positive" attitude toward "euthanasia," and their unconditional obedience to their "Führer." Although they lacked knowledge and experience, they used their influence and their position to assure the success of the killing operation, especially as they obtained personal benefits through their collaboration: promotion, allowances, exemption from service at the front, and ultimately personal power and influence.[41]

After the war, they readily admitted their participation but refused to accept their deeds as murder. They justified their participation by repeating the rationalization derived from Binding and Hoche, portraying the brutal euthanasia killing operation as providing a "mercy death," which "had humane considerations in its favor" and "was based on the ethical principle of sympathy."[42] However, they did not readily admit their culpability in the murder of the Jews, either because they feared retribution from the Allies or because they were less convinced that it was defensible.

Viktor Brack, who fully admitted his involvement in the murder of the handicapped, refused to admit his involvement in the murder of Jews. A Nuremberg interrogation illustrates this. On 23 June 1942, Brack had written a letter to Reich Leader SS Himmler urging the mass sterilization of millions of Jews. Brack based his suggestion on the work of the euthanasia physician Horst Schumann, whose sterilization experiments at Auschwitz had been sponsored by the KdF. Brack suggested that out of the 10 million Jews consigned to death, 2 to 3 million should be used for slave labor, but only if they were sterilized.[43] At Nuremberg, his interrogator confronted him with this letter:[44]

Q: What is your full name?
A: Viktor Brack.
Q: Are you the same Viktor Brack whom I have already interrogated several times?
A: Yes.
Q: Mr. Brack, I have interrogated you exactly four times since the day before yesterday. In each interrogation, I asked only one question, and that was what you know about the sterilization program for Jews. I now ask you again: what do you know about the sterilization program for Jews?
A: State Attorney Rodell, my answer is still the same. I know nothing, absolutely nothing about any kind of sterilization.
Q: Brack, you are not a lawyer, but I believe even you know the meaning of perjury.
A: Yes, yes, naturally.
Q: Good, I shall administer the oath again, in case you have forgotten the last oath you took. Stand up, raise your right hand, and repeat after me: I swear by God the Almighty and All-knowing, that I shall speak the truth, shall not omit anything or add anything, so help me God.

(The witness repeats the oath.)

You do know, that an omission is as serious a violation of your oath as is false testimony.

THE ORIGINS OF NAZI GENOCIDE

A: Yes.

Q: Brack, what do you know about the sterilization program for Jews?

A: Nothing, absolutely nothing.

Q: Mr. Brack, this is a white piece of paper. Put your signature on it, exactly the same way you normally sign.

(The witness signs the paper.)
(Mr. Rodell shows a document to the witness. The document is covered and only a signature is visible.)

Which of these two signatures is yours?

A: Mr. Rodell, both signatures are obviously mine. I recognize and accept the signature on this document as my own.

Q: Viktor Brack, our cat and mouse game is now over. Read this bloody document, this letter is damn criminal. You wrote it and probably forgot to burn it in 1945.

(The witness cries and collapses.)

I am not impressed by an SS general with bloody hands, who first lies arrogantly and now cries remorsefully. You would probably not be sitting here as such an absurd creature, if you had reflected on your odious crimes, which in your case started even before 1933, at the time and not only now. I find it difficult to feel sorry for you, one of the former leaders of Greater Germany, who laughingly watched as heads rolled. . . .

A: Herr Dr., Herr Dr., I know that I have lied to you, but I will now tell you everything, really, the whole truth, definitely, but please do not leave my lies in the official record. Please strike the interrogations in which I lied. I will now truthfully testify.

Q: Good, Brack, I am now ready to start a new interrogation. After you have told me the truth, I will decide whether to strike the interrogations containing your lies, which established your perjury. This is your last opportunity to speak the truth. I only want to point out, that speaking the truth is for your own benefit because, as you can see, your answers depend not only on your words but also on your own documents, which you SS leaders forgot to destroy. To repeat, if you tell me the truth, that is, the whole truth, there will be no reason to save the minutes that contain your lies. I believe that you too will feel better and have fewer misgivings, once you have described things the way they really took place.

A: Will I be indicted?

Q: I do not know that. I am only interested in your testimony, because we want to know exactly what happened in the Third Reich. Have you received an indictment?

A: No.

Q: In that case, I especially recommend that you tell the truth. We are now starting a new interrogation.

This bizarre interrogation shows how the perpetrators attempted to extricate themselves from their own complicity in killing operations. Confronted with irrefutable evidence, Brack was obviously shocked, reevaluated his position, and promised to tell the truth. But although he revealed much, he also continued to lie. As we shall see, he deceived the Nuremberg prosecution about his responsibility for the murder of handicapped Jewish patients, and the truth about their fate emerged only long after Nuremberg. Of course, lying did not help Brack, who was hanged.

Physicians in the civil service were intimate collaborators with the T4 managers in the euthanasia killing operation. Since the KdF could not openly supervise the killings, and since the front organization that was presented to the public did not have the authority to select and transport handicapped patients, T4 needed the support of the government agencies that directed the public health offices as well as public and private hospitals. The physicians heading these agencies did not differ in background and attitude from the T4 managers. They were managers with medical degrees, just as Bohne and Allers were managers with law degrees. Their motives for participating in the killing operation were the same as those of the nonmedical managers. Of course, they also had additional professional motives because the killings involved their patients in their hospitals. But they were as committed to the killings as their nonmedical colleagues. Both career ambitions and ideological commitment motivated them. They drew not only on Nazi ideology but also on the scientific tradition of exclusion.

Herbert Linden, the KdF's contact in the health department of the RMdI, was a key manager of euthanasia; as Brack put it after the war, "He was always there for the entire affair."[45] He was not a practicing physician but a government manager, and his participation in the euthanasia killing operation involved primarily shuffling paper. He had joined the Nazi party in 1925, the same year he received his medical license, and thus had very impressive party credentials. But he was not active in party affairs and had joined none of the party formations; he appears, however, to have been the party's man in the civil service.[46] He actively championed racial and eugenic legislation as an author and a bureaucrat, sat in the inner circle of managers planning the killings, and advanced in his ministry as the expert on excluding and killing the handicapped. His personality and ideology matched that of men like Brack.

He embraced the military virtues young Nazis favored, laughing death in the face to conquer the world.[47]

In many ways, Linden resembled Werner Heyde, the physician in charge of T4's medical department. Both were young men who had made their careers under Nazi rule. Linden had joined the Nazi movement long before 1933, but Heyde made up for his lack of pre-1933 credentials by joining the party and the SS after his meeting with Eicke. Heyde had academic ambitions and used his new party connections to advance at his university.[48] His participation in the killing operation was a natural career move.

Paul Nitsche, Heyde's successor as T4's medical manager, was very different. The director of a leading state hospital and a prominent member of his profession, Nitsche joined T4 because he was ideologically committed to the killing operation. Since he did not join the Nazi party until May 1933, his commitment was based less on Nazi ideology than on his support for racial science and on his vision of "progressive medicine."[49] Born in 1876, he had received his medical license in 1901 and obtained the title of professor in 1925 and therefore was well established and no longer motivated by ambition by the time he joined T4. Unlike Heyde, who fought with Brack about jurisdiction, Nitsche worked smoothly with the T4 managers.[50]

Linden and the central bureaucracy depended on local managers of the health care system to enforce their orders. Physicians in charge of local agencies — such as, for example, Hermann Hans Vellguth, who had joined the Nazi party and the SS before and headed the Vienna public health office after the Anschluß — enthusiastically supported the exclusionary policies from sterilization to killing.[51] Three of the local physician managers deserve special attention: Eugen Stähle, Otto Mauthe, and Ludwig Sprauer.[52] They headed the health care administration in Württemberg and Baden, the area where Grafeneck was located and the euthanasia killings commenced. They helped make the killings in those south German states an unusually successful operation. They mostly completed paperwork, but all three also joined Herbert Linden in a visit to Grafeneck to observe the gassing and cremation procedure.[53]

The internist Eugen Stähle, born in 1890 and a veteran of World War I, headed the health department in the Württemberg Ministry of Interior. An old Nazi and an antisemite, who fought in the postwar Free Corps and joined the party in 1927, he fully supported the killing operation and in late 1939 offered Grafeneck to Linden as a killing center.[54] The gynecologist Otto Mauthe, born in 1892, served as Stähle's deputy for state and private mental hospitals. Unlike Stähle, he had joined the Nazi party in 1933 or 1934, after Hitler's assumption of power, and at that time probably also joined the brown-shirt SA. But there is no evidence that his attitude was softer than his superior's toward the handicapped or Jews.[55]

TABLE 10.2. Uniformed and Nonuniformed German Police Ranks and Equivalent Ranks in the SS and the U.S. Army

Sipo (security police)	Orpo (uniformed police)	SS (including Waffen SS)	U.S. Army
Kriminalassistent	Zugwachmeister	Oberscharführer	Staff sergeant
Kriminaloberassistent	Hauptwachtmeister	Hauptscharführer	Technical sergeant
Kriminalsekretär	Meister	Sturmscharführer	Master sergeant
Kriminalobersekretär	Leutnant	Untersturmführer	Second lieutenant
Kriminalinspektor	Oberleutnant	Obersturmführer	First lieutenant
Kriminalkommissar	Hauptmann	Hauptsturmführer	Captain
Regierungs- und Kriminalrat	Major	Sturmbannführer	Major
Oberregierungs- und Kriminalrat	Oberstleutnant	Obersturmbannführer	Lieutenant colonel
Regierungs- und Kriminaldirektor	Oberst	Standartenführer; Oberführer	Colonel
Kriminaldirigent	Generalmajor	Brigadeführer	Brigadier general
Reichskriminaldirektor	Generalleutnant	Gruppenführer	Major general

Source: NARA Library: SHAEF, G-2 (Counter-Intelligence Subdivision, Evaluation and Dissemination Section), *The German Police*, EDS/G/10, Apr. 1945.

Ludwig Sprauer, born in 1884, received his medical license in 1907 and entered government service in 1918. Serving as a local public health officer in Baden from 1920 to 1934, he joined the Nazi party in 1933 and was appointed in 1934 to head the public health service in the state of Baden. He took his orders directly from Linden and supervised the selection and transfer of Baden's handicapped patients.[56]

The T4 managers in Berlin needed men they could trust to run the killing centers. They selected police officers who were loaned to them by Heydrich's RSHA. (See table 10.2.) These supervisors formed the link between the Berlin managers and the rank and file. They supervised the killings on the spot. Although some of them killed individuals from time to time, and all of them directed and watched the killing process, their primary job was administration. These supervisors were thus both bureaucratic killers and directly involved killers on the scene (*tatnahe Täter*).

The T4 managers appointed the senior nonmedical staff members to run the killing centers, but from the start, authority was divided between them and the physicians-in-charge. Following traditional hierarchical hospital structures, the physicians argued that they should run the centers, and Hitler's order that only they should do the killing appeared to support their claims for preeminence. But the T4 managers tended to prefer their nonmedical appointees, usually police officers, and eventually the physicians had to recognize that "Blankenburg, Vorberg and Allers, and Brack perhaps somewhat less, played up the nonmedical personnel."[57] Even influential and strongwilled physicians like Irmfried Eberl and Rudolf Lonauer soon discovered that they had to share power with nonmedical supervisors. Usually this did not cause serious problems; they always cooperated in their common commitment to the killing enterprise.

Christian Wirth was undoubtedly the most important nonmedical supervisor. Since he was killed in action toward the end of the war, we know about him only through surviving documents and the postwar testimony of fellow perpetrators. Born in 1885, he was relatively old for a senior T4 operative when he joined in 1940, at age fifty-five. He had joined the uniformed police before World War I and had risen by 1939 to the rank of captain of detectives (Kriminalkommissar) with the Stuttgart Kripo. He became a member of the Nazi party before 1923, resigned after the Hitler *Putsch*, and reentered as an "old fighter" in 1931. In 1933 he joined the brown-shirt SA but in 1939 transferred to the SS with the rank of first lieutenant (Obersturmführer).[58]

In 1940 Wirth was detached from the police for service with T4. He was not the only police officer assigned to T4, but he was apparently the most important. Since the handicapped patients of Württemberg were to be among the first victims, it was not unreasonable to select a Stuttgart officer. But we do not know why Wirth was chosen and can only assume that his Stuttgart superiors recommended him as a man with the right qualifications. He participated in the first experimental gassing at Brandenburg, helped set up office procedures at Brandenburg and Grafeneck, and thereafter appeared as a troubleshooter in various other killing centers.[59] But although Wirth seems to have had some supervisory authority over office procedures at almost all killing centers, his most noticeable T4 assignment was his lengthy service as chief of the office staff and director of personnel at Hartheim, where he was intimately involved with all aspects of the killing center operation.

All accounts agree that Wirth was a coarse and brutal man who used any means to assure that the killings functioned smoothly.[60] Once he personally shot and killed four female victims because their physical condition made it inconvenient to send them to the gas chamber.[61] One fellow perpetrator testified that on duty Wirth "was pitiless, and one could easily imagine him capable of shooting a subordinate on the spot."[62] The staff called Wirth "wild Christian."[63] In many ways, he resembled the Hessen hospital administrator Bernotat, another brutal man totally committed to Nazi ideology. It was therefore not surprising that the T4 managers selected Wirth to lead the T4 contingent assigned to the killing centers of the final solution.

Wirth's role at Hartheim was unusually powerful, but in all killing centers, the nonmedical supervisor exercised great authority. He oversaw the paperwork as head of the registry office (Standesamt), directed the killing process as the individual responsible for security, and commanded the junior staff as the director of personnel. Usually the supervisors had been posted to T4 from the police, such as, for example, Franz Reichleitner and Franz Stangl at Hartheim, Jacob Wöger at Grafeneck, Hermann Holzschuh at Grafeneck and Bernburg, Fritz Hirsche at Brandenburg and Bernburg, Gottlieb Hering at Bernburg and Hadamar, and Fritz Tauscher at Sonnenstein. Several of them later followed Wirth to the killing centers in the East.[64]

We know more about Franz Stangl, who was deputy to the chief supervisor at Hartheim and later commandant of Treblinka, than we do about the others; his career can therefore serve as a typical example. Born in 1908 in Altmünster, located in the Salzkammergut region of Upper Austria, he was only thirty-two years old when he joined the T4 killing operation. After completing his public schooling in 1923, he trained to become an artisan, following in the footsteps of his father, who had worked as a carpenter and night watchman. After passing his examination as a weaver in 1927, Stangl moved to Innsbruck in 1930 and applied for an appointment in the Austrian federal police. Accepted in early 1931, he trained for two years at the federal police academy in Linz, received his final appointment as a civil servant in January 1933, and was posted to the metropolitan police (Schutzpolizei) in Linz. Ambitious for advancement, Stangl continued his education by taking practical courses that advanced his police expertise. In 1935 he was promoted to detective in the Kripo office in the town of Wels and was assigned to the political department.

After the incorporation of Austria, Stangl's political department in the Wels Kripo office was absorbed into the Linz Gestapo. In May 1938, Stangl joined the Nazi party and also entered the SS, but apparently he had either belonged to or actively sympathized with the Nazi movement prior to the Anschluß—which was then totally illegal for an Austrian police officer—because he received permission to wear the insignia of an "old fighter," usually reserved for those who had served the movement prior to its assumption of power. Nevertheless, the transition was not particularly smooth for Stangl. He hated to move from Wels to Linz, and he later claimed that he was persecuted by his new boss, Georg Prohaska, the chief of the Linz Gestapo who was imported from Bavaria. If this was true, it did not seem to have limited his usefulness to the Linz Gestapo, as he was sufficiently trusted to serve in the Jewish department (*Judenreferat*) and to travel through Upper Austria

THE ORIGINS OF NAZI GENOCIDE

and the Sudetenland to survey and register Jewish communities. Still, there seemed to have been a personality conflict between Prohaska and Stangl, something not altogether rare in bureaucracies.

In November 1940, Stangl joined T4. At Stangl's postwar trial, the court concluded that he wanted to leave his Linz posting to escape his difficult boss and that he maneuvered an invitation to join T4 through the intervention of Franz Reichleitner, a fellow Austrian Kripo officer from another jurisdiction, who had already been assigned to T4. In a jail cell interview thirty years after he entered T4, Stangl told a different story to a British journalist. He did not mention Reichleitner's intervention to get him the job.[65] This was probably an attempt to hide the fact that he had solicited the invitation, which, as we have seen, was the usual way to obtain a staff job at T4.

Stangl did, however, give the journalist a detailed account of his actual induction and thus provided more information than is usually available.[66] He traveled to Berlin and reported as ordered to the RKPA, which was then Office V of the RSHA. There he was received by Paul Werner, the deputy chief of the RKPA.[67] Werner offered him a job as supervisor in charge of security at a T4 killing center and, using the language usually employed during recruitment, described the euthanasia killing program as a "humanitarian" effort that was "essential, legal, and secret." Stangl claimed that Werner was both polite and insistent, reminding him that if he accepted, he would be able to escape his boss in Linz, which he stated was the reason he accepted the assignment. Stangl next met with Brack, who offered him a choice between Hartheim and Sonnenstein, and Stangl picked the Austrian center of Hartheim near Linz. To permit him to outrank and outshine the local police chief in Alkoven near Hartheim, Stangl was transferred to the uniformed order police and advanced in rank to lieutenant.

We can now attempt to answer the questions why Stangl was offered the job and why he accepted. If he solicited a job through Reichleitner, he got the appointment because he was recommended, but undoubtedly Werner would only have recruited him if he had received a favorable evaluation from Prohaska. If he had not solicited the job, a recommendation from Prohaska would have brought him to Werner's attention. In either event, the conflict between Prohaska and Stangl thus did not prevent Prohaska's support and probably was not the only reason Stangl accepted.

At Hartheim Stangl was Wirth's assistant in charge of security, and later, when Reichleitner succeeded Wirth, he served as Reichleitner's deputy. Later, he was briefly posted to Bernburg to reorganize the office of that killing center. In the spring of 1942 he was ordered to appear at T4 and there was offered a choice: return to Linz or accept a posting to Lublin in the East. Again Stangl accepted the offer to participate in killing operations and led a contingent of T4 staff to the killing centers of the East. There Stangl served first as commandant of Sobibor, where he was succeeded by his Hartheim colleague Reichleitner, and second as commandant of Treblinka.[68]

Our information about Stangl's background and T4 activities is more detailed than the information we have on other supervisors, but his career does not differ substantially from their careers. Jacob Wöger served as supervisor of Grafeneck, one of the two killing centers operational at the very beginning. Wöger was recruited by Gerhard Bohne as early as December 1939.[69] Born the son of a farmer in 1897, Wöger entered local government service, fought in World War I, and joined the Württemberg police in 1922. In 1933 he became a member of both the Nazi party and the SS. By 1936, Wöger had risen to the rank of detective master sergeant (Kriminalsekretär) in the Stuttgart Kripo, the same force from which T4 recruited Wirth, and in 1938 he transferred to the staff of the inspector of the Sipo. While serving with T4, he passed his examination for captain of detectives and was duly promoted. After his service at Grafeneck, he returned to his old police job.[70]

Hermann Holzschuh was Wöger's deputy at Grafeneck. Born the son of a Stuttgart lieutenant of detectives in 1907, Holzschuh entered the Württemberg police and advanced by 1937 to the position of detective technical sergeant (Kriminaloberassistent) in the Stuttgart Kripo. He had joined the Nazi party and the SA in 1933, switching from the SA to the SS in 1939. In February 1940, he was recruited by T4 on the recommendation of his Kripo colleague Wöger, served at Grafeneck as Wöger's deputy, succeeded Wöger in August 1940, and moved to Bernburg as chief registrar in February 1941. He departed Bernburg in April 1941, supposedly over differences with Werner Heyde, and was succeeded there by Stangl. Following in Wöger's footsteps, he soon thereafter left T4 for a posting to the staff of the *Befehlshaber* of the Sipo and SD in Kiev.[71]

We know much less about the other supervisors, but we do know that almost all office chiefs were police officers and presumably members of the SS. With responsibility for record keeping, correspondence, registry, personnel, and security, they were basically in charge of the entire killing process, serving either as the first assistant or as equal to the physician-in-charge. After Wirth had established procedures at the Brandenburg killing center, Fritz Hirsche assumed the position of office chief. He later joined the staff move to Bernburg and also did temporary service in Hartheim early in 1943. Hirsche was a captain of the uniformed police.[72]

The office chief at Sonnenstein was apparently a police officer named Schemel, and his two assistants in charge of the registry office were Fritz Tauscher and Gottlieb Hering.[73] Tauscher was a first lieutenant of the uniformed police, served in Sonnenstein in 1940 and 1941, and was posted to the Belzec killing center in the East during late 1942 or early 1943.[74] Hering was a Kripo detective who eventually reached officer rank. After Sonnenstein, he became office manager at Hartheim and thereafter was posted to the East, where he succeeded Wirth as commandant of Belzec.[75]

Although Hadamar, the last of the killing centers to be established, operated like all the others, it differed because the local provincial hospital administrator, Fritz Bernotat, seems to have retained some influence over the killing operation. His representative at Hadamar was Alfons Klein, who had been at the institution since 1934. Born in 1909, Klein had joined the Nazi party and the SA in 1930 and held local party office after 1934. Bernotat appointed Klein as Hadamar director in 1939, and after 1941, during "wild" euthanasia, Klein occupied the dominant position at Hadamar. Klein apparently helped supervise the renovations that turned Hadamar into a killing center, and thereafter T4 employed him as financial officer during the Hadamar gassing phase.[76]

Why did these police officers participate in killing operations? No definitive answer can be provided. Surviving documents do not tell us, some of the officers could not be asked because they did not survive the war, and those who did survive testified in their own defense and were thus unwilling to reveal damaging information. However, we know enough to permit informed speculation about their motives.

These officers were not forced to participate. Senior staff members were recruited, not conscripted. As decision makers who had to use their own initiative to assure that the killings operated smoothly and to introduce innovations that would improve the operation, supervisors had to be willing partners. Moreover, we know from Stangl's account that the RKPA gave him the option of declining the job. These supervisors accepted their assignment although they knew that it involved mass murder. They not only processed paperwork and hired personnel but also had no difficulty facing the killings directly as participants. And some even accepted the later assignment to join in the larger killing operation in the East.

Although it is hard to imagine, they performed, and indeed even sought, these jobs, at least in part, for professional advancement and material benefits. They believed that accepting the assignments would bring promotion or feared that refusal would retard their careers. They also expected certain benefits: escape from other less protected assignments, placement at the home front near their families, and the material rewards that secret assignments offered. Stangl claimed that he accepted for no other reason than to escape his Linz superior Georg Prohaska. It is revealing, however, that he wanted to get away from Prohaska, the "terrible reactionary from Munich," but was perfectly willing to serve Wirth, the far more terrible man from Stuttgart.[77] After the war, Stangl complained about the *Piefkes* to his British interviewer:

"I hate ... I hate the Germans ... for what they pulled me into," conveniently forgetting that Rudolf Lonauer, his Hartheim boss, and Odilo Globocnik, his boss in Lublin, were both Austrians.[78]

As police and SS officers, these men were, of course, members of a hierarchical organization operating along military lines, and they were thus used to following orders. Although this undoubtedly played a role, Stangl's departure from Linz over his conflict with Prohaska and Holzschuh's departure from Bernburg due to disagreements with Heyde do indicate that they were at times able to put their own interests ahead of the organization.

These police officers were also Nazis and, like the T4 managers, adhered to the ideology of the movement, including absolute obedience to the will of the Führer. As police and SS officers, they undoubtedly also shared the hostility toward "unworthy life." One can therefore assume that they agreed in principle with the goals of the euthanasia killing operation and thereafter with those of the final solution. Still, agreement in principle does not imply willingness to kill; something else was needed. They had to be "hard," a valued condition among Nazis. All seem to have possessed this vaunted masculine virtue. All proved this a second time by accepting new postings to the killing centers in the East. Only Wöger, who was injured in a traffic accident in 1940, did not go east; Holzschuh also avoided posting to the killing centers, but his job with the Sipo in Kiev proved his Nazi "masculinity."

Finally, the supervisors believed, as did the managers, that they were making history, that they were participants at the center of momentous events. They were proud to be a part of the march of history. A good example is Hans-Heinz Schütt, a thirty-eight-year-old white-collar worker who had held various office jobs in the party and the SS and who served in the administration of Grafeneck and later in the Lublin camps. In a letter to his stepbrother on the occasion of the boy's confirmation, Schütt told him that they were living in "an age ... never previously experienced by a German," pointing out that "there is only *one* victor, and this victor will determine the future of Europe, even the entire world. And this victor is Adolf Hitler." Schütt concluded with congratulations and the following addendum: "God's blessings, which accompanied the achievements of the Führer, have proved the truth of our ideology [*Weltanschauung*]. We enter a great, new Germany with the blessings of God but without the prayers of the priests."[79]

Three professionals—the chemists Albert Widmann, August Becker, and Helmut Kallmeyer—provided support services for T4 and occupied positions equivalent to those of the T4 managers and supervisors. These three men did not make policy or administer killing operations; instead, they functioned as specialists who supplied professional services essential for the success of the killings. Because the T4 managers used gas and poison to implement mass killings, they needed the services of chemists familiar with those killing agents. Obviously, the T4 managers had to employ chemists they could trust to undertake such a secret, sensitive assignment. They also needed chemists who could obtain those agents for T4 without arousing suspicion. Himmler's SS and police were the logical place to recruit such professionals. Both Widmann and Becker fulfilled those requirements.

Albert Widmann, the chief of KTI's section for chemical analysis, did not actually work for T4, but he and his office supplied the needed support services. Widmann was involved from the beginning: he took part in early discussions about killing methods, participated in the Brandenburg gassing experiment, tested gassing and dynamiting in occupied Bielorussia, and, through his office, obtained for T4 the required gas and poisons.

Born in 1912 in Stuttgart, the son of a railroad engineer, Widmann studied at the Stuttgart Technical Institute, receiving his certificate in chemical engineering in 1936 and his doctorate in 1938. He was almost immediately hired by KTI chief Walter Heess, who, also a native of Stuttgart, had earlier employed Widmann as a temporary consultant. By 1940, Widmann had been promoted to head the chemistry section. Widmann seems to have been relatively uninvolved in politics, his political affiliations resembling those of many other Germans. After Hitler's assumption of power in January 1933, Widmann, then still a student, in July joined the Nazi motor corps. He was admitted to the Nazi party in May 1937, and after he had joined the KTI, he was transferred in December 1939 from the motor corps to the SS with the rank of second lieutenant.[80]

Widmann provided two separate services for T4. One simply involved paperwork. As the surviving paperwork indicates, he obtained the carbon monoxide gas needed for the killing centers and the medicines needed for killings in children's wards and "wild" euthanasia hospitals.[81] He also shared his technological know-how. Others could supervise and administer, Widmann instructed and experimented. He thus appeared in Brandenburg only to teach the gassing method, and thereafter he visited killing centers only when solutions to technical problems needed to be tested, for example, when the crematorium in Sonnenstein did not function properly.[82] For T4, he tested gassing on animals before recommending it as the means to kill humans. For Arthur Nebe, he experimented with dynamite and also tested ways to recycle gas by piping it from a motor exhaust to the interior of a chamber. Unrelated to these efforts, he conducted fatal experiments on concentration camp prisoners to test poisoned ammunition.[83]

Problem solving was Widmann's specialty, and he did not care what kind of problems were involved. Paul Werner, Nebe's deputy and thus Widmann's superior at the RKPA, provided information on the type of problems the KTI scientists solved. Werner, who claimed to have had no involvement with any killings, told his postwar interrogators that "he once heard" that the KTI had technical problems with extracted teeth from the concentration camps: "Those teeth contained gold, and this involved techniques of separating the gold and placing it at the disposal of the Reich Bank. I still remember, that there was talk that it is technically not that simple to separate the gold from the teeth."[84] There is no evidence that the twenty-eight-year-old Widmann was especially motivated by Nazi ideology. Instead, he saw himself as an expert determined to keep his job. After the war, when prosecutors asked him how killing handicapped people on Nebe's orders in Bielorussia was related to antipartisan warfare, supposedly Nebe's assignment in the East, Widmann's answer revealed his attitude: "I never thought about that question. After Nebe told me that he had orders to kill the mental patients in his area, there was nothing for me to think about. After all, mental patients were also killed in the Reich."[85]

August Becker was older than Widmann. Born in 1900 in Hessen, the son of a factory owner, he was drafted at the end of World War I, studied chemistry and physics at the University of Gießen after the war, and received his doctorate in chemistry in 1933. From 1933 to 1935, he remained at the university as a postgraduate assistant. Becker had joined the Nazi party in September 1930 and the SS in February 1931. Unlike Widmann, he thus joined early and chose to work full-time for the Nazi movement. From February to April 1934, he worked at a temporary job with the Gießen Gestapo office, and in 1935 he left the university to join SS Regiment "Germania" of the SS Special Purpose Troops (the future Waffen SS) as SS staff sergeant (Oberscharführer). Stationed in Arolsen, he remained with his unit until 1938. That year, he was posted to the SD to work in its Office II, later Office VI of the newly created RSHA. Promoted to the rank of SS second lieutenant (Untersturmführer), he was employed as a chemist to detect whether written communications used invisible ink.[86]

In December 1939, following a request from Brack to Himmler, the RSHA loaned Becker to T4 so that he could oversee the technical execution of the gassing process; as he later described it: "I functioned as expert for gassing [*Vergasungsfragen*] during the destruction of mental patients in hospitals and nursing homes."[87] He consulted with Widmann on procedure, attended the experimental gassing in Brandenburg, and thereafter transported the needed containers of carbon monoxide from BASF, the I. G. Farben factory in Ludwigshafen, to the various killing centers.[88] He not only delivered the gas but was often also present during gassings to instruct and advise the physicians.[89] At the Brandenburg gassing experiment, he noticed that Irmfried Eberl opened the gas container too fast and the escaping gas made a hissing sound. Fearful that this noise "would make the victims uneasy," he stepped in and demonstrated how to open the valve slowly and quietly, and "thereafter the killing of the mental patients progressed without further incidents."[90]

As the leading German expert on the gassing of human beings, Becker continued to work in his specialty even after he returned from T4 to the RSHA because Himmler wanted to use the T4 experts for the "huge gassing operation to commence in the East."[91] He was assigned to Office IId, a department dealing with technical matters and headed by Walter Rauff, where he joined with Friedrich Pradel, boss of the RSHA motor pool, to work on the improvement of gas vans. During late 1941 and the first half of 1942, Becker visited all SS Einsatzgruppen operating in the occupied Soviet Union to check, evaluate, and possibly repair the gas vans used to kill Jewish and Gypsy women and children. Whenever possible, during his travels Becker reported to Rauff and Pradel suggestions on how to improve gassing efficiency.[92]

Unlike Widmann and Becker, Helmut Kallmeyer did not come from Himmler's police and SS but was personally recruited by Viktor Brack. Born in Hamburg in 1910, the son of a senior government surveyor, he passed his *Abitur*, the prized graduation certificate, in 1929 and thereafter studied chemistry at various universities, completing his studies at the Berlin Technical Institute with certification in 1939 and the doctorate in 1940. He obtained a job in Berlin with Kodak but was drafted into the navy before he could begin work. Kallmeyer never joined the Nazi party but did belong to the SA, later claiming that as a member of a German sailing club he had been automatically transferred into the brown shirts with the entire club membership.[93]

Kallmeyer served in the navy from September 1939 until September 1941. During Christmas 1940, he married Gertrud Fröse, whom he had met as a student four years earlier at his sailing club. In September 1941, Kallmeyer was released from the navy for special home front duty and thereafter joined the perpetrators of mass murder. His name surfaced immediately after the war in the Nuremberg Medical Trial in a prosecution document used against Brack. In this document, the draft of a letter from Alfred Wetzel of the Reich Ministry of the Occupied Eastern Territories to Heinrich Lohse, the Reich commissar for the Ostland, concerning the "solution of the Jewish question," Wetzel informed Lohse that Brack was prepared to send his people to Riga, "especially his chemist Dr. Kallmeyer," to oversee the construction of gassing installations so that the Jews unable to work could be eliminated with "Brack's devices."[94] Later, German prosecutors investigated whether Kallmeyer had also been in Lublin, where T4 was then collaborating in the establishment of the Belzec, Sobibor, and Treblinka killing centers.[95] Both Kallmeyer and his wife reviewed the events of those years during numerous postwar interrogations, and their testimonies illustrate better than most how the perpetrators did everything to hide their culpability, lying and stonewalling until irrefutable evidence convinced them to revise their accounts.

Kallmeyer told his interrogators that he had no idea why he had been recalled from active service. He had simply followed orders, traveled to Berlin, and reported to the agency that had recalled him. He could not remember the name of the agency but did recall that it was located in a large villa on Tiergarten Straße. There some gentleman, whose name he did not remember, accepted his papers and told him to go home until called. Since his wife was pregnant and delivered a boy in late October, he was happy to comply: "The above mentioned agency continuously deposited my salary into my bank account, and, as I have indicated, I practically did not have to perform any duties in return." Finally, after sitting at home and collecting his salary for at least four months, Kallmeyer "suddenly received directions from this agency to report immediately to Lublin." In January or February 1942 — he was not certain about the exact date — Kallmeyer went to Lublin.

In Lublin, Kallmeyer reported to an agency whose name he said he could not remember and was received by a man whose name he said he could not remember but who wore a uniform that was either military, police, or SS. Told to wait, he spent a week in Lublin, although he claimed he could not remember exactly where, and was then told to return to Berlin. He reported to the agency at Tiergarten Straße and was ordered to start an analysis of drinking water, but before he could do so, he was admitted to a hospital on 28 February 1942 — he did remember that date — with typhus. After recovery, he took a one-month recuperative furlough with pay. When he finally reported to the Tiergarten Straße agency, he was told to forget about drinking water and was assigned to the KTI, where he spent the remainder of the war as a scientific collaborator.

As far as Riga was concerned, Kallmeyer had never heard of such an assignment. In fact, he claimed the name of Riga had first come to his attention at Nuremberg, where he had been shown the Wetzel letter. He told his interrogators that at the time he did not worry about his long, paid inactivity. After all, it was war; he quoted a well-known German saying: "Most of the time a soldier waits in vain."[96]

Kallmeyer's account defies common sense. The facts were different. It is hard to believe that he did not expect the call from Berlin or did not know the agency that requested him. After all, his wife, the former Gertrud Fröse, had worked at the KdF and in 1940 had been Viktor Brack's secretary.[97] Brack had attended Kallmeyer's wedding as a guest, something Kallmeyer eventually admitted, adding that he might even have stood up as a witness (*Trauzeuge*).

Even if Brack had initiated Kallmeyer's recruitment before the stop order and thus had nothing for him to do when he arrived, an interpretation Kallmeyer favored, there was no reason to send him to Lublin without a definite assignment. This occurred at a time when T4 was starting to dispatch specialists to construct the killing centers in the Lublin region. But Kallmeyer only admitted that someone might have told him that he "had been intended for action as a chemist in the East." Although attempts to launch gassings in the Baltic region never materialized, and Kallmeyer probably never went there, the fact that Brack considered "his chemist" Kallmeyer knowledgeable in gassing matters remains significant. Of course, Kallmeyer had heard about Riga before Nuremberg. In a postwar letter from Cuba, Kallmeyer wrote to his lawyer that "the sudden cold weather prevented our departure" for Riga, and he thus eventually admitted that he might have heard something about Riga during 1941.[98] As far as his duties at the KTI were concerned, there, too, his name appeared on documents involving the delivery of gas and poisons to the T4 killing operation.[99]

Gertrud Kallmeyer née Fröse was equally evasive. At first, she denied any knowledge about the euthanasia killings, claiming that she had no contact with Brack after she left the KdF in late 1940. Concerning her husband, she admitted that he had gone to Lublin and told her about Riga, but she insisted that he had never gone there.[100] At a later interrogation, she admitted that she had been aware of the euthanasia program but denied having known any specific details.[101] The postwar German police investigators were not convinced. Citing comments by another witness that there had been a "special relationship of trust" between Brack and his secretary, they believed she was lying: "She did not truthfully report the facts."[102]

Kallmeyer and his wife maintained that in 1940 and 1941 they had known nothing about the euthanasia killings and thus obviously nothing about the killings that were then commencing in the East. But confronted with the testimony of other perpetrators, Gertrud Kallmeyer finally admitted that during 1940 she had been posted to the Grafeneck killing center. But she maintained that she was at Grafeneck before the killings, had only supervised the kitchen and installed a library, and had never met Dr. Horst Schumann, Jacob Wöger, or Hermann Holzschuh.[103] Confronted with other evidence, Gertrud Kallmeyer finally admitted that she might have been at Grafeneck after the killings started and that she might have left her job with Brack later than she had originally claimed, leading the investigative judge to comment that "the witness is so adroit that her constant reference to her weak memory seems dubious."[104] Shortly thereafter, Gertrud Kallmeyer wrote to the court to revise her testimony: "Today I can no longer exclude the possibility that the relationship described by one witness did briefly exist between myself and Dr. Schumann."[105] After the war, the Kallmeyers met and dined with the Schumanns in Ghana, where Horst Schumann was hiding from arrest warrants for his killings in Grafeneck and Sonnenstein and his experiments in Auschwitz.[106]

Although the postwar investigators did not believe their accounts, the involvement of the Kallmeyers with killing operations was never fully proved.[107] Still, the following scenario seems to be a reasonable reconstruction. Brack recruited his secretary's husband as a chemist for T4. Because Gertrud not only knew about the killings but also observed them firsthand at Grafeneck,

Helmut was fully informed about his prospective duties before he accepted the T4 job. He also knew the benefits: the chance to work in his own field for the first time since graduation, assurance of duty away from the front, and time to spend with wife and baby. Brack needed a specialist to aid T4 in the construction of killing centers in the East. August Becker had left, Albert Widmann was busy, and Brack could not get a new chemist from the RSHA. He found Kallmeyer a perfect choice to be the T4 chemist needed to help construct mass gassing facilities in the Lublin region.

The three chemists were not the only experts T4 recruited. The killing operation also needed the services of craftsmen. The best example is Erwin Lambert, master mason and building trades foreman (*Maurerpolier*), who started to work for T4 in January 1940 and joined the T4 staff in the Lublin region in the summer of 1942, eventually following the staff in 1943 to the Trieste region. After the war, Lambert denied involvement. He claimed that he had only "suspected" that the buildings he repaired were to be used for killings. But like other perpetrators, he was eventually forced to reveal more.[108]

Lambert was born in 1909 in Schildow, in the Niederbarnim district, not far from Berlin. His father was killed in World War I; his stepfather owned a construction firm in Schildow. After basic schooling, Lambert became an apprentice, first to a locksmith and then to a mason. After passing his apprentice examination, he attended a school for the building trades in Berlin in the mid-1920s and passed his examination for master mason in the mid-1930s. He was always employed, working as a mason and, after becoming a master mason, as a foreman for various Berlin construction firms. He was not a member of the Nazi party prior to Hitler's assumption of power but joined in March 1933. He never joined any of the party's paramilitary formations but did serve as a party block leader in his native Schildow.[109]

Late in 1939, T4 tried to recruit Lambert, who had been recommended by the local office of the German Labor Front. At first, he hesitated to change jobs or to leave his ailing mother, but in January 1940, he accepted T4's offer. We may well ask why T4 required his services. The construction work needed to transform hospital buildings into killing centers was carried out by workers hired locally.[110] In addition, T4 recruited individual craftsmen for specific tasks. In Hadamar, for example, T4 engaged Fritz Schirwing, a master locksmith who was also Bernotat's brother-in-law, to install the pipes, showers, and fans in the gas chamber.[111] In Berlin, T4 recruited Herbert Kalisch, an electrician working for the General Electric Company, to install the electric power lines in the gas chamber and crematorium at Bernburg and Sonnenstein.[112] Lambert's services as mason were not essential, and it thus appears that he was hired as a construction foreman to supervise other workers. T4 wanted someone on hand to provide the link between headquarters and workers re-

THE ORIGINS OF NAZI GENOCIDE

cruited locally, a trusted specialist to carry out essential tasks. Lambert was "the traveling construction boss of Operation T4." [113]

Lambert was asked to direct the construction work required to turn the villa at number 4 on Tiergarten Straße into T4 headquarters; later, he supervised repairs on the T4 building and on the T4 vacation home in Austria. His primary task, however, was to direct construction at the killing centers, especially the construction of gas chambers and crematoria. Lambert's testimony that he only erected room dividers and installed doors is simply not believable.[114] Since the necessary construction at Brandenburg and Grafeneck had apparently been completed before Lambert joined T4, he obviously worked only at Hartheim, Sonnenstein, Bernburg, and Hadamar, where he served as T4's "expert for the construction of gas chambers." [115]

After the stop order limited the work of the euthanasia killing centers to the murders of 14f13, Lambert was posted to the East, where his career paralleled that of many other members of the T4 staff. But his assignment to the East, and later to Trieste, was often interrupted for further T4 construction jobs in Germany and Austria. He visited the Lublin region three times to construct gas chambers in Treblinka and Sobibor, and he also directed construction work in several forced labor camps nearby.[116] Aided by Ukrainian volunteers and supervising crews of condemned Jewish workers, he rapidly constructed solid facilities: "Using his expert knowledge about gassing installations, Lambert was able rapidly to complete all work on the big gas house [in Treblinka]." [117] Lambert remained an uninvolved expert — even in the East — interested in his work and not in the conditions surrounding that work. According to one survivor account, Lambert avoided looking at dead bodies and treated his Jewish work crew in a professional manner, leading one postwar author to stress his "humane behavior toward the prisoners." [118] After Operation Reinhard closed down, Lambert was posted to Trieste, where, along with the police duties required of all T4 staff members, he continued to follow his profession by installing cremation facilities at the Risiera di San Sabba.[119]

Physicians played an important role in the euthanasia killing operation. We have seen how scientists and physicians advocated the exclusion of those considered "unworthy of life" and how their racial and eugenic theories were absorbed and integrated into the Nazi movement. Using scientists to legitimize their ideology, the Nazi leaders granted them limited control over the implementation of exclusionary policies. Physicians and scientists thus served the state as theorists and experts. During the 1930s, they implemented sterilization legislation against the handicapped and provided expert advice on classifying Jews and Gypsies. As we have seen, once the regime moved from exclusion to extermination in late 1939 — a decision made by political leaders, not expert advisers — physicians helped to manage the killings, while scientists did not hesitate to profit from the enterprise. Scientists and physicians thus proposed, justified, and managed the killings. Some joined the ranks of the bureaucratic killers (*Schreibtischtäter*). But some also became killers on the scene (*tatnahe Täter*).

The move from theory to realization, from advocacy of the "destruction of life unworthy of life" to the actual killing of human beings, was, even for theorists, a giant step. For example, in November 1939, Brack asked Paul Nitsche, a leading advocate of euthanasia, to "establish gas chambers and to assume supervision over their operation." Pointing to his "advanced age" and his distaste for the "secrecy game [*Geheimnistuerei*]," Nitsche refused to supervise a killing center.[1] Of course, once the centers operated, Nitsche and his colleague Heyde could not resist the opportunity to watch a killing procedure.[2]

For the killing jobs, T4 needed physicians who were young, aggressive, and ambitious. Such men staffed the killing centers and the children's killing wards. Of course, older physicians were also involved in killings with injections, tablets, and starvation — but not with gas. But such older physicians — Hermann Pfannmüller at Eglfing-Haar, Valentin Faltlhauser at Kaufbeuren-Irsee, and Adolf Wahlmann at Hadamar — were exceptions and usually gave orders to younger physicians and to nurses who did the actual killing.

Various myths have been created to explain the role of physicians in Nazi killing operations. Authors dealing with Nazi crimes have ascribed to physicians as a group a unique commitment to serve humanity and have thus viewed their participation in these crimes as a particularly egregious fall from grace. The mystification of physicians started early. On one side, they were described as "angels of death," a phrase widely applied to Josef Mengele, who was, after all, only one killer among many at Auschwitz, although he had more scientific training than most and unscrupulously used the latest scientific techniques to gain academic credit from his crimes. On the other side, a tendency developed to dilute the crimes of the physicians by granting them sincere though misguided motives.[3]

In his recent study of the "Nazi doctors," psychiatrist Robert Jay Lifton presented a similar analysis that has been widely accepted. Characterizing physicians as "healers" who "work at the border of life and death," he designated those who participated in the Nazi killing programs as "healers-turned-killers."[4] Lifton described mass murder as "medicalized killing," defining it as "the 'surgical' method of killing large numbers of people by means of a controlled technology making use of highly poisonous gas." Lifton described the motives of the physicians as purely ideological; they became killers because they followed a "biomedical vision," approaching their task as a "therapeutic imperative."[5] In this way, Lifton distinguished between so-called idealists like Karl Brandt, described as an example of a "decent Nazi," and someone like Werner Heyde, described as an SS "hit man" with "psychopathic and sadistic tendencies."[6]

The biographies of the physicians involved might, however, lead to conclusions that are substantially different. Physicians as a group are no more dedicated than other professionals and do not resist crime any better than do chemists, lawyers, or historians. Their status at that time as men with academic degrees was relatively high, but measured by family background and economic position, it did not differ from that of other professionals. In fact, after World War I, the status of medical practitioners and students diminished in Germany, which might help to explain why they "were filled with resentment and hate against the reality of Weimar democracy" and joined the Nazi party in substantial numbers.[7]

Of course, it is undoubtedly true that the participating physicians believed in the racial and eugenic goals of the Nazi regime. As the geneticist Benno Müller-Hill has pointed out, biological and social scientists, and their students, championed the doctrine of human inequality and thus encouraged, reinforced, and supported policies of exclusion and extermination.[8] But like the managers, physicians collaborated in killing operations for many personal reasons unrelated to their ideological commitment. The example of Gottfried Ewald has shown that a physician could refuse to participate in killings even if he subscribed to the ideology of racial science. Whatever view each held on racial and physical purity, individual physicians had to make a conscious choice to do the killings; in fact, only some chose to follow their "biomedical vision" into the killing centers.

The motives that led these physicians to involve themselves in killing operations probably differed from person to person. But the evidence does not support a conclusion that differentiates between the motives of "idealists" like Brandt and storm troopers like Heyde, that is, between Brandt's lofty aims and Heyde's brutal behavior. The differences between such men primarily reflect social class and manners and do not tell us a great deal about their motives. In the same way, Heyde differed in background, training, and decorum from his successor Nitsche, but the two men did not differ in the way they carried out their killing tasks.

These tasks involved murder pure and simple, and physicians did not commit murder differently than did their less-educated collaborators. The term "medicalized killing" is thus misleading. In the euthanasia killing centers, the physicians administered death, and in places like Auschwitz, other physicians did the same. But the technique of mass murder through the use of gas had nothing to do with medicine. Mass murder did not become preventive medicine just because Nazi ideologues borrowed their language from medicine to describe their extermination policies as necessary surgery. Although Hitler ordered that only physicians could do the killing, everyone knew that death in the gas chamber was not a medical procedure. As we have already seen, Georg Renno, the Hartheim physician, fully understood this and told Werner Heyde, "I did not study medicine to service a gas valve."[9] In fact, members of the RSHA and not physicians first advanced the idea of using gas, while supervisors, mostly police officers, developed the technique of gassing and cremating human beings.

In the months following the end of the war, the Allied armies who liberated the hospitals and camps described involved physicians without postwar mystification about their motives and deeds. The 2 July 1945 American intelligence report about the Kaufbeuren hospital, finally liberated, as we have seen, two months after the end of the war, had the handwritten heading, "Medical Extermination Camp at Kaufbeuren, Bavaria," and was probably close to the truth when it described the physicians and nurses as follows:

A wholesale extermination plant functioned to this date within less than half a mile from the Military Government C.I.C. and M.P. Headquarters in this idyllic Swabian town and virtually every inhabitant was fully aware of the fact that human beings were both used as guinea pigs and were systematically butchered. The perpetrators or passive collaborators involved were in no way conscious of their crimes, they were *Germans* and not *Nazis*. Among them were Catholic sisters. The chief nurse who had confessed without coercion, that she had murdered "approximately" 210 children in the course of two years by intramuscular injection, asked simply "will anything happen to me?"...

... Observers found, in an uncooled morgue stinking bodies of men and women who had died twelve hours to three days before. Their weight was

THE ORIGINS OF NAZI GENOCIDE

between 26 and 33 kilos. Among the children still living was a ten years old boy whose weight was less than 10 Kilos and whose legs at the calf had a diameter of 2½ inches. . . .

. . . Dr. Valentin Faltlhauser, Obermedizinalrat, a civilian medical grade roughly corresponding to a Colonel in State Service, since 1919, aged sixty-nine, was in charge and has been arrested. Dr. Lothar Gärtner, second in charge, aged forty-three, and with the institution since January 1, 1930, committed suicide by hanging himself on the wire of a bed lamp. Arrested also were three other doctors, [and] the food administrator, Fanziska Vill, who was secretary to Dr. Faltlhauser, and mistress of Dr. Gärtner.[10]

The young physicians who served in the killing centers or attended the children's wards were simply killers; that they had medical degrees is quite beside the point. As we have seen, the supervisors ran the killing centers, although some physicians contested or shared authority. The centers did not actually need physicians. As Renno pointed out, one did not need a medical degree to open a gas valve, and even to do that correctly, the physicians had to be instructed by the chemists Widmann and Becker.

There were, of course, reasons for the presence of physicians. They were needed to check the medical records that arrived with the victims so that serious errors in selection could be avoided. They were also needed to determine what fraudulent diagnosis would be most credible on the death certificates, although sometimes the offices established routine causes to insert.[11] Finally, they were needed to give the killing center the appearance of a regular hospital to the outside world. But these reasons alone do not explain why physicians played such a large role at the euthanasia killing centers. One reason was Hitler's order that only physicians should kill.[12] Second, physicians and managers engaged in a turf war, exemplified by the conflict between Brack and Heyde.[13] Needed or not, the physicians would not abandon their prerogatives in the killing process to the nonmedical managers.

Fourteen young physicians served in the killing centers between January 1940 and August 1941.[14] Of these, four served as physicians-in-charge: Ernst Baumhard, Irmfried Eberl, Rudolf Lonauer, and Horst Schumann. Eberl was in charge first at Brandenburg and then at Bernburg; Lonauer at Hartheim; and Schumann first at Grafeneck and then at Sonnenstein. Baumhard, who first served as Schumann's assistant at Grafeneck, was later in charge at Hadamar.

Baumhard, about whom little information is available, left T4 in the summer of 1941 to enter the navy; he was killed in the war.[15] Eberl hanged himself in early 1948 in his jail cell.[16] Lonauer took his life on 5 May 1945.[17] Schumann survived, fled to Africa in 1951, was extradited to Germany in 1966, was released in 1971 "due to illness," and died in 1983.[18]

These physicians-in-charge at killing centers were in their early thirties: Schumann was born in 1906, Lonauer in 1907, Eberl in 1910, and Baumhard in 1911. They received their medical licenses in the 1930s: Lonauer in 1931, Schumann in 1932, Eberl in 1935, and Baumhard only in 1939. All three also completed their doctorates. Only Lonauer certified in a specialty, receiving his specialization certification in psychiatry in 1937. Eberl and Lonauer were Austrians. Schumann joined the Nazi party in early 1930 and the SA in 1932. Lonauer joined the Austrian Nazi party in 1931, left in 1932, and reentered in 1933; he was also a member of the SS, reaching the rank of SS captain (Hauptsturmführer) in 1942. Eberl joined the party in Austria in 1931, and no evidence exists that he also joined one of its formations. Baumhard joined the party in 1937.[19]

Schumann was the son of a physician from Halle on the Saale River in the eastern part of Germany. The father, a nationalist and a conservative, influenced the son, who followed his father into a right-wing fraternity and into the Nazi party. Schumann did his residency in internal medicine from 1931 to 1934 and then entered the civil service as a physician with the public health office in Halle. Shortly before the war, he was drafted as a medical officer into the air force. Soon thereafter, in early October 1939, Schumann was summoned to the KdF, where Brack informed him about the euthanasia killing operation and asked him to join. Schumann accepted and was appointed physician-in-charge at Grafeneck, interrupting his service for about four weeks in April 1940 to take a course in psychiatry with Werner Heyde at Würzburg. From Grafeneck, Schumann moved to Sonnenstein.[20]

Lonauer was born the son of an Austrian civil servant in Linz. His father had supported the Greater German movement and had also joined the Nazi party. His son followed him into the party and also joined the SS. Lonauer's wife, a native of Graz, was supposed to have been a fanatic Nazi who influenced Lonauer; they proved their family commitment to the Nazi cause at the end of the war with a joint suicide that also included their two children. Certified in psychiatry, and a member of the movement during the period of illegality, which gave him impeccable Nazi credentials, Lonauer was appointed after the Anschluß director of the Niedernhart state hospital in Linz. In 1940 he was made physician-in-charge at nearby Hartheim, and except for a period with the Wehrmacht from September 1943 to November 1944, he headed both Niedernhart and Hartheim until the end of the war.[21]

Eberl was born in Bregenz in the Vorarlberg province of Austria, attended the University of Innsbruck, and received his medical license and his doctorate in 1935. Thereafter, he completed his training at various hospitals in Innsbruck and Vienna in forensic medicine, tuberculosis, and gynecology. In 1936 Eberl moved to Germany; in his vita, he claimed that as a member of the illegal Nazi movement, he was prevented by the Austrian government from obtaining a hospital appointment. In Germany, he at first worked in Dresden and then went to Dessau. There he was employed at the city hospital, substituted in a private practice, and headed the department of public health for the local Nazi party regional office. In March 1937, he received permanent medical certification in Germany, and in May 1937, he was granted official permission to use the doctor title. In October 1937, he was appointed physician with the emergency medical services (Rettungsamt) of the city of Berlin. He joined T4 early and was present at the Brandenburg gassing experiment as the institutional director, later moving from there to Bernburg.[22]

In June 1938, Eberl married Ruth Rehm. She was born in 1907 in Ulm, Bavaria, and received her schooling in Erfurt and Magdeburg. She studied "scientific graphology" for two years, passed her examination in 1932, and joined the Nazi party that September. After a year of independent employment as a graphologist, she worked for the Nazi movement in Magdeburg, Erfurt, and Weimar and, finally, for the German Labor Front in Berlin. She was killed in an air raid in July 1944.[23] She was a strong and determined supporter of the Nazi movement who did not hesitate to denounce fellow Germans to the Gestapo.[24]

We must now ask how T4 selected these physicians. They were each probably recommended by someone in the circle of senior scientists and physicians assembled by T4 to help plan the killing operation.[25] Of course, they sought men committed to Nazi ideology and the scientific theories about eugenics and race. As the refusal by Nitsche has shown, older men with established careers did not want to take such jobs. T4 therefore recruited younger men who still needed to establish themselves. Such men had to be ambitious for advancement in the new Germany and thus willing to take on a job that they considered more important than fighting at the front. Candidates also had to be vetted for reliability, which was probably done through the Nazi party organizations.

Three physicians-in-charge—Lonauer, Schumann, and Eberl—met these criteria. All three were already civil servants and party stalwarts. As director of Niedernhart and thus well known to local Nazi leaders, Lonauer was a natural choice for physician-in-charge at nearby Hartheim. Schumann had not been the first choice for Grafeneck. That candidate had been an SS physician named Werner Kirchert who refused the job but recommended Schumann.[26] Eberl, the displaced Austrian trying to get a foothold in Germany, was another obvious choice. Of course, the men had to be convinced to accept the position. Brack and Heyde recruited them, and part of their inducement was the promise of professional advancement. Although their duties were actually analogous to those of a person in charge of a slaughterhouse, they were obviously attracted by the status of a state hospital director, the fraudulent title they would hold. The possibility that they could conduct scientific research at the killing centers was another attraction. This did not happen, however, and Eberl later complained that Heyde's promises that the medical staff of the killing centers would hold seminars, engage in research, and employ pathologists did not materialize.[27]

Killing center reality tested the physicians' commitment to their theory of destruction. Some physicians like Ernst Baumhard eventually decided to leave for the armed forces, but others decided to stay and turn mass murder into a profession. Three physicians-in-charge chose to continue mass murder after the stop order. Both Schumann and Lonauer selected concentration camp prisoners in the 14f13 operation and then supervised the murders of the selected prisoners in their own killing centers. Lonauer continued to murder victims at Hartheim, where throughout the war, concentration camp prisoners were gassed and where he maintained cordial relations with the Mauthausen concentration camp staff next door.[28] Schumann left Sonnenstein in 1942 to conduct X-ray experiments at Auschwitz to discover how human beings could be rapidly sterilized.[29] And as we shall see, Eberl served as the first commandant of Treblinka.

Ten other physicians, assistants to the physicians-in-charge, worked in the killing centers. Of these, Friedrich Berner, who worked in Hadamar, and Günther Hennecke, who worked in Grafeneck and Hadamar, left T4 and were killed during the war.[30] Kurt Schmalenbach, who was also killed, had a longer T4 career. Schmalenbach had been Nitsche's assistant at Sonnenstein before the war and before that institution became a killing center. He probably joined T4 on Nitsche's recommendation, assisted Schumann at Sonnenstein, and later succeeded him for a brief stint as physician-in-charge. Schmalenbach also served at T4 headquarters and was one of the traveling physicians of the 14f13 operation.[31]

The other seven physicians all survived the war to face judicial proceedings: Kurt Borm, Heinrich Bunke, Klaus Endruweit, Hans-Bodo Gorgaß, Georg Renno, Aquilin Ullrich, and Ewald Worthmann. They were all very young in 1940. Three were approximately the same age as the physicians-in-charge: Renno was thirty-three, and Borm and Gorgaß were each thirty-one years old. The others were younger: Worthmann was twenty-nine, Endruweit was twenty-seven, and Bunke and Ullrich were each twenty-six years old. More important, they were very recent graduates when they joined T4 in 1940. The physicians-in-charge had received their medical licenses in 1931 (Lonauer), 1932 (Schumann), and 1935 (Eberl). Of the seven assistants, only Renno, who had received his license as early as 1933, and Gorgaß, who had been licensed in 1937, were equally qualified. Of the others, Borm received his license in September 1938, Worthmann in January 1939, and Bunke, Endruweit, and Ullrich received emergency licenses (*Notapprobation*) in 1939 after the war had started.

All seven did, however, have adequate, though not overwhelming, party credentials, but this was undoubtedly determined by their ages. Renno was the oldest and had been a member of the movement even before the Nazi assumption of power. He had joined the National Socialist German Student Union (Nationalsozialistischer Deutscher Studentenbund, or NSDStB) in 1929, the party in 1930, and the SS in 1931. Borm was almost as old as Renno and had also joined early, becoming a member of the party in 1930 and of the SS in 1933. Gorgaß was as old as Borm but had joined the party only in 1937; he was also a member of the brown-shirt SA. The other four were younger, and their careers in the movement were therefore rather brief. Bunke joined the party in 1937. Endruweit belonged to the Hitler Youth, although there is some evidence that he had also joined the NSDStB and the SA in 1933 or 1934. Ullrich joined the NSDStB in 1934 and the party in 1937, and he might also have belonged to the SA and Hitler Youth. Worthmann joined the SA in 1933 and the party in 1937.[32]

Kurt Borm was the only son of a civil servant who headed the welfare office in Berlin-Rummelsburg. Borm studied at the University of Berlin and was a student of Karl Bonhoeffer's. He interned in internal medicine at one of the Berlin city hospitals. With his new medical license in hand, he entered the SS Guard Regiment Adolf Hitler as medical officer in September 1939 and served there until he joined T4 in November 1940.[33]

Aquilin Ullrich was the youngest of five children. His father taught in a classical secondary school (*Gymnasium*). He studied at Munich, Freiburg, and finally Würzburg. In 1938 he led an anthropological study group, which included his friends Endruweit and Worthmann, to Bessarabia to study ethnic German settlements. At the start of the war, he joined a Wehrmacht medical unit, first as a noncommissioned officer and then, after passing his emergency license examination, as a medical officer, but soon thereafter, he transferred to T4.[34]

Heinrich Bunke was the son of a schoolteacher. He studied at Göttingen, Kiel, Munich, and Freiburg, where he met Ullrich. He joined the Wehrmacht at the start of the war, passed his emergency medical examination in Kiel in November 1939, and was promoted to medical officer at Christmas. In the late summer of 1940, he joined T4.[35] Klaus Endruweit was born in Tilsit in East Prussia; his father was a teacher of deaf-mutes (*Taubstummenoberlehrer*). He studied at Munich, where he met Ullrich, and Berlin and finished at Würzburg. He joined the medical corps, passed his emergency examination, and served as medical officer in the French campaign, joining T4 in November 1940.[36] Ewald Worthmann, another friend of Ullrich's, studied at Hamburg, Munich, and Berlin and with Werner Heyde at Würzburg, where he received his doctorate with a thesis in race hygiene late in 1938.[37]

Georg Renno had completed his medical studies by 1933 and thus held a regular medical appointment during the 1930s. In 1933 he obtained a civil service job as junior physician at the state hospital at Leipzig-Dösen; Paul Nitsche headed this institution during the 1920s and again after 1 January 1940. On the side, Renno served as physician for his SS unit with the rank of second lieutenant (Untersturmführer). At the start of euthanasia discussions, Nitsche at Leipzig-Dösen tried out a killing method using injections of medication to kill about sixty patients, a method that would be used in the children's wards and the hospitals of "wild" euthanasia. For this experiment, Nitsche picked two junior physicians, one of whom was Georg Renno. In May 1940, Renno joined T4.[38]

Hans-Bodo Gorgaß received his medical education at the University of Leipzig and, after passing his examination in 1935, in 1936 also obtained civil service employment as a physician in the state institution system of Hessen-Nassau, the domain of Fritz Bernotat. He served first at Eichberg and in 1938, at the young age of twenty-nine, was appointed senior physician at Kalmenhof. Drafted in late 1939, he joined T4 in 1940.[39]

It is not difficult to see why these men were selected. They were chosen because they were available, as were most junior T4 staff members. They got their jobs through word-of-mouth recommendations. Ullrich, Endruweit, and Worthmann had studied at Würzburg and were thus known to Werner Heyde, the chief of the T4 Medical Office. We do not know who was approached first, but both Worthmann and Ullrich joined early. After the war, Ullrich reported that he was brought by the Würzburg Nazi student leader to meet Heyde and that Heyde asked him to join the killing operation. Endruweit joined somewhat later, as did Bunke, probably on his friend Ullrich's recommendation.[40]

Of course, all had the required party credentials, but even failure to have such credentials did not always pose a problem. Schmalenbach was already working for T4 while the KdF was trying to discover his standing in the Nazi movement. His papers could not be found by the party's offices, and he did not get a clean bill of health as a Nazi until the summer of 1941.[41]

After joining, each of the young physicians went to Berlin for their assignments. Ullrich was received by Blankenburg, who drove him to the Brandenburg killing center, where he explained the killing procedure. There Ullrich served as Eberl's assistant. Later he served at T4 headquarters and also joined panels of physicians selecting patients at the Bethel hospital.[42] Bunke was met by Heyde and Nitsche and thereafter assisted Eberl first in Brandenburg and then in Bernburg.[43] Endruweit was received by Hefelmann and assigned to Sonnenstein.[44]

Borm's assignment to T4 was probably due to his SS membership and his service with the Waffen SS, because SS Reich Physician Grawitz helped staff T4. But Borm's release to the KdF from the Waffen SS was designated as "leave [*Beurlaubung*]" and was not reclassified a "military command assignment [*Kommandierung*]" until July 1942, thus underlining that acceptance of the job was voluntary.[45]

Renno, another SS member, was not assigned by the SS but recruited by Nitsche, whom he had already assisted killing patients at Leipzig-Dösen. He was simply posted as physician to the Niedernhart hospital in Linz and, as such, automatically also assumed, as did Lonauer, the position of Hartheim physician.[46] From October 1941 until February 1942, Renno also did a stint in the children's killing ward at Waldniel.[47]

Gorgaß was probably recommended by Bernotat, who wanted some control over operations at Hadamar. After his release from the Wehrmacht, Gorgaß reported to Bernotat in Wiesbaden, who told him that he must accept the job. Interviewed by Brack in Berlin, Gorgaß accepted and was then sent to Sonnenstein and Hartheim for training. Thereafter, he assumed his post at Hadamar. During his training, he also accompanied Schumann to Buchenwald to observe the 14f13 procedure.[48]

We must ask why these young physicians accepted the assignments. They did have a choice; even posting by the SS was not compulsory. They could have refused the assignments, and they could even have asked to be excused after they had started. They did not refuse. They did, of course, believe in the ideology that promoted the "destruction of life unworthy of life."[49] But even if commitment to this idea was one motivation, it alone cannot explain their actions. As we have seen, at least one SS physician, who must also have believed in this ideology, did refuse. Pressure applied by T4 to accept and continue the jobs is also a poor explanation. True, Bernotat told Gorgaß that he must accept the job, but Brack later did not pressure him at all.[50] All agreed after the war that there had not been any extraordinary pressure. Gorgaß argued at his trial that he feared for his wife and family, but he did not indicate why he was afraid.[51] It seems more likely that he was afraid they would suffer "inconveniences," as suggested by the long correspondence involving his wife's privileges at Kalmenhof after he had left his job there for his T4 assignment.[52]

Career considerations and personal profit seem to have motivated these young physicians. They were just starting their careers; some had virtually no previous experience as fully certified physicians. They were impressed by the senior physicians associated with T4; Gorgaß mentioned especially Paul Nitsche, who headed the professional association of psychiatrists and neurologists, and the professors Werner Heyde and Carl Schneider.[53] Bunke was also impressed that holders of university chairs were involved with T4, and he testified after the war that in the Wehrmacht he would have been assigned fewer medical duties than in T4, which "would provide for me the opportunity to collaborate with experienced professors, to do scientific work, and to complete my education."[54] Although major research opportunities never became available, Bunke did get leave to assist Julius Hallervorden at Berlin-Buch with research on brains acquired through the killing operation.[55] And Endruweit received a three-month furlough to complete his doctorate.[56]

They could have reported for front-line duty, where they would have gained more experience as physicians, although not experience that would further their careers. They wanted to advance in their field, in the civil service, and in the party structure. Work for the KdF would do so, while front-line duty would not and would be far more dangerous.

How well does the label "healers-turned-killers" fit the killing center physicians? It might appear to fit them best. But most of them had not had a great deal of experience as "healers" and did not differ from their associates, the chemists and policemen, who also turned into killers. Their training in medicine and their ambition as physicians did not make them different from their nonmedical colleagues. To convince them to join, the T4 managers used the same clichés about "mercy death" and "euthanasia law" employed to persuade the nonmedical supervisors. If they objected to their killing task, they did so, as did Renno, because opening gas valves was beneath their dignity.

The fourteen physicians in the killing centers were the most visible but not the only T4 killers. A list of participating physicians used by T4 for internal purposes contains about sixty names, many with overlapping functions.[57] Although the list is not fully accurate because it does not reflect movement of personnel—for example, Schmalenbach is listed under headquarters and not under killing centers—it provides a fairly good idea of the number of physicians needed to run the killing operation. The majority of physicians, about thirty-nine, served as medical experts selecting victims by evaluating questionnaires. The list shows twelve working at headquarters, and, omitting Schmalenbach, thirteen at the killing centers. An additional nine are listed under "research" at the Görden and Heidelberg research stations. The list does not include the children's wards, which would add at least twenty-five physicians.[58] The twelve physicians known to have participated in the 14f13 operation are not listed separately, but their names do appear under other headings. The list also does not include the unknown number of physicians involved in the decentralized killings of "wild" euthanasia. And it certainly does not include the bureaucrats with medical degrees in the RMdI, the state ministries, and the local public health offices.

The physicians in the euthanasia killing centers functioned as did those in charge of the killing centers in the East; the operation of the euthanasia gassing institutions of Brandenburg, Grafeneck, Hartheim, Bernburg, Sonnenstein, and Hadamar did not differ from that of the larger killing camps of Chelmno, Belzec, Sobibor, and Treblinka. In these centers, the victims were "processed," killed as soon as they arrived. Both the physicians in the former and the supervisors in the latter were merely technicians of mass murder. In contrast, the physicians in the children's wards and the institutions of "wild" euthanasia functioned as did those running the concentration camps. At their hospitals, they incarcerated patients, fed them poorly, worked them hard, applied procedures that could be considered torture, and killed some patients either on orders from Berlin or for arbitrary personal reasons.

Besides the killing centers, other T4 killing operations employed many different physicians. Two such physicians, who headed hospitals that resembled concentration camps, can serve as examples: Hermann Pfannmüller at Eglfing-Haar and Friedrich Mennecke at Eichberg. We have already discussed their work for T4 and thus will concentrate here only on their roles as perpetrators.

Pfannmüller appeared as an unusually unpleasant criminal to his postwar Allied interrogators. In 1947 the legal consultant to the U.S. Military Tribunals at Nuremberg took the unusual step of transmitting from the Americans to the Bavarian Ministry of Interior "the displeasure that the Bavarian courts had not yet moved against" this euthanasia killer, suggesting that Pfannmüller was still at liberty.[59] He denied responsibility for his actions, evaded all answers, and insulted his interrogators; one American prosecutor exclaimed, "I don't want to hear any more quibbling from you."[60] As we have seen, he forcefully rejected any implication that he had "fat hands" as his only response to the devastating testimony by Ludwig Lehner that he starved children at Eglfing-Haar.[61] The nurse Josefine Noichl testified in a postwar German court that Pfannmüller had kicked an adult patient down the stairs and slapped a retarded child for spilling his milk; he denied this, but the judge found the account "believable."[62] Pfannmüller's American interrogators were shocked that he could not even remember how many children he had killed, and his postwar successor as institutional director described him as a man committed to "racial insanity."[63]

Pfannmüller was not one of T4's young men but, like Nitsche, an established physician. Born in 1886, he had completed his medical training and had entered the civil service before World War I, serving since 1913 as a physician in various Bavarian state hospitals.[64] He later testified that his outlook had always been *völkisch*, and he probably absorbed the doctrine of racial hygiene in his student days.[65] He joined the Nazi party in 1922 for only a few years, later providing two contradictory reasons for his resignation: he either left in 1923 over "personal differences" with Julius Streicher or in 1925 because the government of Franconia ordered civil servants to do so. He reentered the party and also joined the SA in 1933 and in the mid-1930s headed the Augsburg office for race and heredity.[66] In 1938 he was appointed director of the Eglfing-Haar state hospital, an institution with about 3,000 beds and a staff of fifteen physicians.[67]

Pfannmüller's party connections and ideological commitment probably had something to do with his rise to the directorship, but his years of service placed him in line for such an appointment even if he had possessed less impressive party credentials. He willingly placed his institution at the disposal of T4, running a children's ward, transit institution, and hospital of "wild" euthanasia and also serving as an expert who, paid by the piece, processed questionnaires in record time.[68]

It is easy to dismiss Pfannmüller as a typical Nazi bully, a drifter who came into his own under the Nazi regime like Eicke and the other concentration camp chiefs he resembles. But he was an established psychiatrist and civil servant. True, he was brutal and insensitive, but sensitivity was not a quality most German civil servants possessed. He acted from ideological motives and because he accepted higher authority, telling his postwar judges, "I didn't feel responsible since the orders came from other sources."[69] His ideology was a mixture of Nazi clichés and the scientific race hygiene theories to which most of his colleagues subscribed. Without any psychological or moral qualms about his deeds, he continued, even after the war, to hold the views he had absorbed in his youth. As he told his postwar judges: "For me the term *völkisch* means national, and the term Aryan means that Germans must be in charge. Only those of German descent can be Aryans. I look upon Jews as a different race, one that cannot represent Germandom."[70]

Mennecke emerged from the war with an equally unsavory reputation. Much younger than Pfannmüller, his activities during the war paralleled those of his older colleague. He served as director of the Eichberg state hospital, which housed a children's ward and also functioned as a transit institution and a hospital for "wild" euthanasia. He also served as a medical expert, selecting between 2,000 and 3,000 victims, and was one of the traveling T4 physicians of the 14f13 operation.[71] Furthermore, he performed these duties without any doubts, supremely self-confident and self-absorbed. After the war, however, as Mennecke faced imprisonment and possible death, he did finally express remorse, although in his self-pitying statement he still tried to obscure his own responsibility: "I deeply regret the fact that in 1940 I was drawn into this program. But when, after the collapse, the whole extent of the extermination of human beings became public knowledge of which I had known nothing up to that date, I was ashamed that I had ever had any part in this program, even if in a subordinate position, and I am still ashamed today. That is what I have to say."[72]

We know a great deal about Mennecke. In addition to his postwar interrogations and his trial testimony, his voluminous correspondence with his wife survived the war. As we have seen earlier, he constantly wrote letters to his wife, even from the concentration camps, not only describing his activities but also revealing his thoughts.[73]

Mennecke was born in 1904 into a working-class family. His father returned from the war severely wounded and died in 1923. An uncle helped support the family but could offer financial help only for the education of Mennecke's older brother. After completing his secondary education in 1923, Mennecke thus worked in the business world for four years while his brother studied law. Only after his brother's graduation did Mennecke begin his study of medicine. Completing his doctorate at Göttingen, he received his medical license in 1935.[74] These early experiences probably had something to do with Mennecke's drive for advancement and status.

As a student, Mennecke joined the Nazi party at Göttingen in May 1932 and, after the Nazi assumption of power, used his party affiliation to advance his career. Equally important, he had also joined the SS, rising by 1940 to the rank of captain (Hauptsturmführer), which also worked to his advantage.[75]

After completing his internship and residency, Mennecke obtained a job at Eichberg early in 1936; the director at the time suspected that Bernotat had appointed him because of his party credentials. In January 1939, he assumed the position of director at Eichberg; his career under Bernotat had been even more spectacular than that of Gorgaß.[76] In 1937 he married Eva Wehlan, a medical laboratory assistant.[77]

In February 1940, Mennecke attended a meeting of medical experts at T4 headquarters in Berlin. He later claimed that his name must have been supplied by his local SS unit, but it seems equally likely that he was recommended by Bernotat. At the meeting, he agreed to serve as a medical expert. It seemed an obvious decision for an ambitious thirty-six-year-old physician who had been elevated to the post of director of a major state hospital on the basis of his political connections and who would hardly have dared to offend his political bosses. In addition, he was impressed by the presence of senior physicians, who were either professors or institutional directors, and obviously looked forward to a profitable association. One advantage came immediately: Werner Heyde arranged that he receive his certification in psychiatry.[78]

Mennecke performed a variety of services for T4. He served as a medical expert, evaluating questionnaires and selecting victims. He traveled with panels of physicians to select victims in various hospitals. And he served as one of the physicians assigned to the 14f13 operation, visiting various concentration camps in his SS uniform to help select victims. Finally, he placed his hospital at the disposal of T4, something Bernotat no doubt approved. Eichberg served as a transit institution and later as a "wild" euthanasia hospital. It also hosted a children's killing ward, which was administered by Walter Schmidt, an assistant physician at Eichberg and also an SS member. Finally, Eichberg supplied Carl Schneider's research station at the University of Heidelberg with brains from children killed at Eichberg, which were utilized in research studies.[79]

These activities brought a great deal of satisfaction to the ambitious Mennecke. As we have seen from the letters written during his 14f13 trips, he enjoyed the travel, the attention, and the food and companionship and gave little thought to his victims. His letters are filled with news about how his paperwork was processed, focusing on the form instead of the substance of his deeds; they also describe his gratification at mingling with the important men of the KdF.[80] Mennecke felt he had achieved success at the nexus of politics, medicine, and research, quite an accomplishment for a young physician whose abilities in medicine and research had been judged mediocre by his first Eichberg medical boss.[81]

Mennecke's motives for participating in the killing operation — if he even thought about it — were a mixture of ideology, careerism, and greed. Obviously, he accepted and affirmed the tenets of Nazi belief, especially as it corresponded to the theories espoused by his senior professional colleagues. He also wanted to advance his career. He not only obtained his specialty certification but also attended courses offered by Carl Schneider, even arranging for his wife to receive money to attend.[82] And like many other perpetrators, he enjoyed the privileges and the money T4 distributed.[83] Mennecke belonged to that circle of managers and physicians who, on their many inspection trips around the country, expected to enjoy their duty; on one of these traveling commissions of physicians, members complained that local officials were attacking the operation because they had assigned them poor accommodations.[84]

As with many other young T4 physicians, Mennecke's hopes for advancement did not materialize. A dispute with Bernotat led to Mennecke's removal from Eichberg late in 1942. Although Mennecke remained the titular director, Bernotat used his party connections to get him drafted and sent to the front.[85]

Mennecke did not, however, cut his ties to T4; he maintained a correspondence with T4 managers and attended T4 meetings. He desperately tried to obtain a position as director at a different institution, and the T4 managers, especially Nitsche, wanted to place him elsewhere, just as they tried to secure jobs for other T4 collaborators. But he never obtained another director's job.[86] The KdF was not all-powerful; it had to compete with others in the party and in the state. Appointment to government jobs involved various local and national agencies, and negotiations often dragged on for a long time. For example, in the late spring of 1944, competition started for the open pediatrics chair at the University of Vienna. Werner Catel of Leipzig, one of the T4 inner circle, was a leading competitor. The university faculty, its rector, and its Nazi party student organization, as well as the city of Vienna, were involved in the negotiations, and the final decision was to be made by the Reich Ministry for Science and Education. Max de Crinis, a key member of the T4 circle, served as adviser to the ministry and obviously backed Catel. Still, the negotiations

THE ORIGINS OF NAZI GENOCIDE

dragged into March 1945, and soon thereafter, Germany's defeat made the matter moot.[87]

The young physicians participated in part because their teachers advocated the killings and helped formulate policy.[88] But these younger men, and not their older colleagues, had to carry out those policies, becoming the true technicians of mass murder. Older colleagues and senior managers could provide them only with justifications taken from Binding and Hoche and similar works, updating them with recent Nazi doctrines. Brack and other managers gave physicians and staff at killing centers pep talks about "personal cleanliness [*persönliche Sauberkeit*]," "moral fiber [*charakterliche Anständigkeit*]," and "inner conviction worthy of euthanasia [*innere Haltung, die der Euthanasie wert sei*]," which were couched in language dear to the German middle class but only reflected the "pathetic clichés of the semi-literate."[89] Such ideological clichés obviously followed language rules that were used in all Nazi killing operations. The euphemism "decontaminated [*Desinfiziert*]" was thus always used in place of the more accurate word "killed."[90] It is not surprising that Georg Renno told his postwar interrogators that "in those days we did not talk about killing centers [*Tötungsanstalten*], but only about euthanasia institutions [*Euthanasieanstalten*]," and also complained that "in those days we only said euthanasia physician [*Euthanasiearzt*]."[91]

In hospitals and children's wards, but not in the killing centers, nurses, both males and females, collaborated as essential helpmates with the murdering physicians.[92] After the war, nurses were often tried together with the physicians they had assisted.[93] This collaboration was usually voluntary. The physicians were given the choice of accepting or declining, and they in turn gave that choice to their nurses.[94] But in the hierarchical German hospital system, as in that of most other countries, nurses were trained to obey physicians and often had a dependent relationship with the physicians they assisted. Although this was hardly an excuse for following orders to kill, as the refusal of some to do so proves, it does help explain the motives of some nurses.

Many nurses, especially in the hospitals that served as transit or final stations during "wild" euthanasia, were ideologically motivated and indifferent to human life.[95] But other nurses had no ideological motives. The career of the nurse Anna Katschenka, who killed children at the Am Spiegelgrund hospital in Vienna, can serve as an example of nurses who were not ideologically motivated.

Katschenka was born in Vienna in 1905, the daughter of a printer who was active in socialist and union affairs. She attended the public schools and thereafter nursing school for three years, graduating with excellent grades in 1927. From the date of graduation until 1941, she worked in three Vienna hospitals and was considered a valuable nurse in each of them: the maternity wing of the Brigitta hospital, the infectious diseases ward of the Carolingian children's hospital, and an old-age home.

Katschenka never joined the Nazi party or any of its affiliates. Her family had been associated with the Austrian Social Democratic party, and the defeat of the socialists in 1934 caused her anxiety. The Anschluß in 1938 also led to a period of apprehension. She had married a Jewish medical student in 1929, but one year later, the marriage ended, without children, in divorce. She suffered from mild depression after the Anschluß, and her hospital therefore sent her for treatment to the psychiatrist Erwin Jekelius. He helped her overcome her depression, and she formed an attachment to him. In 1941 she heard that nurses were needed at Am Spiegelgrund, where Jekelius served as chief, and she switched jobs. She came with experience at a children's hospital, although she had never worked with handicapped children.

At Am Spiegelgrund, Jekelius told her about children's euthanasia and asked her to administer the medication. She agreed and after the war told her interrogators that Jekelius had assured her that only absolutely hopeless children would be killed. After Jekelius left for the Wehrmacht, she kept in contact and even visited him; she also continued to kill children on the orders of his successor, Ernst Illing. A postwar psychiatric evaluation found Katschenka intelligent and sane but also found that she was impressionable and easily influenced and that she had maintained a dependent relationship with Jekelius.[96]

The killing centers operated differently. There nurses and physicians practiced no medicine. Still, the T4 managers and their supervisors needed staff to run the killing centers and, for that purpose, hired nurses, laborers, janitors, and secretaries. T4 usually used the technical method of the emergency service assignment (*Notdienstverpflichtung*) to hire the rank-and-file staff.[97] Although this method of labor assignment was compulsory, it provided for a system of appeals, something the T4 managers could not afford if they wanted to keep the operation secret. T4 required voluntary participation, and no one was forced to join the killing operation.[98]

Rank-and-file members were usually not specifically recruited. Since T4 was looking for people able to do physical labor, office work, and janitorial services, who did not need supervisory or technical skills, the persons selected were basically interchangeable. Of course, the T4 managers sought individuals they could trust. The selection criteria were nevertheless simple. They chose persons who were recommended, knew someone already inside, or had party credentials. T4 relied on the bureaucracy to recommend candidates, circulating job announcements for "trustworthy party members" to various party and government offices.[99] Thus the mason Erwin Lambert was recommended by the Labor Front, and August Miete, who later also went to Treblinka and Trieste, was told to apply to Grafeneck by his local chamber of agriculture.[100]

T4 also preferred candidates whose friends were already part of the killing operation, thus permitting insiders to vouch for newcomers. This was apparently the way Franz Suchomel and Franz Wolf, who later served in Hadamar, Sobibor, Treblinka, and Trieste, entered T4.[101] Most often, however, the news about jobs circulated by word of mouth. Thus, for example, Margit Troller heard that the Linz Nazi party regional office was looking for people to fill jobs at an agency outside the city; she applied and was hired as a clerk for Hartheim.[102]

Most rank-and-file staff members were hired on the local level. To staff Hartheim, for example, T4 used the office of Gauleiter August Eigruber, the Nazi party regional leader for Upper Austria (then known as Upper Danube). The job of finding people was apparently given to the regional inspector Stefan Schachermeyer, who also arranged the necessary paperwork. Candidates usually had a brief interview in Linz with T4 representatives from Berlin—Brack, Kaufmann, and others—as well as an interview with the local people, Rudolf Lonauer and Christian Wirth.[103]

This relatively lax selection system was based on the assumption that party members could be trusted, especially if other party members vouched for them. Sometimes, however, they needed to hire someone with special skills who did not have such recommendations. At that point, T4 had to investigate. Thus the electrician Herbert Kalisch was interviewed by the Gestapo before T4 would complete the hiring process.[104]

Obviously, candidates selected to do the most sensitive killing work had to be chosen carefully. This applied to the men who had to remove the bodies from the gas chamber, break out the teeth containing gold, and cremate the corpses. They were known as stokers (*Brenner*) and also, in the euphemistic language of euthanasia, as decontaminators (*Desinfektoren*). Some of them exercised influence in the killing center because their job placed them at the center of the secret killing enterprise. As we have seen, in Hartheim, for example, senior stoker (*Oberbrenner*) Valasta often administered the gas and oversaw the gassing in place of the physician.[105]

T4 usually picked members of the SS to serve as stokers. In Brandenburg, there were seven SS stokers and ten SS guards who sometimes also worked as stokers; in Bernburg, there were also seven SS stokers and, for a short time, nine; and in Sonnenstein, there were two SS stokers.[106] But not every stoker came with an SS background. One Hartheim stoker can serve as a good example of the idiosyncrasy of the hiring process.

The Austrian Vinzenz Nohel, born in Moravia in 1902, was trained as a mechanic but was frequently unemployed. In 1939 he earned 25 RM per week to support his wife and four children and was thus always "looking to earn more money." Although his postwar interrogation does not indicate whether he was a member of the Nazi party, his brother was an old party member and an SA brigadier general (Brigadeführer). Nohel hoped that this brother, who returned to Austria from the Reich after the Anschluß, would help him obtain a better-paying job, but at first, the brother did not help him. Finally, late in 1939 or early in 1940, his brother invited Nohel to his Linz office and took him to meet T4's Kaufmann, who hired Nohel to work in the Hartheim killing center. During his postwar interrogation, Nohel described the hiring procedure: "I went with my brother, and several other men looking for work, to the government building to see a certain Kaufmann. There I was asked about my current wages. They laughed when I told them that I had been earning 25 RM per week. They then told me and the others that we would be sent to Hartheim and that we would earn more money."

In Hartheim, Nohel was assigned work as a stoker, and he remained there until the end. He did receive the promised higher wages: 170 RM per month, plus a 50 RM family separation allowance, a 35 RM stoker's allowance, and a 35 RM premium for keeping quiet. Further, "because the work [as stoker] was very strenuous and nerve-shattering, we also received a ¼ liter schnapps every day." [107]

Not every staff member directly involved in the actual killings worked as a stoker. Other jobs had to be done around the gas chambers and crematoria. Heinrich Barbl, an Austrian metalworker who joined the Nazi party and the SS after the Anschluß, was posted to Hartheim during the period of construction. After the killing center began operation, he worked next to the crematorium as a *Stanzer*, stamping letters into sheet metal to form nameplates that were attached to urns. Every day he filled the urns with ashes — any ashes — to mail to relatives.[108] Like the stokers, he worked every day next to the killings; Georg Renno recalled after the war that Barbl always drank a lot of alcohol.[109] In 1942 he was posted to the East and served at Belzec and Sobibor.

Heinrich Unverhau was a north German who had been a metalworker but, after an industrial accident, became first a musician and then a male nurse. A member of the Nazi party and the SA, he was recruited by T4 and assigned to Grafeneck and Hadamar. There he accompanied patient transports to the killing centers, administered injections of sedatives, brought patients into the gas chambers, and helped ventilate the chambers after the patients had been killed. He thus participated directly in the killing process and after the stop order moved East to help staff Belzec.[110]

Hermann Merta had been a male nurse in the Ybbs hospital of the city of Vienna. In 1940 Christian Wirth came to Ybbs to recruit nurses, and Merta volunteered without knowing what kind of work was involved because he was told "that then I would not have to join the Wehrmacht." He later claimed that after arriving at Hartheim he wanted to reconsider but was told that it was too late. At any rate, he did his work. He was assigned to accompany victims transferred to Hartheim from various institutions, a job often given to nurses with experience in pacifying and controlling patients. But there was no absolute division of labor in the killing centers, and he was at times also called upon to remove bodies from the gas chamber and to help prepare urns for shipment to relatives. He also profited from the personal property of killed victims; he admitted that Wirth gave him two suits and several hand-kerchiefs.[111] Merta was not the only one to profit in this way. Karl Harrer, another male nurse who accompanied victims to Hartheim, told postwar in-terrogators: "Several times I received from Captain Wirth goods left behind by the mental patients, for example a coat, a suit, and similar items."[112]

Maria Appinger was born in 1903 in Nuremberg; her father was an engi-neer. After completing school, she kept house for her parents until she was twenty-five years old and then attended nursing school in Berlin. After two years as a private nurse, she was hired by the Wittenauer hospital complex and remained there until her recruitment by T4. In December 1939, Appinger, who had joined the Nazi party in January 1932, received her emergency post-ing through the Berlin police. On 4 January 1940, she joined other recruited nurses at the Columbus House, T4 headquarters at the time, and they were all informed about the nature of their T4 assignments. Apparently no one ob-jected, and they were posted to Grafeneck. Appinger worked at Grafeneck until May 1940 and was then transferred to Sonnenstein, remaining there until the middle of 1942. After five months in Minsk, she was posted to a children's killing ward but left nursing in 1943. At both Grafeneck and Sonnenstein, Ap-pinger accompanied transferred victims on the buses and trains that brought them to the killing centers and, after arrival, took them to the "anteroom of the gas chamber."[113]

A number of female nurses from the Ybbs hospital claimed after the war that they were transferred to Hartheim against their will. According to their story, in November 1940, several police officers representing the city of Vienna arrived at Ybbs and asked for volunteers to transfer to another institution. They wanted only unmarried nurses. When no one volunteered, they picked a number of single nurses and issued emergency service assignments. Unable to avoid the assignment, the nurses reported to Hartheim, where they discov-ered the purpose of that killing center. They were threatened with incarcera-tion in a concentration camp if they refused. Without their knowledge, they were later also enrolled in the Nazi party. At Hartheim, they were assigned to cook and clean; one of them told her postwar interrogator: "In my entire life, I did not work as hard as I did there." But at times, they also had to accom-pany and undress victims.[114]

These claims raise questions that have plagued most postwar trials of Nazi criminals. Most defendants insisted that they cooperated only under duress. But after almost fifty years of postwar proceedings, proof has not been pro-vided in a single case that someone who refused to participate in killing operations was shot, incarcerated, or penalized in any way, except perhaps through transfer to the front, which was, after all, the destiny of most German soldiers.[115] But it is possible that putative duress did apply, that is, these young, impressionable nurses might have believed that the intimidating Christian Wirth would place them in a concentration camp.[116]

Punishment, even incarceration in a concentration camp, was, however, a real possibility if members of the staff talked about the killings to outsiders. All employees had to sign an oath of silence. The threat of incarceration undoubtedly applied to talking but not to refusing. The nurse Merta told his postwar interrogators that he was afraid to request a discharge because if his superiors thought he would talk, they might kill him.[117] The nurses had been told "whoever talks will be taken to the Gestapo and placed against the wall."[118] One secretary at Grafeneck was committed to a concentration camp by Viktor Brack because she talked about her work but was released through the intervention of Werner Heyde.[119] Whatever the truth of such stories, they had nothing to do with a refusal to kill.

The claim that nurses were enrolled in the Nazi party without personally applying is also dubious. The Nazis were selective about membership, and usually admission followed application only after the applicant was investigated. Of course, it is reasonable to assume that the nurses were readily admitted, but not if they did not apply. At least one nurse testified that "in Hartheim there was no direct coercion to join the party."[120]

We might also ask how difficult it actually was to decline work at the killing centers. It is hard to tell because virtually no one openly refused. There is, however, testimony that staff members who wanted to leave were told to approach the T4 manager Adolf Kaufmann, who obtained their discharge within two weeks.[121] The male nurse Franz Sitter from Ybbs volunteered for Hartheim in October 1940 without knowing details about the job. After Wirth informed him and swore him to secrecy, Sitter decided to refuse. He asked to see Lonauer and demanded to be released. Lonauer tried to talk him out of it, pointing to the "financial advantages" and to the draft deferment. Sitter insisted and was returned to Ybbs. He was drafted in February 1941.[122] Other nurses found other ways to leave. One became pregnant and was discharged.[123] Another volunteered for the Wehrmacht and could therefore leave.[124]

Other accounts indicate that threats of being "put against the wall" were not serious. Emil Reisenberger, a mechanic, was given an emergency service assignment to Hartheim and was employed there as a janitor. He was a former member of the Austrian Social Democratic party and also of its paramilitary arm, the socialist *Schutzbund*, who joined the SA and the Nazi party in 1938. He remained attached to his socialist past, however, and found the work at Hartheim "repulsive." He argued with coworkers, was denounced

THE ORIGINS OF NAZI GENOCIDE

and demoted, and then was caught in a serious infraction: he had shown a friend around the building. Afraid that he would be "put against the wall," he went to his room and shot himself. While waiting for the ambulance, he was warned to say that the shooting was an accident. Released from the Linz hospital after four weeks, he was granted sick leave. After his return, Blankenburg and Lonauer told him that he would be sent to a concentration camp for six months. But this never happened; instead, he was discharged and, soon thereafter, was drafted.[125]

Matthias Buchberger, another Hartheim staff member, told his postwar interrogator that he was "deeply opposed to the actions of his superiors against defenseless victims" and that "although I was a Nazi, I absolutely rejected this." Lonauer asked him to serve as a stoker, but he refused, explaining that he was "not fitted for such a job due to my loathing of corpses." He was excused and assigned to cleaning the yard and the stables.[126]

Many staff members, however, were willing to do their assigned work. We may remember the Hadamar secretary who worked with a box of teeth on her desk.[127] These staff members worked day after day in a factory with only one product: corpses of murdered human beings. An atmosphere of licentiousness rapidly developed, an attitude that "anything goes." One constantly used stimulus was alcohol, which was freely distributed by the supervisors. One staff member assigned to Hartheim as a photographer found that the stench of burning flesh made it impossible for him to keep any food in his stomach. Wirth prescribed alcohol, and thereafter the photographer was always drunk.[128] Reports abounded of drunken orgies, numerous sexual liaisons, brawling and bullying, and stealing the property of victims.[129] The toleration of such behavior by T4 had led to the resignation of Gerhard Bohne, but the managers knew that they could not impose too many restrictions on those assigned to the secret killings.[130] After all, the important task was killing, and the job of manager was to assure that the staff members served the killing process. And so the killings continued.

After the stop order, almost a hundred supervisors and staff members were posted to the camps of Operation Reinhard—Belzec, Sobibor, and Treblinka. Some of the staff had been stokers and others had transported, undressed, and led patients to the gas chambers. But many had never been assigned to work with patients or near gas chambers. All of them, however, had been intimately involved in the killing process. Because some of those transferred to the East were placed on trial after the war, we know a fair amount about them. We have already examined the supervisors and experts who served in the East; we must now look at the rank-and-file staff members who were posted to the killing centers of Operation Reinhard.

Taking as a sample eighteen staff members posted to the East, we find that nothing distinguished them from the T4 colleagues who remained behind.

Their backgrounds, party affiliation, and T4 jobs did not differ from those of the others. Franz Hödl can serve as an example. Born in 1905 in Austria, he joined the Nazi party in Linz in 1937 before, and the SS just after, the Anschluß. His party affiliation probably got him a job as driver for a car company in Upper Austria. In 1940 he was recruited, as were most other killing center staff members, by the Nazi party regional office for work in Hartheim. At the killing center, he drove the bus that brought patients to Hartheim castle and probably also supervised them during their registration and undressing. After his 1942 transfer to Lublin, he supposedly served as driver for the office of SS and Police Leader Globocnik. In Trieste, he was Franz Stangl's driver.[131]

Nothing in the background of Willi Mentz could have predicted that he would be considered by Treblinka prisoners an "animal and sadist" and "one of the worst murderers" among the German staff.[132] Mentz was born in 1904 into a working-class family in the province of Posen, which reverted to Poland in 1919 and was incorporated into the Reich as the Wartheland in 1939. After eight years of public schooling, he worked first as an unskilled laborer in a factory where his father was foreman, later as a miner, and eventually as a master milker. He joined the Nazi party in the fall of 1932 but did not belong to any of its formations. He attempted to join the police but was not accepted. In 1940 the agricultural labor exchange in Münster offered him a job at the Grafeneck castle as milker, and he accepted, taking care of cows and swine at both Grafeneck and Hadamar. Obviously, he knew about the killings and watched the killing process, but supposedly his job did not require his personal involvement. In July 1942, he went to the East, serving in Treblinka, Sobibor, and later Trieste. In Treblinka, where the prisoners referred to him as "Frankenstein," he supervised at first the burning of bodies in the "upper camp" and later shot mothers and their children at the so-called infirmary.[133]

Robert Jührs, born in 1911 in Frankfurt, was another staff member whose background would not have led us to predict his service with T4 and Operation Reinhard. His father, an interior decorator, died as an inmate of the Herborn state hospital when Jührs was four years old, and he was raised by his mother. After attending eight years of public school, he served as a cooper apprentice, but an accident forced him to give up this career, and thereafter he took jobs as an unskilled worker. During the 1930s, he was in turn an usher at the Frankfurt opera, a janitor, and a file clerk for the Winter Relief Lottery and then for the Hessen labor exchange. Recruited to Hadamar in June 1941, he was posted in the summer of 1942 to Belzec, Sobibor, and later Trieste. He joined the Nazi party in 1930 and belonged to the SA from 1929 to 1935.[134]

Two staff members in our sample had served as cooks and thus were not directly involved in the T4 killings; but both were SS members. Gustav Münzberger, born in 1903, was one of T4's Sudeten German members. His father was a master carpenter, and Münzberger worked in his father's shop after

THE ORIGINS OF NAZI GENOCIDE

he passed his carpenter apprentice examination. He took over his father's shop in 1931. He served for two years in the Czech army in the early 1920s and again in the fall of 1938. Although he had only belonged to the Sudeten German gymnastics association, which indicated his ethnic allegiance but not necessarily his political commitment, he joined the SS late in 1938, after the incorporation of the Sudetenland, and the Nazi party in 1940. Posted to Sonnenstein in 1940, he served there as assistant cook until 1942, when he left for training at Trawniki and then service at Treblinka and later Trieste.[135] In Treblinka, Münzberger was in charge of the gas chamber; usually drunk, he stood at the door, using his whip to drive the victims into the chamber.[136]

The other cook was the infamous Kurt Franz, the last commandant of Treblinka, who considered his dog more "human" than he did the Jewish prisoners and who ordered his Saint Bernard, named Barry, to attack prisoners using the command, "Human, bite the dog [*Mensch, faß den Hund*]."[137] Born in 1914 in Düsseldorf, Franz attended public school from 1920 to 1928 and then worked as a messenger. In 1929 he started an apprenticeship as a cook, first at the Düsseldorf Hirschquelle restaurant and then at the Hotel Wittelsbacher Hof. His father, who was a salesman, died early, and his mother, who was a "very observant Catholic," married a man with a strong right-wing nationalist outlook. Franz joined various right-wing national groups and served in the voluntary labor corps. After training with a master butcher for one year, he fulfilled his military obligation from 1935 to 1937 and, after his discharge, joined the SS in October 1937. He was posted to the Third Death Head Regiment Thuringia at Weimar for training and thereafter served as cook and guard at the Buchenwald concentration camp, advancing to the rank of corporal (Unterscharführer). Franz joined T4 in late 1939 and worked as a cook at Grafeneck, Brandenburg, Hartheim, and Sonnenstein. In late 1941, he was assigned as cook to T4 headquarters. Promoted to staff sergeant (Oberscharführer) on 20 April 1942, Franz went to Lublin in the spring of 1942, first to Belzec and then Treblinka, where he was promoted to second lieutenant (Untersturmführer) in June 1943. Thereafter, he served in Trieste.[138]

Several staff members were T4 photographers, since patients had to be photographed before they were killed: Franz Rum, Franz Wolf, and Franz Suchomel. We do not know why they were selected for service in the East. Nothing in their backgrounds or T4 service indicated that they were particularly capable killers. They had no strong party credentials, had not been members of the SS, and had not been directly involved in the killings at T4. They had been recruited into T4 through friends, and these connections might explain their posting to the East.

Franz Rum was born the son of a carpenter in Berlin in 1890. After eight years of public school, he passed his apprentice examination as a waiter in 1909. He worked as a waiter in France, England, and Berlin and, after service in World War I, was "waiter, night train porter, saloon owner, and owner of a laundry." An acquaintance recommended him to T4, and there he worked in the photo laboratory in Berlin. In 1942 he was posted to Treblinka, Sobibor, and later Trieste. Rum had joined the Nazi party in March 1933, a time when many Germans joined the movement that had come to power two months earlier.[139]

Franz Wolf, born in 1907 in Krumau on the Moldau River, was another Sudeten German. His father was a photographer who owned his own shop. After eight years of public school, Wolf studied to be a forest ranger. Unable to find a job, he turned to photography and worked for his father. He served in the Czech army in the late 1920s and again in the fall of 1938. Drafted by the Wehrmacht in August 1939, he fought in the Polish and French campaigns. In the fall of 1940, he was recruited by T4 on the recommendation of Franz Wagner, who had trained in the shop of Wolf's father. He worked as a photographer at Hadamar, at T4 headquarters, and at Carl Schneider's Heidelberg clinic. Together with his brother Josef, who also worked for T4, he was thereafter posted to Sobibor and later to Trieste. His brother was killed in Sobibor during the Jewish uprising. Wolf was a member of Konrad Henlein's Sudeten German party, and although there is no proof, he later probably joined the Nazi party.[140]

Franz Suchomel, familiar to us from his role in Claude Lanzman's 1985 documentary *Shoah*, was another Sudeten German from Krumau, where he was born in 1907. His father owned a tailor shop, and Suchomel became a tailor, worked in his father's shop, and took over the family business in 1936. He served in the Czech army in the late 1920s and again in the fall of 1938. He was a practicing Catholic. His politics were pro-German, and he had joined the Sudeten German party. After the incorporation of the Sudetenland, he joined the Nazi motor corps but not the party itself. He served in the Wehrmacht in 1940 but was discharged after the French campaign to run his tailor shop. Early in 1941, he was recruited by T4, probably through the recommendation of the other T4 staff members from Krumau, and like them, he was assigned as a photographer. He developed pictures of patients taken before they were killed, first at T4 headquarters and then at Hadamar. In August 1942, he was posted to Treblinka, then Sobibor, and later Trieste.[141]

Only four of our sample served as T4 stokers, removing dead bodies from the gas chambers, breaking out gold teeth, burning the bodies, and doing other jobs around the gas chambers and the crematoria. Although the job of stoker was probably the best preparation for work in the East, it is significant that not every stoker was transferred to Lublin. In addition, one member of our sample, the Austrian Heinrich Barbl, whose work at Hartheim we have already discussed, had served as a *Stanzer* in the killing center's crematorium room. He was selected for service in the East and posted to Belzec and Sobibor.[142]

Karl Frenzel, the first stoker in our sample, was born in 1911 in the province of Brandenburg, went to public school in Oranienburg from 1918 to 1926, and passed his apprentice examination as a carpenter in 1930. Thereafter, he was first unemployed and later worked as a butcher. His father had worked for the railroad and had served as a local official of the Social Democratic party, but his brother was a Nazi. Frenzel, who had been a member of the socialist carpenter's union, joined the Nazi party and the SA in August 1930; his father joined in 1934. He served as an auxiliary police officer in SA uniform during the summer of 1933 and thereafter obtained jobs through his party connections, first as carpenter and later as a building custodian. At the start of the war, he was drafted into the Reich Labor Service but was soon released because he had many children to support. Since his brothers were in the army, he felt left out of the action and thus applied for military duty through his SA unit. Instead, he was assigned a job with T4; later, when he was called up by the Wehrmacht, T4 was able to reclaim him. When he reported to the Columbus House in late 1939, he and his fellow recruits were first checked for political reliability and then had to watch films showing the supposed degeneration of the handicapped. He was posted to serve in the laundry and as a guard at Grafeneck, then as a construction worker at Bernburg, and finally as a stoker at Hadamar. In April 1942, he was posted to Sobibor and later to Trieste.[143]

Werner Dubois, the second stoker, was born in Wuppertal in the Ruhr in 1913. His father, a printer, returned from World War I severely wounded, and Dubois was raised by his grandmother. After eight years of public school, he worked as a cabinetmaker, started but did not complete an apprenticeship as a brushmaker, took a course in agriculture, and then worked on the land near Frankfurt on the Oder until 1933. Dubois joined the SA in July 1933, entered the Labor Service, and then returned to work on the land. He joined the Nazi party motor corps, took a course and passed his examination as a driver, and applied unsuccessfully for a job as a driver with the SS Guard Regiment Adolf Hitler. In January 1937, he became a member of the SS Death Head Unit Brandenburg and joined the Nazi party and the SS. After training in Oranienburg, he was attached as a driver to an SS motor unit at the Sachsenhausen concentration camp. In the fall of 1939, Dubois was recruited by T4, together with his friend Lorenz Hackenholt, who would later operate the diesel engine at the Belzec gas chambers.[144] Dubois drove the buses that took patients to the Grafeneck, Brandenburg, Hadamar, and Bernburg killing centers. He also transported corpses and urns and worked as a stoker. In early 1942, he served as a T4 driver with the national transport construction agency, Organization Todt, in Russia. Thereafter, he was posted to Belzec and

Sobibor, where he was seriously injured during the Jewish uprising. In February 1944, he was assigned to Trieste.[145]

August Miete, the third stoker, was born in 1908 in Westphalia and worked on the family farm. In 1940, the year he joined the Nazi party, the Münster agriculture chamber advised him about a job at Grafeneck, and he accepted an offer to work on the farm attached to the killing center. At Hadamar, however, he worked as a stoker. In 1942 he went to Treblinka and later to Trieste.[146] Little in his background gave any indication that at Treblinka, where he was one of those shooting newly arrived prisoners in the so-called infirmary, the Jewish inmates would call him the "angel of death."[147]

Six of our sample were male nurses, but their work for T4 had little to do with medicine. Ernst Zierke was born in 1905, the son of a railroad worker who died in 1917. After eight years of public school, he worked as a woodcutter on several estates but in 1930 found himself unemployed. That year, he joined the Nazi party and the SA. He trained as a male nurse at the Neuruppin hospital and eventually received a permanent civil service appointment. In late 1939, he was recruited by T4 and was assigned first to Grafeneck and then to Hadamar to accompany patients transported to the killing centers. In late 1941, he also worked at the Eichberg hospital. After joining T4's Organization Todt trip to Russia between January and March 1942, he returned to Eichberg. That summer, he was posted to Belzec and Sobibor and later to Trieste.[148]

Heinrich Arthur Matthes was born in 1902 in the Leipzig district, the son of a senior male nurse. After eight years of public school, he became a tailor but changed careers to become a nurse. He trained at Sonnenstein and took his examination there, working thereafter at the Arnsdorf and Bräunsdorf hospitals. He joined the SA in 1934 and applied for membership in the Nazi party in 1937, but the records do not show whether he was accepted. Matthes served in the early campaigns of World War II but was then recruited by T4. He worked in the T4 photo laboratory and served in the T4 unit with Organization Todt in Russia. He was then posted to Treblinka, in command of the upper camp, where the gassing and burning took place, then to Sobibor, and later to Trieste.[149]

Otto Stadie was born in Berlin in 1897, the son of a stock clerk. He completed eight years of public school and then worked as a messenger. Thereafter, he worked at Dr. Bernstein's Berlin clinic for skin and venereal diseases and received his training as a male nurse at this Jewish-owned clinic. He served as a medic in World War I and, after the war, settled in Breslau. After some years of unemployment, he obtained a job as a nurse at the Wuhlheide city hospital in Berlin and remained there until the war began. He had joined the Nazi party and the SA in 1933. In 1939 he was drafted as a medic and served during the Polish and French campaigns. He was then recruited by T4 and assigned to Bernburg as a bus driver accompanying patient transports.

In 1942 he was posted to Treblinka, where he served as Franz Stangl's orderly, and then to Trieste.[150]

Otto Horn was born in 1903 in the Leipzig district, "the son of the female worker Emma Ida Horn," and was raised by maternal grandparents. After eight years of public school, he was first a factory worker and then an agricultural laborer. In 1926 he began training as a nurse, passed his examination at Sonnenstein, and worked as a nurse in Leipzig-Dösen and Arnsdorf. He joined the Nazi party in 1937. During World War II, he was drafted as a medic and served in the Polish and French campaigns. He was stationed late in 1940 in the Wartheland. He fought at the opening of the Russian campaign, where he probably observed the killings of the Einsatzgruppen, but was then discharged to his job at Arnsdorf. Recruited by T4, he was assigned to Sonnenstein but possibly arrived there after the stop order. He then worked at T4 headquarters photocopying and filing medical records. Recalled to the Wehrmacht, he was soon reclaimed by T4 for filing records. After posting to the T4 unit with Organization Todt in Russia, he was sent for training to Trawniki and thereafter to Treblinka and then Trieste.[151]

Willy Grossmann was born in 1901 in Saxony, the son of a mason. After finishing school, he worked in a factory. In the late 1920s, he trained to be a male nurse at hospitals in Pirna and Zwickau and thereafter worked as a nurse. He was drafted into the Dresden police in 1939 and assigned to Sonnenstein, where he supposedly worked as the doorman. After serving in the T4 unit with Organization Todt in Russia, he was posted to Treblinka and then Trieste.[152]

We have already discussed Heinrich Unverhau, the last of our eighteen-man sample, who was born in 1911 in the Goslar district in the Harz mountains. He played with the city orchestras of Königslutter and Neuruppin as well as with the orchestras of the Steel Helmet veteran's organization and the SA before he became a male nurse at the Teupitz and Neuruppin hospitals. He worked for T4 at Grafeneck and Hadamar, served in T4's unit with Organization Todt in Russia, and was finally assigned to Belzec and later to Trieste.[153]

We must now ask whether these men knew before they arrived in Lublin the nature of the task they would have to perform. After the war, they almost all denied such knowledge, claiming that they were not told until they had already arrived in Lublin. Even senior members of T4 denied any knowledge. Brandt and Nitsche denied ever knowing anything.[154] Brack claimed he knew nothing until he was told by Himmler in April 1942 and even maintained that Bouhler did not discover the truth until May.[155]

None of these denials is believable. It seems only reasonable to conclude that the men were briefed, and some evidence suggests that this was the procedure followed. Franz Stangl told the journalist Gitta Sereny after the war that he was in charge of a group of twenty T4 staff members traveling to

Lublin, and when Sereny asked whether he knew what their task would be, he answered: "Later I found out that three or four of them had known, but at the time they said nothing—they didn't let on."[156] Alfred Ittner, a T4 book-keeper who later had a serious disagreement with Stangl, was one of the men in Stangl's group. Ittner later testified that he did know the nature of the job waiting for them in Lublin because a T4 manager, either Robert Lorent or Fritz Schmiedel, had told him that he would be assigned as business manager to a camp in Poland where Jews would be "systematically killed."[157] It is very unlikely that Stangl and the others did not know.

We must also ask why they accepted the job and why they remained even after they witnessed the horror of these camps. After the war, most of them claimed that they were under orders and could not refuse, but that is also unbelievable. The physician Kurt Borm testified that Blankenburg asked him to serve in Lublin and that, knowing about the killing of Jews in the Lublin camps, he refused without suffering any consequences.[158]

Some T4 staff members sought and received transfers. However, such efforts had nothing to do with moral objections. Alfred Ittner, who apparently had no scruples about serving as business manager at Treblinka, was reassigned by Stangl to supervise the mass burials, supposedly because he refused to misappropriate funds for Stangl's use. Ittner complained to T4 about this assignment and managed to have himself recalled.[159] Hans-Heinz Schütt, who strongly supported the euthanasia killings, hinting in a letter to his brother at his involvement in great tasks, did not like the atmosphere in the Eastern camps after he was transferred there as a business manager. He spent as little time as possible in Sobibor, staying in nearby Chelm to make his purchases for the camp. He complained to T4 and eventually managed to be posted back to the Waffen SS for front duty.[160]

The fear that requests to leave would result in death, an excuse for partici-pation that was advanced after the war, was unwarranted. Erich Lachmann, a police auxiliary assigned from Trawniki to Sobibor—one of the few staff members without previous association with T4—deserted with his Polish girlfriend in the winter of 1942–43 and was arrested several months later in Warsaw. He was sentenced by an SS and police court to six years in prison; released in April 1945 for the final battle, he was captured by Soviet troops and survived the war.[161] This shows that even the crime of desertion did not necessarily bring the death sentence.

Finally, we must ask why these men were selected. Except for a few super-visors and experts, the men transferred from T4 to Lublin were rank-and-file members of the euthanasia killing program. They had probably been selected because their superiors believed them capable of the killings expected in the East, because they had conscientiously fulfilled their duties in T4, or simply because one of the T4 chiefs had noticed them. Although most had solid Nazi party credentials, a few did not. A substantial number were members of the SS and the SA, some even with concentration camp experience, but many had no such backgrounds. Many had gained killing experience working as stokers or accompanying patients, but others had only taken care of farm animals, done the cooking, or developed photographs. In the end, we do not know why these men were picked. We must also wonder why some of these men, especially those who did not serve in the SS or as stokers, behaved in such a brutal fashion in the East. One reason may be that no one placed limitations on their actions. In Germany, they had to work hard cooking, cleaning, and building, not to mention burning bodies. In the East, all of them became supervisors; moreover, they became masters over life and death.[162]

When all is said and done, we are still unable to grasp the reasons that seemingly normal men and women were able to commit such extraordinary crimes. Neither ideology nor self-interest is a satisfactory explanation for such behavior. Those killers belonged to that time and place. Attempts to replicate their actions in the laboratory must fail, even if experiments seem to show, as did the one by Stanley Milgram, that ordinary men anywhere can commit such crimes.[163] But there is a fundamental difference between the antiseptic experimental setting and the grisly reality of the killing fields and the killing centers. The T4 killers confronted real human beings as victims, saw their agony, experienced the blood and gore of the killing process. In Milgram's social science experiment, the subjects might have lacked the imagination to understand the pain they could inflict, but the Nazi killers, even if they were entirely lacking in imagination, could not avoid knowing what they were doing. They could see how their actions affected real human beings. They understood the consequences of their deeds.

Chapter 12

Excluding Gypsies

The handicapped were the first but not the last victims of Nazi genocide. The mass murder of the handicapped was rapidly followed by the mass murder of Jews and Gypsies. Nazi ideology and race science had always targeted not only the so-called degenerate portion of the *Volk*, that is, the handicapped, but also the members of so-called alien and inferior races. In Germany and Central Europe, those aliens were Jews and Gypsies. Although both minorities had resided in Central Europe for centuries, and had become citizens, the public continued to consider them alien races.

Of course, some non-Caucasian persons did live in Central Europe, but their numbers were small, they were usually individuals holding foreign citizenship, and they stood under the protection of foreign governments. One small group of non-Caucasians, however, did not have this kind of protection. They were children, usually illegitimate, of German mothers and colonial soldiers in the Allied armies that had occupied the Rhineland after World War I. The Germans disapproved of these fathers as so-called colored people; most were black French soldiers from North Africa, especially Morocco, but a few were Asians and at least one was an African American. Copying the language first introduced by Eugen Fischer, the Germans called the children "Rhineland bastards."[1]

Even before the Nazis came to power, German politicians and scientists deplored the presence of colored hybrids on German soil; German antagonism was intensified by the fact that these children were the offspring of hated occupiers.[2] After Hitler's appointment as chancellor, the German government decided to move against these children, who ranged in age from four to fifteen. First, the regime believed it necessary to define and count the members of the group. As we have seen, definition was essential to assure the noninvolved members of the majority that they were not threatened by exclusion. At first, the figures were inflated; eventually the experts collected data on just 385 children.[3]

The Prussian Ministry of Interior thereupon commissioned a race scientist to scrutinize and classify the children. In the summer of 1933, Wolfgang Abel, head of the department on race in Eugen Fischer's Kaiser Wilhelm Institute for Anthropology, undertook this scientific investigation. Abel's sample was small, but his conclusions were definitive and hostile. With his measurements of the children, he attempted to prove their inferiority by cataloging such physical deformities as flat feet and such psychological aberrations as "preference for life on the street [*Vorliebe für Strassenleben*]."[4]

To solve Germany's colored minority problem, the RMdI assembled teams of experts who, between 1933 and 1937, attended meetings and sat on commissions and subcommittees. The panel of experts included many of the bureaucrats and scientists discussed earlier, such as Gerhard Wagner, Arthur Gütt, Herbert Linden, Walter Gross, Hans F. K. Günther, Eugen Fischer, Fritz Lenz, and Ernst Rüdin.[5]

These experts explored various means of ridding Germany of this undesirable element; they settled on sterilization. Apprehensive about foreign reaction, they postponed implementation until 1937. The sterilization law did not, however, permit sterilization of children whose only hereditary disease was their race. The ministry decided to sterilize them secretly in violation of the law. As we have seen, this was not the only example of the regime's secret and illegal pursuit of its ideological goals.

The Gestapo was in charge of collecting the children. The children were first examined by a board of race scientists to determine whether they were indeed the offspring of an alien race and then sterilized in local hospitals.[6] The exclusion of this small colored minority was thus achieved without arousing widespread attention or requiring special legislation. But the results were final; the colored children had been excluded from the German national community by the most radical means available in 1937.

The Nazi regime moved just as rapidly during the 1930s to exclude Jews and Gypsies from the national community, while the race scientists labored to define and register the two excluded groups. Nazi anti-Jewish policies of the 1930s have been covered in the literature in great detail.[7] In contrast, the policies invoked against Gypsies are relatively unknown.

Prejudice and intermittent persecution had confronted Gypsies since their arrival in Europe in about the thirteenth century. These traditional prejudices did not disappear with the Enlightenment. In fact, Gypsies could purchase acceptance only by renunciation of their culture and life-style, in the same way that the Enlightenment demanded that Jews renounce their post-Biblical practices in exchange for equality.[8] The nineteenth and early twentieth centuries witnessed both attempts at assimilation by the minority and continued persecution by the majority. In Germany and Austria, large numbers of Gypsies established permanent residences and pursued regular occupations, but this reality could not overcome the stereotype of Gypsies as vagabonds, thieves, pickpockets, swindlers, beggars, and fortune-tellers.[9] Furthermore, popular opinion about nomadic Gypsies failed to recognize Gypsy tradition, including a family structure different from that of non-Gypsies, and Gypsy occupational structure, which was heavily based on trades that required circuit riding. Moreover, as a "dark-skinned" people, Gypsies suffered from color prejudice.

At the beginning of the twentieth century, the German state governments handed control over Gypsies to the police. Governments found the appearance of groups of Gypsies particularly threatening and therefore issued regulations designed to control them, discourage them from traveling and pursuing itinerant occupations, or expel them. In 1899, for example, the state of Bavaria established an Information Agency on Gypsies at Munich police headquarters to collect data, including genealogies, photographs, and fingerprints.[10] In 1906 the Prussian Ministry of Interior issued detailed guidelines on how police authorities should deal with Gypsies. All foreign Gypsies were to be deported. German Gypsies were to be placed under police surveillance if they could not prove local residency and occupation. All attempts were to be made to break up "Gypsy gangs." The police were to pay special attention to how Gypsies treated horses, and welfare organizations were to seize any Gypsy children perceived to be neglected. The police were not to issue Gypsies identity papers or trade permits unless absolutely necessary.[11]

Although the Weimar Republic guaranteed full citizenship rights to Gypsies, police harassment did not stop. In an attempt to prevent female Gypsies from practicing professions like fortune-telling that were presumably their province, a Prussian decree of 1920 prohibited Gypsy girls and women from staying in spas and resorts, a restriction that would be issued against Jews in the Nazi period.[12] In 1927 the Prussian Ministry of Interior ordered the fingerprinting of every Gypsy above the age of six who could not prove to the police that he or she had a fixed domicile. The police issued certificates to those they had fingerprinted, and these certificates became part of every Gypsy's identity papers.[13]

As the Nazis assumed power, the fate of the Gypsy minority would radically change. The Gypsy minority of 30,000 to 35,000 was extremely small, representing only about .05 percent of the 1933 German population, and the proportion of Gypsies in Austria was approximately the same. Different groups of Gypsies, in German, *Zigeuner*, used different names to designate themselves; usually the name referred to the language the group spoke. The members of the largest European Gypsy group were therefore known as Roma, speaking the Romani language. In Germany, however, the largest Gypsy group was called Sinti, deriving from its members' language, which originated in the Sind region of India. In Austria, Roma Gypsies were more numerous; 8,000 Roma and 4,000 Sinti resided in Austria. In addition, linguistic subgroups existed, such as, for example, the Lalleri, who were generally considered Sinti. Further, some Gypsies designated themselves by their profession, although they also belonged to one of the language groups. For example, the Roma Gypsies in Austria involved in itinerant horse trading called themselves Lowara.[14] By 1933, a majority of German and Austrian Gypsies had regular domiciles and occupations, although some of these occupations—for example, circuit-riding horse traders and circus performers—were itinerant trades (*Wandergewerbe*).[15]

At first, the Nazi regime merely intensified already existing anti-Gypsy regulations. But the old regulations, though based on stereotypes, attempted to control behavior and thus distinguished between migrant and domiciled Gypsies. As a law-and-order regime, the Nazi government continued to recognize this distinction, concentrating on migrant Gypsies as so-called *Asoziale* who posed a threat to social stability. But the regime had wider aims. As we have seen, its leaders believed that certain behavior was hereditary. They therefore commissioned scientific studies to determine which groups manifested antisocial behavior. In addition, they believed that behavior was linked to race and that membership in some races caused deviant behavior. In the case of Gypsies, scientists and police officials in Nazi Germany believed that their alien racial traits produced criminality. Therefore, to determine a person's criminality, it was sufficient to classify that individual as a Gypsy. Of course, as in the case of the handicapped, classification as a Gypsy had to be "scientific."

Robert Ritter was the race scientist chosen to direct the classification of the Gypsies. Born in 1901 in Aachen, the son of a naval officer, Ritter attended secondary school at an elite Berlin *Gymnasium* and at the Prussian military academy. Before graduation in 1921, he fought with the postwar Free Corps on Germany's eastern border and worked with nationalistic youth groups. As was then customary, Ritter studied at a number of universities and in 1927 received his doctorate in educational psychology at the University of Munich. Continuing his studies in child psychology, Ritter pursued a medical degree and in 1930 received his doctorate in medicine at Heidelberg. He obtained his medical license in 1930 and his specialist certification in child psychiatry in 1934. He did his residency at hospitals in Paris, Zurich, and Berlin and as a staff member at the University Psychiatric Clinic in Tübingen, where he received his *Habilitation* in 1936. Ritter's work during those years focused on antisocial youth, and he established himself with the publication in 1936 of a study tracing ten generations of families considered to be vagabonds and thieves.[16]

Ritter's background, education, and experience indicated his strong nationalist outlook. Further, his research interests revealed his *völkisch* leanings. He appeared not to have joined the Nazi movement during the Weimar Republic, and there is no evidence that he joined the Nazi party later. He did, however, apparently occupy a position as a child psychiatrist with the Hitler

Youth.[17] Ritter's career provides evidence that at least some of the scientific work that led to exclusion and eventually to murder was done by Germans without close party connections.

Between 1936 and 1941, Ritter and a small staff conducted eugenic research in the southwest German region of Swabia. He investigated family histories of vagabonds and swindlers (*Gauner*), especially "those of alien race" and their hybrid offspring (*fremdrassige Bastarde*).[18] This research was financed by the DFG, after Ritter's work had been highly recommended to the DFG by a select group, including Ernst Rüdin, director of the Kaiser Wilhelm Institute for Psychiatry, Hans Reiter, head of the Reich Health Office, and Arthur Gütt and Herbert Linden of the RMdI.[19] By 1940 Ritter could report to the DFG that his research had broadened as his team investigated ethnic Germans from the Baltic, traveling population groups in the southern and western regions of Germany, a Jewish population group, emphasizing its "influence on the German population and environment through hereditary impact resulting from mixed marriages" and its difference from "Polish and Galician Jews," and, most important, *all* "Gypsy tribes" in Germany and Austria.[20]

In 1936 Ritter was appointed to head the newly created Eugenic and Population Biological Research Station of the Reich Health Office (Rassenhygienische und Bevölkerungsbiologische Forschungsstelle des Reichsgesundheitsamtes) and thereafter directed his research team from that agency. At first, he directed the research station from Tübingen, but in 1938 he moved the station to Berlin. In 1941, as conducting research about Gypsies yielded to implementing practical measures against them, Ritter also became chief of the newly created Criminal Biological Institute of the Security Police (Kriminalbiologisches Institut der Sicherheitspolizei). This institute was located within detective headquarters, the RKPA, then Office V of the RSHA.[21]

Ritter's team of researchers included a number of younger race scientists; the most important were Eva Justin, Adolf Würth, and Sophie Ehrhardt.[22] Eva Justin was born in 1909 in Dresden, the daughter of a railroad official. After passing her academic secondary school final examination, the *Abitur*, she trained as a nurse, met Ritter, and went to work in his eugenic laboratory at the Tübingen university clinic. She later followed Ritter from Tübingen to Berlin and helped conduct most of his research on Gypsies.[23] In the records of the DFG, she is listed as research assistant for Ritter's grants.[24] Although she had not followed the regular university procedures for a degree, she received her doctorate in anthropology at Berlin in 1943. Her application for admission to candidacy was backed by Eugen Fischer, and as references, she listed three influential representatives of the regime: Hans Reiter of the Reich Health Office, Herbert Linden of the RMdI, and Paul Werner, deputy chief of the RKPA.[25]

For her dissertation, Justin wrote a report on her work involving Gypsy children, who arrived in Auschwitz at the time her thesis was published.[26] Since Ritter did not hold a university appointment that permitted him to supervise doctoral candidates, the ethnologist Richard Thurnwald, one of the founders of race science, served as her sponsor, while Eugen Fischer and Ritter served as cosponsors.[27]

Adolf Würth was born in 1905 in Baden-Württemberg, the son of a businessman, studied medicine after graduation from secondary school, switched to anthropology, and received his doctorate in 1936 under Fischer in Berlin. He met Ritter, who told him that he needed an anthropologist. Würth applied to the Reich Health Office and was assigned to Ritter's team in Tübingen. Würth remained with Ritter until the Wehrmacht drafted him in June 1940 but returned for about a month in 1941. Würth was not a member of the Nazi party.[28]

Sophie Ehrhardt was born in Russia in 1902. After receiving a master's degree in zoology, she completed her doctorate in anthropology in 1930 under Theodor Mollison, who had also sponsored Josef Mengele's doctorate, and remained in Munich as his assistant. In 1935 Ehrhardt became Hans F. K. Günther's assistant. In 1937 she joined Ritter's Tübingen research team. She followed Ritter to Berlin and continued her own research; for example, she studied Gypsies in East Prussia in 1939–40 and Jews in the Lodz ghetto in 1940.[29]

Ritter's research had started with a relatively modest eugenic investigation for his *Habilitation*, the certification essential for a university career. But he enlarged the topic from a small group of families, some of them Gypsies, to a much larger sample of the Gypsy population. His work was considered important by the regime, and he therefore received solid financial support from the DFG and government support when his team was institutionalized as a research station of the Reich Health Office. Since his research also became an important foundation for the implementation of anti-Gypsy policies, his team's work was also absorbed by the RKPA of Heydrich's RSHA.

The research conducted by Ritter and his associates was designed to produce genealogies of all Gypsies, tracing members of extended families, marriages to outsiders, physical health, education, criminal record, and social adjustment.[30] Ritter attempted to improve upon Henry H. Goddard's genealogical study of the American Kallikak family, which had occupied a place of central importance in the history of eugenic research.[31] But following traditional eugenic research practices, which were beginning to lose credibility in the United States, Ritter's team was only able to accumulate more data. Eventually, they classified about 30,000 Gypsies, creating genealogical charts accompanied by case histories with photographs, official documents, measurements, and other physical evidence.[32]

Considering their eugenic research approach, race-conscious outlook, and anti-Gypsy prejudice, it is not surprising that Ritter and his team concluded that Gypsies as a group were degenerate, criminal, and *asozial* and that this condition was hereditary. They also believed that the Gypsy urge to travel was inherited, just as the American eugenicist Charles Benedict Davenport had believed in a Mendelian gene for "nomadism."[33] At first, Ritter considered his study of Gypsies part of his investigation of degenerate, criminal, and anti-social elements and thus created a distinction between hybrids, who inter-mingled with the general population, and "pure" Gypsies, who continued to follow their undiluted traditions. Although Ritter categorized Gypsy hybrids (*Zigeunermischlinge*) as antisocial, he viewed pure Gypsies not as antisocial but as a people following their traditional ways in a changed environment. Ritter used the popular romantic image of Gypsies to describe these pure Gypsies, a concept similar to that of the "noble savage." Obviously, this idea logically led to the notion of establishing a Gypsy reservation.[34] At any rate, Ritter classified about 90 percent of all Gypsies as hybrids.[35]

Ritter's co-optation by the government reveals that the Nazi regime con-sidered his research both valuable and useful. Because *Rechtssicherheit* de-manded a clear definition of groups to be excluded, government agencies required Ritter's services. The police needed detailed information about the supposed criminality of Gypsies because decrees against antisocial elements initially provided the best means of excluding them. They also needed in-formation about their citizenship because foreign Gypsies could simply be expelled, and Ritter provided supposed facts that could be used to challenge the German citizenship of Gypsies.[36] Although most Roma were sufficiently dark skinned to be easily identified, agencies needed further information be-cause many Sinti were as light skinned as other Germans and could not be so easily identified; the police thus required expert evaluations before classifying suspects as Gypsies.[37]

Eventually, as the regime moved toward the exclusion of Gypsies as a race, officials needed to know how to distinguish between Gypsies and other Ger-mans. Furthermore, as they sought to justify their actions, German policy makers continued to equate the so-called Gypsy problem with the fight against criminality, just as the so-called Jewish problem was seen as a fight against financial corruption and political subversion and the problem of the handicapped as a fight against degeneration. In a 1940 letter support-ing one of Ritter's applications for DFG funding, Paul Werner represented pragmatic thinking at the RSHA: "The Gypsy problem is currently of the highest priority as a principal part of the entire social problem. Although the Gypsy problem is primarily a racial problem, its practical implications in-volve largely the problem posed by antisocial elements."[38]

The definition of excluded groups and the classification of its members proved difficult. We have seen that the definition of the handicapped was flexible and that attempts to classify members of that group scientifically on the basis of questionnaires were ultimately arbitrary. Similarly, the regime eventually settled on a pragmatic solution to the problem of defining and classifying German and Austrian Jews.

The Jewish group was far too large to permit individual anthropological investigations. The regime thus settled on simple genealogical proof of membership. The status of grandparents (and.for members of the SS, even more remote ancestors) determined membership of offspring, and that status depended on the registered religion of the grandparents. Based on this evidence, which primarily promoted the field of genealogical research, policy makers and race scientists established presumed scientific categories of hybrids of the first and second degree. Anthropological verification was provided only for those challenging the classification at their own expense. Usually challengers rested their cases on claims of illegitimacy, insisting that the parent listed on the birth certificate was not the actual parent. These anthropological investigations, usually based on hearsay and photographs, were often inaccurate in the days before DNA testing.[39]

Ritter's studies of Gypsies had no greater scientific validity than did the anthropological investigations of Jewish hybrids. Still, he classified most of the German and many of the Austrian Gypsies on a scale ranging from pure Gypsy to non-Gypsy. Their files were marked with "Z" for Gypsy (*Zigeuner*) or "NZ" for non-Gypsy. For the overwhelming majority, however, the classification was "ZM" for Gypsy hybrid (*Zigeunermischling*). Hybrids were then further labeled with a plus or a minus sign, so that "ZM+" stood for a hybrid with mostly Gypsy "blood," while "ZM−" stood for a hybrid with mostly German "blood."[40]

In the first years of the regime, the Nazi leaders concentrated on the exclusion of its enemies from the public arena, including the civil service, publishing, entertainment, and the arts. Since the elimination of imagined Jewish overrepresentation in public life had been a major campaign issue for the German right, this policy, exemplified by the April 1933 Law for the Restoration of the Professional Civil Service, was directed primarily against Jews.[41]

This did not mean, however, that the Nazis neglected other targeted groups; at about the same time, the regime moved against the handicapped with the July 1933 sterilization law. But as far as Gypsies were concerned, no new legislation was immediately necessary. The pre-Nazi decrees were sufficient to deal with Gypsies, and new provisions of the penal code covering all criminal convictions could also be applied. Special powers of arbitrary arrest granted to the police led to the commitment of numerous Gypsies to the concentration camps. Decrees issued in 1934 authorizing the police to expel eastern European Jews, the so-called *Ostjuden*, were also used to expel Gypsies who could not prove their German citizenship.[42] In the same way, the

Law for the Prevention of Offspring with Hereditary Diseases was used to sterilize Gypsies. We do not know exactly how many Gypsies were sterilized, but we do know that the numbers were large enough to support the conclusion that sterilization of Gypsies was a calculated policy. Sterilization for such racial reasons was illegal, as we have seen in the earlier discussion of colored children in the Rhineland. In that case, the authorities were afraid to use the sterilization law, probably because of possible international reaction, and sterilized the children outside the law. In the case of Gypsies, no foreign complications were expected, and the victims were simply designated as "feebleminded" to comply with the law.[43]

Nevertheless, existing legislation alone did not long satisfy the Nazi regime. Local demands for tighter controls produced results. In 1935 the police began to confine a growing number of German Gypsies in newly created municipal Gypsy camps (*Zigeunerlager*). A result of local initiatives, these camps were created and paid for by municipal governments and local welfare offices.[44] The camps were designed for itinerant Gypsies who moved from job to job using wagons as mobile homes (*Wohnwagen*). Prior to the creation of these camps, Gypsies usually rented spaces in private campgrounds, where poor sanitary conditions often accompanied high rents. But the owners of these private camping areas did not restrict the movements or occupations of their tenants, leading to protests from local citizens. In Frankfurt, for example, the district office of the Nazi party complained to the chief of police about the continued presence of Gypsies at a private campground: "Unfortunately the rabble [*Gesindel*] is still residing in Kruppstraße, and so far no indications of departure can be noticed. Meanwhile, complaints from pedestrians taking a stroll [*Spaziergänger*] have not diminished, and frequently one can now also see that the Gypsies are stealing wood at the Enkheimer copse."[45]

The first Gypsy camp created by the government was probably established in Cologne. It opened in early 1935 and held about 300 persons by August and twice that many by 1937. All Gypsies living in mobile homes in the Cologne region, as well as those arriving after the camp was opened, were forced to move their wagons to the camp. In addition, Gypsies receiving welfare were taken to the camp even if they were residing in a fixed domicile. No non-Gypsy was permitted to enter the camp, but Gypsies could leave to pursue their occupations. After 1937, they could leave only during the day. The camp was surrounded by barbed wire, and all persons entering or leaving through the only gate had to report to the guard. Occasionally the police would initiate sweeps to control identity papers.[46]

Similar camps were established in many other German cities, and all operated under similar, though sometimes harsher, rules. In Düsseldorf, for example, non-Gypsies could not even enter the camp to visit incarcerated relatives, and even conversations through the barbed wire were prohibited.

Gypsies could leave the camp only with the permission of the guard, although generally they were allowed to go to work in the city. Living conditions were primitive; at times, there was no electricity. The Gypsies received no welfare payments but had to pay rent to the city for the camp accommodations.[47]

The largest Gypsy camp was established at a sewage dump adjacent to the municipal cemetery in the Berlin suburb of Marzahn. It was designed to remove Gypsies from public view during the 1936 Olympic summer games. To accomplish this purpose, the chief of the Berlin police conducted raids throughout Prussia to arrest all Gypsies prior to the games; on 16 July 1936, the police arrested 600 Gypsies in Berlin and marched them to the campsite under guard. The camp, consisting of 130 caravans condemned as uninhabitable by the Reich Labor Service, was guarded by a detachment of the metropolitan police (Schutzpolizei). With only three water pumps and two toilets, hygienic facilities at Berlin-Marzahn were totally inadequate; in March 1938, city authorities reported 170 cases of communicable diseases.[48]

The Gypsy camps were only an interim solution. These early camps resembled ghettos, especially those established for Jews in small Polish towns after 1939. In time, conditions in the camps would deteriorate, and tighter controls would be imposed as the regime moved toward more radical solutions.

In Austria after the Anschluß, camps established for Gypsies were from the beginning more coercive, resembling the forced labor camps established during the war in the East more than they resembled small ghettos. The two largest Austrian camps were Maxglan (earlier Leopoldskron) in Salzburg and Lackenbach in Burgenland.

The Salzburg camp was established in 1939 to hold Gypsies entering the federal state from Germany and from other parts of Austria, though Salzburg tried to drive Gypsies across its border into the territory of Tyrol, a tactic duplicated by its neighbor.[49] Unlike the German camps, the Salzburg camp prohibited mobile homes; between 300 and 400 incarcerated Gypsies were housed in barracks. Space, sanitation, and living conditions were as primitive as in the German camps. Gypsies were permitted to leave the camps only on public business. More important, they were subjected to forced labor. Male Gypsies were assigned to construction projects, and female Gypsies mostly to work inside the camp.[50] Both sexes also served as a pool of available talent for other Nazi projects. For example, Leni Riefenstahl commandeered them to use as extras in the motion picture *Tiefland*, filmed in the hills around Salzburg.[51]

The Lackenbach Gypsy camp in Burgenland was the largest such camp in either Germany or Austria. Established in 1940 to house the Gypsies in the Austrian border regions, it eventually received Gypsies from other areas, including some transferred from the Mauthausen concentration camp. The camp held at least 3,000 Gypsies over the period of its existence. Similar to the Salzburg camp, it also resembled a concentration camp in structure. For example, the camp commandant installed inmate functionaries to carry out his orders and imposed corporal punishment to have them obeyed. The camp's living conditions were also primitive, resulting at one time in a major typhus epidemic. The camp operated until liberation at the end of the war, but few of its inmates lived to see that day.[52]

Increasingly harsh measures against the Gypsies were, however, only preliminary solutions (*Gegenwartslösung*). The German bureaucracy wanted a permanent solution (*restlose Lösung*) or a radical solution (*Radikallösung*) to what they called the Gypsy problem (*Zigeunerproblem*).[53] But such a solution continued to elude them for some time. As we know, eventually mass murder was to be the "final" solution, but they did not know that as they worked on their problem during the 1930s. In the same way, before the decision to kill them was made, the bureaucracy saw sterilization as the solution to the supposed problem of the handicapped. Similarly, they initially believed that emigration was the solution to the Jewish problem.

During the 1930s, the bureaucracy envisioned a "Gypsy law [*Zigeunergesetz*]" as the vehicle for the permanent solution to the Gypsy problem. Preparations for such a law were the province of the RMdI, and in 1936 the specialist who had worked on it, Senior Councillor (Oberregierungsrat) Zindel, reported his preliminary findings to State Secretary Hans Pfundtner. He pointed out that the "fight against the Gypsy plague" was international and that some progress had been made through efforts coordinated by Interpol. Still, he believed that a complete solution, for both Germany and the rest of the world, would not be possible in the near future.

Conceding that incarceration of all Gypsies might not be feasible, Zindel pointed out that one aim of policy was to force Gypsies to settle down in one place, but this objective was difficult to achieve because of Gypsies' inherent travel lust (*Wandertrieb*). But even if they could be forced to stop wandering and stay in one place, Zindel argued, that too would have disadvantages: "One must have serious misgivings—from a racial political viewpoint—about the integration of Gypsies into the population." Moreover, Zindel pointed out, attempts at assimilation "will drive the Gypsy—because of his inherent nature—almost without exception into criminal behavior, and in this situation into truly serious crime."

Zindel then listed various choices, each an alternative to assimilation. The best option, he maintained, would be to force Gypsies onto reservations, but "no community will tolerate such breeding ground for murder, manslaughter, and crimes of all kinds." Another possibility, Zindel continued, would be to compel them to leave the country, but because deportation was legal only for foreigners, that was not feasible. Total surveillance was the final option,

THE ORIGINS OF NAZI GENOCIDE

including incarceration of "dangerous" Gypsies in concentration camps. This was the best of the possible choices at the time. To implement incarceration, Zindel pointed out, it would be essential to identify and register all Gypsies. Registration would have to be the first step toward a solution. As we have seen, Ritter and his associates undertook this task soon thereafter.[54]

In the interim, the RMdI on 6 June 1936 — three months after Zindel's report — issued an advisory to police and local authorities on how to "fight the Gypsy plague." It formalized the various regulations that had already been implemented on the local level, including the deportation of foreign Gypsies, restrictions on the issuance of trade licenses, surveillance and control over traveling Gypsies, registration and fingerprinting, and large-scale roundups.[55] After the Anschluß, German regulations concerning Gypsies, just as those for Jews and the handicapped, were introduced in Austria.[56] In addition, about 3,000 male and female Gypsies were arrested in Burgenland and committed to the Dachau and Ravensbrück concentration camps.[57]

A Gypsy law was never enacted. Events outpaced legislation, as the Nazi regime consistently escalated persecution, embracing ever more radical solutions. A Gypsy law that legislated such solutions could not be issued because radical solutions were kept secret and never placed in the public record. Thus Hitler prohibited the promulgation of a euthanasia law, and nothing was ever added to the public record about the real solution to the Jewish problem. Final solutions — against the handicapped, Jews, and Gypsies — remained secret administrative acts.

Without a law defining jurisdiction and procedures, anti-Gypsy affairs continued to be administered by various agencies, such as, for example, the Reich Health Office of the RMdI and, on the local level, the government welfare offices. In terms of welfare, the similarity between the treatment of Jews and Gypsies is glaringly clear, as we can see from the correspondence between local welfare offices and the DGT.[58] The Tenth Decree to the Reich Citizenship Law, issued on 4 July 1939 and announcing the creation of the Reich Association of Jews in Germany (Reichsvereinigung der Juden in Deutschland), shifted the responsibility for welfare for Jews from the public welfare agencies to the Reich Association.[59] But Gypsies had no recognized organization with funds to provide for indigents. Public welfare agencies thus had to keep Gypsies on their rolls. In the same way, the welfare agencies were forced to continue payments to Jews if the Reich Association did not have sufficient funds or if Jewish war invalids were involved.[60]

Obviously, continued payments did not imply special status but only the absence of a public, legal basis for withholding support from qualified individuals. Any payment to Gypsies was seen as burdensome, especially support for "unwanted" women and children placed on the welfare rolls after their husbands and sons had been sent to concentration camps. Welfare agencies attempted to evade their responsibility. At first, they tried to treat Gypsies like Jews but found that without a Gypsy association, regulations denying them public welfare could not be applied. Then some local welfare agencies simply cut payments in half, while others implemented rules designed to apply to antisocial elements.[61]

Coordination of Gypsy affairs, what the Germans called *Federführung*, rested with Reinhard Heydrich's Sipo, especially Arthur Nebe's RKPA, successor to the police agencies that had traditionally controlled Gypsy affairs. For coordination purposes, the Kripo used the Central Office to Combat the Gypsy Pest (Zentralstelle zur Bekämpfung des Zigeunerunwesens), located at the Munich police headquarters, which was a continuation of the Gypsy bureau established by the Bavarian police in 1926.[62] In October 1938, the Gypsy bureau was moved from Munich to Berlin.[63] Renamed the Reich Headquarters to Combat the Gypsy Pest (Reichszentrale zur Bekämpfung des Zigeunerunwesens), it was placed within the RKPA. There the police developed a national data bank on Gypsies in collaboration with Ritter's research team at the Reich Health Office, establishing special Gypsy bureaus at local Kripo offices.[64] Rules for the implementation of anti-Gypsy policy were passed from the RKPA to local agencies through circulars issued by the RMdI, the Reich leader SS and chief of the German police, or the RKPA.[65]

Because a definitive solution to the Gypsy problem had been postponed, the police could only tighten controls, while the RMdI commissioned Ritter's group to register and classify all Gypsies; in 1941 the police created for Ritter the Criminal Biological Institute. Controls placed on Gypsies included deportation and restriction to Gypsy camps. In addition, numerous Gypsies were sent to the concentration camps, a procedure made easy by a RMdI decree issued on 14 December 1937 instituting preventive arrest.[66] On the basis of this decree, the RKPA circulated guidelines for preventive arrest that included a definition of persons to be considered *asozial* and thus subject to incarceration, listing as one example of such persons the entire Gypsy minority.[67] Gypsies were also targeted by special decrees prohibiting what was considered to be typical Gypsy occupations. Thus an RKPA circular to local Kripo offices ordered them to commit to camps all female Gypsies who had ever been engaged in fortune-telling.[68]

The Nuremberg racial laws provided the most comprehensive means of excluding Gypsies. Directed primarily against Jews, the racial laws were enacted on Hitler's sudden orders during the 1935 Nuremberg party meeting, before the bureaucracy was ready to codify exclusion. Although Gypsies were not specifically mentioned, the laws did in fact apply to them. This was made clear in the commentaries on the laws—written by senior members of the RMdI and published by a house closely linked to the Nazi party—which were cited by the bureaucracy as authoritative guides to the intent of the lawgiver.

THE ORIGINS OF NAZI GENOCIDE

These commentaries classified Gypsies, along with Jews and blacks, as racially distinctive minorities with "alien blood [artfremdes Blut]."[69] Administrative regulations soon extended the draconian antimiscegenation prohibition of the racial laws to "Gypsies, Negroes, and their bastard offspring."[70] The convoluted regulations governing Jewish hybrids with "quarter" or "half" Jewish ancestry were also applied to Gypsies.[71] In the same way, limitations on voting rights imposed on Jews were also applied to Gypsies, who, for example, were prohibited from participating in the 1938 plebiscite on the reunification of Austria with the German Reich.[72]

When Germany launched World War II in September 1939, the severity of policies against all targeted biological minorities intensified. As we have seen, before the war the handicapped had been institutionalized and sterilized. Jews had in turn been fired from jobs in the public sector, driven from the professions, and excluded from the economy through the Aryanization of businesses. Excluded from social and cultural life, they had been forced to carry special identity cards and to take additional "Jewish" first names. All this had been accomplished through dry, bureaucratic procedures, interrupted only once by the mass expulsion of Jews with Polish citizenship in October 1938, followed by the organized violence against Jews of November 1938. Similarly, Gypsies had been excluded from public jobs and social life. They had been prohibited from practicing most of their traditional occupations. They had been registered and classified and on that basis issued special identity papers. Large numbers had been incarcerated in Gypsy camps and concentration camps. And after the start of the war, Gypsies still at liberty within the German Reich were placed under the same exclusionary regulations as were Jews, including elimination of most schooling for children, denial of social benefits, imposition of compulsory labor, and exclusion from public facilities.[73]

These exclusionary policies of the 1930s were as radical as time and place permitted, but they did not fulfill the aims of Nazi leaders to exclude biological minorities. Foreign policy considerations, concerns for the domestic economy, and doubts about public opinion acted to constrain their imagination. But pronouncements on all levels revealed that exclusion was only a first step to a solution. Those responsible for the institutionalized handicapped talked about decimating the patient population. Bureaucrats and propagandists called for a total solution to the Gypsy problem. And Hitler himself warned the Jews about more radical solutions.

War provided Nazi leaders with the opportunity to proceed with more radical solutions. In the fall of 1939, the regime initiated a policy of murdering institutionalized patients. Hitler and his circle apparently believed that under cover of war they could get away with mass murder of the handicapped. This perception that they were free to murder did not yet extend to Jews and Gypsies, and old policies of exclusion continued to be applied against them. The goal of anti-Gypsy policy during the 1930s was registration and surveillance and, as war approached, increased incarceration of Gypsies. The goal of anti-Jewish policy centered initially on Jewish emigration, and as war approached, the regime applied greater pressure upon Jews to force them to leave Germany.[74]

These early anti-Jewish and anti-Gypsy policies did not immediately escalate when war began. Without guidance from above, the bureaucracy pursued chimeric projects. For a time, it considered shipping Jews to Madagascar, an impractical plan that occupied numerous officials while the far more workable killing program was being implemented against the handicapped. In the period between the start of the war on 1 September 1939 and the invasion of the Soviet Union on 22 June 1941, the bureaucracy waited for its Führer's decision; in the meantime, it considered deportation to Poland a possible solution. There the Germans had begun to kill the handicapped, imposed ghettoization and forced labor on Jews, and inflicted killing, incarceration, and forced labor on Gypsies.

The first attempt to deport Jews to the General Government of Poland was made in October 1939 as part of the scheme to relegate Jews to a reservation in the Lublin region. This deportation effort failed because Poland had no room for massive settlements, especially if ethnic Germans from the Baltic region, then occupied by the Soviet Union, were to be resettled in Poland. As a first step, Adolf Eichmann and his staff in October 1939 organized deportations from Mährisch-Ostrau in the Protectorate, from Kattowitz in Silesia, and from Vienna. The transports went to Nisko on the San River, a camp of barracks without accommodations for large numbers of deported persons. The Gestapo deported about 5,000 Jews in two sets of transports before Himmler canceled the scheme.[75]

In 1940 and early 1941, the deportation of Jews was locally inspired. Deportations were no longer officially linked to the so-called Lublin reservation plan that had been abandoned, although German officials continued to mention it in the same breath with the equally discredited Madagascar scheme. Henceforth, the official reason advanced for the deportations would be the need of the German population for housing occupied by Jews. In February 1940, the Gestapo arrested the Jews of Stettin, who numbered about 1,200, as well as about 160 Jews from Schneidemühl, deporting all of them to the Lublin region in the General Government.[76]

Deportations also took place on Germany's western border. In occupied Alsace and Lorraine, the German administration decided to ship Jews, Gypsies, the handicapped, and blacks across the border into France.[77] Using this opportunity to breach the French border, the regional Nazi party leaders in Baden and the Palatinate rounded up all Jews, about 7,000 to 8,000, and on 22 and 23 October 1940 shipped them to France, where French authorities interned most of them in the notorious Gurs camp in the foothills of the Pyrenees.[78] Finally, at the urging of the Nazi leader in Austria, the Gestapo in February and March 1941 deported about 5,000 Jews from Vienna to Lublin before the protest of the German rulers in the General Government stopped further transports.[79]

The haphazard deportations included Gypsies. On 17 October 1939, the RKPA circulated a secret order to Kripo offices prohibiting all Gypsies and Gypsy hybrids not already interned in camps from changing their registered domiciles, a measure essential for implementing their deportation.[80] That month, as Jews were being assembled in Austria, in the Protectorate, and in Silesia for deportation to Nisko, the RKPA decided to add Gypsies to the Nisko transports. On 13 October, Arthur Nebe cabled Eichmann to ask "when he could dispatch the Berlin Gypsies."[81] Eichmann replied that "three or four train cars of Gypsies could be attached" to the Vienna transport and thereafter "a few train cars" could be attached to each departing transport.[82] This opportunity provided the possibility of vast deportations of Gypsies; a memo from Eichmann's office in Vienna devoted to the deportation of Jews included an addendum: "The Gypsies residing in the Ostmark [Austria] will be added to the deportation operation in special railroad wagons."[83] The collapse of the Nisko scheme precluded these Gypsy deportations.

Undaunted, the RKPA continued to explore ways to deport Gypsies. On 27 April 1940, Reinhard Heydrich informed local police and other government agencies that "the first transport of 2,500 Gypsies to the General Government — consisting of extended families [Sippen] — will be dispatched in the middle of May." These Gypsy families were to be collected within the territories of Kripo central offices in Hamburg, Bremen, Cologne, Düsseldorf, Hanover, Frankfurt, and Stuttgart. The offices in Hamburg and Bremen were responsible for collecting 1,000 Gypsies, those in Cologne, Düsseldorf, and Hanover for another 1,000, and those in Frankfurt and Stuttgart for the remaining 500. Those gathered were to be assembled in Hamburg, Cologne, and Stuttgart. To support the police at the assembly camps, representatives of the RKPA and the Reich Health Office arrived at the camps on 14 May.[84]

On the same day, the RKPA issued guidelines for the deportations, which resembled those later issued for the deportation of German Jews. The guidelines exempted from deportation those who were over seventy years old, pregnant women if in the seventh month or later, and those physically incapable of travel. Gypsies married to German non-Gypsies and close Gypsy relatives of serving soldiers were also exempt. Further, Gypsies who owned real estate or a large amount of other property were not included because at the time there was no legal means of confiscating either real or personal property. Finally, Gypsies who could prove that they were foreign nationals could not be deported. Each deported Gypsy was permitted to take only 50 kilos of luggage and Polish currency worth 10 RM. All other money, securities, and jewelry— except wedding rings—were to remain behind. At the assembly points, all Gypsies were to be photographed and fingerprinted, and consecutive numbers were to be painted on their forearms. Gypsies were required to turn in all personal and identity papers, for which they were to receive a receipt.[85]

The Gypsy transports left in late May 1940 as scheduled for the General Government. The Kripo exceeded its quota; 2,800 Gypsies were actually deported. At the assembly points, members of Ritter's team checked the classification of Gypsies scheduled for deportation to assure accuracy, a job similar to that of the physicians who checked medical records in the euthanasia killing centers to prevent embarrassing errors. At the Württemberg state prison of Hohenasperg, designed as the assembly point for Gypsies collected by the Kripo offices in Stuttgart and Frankfurt, Ritter's collaborator Adolf Würth did the paperwork and released twenty-two persons who had not been properly classified as Gypsies.[86]

These were the only Gypsy deportations of 1940. Further transports had been planned—and, for Austria, had already been announced for August 1940—but the administration of the General Government had successfully opposed the potential dumping of Gypsies and Jews there.[87] The deportations would not resume until after the German invasion of the Soviet Union. But by then, Hitler and his clique of Nazi leaders had decided to implement a final solution for both Jews and Gypsies.

Chapter 13

Killing Handicapped Jews

At Nuremberg, Viktor Brack swore under oath that no hand-icapped Jewish patient died in the euthanasia killing centers.[1] He lied. Karl Brandt also lied at Nuremberg, claiming that he knew nothing about the fate of handicapped Jews.[2] Physicians involved in the killing of handicapped Jews — Hermann Pfannmüller, for example — also lied when asked about their Jewish patients.[3] All these lies were part of an elaborate scheme to falsify the record. And the liars succeeded, at Nuremberg and thereafter, in deceiving prosecutors, judges, and historians.[4] Even today, their lies continue to circulate and to obscure our understanding of the fate of handicapped Jews. But the murder of handicapped Jewish patients — which began about a year before the mass murder of Jews commenced in the occupied Soviet Union — formed an important link between euthanasia and the final solution.[5]

The treatment of institutionalized handicapped Jews in Germany deteriorated steadily after 1933. The overwhelming majority of such patients were in non-Jewish German or Austrian hospitals. Of course, many were there because they had been hospitalized before 1933; others were there because they lived in the area the hospital served or because it offered particular services.[6] In any event, there were very few Jewish hospitals for handicapped patients. Only one Jewish institution served as a psychiatric hospital. The Jacoby Hospital and Nursing Home (Jacoby'sche Heil- und Pflegeanstalt), located in Sayn (today Bendorf-Sayn) near Koblenz on the Rhine, was founded by Meir Jacoby in 1869 and was administered by the Jacoby family until World War II, toward the end by the founder's grandsons, both physicians.[7] Late in 1939, the institution was acquired by the Reich Association of Jews in Germany.[8] Additional beds were available in the psychiatric ward of the Berlin Jewish hospital and in the Jewish ward of the Lohr hospital in Bavaria, and throughout the country, Jewish communities maintained a number of old-age and nursing homes that also contained patients with disabilities.[9]

By 1939, the efforts of the German government to exclude German and Austrian Jews had succeeded in isolating and impoverishing the Jewish population. Driven from public life, the professions, and the economy, Jews were stigmatized by the requirement that their special identity cards be stamped with a large "J" as well as the compulsory addition of an extra first name, "Israel" for men and "Sara" for women, all long before they were forced to wear the yellow star of David in September 1941. In response to these exclusionary measures, large numbers of Jews emigrated, shrinking the economic base of the Jewish community and leaving behind an overaged population. The regime continued to exert pressure, forcing Jewish communities to assume, in addition to their traditional obligations concerning religion and culture, all responsibility for the education, health, and welfare of their members. Furthermore, the German police exercised supervision over these activities. Still, treatment of Jews was not yet completely arbitrary. Except for the imposition of exclusionary restrictions, the traditional legal structure governing public services and economic relations continued in force. Further, the civil service was not certain how to treat Jewish hybrids (*Mischlinge*) and Jews in mixed marriages.

On 19 November 1938, the Reich ministers of interior, labor, and finance issued a joint decree, effective at the start of 1939, excluding Jews from public assistance. Henceforth, Jews were entitled to assistance only from Jewish welfare agencies, but if those private agencies were unable to pay the full amount, public welfare would continue to provide Jews with assistance for "shelter, food, clothing, nursing care, aid for the infirm, as well as pregnant women, maternity cases, midwife services, medical treatment as needed, and burial if necessary." This exclusion from public welfare did not, however, apply to seriously wounded (*schwerkriegsbeschädigte*) veterans of World War I.[10] On 4 July 1939, the Tenth Decree to the Reich Citizenship Law transformed the somewhat independent Reich Representation of Jews in Germany (Reichsvertretung) into the Reich Association of Jews in Germany (Reichsvereinigung) and imposed on it the obligation to finance Jewish education and welfare.[11] The question of welfare for Jews in mixed marriages was left open and continued to occupy the German bureaucracy.[12]

Local public welfare offices did everything to remove Jews from the safety net of public assistance and shift the financial burden to private Jewish welfare agencies financed by the Reich Association. This decision to require private citizens to perform the public function of protecting the needy applied also to institutionalized handicapped Jews, except for those who had been committed by the courts or the police.[13] Until 1939, the cost of institutional care had been borne by government for many Jews, even for those in Jewish institutions. For example, two German public welfare agencies had jointly paid for the institutionalization of the Jewish patient Max Ledermann and after the decree of 1938 fought over how these payments should be discontinued.

Born in Dresden in 1902, Ledermann was placed by his father, then residing in Zwickau, in an institution in 1920 and in 1923 was transferred to the Jewish Nursing Home for the Feebleminded in Berlin-Weissensee. After 1930, the father was no longer able to pay for his son's care, and the Berlin welfare agency assumed responsibility but passed the cost on to the Zwickau welfare agency. Zwickau discontinued payment for the year 1939 because the November 1938 decree required local Jewish welfare agencies to pay for Ledermann.

THE ORIGINS OF NAZI GENOCIDE

The Berlin welfare agency, however, continued payment because the Jewish welfare agency did not have the funds. The situation changed on 1 May 1939 when the city reached an agreement with the Berlin Jewish community that henceforth its welfare agency would pay for institutionalized patients while the city would continue welfare for all others.[14] Berlin wanted Zwickau to pay Ledermann's support for the first four months of 1939, but Zwickau refused, arguing that "what is possible after 1 May 1939 should have been possible earlier." To make the point absolutely clear, Zwickau's chief of welfare added the following argument: "The Lord Mayor of Berlin has been convinced that the Berlin Jewish community has no funds, but I cannot believe that this is true. The government has repeatedly announced that Jews in Germany possess on average four times as much wealth as members of the German national community. Therefore, the Jewish community should have been able, without much trouble, to get the funds needed for welfare for their racial brethren." These arguments apparently convinced the DGT, which had been called upon to serve as arbiter, because it sided with Zwickau.[15]

For handicapped Jewish patients in public institutions, the decision concerning welfare posed new problems. This was especially true in those tragic cases where relatives had left Germany. As Jewish emigration accelerated, families left the country but were not able to take along their institutionalized relatives.[16] Emigrating Jews paid state agencies for perpetual care of their remaining relatives in state hospitals. Since Jews often did not have sufficient liquid capital, they found imaginative ways to provide for their relatives. For example, the relatives of a Jewish woman in a state hospital in the Prussian province of Hanover provided for her care in the following way. They sold their house to a German for 21,200 RM, and the buyer committed himself to pay 5,000 RM to the state hospital agency. But since he did not have the entire amount in cash, the agency took a mortgage for the remainder, amortized at 1 percent and with interest at 4.5 percent.[17]

In another case, a senior cantor wanted to provide for his institutionalized daughter as he prepared to follow his other children, who had already emigrated. The daughter was a patient in the Swabian Ursberg hospital, but the Hanover agency would be responsible for her because she had lived in Hanover before entering the Swabian institution. The father agreed to turn over his 10,000 RM life insurance policy to the agency, with the permission of the Jewish organization that had paid his premiums, and to pay all premiums through 1939. The Hanover agency would then pay the premiums until the policy matured. The father agreed that after emigration he would notify Hanover once a year that he was still alive. He also promised to arrange for notification should he die before age sixty-five.[18]

But handicapped Jews without relatives to pay their hospital expenses continued to be supported by the government, unless private Jewish welfare organizations could pay for them. Thus the welfare office of the Delitzsch county district inquired about payment for Hans Freimann, a patient in the Uchtspringe state hospital in the Prussian province of Saxony. His mother had died in 1932, and his father had emigrated. Freimann was the responsibility of the county, and since there was no Jewish welfare society in Delitzsch, the public welfare office wanted to know who would pay.[19] This also applied to handicapped Jews in hospitals in the south German state of Baden because in October 1940 the entire Baden Jewish community had been deported to France and there was no Jewish welfare to pay for Jewish patients left behind.[20]

The German authorities were not motivated by humane considerations or common sense in those instances in which public money continued to be made available to Jews but solely by the dictates of the letter of the positive law. But whenever possible, the law was construed to shift the burden from government to private Jewish agencies, as one bizarre case readily reveals. Theodor "Israel" Wassermann received from public welfare a monthly stipend of 62.90 RM after his two sons, both Jewish hybrids, were drafted into the Wehrmacht. When both sons were killed in the French campaign in 1940, the father became eligible for higher subsidies. The RMdI, however, ruled that the law required that the increased payments had to be paid by the Reich Association. The German government thus imposed financial obligations on impoverished Jewish welfare agencies for soldiers killed in the service of Reich and Führer while dodging the obvious responsibilities of the German state.[21]

Jews in mixed marriages were exempted from these exclusionary provisions, but this did not apply if the couple had divorced or if the German partner had died. Wassermann was apparently no longer married, and the law's exemption, which referred to Jews "living" in a mixed marriage, thus did not apply. However, an order of the Führer later exempted any Jew who had ever been a partner in a mixed marriage if "the only son was killed in the current war."[22]

The limitation of welfare payments was not the only form of exclusion confronting institutionalized Jewish patients during the 1930s. Private institutions also began to discriminate against them. Most private institutions in Germany were church related, belonging either to the Catholic Charity Association or the Protestant Home Mission. These private Christian hospitals had always admitted Jews; in addition, some of their Christian patients had been classified as Jews under the Nuremberg racial laws. In the late 1930s, many of these private hospitals began to exclude Jews.

In March 1937, the German Supreme Administrative Court for Finances issued a decision concerning the tax-exempt status of nonprofit institutions. Its ruling included the statement that "nonprofit exemption cannot be granted to institutions and for purposes designed to benefit Jews."[23] Although this ruling was issued in a case involving a Jewish nonprofit institution, private Christian hospitals claimed that possible loss of nonprofit status made it impossible for them to keep or accept Jewish patients. Thus, private hospitals in Silesia and Württemberg refused to admit Jews and asked the state agency to remove those previously admitted.[24]

The policy of the Alsterdorfer Institutions in Hamburg, a hospital complex of the Protestant Home Mission, is an example of how private Christian nonprofit institutions attempted to rid themselves of their Jewish patients. On 11 August 1937, after the hospital had refused to accept Irene Tobias, a two-year-old feebleminded girl, because she was Jewish, the medical department of the Hamburg health and welfare office asked the hospital to explain its policy concerning Jews. The government agency wanted to know whether it intended to refuse all future Jewish patients.[25]

The Alsterdorfer Institutions replied on 21 August. The hospital director, Pastor Friedrich Lensch, responded that the March 1937 decision on tax exemption had forced the hospital to exclude the Jewish child or face the loss of its tax-exempt status and that it had asked the central office of the Home Mission for advice on how to proceed. The hospital said that it would henceforth accept Jewish patients only if the government certified that such admissions would not affect its tax-exempt status: "We obviously cannot afford to let the presence of some Jewish patients, about 20 among 1,500, cost our institution its nonprofit and charitable status."[26]

In January 1938, the Psychiatric Clinic of Hamburg University Hospital filed a requested report on Irene Tobias with the Hamburg health and welfare office, providing a diagnosis of "severe retardation and epilepsy."[27] The health and welfare office thereupon approached the Ricklinger Institutions in Holstein, another hospital of the Home Mission, about taking Tobias, informing them at the same time that the Alsterdorfer Institutions, actually the best place for the child, had refused admittance.[28] The Schleswig-Holstein office of the Home Mission then wrote to Pastor Lensch, asking the reason for the refusal, because it wanted to act in concert with his institution on fundamental questions.[29] In his reply, Lensch explained the tax-exemption reasons for refusing Jewish patients and urged his colleague to join his institution in refusing to accept or retain Jews.[30]

Starting in September 1937, the Alsterdorfer Institutions urged the Hamburg health and welfare office to transfer all Jewish patients to state homes and hospitals. Lensch supplied the health office with a list of his Jewish patients as well as a list of state institutions that ought to receive them. When the health office hesitated, he persisted, urged it to act, and offered to take German patients if it would take his Jewish patients. His persistence paid off. In late October 1938, most Jewish patients were transferred from the Alsterdorfer Institutions to the Langenhorn state hospital and the Farmsen and Oberalten-allee state homes. The few that remained were transferred soon thereafter, and the Alsterdorfer Institutions were finally cleared of Jews.[31]

By that time, the tax-exempt status of private institutions with Jewish patients was no longer threatened because the Reich Ministry of Finance had already ruled that acceptance of Jews transferred at the request of government agencies would not affect that status.[32] In any event, as postwar evidence suggests, the bureaucratic exchanges were a sham; Pastor Friedrich Lensch, the Alsterdorfer director, was determined to remove his Jewish patients and used the tax-exemption issue only as a pretext.[33]

In June 1938, the German government launched another attack against Jewish patients in German hospitals. New regulations governing Jewish patients were added to an RMdI circular, signed by Hans Pfundtner, dealing with general hospital conditions. Pointing to the supposed "danger of race defilement [Rassenschande]," the RMdI demanded that Jews "be physically separated from patients of German or related blood" and that particular attention be paid to enforcement at state hospitals and nursing homes.[34]

This bureaucratic order, designed to apply the Nuremberg racial laws with utmost stringency, caused consternation in government agencies that administered state hospitals. Although the administrators agreed with the goal of the order, they argued that race defilement was impossible because male and female patients were housed in separate wards. They also objected to the financial burden physical separation would impose on their hospitals.[35] Even the most rabid Nazi administrator, Fritz Bernotat of Hessen-Nassau in Wiesbaden, raised these objections, at the same time indicating that he had already done his best to create separate wards when the numbers justified such action.[36] Nevertheless, local agencies moved to comply. In the province of Hanover, the government agency thus required each hospital to report the number of Jewish patients and to prepare for each a file card that described the contact between that patient and all German patients.[37]

In the south German state of Württemberg, the concentration of Jews in one or two institutions was considered the best way to separate Jewish from German patients. Unlike Prussia, where special provincial agencies oversaw state hospitals and nursing homes for the handicapped, in Württemberg such supervision was the responsibility of the Ministry of Interior. There Eugen Stähle served as chief medical officer; Otto Mauthe was his specialist for state hospitals and psychiatric services. As we have seen, Stähle and Mauthe were intimately involved with the euthanasia killings and totally committed to promoting the goals of the Nazi regime.

In Württemberg as elsewhere, hospitals and homes refused to admit Jewish patients, and in March and April 1939, the Jewish welfare agency in Stuttgart asked the Württemberg Ministry of Interior to decide where to place Jewish patients.[38] The ministry did not reply but started negotiations with hospitals to resolve the problem. At any rate, state hospitals also approached the ministry for a decision. The state hospital at Weinsberg thus notified the ministry in May 1939 that it feared that relatives of German patients would protest if they continued to share quarters with Jews, adding that although "such protests have not yet occurred, they can do so any day." [39]

Late in May 1939, the ministry decided to concentrate Jewish patients at the Württemberg state hospital at Zwiefalten, where special Jewish wards would be established. Mauthe privately informed various hospital directors of the decision, and shortly thereafter Stähle authorized letters to be sent to hospitals setting forth the new policy.[40] Almost immediately, Württemberg institutions requested permission to transfer their Jewish patients to Zwiefalten.[41] But transfers were not as simple as the ministry had imagined. On 31 May 1939, the Zwiefalten hospital complained that it was overcrowded and made further admissions of Jewish patients contingent on an increase in staff and available beds. The ministry postponed a decision, meanwhile considering whether deadlines for the transfers could be suspended until other ways to ease Zwiefalten's staff shortage could be explored.[42]

On 24 June 1939, Mauthe informed a meeting of Württemberg psychiatrists that the transfer of Jewish patients to Zwiefalten would take place "over time." [43] The ministry also had to modify its decision that transfer to Zwiefalten would apply to all Jewish patients. Zwiefalten was a state hospital with facilities for mental patients and was not suitable for patients who did not suffer from a mental illness.[44] The ministry agreed and informed institutions that "the state hospital at Zwiefalten can obviously only accept patients who must be placed into a mental institution." [45] After several months, the ministry eventually decided that Jewish mental patients would be concentrated at Zwiefalten and Jewish patients suffering from feeblemindedness, epilepsy, or other nonmental disabilities would be concentrated at the Catholic nursing home at Heggbach.[46] Finally, in December 1939, the ministry informed the Jewish welfare agency of the new policy: "Until further notice, in Württemberg Jews suffering from mental illness will be placed at the Zwiefalten state hospital and Jews suffering from feeblemindedness at the Heggbach nursing home." [47]

A surviving document reveals the callous disregard exhibited by ministry officials toward Jewish patients and their relatives. On 18 April 1940, Hanne Leus petitioned the ministry on behalf of her sister, Charlotte Schulheimer, who had been transferred from a local psychiatric clinic in Göppingen to the Weinsberg state hospital. Leus feared that the transfer would retard her sister's promising recovery from depression and requested that she be returned to Göppingen at her own expense. On the letter, one ministry official, probably Otto Mauthe, wrote a memo about this request, noting that "forty patients were transferred to Weinsberg, including one Jewish woman, and it is significant that from that side we immediately receive a petition to reverse the transfer." He urged that the petition be rejected on principle but that a transfer to a Jewish institution at the patient's expense could be permitted.

On the same letter, another ministry bureaucrat, probably Eugen Stähle, added his handwritten comment, displaying his antisemitic outrage at the request in less than elegant language:

> Away! And the women and children of the German men killed in battle! This scum is the author of the war and does not deserve pity! Look at the Polish campaign!![48]

The onset of the euthanasia killings in 1940 would obviously affect handicapped Jewish patients. Similarly, institutionalized Jewish patients had not been exempted from the compulsory sterilization law. Thus evidence shows that at least one Jewish woman was sterilized in the Hamburg Alsterdorfer Institutions and at least one Jewish man in the Brandenburg state hospital at Teupitz.[49] And in 1938 the restrictions imposed on the admittance of Jewish patients to German hospitals was specifically waived for those admitted for compulsory sterilization.[50]

It is inconceivable that handicapped Jews would not have been included in the euthanasia killing operation, but that is exactly what Brack and other T4 functionaries maintained at Nuremberg. They argued that Jews were excluded from the benefit of "mercy death" granted German handicapped patients. But they could not deny that in 1940 groups of Jewish patients were transported from German institutions and did not return, as demonstrated by prosecution documents submitted at Nuremberg by the United States that included the transport list of Jews taken from Eglfing-Haar.[51] The T4 functionaries were, nevertheless, able to obscure the fate of handicapped Jewish patients, and their deception has continued to mislead historians.[52] Every statement the T4 defendants and witnesses made at Nuremberg about Jewish patients was simply not true.

Jews were victims of the euthanasia killings from the very beginning. Although they had been excluded from any therapy that could be considered positive, they had been included in every type of negative therapy. Regardless of talk about "mercy death," the regime viewed euthanasia as the most radical form of exclusion, and Jews were therefore never exempted from this negative type of selection. The number of Jews killed by T4 can no longer be reconstructed but undoubtedly totaled several thousand. Early in 1940, the Reich Association of Jews in Germany estimated that there were "at least" 2,500 Jews in German public institutions. Since this number represented the lowest possible verifiable figure, and since it did not include Jewish patients in Austria and in private institutions (as well as Jewish hybrids and Jews in

THE ORIGINS OF NAZI GENOCIDE

mixed marriages who were not members of the Reich Association), one can estimate that about 4,000, perhaps even 5,000, Jews became victims of the euthanasia killings.[53]

The memorial book for murdered Baden and Württemberg Jews, compiled by the Württemberg state archive, lists twenty-six handicapped Jewish patients who were killed in Grafeneck.[54] The first Jewish victim, Berta Mändle, died in Grafeneck on 7 February 1940.[55] The last two, Flora Katz and Korin Breisacher, died there on 17 December 1940.[56] In addition, a number of other patients are listed with the place of death unknown. The dates when they were transferred suggest, at least for some of them, that they were murdered in one of the killing centers but not as part of a Jewish transport. For example, Moritz Gundelfinger was transferred from the Markgröningen hospital on 26 November 1940, and his brother was notified of his death.[57]

Württemberg was not the only region where Jewish patients were killed as individuals. The first transport of handicapped patients left Eglfing-Haar on 18 January 1940 for Grafeneck, where the twenty-five men in that transport were killed. Ludwig "Israel" Alexander was the first person and the only Jew listed on the Eglfing-Haar transport list.[58] The name "Israel," which all male Jews were forced to take on after 1 January 1939, indicates that Alexander was considered Jewish under the Nuremberg racial laws. Alexander was thus probably the first handicapped Jewish patient murdered in the gas chamber of one of the euthanasia killing centers. Scattered documents reveal other individual Jewish patients murdered in the T4 killing centers. For example, a surviving letter from the Halle welfare office inquired on 6 January 1942 whether it could obtain from the Reich Association retroactive payment for the upkeep of Alfred "Israel" Löwe, a patient at the Altscherbitz hospital in the Prussian province of Saxony. The Halle office mentions in passing that Löwe "died on 11 December 1940" in the Bernburg killing center.[59]

Handicapped Jewish patients in German institutions, including those married to Germans and those with only partial Jewish ancestry, could obviously have been selected because they were handicapped, without regard to ancestry, as were their non-Jewish fellow patients. As we have seen, questionnaires were filled out for all handicapped patients, including Jews, and the selection of Jews on an individual basis could and did proceed in the same way as the selection of non-Jews. But this process was slow, and some Jews—those in institutions not immediately slated for transfer—would be killed relatively late. The process was also not foolproof; some Jewish patients might have survived. Apparently, the T4 managers thought that following standard procedures for killing the handicapped was too slow and too uncertain, and they decided to change policy and transfer and kill Jews as a group, not on the basis of evaluated questionnaires but simply because they were Jews.[60]

The decision systematically to murder handicapped Jewish patients still in

German hospitals was apparently made in March or April 1940. At that time, the Gestapo as well as T4 started to collect statistics on institutionalized Jewish patients. In late March or early April, local offices of the Gestapo began to demand that Jewish communities provide them monthly reports on the number of Jewish patients and soon thereafter also requested that all monthly changes be reported.[61] On 15 April 1940, Herbert Linden of the RMdI asked all local authorities to report the numbers of Jewish patients. His letter to state and provincial agencies administering state hospitals and nursing homes required them to submit within three weeks lists of Jewish patients "suffering from mental illness or feeblemindedness."[62]

The various state agencies complied, although some did not meet the ministry's three-week deadline. In Hamburg, the administration did not mail its request for information to the hospitals and homes until 21 May 1940. It received most answers immediately, the last one on 1 June.[63] On 12 June, Linden reminded the Hamburg administration that he still had not received its list of Jewish patients.[64] On 25 June, Hamburg forwarded a list of Jewish patients to the RMdI.[65] Five Hamburg institutions did not have any Jews; as we have seen, the Alsterdorfer Institutions, one of the five, had transferred their Jewish patients to other Hamburg hospitals. Three homes together reported thirty-two Jews, and the university clinic reported five Jewish patients. The state hospital at Langenhorn reported the largest number of Jews: thirty men and thirty-six women.[66]

The purpose of Linden's circular soon became apparent. Jewish patients in various hospitals and homes were transferred to a small number of institutions serving as assembly centers. From there, they were collected by T4's Gekrat and transported to the killing centers. This happened first in the Prussian province of Brandenburg and the city of Berlin, where Jewish patients were assembled in the hospital complex Berlin-Buch, from which they were moved in a number of transports during June and July 1940.

A few surviving documents record this process. Five days after Linden mailed his circular on 15 April 1940, the Potsdam district governor (Regierungspräsident) asked the Neuruppin hospital in the province of Brandenburg to report its Jewish patients.[67] On 7 June, T4's Gekrat informed Neuruppin that on 20 June it would pick up about sixty-five Jewish patients.[68] The record does not reveal whether these patients were actually collected or where they were taken. But on 12 July, the Brandenburg agency overseeing hospitals and homes notified its institutions that the city of Berlin had finally agreed to accept all Brandenburg Jewish patients. The agreement provided for their transfer to the Berlin-Buch hospital complex. Using language that would reappear in later circulars in other cities, the agreement specified exactly who would be included: "All patients from Brandenburg and Berlin, both those on welfare and those paying for their own keep, are to be included. But they must be 100 percent Jews [*Volljuden*], with German or Polish citizenship or stateless persons. Jewish hybrids [*Mischlinge*] of any degree as well as persons with citizenship elsewhere (for example, Romanians, Czechs, Hungarians, etc.) are excluded. This must be followed exactly." [69] In response to this request, the Neuruppin institution transferred Jewish patients to Buch on 18 July. [70] Of course, they did not remain there. Almost immediately, Buch sent Neuruppin a list of forty-one Neuruppin male Jewish patients transferred from Buch on 20 July and eighteen Neuruppin female Jewish patients transferred on 22 July. [71]

This pattern was repeated in numerous places. In north Germany, the transfer of Jewish patients to the assembly center at the Langenhorn hospital complex in Hamburg started early in September 1940. On 30 August 1940, the RMdI wrote to the provincial administration in Schleswig-Holstein about the transfer of Jewish patients, and on 3 September this circular was passed on to the government agency supervising hospitals and homes, which in turn notified hospitals on 6 September. The RMdI provided a justification for these transfers: "The continuing situation where Jews are quartered together with Germans in state hospitals and nursing homes can no longer be accepted, because this has generated complaints both from the nursing staff and from relatives of German patients." This justification was an obvious invention, as there is no surviving record of such complaints. The RMdI used the same guidelines applied at Berlin-Buch to define the group to be included, again warning that hybrids and foreign nationals had to be exempted. The Jewish patients were to be moved to Langenhorn no later than 18 September, and they would be transferred from there on 23 September. The ministry circular did not reveal the final destination for these transfers, stating only that they would be taken from Langenhorn "to an assembly center [*Sammelanstalt*]." [72]

Local hospitals responded rapidly. On 10 September, the Neustadt hospital in Holstein thus reported to the administration that eleven Jewish patients were ready for transfer, supplying their names and dates and places of birth. [73] They were moved to Hamburg on 12 and 13 September, and on 14 September, Neustadt sent their records to Langenhorn. [74] On 23 September, these Neustadt Jewish patients, together with Jewish patients from Hamburg and other north German cities, were picked up by Gekrat according to plan. [75]

In Bavaria, the Eglfing-Haar hospital served as an assembly center for Jewish patients. We can follow the process using documents involving the Jewish patients at the Bavarian state hospital and nursing home in Lohr on the Main. On 4 September 1940, the Bavarian Ministry of Interior informed the Lohr institution that all Jewish patients had to be transferred to Eglfing-Haar on 14 September, adding the usual restrictions against the transfer of hybrids and foreign Jews. [76] The transport of nineteen Jewish patients actually left Lohr by train on 16 September and reached Eglfing-Haar on the same day. [77]

At Eglfing-Haar, Jewish patients from all Bavarian hospitals were assembled in the middle of September and quartered in two isolated buildings. One male nurse later described these Jewish patients: "There were many elderly gentlemen, including a city councilman from the Rhineland, businesspeople, lawyers, an acquaintance of Thomas Mann," as well as "frail, elderly ladies" and "a boy from Gmund whose parents had escaped to England."[78] On 20 September, Gekrat collected these handicapped Jewish patients: 33 Eglfing-Haar patients and 158 patients from other Bavarian institutions, for a total of 191.[79] That day, the Eglfing-Haar director, Hermann Pfannmüller, sent the list of transferred Jews to the Ministry of Interior in Munich, summarizing the results of the day's work: "I herewith report to the State Ministry that henceforth my institution will accommodate only Aryan mental patients."[80]

The same process took place in other regions. For example, in Austria 400 Jewish patients were collected at the Vienna Am Steinhof hospital and were moved from there as a group at the end of August 1940.[81]

The Wunstorf state hospital in the Prussian province of Hanover became the assembly center for twenty-five institutions in northwest Germany. The process started on 30 August 1940, as elsewhere, with a letter from the RMdI announcing the imminent transfer of Jewish patients.[82] On 10 September, Herbert Linden of the RMdI followed up a telephone conversation by sending an express letter to the governor of Hanover, listing the institutions and the number of their Jewish patients scheduled to be transferred to Wunstorf.[83] Everything went according to plan, and on 27 September Gekrat picked up the 158 Jewish patients collected from twenty-five institutions and assembled at Wunstorf.[84]

In the Kassel district of Hessen-Nassau, the Jewish patients were assembled in the Giessen state hospital after the arrival of the RMdI circular of 30 August 1940. Jewish patients from several hospitals were transferred to Giessen on 25 September, and all were collected by Gekrat from Giessen on 1 October.[85]

Jewish patients were not all transferred at the same time. For example, in the Rhineland, they were not collected until February 1941. On 15 January, Gekrat informed Dr. Hertz's Private Clinic in Bonn that the RMdI had issued orders that the clinic's Jewish patients had to be transferred to the Andernach state hospital and that the Gekrat organization would provide transportation.[86] On 29 January, the public health office in Bonn provided the clinic with the RMdI guidelines on whom to include.[87] Finally, on 10 February, five Jewish patients were sent from Bonn to Andernach.[88] The next day, these five patients, together with forty-seven Jewish patients from other institutions, were transferred in a Gekrat transport.[89]

The handicapped Jewish patients who had been assigned to these Jewish transports had been chosen not on the basis of their questionnaires but solely on the basis of lists compiled by institutions in response to the RMdI circular. Although we know that these transports went directly to the euthanasia killing centers, none of the surviving official documents from 1940 provides a specific destination, mentioning only "transfer to an assembly center," supposedly an institution where Jewish patients would no longer mingle with Germans. But this changed as paperwork began to accumulate. Soon relatives, welfare offices, insurance companies, and the courts inquired about the Jewish patients who had disappeared. At first, the institutions stonewalled, replying only that on orders of the ministry the patient had been transferred to another institution with a Jewish transport, adding, "The name of that institution is not known." [90]

The correspondence of the Wunstorf hospital, from which handicapped Jewish patients were transferred to an unknown destination on 27 September 1940, provides some indication of the policy developed to deal with such inquiries.[91] The hospital received letters from relatives in various German cities and several foreign countries. On 27 September, the day the patients left Wunstorf, a patient's sister wrote from Soest near Münster: "At the request of my mother, I beg for information about the condition of my sister, Martha Sara Hirsch from Soest. We would like to know how she is doing and how well she has taken the transfer. How long will she be in your institutions, and where will she end up? Return postage enclosed." On 1 October, a patient's brother wrote from the Netherlands: "I received the news that my brother, Josef Frankenstein, has been transferred, since I have not heard from him in some time. How is his health? Hopefully all is well. Does my brother do his work assignment well? What kind of work does he do? Aunt Henriette and his sister Leni send their heartfelt greetings." On 14 October, Liselotte Rosenholz from Hanover wrote about her son: "On 21 September my son Heinz Israel was moved to your place from Rothenburg, so that with other patients he could be transferred elsewhere. As I have not received any news about where my dear little Heinz [Heinzchen] has ended up, you can imagine my distress. Please permit me the inquiry, whether you can tell me to where the patients have been moved."

On 3 November, Werner "Israel" Feld, the blind father of a patient, wrote from Berlin: "I respectfully ask whether my son is still with you or to where he has been moved. As a father it is terrible not to know the fate of one's child. I know the sad state of his health, and am prepared for anything." And on 25 December, Heinz "Israel" Stern wrote from Frankfurt: "Dear Josef! We have not heard from you in such a long time, and I have just heard from Göttingen that you are now in Wunstorf. Why don't you write us any more? If you need something, please let us know. I am enclosing postage, please send news soon."

The Wunstorf answer to these and all other letters was the same: the institution denied knowledge about the location of the Jewish patients. Indeed, officially the institution did not know what had happened to the patients; T4's

Gekrat did not provide that information. But unofficially, by word of mouth, Gekrat apparently did set down rules on how to reply to inquiries. First, the institution simply replied that the destination was unknown. Second, Wunstorf referred those who inquired about patients to the Hanover office of the Reich Association of Jews in Germany, but the Reich Association also had no information. Third, Wunstorf referred everyone to Gekrat, providing the address of T4's transport company. Gekrat did not, however, answer inquiries.

Gekrat did provide the institution with a fallback position, permitting Wunstorf to mention in some letters that the Jewish patients had been transferred to an institution in the General Government, at times alluding also to the Lublin region. On 16 December 1940, Wunstorf even provided the name of the "Cholm hospital near Lublin" to someone making an inquiry, an address the institution had obviously received from Gekrat. The Reich Association heard these rumors and wrote to Lublin to inquire about the Jewish patients, only to be told that all Lublin patients had been moved to Warsaw and Cracow but not whether any Jews were included.[92]

The supposed destination in the Lublin region served not only as camouflage for Gekrat but also as a means to extort money. Those supporting Jewish patients—relatives, welfare offices, insurance agencies, and the Reich Association—stopped payment for bed and board as of the day the patients were transferred. Because T4 wanted to continue receiving funds following the transfer, it had to provide some answers to their inquiries. Thus Gekrat wrote to the state hospital in Lohr on 21 February 1941, requesting the names of those financially responsible for the Jews deported from Lohr on 16 September 1940. Gekrat claimed to represent the institutions that had received these Jewish patients, who naturally wanted to collect payment due for bed and board. In this letter, Gekrat mentioned that these institutions were all located in the General Government.[93] Thus citing the General Government as the final destination served as camouflage for the collection of unearned fees.

This argument sounded plausible. After all, the deportations to Nisko in the General Government had taken place in October 1939, and the deportation of the Stettin Jews to the Lublin region had occurred in February 1940. It was therefore known that Jews had been deported and that their destination had been Poland. As we have seen, Viktor Brack and other T4 functionaries argued at Nuremberg that Poland had been the destination of the Jewish patients and that they had not been killed in the euthanasia program, an argument they later repeated to German courts.[94]

But the fiction that Jewish patients were living at some Polish institution could not be maintained for long. Eventually, relatives and public agencies received death notices, as had the relatives of murdered German patients. But these notices did not come from killing centers inside Germany. They arrived from occupied Poland on stationery with the heading, "Mental Asylum

THE ORIGINS OF NAZI GENOCIDE

Chelm, Post Office Lublin" (Irrenanstalt Chelm, Post Lublin). Further correspondence was usually answered by "Local Police Office, Chelm II" (Die Ortspolizeibehörde, Chelm II). The stationery was not, however, always exactly the same. Sometimes the name was "Cholm" and not "Chelm"; however, other words, print, placement, and looks were identical.[95]

Unlike the condolence letters sent to murdered German patients, those from Chelm were brief and to the point. They noted only that the person had died, providing the date and cause of death. Two copies of the death certificate, certified by the registry officer at Chelm II or Cholm II, were enclosed. The death notices were spread out from November 1940 to March 1941. Obviously, T4 collected payment for patient expenses during the time between transfer and death notification.

Chelm death notices were sent not only to relatives but also to various public agencies, especially those with financial responsibility for the patients.[96] With true Germanic thoroughness, death notices were entered by local registry offices on the permanent birth records of the murdered Jewish patients. Thus the notice "died Chelm II" or "died Cholm II" with the date was entered on nineteenth-century birth records, usually just below the 1939 notice that the person had added "Israel" or "Sara" to his or her name.[97]

The entire enterprise was a fabrication that existed only on paper. Still, the idea that Jewish patients were transported to Polish hospitals and that they either died or were killed there dominated postwar historiography and continues to be believed to this day. Even accounts that do not accept this deception still maintain that some patients might possibly have been sent to Poland.[98] But this is simply not true. No handicapped Jewish patients transported by Gekrat ever arrived in Poland. In fact, no Chelm hospital existed to receive patients in 1940. On 12 January 1940, the Germans had killed all patients at the psychiatric hospital in Chelm, and it was closed for the remainder of the war.[99] Although it is not possible to trace every transport of transferred Jewish patients, we do know the destination of several large transports, and the evidence that they went directly to one of the euthanasia killing centers is incontrovertible.

The evidence includes an eyewitness account of the murder of Jewish patients from Berlin-Buch at the Brandenburg killing center. As we have seen, handicapped Jews were collected at Buch and transferred from there in the summer of 1940. There were several such transports, most of which apparently occurred in July 1940, although one document reveals that transfers had taken place as early as June 1940. Thus in November 1940, the Berlin central welfare office notified local welfare offices that "during a special operation [Sonderaktion] almost all Jewish mental patients from institutions in the Reich capital and in the province of Brandenburg were transferred to the General Government during the month of July 1940."[100]

The eyewitness account of the murder of Jewish patients comes from Herbert Kalisch, the T4 electrician, who was interrogated in 1960 and 1961 by German prosecutors.[101] On one occasion, he accompanied a transport of patients, and he testified that "as far as I remember, it was still in June 1940." The T4 people wore either white coats to look like hospital staff or green uniforms to resemble the police.

> We drove in six large buses of the Reich railroads to the mental hospital Buch near Berlin, and there collected about 100 women with children and about 100 men, all members of the Jewish race.... The transport went to the city of Brandenburg on the Havel, to the old prison in the center of the city, which, being empty, had been remodeled into a crematorium. After arrival at the prison, the persons were put in cells, separated by gender. Still on the same day, immediately after arrival, about twenty persons at a time were taken from the cells. The persons were undressed completely, as they were told that they would be taken to another building for bathing and delousing. First they took women and children for gassing. To pacify these patients, physicians gave them a cursory examination. Thereafter, they were placed in a room with wooden benches, which looked, more or less, like a shower room. But before they entered the room, they were marked with consecutive numbers. The doors were locked as soon as the prescribed number of persons had entered the "shower room." At the ceiling were shower heads through which gas entered the room. The gas was ventilated after fifteen to twenty minutes, as soon as one had discovered by looking through the peep-hole that all people inside were no longer alive. As the earlier examination had noted which persons had gold teeth, these persons could now be discovered by their marked number. The gold teeth were pulled from the dead people. Thereupon SS men stationed at the prison carried the dead people from the "shower room" and took them to the crematorium. On that very day, the entire transport was eliminated in this fashion.[102]

At a later interrogation, Kalisch enlarged on his testimony: "The transport that was gassed in the gas chamber of the former prison in Brandenburg on the Havel in about June 1940 contained only Jews, who I would estimate were men and women between the ages of eighteen and fifty-five."[103]

Kalisch's eyewitness testimony is not the only evidence we possess that Jewish patients were gassed on German soil. The 1940 pocket diary of Irmfried Eberl survived the war. As physician-in-charge at Brandenburg, Eberl noted the arrival of transports for gassing, often listing the number of victims and usually indicating the composition by using the capital letter "M" for men (*Männer*), "F" for women (*Frauen*), and "J" for Jews (*Juden*). The diary contains a relatively large number of "J" entries, and some match exactly the schedule of transfers known to us. As we have seen, handicapped Jewish patients from north Germany were collected at Langenhorn in Hamburg and were transferred from there on 23 September 1940. Gekrat took them directly to Brandenburg, and they were killed there on that very day. In his pocket diary, Eberl entered for Monday, 23 September, "Hamburg-Langenhorn J." We also know that the Jewish patients from northwest Germany, collected at Wunstorf in the province of Hanover, were transferred on 27 September 1940. They too were killed at Brandenburg on that very day. For Friday, 27 September, Eberl entered "Hannover-Wunstorf J." [104]

Once the decision had been made to kill the Jewish patients as a group, T4 apparently intended simply to have them disappear. Thus "transferred to the General Government" was to serve as the last announcement, just as later the final news about deported German Jews was often the notice that they had been sent "to the East." But greed—the determination to enrich the T4 organization by collecting payment for the bed and board of transferred Jewish patients—inspired the T4 managers to invent the Chelm institutional address.

In a memo about the Bernburg killing center, Eberl described the method he followed to process a transport, including the necessary paperwork. As an aside, he mentioned that the T4 Central Office did not want to register any concentration camp prisoners killed in Operation 14f13, a procedure he opposed, adding, "In these cases I point to my experiences with Jewish transports in the year 1940. There the Berlin central office also did not want any registration, but I ordered this done anyhow at Brandenburg, and it was later shown that this was the correct procedure." [105]

The reason T4 later appreciated Eberl's meticulous record keeping was its need to obtain names and addresses so that it could fraudulently bill the individual or agency responsible for a patient's care. T4 needed to know which institutions patients had come from and who was responsible for payments. At other killing centers, this information was more difficult to obtain. Thus T4 did not know the names and addresses of those who supported the Jewish patients from Eglfing-Haar, probably killed not at Brandenburg but at either Grafeneck or Hartheim, and, as in the Gekrat letter to Lohr, had to seek them later.

Since the handicapped Jewish patients were killed on the same day that they were transferred, a postdated death notice permitted T4 to collect money for several months after the patients were already dead, thus defrauding relatives, insurance companies, and welfare offices. For example, Toni Louise Lippmann disappeared from Buch in July 1940, and the family received the Chelm death notice on 6 January 1941, permitting T4 to collect money for about five months. [106] Chelm death notices for Jewish patients who had been transferred from Neustadt in Holstein to Langenhorn and then transported from there on 23 September 1940 arrived between 4 December 1940 and

31 March 1941. T4 thus collected between two and six months' extra payment.[107]

In the case of murdered non-Jewish patients, T4 was relatively fast in sending death notices because it wanted to avoid popular unrest, but with Jewish patients, it was able to disregard completely the feelings of relatives without fear of repercussions. Thus on 13 August 1940, Charlotte Graetz in Berlin-Charlottenburg inquired about her aunt, Eva "Sara" Lichtenstein née Graff. On 15 August, the Buch hospital replied that her aunt was transferred on 15 July 1940 and that she would eventually get information from the receiving institution. On 7 November, Graetz wrote again, this time to the Central Health Office in Berlin, which replied on 14 November that her aunt had been transferred with "numerous other Jewish patients" and that they had been moved "to the General Government Warsaw." The health office added that she could obtain more information from Gekrat. Finally, on 17 February 1941, Chelm wrote to Graetz that her aunt had died on 16 February and enclosed a death certificate.[108]

On 7 November 1940, Chelm notified Flora Tauber in Vienna that her son had died the previous day: "We must inform you, that your son, Alfred Israel Tauber, who had been here for some time, has died here. For possible use, we are enclosing two certified copies of the death certificate." Tauber was no doubt a Jewish patient transferred from Am Steinhof in late August 1940. We do not know when the mother actually received the Chelm letter, but on 2 December, she wrote to the Lublin post office box number listed on the Chelm stationery—a box number that undoubtedly was a cover for T4 in Berlin—concerning her son's burial. The Chelm II police replied on 7 April 1941 that her letter had not arrived until 12 December, which failed to explain why the reply took an extra three months. In any event, the letter informed the mother that the urn containing her son's ashes had already been buried in the institution's cemetery "on orders from higher offices." Flora Tauber persisted. On 16 April 1941, she again wrote to Chelm, this time about her son's grave, requesting a memorial plaque. The Chelm II police answered on 14 May that they could not accommodate her wishes. Since the institution cared for the grave at no cost to her, she was advised to wait until the end of the war when there might be a possibility of erecting such a plaque. This was the last of the surviving letters, thus ending this bizarre correspondence.[109]

The entire Chelm enterprise, designed to enrich T4's coffers, was completely amateurish. The letterhead was simple and did not have the normal appearance of a German institutional letterhead. In any event, it was not clear why a Polish institution near Lublin would use a German letterhead. Further, the confusion over the name, sometimes spelled Chelm and sometimes Cholm, indicated that as far as forgery was concerned, the T4 people were dilettantes. Still, no one, including German government agencies, seemed to

THE ORIGINS OF NAZI GENOCIDE

notice these discrepancies. The same was true about the way payment was collected. The Chelm institution near Lublin asked that monies due be paid into "Post Office Account Berlin No. 17050," without explaining why a Polish institution would have an account in Berlin.[110]

The fraudulent letters were actually written in Berlin. They were the responsibility of T4's liquidation office, located at the Columbus House. At first headed by Fritz Hirsche and later by Gerhard Simon, the liquidation office took care of the paperwork left over from killing operations. One of its departments, headed by Arnold Behrens and designated XY, dealt with the Chelm notices.[111] T4 probably had an agreement with the German post office to redirect letters sent to Chelm post office box 822 in Lublin but did not mail Chelm letters directly from Berlin. A T4 courier took them to Lublin for mailing so that the Lublin post office cancellation would appear on the letter. The T4 courier Erich Fettke, who transported documents between the killing centers and T4 headquarters in Germany and later also between Berlin and the Lublin killing centers of Operation Reinhard, was probably the courier for the Chelm mailing.[112]

The Chelm enterprise demonstrates how secret government activities can get out of hand. T4 had orders to kill the Jewish patients, but its decision to manufacture the Chelm notices to make money was probably not specifically sanctioned from above. Considering the phobia about secrecy and the fear that the KdF would be exposed, the amateurish forgery enterprise presented serious dangers to such a secret project. The decision to proceed with the scheme shows not only how greed operated but also that T4 felt immune from normal bureaucratic constraints. This is illustrated by one recorded misuse of the forgery equipment.

A certain Richard Kochan worked for T4 at the Columbus House. Arrested in August 1942 by the Gestapo, Kochan was tried by the Berlin Special Court (Sondergericht), which had jurisdiction over political crimes. He was convicted and sentenced to death on 10 February 1943 and executed at Plötzensee prison on 16 March. The charge of fraud and deception was vague, and at the trial, the defendant was prohibited from explaining his crime and the judges were prevented from asking questions. With the aid of two secretaries at the KdF, who testified at his trial, Kochan had used forged papers to impersonate a police officer and to enrich himself. Kochan and other T4 employees apparently used various forged documents to obtain special privileges, including free travel on the railroad and free deck chairs at the beach. Kochan also appears to have used forged identity papers to convince Jews that he could get them exit visas for money. These were all minor offenses, but the secrecy of his trial and the severity of his sentence reveals that the KdF recognized that such a case threatened the secret enterprise.[113]

The decision to kill the handicapped Jewish patients formed an important link between euthanasia and the final solution because it reveals the accelerated efforts to draw more targeted groups into the killing enterprise. Although we have no documentary evidence about who made the decision to transfer and kill Jewish patients as a group, the determination to depart from normal routine had to have been decided by Hitler's two plenipotentiaries for euthanasia, Karl Brandt and Philipp Bouhler. And because they held their decision-making sessions at Hitler's headquarters, it is likely that the Führer was consulted before the order to kill handicapped Jews as a group was issued.[114] Late in June 1941, the German killing operations expanded to include all Jews. Until then, the handicapped Jewish patients in Germany and Austria had been the only group of Jewish victims. The decision to kill handicapped Jewish patients as a group, made in the spring of 1940 at the highest level, foreshadowed, possibly foreordained, the final solution of 1941.

The patients in the Jewish hospital at Bendorf-Sayn had not been included in the killing operation against handicapped Jewish patients. Since they had already been isolated from German society, they did not require immediate attention. On 12 December 1940, after most Jewish handicapped patients in German hospitals had already been murdered, Herbert Linden of the RMdI decreed that henceforth Jewish patients were to be admitted only to the Bendorf-Sayn hospital of the Reich Association.[115] However, this decree was never widely applied; Bendorf-Sayn did not have the facilities to accept all Jewish patients, and those who had hoped that all Jews could be placed in a Jewish institution were disappointed.[116] Jewish patients who had somehow escaped the group transfers, or those who were newly admitted, had to be retained for the moment in German institutions.[117]

In addition, Jews committed by the courts could not be sent to Bendorf-Sayn because private institutions could not exercise government functions.[118] On 6 February 1942, the RJM therefore issued a directive to all attorneys general, ordering that henceforth all Jews committed to state institutions in each region had to be placed into designated hospitals. Those listed were well-known euthanasia centers: Langenhorn, Görden, Tapiau, Am Steinhof, and Eglfing-Haar.[119]

The systematic deportation of German and Austrian Jews commenced in October 1941.[120] Thereafter, Jewish patients were simply added to the regular deportation transports to the East.[121] Thus handicapped Jewish patients in Bendorf-Sayn were added to the Jewish deportations from Koblenz on 22 March, 30 April, 15 June, and 27 July 1942.[122] After the deportations, the Bendorf-Sayn hospital was empty; only three staff members living in mixed marriages, including the physician Wilhelm Rosenau, remained. The building complex was seized, and after much bureaucratic infighting between the city of Koblenz, the Gestapo, and various Nazi party agencies, it was used as an alternate hospital facility for Koblenz.[123]

THE ORIGINS OF NAZI GENOCIDE

Jewish staff and patients were deported to the Lublin region, where they were commingled with all other Jews and shared their fate.[124] The handicapped were especially vulnerable because of their visibility. Local Nazis certainly noticed them. The Nazi propagandist who reported that among Jews arriving in the Lublin region were "eighty-nine total idiots [Vollidioten]" might well have been referring to Bendorf-Sayn patients.[125] Such accounts from the East probably misled historians to conclude that the arrival in Poland in 1942 of handicapped Jews validated the argument in favor of Poland as the destination for the handicapped Jews transferred by Gekrat in 1940.[126] But these deportations of 1941–42 had nothing to do with T4 and were totally unrelated to the supposed 1940 transports to Chelm or Cholm. Instead, they were part of the mass deportation of German Jews to the East, where the handicapped Jewish patients deported in 1942 from Bendorf-Sayn were to be killed along with all other deported Jews.

Despite the killings and deportations, handicapped Jewish patients continued to appear from time to time in various German hospitals. Herbert Linden therefore issued another circular on 10 November 1942, announcing that the Jewish institution at Bendorf-Sayn was closed and that henceforth all Jewish patients were to be sent to the Jewish hospital in Berlin.[127] But even this final command could not be fully implemented; the Jewish hospital in Berlin's Iranische Straße did not have enough room to accommodate any more patients.[128] In any event, by that time the issue was largely moot. The deportation of the German and Austrian Jews was in full swing, and soon few Jews would be left in Germany and Austria. The fact that the slaughter of the Jews had begun with the murder of handicapped German and Austrian Jews was forgotten as the killing frenzy in the East engulfed vast numbers of Jews from all European countries.

Chapter 14 The Final Solution

On 22 June 1941, the German Wehrmacht invaded the Soviet Union, and the Nazi regime embarked on its second, and far more ambitious, killing operation. Mobile operational units of the SS, the Einsatzgruppen of the Sipo and SD, crossed the Soviet border immediately after the battle troops. In the occupied territory of the Soviet Union, these units shot large numbers of civilians in mass executions.[1] Their primary task was the murder of all Jews on Soviet soil.[2] They also murdered all Gypsies and, wherever possible, the handicapped.[3] The quartermaster of the German army, General Eduard Wagner, thus recorded in September 1941: "Russians consider the feebleminded holy. Nevertheless, killing necessary."[4]

The Germans labeled the murder of Soviet Jews, and the subsequent murder of all Jews within their jurisdiction, as the final solution of the European Jewish question (*Endlösung der europäischen Judenfrage*).[5] The term "final solution," used in the contemporaneous protocol of Reinhard Heydrich's Wannsee conference, has come to stand for the mass murder of Jews, although Hermann Göring in his letter of authorization referred both to "final solution [*Endlösung*]" and to "total solution [*Gesamtlösung*]."[6]

Historians investigating Nazi genocide have long debated who gave the order to kill all Jews, when it was issued, and how it was transmitted.[7] Even though the specific mechanism, including the approximate date, has been a matter of contention, there now appears to be general agreement that Hitler had a deciding voice, although no one has ever discovered, or is likely to discover, a smoking gun.

The chronology of Nazi killing operations provides a road map for those seeking answers to these questions. The murder of the handicapped preceded the murder of Jews and Gypsies, and it is therefore reasonable to conclude that T4's killing operation served as a model for the final solution. The success of the euthanasia policy convinced the Nazi leadership that mass murder was technically feasible, that ordinary men and women were willing to kill large numbers of innocent human beings, and that the bureaucracy would cooperate in such an unprecedented enterprise.

Just as race scientists, psychiatrists, and party ideologues had advocated killing the handicapped even before the killings commenced, German police officers and government administrators in the East proposed killing the Jews before the final solution started.[8] But nothing so radical or unprecedented could be initiated without Hitler's approval. There is no reason to believe that the decision-making process that led to the final solution was substantially different from the one that preceded the euthanasia killings. The decision-making process thus illustrates the linkage between the two killing operations.

As Hans Heinrich Lammers testified at Nuremberg, Hitler gave a direct verbal order to start the T4 killing operation, and as we have seen, the KdF moved quickly to implement this order. But, in the best tradition of CYA (Cover Your Ass), the bureaucrats of the KdF insisted upon written authorization from their Führer both for their own protection and to assure the collaboration of physicians and government agencies. The KdF prepared the text of the authorization, and, backdating it to the day the war had started, Hitler signed it in October 1939.[9]

It seems eminently reasonable to assume that the decision to implement the final solution would have been made in the same way. Although no testimony has survived to document this, Hitler apparently again gave verbal orders, this time commissioning Heinrich Himmler and his SS and police to kill the Jews.[10] However, unlike euthanasia, there was no written authorization. The reasons for this are not difficult to fathom. Too many people had read Hitler's euthanasia authorization, and such widespread knowledge could have implicated him in the T4 killings; obviously, he refused to sign another such document. In addition, the loyal SS could hardly attempt CYA by asking their Führer for an authorization. Still, Heydrich, whose RSHA had to implement the order Hitler gave to Himmler, needed some written commission to compel the cooperation of other government agencies. Hermann Göring therefore supplied a retroactive sanction in a letter dated 31 July 1941 when he authorized Heydrich to "undertake organizational, technical, and financial preparations" for the murder of the European Jews.[11] Just as Hitler did not write but only signed the letter to Brandt and Bouhler prepared by the KdF, Göring did not initiate but only signed the authorization prepared and submitted by Heydrich.[12]

We have no such details about the decision to kill the Gypsies. They were deemed so marginal that their murder provoked no intra-agency rivalries and thus required no written authorization. Nevertheless, even on what was considered a relatively minor policy decision, Hitler was forced to serve as the final arbiter of the Gypsies' fate. For example, in 1942 Martin Bormann discovered that the Reich leader SS had exempted certain pure Gypsies so that research on their "valuable Teutonic practices" could be completed. On 3 December 1942, Bormann complained about this arbitrary change in policy in a letter to Himmler. On the front of this letter, Himmler added a handwritten comment that he would have to prepare data concerning the Gypsies for Hitler.[13]

We do not know the date Hitler issued his order to kill the Jews. Obviously, that order had to precede the killings and Göring's letter, and most historians accept the spring of 1941 as the earliest possible time. But the decision on the highest level to kill handicapped Jewish patients as a group provides at least some indication that a preliminary decision might already have been reached in the spring of 1940. Further, although Hitler believed that the cover of war would make radical exclusion through killing operations possible—which he emphasized by backdating his euthanasia authorization to the day the war began—he nevertheless did not issue a definite order until he was certain that such an ambitious killing enterprise was feasible. But when international conditions, the progress of the war, and the killing capabilities demonstrated by euthanasia made radical exclusion attainable, Jews as a group were included in the killing operations.[14]

Once the order had been given, the SS Einsatzgruppen served as the first means of implementation. In the first sweep through the Soviet Union in 1941 and early 1942, most Soviet Jews were shot; only those able to work for the Germans were permitted to live and relegated to ghettos and camps.[15] But this primitive method of shooting the victims was too public. It also posed logistic problems for the killers, requiring a large killing staff and imposing a psychological burden on the shooters. The SS and police, therefore, soon began to search for a better killing method. They soon turned to the euthanasia program as a model. But carbon monoxide tanks were too expensive, and a dependable supply from distant factories could not be assured. The RSHA motor pool therefore combined the T4 gas van used in the Wartheland with the killing method Albert Widmann had discovered in Bielorussia to develop a gas van, which, like a perpetual motion machine, recycled exhaust fumes to kill its human cargo.[16] And as we have seen, August Becker traveled throughout the Soviet Union to study and perfect these special vans (*Sonderwagen*).

Himmler's men eventually realized, just as the T4 killers had discovered several years earlier, that it was more efficient to bring the victims to a central killing place. It was only logical that these places would be modeled on the T4 centers. (See table 14.1.) But the killers had also learned from the public response to euthanasia that such installations should not be established inside Germany. Therefore, the first killing center of the final solution began functioning in December 1941 at Chelmno (Kulmhof in German) in the Wartheland. Although it was a stationary killing center, it used the gas vans already tested by the Einsatzgruppen. To make use of previous T4 experience, the HSSPF in Posen assigned Herbert Lange, who had used vans to kill the handicapped in the Wartheland and at Soldau, to operate Chelmno.[17]

At the same time, Himmler commissioned Odilo Globocnik, the SSPF in Lublin, to kill the Jews of Poland, an undertaking later named Operation Reinhard in honor of the assassinated Heydrich. To accomplish his mission, Globocnik established three killing centers in the Lublin region—the Belzec, Sobibor, and Treblinka extermination camps—which started to operate, one

TABLE 14.1. The Killing Centers of the Final Solution

Killing center	Jurisdiction	Killing method	Minimum number of victims	Selection for labor
Chelmno (Kulmhof), 1941–42, 1944	HSSPF Posen	Gas van, carbon monoxide	152,000	No
Belzec, 1942	SSPF Lublin and T4	Gas chamber, carbon monoxide	600,000	No
Sobibor, 1942–43	SSPF Lublin and T4	Gas chamber, carbon monoxide	250,000	No
Treblinka, 1942–43	SSPF Lublin and T4	Gas chamber, carbon monoxide	900,000	No
Majdanek, 1942–44	WVHA	Gas chamber, carbon monoxide and Zyklon B	60,000	Yes
Auschwitz-Birkenau, 1942–44	WVHA	Gas chamber, Zyklon B	1,100,000	Yes

Sources: Ino Arndt and Wolfgang Scheffler, "Organisierter Massenmord an Juden in nationalsozialistischen Vernichtungslagern," *Vierteljahrshefte für Zeitgeschichte* 24 (1976): 105–35; Adalbert Rückerl, *NS-Vernichtungslager im Spiegel deutscher Strafprozesse* (Munich: Deutscher Taschenbuch Verlag, 1977); LG Düsseldorf, Urteil Hermann Hackmann, 8 Ks 1/75, 30 June 1981, pp. 89–90; Franciszek Piper, *Die Zahl der Opfer von Auschwitz,* trans. Jochen August (Oswiecim: Verlag Staatliches Museum, 1993).

after the other, in the spring and summer of 1942. Unlike Chelmno, the camps of Operation Reinhard used stationary gas chambers, in which a diesel motor propelled gas fumes into the chambers.[18]

Because the killing task was so massive, Himmler also selected some of his concentration camps to serve as killing centers. He chose the newly established camp at Auschwitz in Upper Silesia and the so-called POW camp at Majdanek, a suburb of Lublin, to perform the killing function. Operating under the authority of the Inspectorate of the Concentration Camps, by 1942 part of Oswald Pohl's Central Office for Economy and Administration (Wirtschaftsverwaltungshauptamt, or WVHA), Auschwitz and Majdanek remained concentration camps while also running the killing centers as part of their operation. At Auschwitz, the killing center was located at Birkenau, also known as Auschwitz II. The agent used to kill the victims differed slightly at Auschwitz, where the SS replaced carbon monoxide with hydrogen cyanide, known under the trade name Zyklon B, which was already in use as a pesticide in all concentration camps to fumigate barracks.[19]

The killing program against Jews and Gypsies initially involved only those residing in the occupied Soviet Union, but as killing centers opened first in Chelmno and then elsewhere, the operation expanded within six months to include those residing in occupied Poland. But this was only the beginning. Although Heydrich's RSHA, the agency in charge of all deportations, had plans for an orderly sequence of deportations starting in the West, Hitler forced a change in plans when in the fall of 1941 he demanded that systematic deportation of the German Jews start immediately.[20] The deportation of German and Austrian Jews and Gypsies reveals the true intentions of the killers and the limitations reality continued to impose on their activities. In the rest of Europe, both among Germany's allies and in the occupied west, the Germans still had to consider local conditions.[21] But in the German Reich, as in the occupied East, no such limitations faced the killers.

The requirement that Jews wear the star of David on their clothing, decreed on 1 September 1941 and to take effect on 15 September, was the signal for the start of deportations from Germany, Austria, and the Protectorate; the first transports left in October 1941. The deportations were directed and coordinated by RSHA Office IV, the Gestapo, and, within it, the Jewish department (*Judenreferat*), headed by Adolf Eichmann and designated RSHA IVb4.[22]

The first deportations, which took place between 15 October and 2 November, involved about 20,000 Jews from Berlin, Vienna, Prague, Cologne, Düsseldorf, Frankfurt, Hamburg, and Luxembourg and went only as far as the Lodz ghetto. Lodz was not a logical destination for these transports because it was located in the incorporated Wartheland and thus was technically within the borders of the Reich. The deported German Jews were still German citizens with rights to property and pensions. To prevent deported Jews from retaining these rights, the Gestapo used several 1933 anticommunist laws to declare each deported Jew a subversive who had forfeited his or her citizenship, pension, and property rights.[23] This was a time-consuming process, however, that involved a great deal of paperwork. Therefore, the RMdI issued the Eleventh Decree to the Reich Citizenship Law on 25 November 1941, which provided for automatic loss of citizenship and confiscation of property if a German Jew took up residence in a foreign country; involuntary deportation to territories occupied by the Wehrmacht constituted such a change of address.[24]

The German governor of the Wartheland, Arthur Greiser, did not want additional Jews, and Himmler had to persuade him to accept them. Under pressure to complete the deportations on Hitler's schedule, Himmler wrote Greiser on 18 September 1941, promising that if he accepted these transports, the Jews would be "moved farther east next spring."[25] But considering that Greiser was then in the process of creating the Chelmno killing center and that the RSHA would soon delegate its man Herbert Lange to command there, we must assume that Himmler meant "killing" not "moving."[26] Many

THE ORIGINS OF NAZI GENOCIDE

of the German, Austrian, and Czech Jews deported to Lodz died in the ghetto of starvation, exposure, and disease, but the majority were killed in Chelmno during the spring and fall of 1942. Those remaining were sent to Auschwitz when the ghetto was finally dissolved in August 1944.

On 8 November 1941, the second phase of German Jewish deportations commenced. During November and December (and intermittently during 1942), about 22,000 Jews were deported from various German, Austrian, and Czech cities. The destination was the Ostland, the administrative region that included Lithuania, Latvia, Estonia, and Bielorussia. Out of a total of twenty-two transports, ten went to Riga, seven to Minsk, and five to Kovno. The Ostland was a territory where the Einsatzgruppen operated, and the arriving German Jews were thus subject to murder by these SS killing squads. Although most of the new arrivals were placed into German Jewish ghettos in Riga and Minsk, the members of some transports were killed on arrival. In Kovno, SS Colonel (Standartenführer) Karl Jäger's Einsatzkommando 3 (one of the commandos operating under Franz Stahlecker's Einsatzgruppe A) killed all German Jews upon arrival. They were shot in Fort No. 9 outside the city, the first deported German Jews murdered as part of the final solution. Their deaths were recorded in Jäger's report to his commanding officer:

25 November 1941, Kovno Fort IX: Jews 1,159, female Jews 1,600, Jewish children 175, total 2,934 (resettlers from Berlin, Munich, and Frankfurt). 29 November 1941, Kovno Fort IX: Jews 693, female Jews 1,155, Jewish children 152, total 2,000 (resettlers from Vienna and Breslau).[27]

In the same way, the first transport of German Jews to arrive in Riga never reached the ghetto. It left Berlin on 27 November 1941 and arrived in Riga on 30 November, the day Einsatzkommando 2 killed most of the remaining Latvian Jews in the city. The arriving Jews from Berlin were taken directly to Rumbuli forest, where they were executed early in the morning before the operation against the Latvian Jews began.[28]

During the spring of 1942, and somewhat less during the fall of that year, trains continued to arrive in the Ostland. Almost all Jews on those transports were killed upon arrival. In 1942 the Eichmann office made some changes in the deportation procedure. The Theresienstadt ghetto in the Protectorate was established to serve as a transit camp for Czech Jews but was also used as a destination for German and Austrian Jews over sixty-five years old and their spouses if over fifty-five. Theresienstadt also held other persons exempted from deportation to the East, including those with high military decorations or important international connections, Jewish hybrids, and Jewish partners in mixed marriages. But transports to Theresienstadt did not cross the borders of the Reich, and the Eleventh Decree therefore could not be invoked to confiscate property. Nevertheless, the RSHA found an ingenious way to seize the property of those deported to Theresienstadt. Imitating the method used to finance care in a nursing home, the Gestapo forced old people to sign a contract (*Heimkaufvertrag*) with the Reich Association of Jews by which they gave up all their property in return for "perpetual care" in Theresienstadt.[29] This hoax generated large sums for the RSHA, which took the money from the Reich Association; the deported Jews received, in return, miserable conditions in Theresienstadt and later a journey to the East.

In the third phase of German Jewish deportations, deportees were shipped during 1942 to the Lublin region in the General Government. Many of the arriving Jews were dumped into small ghettos or labor camps; Izbica, Piaski, and Trawniki were the most frequent destinations. There the German Jews shared the eventual fate of the Polish Jews. Some transports, however, went directly to the killing centers of Operation Reinhard. Starting early in 1943, German Jewish transports went directly to Auschwitz.

The German Jewish deportations demonstrated the determination of the Nazi regime to murder Jews as rapidly as possible. As in the euthanasia killings, however, the regime encountered problems and made mistakes. For example, in October 1941, a meeting of Gestapo representatives in Eichmann's office discussed procedures for the deportations. Although Eichmann seems to have ordered the exemption of hybrid Jews, Jews in mixed marriages, and Jews over sixty years, local Gestapo offices disregarded these directives during the winter of 1941, putting many older Jews on the transport lists to Lodz and the Ostland.[30] Obviously, the deportation of Jewish men and women in their seventies and eighties discredited the public explanation that Jews went East to do heavy labor. The error was soon corrected by the simple device of sending older Jews to the East via Theresienstadt. The problem of how to confiscate Jewish property was only solved with the Eleventh Decree after the deportations of the first phase. And, as the discussions at the Wannsee conference and those that followed showed, the problem of how to deal with Jewish hybrids and mixed marriages occupied the bureaucracy until the end of the war.[31]

The final solution applied to Gypsies as well as Jews. As we have seen, the SS Einsatzgruppen shot them alongside Jews. In Germany and Austria, large numbers of Gypsies had already been incarcerated in Gypsy camps, and others had been deported to Poland. And just as the European Jews were either deported to the East by the Germans or killed locally by Germany's allies, Gypsies everywhere faced death at the hands of the Germans or their local collaborators. In the Protectorate, Gypsies were incarcerated in camps— Lety in Bohemia and Hodonin in Moravia—where forced labor, malnutrition, and disease killed many; those remaining were deported to Auschwitz. In Croatia, a German ally, almost all Gypsies were murdered. In the Netherlands and in Belgium, both under German occupation, almost all Gypsies were deported to the East.[32]

By the time the war against the Soviet Union started, only a relatively small number of Gypsies—about 30,000—remained in Germany and Austria. Almost immediately, the police moved to incarcerate more Gypsies; thus the RKPA "suggested" that Gypsies in East Prussia be placed in a camp near Königsberg.[33] In November 1941, as the Jewish deportations started, the RKPA decided to add Gypsies to the Jewish transports. Himmler had at first proposed to Greiser the deportation of 60,000 people to the Wartheland, but realities forced him to lower the number. In the end, only 20,000 Jews were deported to the Lodz ghetto, and the RKPA was able to add 5,007 Gypsies to this wave of deportations.[34]

The fate of Gypsies deported to Lodz was almost immediate death. Placed in a small area of the ghetto, completely separated from the Jewish section, the Gypsy population of the ghetto was decimated by overcrowding, starvation, and epidemics.[35] The survivors were deported to the Chelmno killing center early in 1942, where they were murdered alongside Jews.[36] A group of 120 Gypsies, sent from Lodz to Posen to work in munitions factories, also did not survive the war.[37]

We have little information about Gypsy deportations during 1942. We do know that many Gypsies from the East, as well as some from the Reich, were incarcerated in Polish ghettos, including the one in Warsaw, and that they were murdered in the killing centers of Operation Reinhard.[38]

During 1941 and 1942, regulations restricting and labeling German and Austrian Gypsies multiplied. In April 1941, Kripo and government offices were ordered to identify the draft records of Gypsies before turning them over to draft offices.[39] In June, the RMdI reinterpreted the Nuremberg racial laws, canceling permission for Gypsies with three German grandparents to marry Germans.[40] In October, the police were ordered to indicate on the registry cards maintained for every German whether the person was a Gypsy or Gypsy hybrid.[41] In November, the RSHA circulated an education ministry rule excluding Gypsy children from the public schools if they were not German citizens. As far as those with German citizenship were concerned, the ministry found that since not enough such children existed to warrant separate schools, they had to be accepted but could nonetheless be excluded if they "presented a moral or other danger to German fellow students."[42] In February 1942, Gypsies were excluded from service as air raid wardens or in civil defense rescue squads.[43] On 13 March 1942, the Reich Ministry of Labor decreed that henceforth the rules governing the social and economic status of Jews would also apply to Gypsies, thereby extending the decree of 3 October 1941 concerning "the employment of Jews" to Gypsies. The regulations suspended weekend and holiday pay for Gypsies and disqualified them from receiving overtime pay and all other entitlements, such as workmen's compensation, death benefits, and supplemental child welfare payments.[44] And in July 1942, the Supreme Command of the Wehrmacht excluded Gypsies from active military service.[45]

Finally, on 16 December 1942, Himmler ordered the total deportation of Gypsies from the German Reich to Auschwitz.[46] On 26 September 1942, nearly three months before Himmler's decree, 200 Gypsies were transferred from Buchenwald to the Auschwitz concentration camp and assigned to build the new Gypsy enclosure at Birkenau, eventually designated BIIe and commonly known as the Gypsy camp (Zigeunerlager). The first transport of German Gypsies arrived at this newly erected camp on 26 February 1943. Gypsies from other countries in occupied Europe arrived there after 7 March 1943.[47] Transports from Germany and Austria arrived during the month of March 1943.[48] In the Birkenau Gypsy camp, men were not separated from women and children, and the Gypsy camp was thus a family camp. This was an extremely unusual privilege, which had been granted only once before, in the case of the 1943 Birkenau family camp (Familienlager) for Jews from Theresienstadt. But the final fate of the Gypsies did not differ from that of the Theresienstadt Jews. In the end, the surviving Gypsies were murdered in the Birkenau gas chambers on 2 August 1944. About 20,000 Gypsies were killed in the seventeen months of the Birkenau Gypsy camp's existence.[49]

The Gypsies remaining in Germany and Austria had a choice between deportation and sterilization, and the RKPA enforced this provision.[50] In any event, compulsory sterilization had always been considered a possible alternative to killing. In 1940 Leonardo Conti had thus advocated mass sterilization of all Gypsies.[51] And the same method had also been proposed for Jews. In June 1942, Viktor Brack had suggested to Himmler that instead of killing all Jews, 2 to 3 million could be used as a labor force as long as they were first sterilized.[52] But the sterilization of millions could not be carried out by traditional means, and the SS therefore searched for a way to make sterilization fast and cheap. For this purpose, T4 dispatched one of its physicians, Horst Schumann, to conduct sterilization experiments at Auschwitz.[53] But no easy way was ever discovered.

Himmler's Auschwitz decree, condemning Gypsies to the concentration camps and certain death, provided for exceptions. The decree exempted "racially pure Sinti and Lalleri Gypsies." This exemption has misled some historians into believing that the Nazi regime considered some Gypsies to be Aryan relatives who must not be destroyed. But these theoretical exemptions never became reality. At the time Himmler issued his exemption, for example, Lalleri Gypsies held at the Berlin-Marzahn camp were deported to Auschwitz.[54]

In October 1942, Himmler issued a decree appointing nine Gypsy men as

THE ORIGINS OF NAZI GENOCIDE

so-called speakers, eight pure Sinti and one Lalleri. They were to identify pure Sinti and Lalleri and some "good hybrids" for exemption. Himmler intended to permit these pure Sinti and Lalleri to wander within a "designated area" and to follow their "customs and habits." [55] It was obviously one of Himmler's pet ideas to keep a few Gypsies, those he thought most representative of their kind, as living museum pieces on a reservation he would select and supervise. While some Nazi leaders were assembling Jewish books and artifacts to display after the Jews had disappeared, Himmler chose to collect living specimens to exhibit after the Gypsies had disappeared. As we have seen, Bormann objected to Himmler's plan, and the matter was referred to Hitler. Himmler apparently convinced Hitler and was thus able to exempt the pure Sinti and Lalleri from his Auschwitz decree. This decree, issued only thirteen days after the Bormann letter, also indicates that the conflict forced him to prove his anti-Gypsy commitment by moving rapidly against all other Gypsies.

The reality was altogether different from the wording of the decree. The local Kripo offices, responsible for the deportations to Auschwitz, did not pay much attention to the exemptions. The lists provided by the speakers were disregarded, and the Kripo usually made the selections. [56] How can we explain this confusion?

Until Himmler's intervention, anti-Gypsy policy had been based largely on the work of the race scientist Robert Ritter and his staff. They had registered the Gypsies and had provided the racial categories that determined police actions. Working in close cooperation with the RKPA, Ritter had provided the scientific basis for radical exclusion, favored in both the RMdI and the RSHA. Ritter had classified almost all Gypsies as undesirable hybrids and had also considered pure Gypsies as inferior stock. His evaluation of the Lalleri, for example, had not been positive. [57] But Ritter was an outsider, not a member of the SS, whose influence was based on his position as an expert with the RMdI and the RKPA. Within the SS there emerged rival researchers, grouped around the SS Ahnenerbe, the office dealing with the study of ancestral heritage. They wanted to enter this field of research but were faced with obstacles because Ritter monopolized the field; he had the resources, including experienced assistants, funding from the DFG, and access to the living research material.

In their move to replace Ritter, the Ahnenerbe people in the SS apparently convinced Himmler that Ritter's approach had overlooked the Aryan heritage of pure Gypsies, and they seem to have persuaded the Reich leader SS to propose the reservation idea, which appealed to Himmler's romanticism and, once implemented, obviously would have created vast SS research opportunities. [58] But the SS and police needed Ritter to implement the Auschwitz decree and all other anti-Gypsy legislation because only he had the resources to provide the needed racial evaluations. It is therefore not surprising that in January 1943, after Himmler had exempted pure Lalleri for his reservation, the RSHA announced that "previous investigations have found that no racially pure Lalleri Gypsies can be found in the territory of the Reich."[59]

Within the overall plan to exterminate the biological enemy, different segments of the bureaucracy fought each other over ways to implement exclusion and murder. During the 1930s, party and ministry bureaucrats had differed over how the sterilization laws should be applied. During the 1940s, the government and the SS differed over how the Jewish hybrids should be treated and how Jewish labor should be exploited. In the same way, different groups within the SS empire fought over the fate of the infinitesimally small numbers of supposedly pure Lalleri Gypsies. In the end, the drive to exterminate triumphed.

Two examples, one for Gypsies and one for Jews, both involving children, testify to the determination of German bureaucrats and scientists to destroy all members of alien races. Since the late 1930s, the government agencies responsible for administering welfare for children had tried to exclude, or at least isolate, Jewish and Gypsy children. These children were minors who had been made wards of the state by the courts or government agencies. The reasons they were made wards, sometimes fabricated, were, among others, juvenile delinquency, inability of a single parent to care for the child, or commitment of parents to a concentration camp.[60]

Württemberg, the south German state that had pioneered the isolation of handicapped Jewish patients, ordered in November 1938 that all Gypsy children in Württemberg homes be concentrated at the Catholic St. Joseph's Home (St. Josefspflege) in Mulfingen.[61] This isolation of Gypsy children was directed by the physician in charge of minors in Württemberg homes, Max Eyrich, who at the start of euthanasia had traveled with Otto Mauthe to various institutions to supervise the rapid completion of all questionnaires.[62]

After Himmler had issued his Auschwitz decree, at a time when even pregnant Gypsy girls were sent to Auschwitz, the Mulfingen children should have been deported.[63] Robert Ritter, however, apparently had the children's deportation postponed to enable him and his staff to study them. As we have seen, his assistant, Eva Justin, even used her Mulfingen research for her doctoral dissertation at the University of Berlin. This delay did not help the children, however. Surviving records show that thirty-nine Mulfingen children — twenty boys and nineteen girls — were registered in Auschwitz on 12 May 1944.[64]

By 1943 few Jewish children were still at liberty in Germany, but most Jewish hybrid children (Mischlingskinder) had not been deported to the East. Although practical considerations exempted Jewish hybrid children until the end, those found in homes as wards of the state were sufficiently exposed and expendable to face a fate similar to that of Gypsy children. Although the documentation about this part of the final solution has almost completely disappeared, we do know about one small group of Jewish hybrid children. During the postwar trial of the Hadamar killers, the mother of one partly Jewish child reported the murder of her fourteen-year-old daughter Ingeborg.[65] This led to the discovery that during 1943 and 1944 there had been a special ward for Jewish hybrid children at Hadamar.[66]

On 15 April 1943, Herbert Linden's office at the RMdI asked Fritz Bernotat to create at Hadamar a ward for Jewish hybrid children. This ward would eventually receive children from all parts of the Reich but started by admitting children from local Hessen homes.[67] Bernotat immediately established this ward, camouflaging its purpose by calling it an "educational home." He also moved rapidly to have children from local hospitals and homes transferred.[68] For example, on 15 May, he requested that Eichberg report within five days all partly Jewish minors; on 19 May, Walter Schmidt reported two such children.[69] Children eventually also arrived from other parts of Germany. Thus the government of Braunschweig ordered two partly Jewish boys transferred from one of its institutions to Hadamar after the Reich Association of Jews had failed to move them to the Berlin Jewish hospital.[70]

We do not know the exact number of Jewish children transferred to Hadamar during 1943 and 1944, but we do know that most were healthy and that they were sent to Hadamar because they were partly Jewish. Because the deportation guidelines exempted these children, the bureaucracy of the RMdI, not the RSHA, decided to destroy at least those Jewish hybrids in its control as wards of the state. At Hadamar, these healthy children were killed with injections.[71]

We have now seen, again and again, the linkage between the killing operations against the handicapped, Jews, and Gypsies. Interpretations about the three operations have changed over the years. At the time, the murder of the handicapped led to public opposition, while the murder of Jews, and even more so Gypsies, failed to produce public opposition. Since the war, however, public interest has focused on the murder of Jews, while the murder of the handicapped and Gypsies has received little attention until recently.[72] But one cannot explain any one of these Nazi killing operations without explaining the others. Together they represented Nazi genocide.

The linkage between the three killing operations was, as we have seen, ideological, based on the belief in human inequality and on the determination to cleanse the gene pool of the German nation. But collaboration between different segments of the bureaucracy also established linkage. Although the KdF directed the euthanasia killings in collaboration with the RMdI, the SS and police provided logistic support without assuming direct responsibility.[73] The SS supplied technical aid and junior staff in the Reich, and its units did the killing on Germany's eastern border. But collaboration went further. For example, the work of the health and the police bureaucracies meshed to snare individuals who might otherwise have been able to escape. Thus the Vienna SS made sure that the city's health department committed Marie Wlach, a half-blind homeless person whose husband was in a concentration camp, to the Am Steinhof hospital. Wlach was married to a Jew.[74]

Just as the SS had assisted the KdF in managing euthanasia, the KdF offered its expertise to the SS in solving the problems of the final solution. As the SS was searching for better means to implement the killings in the East, it chose to use the methods tried and tested in the euthanasia program. Chemists previously associated with T4 — Albert Widmann and August Becker — aided the Einsatzgruppen leadership in testing the feasibility of killing with explosives and with gas. Methods formerly utilized to kill the handicapped in East Prussia were applied by the same SS unit — the Lange Commando — in the first killing center for Jews and Gypsies at Chelmno. And as the Alfred Wetzel letter about Riga proposing the use of "Brack's devices" and the services of T4 chemist Helmut Kallmeyer has shown, the KdF also offered its technical support for various other local killing operations. We can thus see that the KdF served as godfather to the emerging efforts to rationalize the final solution.

It is therefore not surprising that the KdF also served as a resource for the massive killing enterprise known as Operation Reinhard. When Himmler commissioned the Lublin SSPF Odilo Globocnik to kill the Polish Jews, probably in late July 1941, Globocnik needed the experienced staff of T4 to carry out this assignment.[75] Since the staffs of the T4 killing centers were no longer needed after the cessation of gassing, the KdF leadership wanted to keep them together as a group for use once euthanasia killings could start again.[76] The KdF thus had a special interest in finding employment for its staff members.

Before the use of T4's staff in the killing centers of Operation Reinhard could materialize, the KdF arranged for its members to be sent behind the front lines in the Soviet Union.[77] At Nuremberg, Brack testified that in late 1941, Fritz Todt, Speer's predecessor as Reich minister of armaments, told Hitler that housing and health services for the troops in the East needed radical improvement, and the Führer thereupon ordered that all medical institutions supply aid. Bouhler readily organized T4 units for volunteer service in the East under the umbrella of the national transportation construction agency known as Organization Todt.[78] In January 1942, several groups of T4's staff, both men and women, one under the command of Viktor Brack, left for the East.[79] From the letters of the physician Irmfried Eberl, who commanded another unit, we know the names of some of the other T4 physicians assigned to these units: Kurt Borm, Hans-Bodo Gorgaß, Kurt Schmalenbach, Horst Schumann, and Aquilin Ullrich.[80]

The exact assignment of the T4 people in the East has never been absolutely clear. It is, of course, possible that Bouhler sent them east to keep them busy and to contribute to the welfare of the troops, and nothing in the Eberl letters or in postwar testimony contradicts this interpretation. The Eberl group, for example, set up medical stations in Minsk and towns nearby to take care of wounded troops who arrived there from the front lines.[81] But there has always been some suspicion that their task was more sinister. At least some anecdotal evidence suggests that the T4 physicians and nurses gave deadly injections to brain-damaged German soldiers.[82] In any event, the assignment with Organization Todt was only temporary, and the T4 people continued to maintain group cohesion; Karl Brandt intervened when local authorities caused difficulties, and the staff remaining at home sent cigarettes and other items via the KdF offices.[83] Moreover, the units designed to aid wounded soldiers apparently included not only Brack but also a junior member of Karl Brandt's staff.[84]

While the T4 staff was occupied in Russia, plans to construct killing centers in the Lublin region of eastern Poland progressed. Globocnik had to decide what method to use to kill large numbers of human beings. The decision had been made to employ some form of gassing, and the KdF was the organization with the experience and staff to accomplish the gigantic task of creating the necessary facilities. In September 1941, Philipp Bouhler and Viktor Brack visited Globocnik in Lublin, where they observed the construction of "labor camps."[85] Although at Nuremberg Brack denied that this visit had anything to do with the final solution, it seems likely that they discussed their future collaboration and that the "labor camp" they inspected was in fact the site of the future Belzec killing center.[86]

During the winter of 1941–42, a number of T4 men visited Lublin, and there can be no doubt that their sojourns there were connected with the construction of killing centers. We have seen that the T4 chemist Helmut Kallmeyer visited Lublin in January or February 1942. Christian Wirth was also in Lublin in late fall or early winter 1941, which is the only reasonable explanation for why this T4 troubleshooter did not accompany the T4 groups assigned to Organization Todt in Russia.[87]

Expert advice on the design and construction of killing centers was not the only KdF contribution. Unlike the concentration camps, which had the staffs and organization to implement mass murder, Globocnik needed staff to run his killing centers. He therefore subcontracted to T4 the running of the killing centers of Operation Reinhard. The T4 staff returned from Russia in April 1942 and were soon thereafter posted to Lublin. In the second half of April, Globocnik conferred with Bouhler and Brack in Berlin, and they probably settled all remaining questions about the KdF's role in Operation Reinhard.[88] Eventually, T4 men composed almost the entire personnel of the extermination camps of Operation Reinhard. The first group left in April, and further staff members were posted east in June 1942.[89] Altogether, at least ninety T4 men were assigned to Belzec, Sobibor, and Treblinka.[90]

The T4 men usually arrived in small groups. Those without military experience first received rudimentary training at Trawniki; others went directly to their assignments.[91] All had to sign a declaration swearing to keep the secret of the killing operation.[92] The killing centers they ran in the Lublin region were modeled on those they had left in the Reich. But the much larger enterprise created conditions far worse than had existed in Germany. Of course, as we have seen, brutalization and corruption of staff members had also been a by-product of the euthanasia killing enterprise. But at home some restraints upon the killers still operated. Such restraints no longer applied in the East, especially as the sheer numbers of victims overwhelmed the machine of destruction. Sadism, torture, and corruption reached previously unimaginable proportions in Belzec, Sobibor, and Treblinka. An American judge would years later describe one of these camps as a "human abattoir."[93] Even Bouhler worried that "the absolute degradation and brutalization of the people involved" would make the T4 staff assigned to Lublin no longer fit for the job of euthanasia inside the borders of the Reich.[94]

Running the killing centers in the East was a joint enterprise. Globocnik as Lublin SSPF was the military superior of the T4 staff; his office directed the deportations, provided the infrastructure, including the Ukrainian guards, and disposed of the accumulated loot. But in all respects, the staff remained a T4 unit. The KdF did not relinquish authority in personnel matters, including the right to alter assignments. T4 continued to pay the staff members' wages and supplemental allowances and also sent them to the T4 vacation home in Austria; it delivered their mail, both letters and packages, which arrived in Lublin by courier.[95] Each staff member had two addresses. As Irmfried Eberl wrote his wife, private letters were to be mailed to the "SS Special Commando, Treblinka near Malkinia" but packages should be sent to the following address: "Berlin W 35, Tiergarten Straße 4 (Operation East)."[96]

The supervision of the KdF was not restricted to paperwork from a distance. Leading KdF functionaries, including Bouhler and Blankenburg, visited the camps, and the T4 business manager Dietrich Allers was seen at Belzec.[97] Christian Wirth, the most brutal of the T4 supervisors, was promoted from commandant of Belzec to the position of inspector over all three killing centers of Operation Reinhard, thus exercising authority just below Globocnik's general control over all T4 operations in Lublin.[98]

After Operation Reinhard ended in 1943, the T4 staff remained together as a group, following Globocnik to the Adriatic coast. Wirth served as their commander, and after he was killed, T4 manager Allers assumed command. Serving as a security force, the staff members again attempted to establish a killing center. They transformed an old rice factory in Trieste, the Risiera di San Sabba, into a camp for interrogation of suspected partisans and for Jews in transit to Auschwitz. Some evidence exists that prisoners at San Sabba were

THE ORIGINS OF NAZI GENOCIDE

killed by gas and their bodies burned in a crematorium. But time was running out, and San Sabba never grew into a major killing center.[99]

Only one physician — Irmfried Eberl — was assigned to the camps of Operation Reinhard. He was one of the three senior physicians-in-charge at the euthanasia killing centers. Horst Schumann was already assigned to sterilization experiments at Auschwitz. Rudolf Lonauer could not be spared because Hartheim fulfilled a major responsibility under 14f13 and in conjunction with Mauthausen. Eberl's selection was therefore not illogical. For about two months, during July and August 1942, he served as the commandant of Treblinka. Late in August, or early in September, Globocnik relieved him of his command and he returned to Germany, where he again assumed command of the Bernburg killing center. The reason usually given was his inability to manage the Treblinka killing operation. Descriptions of the disorder in Treblinka under his management included accounts of dead bodies found everywhere, indiscriminate shootings by Ukrainian guards, and the dissolute behavior of the T4 staff.[100]

True, the numbers of victims killed daily at Treblinka were very large and the speed with which they were killed was very fast; Eberl wrote his wife, "The pace in Treblinka is truly breathtaking." [101] It is thus possible that Eberl was unable to handle the job. But it is surprising that Eberl, who has often been described as precise in his management of Brandenburg and Bernburg, was not able to direct operations as well as Franz Stangl, who succeeded him at Treblinka. It is, of course, possible that Eberl was good only at record keeping, as he showed in his meticulous handling of killing statistics, including those of handicapped Jewish patients, but was not capable of running a large killing operation with military precision.

There are, however, other possible explanations. One could be the rivalry between the physicians and the nonmedical staff. We have seen that the T4 managers favored the supervisors over the physicians. Globocnik might have shared this preference for police officers. Apparently, he was traveling with both Blankenburg and Wirth when he dismissed Eberl.[102] It is quite possible that Wirth, who dominated everyone around him, would have considered Eberl, with authority equal to his own, as a rival and would have wanted to replace him with one of his Hartheim people.

Eberl's independence also might have led to conflict on another front. Globocnik's massive killing operation yielded unbelievable wealth. His final accounting gives some indication of the money and jewelry collected from the victims, even without counting the gold from the teeth of those murdered.[103] These valuables went to the SS, but there is evidence that T4 shared in the bounty and that gold from teeth was collected at T4 in Berlin and processed by the KTI. [104] Some evidence suggests that Eberl did not share the valuables he collected with the Lublin SSPF, which might well have been the reason he was replaced.[105] In any event, the killing centers of Operation Reinhard functioned well despite the absence of physicians after Eberl's departure.

The killing technique was the most important contribution made by the T4 euthanasia program to the final solution. This technique involved both the hardware and the software of the killing process. It encompassed not only gas chambers and crematoria, but also the method developed to lure victims into these chambers, to kill them on an assembly line, and to process their corpses. These techniques, including the extraction of teeth and bridgework containing gold, were developed by T4 and exported to the East.

As we have seen, there were obvious differences. For example, the euthanasia killing centers located within the Reich used gas tanks from I. G. Farben with pure carbon monoxide, while centers in the East, where it was too expensive and time-consuming to obtain such tanks, utilized impure exhaust fumes from diesel engines. But the similarities are far more important than the differences.

First, subterfuge was used to fool the victims upon arrival with the appearance of normality. In the euthanasia centers, physicians and nurses checking medical files made the killing center look like a regular hospital, while in the camps of Operation Reinhard, the trappings of the reception area and the welcoming speech by a staff member made the killing center look like a labor camp. The victims were told in both places that they had to take showers for hygienic reasons, and the gas chambers were disguised as shower rooms, while the belongings of the victims were carefully collected and registered to maintain the illusion of normality. In both places, but especially in the East, the practice of assembly line mass murder did, however, produce a callous barbarity that usually vitiated all attempts to deceive the victims.

Second, in both the Reich and the East, the victims were crowded into the gas chamber, and their corpses were burned immediately after they had been killed. In the Reich, they used mobile crematoria; in the East, they utilized outdoor burning. At home, the German staff had to remove and burn the corpses; in Poland, they supervised Jewish prisoners who did the job. But in both places, they robbed the corpses. The system of stealing gold teeth and gold bridgework from the corpses of the murdered victims was first introduced in the euthanasia killing centers and then copied in the extermination camps of Operation Reinhard.[106]

In Birkenau, the killing center at Auschwitz, the SS staff improved upon the extermination technique first used in the euthanasia killings. They introduced Zyklon B, which acted faster, and constructed a killing plant combining gas chambers and stationary crematoria in one building. They also identified and selected those still able to work so that they could exploit their labor before killing them.[107] But even this had already been practiced by the euthanasia killers, who postponed the deaths of those handicapped patients still able to work.[108]

At Auschwitz-Birkenau, and also at Majdanek, the SS did not need the help of T4 specialists. The T4 technique was a basically simple German invention, one that any organization could learn to use. The concentration camps possessed both the organization and the manpower, as well as a commitment to savage brutality, to execute the killing task.

Birkenau did, however, employ physicians. Some have argued that the use of physicians in both the euthanasia killing centers and at Birkenau proves that they were an essential part of the killing process, even that their presence meant that these were "medicalized killings."[109] But their presence has a much simpler explanation. The T4 killing operation needed physicians because the German health care system served as the setting and produced the victims. But although the presence of physicians was essential in the wards of children's and "wild" euthanasia, where the setting was that of a hospital, nothing required their presence in the T4 killing centers. The reasons for their presence in these centers was Hitler's specific authorization, the attempt to deceive the victims, the need to process medical files, and the unwillingness of the medical leadership to relinquish authority to nonmedical managers and supervisors. Physicians were not essential, however, for the smooth operation of a killing center; the success of Belzec, Chelmno, Sobibor, and Treblinka at killing without the benefit of physicians proves that they were not an essential component of the process. We must therefore ask why physicians were used at Auschwitz-Birkenau.

The Birkenau killing center was attached to the concentration camp of Auschwitz and therefore under the control of the Inspectorate of the Concentration Camps, which was, in turn, a component of Oswald Pohl's WVHA. Unlike the RSHA, which saw the murder of all Jews and Gypsies as its primary task, the WVHA wanted to use as many concentration camp prisoners as possible as forced laborers in Germany's war industries. To accomplish this, the SS at Auschwitz instituted the infamous "selections," where they separated men and women still able to work from those consigned to the gas chambers. The conduct of these selections was the primary contribution of SS physicians to the Birkenau killing process; their unethical anthropological and medical research was only a private sideline. In the concentration camps, the office of the SS physician was one among many competing SS offices, each with an assigned task. The killing center did not fit into that established structure, and men had to be reassigned to various aspects of the killing process. The task of selecting those still healthy enough to do work was assigned to physicians for two reasons. First, they were available. Almost any SS functionary could, and sometimes did, conduct selections. The presence of SS physicians, who did not have to be imported for this task, made their use convenient, especially as the camp did not have a surplus of SS officers. Second, since various offices within the camp system tended to compete with each other, the SS physicians were loath to abdicate their authority to other SS offices. The assignment of physicians to the "selections" thus only reflected a normal bureaucratic division of labor.[110] The idea that SS physicians were employed because they brought to the task special skills as race scientists did not apply. As Müller-Hill has pointed out, even though the SS physicians were the students of the race scientists, it was not necessary to be an anthropologist "to select old people, mothers, and children."[111]

————

In the postwar world, Auschwitz has come to symbolize genocide in the twentieth century. But Auschwitz was only the last, most perfect Nazi killing center. The entire killing enterprise had started in January 1940 with the murder of the most helpless human beings, institutionalized handicapped patients, had expanded in 1941 to include Jews and Gypsies, and had by 1945 cost the lives of at least 6 million men, women, and children.

NOTES

ABBREVIATIONS

In addition to the abbreviations used in the text, the following abbreviations are used in the notes.

AMM	Archiv und Museum Mauthausen, Vienna
AVA	Allgemeines Verwaltungsarchiv, Vienna
BAK	Bundesarchiv Koblenz
BA-MA	Bundesarchiv-Militärarchiv, Freiburg im Breisgau
BDC	Berlin Document Center
DÖW	Dokumentationsarchiv des österreichischen Widerstandes, Vienna
GStA	Generalstaatsanwalt (attorney general)
GStA DDR	Generalstaatsanwalt der Deutschen Demokratischen Republik, Berlin
GStA Frankfurt	Generalstaatsanwalt Frankfurt (Staatsanwaltschaft bei dem Oberlandesgericht)
HHStA	Hessisches Hauptstaatsarchiv, Wiesbaden
HStA Düsseldorf	Hauptstaatsarchiv Düsseldorf
HStA Stuttgart	Hauptstaatsarchiv Stuttgart
JuNSV	Adelheid L. Rüter-Ehlermann and C. F. Rüter, eds., *Justiz und NS-Verbrechen: Sammlung deutscher Strafurteile wegen nationalsozialistischer Tötungsverbrechen*, 22 vols. (Amsterdam: University Press Amsterdam, 1968–81)
LA Berlin	Landesarchiv Berlin
LG	Landgericht (District Court [Germany]); Landesgericht (Austria)
NARA	National Archives and Records Administration, National Archives Building, Washington, D.C.
NARA Suitland	National Archives and Records Administration, Suitland (Maryland) Records Branch
OLG	Oberlandesgericht (Circuit [Appeals] Court)
OStA	Oberstaatsanwalt (senior state attorney)
StA	Staatsanwalt/Staatsanwaltschaft (state attorney/state attorney's office)
StA Düsseldorf	Staatsanwaltschaft bei dem Landgericht Düsseldorf
StA Hamburg	Staatsanwaltschaft bei dem Landgericht Hamburg
StA Köln	Staatsanwaltschaft bei dem Landgericht Köln

StA München I	Staatsanwaltschaft bei dem Landgericht München I
StArch Sigmaringen	Staatsarchiv Sigmaringen
StA Stuttgart	Staatsanwaltschaft bei dem Landgericht Stuttgart
StGB	*Strafgesetzbuch*
StS	Staatssekretär (state secretary)
TWC	*Trials of War Criminals before the Nuremberg Military Tribunals under Control Council Law No. 10* (Green Series), 14 vols. (Washington, D.C.: Government Printing Office, 1950–52)
VG	Volksgericht (People's Court [Austria])
Yivo	Yivo Institute for Jewish Research, New York
ZStL	Zentrale Stelle der Landesjustizverwaltungen, Ludwigsburg

CHAPTER ONE

1. See *Hundert Jahre deutscher Rassismus*; Proctor, *Racial Hygiene*; and Mosse, *Toward the Final Solution*.

2. See Müller-Hill, *Tödliche Wissenschaft*.

3. I have based this discussion on the analysis (and works cited) in Gould, *Mismeasure of Man*.

4. See Bergmann, Czarnowski, and Ehmann, "Objekte humangenetischer Forschung," p. 122.

5. Cited in Gould, *Mismeasure of Man*, p. 83.

6. Ibid., pp. 242–43 (quote on p. 28). On the construction of hierarchies, see Allen, "Misuse of Biological Hierarchies," pp. 105–7.

7. Cited in Gould, *Mismeasure of Man*, p. 104.

8. Cited ibid., p. 103.

9. Ibid., p. 115.

10. Ibid., p. 31.

11. Ibid., p. 147.

12. Proctor, *Racial Hygiene*, pp. 30–38.

13. Graham, "Science and Values," p. 1135; Gould, *Mismeasure of Man*, p. 162; Proctor, *Racial Hygiene*, p. 34.

14. Gould, *Mismeasure of Man*, p. 162. See also Müller-Hill, "Selektion," pp. 138–39.

15. Gould, *Mismeasure of Man*, pp. 113–22.

16. Cited ibid., p. 134.

17. Cited ibid., p. 138.

18. Cited ibid., p. 139.

19. Cited ibid., p. 134.

20. Cited ibid., p. 126.

21. Cited in Klee, *"Euthanasie" im NS-Staat*, p. 360. Unless otherwise noted, all translations are my own.

22. Gould, *Mismeasure of Man*, pp. 146–57.

23. Ibid., pp. 234–320.

24. Cited ibid., p. 310n.

25. Ibid., pp. 158–59. In Germany, the highest grade of feeblemindedness (*Schwachsinn*),

equivalent to the American "moron," was called *Debilität* from the French *débile*, while the other two grades—*Imbezillität* and *Idiotie*—are direct equivalents of the American labels. See Gütt, Rüdin, and Ruttke, *Gesetz zur Verhütung erbkranken Nachwuchses* (2d rev. ed.), p. 119.

26. Cited in Allen, "Eugenics Record Office," p. 225.
27. Ibid., pp. 244–45.
28. Ibid., pp. 226–27, 255, 260–64.
29. Ibid., pp. 243, 246.
30. Gould, *Mismeasure of Man*, pp. 234–39.
31. Ibid., pp. 192–94.
32. Ibid., pp. 195–99.
33. Ibid., p. 199.
34. Ibid., pp. 157–58, 161.
35. On the genius project, see ibid., pp. 183–88.
36. Cited ibid., p. 183.
37. Ibid., pp. 160–61.
38. Cited ibid., p. 181.
39. Cited ibid., p. 161. On the connection between Goddard and the ERO, see Allen, "Eugenics Record Office," p. 242.
40. Gould, *Mismeasure of Man*, p. 197.
41. Allen, "Eugenics Record Office," p. 248.
42. Cited in Gould, *Mismeasure of Man*, p. 225.
43. Allen, "Eugenics Record Office," pp. 242–43.
44. Gould, *Mismeasure of Man*, pp. 217–22, 225–30.
45. Ibid., pp. 235–36.
46. Ibid., p. 322; Müller-Hill, "Selektion," pp. 153–55. See also Graham, "Science and Values," pp. 1157–64.
47. Gould, *Mismeasure of Man*, pp. 293–96.
48. Allen, "Eugenics Record Office," pp. 247–48.
49. Cited in Gould, *Mismeasure of Man*, pp. 164, 181.
50. Allen, "Eugenics Record Office," p. 258.
51. Cited in Gould, *Mismeasure of Man*, p. 164.
52. Allen, "Misuse of Biological Hierarchies," p. 122.
53. *Buck v. Bell*, 274 U.S. 200 (1927).
54. Ibid., p. 202.
55. Ibid., p. 207.
56. See, for example, Allen, "Misuse of Biological Hierarchies," pp. 125–26, and "Eugenics Record Office," pp. 250–53; and Gould, *Mismeasure of Man*, p. 22.
57. Proctor, *Racial Hygiene*, p. 8; Weiss, "Race Hygiene Movement," pp. 197, 209; Müller-Hill, "Selektion," p. 139; Thom and Caregorodcev, *Medizin unterm Hakenkreuz*, p. 130.
58. Bergmann, Czarnowski, and Ehmann, "Objekte humangenetischer Forschung," p. 122.
59. Graham, "Science and Values," pp. 1134–36; Schmuhl, *Rassenhygiene, Nationalsozialismus, Euthanasie*, pp. 31–32, 58.
60. Weiss, "Race Hygiene Movement," p. 210; Graham, "Science and Values," p. 1136; Müller-Hill, "Selektion," p. 139.
61. Weiss, "Race Hygiene Movement," pp. 206–9.
62. Ibid., p. 212.
63. Ibid., p. 201; Bergmann, Czarnowski, and Ehmann, "Objekte humangenetischer Forschung," p. 122.

64. Weiss, "Race Hygiene Movement," p. 212.

65. Ibid., pp. 210–11; Bergmann, Czarnowski, and Ehmann, "Objekte humangenetischer Forschung," p. 123.

66. Roth, "Alfred Grotjahn," pp. 31–56.

67. Graham, "Science and Values," p. 1140.

68. Ibid., pp. 1142–43.

69. Weiss, "Race Hygiene Movement," p. 195. See also Kühl, *Nazi Connection*, chap. 6.

70. Weiss, "Race Hygiene Movement," p. 194; Proctor, *Racial Hygiene*, pp. 20–30, 55–56.

71. Weiss, "Race Hygiene Movement," pp. 202, 226–28.

72. Graham, "Science and Values," pp. 1138–39; Weiss, "Race Hygiene Movement," p. 201.

73. Weiss, "Race Hygiene Movement," p. 222.

74. Ibid., pp. 226–28.

75. Ibid., p. 194; Kühl, *Nazi Connection*, p. 71.

76. See Bridgman, *Revolt of the Hereros*.

77. Bergmann, Czarnowski, and Ehmann, "Objekte humangenetischer Forschung," pp. 129–30.

78. Bridgman, *Revolt of the Hereros*, p. 25. See also Bergmann, Czarnowski, and Ehmann, "Objekte humangenetischer Forschung," pp. 127–28.

79. Bergmann, Czarnowski, and Ehmann, "Objekte humangenetischer Forschung," pp. 128, 131.

80. Cited in Pross and Aly, *Wert des Menschen*, p. 98. See also *Hundert Jahre deutscher Rassismus*, pp. 22–23.

81. Cited in Bergmann, Czarnowski, and Ehmann, "Objekte humangenetischer Forschung," p. 128.

82. Ibid., p. 130.

83. For the *völkisch* movements, see Mosse, *Crisis of German Ideology*; Stern, *Politics of Cultural Despair*; and Waite, *Vanguard of Nazism*.

84. Weiss, "Race Hygiene Movement," pp. 214, 219.

85. Ibid., pp. 214, 221; *Hundert Jahre deutscher Rassismus*, p. 78.

86. Cited in Graham, "Science and Values," p. 1143, n. 24.

87. Bergmann, Czarnowski, and Ehmann, "Objekte humangenetischer Forschung," pp. 121, 124.

88. Weiss, "Race Hygiene Movement," pp. 207, 221, 226; Thom and Caregorodcev, *Medizin unterm Hakenkreuz*, p. 139.

89. Weiss, "Race Hygiene Movement," p. 232; Bergmann, Czarnowski, and Ehmann, "Objekte humangenetischer Forschung," p. 125; Müller-Hill, "Selektion," p. 141. On Verschuer's research, see BAK, R73/15341–42.

90. BDC, NSDAP master file. See also Weinreich, *Hitler's Professors*, p. 270.

91. Weiss, "Race Hygiene Movement," p. 221; Proctor, *Racial Hygiene*, p. 80. See also Weindling, *Health, Race, and German Politics*, p. 339, chart.

92. Erwin Baur, Eugen Fischer, and Fritz Lenz, *Grundriß der menschlichen Erblichkeitslehre und Rassenkunde* (Munich, 1921). The third revised edition appeared in two volumes as *Grundriß der menschlichen Erblichkeitslehre und Rassenhygiene* (Munich, 1927–31), with the original work as volume 1 entitled *Menschliche Erblichkeitslehre* (1927), and volume 2 by Lenz entitled *Menschliche Auslese und Rassenhygiene* (1931). The fifth revised edition appeared as *Menschliche Erblehre und Rassenhygiene* (Munich, 1940). J. F. Lehmann published all editions. An English edition of volume 1 appeared as *Human Heredity*, trans. Eden Paul and Cedar Paul (New York, 1931). See also Müller-Hill, *Tödliche Wissenschaft*, p. 12; Weiss, "Race Hygiene Movement," p. 214; Bergmann, Czarnowski, and Ehmann, "Objekte humangenetischer Forschung," p. 126; and *Hundert Jahre deutscher Rassismus*, pp. 75–79.

93. *Hundert Jahre deutscher Rassismus*, p. 77; Gilsenbach, "Erwin Baur," pp. 184–97.

94. Müller-Hill, "Selektion," p. 142; Bergmann, Czarnowski, and Ehmann, "Objekte humangenetischer Forschung," p. 126.

95. See Weindling, *Health, Race, and German Politics*, pp. 515–17, chart.

96. Weiss, "Race Hygiene Movement," p. 221; Macrakis, *Surviving the Swastika*, pp. 125–30. See also BAK, R73/14095, concerning projects of the Rüdin institute.

97. Bergmann, Czarnowski, and Ehmann, "Objekte humangenetischer Forschung," pp. 124–25; Macrakis, *Surviving the Swastika*, pp. 125–30.

98. Weiss, "Race Hygiene Movement," p. 216.

99. Bergmann, Czarnowski, and Ehmann, "Objekte humangenetischer Forschung," pp. 131–32.

100. Müller-Hill, "Selektion," p. 144.

101. Ibid.

102. Cited ibid., p. 141.

103. Binding did not use the term *Schwachsinn* for feeblemindedness but instead used the less scientific and less specific term *Blödsinnig*. Hoche used the same term. Binding and Hoche, *Vernichtung lebensunwerten Lebens*, pp. 31, 51.

104. Ibid., p. 45.

105. See Weindling, *Health, Race, and German Politics*, pp. 393–98.

106. Binding and Hoche, *Vernichtung lebensunwerten Lebens*, pp. 6–16.

107. Ibid., pp. 16–17.

108. Ibid., pp. 27–28.

109. Ibid., p. 27.

110. Ibid., pp. 29–32.

111. Ibid., pp. 47, 51, 55.

112. Ibid., pp. 54–55.

113. Ibid., pp. 45–47, 49–50.

114. Ibid., pp. 47–48.

115. Ibid., pp. 48–49.

116. Ibid., pp. 35–36.

117. Ibid., p. 37.

118. Ibid., pp. 39–40.

119. See Hafner and Winau, "Karl Binding und Alfred Hoche," p. 233, n. 46.

120. Ibid., p. 252.

121. Weiss, "Race Hygiene Movement," p. 234.

122. Compare, for example, the language about "blood" used in the Nuremberg racial laws. See also Kater, "Gesundheitsführung," p. 350.

123. See, for example, Aly, "Der saubere und der schmutzige Fortschritt," pp. 9–78.

124. Cited in Pross and Aly, *Wert des Menschen*, p. 92.

125. Cited in DÖW, file 19134: VG bei dem LG Wien, Urteil Maximilian Thaller, Vg 11e Vr 5502/46 (Hv 328/48), 25 Oct. 1948. See also Roth, "Ein Mustergau gegen die Armen, Leistungsschwachen und 'Gemeinschaftsunfähigen,'" in Ebbinghaus, Kaupen-Haas, and Roth, *Heilen und Vernichten im Mustergau Hamburg*, pp. 7–17. For evidence on the treatment of the *Asozialen* during the war, see the documents in DÖW, file E19198, Reichsgau Wien, Hauptgesundheitsamt. See also Müller-Hill, "Selektion," pp. 147–48.

126. See Walk, *Sonderrecht für die Juden*, p. 146, no. 81.

127. StA Hamburg, Verfahren Friedrich Lensch und Kurt Struve, 147 Js 58/67, Gesundheitsbehörde Bd. 1: memo from psychiatrist Holm, "Verpflegung, insbesondere Butterausgabe an die Kranken der Klinik Eilbeckthal," 22 Nov. 1937; BAK, R36/881: Verpflegungskosten in Heil- und Pflegeanstalten, 28 Feb. 1939. See also Weiss, "Race Hygiene

Movement," pp. 223–24, and Ebbinghaus, "Kostensenkung, 'Aktive Therapie' und Vernichtung," in Ebbinghaus, Kaupen-Haas, and Roth, *Heilen und Vernichten im Mustergau Hamburg*, pp. 136–46.

128. ZStL, Heidelberg Docs. 127,084, 127,088: copy of "Die Krankenanstalten in der Kriegsernährungswirtschaft," in *Für das gesamte Krankenhauswesen*, Heft 3, and cover letter from Paul Nitsche to Hans Heinze, 30 Oct. 1942. The so-called Heidelberg Documents contain papers of Professor Paul Nitsche, the last medical chief of adult euthanasia. See also chap. 5, n. 99, below.

129. See Broszat, "Konzentrationslager," pp. 66–72, 76–78; Friedlander, "Nazi Concentration Camps," pp. 41–42; Pingel, *Häftlinge unter SS-Herrschaft*, pp. 70–74; Tuchel, *Konzentrationslager*, p. 155, n. 134; and Drobisch and Wieland, *System der NS-Konzentrationslager*, pp. 199–204.

130. ZStL, Heidelberg Docs. 127,947–50: Otto Hebold to Paul Nitsche, 23 Mar. 1944, and Nitsche note, 29 Mar. 1944.

131. See Bock, *Zwangssterilisation*, and Nowak, *"Euthanasie" und Sterilisierung*. See also Weiss, "Race Hygiene Movement," pp. 225, 229.

132. See Bergmann, Czarnowski, and Ehmann, "Objekte humangenetischer Forschung," p. 132, and Pommerin, *"Sterilisierung der Rheinlandbastarde."*

133. See Müller-Hill, *Tödliche Wissenschaft*, pp. 59–61; Hohmann, *Ritter und die Erben der Kriminalbiologie*; Brucker-Boroujerdi and Wippermann, " 'Zigeunerlager' Berlin-Marzahn"; Hase-Mihalik and Kreuzkamp, *Du kriegst auch einen schönen Wohnwagen*; and Milton, "Gypsies and the Holocaust."

134. For the anti-Jewish policies of the Nazi regime during the 1930s, see Adam, *Judenpolitik*, and Schleunes, *Twisted Road to Auschwitz*. For an example of harassment, see the files in BAK, R36/2118, concerning the campaign to prevent the burial of Jews in German cemeteries.

135. Müller-Hill, "Selektion," pp. 144, 146.

136. Ibid., p. 145.

137. BAK, R18/5518: "Mitschrift über die Besprechung am 15. Juni 1937 betr. Fragen der unehelichen Mutterschaft."

138. See Beyerchen, *Scientists under Hitler*, and Macrakis, *Surviving the Swastika*.

139. Bergmann, Czarnowski, and Ehmann, "Objekte humangenetischer Forschung," pp. 131–32; Weiss, "Race Hygiene Movement," pp. 226–28.

140. Thom and Caregorodcev, *Medizin unterm Hakenkreuz*, pp. 139–40.

141. See Bergmann, Czarnowski, and Ehmann, "Objekte humangenetischer Forschung," p. 124, and Weinreich, *Hitler's Professors*, pp. 269–70. See also BAK, R73/15341: DFG Vermerk, 6 Dec. 1935, concerning Gütt's support for race hygiene research.

142. Weiss, "Race Hygiene Movement," p. 228.

143. Ibid., p. 233; Bergmann, Czarnowski, and Ehmann, "Objekte humangenetischer Forschung," p. 124. See also BAK, R73/15341: Verschuer memo for DFG, 16 Nov. 1936.

144. Bergmann, Czarnowski, and Ehmann, "Objekte humangenetischer Forschung," p. 132; Müller-Hill, "Selektion," p. 144.

145. On Nazi language, see Klemperer, *LTI: Aus dem Notizbuch eines Philologen*.

146. Müller-Hill, "Selektion," pp. 146–47.

147. Weiss, "Rassenhygienische Bewegung," p. 170.

148. See BAK, R18/1022, 1023, Fürsorge für Juden und Zigeuner.

149. For early postwar accounts of the killing of handicapped patients, see Mitscherlich and Mielke, *Medizin ohne Menschlichkeit*, and Platen-Hallermund, *Die Tötung Geisteskranker*. For a later account, based also on postwar trials in West Germany, see Kaul, *Nazimordaktion T4*. The three recent works by Ernst Klee provide the most detailed account: *"Euthanasie" im NS-Staat*, *Dokumente*, and *Was sie taten—Was sie wurden*.

150. See Emmerich, "Forensische Psychiatrie," and Grode, *"Sonderbehandlung 14f13."*

151. See Reitlinger, *Final Solution*; Hilberg, *Destruction*; and Adler, *Der verwaltete Mensch*.

152. See Zimmermann, *Verfolgt, Vertrieben, Vernichtet*; Zülch, *In Auschwitz vergast*; Thurner, *Zigeuner in Österreich*; and Milton, "Context of the Holocaust." See also BAK, R73/14005: DFG files on Robert Ritter.

153. U.S. Military Tribunal, Transcript of the Proceedings in Case 1, p. 1513.

154. StA Düsseldorf, Anklageschrift Kurt Franz, 8 Js 10904/59, 29 Jan. 1963, p. 98.

CHAPTER TWO

1. On the Nazi party's racial and eugenic program, see Adam, *Judenpolitik*, pp. 19–38; Bock, *Zwangssterilisation*, pp. 23–27; and Nowak, *"Euthanasie" und Sterilisierung*, pp. 34–38. See also Gütt, Linden, and Maßfeller, *Blutschutz- und Ehegesundheitsgesetz* (1st ed.), p. v.

2. For the support physicians and civil servants provided for this eugenic legislation, see BAK, R18/5585: Oberregierungsrat Dr. med. Linden, Berlin, "Die praktische Anwendung des Gesetzes zur Verhütung erbkranken Nachwuchses."

3. *Reichsgesetzblatt* 1933, 1:529.

4. *Reichsgesetzblatt* 1935, 1:1246.

5. For an English translation of the eugenic legislation, see Control Commission for Germany (British Element), "Nazi Health Laws." The German authorities also published an English translation of this legislation: Reichsausschuß für Volksgesundheitsdienst, *Law for the Prevention of Hereditarily Diseased Offspring*.

6. Gütt, Rüdin, and Ruttke, *Gesetz zur Verhütung erbkranken Nachwuchses* (1st ed.), p. 6.

7. *Reichsgesetzblatt* 1933, 1:995, 1000, English translation and explanation in *Statutory Criminal Law of Germany*, pp. 19, 27–32.

8. StGB §20a, §42a–m.

9. Walk, *Sonderrecht für die Juden*.

10. "Gesetz zur Wiederherstellung des Berufsbeamtentums," *Reichsgesetzblatt* 1933, 1: 175. See also Walk, *Sonderrecht für die Juden*, p. 12, no. 46.

11. The various decrees and regulations are listed chronologically in Walk, *Sonderrecht für die Juden*.

12. "Reichsbürgergesetz" and "Gesetz zum Schutze des deutschen Blutes und der deutschen Ehre," *Reichsgesetzblatt* 1935, 1:1146. See also Walk, *Sonderrecht für die Juden*, p. 127, nos. 636–37. Facsimile reproduction in Eschwege, *Kennzeichen J*, pp. 79–80.

13. Gütt, Linden, and Maßfeller, *Blutschutz- und Ehegesundheitsgesetz* (1st ed.), pp. 21, 259ff.

14. Adam, *Judenpolitik*, pp. 125–31; Schleunes, *Twisted Road to Auschwitz*, pp. 121–25.

15. Cited in Gütt, Linden, and Maßfeller, *Blutschutz- und Ehegesundheitsgesetz* (1st ed.), p. 21. The German words used to define the status of blood were *artverwandt* for "related" and *artfremd* for "alien."

16. Ibid., p. 22.

17. *Reichsgesetzblatt* 1935, 1:1334. See also Gütt, Linden, and Maßfeller, *Blutschutz- und Ehegesundheitsgesetz* (1st ed.), pp. 225ff.

18. Gütt, Linden, and Maßfeller, *Blutschutz- und Ehegesundheitsgesetz* (1st ed.), p. 16.

19. *Reichsgesetzblatt* 1935, 1:1333.

20. See BAK, R18/5584: Dienstversammlung der Medizinaldezernenten des RMdI, 2–3 Apr. 1936; Gütt, Linden, and Maßfeller, *Blutschutz- und Ehegesundheitsgesetz* (1st ed.), pp. 21ff.; and Bergmann, Czarnowski, and Ehmann, "Objekte humangenetischer Forschung," p. 131.

21. See the collection of anti-Gypsy laws, decrees, and regulations in StA Hamburg, Ver-

fahren Ruth Kellermann, 2200 Js 2/84. For traditional anti-Gypsy police powers, see, for example, ibid.: decree of Prussian Ministry of Interior (sig. von Bethmann-Hollweg), Verfügung btr. die Bekämpfung des Zigeunerunwesens, 17 Feb. 1906.

22. Ibid.: decree of Reich and Prussian Ministry of Interior, Bekämpfung der Zigeunerplage, 6 June 1936, and decree (sig. Frick), "Vorbeugende Verbrechensbekämpfung durch die Polizei," 14 Dec. 1937.

23. See Calvelli-Adorno, "Rassische Verfolgung der Zigeuner."

24. Walk, *Sonderrecht für die Juden*, p. 146, no. 81.

25. See Kater, *Doctors under Hitler*, p. 182, and Bergmann, Czarnowski, and Ehmann, "Objekte humangenetischer Forschung," p. 131. See also Noakes, "Judenmischlinge."

26. *Reichsgesetzblatt* 1933, 1:529, English translation in Control Commission for Germany (British Element), "Nazi Health Laws," pp. 1–5. See also Vogel, "Gesetz zur Verhütung erbkranken Nachwuchses."

27. Bock, *Zwangssterilisation*, pp. 80–87; Nowak, *"Euthanasie" und Sterilisierung*, pp. 64–65.

28. *Reichsgesetzblatt* 1933, 1:529, English translation in Control Commission for Germany (British Element), "Nazi Health Laws," pp. 1–5.

29. For a discussion of the categories defined as hereditary diseases, see Gütt, Rüdin, and Ruttke, *Gesetz zur Verhütung erbkranken Nachwuchses* (1st ed.), pp. 119ff.

30. The German medical press announced in 1935 that 205 hereditary health courts and 31 appellate courts of hereditary health had been established. Cited in Proctor, *Racial Hygiene*, p. 361, n. 33.

31. See DÖW, file E19198, Reichsgau Wien, Hauptgesundheitsamt, for a sample form ordering an individual to report for sterilization. The form concludes with the following warning: "You are explicitly advised that the operation can also be performed against your will."

32. Nowak, *"Euthanasie" und Sterilisierung*, p. 65.

33. Bock, *Zwangssterilisation*, p. 232.

34. Results of sterilization proceedings, based on statistics accumulated by the RJM, were collected by the RMdI and can be found in BAK, R18/5585.

35. See also Proctor, *Racial Hygiene*, pp. 107–8.

36. For the regulations limiting sterilization during the war, see RMdI decree, 31 Aug. 1939 (*Reichsgesetzblatt* 1:1560), and the various RMdI circulars of implementation and clarification (NARA Suitland, Heidelberg Docs. 126,804–9, 126,811–12A, 126,813–15A, 127,504–9).

37. BA-MA, H20/463, 465: report on the Protectorate, Sept. 1942, p. 2. See also NARA Suitland, Heidelberg Docs. 126,822–24.

38. For a good summation and evaluation of all surviving statistics on sterilizations, see Bock, *Zwangssterilisation*, pp. 230–46.

39. A collection of amendments and regulations (prepared after the Anschluß for the information of Austrian health authorities) can be found in AVA, Bürckel Akte, file 2354, and DÖW, file E19198, Reichsgau Wien, Hauptgesundheitsamt.

40. *Reichsgesetzblatt* 1933, 1:1021, English translation in Control Commission for Germany (British Element), "Nazi Health Laws," pp. 8ff.

41. BAK, R18/5585: circular 21/34 from NSDAP Amt für Volksgesundheit und NS-Ärztebund (sig. Gerhard Wagner), 13 Sept. 1934.

42. First amendment of 26 June 1935, *Reichsgesetzblatt* 1935, 1:773.

43. First regulation of 5 Dec. 1935, §1 (*Reichsgesetzblatt* 1933, 1:1021), English translation in Control Commission for Germany (British Element), "Nazi Health Laws," p. 8. See also Proctor, *Racial Hygiene*, pp. 108–12, for a discussion of how the medical profession mastered the technical problems of mass sterilization.

44. Second amendment of 4 Feb. 1936, *Reichsgesetzblatt* 1936, 1:119, English translation in Control Commission for Germany (British Element), "Nazi Health Laws," p. 8; fifth regulation of 25 Feb. 1936, *Reichsgesetzblatt* 1936, 1:122, English translation in Control Commission for Germany (British Element), "Nazi Health Laws," p. 23.

45. Article 42k of the German penal code (StGB §42k), English translation in *Statutory Criminal·Law of Germany*, pp. 30–31.

46. First amendment of 26 June 1935, *Reichsgesetzblatt* 1935, 1:773. The reference to homosexuals is based on article 175 of the German penal code (StGB §175) (sodomy and bestiality [*Widernatürliche Unzucht*]), English translation in *Statutory Criminal Law of Germany*, p. 114.

47. Bock, *Zwangssterilisation*, p. 95.

48. *Reichsgesetzblatt* 1935, 1:1246, English translation in Control Commission for Germany (British Element), "Nazi Health Laws," pp. 33–34.

49. See Gerhard Friese, *Das Ehegesundheitsgesetz*, Schriftenreihe des Reichsausschusses für Volksgesundheitsdienst, no. 17 (Berlin, 1938), pp. 9–12 (copy in AVA, Bürckel Akte, file 2354).

50. First regulation of 29 Nov. 1935, *Reichsgesetzblatt* 1935, 1:1419, English translation in Control Commission for Germany (British Element), "Nazi Health Laws," pp. 35–40.

51. Sample tests can be found in BAK, R18/5585; DÖW, file 1862; and AVA, Bürckel Akte, file 2354.

52. DÖW, file E18620: Antrag auf Unfruchtbarmachung, Solbad Hall, 22 Mar. 1943.

53. BAK, R18/5585: Erbgesundheitsgericht Gera, Beschluß vom 21. Mai 1937.

54. Ibid.: Erbgesundheitsobergericht Jena, Beschluß vom 4. August 1937. See also ibid.: RJM to Oberlandesgerichtspräsidenten, 22 Apr. 1936, urging that proceedings should not be limited only to written records.

55. Ibid.: memo, Munich, 10 June 1937. The memo was probably composed by someone on the staff of Gerhard Wagner, the Reich physician leader.

56. ZStL, Bd. 513: memo from Dr. Irmfried Eberl concerning Johannes Schmidt, n.d.

57. The term "Heil- und Pflegeanstalt" was introduced in Germany in the 1920s as part of a reform of mental hospitals, previously known as "Irrenanstalten" (lunatic asylums). As the name implies, these institutions were to combine confinement, rehabilitation, and long-term care and did not treat only mental patients. On the translation of the name, see Note on Language.

58. BAK, R36/1373: circular from the RMdI (sig. Gütt) to Landesregierungen, "Betr. Erbbiologische Bestandsaufnahme in Heil- und Pflegeanstalten," 8 Jan. 1936.

59. Ibid.: RMdI to DGT, 27 June 1936.

60. Ibid.: circular from the RMdI (sig. Gütt) to Landesregierungen, "Betr. Erbbiologische Bestandsaufnahme in Heil- und Pflegeanstalten," 8 Jan. 1936.

61. Reports from the Prussian provinces (and the city of Berlin) and from some individual institutions, as well as the DGT's summaries, ibid.: "Akten betr. Ergebnis der Sterilisationsmaßnahmen in den Heil- und Pflegeanstalten."

62. See Adam, *Judenpolitik*, for a similar struggle between state and party over control of the policies against Jews.

63. BAK, R18/5585: Gerhard Wagner to Hitler, 29 May 1937, with forty-six-page memo attached.

64. BAK, R18/5586: "Vorläufige Stellungnahme zu den Ausführungen des Reichsärzteführers Dr. Wagner" (forty-page memo).

65. BAK, R18/5585: Ergebnis des Vortrages bei dem Führer am 14. Juni 1937 in Gegenwart von Reichsleiter Bormann.

66. See ibid. for correspondence between Hans Heinrich Lammers, Hans Pfundtner, and Gerhard Wagner, 1937–38.

67. See the correspondence in AVA, Bürckel Akte, file 2354.

68. Ibid.: RMdI decree, 11 Dec. 1939.

69. BDC, dossier Leonardo Conti.

CHAPTER THREE

1. GStA Frankfurt, Anklage Werner Heyde, Gerhard Bohne und Hans Hefelmann, Ks 2/63 (GStA), Js 17/59 (GStA), 22 May 1962, p. 40; U.S. Military Tribunal, Transcript of the Proceedings in Case 1, p. 2482 (testimony Karl Brandt).

2. StA Stuttgart, Verfahren Albert Widmann, Ks 19/62 (19 Js 328/60): interrogation of Werner Catel by StA Hannover (Bd. VI, 2 Js 237/56), 14 May 1962, p. 2; U.S. Military Tribunal, Transcript of the Proceedings in Case 1, pp. 2398–99 (testimony Karl Brandt). Both Catel and Brand described the same malformations. Catel remembered convulsions; Brandt did not. Catel commented that the child was "apparently" blind but did not mention mental retardation. Brandt was certain about the blindness; about retardation, he testified that the child "was … an idiot — at least it seemed to be an idiot."

3. StA Stuttgart, Verfahren Widmann, Ks 19/62 (19 Js 328/60): interrogation of Werner Catel by StA Hannover (Bd. VI, 2 Js 237/56), 14 May 1962, p. 2.

4. U.S. Military Tribunal, Transcript of the Proceedings in Case 1, pp. 2398–99 (testimony Karl Brandt).

5. Ibid. Catel later claimed that he was on vacation and did not participate in this decision. See StA Stuttgart, Verfahren Widmann, Ks 19/62 (19 Js 328/60): interrogation of Werner Catel by StA Hannover (Bd. VI, 2 Js 237/56), 14 May 1962, p. 2.

6. GStA Frankfurt, Anklage Heyde, Bohne und Hefelmann, Ks 2/63 (GStA), Js 17/59 (GStA), 22 May 1962, pp. 53–54 (testimony Hans Hefelmann).

7. For a similar analysis, see StA Hamburg, Anklage Friedrich Lensch und Kurt Struve, 147 Js 58/67, 24 Apr. 1973, p. 94.

8. Ibid., p. 93. The name does not actually apply until somewhat later. At this time, the Munich headquarters was headed by Rudolf Hess and was known as the Office of the Deputy of the Führer. After Hess's flight to England in 1940, the chief of staff, Martin Bormann, took his place, and the headquarters was then known as the Nazi Party Chancellery.

9. BDC, dossier Hans Hefelmann: Nazi party membership file card; GStA Frankfurt, Anklage Heyde, Bohne und Hefelmann, Ks 2/63 (GStA), Js 17/59 (GStA), 22 May 1962, pp. 21–24.

10. BDC, dossier Hans Hefelmann: recommendation for award, 30 Mar. 1943.

11. BDC, dossier Richard von Hegener: Nazi party membership file card and recommendation for award, 30 Mar. 1943; BAK, NL263, Nachlaß Rheindorf: Landeskriminalpolizeiabteilung Mecklenburg, Anklage Richard von Hegener, 5-0/410/47/B1, 5-0/339/49/B1, Schwerin, 9 Sept. 1949; ZStL, Sammlung Verschiedenes, Bd. 18: LG Magdeburg, Urteil Richard von Hegener, 11 KLs 139/51, 20 Feb. 1952.

12. The information about planning and early implementation of children's euthanasia comes from the interrogation of Hans Hefelmann, available at the offices of the Staatsanwaltschaft bei dem Oberlandesgericht Frankfurt. His verbose testimony was obviously self-serving and cannot always be trusted. Crucial portions of Hefelmann's testimony are cited in GStA Frankfurt, Anklage Heyde, Bohne und Hefelmann, Ks 2/63 (GStA), Js 17/59 (GStA), 22 May 1962. I have based my reconstruction of these planning sessions on this (Heyde) indictment, as well as on StA Hamburg, Anklage Lensch und Struve, 147 Js 58/67, 24 Apr. 1973.

13. For administrative purposes, the German Reich retained its federal structure even under the Nazi regime. The various federal states were known as *Länder*. Only the largest of these, especially the giant state of Prussia, were subdivided into provinces. Incorporated

Austria, thereafter a kind of federal state renamed Ostmark, also remained subdivided into provinces. The Prussian provinces were subdivided into districts (*Regierungsbezirke*). For the administrative relationship between public health on the national and on the local level, see, for example, Nuremberg Doc. PS-3896 (affidavit Dr. Ludwig Sprauer), where this chief public health officer in the state of Baden describes himself as a subordinate of the RMdI.

14. BDC, dossier Arthur Gütt; BAK, R18/3356: circular from Wilhelm Frick, 31 Aug. 1939, concerning Gütt's retirement; BAK, R18/5583: Kopfstärke der Gesundheitsabteilung, 1933–39.

15. See BAK, R18/5585, for reviews in legal and scientific journals of his coauthored commentary on the sterilization law (Gütt, Rüdin, and Ruttke, *Gesetz zur Verhütung erbkranken Nachwuchses*). He also coauthored a commentary on the Nuremberg racial laws and the Marriage Health Law (Gütt, Linden, and Maßfeller, *Blutschutz- und Ehegesundheitsgesetz*).

16. BAK, R18/5583: Kopfstärke der Gesundheitsabteilung. The files of the RMdI at BAK (R18) do not contain a prewar breakdown of department sections (*Referate*), and thus Linden's responsibilities can only be surmised on the basis of his involvement in euthanasia and his wartime responsibilities. (For Linden's wartime duties, see BAK, R18/3356: chart of Unterabteilung I.) Linden was coauthor with Gütt and Maßfeller of *Blutschutz- und Ehegesundheitsgesetz*.

17. BDC, dossier Herbert Linden: Reichsärztekammer file card.

18. Ibid.: membership record in the Reichsbund der Deutschen Beamten, including information on Linden's party membership. Linden's Nazi party membership file card could not be located in the BDC; there were also no personnel records for Linden in the BDC's SA and SS collections.

19. Standesamt Berlin-Zehlendorf: death record 977, 11 May 1945.

20. GStA Frankfurt, Anklage Heyde, Bohne und Hefelmann, Ks 2/63 (GStA), Js 17/59 (GStA), 22 May 1962, pp. 56a–57; StA Hamburg, Anklage Lensch und Struve, 147 Js 58/67, 24 Apr. 1973, pp. 101–3.

21. Personal data, including party membership file cards, medical certification, and similar information, for Werner Catel, Hans Heinze, Hellmuth Unger, and Ernst Wentzler can be found in their BDC dossiers. See also Klee, "*Euthanasie*" *im NS-Staat*, p. 79. On euthanasia films, see Roth, "Filmpropaganda."

22. StA Hamburg, Sachsstandsvermerk, 147 Js 58/67, 25 Feb. 1970, p. 38; StA Hamburg, Anklage Lensch und Struve, 147 Js 58/67, 24 Apr. 1973, pp. 103, 127.

23. StA Hamburg, Anklage Wilhelm Bayer, Werner Catel, 14 Js 265/48, 7 Feb. 1949, pp. 22–23.

24. U.S. Military Tribunal, Transcript of the Proceedings in Case 1, p. 2494.

25. BAK, R18/5586: RMdI Runderlaß, 18 Aug. 1939.

26. The German secrecy designation was "streng vertraulich!" The origins of the decree in Department IV can be seen from the reference number: IV b 3088/39-1079 Mi. Stuckart signed the circulated decree "In Vertretung."

27. See LA Berlin, Rep. 214, Acc. 2740, Nr. 154–55, and AVA, Bürckel Akte, file 2350, for copies of RMdI decree, 18 Aug. 1939, and reporting form.

28. StA Hamburg, Anklage Lensch und Struve, 147 Js 58/67, 24 Apr. 1973, pp. 114–16: text of RMdI decree, 7 June 1940.

29. Text of Meldebogen in GStA Frankfurt, Anklage Heyde, Bohne und Hefelmann, Ks 2/63 (GStA), Js 17/59 (GStA), 22 May 1962, pp. 69–72, and StA Hamburg, Anklage Lensch und Struve, 147 Js 58/67, 24 Apr. 1973, pp. 110–14.

30. StA Hamburg, Sachsstandsvermerk, 147 Js 58/67, 25 Feb. 1970, p. 38.

31. StA Hamburg, Anklage Bayer, Catel, 14 Js 265/48, 7 Feb. 1949, pp. 23–24.

32. See StArch Sigmaringen, Wü 29/3, Acc. 33/1973, Nr. 1752: StA Tübingen, Anklage

Otto Mauthe, 1 Js 85–87/47, 4 Jan. 1949, p. 15; DÖW, file E19198: circular from Reichsgau Wien, Hauptgesundheitsamt (sig. Dr. Vellguth), 15 Nov. 1941.

33. Nuremberg Doc. NO-2758: primitive organizational chart of the Reich Committee's procedures (draft drawn by Viktor Brack in jail at Nuremberg).

34. See StA Hamburg, Anklage Bayer, Catel, 14 Js 265/48, 7 Feb. 1949, pp. 51–52. On Catel, see also Schultz, "Werner Catel."

35. GStA Frankfurt, Anklage Heyde, Bohne und Hefelmann, Ks 2/63 (GStA), Js 17/59 (GStA), 22 May 1962, p. 95.

36. Ibid., pp. 90–95; StA Hamburg, Anklage Lensch und Struve, 147 Js 58/67, 24 Apr. 1973, pp. 130–33.

37. LA Berlin, Rep. 214, Acc. 2740, Nr. 154–55: RMdI decree, 1 July 1940.

38. StA Hamburg, Anklage Lensch und Struve, 147 Js 58/67, 24 Apr. 1973, pp. 117–19: text of RMdI decree, 18 June 1940; LA Berlin, Rep. 214, Acc. 2740, Nr. 154–55: Ministerialblatt of the Reich and Prussian Ministry of Interior, 26 June 1940.

39. LA Berlin, Rep. 214, Acc. 2740, Nr. 154–55: Amtsarzt und Leiter des Gesundheits- amtes to Polizeipräsident Berlin, 14 Aug. 1940, with second letter to Görden attached.

40. On costs, see StA Hamburg, Anklage Bayer, Catel, 14 Js 265/48, 7 Feb. 1949, p. 22: RMdI decrees, 30 May 1941, 10 July 1942; LA Berlin, Rep. 214, Acc. 2740, Nr. 154–55: *Dienst- blatt* (Berlin, 1940), Teil VII, Allgemeine Wohlfahrt, Jugendwohlfahrt, Gesundheitswesen, Leibesübungen, VII/135, VII/148.

41. For collaboration between the KdF and local authorities concerning the establish- ment of children's wards, see, for example, StArch Sigmaringen, Wü 29/3, Acc. 33/1973, Nr. 1752: StA Tübingen, Anklage Mauthe, 1 Js 85–87/47, 4 Jan. 1949, pp. 16r–17, and LG Tübin- gen, Urteil Otto Mauthe, Ks 6/49, 5 July 1949, p. 11.

42. Nuremberg Doc. NO-1313: Dr. F. Hoelzel to Hermann Pfannmüller, 28 Aug. 1940. See also ibid. PS-3823: affidavit Dr. Eidam, 5 May 1945, and StA Köln, Verfahren Dr. Alfred Leu, 24 Ks 1/51 (24 Js 642/51): interrogation Franz Schlund, 31 Oct. 1951.

43. See, for example, DÖW, file 19209, Personalakten Dr. Erwin Jekelius: memo, Reichs- gau Wien, Hauptgesundheitsamt, 26 Mar. 1941, showing that Jekelius planned to attend a meeting near Dresden called by the Reich Committee and, immediately thereafter, a meet- ing on adult euthanasia in Berlin.

44. See table 3.4. Hans Hefelmann named a number of additional children's wards in his interrogation (GStA Frankfurt), bringing the number to thirty wards. See Klee, *"Eutha- nasie" im NS-Staat*, pp. 300, 302.

45. See BAK, R18/3768, for a list of all German institutions holding patients eligible for euthanasia. The list is arranged by federal states and Prussian and Austrian provinces; it provides information about the status (public, private, etc.) and function (hospital, uni- versity clinic, rehabilitation center for alcoholics, etc.) of each institution.

46. LG Düsseldorf, Urteil Walter Creutz, 8 KLs 8/48, 27 Jan. 1950, pp. 5–6, 17–20.

47. On research at Görden, see, for example, ZStL, Heidelberg Docs. 127,050–155: Hans Heinze, "Bericht über die bisherige Tätigkeit der Beobachtungs- und Forschungsabteilung bei der Landesanstalt Görden," 9 Sept. 1942.

48. GStA Frankfurt, Anklage Aquilin Ullrich, Heinrich Bunke, Kurt Borm und Klaus Endruweit, Js 15/61 (GStA), 15 Jan. 1965, p. 232 (testimony Heinrich Bunke).

49. StA Wien, Anklage Ernst Illing, Marianne Türk und Margarete Hübsch, 15 St 9103/45, 18 June 1946; VG bei dem LG Wien, Urteil Ernst Illing, Marianne Türk und Margarete Hübsch, Vg 1a Vr 2365/45 (Hv 1208/46), 18 July 1946. Both indictment and de- cision can be found in DÖW, file 4974, English translation available as Nuremberg Doc. NO-317. See also DÖW, file 18282: VG bei dem LG Wien, Urteil Anna Katschenka, Vg 12g Vr 5442/46 (Hv 301/48), 9 Apr. 1948.

50. On Jekelius, see BDC, dossier Erwin Jekelius: Reichsärztekammer file card and Nazi

party membership file card; DÖW, file E19209, Personalakten Dr. Erwin Jekelius. On Illing, see BDC, dossier Ernst Illing: Reichsärztekammer file card, Nazi party membership file card, and Personalakten Illing of the Reichsministerium für Wissenschaft, Erziehung und Volksbildung.

51. On Illing's position as assistant to Heinze, see ZStL, Heidelberg Docs. 127,116–17: Heinze memo, 18 Mar. 1942. On Illing's transfer from Görden to Am Spiegelgrund, see DÖW, file E19292: correspondence and memos of Gemeindeverwaltung des Reichsgaues Wien, 1942–43, esp. Hauptabteilung E, Gesundheitswesen und Volkspflege, Anstaltenamt, E 9 Personalabteilung to Landesanstalt Görden, 5 Aug. 1942, and Oberpräsident der Provinz Mark Brandenburg (Verwaltung des Provinzialverbandes), 5 Oct. 1942.

52. DÖW, file E19292: Reich Committee to Ernst Illing, 27 June 1942.

53. See Schmidt, *Selektion in der Heilanstalt*, pp. 99–131.

54. StA München I, Anklage Hermann Pfannmüller, 1b Js 1791/47, 16 June 1948; LG München I, Urteil Hermann Pfannmüller, 1 Ks 10/49, 5 Nov. 1949; *JuNSV*, vol. 8, no. 271: LG München I, Urteil Pfannmüller, 1 Ks 10/49, 15 Mar. 1951.

55. BDC, dossier Hermann Pfannmüller: Reichsärztekammer file card and Nazi party membership file card; NARA, RG 238: interrogation Hermann Pfannmüller, 5 Sept. 1945, pp. 1–2; StA München I, Verfahren Hermann Pfannmüller, 1 Ks 10/49 (1b Js 1791/47): Protokoll der öffentlichen Sitzung des Schwurgerichts bei dem LG München I, 19 Oct. 1949, pp. 4–7.

56. NARA, RG 238: interrogation Hermann Pfannmüller, 5 Sept. 1945, pp. 1–2; StA München I, Anklage Pfannmüller, 1b Js 1791/47, 16 June 1948; StA München I, Verfahren Pfannmüller, 1 Ks 10/49 (1b Js 1791/47): Protokoll der öffentlichen Sitzung des Schwurgerichts bei dem LG München I, 19 Oct. 1949, pp. 6–7.

57. Nuremberg Doc. NO-863: voluntary testimony, Ludwig Lehner, London, 25 Aug. 1946, repeated (with some stylistic changes) as sworn affidavit for U.S. Office of Chief of Council for War Crimes, St. Wolfgang, Wasserburg on the Inn, Upper Bavaria, 30 Mar. 1947. See also U.S. Military Tribunal, Transcript of the Proceedings in Case 1, pp. 1538–39. Lehner repeated this testimony at Pfannmüller's German trial, and Pfannmüller and his witnesses denied these events. See StA München I, Verfahren Pfannmüller, 1 Ks 10/49 (1b Js 1791/47): Protokoll der öffentlichen Sitzung des Schwurgerichts bei dem LG München I, 25 Oct. 1949, pp. 61–65.

58. U.S. Military Tribunal, Transcript of the Proceedings in Case 1, pp. 7305–6.

59. "Die Einschläferung der Kinder war die sauberste Euthanasie." StA München I, Verfahren Pfannmüller, 1 Ks 10/49 (1b Js 1791/47): Protokoll der öffentlichen Sitzung des Schwurgerichts bei dem LG München I, 19 Oct. 1949, p. 12.

60. BDC, dossier Fritz Bernotat. Bernotat was born in 1890 and joined the Nazi party in 1928 and the SS in 1932. For an evaluation of his impact on patient care in Hessen-Nassau, see HHStA, 461/32442/3: LG Frankfurt, Urteil Friedrich Mennecke, Walter Schmidt, 4 KLs 15/46, 21 Dec. 1946 (also in *JuNSV*, vol. 1, no. 011), and report by Dr. Schrader to U.S. Military Government, n.d. (report requested 21 Apr. 1945), concerning conditions in state institutions of the Wiesbaden district; and NARA, RG 238, Microfilm Publication M-1019, roll 46: interrogation Friedrich Mennecke, 11 Jan. 1947.

61. HHStA, 461/32442/2: StA Frankfurt, interrogation Friedrich Mennecke, 6 May 1946.

62. On Mennecke, see BDC, dossier Friedrich Mennecke: Reichsärztekammer file card and copies of medical degree and medical license, Nazi party membership file card, and SS Personalakten, and NARA, RG 238, Microfilm Publication M-1019, roll 46: interrogation Friedrich Mennecke, 11 Jan. 1947, pp. 1–4. On Schmidt, see BDC, dossier Walter Eugen Schmidt: Reichsärztekammer file card, Nazi party membership file card, and SS Personalakten, and NARA, RG 238, Microfilm Publication M-1019, roll 52: interrogation Walter Schmidt, 11 Jan. 1946, pp. 1–3. On the interaction between Mennecke and Schmidt, see

their confrontation at their postwar trial in HHStA, 461/32442/4: LG Frankfurt, Verfahren Friedrich Mennecke, Walter Schmidt, 4 KLs 15/46 (4a Js 13/46), Protokoll der öffentlichen Sitzung der 4. Strafkammer, 3 Dec. 1946, pp. 21–28. See also HHStA, 461/32442/3: StA Frankfurt, Anklage Friedrich Mennecke, Walter Schmidt, 4a Js 13/46, 7 Oct. 1946, pp. 3–5, and U.S. Military Tribunal, Transcript of the Proceedings in Case 1, pp. 1833–34, 1837, 1866–1945.

63. GStA Frankfurt, Sammlung Euthanasie: Walter Schmidt to Friedrich Mennecke, 23 Dec. 1941, 9 Jan. 1942.

64. *JuNSV*, vol. 1, no. 014: LG Frankfurt, Urteil Hermann Wesse, Mathilde Weber, 4 Ks 1/48, 30 Jan. 1947; *JuNSV*, vol. 4, no. 117: LG Frankfurt, Urteil Mathilde Weber, 4 KLs 18/46, 9 Feb. 1949. See also Sick, *"Euthanasie" im Nationalsozialismus am Beispiel des Kalmenhofs*.

65. HHStA, 461/32442/2: Hermann Wesse to Richard von Hegener, 12 May 1944, announcing assumption of duties in Kalmenhof-Idstein.

66. On Faltlhauser's Nazi party membership, see BDC, dossier Valentin Faltlhauser; on his participation in euthanasia, see ZStL, Heidelberg Docs. 127,890–93.

67. Nuremberg Doc. PS-1696.

68. StArch Sigmaringen, Wü 29/3, Acc. 33/1973, Nr. 1752: StA Tübingen, Anklage Mauthe, 1 Js 85–87/47, 4 Jan. 1949, p. 2r. See also BDC, dossiers Otto Mauthe and Eugen Stähle.

69. StArch Sigmaringen, Wü 29/3, Acc. 33/1973, Nr. 1752: StA Tübingen, Anklage Mauthe, 1 Js 85–87/47, 4 Jan. 1949, pp. 16r–17.

70. *JuNSV*, vol. 6, no. 211: LG Freiburg, Urteil Josef Artur Schreck und Ludwig Sprauer, 1 Ks 5/48, 16 Nov. 1948.

71. GStA Frankfurt, Verfahren Heyde, Bohne und Hefelmann, Ks 2/63 (GStA), Js 17/59 (GStA): interrogation Dr. J. R., 17 May 1961.

72. DÖW, file E18370/1: StA Frankfurt, Js 18/61 (GStA), interrogation Georg Renno, 1 Feb. 1965, pp. 1–2; BDC, dossier Georg Renno.

73. DÖW, file E18370/1: StA Frankfurt, Js 18/61 (GStA), interrogation Georg Renno, 1 Feb. 1965, p. 2.

74. BDC, dossier Hermann Wesse.

75. StA Düsseldorf, Anklage Walter Creutz, 8 Js 116/47, 23 Jan. 1948, pp. 25–27; LG Düsseldorf, Urteil Walter Creutz, 8 KLs 8/48, 24 Nov. 1948, pp. 17–20.

76. StA Köln, Verfahren Leu, 24 Ks 1/51 (24 Js 642/51): interrogation Dr. Walter Medow, 5 Nov. 1951, interrogation Dr. Hans Wiepking, 30 Oct. 1951, and interrogation Dr. Hans-Heinrich Braunroth, 2 Nov. 1951.

77. LG Schwerin, Urteil Hans-Heinrich Braunroth, 1 KLs 3/46, 16 Aug. 1946; LG Köln, Urteil Alfred Leu, 24 Ks 1/51, 24 Oct. 1951; LG Köln, Urteil Alfred Leu, 24 Ks 1/51, 4 Dec. 1953.

78. StA Hamburg, Anklage Bayer, Catel, 14 Js 265/48, 7 Feb. 1949, pp. 11–12, 25–26.

79. Ibid., p. 27.

80. See Nuremberg Doc. PS-3816: affidavit Dr. Gerhard Schmidt, 28 Mar. 1946; U.S. Military Tribunal, Transcript of the Proceedings in Case 1, p. 2433 (testimony Karl Brandt), pp. 7305–6 (testimony Hermann Pfannmüller); Schmidt, *Selektion in der Heilanstalt*, pp. 132–49; and Klee, *"Euthanasie" im NS-Staat*, pp. 429–32.

81. StA Hamburg, Anklage Lensch und Struve, 147 Js 58/67, 24 Apr. 1973, p. 154.

82. NARA, RG 238, Microfilm Publication M-1019, roll 52: interrogation Hermann Pfannmüller, 21 Sept. 1946, pp. 23–24.

83. StA Hamburg, Anklage Bayer, Catel, 14 Js 265/48, 7 Feb. 1949, p. 27.

84. DÖW, file 18282: LG Wien, interrogation Marianne Türk, 25 Jan. 1946. See also Schmidt, *Selektion in der Heilanstalt*, p. 115.

85. GStA Frankfurt, Anklage Heyde, Bohne und Hefelmann, Ks 2/63 (GStA), Js 17/59 (GStA), 22 May 1962, pp. 144–45 (testimony of senior Kaufbeuren nurse).

86. For a chemical analysis of these medicines and a description, including normal medical usage, usual dosage, and dosage required for killing, see StA Hamburg, Verfahren Lensch und Struve, 147 Js 58/67: Gutachten Jozef Radzicki (German translation), pp. 19–26.

87. See, for example, Nuremberg Doc. PS-3824: autopsy report on Emil Ruf in Eglfing-Haar, 20 Apr. 1942.

88. U.S. Military Tribunal, Transcript of the Proceedings in Case 1, p. 7392.

89. For a brief description, see Henry Friedlander, "The SS and Police," in Grobman, Landes, and Milton, *Genocide*, pp. 150–54.

90. For the organization and personnel of the RKPA and the KTI, see BAK, R58/473, and ZStL, Bd. 141.

91. BDC, dossier Albert Widmann. Widmann had joined the SS in December 1939 with the rank of second lieutenant (Untersturmführer) and had been promoted by 1944 to the rank of major (Sturmbannführer). See also LG Düsseldorf, Urteil Albert Widmann, 8 Ks 1/61, 16 May 1961.

92. StA Düsseldorf, Verfahren Albert Widmann, 8 Ks 1/61 (8 Js 7212/59): interrogation Albert Widmann, 12 Jan. 1960, and interrogation of KdF female clerk I. R., 14 Oct. 1959; StA Stuttgart, Verfahren Widmann, Ks 19/62 (19 Js 328/60): Landeskriminalamt Baden-Württemberg, Sonderkommission Zentrale Stelle, report on interrogations, 29 June 1961, interrogation of KdF female clerk I. L.

93. See BAK, R58/1059, for letters, memos, and receipts from and to KTI Abteilung Chemie (Widmann), Reichsausschuß, Hauptsanitätslager der Waffen SS, and the following institutions: Städt. Krankenhäuser und Kinderheime Stuttgart (Oberärztin Dr. Schütte); Heil- und Pflegeanstalt Ansbach; Landesanstalt Görden (Dr. Heinze); Landesheilanstalt Eichberg (Dr. Schmidt); Landesheilanstalt Groß-Schweidnitz über Löbau in Sachsen (Dr. Mittag); Landesheilanstalt Uchtspringe, Altmark (Dr. Beese); and Heilerziehungsanstalt Kalmenhof-Idstein (Dr. Grossmann). See also ZStL, Bd. 141: Reichsarzt SS und Polizei, Sanitätszeugmeister, KTI receipt of medicines received (listing twenty-six items).

94. StA Hamburg, Anklage Bayer, Catel, 14 Js 265/48, 7 Feb. 1949, pp. 24, 40; StArch Sigmaringen, Wü 29/3, Acc. 33/1973, Nr. 1752: StA Tübingen, Anklage Mauthe, 1 Js 85–87/47, 4 Jan. 1949, p. 2r. See also correspondence between Reich Committee and Thuringian Ministry of Interior in ZStL, Sammlung Verschiedenes, Bd. 132.

95. StArch Sigmaringen, Wü 29/3, Acc. 33/1973, Nr. 1752: LG Tübingen, Urteil Mauthe, Ks 6/49, 5 July 1949, p. 11.

96. HHStA, 461/32442/4: list of children with date transferred and date of death.

97. See, for example, Nuremberg Doc. NO-3355: Hermann Pfannmüller to Reich Committee, 17 Jan. 1941, reporting three children already patients at Eglfing-Haar.

98. HHStA, 461/32442/4: interrogation of Frankfurt public health officer, 22 Jan. 1947. See also StA Hamburg, Anklage Bayer, Catel, 14 Js 265/48, 7 Feb. 1949, p. 40. For a copy of the form letter sent by the Reich Committee to the local public health authorities requesting the transfer of children, see GStA Frankfurt, Anklage Heyde, Bohne und Hefelmann, Ks 2/63 (GStA), Js 17/59 (GStA), 22 May 1962, pp. 98–99.

99. HHStA, 461/32442/4: LG Frankfurt, Verfahren Mennecke, Schmidt, 4 KLs 15/46 (4a Js 13/46), Protokoll der öffentlichen Sitzung der 4. Strafkammer, 9 Dec. 1946, p. 13 (testimony Walter Schmidt).

100. StA Hamburg, Anklage Bayer, Catel, 14 Js 265/48, 7 Feb. 1949, pp. 22–23.

101. See Schmidt, *Selektion in der Heilanstalt*, pp. 106–8, for conclusions based on Eglfing-Haar medical records.

102. U.S. Military Tribunal, Transcript of the Proceedings in Case 1, p. 7314 (testimony

Hermann Pfannmüller); NARA, RG 238, Microfilm Publication M-1019, roll 52: interrogation Walter Schmidt, 11 Jan. 1946, p. 14.

103. See HHStA, 461/32442/12, for a sample authorization. This particular authorization for "treatment," on stationery of the Reich Committee and dated 29 January 1945, is addressed to Dr. Walter Schmidt in Eichberg and signed by Richard von Hegener.

104. U.S. Military Tribunal, Transcript of the Proceedings in Case 1, p. 1837.

105. See the list of medical conditions to be reported to the Reich Committee in BAK, R18/5586: RMdI decree, 18 Aug. 1939.

106. See, for example, Schmidt, *Selektion in der Heilanstalt*, pp. 110–13.

107. Werner Heyde cited in Klee, *"Euthanasie" im NS-Staat*, pp. 295, 298.

108. GStA Frankfurt, Anklage Heyde, Bohne und Hefelmann, Ks 2/63 (GStA), Js 17/59 (GStA), 22 May 1962, p. 105.

109. See, for example, GStA Frankfurt, Sammlung Euthanasie: RAG (Medizinalrat Müller) to Anstalt Liebenau, 15 Mar. 1941, and HHStA, 461/32442/1: report by Dr. Elisabeth Vigano, 9 Aug. 1945.

110. See, for example, Aly, "Medizin gegen Unbrauchbare," pp. 35–38.

111. See, for example, DÖW, file 19209: "Gutachten über den Vortrag Dr. Jekelius," 3 Nov. 1943, showing the poor scientific caliber of at least one of these physicians.

112. See the BDC dossiers of Hans Heinze, Ernst Illing, Erwin Jekelius, Friedrich Mennecke, Hermann Pfannmüller, Georg Renno, Walter Schmidt, and Hermann Wesse.

113. HHStA, 461/32442/14: Friedrich Mennecke to Ärztekammer Hessen-Nassau, 25 Feb. 1940, applying for certification in psychiatry and neurology, and partial draft of letter from Mennecke to Herbert Linden, n.d. [1940], with reference to discussions with Viktor Brack and Werner Heyde about his certification.

114. BA-MA, H20/463, 465: Prof. Dr. Carl Schneider, Bericht über einen Besuch in der Heil- und Pflegeanstalt Eichberg, 11 Feb. 1943.

115. HHStA, 461/32442/2: Walter Schmidt to Reich Committee, 15 May 1944.

116. See, for example, HHStA, 461/32442/4: Walter Schmidt to Friedrich Mennecke, 9 Jan. 1942, and HHStA, 461/32442/12: Reich Committee to Walter Schmidt, 18 Nov. 1943. See also HHStA, 461/32442/1: interrogation of nurse Katharina Kallmünzer, 20 Mar. 1946, who received a onetime bonus of 100 RM and thereafter a supplement of 25 RM each month.

117. See Müller-Hill, *Tödliche Wissenschaft*, pp. 68–75.

118. See ZStL, Heidelberg Docs. 127,973–74: Paul Nitsche to Carl Schneider, 3 Dec. 1943; HHStA, 461/32442/4-12-13, for correspondence from Heidelberg clinic to Eichberg, esp. Fritz Bernotat to Eichberg, 27 May 1942. The Eichberg telephone operator recalled after the war that "Heidelberg physicians brought children and also took children away" (HHStA, 461/32442/1: interrogation, 27 July 1945). See also BA-MA, H20/463, 465: Carl Schneider, Bericht über einen Besuch in der Heil- und Pflegeanstalt Eichberg, 11 Feb. 1943.

119. Chroust, *Friedrich Mennecke*, pp. 343–438.

120. RMdI decree (sig. Conti), 20 Sept. 1941, text in GStA Frankfurt, Anklage Heyde, Bohne und Hefelmann, Ks 2/63 (GStA), Js 17/59 (GStA), 22 May 1962, pp. 100–104.

121. See, for example, HHStA, 461/32442/1: interrogation of hairdresser E. G., 3 Oct. 1945, about pressure exerted on her by the public health office to commit her infant to Eichberg.

122. GStA Frankfurt, Anklage Heyde, Bohne und Hefelmann, Ks 2/63 (GStA), Js 17/59 (GStA), 22 May 1962, pp. 110–12.

123. Ibid., pp. 112–15.

124. Aly, "Medizin gegen Unbrauchbare," pp. 12–13, 34.

125. See, for example, HHStA, 461/32442/12: Reich Committee to Walter Schmidt, 16 Nov. 1943, and Schmidt to Reich Committee, 27 Nov. 1943. See also HHStA, 461/32442/4: interrogation of deputy director of Frankfurt Gesundheitsamt, 25 Jan. 1947.

126. For a petition, see HHStA, 461/32442/12: letter from a mother to Eichberg, 5 Mar. 1944. For denunciations, see Nuremberg Doc. NO-2253: affidavit of Hugo Suchomel, 21 Feb. 1947, and HHStA, 461/32442/12: Johann Risch to Walter Schmidt, 29 Feb. 1944. For subterfuge, see HHStA, 461/32442/3: Eichberg to Otto Stroh, 11 Sept. 1944, and Otto Stroh to Frankfurter Strafkammer, 8 Dec. 1946.

127. See, for example, GStA Frankfurt, Eberl Akten, I/152a, 1:123: Irmfried Eberl to Paul Nitsche, 4 Dec. 1942, requesting permission to include infant relative of colleague, the Ehrenzeichenträger Albert Geis, in children's euthanasia. See also Klee, *"Euthanasie" im NS-Staat*, pp. 307–8.

128. StA Hamburg, Anklage Bayer, Catel, 14 Js 265/48, 7 Feb. 1949, p. 27. See also U.S. Military Tribunal, Transcript of the Proceedings in Case 1, pp. 7715–16, 7749–53 (testimony Viktor Brack).

129. U.S. Military Tribunal, Transcript of the Proceedings in Case 1, p. 7394. At his German trial, Pfannmüller was not forced to admit that he had lied to the parents. See StA München I, Verfahren Pfannmüller, 1 Ks 10/49 (1b Js 1791/47): Protokoll der öffentlichen Sitzung des Schwurgerichts bei dem LG München I, 19 Oct. 1949, p. 13.

130. U.S. Military Tribunal, Transcript of the Proceedings in Case 1, pp. 2432, 2531 (testimony Karl Brandt).

131. StA Hamburg, Anklage Lensch und Struve, 147 Js 58/67, 24 Apr. 1973, pp. 129–30; HHStA, 461/32442/1: report by Dr. Elisabeth Vigano, 9 Aug. 1945.

132. U.S. Military Tribunal, Transcript of the Proceedings in Case 1, p. 2493 (testimony Karl Brandt).

133. GStA Frankfurt, Anklage Heyde, Bohne und Hefelmann, Ks 2/63 (GStA), Js 17/59 (GStA), 22 May 1962, p. 177.

CHAPTER FOUR

1. Schmidt, *Selektion in der Heilanstalt*, p. 24.

2. U.S. Military Tribunal, Transcript of the Proceedings in Case 1, p. 1513.

3. See, for example, Thom and Caregorodcev, *Medizin unterm Hakenkreuz*, pp. 130–31.

4. GStA Frankfurt, Anklage Reinhold Vorberg und Dietrich Allers, Js 20/61 (GStA), 15 Feb. 1966, p. 11 (testimony Otto Mauthe, 15 Nov. 1961).

5. NARA, RG 238, Microfilm Publication M-1019, roll 46: interrogation Friedrich Mennecke, 11 Jan. 1947, p. 23.

6. BAK, R18/3356: RMdI circular (sig. Wilhelm Frick), 31 Aug. 1939.

7. U.S. Military Tribunal, Transcript of the Proceedings in Case 1, p. 2668 (testimony Hans Heinrich Lammers). See also GStA Frankfurt, Anklage Werner Heyde, Gerhard Bohne und Hans Hefelmann, Ks 2/63 (GStA), Js 17/59 (GStA), 22 May 1962, pp. 178–79.

8. For an example of this type of postwar testimony, see U.S. Military Tribunal, Transcript of the Proceedings in Case 1, pp. 7299–300 (testimony Hermann Pfannmüller). See also Platen-Hallermund, *Die Tötung Geisteskranker*, pp. 25–26.

9. U.S. Military Tribunal, Transcript of the Proceedings in Case 1, p. 2669 (testimony Hans Heinrich Lammers).

10. Ibid., pp. 7555–57 (testimony Viktor Brack). See also GStA Frankfurt, Anklage Heyde, Bohne und Hefelmann, Ks 2/63 (GStA), Js 17/59 (GStA), 22 May 1962, pp. 180–85; GStA Frankfurt, Anklage Vorberg und Allers, Js 20/61 (GStA), 15 Feb. 1966, pp. 21–22.

11. U.S. Military Tribunal, Transcript of the Proceedings in Case 1, p. 2396 (testimony Karl Brandt).

12. Ibid., p. 7557 (testimony Viktor Brack).

13. Ibid., pp. 2396, 2400–2401 (testimony Karl Brandt), p. 2668 (testimony Hans Heinrich Lammers).

14. Ibid., pp. 7555–57 (testimony Viktor Brack); GStA Frankfurt, Anklage Heyde, Bohne und Hefelmann, Ks 2/63 (GStA), Js 17/59 (GStA), 22 May 1962, pp. 182–83.

15. U.S. Military Tribunal, Transcript of the Proceedings in Case 1, p. 7565 (testimony Viktor Brack).

16. NARA, RG 238: interrogation Karl Brandt, 1 Oct. 1945 P.M., p. 4.

17. BAK, R18/3356: RMdI circular, 31 Aug. 1939 (sig. Wilhelm Frick).

18. See BAK, R18/3672, for his promotion and the creation of the new subdepartment. For his appointment as plenipotentiary, see BAK, R18/3768, and GStA Frankfurt, Sammlung Euthanasie: RMdI, 23 Oct. 1941, Bestellung eines Reichsbeauftragten für die Heil- u. Pflegeanstalten (*Reichsgesetzblatt* 1941, 1:653).

19. U.S. Military Tribunal, Transcript of the Proceedings in Case 1, pp. 7558–59 (testimony Viktor Brack).

20. BDC, dossier Werner Heyde: Reichsärztekammer file card.

21. Ibid.: letter of reference from Prof. Dr. Reichardt, Psychiatrische und Nervenklinik der Universität, Würzburg, 25 May 1936, and Lebenslauf Heyde, n.d.

22. BDC, dossier Theodor Eicke: Eicke to Heinrich Himmler, 22, 29 Mar. 1933, and Lebenslauf Eicke, 15 Mar. 1937.

23. Ibid.: Werner Heyde to Heinrich Himmler, 22 Apr. 1933, and Eicke to Himmler, 16 May 1933. For a facsimile publication of the Heyde-Eicke-Himmler correspondence, see Friedlander and Milton, *Berlin Document Center*, vol. 1, docs. 109–11. On homosexual behavior, see BDC, dossier Werner Heyde: SS court decision concerning accusation against Heyde under article 175 of the penal code (StGB §175, prohibition of sodomy), 24 Oct. 1939.

24. See Sydnor, *Soldiers of Destruction*, chap. 1.

25. BDC, dossier Werner Heyde: Lebenslauf Heyde, n.d.

26. Ibid.: Nazi party membership file card and SS Karteikarte.

27. See ibid.: Lebenslauf Heyde, n.d., where Heyde mentions his conflicts before 1933 with the Jewish senior physician.

28. Ibid.: letter of reference from Prof. Dr. Reichardt, Psychiatrische und Nervenklinik der Universität, Würzburg, 25 May 1936, and Lebenslauf Heyde, n.d.

29. Ibid.: SS Führungshauptamt to SS Personalhauptamt, 12 June 1941.

30. U.S. Military Tribunal, Transcript of the Proceedings in Case 1, pp. 7558–59 (testimony Viktor Brack).

31. GStA Frankfurt, Anklage Vorberg und Allers, Js 20/61 (GStA), 15 Feb. 1966, pp. 22–24; GStA Frankfurt, Anklage Heyde, Bohne und Hefelmann, Ks 2/63 (GStA), Js 17/59 (GStA), 22 May 1962, pp. 188–89; LG Dresden, Urteil Hermann Paul Nitsche, 1 Ks 58/47, 7 July 1947, p. 3.

32. U.S. Military Tribunal, Transcript of the Proceedings in Case 1, p. 7565 (testimony Viktor Brack); StA München I, Verfahren Hermann Pfannmüller, 1 Ks 10/49 (1b Js 1791/47): Protokoll der öffentlichen Sitzung des Schwurgerichts bei dem LG München I, 19 Oct. 1949, p. 8.

33. GStA Frankfurt, Anklage Heyde, Bohne und Hefelmann, Ks 2/63 (GStA), Js 17/59 (GStA), 22 May 1962, pp. 190–97; GStA Frankfurt, Anklage Vorberg und Allers, Js 20/61 (GStA), 15 Feb. 1966, pp. 22–24.

34. U.S. Military Tribunal, Transcript of the Proceedings in Case 1, pp. 7560–61 (testimony Viktor Brack).

35. StGB §211 (murder), §212 (manslaughter), English translation in *Statutory Criminal Law of Germany*, p. 128.

36. U.S. Military Tribunal, Transcript of the Proceedings in Case 1, pp. 2669–71 (testimony Hans Heinrich Lammers).

37. See ZStL, Heidelberg Docs. 126,659–90. See also Roth and Aly, "Diskussion über

die Legalisierung der nationalsozialistischen Anstaltsmorde," and "Das 'Gesetz über die Sterbehilfe bei unheilbar Kranken.'"

38. NARA, RG 238: interrogation Karl Brandt, 1 Oct. 1945 P.M., p. 3.

39. GStA Frankfurt, Anklage Heyde, Bohne und Hefelmann, Ks 2/63 (GStA), Js 17/59 (GStA), 22 May 1962, pp. 201–6. The language of this authorization, which was sufficiently flexible to permit inclusion of patients suffering from other than mental disabilities, was probably prepared by a committee, including leading psychiatrists such as Max de Crinis. See also Dressen, "Euthanasie," pp. 31, 304, n. 18.

40. Platen-Hallermund, *Die Tötung Geisteskranker*, p. 21; U.S. Military Tribunal, Transcript of the Proceedings in Case 1, pp. 2369, 2402 (testimony Karl Brandt).

41. Platen-Hallermund, *Die Tötung Geisteskranker*, p. 18; U.S. Military Tribunal, Transcript of the Proceedings in Case 1, pp. 2678–90 (testimony Hans Heinrich Lammers).

42. See, for example, StA Köln, Anklage Alfred Leu, 24 Js 527/50, 10 July 1951, p. 5.

43. Nuremberg Doc. PS-630 (also in BAK, R22/4209).

44. See LA Berlin, Bauakten, Tiergartenstraße 4: Zeichnung T4 zum Neubau eines Wohnhauses sowie eines Bureaugebäudes auf dem Grundstück Tiergartenstraße Nr. 4 Herrn Banquier Weissbach gehörig.

45. U.S. Military Tribunal, Transcript of the Proceedings in Case 1, p. 2413 (testimony Karl Brandt). See also the documentary evidence of consultations with Hitler: ZStL, Heidelberg Docs. 127,398–99: Entscheidungen der beiden Euthanasiebeauftragten hinsichtlich der bei der Begutachtung anzulegenden Maßstäbe, unter Einbeziehung der Ergebnisse der Besprechungen in Berchtesgaden vom 10. 3. 1941; ibid. 127,400–401: Entscheidungen der beiden Euthanasiebeauftragten hinsichtlich der bei der Begutachtung anzulegenden Maßstäbe, 30 Jan. 1941. Both documents have been published in Tuchel, *Beiträge und Dokumente*, pp. 62–66.

46. See BDC, dossier Karl Brandt: Reichsärztekammer file card, Nazi party membership file card, SS Karteikarte, and Lebenslauf. For Brandt's biography, see also Nuremberg Doc. NO-475 (affidavit Karl Brandt), and U.S. Military Tribunal, Transcript of the Proceedings in Case 1, pp. 2301–13. For his lack of involvement, see ibid., p. 2413 (testimony Karl Brandt). For his activities as plenipotentiary, see BAK, R18/3810.

47. For biographical details about Bouhler, see BDC, dossier Philipp Bouhler: SS Karteikarte and Führer-Fragebogen.

48. Nuremberg Doc. NO-834 and BAK, R22/4209: Philipp Bouhler to Franz Gürtner, 5 Sept. 1940.

49. BDC, dossier Viktor Brack: Nazi party membership file card, SS personnel records, and handwritten Lebenslauf; Nuremberg Docs. NO-426, NO-820 (affidavits Viktor Brack); NARA, RG 238, Microfilm Publication M-1019, roll 8: interrogation Viktor Brack, 4 Sept. 1946 A.M., pp. 1–3, and 4 Dec. 1946, pp. 1–8; U.S. Military Tribunal, Transcript of the Proceedings in Case 1, pp. 7413–72 (testimony Viktor Brack); Friedlander and Milton, *Berlin Document Center*, vol. 1, doc. 59 (handwritten Lebenslauf).

50. U.S. Military Tribunal, Transcript of the Proceedings in Case 1, pp. 7532–33 (testimony Viktor Brack).

51. Klee, *Dokumente*, p. 20.

52. Ibid., p. 17.

53. Nuremberg Doc. NO-426 (affidavit Viktor Brack); NARA, RG 238, Microfilm Publication M-1019, roll 8: interrogation Viktor Brack, 4 Sept. 1946 A.M., p. 1; GStA Frankfurt, Sammlung Euthanasie: Viktor Brack to Heinrich Himmler, 6 July 1942.

54. BDC, dossier Werner Blankenburg: Nazi party membership file card and SA Personalfragebogen.

55. GStA Frankfurt, Anklage Vorberg und Allers, Js 20/61 (GStA), 15 Feb. 1966, pp. 267–

71; LG Frankfurt, Urteil Reinhold Vorberg und Dietrich Allers, Ks 2/66 (GStA), 20 Dec. 1968, pp. 2–5. See also NARA, RG 238, Microfilm Publication M-1019, roll 8: interrogation Viktor Brack, 4 Sept. 1946 P.M.

56. BDC, dossier Reinhold Vorberg: Nazi party membership file card.

57. See also Nuremberg Docs. NO-253, NO-2758, and Klee, *"Euthanasie" im NS-Staat*, pp. 168–69.

58. GStA Frankfurt, Anklage Vorberg und Allers, Js 20/61 (GStA), 15 Feb. 1966, pp. 36–37.

59. BDC, dossier Gerhard Bohne: RuSHA-Fragebogen, Parteistatistische Erhebung, Nazi party membership file card, and handwritten Lebenslauf.

60. Klee, *"Euthanasie" im NS-Staat*, p. 173. See also GStA Frankfurt, Sammlung Euthanasie: Viktor Brack to Heinrich Himmler, 6 July 1942.

61. BDC, dossier Dietrich Allers: Nazi party membership file card and Personalbogen.

62. GStA Frankfurt, Anklage Vorberg und Allers, Js 20/61 (GStA), 15 Feb. 1966, p. 272; LG Frankfurt, Urteil Vorberg und Allers, Ks 2/66 (GStA), 20 Dec. 1968, pp. 5–9. See also NARA, RG 238, Microfilm Publication M-1019, roll 8: interrogation Viktor Brack, 4 Sept. 1946 P.M.

63. GStA Frankfurt, Anklage Heyde, Bohne und Hefelmann, Ks 2/63 (GStA), Js 17/59 (GStA), 22 May 1962, p. 693 (testimony Hans Hefelmann). See also BDC, dossier Werner Heyde: SS court decision concerning accusation against Heyde under StGB §175, 24 Oct. 1939, and notation on his SS Karteikarte.

64. BDC, dossier Paul Nitsche: Reichsärztekammer file card and Nazi party membership file card; GStA DDR (StA Dresden), Verfahren Paul Nitsche, (S) 1 Ks 58/47 (1/47), Bd. 1: German translation of Soviet interrogation of Paul Nitsche, n.d., and interrogation Paul Nitsche, 25 Mar., 12 Apr. 1946. See also LG Dresden, Urteil Nitsche, 1 Ks 58/47, 7 July 1947, esp. p. 3.

65. GStA Frankfurt, Anklage Vorberg und Allers, Js 20/61 (GStA), 15 Feb. 1966, pp. 38–41.

66. Ibid., pp. 41–43.

67. BDC, dossier Friedrich Robert Lorent: SA Führer-Fragebogen; NARA, RG 238, Microfilm Publication M-1019, roll 8: interrogation Viktor Brack, 4 Sept. 1946 P.M.; GStA Frankfurt, Anklage Georg Renno, Hans-Joachim Becker und Friedrich Robert Lorent, Js 18/61 (GStA), Js 7/63 (GStA), Js 5/65 (GStA), 7 Nov. 1967, pp. 87–99; LG Frankfurt, Urteil Hans-Joachim Becker und Friedrich Robert Lorent, Ks 1/69 (GStA), 27 May 1970, pp. 6–10.

68. NARA, RG 238, Microfilm Publication M-1019, roll 8: interrogation Viktor Brack, 4 Sept. 1946 P.M., pp. 16–17.

69. GStA Frankfurt, Anklage Vorberg und Allers, Js 20/61 (GStA), 15 Feb. 1966, p. 43; GStA Frankfurt, Anklage Renno, Becker und Lorent, Js 18/61 (GStA), Js 7/63 (GStA), Js 5/65 (GStA), 7 Nov. 1967, p. 39.

70. See, for example, GStA Frankfurt, Anklage Renno, Becker und Lorent, Js 18/61 (GStA), Js 7/63 (GStA), Js 5/65 (GStA), 7 Nov. 1967, p. 38.

71. GStA Frankfurt, Anklage Vorberg und Allers, Js 20/61 (GStA), 15 Feb. 1966, p. 43; GStA Frankfurt, Anklage Renno, Becker und Lorent, Js 18/61 (GStA), Js 7/63 (GStA), Js 5/65 (GStA), 7 Nov. 1967, pp. 37–41.

72. GStA Frankfurt, Anklage Renno, Becker und Lorent, Js 18/61 (GStA), Js 7/63 (GStA), Js 5/65 (GStA), 7 Nov. 1967, p. 90.

73. Klee, *Dokumente*, p. 25.

74. GStA Frankfurt, Anklage Renno, Becker und Lorent, Js 18/61 (GStA), Js 7/63 (GStA), Js 5/65 (GStA), 7 Nov. 1967, pp. 44–45.

75. Ibid., p. 45. For sample written secrecy oaths, see Nuremberg Docs. NO-1311, NO-1312.

76. GStA Frankfurt, Anklage Adolf Gustav Kaufmann, Js 16/63 (GStA), 27 June 1966, pp. 3–8. See also BDC, dossier Adolf Gustav Kaufmann.

77. GStA Frankfurt, Anklage Kaufmann, Js 16/63 (GStA), 27 June 1966, pp. 21–36.

78. See Nuremberg Doc. NO-2758 (primitive organizational chart drawn by Viktor Brack in jail at Nuremberg), for a visual representation of the interaction between KdF, T4, and the front organizations.

79. GStA Frankfurt, Anklage Vorberg und Allers, Js 20/61 (GStA), 15 Feb. 1966, pp. 47–48.

80. Ibid., pp. 48–49.

81. Ibid., pp. 49–50.

82. See ZStL, Sammlung Verschiedenes, Bd. 56: copy of registration of incorporation for Gemeinnützige Kranken-Transport G.m.b.H. from Handelsregister Berlin-Charlottenburg.

83. GStA Frankfurt, Anklage Vorberg und Allers, Js 20/61 (GStA), 15 Feb. 1966, p. 52.

84. LG Frankfurt, Urteil Becker und Lorent, Ks 1/69 (GStA), 27 May 1970, pp. 3–5; BDC, dossier Hans-Joachim Becker: party correspondence.

85. GStA Frankfurt, Anklage Renno, Becker und Lorent, Js 18/61 (GStA), Js 7/63 (GStA), Js 5/65 (GStA), 7 Nov. 1967, pp. 79–86.

86. NARA, RG 238, Microfilm Publication M-1019, roll 46: interrogation Friedrich Mennecke, 11 Jan. 1947, pp. 6–9.

87. GStA Frankfurt, Sammlung Euthanasie: RMdI decree, 21 Sept. 1939.

88. StA Hamburg, Verfahren Friedrich Lensch und Kurt Struve, 147 Js 58/67, Gesundheitsbehörde Bd. 1: Reichsstatthalter in Hamburg to RMdI, 14 Oct. 1939.

89. Ibid.: Verzeichnis der Heil- u. Pflegeanstalten zum Runderlaß des Reichsministers des Innern vom 21. September 1939.

90. NARA, RG 238: interrogation Karl Brandt, 1 Oct. 1945 P.M., p. 5; U.S. Military Tribunal, Transcript of the Proceedings in Case 1, p. 1872 (testimony Friedrich Mennecke).

91. GStA Frankfurt, Sammlung Euthanasie: RMdI to Weißenau, 9 Oct. 1939; Nuremberg Doc. PS-3871: RMdI to Dr. Hertz'sche Privatklinik, Bonn, 11 June 1940; StA Hamburg, Verfahren Lensch und Struve, 147 Js 58/67, Gesundheitsbehörde Bd. 1: RMdI to Reichsstatthalter, 30 June 1940.

92. For facsimile examples of Meldebogen 2, see StA Hamburg, Verfahren Lensch und Struve, 147 Js 58/67, Gesundheitsbehörde Bd. 1; GStA Frankfurt, Anklage Vorberg und Allers, Js 20/61 (GStA), 15 Feb. 1966, p. 64; and Friedlander and Milton, *Bundesarchiv*, doc. 57.

93. For a facsimile example of Meldebogen 1, see GStA Frankfurt, Anklage Vorberg und Allers, Js 20/61 (GStA), 15 Feb. 1966, p. 62.

94. For facsimile examples of the revised Meldebogen 1, see DÖW, file 18229; StA Hamburg, Verfahren Lensch und Struve, 147 Js 58/67, Gesundheitsbehörde Bd. 1; and Friedlander and Milton, *Bundesarchiv*, doc. 57.

95. For facsimile examples of the Merkblatt, see Nuremberg Doc. PS-3871; StA Hamburg, Verfahren Lensch und Struve, 147 Js 58/67, Gesundheitsbehörde Bd. 1; and Friedlander and Milton, *Bundesarchiv*, doc. 57.

96. For copies of the additional instructions, see Nuremberg Docs. NO-825, PS-3871, and StA Hamburg, Verfahren Lensch und Struve, 147 Js 58/67, Gesundheitsbehörde Bd. 1.

97. See, for example, GStA Frankfurt, Anklage Heyde, Bohne und Hefelmann, Ks 2/63 (GStA), Js 17/59 (GStA), 22 May 1962, pp. 214–17; *JuNSV*, vol. 6, no. 211: LG Freiburg, Urteil Josef Artur Schreck und Ludwig Sprauer, 1 Ks 5/48, 16 Nov. 1948.

98. See Nuremberg Doc. NO-817: affidavit Dr. Otto Gutekunst, 20 Nov. 1946.

99. U.S. Military Tribunal, Transcript of the Proceedings in Case 1, pp. 7572–73 (testimony Viktor Brack).

100. See, for example, NARA, RG 238: interrogation Hermann Pfannmüller, 18 Sept. 1945, on earlier contacts between Linden and Pfannmüller.

101. BDC, dossier Prof. Dr. Gottfried Ewald: NSDAP Gauleitung Süd-Hannover-Braun-

schweig to NSDAP Kreisleitung Göttingen, 11 Sept. 1939, concerning KdF request for political evaluation of Ewald.

102. On the lack of resistance, see also Klee, *"Euthanasie" im NS-Staat*, pp. 218–19.

103. See, for example, *JuNSV*, vol. 7, no. 225: LG Koblenz, Urteil 9/5 KLs 41/48, 28 July 1950.

104. See NARA, RG 238, Microfilm Publication M-1019, roll 65: interrogation Walter Schmidt, 11 Jan. 1947, pp. 4–11, about "signing declarations" on secrecy; U.S. Military Tribunal, Transcript of the Proceedings in Case 1, p. 7341 (testimony Hermann Pfannmüller), about "shaking hands" on secrecy; ibid., p. 1925 (testimony Friedrich Mennecke), about receiving "no written appointment"; and ibid., p. 7317 (testimony Hermann Pfannmüller), about receiving "written appointment" from the RMdI.

105. GStA Frankfurt, Anklage Heyde, Bohne und Hefelmann, Ks 2/63 (GStA), Js 17/59 (GStA), 22 May 1962, pp. 552–53.

106. Klee, *"Euthanasie" im NS-Staat*, p. 224.

107. GStA Frankfurt, Anklage Heyde, Bohne und Hefelmann, Ks 2/63 (GStA), Js 17/59 (GStA), 22 May 1962, pp. 553–56.

108. BDC, dossier Ewald. The surviving documents do not reveal the formal reasons Ewald was denied party membership. Lifton, *Nazi Doctors*, p. 85, maintains that his rejection "turned out to be related to Ewald's First World War injury, which had led to amputation of one of his forearms." The documents do not, however, support this interpretation. Pointing to one Nazi party evaluation that lists Ewald as a "militarily disabled one-armed person," Lifton views this comment as pejorative and implies that this was the reason for rejection. But the German term *kriegsbeschädigter Einarmer*, which I would translate as "one-armed disabled war veteran," is hardly pejorative. I believe that it is far more likely that Ewald's application for party membership was rejected because he had belonged to the right-wing Free Corps movement, then a rival of the Nazi party. Compare also Kater, *Doctors under Hitler*, p. 147.

109. GStA Frankfurt, Anklage Heyde, Bohne und Hefelmann, Ks 2/63 (GStA), Js 17/59 (GStA), 22 May 1962, pp. 557–72.

110. Klee, *"Euthanasie" im NS-Staat*, p. 226.

111. HHStA, 461/32442/4: LG Frankfurt, Verfahren Friedrich Mennecke, Walter Schmidt, 4 KLs 15/46 (4a Js 13/46), Protokoll der öffentlichen Sitzung der 4. Strafkammer, 2 Dec. 1946, pp. 2–6. See also NARA, RG 238, Microfilm Publication M-1019, roll 46: interrogation Friedrich Mennecke, 11 Jan. 1947, p. 6.

112. U.S. Military Tribunal, Transcript of the Proceedings in Case 1, p. 1869.

113. ZStL, Heidelberg Docs. 127,890–93. See also GStA Frankfurt, Anklage Vorberg und Allers, Js 20/61 (GStA), 15 Feb. 1966, p. 39.

114. U.S. Military Tribunal, Transcript of the Proceedings in Case 1, pp. 2415–16 (testimony Karl Brandt).

115. Ibid., p. 7325 (testimony Hermann Pfannmüller).

116. Ibid., p. 1924.

117. GStA Frankfurt, Anklage Heyde, Bohne und Hefelmann, Ks 2/63 (GStA), Js 17/59 (GStA), 22 May 1962, pp. 435–37. See also GStA Frankfurt, Anklage Vorberg und Allers, Js 20/61 (GStA), 15 Feb. 1966, p. 38; GStA Frankfurt, Anklage Horst Schumann, Js 18/67 (GStA), 12 Dec. 1969, p. 61; and LG Dresden, Urteil Nitsche, 1 Ks 58/47, 7 July 1947, p. 3.

118. See, for example, the BDC Reichsärztekammer file cards for Kurt Borm, Heinrich Bunke, Irmfried Eberl, Klaus Endruweit, Emil Gelny, Hans-Bodo Gorgaß, Friedrich Mennecke, Georg Renno, Walter Eugen Schmidt, Horst Schumann, Hilde Wernicke, and Hermann Wesse.

119. See Thom and Caregorodcev, *Medizin unterm Hakenkreuz*, p. 127. See also Lockot, *Erinnern und Durcharbeiten*; Cocks, *Psychotherapy*; Baader and Schultz, *Medizin und*

Nationalsozialismus; and Kudlien et al., *Ärzte im Nationalsozialismus*. See also NARA Suitland, Heidelberg Docs. 124,887–93, 124,968–69, and ZStL, Heidelberg Docs. 124,894–96, concerning the failed attempts at collaboration between psychotherapists led by Prof. Matthias Heinrich Göring, Hermann's cousin, and the professional association of psychiatrists and neurologists (Gesellschaft deutscher Psychiater und Neurologen).

120. NARA Suitland, Heidelberg Docs. 127,403–5: memo from Prof. Dr. Carl Schneider (Heidelberg), 25 Mar. 1941.

121. Ibid. 124,942–43: Paul Nitsche to Ernst Rüdin, 17 July 1941.

122. U.S. Military Tribunal, Transcript of the Proceedings in Case 1, p. 2520 (testimony Karl Brandt).

123. Ibid., pp. 7381, 7384. For the RAG-Pfannmüller correspondence, see Nuremberg Docs. NO-1129, NO-1130. See also GStA Frankfurt, Anklage Vorberg und Allers, Js 20/61 (GStA), 15 Feb. 1966, p. 82, and Richarz, *Heilen, Pflegen, Töten*, p. 149, chart.

124. U.S. Military Tribunal, Transcript of the Proceedings in Case 1, p. 1880. Mennecke testified that he could not remember the exact number but estimated that he evaluated at least 2,000–3,000 patients.

125. Ibid., p. 1922.

126. GStA Frankfurt, Anklage Vorberg und Allers, Js 20/61 (GStA), 15 Feb. 1966, pp. 26–27.

127. See Schmidt, *Selektion in der Heilanstalt*, pp. 46–49. For the inclusion of senile patients collected in poorhouses in Tyrol-Voralberg, see DÖW, file 19196/2: StA Innsbruck, Anklage Hans Czermak, St 3782/48, 26 July 1949.

128. *JuNSV*, vol. 6, no. 211: LG Freiburg, Urteil Schreck und Sprauer, 1 Ks 5/48, 16 Nov. 1948.

129. GStA Frankfurt, Anklage Vorberg und Allers, Js 20/61 (GStA), 15 Feb. 1966, pp. 26–27.

130. ZStL, Heidelberg Docs. 127,398–99: Entscheidungen der beiden Euthanasiebeauftragten hinsichtlich der bei der Begutachtung anzulegenden Maßstäbe, unter Einbeziehung der Ergebnisse der Besprechungen in Berchtesgaden vom 10. 3. 1941; ibid. 127,400–401: Entscheidungen der beiden Euthanasiebeauftragten hinsichtlich der bei der Begutachtung anzulegenden Maßstäbe, 30 Jan. 1941.

131. NARA, RG 238, Microfilm Publication M-1019, roll 46: interrogation Friedrich Mennecke, 11 Jan. 1947, pp. 6–9.

132. See also Schmidt, *Selektion in der Heilanstalt*, pp. 68–69.

133. U.S. Military Tribunal, Transcript of the Proceedings in Case 1, p. 7696.

134. See ibid., pp. 2413, 2527 (testimony Karl Brandt), pp. 7603, 7664–65 (testimony Viktor Brack).

135. See, for example, Klee, *"Euthanasie" im NS-Staat*, pp. 143–45, 187.

136. Herbert Linden to Oberpräsident Hannover, 26 July 1940, cited in GStA Frankfurt, Anklage Vorberg und Allers, Js 20/61 (GStA), 15 Feb. 1966, p. 70.

137. U.S. Military Tribunal, Transcript of the Proceedings in Case 1, pp. 2506, 2510, 2515–16. See also ZStL, Heidelberg Doc. 127,398.

138. U.S. Military Tribunal, Transcript of the Proceedings in Case 1, pp. 7571–72 (testimony Viktor Brack).

139. StA Hamburg, Verfahren Lensch und Struve, 147 Js 58/67, Gesundheitsbehörde Bd. 1: reporting form for institutions, Aug. 1940.

140. U.S. Military Tribunal, Transcript of the Proceedings in Case 1, p. 1906 (testimony Friedrich Mennecke).

141. See, for example, GStA Frankfurt, Anklage Heyde, Bohne und Hefelmann, Ks 2/63 (GStA), Js 17/59 (GStA), 22 May 1962, pp. 318–43; GStA Frankfurt, Anklage Vorberg und Allers, Js 20/61 (GStA), 15 Feb. 1966, pp. 39–40; GStA Frankfurt, Eberl Akten, I/209, 1:

156: Oberpräsident (Verwaltung des Provinzialverbandes), Merseburg, granting authority to Dr. Eberl to review patients (*Nachuntersuchungen*) in various local institutions, 14 May 1941; GStA Frankfurt, Sammlung Euthanasie: Dr. Hebold to Privatanstalt "Christophs-bad," Göppingen-Württemberg, 11 Nov. 1941, about review and registration of patients at Zwiefalten and Göppingen; DÖW, file E18370/2: report of Bezirksgendarmeriekommando Kirchdorf a/K., Oberösterreich, 15 Aug. 1946, about selection of patients in local institution by Dr. Rudolf Lonauer; DÖW, file 11440: VG bei dem LG Innsbruck, Urteil Hans Czermak, Vg 10 Vr 4740/47, 1 Dec. 1949, concerning selections by physicians Friedrich Mennecke, Rudolf Lonauer, and Georg Renno in the small institutions of Tyrol-Voralberg; DÖW, file E18370/3: Bezirksgericht Ybbs, interrogations of Theresia Helmreich, 21 Mar. 1946, Franz Stempfl, 22 Mar. 1946, and Aron Heindl, 20 Mar. 1946, for the way a T4 panel of physicians in 1940 combed through the Austrian mental hospital in Ybbs; HHStA, 461/32442/12: Friedrich Mennecke to Walter Schmidt, 29 June 1940, about Mennecke's work with panels of physicians in Austrian institutions; HHStA, 461/32442/3: StA Frankfurt, Anklage Mennecke, Schmidt, 7 Oct. 1946, 4a Js 13/46, p. 15, for an account of Mennecke's travels; and ZStL, Bd. 513: Diakonissenanstalt Neuendettelsau to RMdI and Bayerisches MdI, 7 Oct. 1940, protesting visit of a T4 panel of physicians headed by Theo Steinmeyer.

142. GStA Frankfurt, Anklage Heyde, Bohne und Hefelmann, Ks 2/63 (GStA), Js 17/59 (GStA), 22 May 1962, pp. 343–48. See also U.S. Military Tribunal, Transcript of the Proceedings in Case 1, pp. 7377–80 (testimony Hermann Pfannmüller).

143. U.S. Military Tribunal, Transcript of the Proceedings in Case 1, p. 1908 (testimony Friedrich Mennecke).

144. GStA Frankfurt, Anklage Heyde, Bohne und Hefelmann, Ks 2/63 (GStA), Js 17/59 (GStA), 22 May 1962, pp. 346–47.

145. GStA Frankfurt, Sammlung Euthanasie: circular from Baden minister of the interior (Sprauer) to various institutions, 2 Apr. 1940.

146. See, for example, Nuremberg Doc. NO-3358: Eglfing-Haar "Transport-Liste Nr. 23."

147. See, for example, ibid. NO-1131, NO-1132, NO-1133, NO-1134: Bayerisches MdI to Heil- und Pflegeanstalt Eglfing-Haar, 18 Oct., 12 Nov. 1940, 14 Jan., 13 Feb. 1941.

148. GStA Frankfurt, Sammlung Euthanasie: Baden MdI (Sprauer) to Kreispflegeanstalt Hub, 8 Feb. 1940; GStA Frankfurt, Anklage Vorberg und Allers, Js 20/61 (GStA), 15 Feb. 1966, pp. 87–88; GStA Frankfurt, Anklage Heyde, Bohne und Hefelmann, Ks 2/63 (GStA), Js 17/59 (GStA), 22 May 1962, pp. 372–73. See sample "property declaration of patient [*Eigentumsnachweis des Kranken*]," copy from DDR archives, kindly provided by Dr. Götz Aly, Berlin.

149. For transmission of lists, see, for example, Gemeinnützige Kranken-Transport G.m.b.H. to Brandenburgische Landesanstalt Neuruppin, 7 June 1940, copy from DDR archives, kindly provided by Dr. Götz Aly, Berlin. For the visit of the Transportleiter to institutions, see GStA Frankfurt, Anklage Vorberg und Allers, Js 20/61 (GStA), 15 Feb. 1966, pp. 88–89.

150. GStA Frankfurt, Anklage Vorberg und Allers, Js 20/61 (GStA), 15 Feb. 1966, p. 89. See also GStA Frankfurt, Sammlung Euthanasie: Dr. Wilhelm Weskott, Weissenau, to Württemberg MdI (Stähle), 12 July 1940.

151. See Nuremberg Docs. NO-1134, NO-1135, for sample receipts from Gekrat for patients collected from Eglfing-Haar.

152. Ibid., D-906: report, 24 Feb. 1941.

153. U.S. Military Tribunal, Transcript of the Proceedings in Case 1, pp. 2426–27 (testimony Karl Brandt).

154. Ibid., p. 2427 (testimony Karl Brandt).

155. GStA Frankfurt, Sammlung Euthanasie: Heil- und Pflegeanstalt in Stetten i.R. (L.

Schlaich) to Württemberg MdI, 14 Sept. 1940, and Gemeinnützige Stiftung für Anstalts-pflege to Heil- und Pflegeanstalt Wiesloch, 13 Feb. 1941.

156. For a sample letter and for correspondence by a relative with a surrendering insti-tution and Gekrat, see the Schramm file in HHStA 461/32061/18.

157. For sample letters, see DÖW, file E18229, and HHStA 461/32061/18.

158. For sample notifications, see Nuremberg Docs. PS-628, NO-520, NO-828, NO-840; BAK, R22/5021; HHStA 461/32061/18; and DÖW, file E18229.

159. U.S. Military Tribunal, Transcript of the Proceedings in Case 1, p. 2432 (testimony Karl Brandt).

160. See chapter 5, esp. table 5.3.

CHAPTER FIVE

1. Leo Alexander was the first to apply the term "killing center" to the places where patients were killed in gas chambers. See his "Medical Science under Dictatorship," p. 40. In the German literature they are often called "euthanasia institution [*Euthanasie-Anstalt*]."

The term "killing center" best describes the places where human beings were killed in a process that copied factory production. I have therefore also used it for the camps in the East where the Nazis copied the euthanasia killing center method to murder Jews and Gypsies, as well as the term "extermination camp [*Vernichtungslager*]" used in the German literature, which also describes those places correctly. For the mass execution sites by shooting, the term "killing field" provides a correct description.

I have refused to employ the term "death camp," widely used in popular literature and also in many scholarly works, because it does not distinguish between the factory pro-cess of mass murder and concentration camps where large numbers of inmates died from forced labor, starvation, and disease.

2. NARA, RG 238: interrogation Karl Brandt, 1 Oct. 1945 P.M., p. 7.

3. See, for example, the story of the personal experience with gas by the Kripo chief Arthur Nebe in StA Stuttgart, Verfahren Albert Widmann, Ks 19/62 (19 Js 328/60): Öffent-liche Sitzung des Schwurgerichts, Hauptverhandlung, Aug.–Sept. 1967, p. 11.

4. StA Düsseldorf, Verfahren Albert Widmann, 8 Ks 1/61 (8 Js 7212/59): interrogation Albert Widmann, 15 Jan. 1960, pp. 2–3.

5. NARA, RG 238: interrogation Karl Brandt, 1 Oct. 1945 P.M., p. 7.

6. Ibid., p. 8. Undoubtedly Brandt had remembered the arguments advanced twenty years earlier by the lawyer Karl Binding to justify euthanasia, including his proscription that death must be "absolutely painless" and can "only be administered by an expert." Binding and Hoche, *Vernichtung lebensunwerten Lebens*, p. 37.

7. "Was willst Du denn, es geht doch." StA Düsseldorf, Verfahren Widmann, 8 Ks 1/61 (8 Js 7212/59): interrogation Albert Widmann, 15 Jan. 1960, p. 2.

8. Ibid.: interrogation Albert Widmann, 11 Jan. 1960, p. 7.

9. GStA Frankfurt, Anklage Aquilin Ullrich, Heinrich Bunke, Kurt Borm und Klaus Endruweit, Js 15/61 (GStA), 15 Jan. 1965, pp. 175–76.

10. Ibid., pp. 176–77.

11. See U.S. Military Tribunal, Transcript of the Proceedings in Case 1, p. 7645 (testimony Viktor Brack); StA Stuttgart, Verfahren Widmann, Ks 19/62 (19 Js 328/60): interrogation August Becker, 4 Apr. 1960.

12. GStA Frankfurt, Anklage Werner Heyde, Gerhard Bohne und Hans Hefelmann, Ks 2/63 (GStA), Js 17/59 (GStA), 22 May 1962, pp. 290–93 (interrogation Werner Heyde), pp. 293–98 (interrogation August Becker).

13. LG Dresden, Urteil Hermann Paul Nitsche, 1 Ks 58/47, 7 July 1947, p. 3.

14. NARA, RG 238: interrogation Karl Brandt, 1 Oct. 1945 P.M., p. 13.

15. GStA Frankfurt, Anklage Heyde, Bohne und Hefelmann, Ks 2/63 (GStA), Js 17/59 (GStA), 22 May 1962, pp. 287–99; U.S. Military Tribunal, Transcript of the Proceedings in Case 1, p. 7645 (testimony Viktor Brack); StA Stuttgart, Anklage Albert Widmann und August Becker, (19) 13 Js 328/60, 29 Aug. 1962, pp. 39–41; StA Stuttgart, Verfahren Widmann, Ks 19/62 (19 Js 328/60): interrogation August Becker, 4 Apr. 1960.

16. U.S. Military Tribunal, Transcript of the Proceedings in Case 1, p. 7648 (testimony Viktor Brack); GStA Frankfurt, Anklage Reinhold Vorberg und Dietrich Allers, Js 20/61 (GStA), 15 Feb. 1966, pp. 55–58; GStA Frankfurt, Anklage Heyde, Bohne und Hefelmann, Ks 2/63 (GStA), Js 17/59 (GStA), 22 May 1962, pp. 261–87; GStA Frankfurt, Anklage Horst Schumann, Js 18/67 (GStA), 12 Dec. 1969, p. 86; StA Hamburg, Anklage Friedrich Lensch und Kurt Struve, 147 Js 58/67, 24 Apr. 1973, pp. 201–31.

17. GStA Frankfurt, Anklage Georg Renno, Hans-Joachim Becker und Friedrich Robert Lorent, Js 18/61 (GStA), Js 7/63 (GStA), Js 5/65 (GStA), 7 Nov. 1967, pp. 42–43.

18. U.S. Military Tribunal, Transcript of the Proceedings in Case 1, p. 7652.

19. Although we have seen that the killing center at Brandenburg was operational for the experimental gassing in January 1940 at the latest, the first "regular" gassing of patients does not seem to have taken place prior to February 1940. See NARA, RG 338, Microfilm Publication T-1021, roll 18, "Hartheim Statistics," p. 2.

20. I have not been able to discover how and from whom T4 obtained this facility as either owner or tenant.

21. GStA Frankfurt, Anklage Adolf Gustav Kaufmann, Js 16/63 (GStA), 27 June 1966, p. 29; GStA Frankfurt, Anklage Ullrich, Bunke, Borm und Endruweit, Js 15/61 (GStA), 15 Jan. 1965, p. 179.

22. GStA Frankfurt, Anklage Ullrich, Bunke, Borm und Endruweit, Js 15/61 (GStA), 15 Jan. 1965, pp. 176–77.

23. Ibid., pp. 177–78, 183–84 (testimony Erich Sporleder).

24. Ibid., pp. 176, 179.

25. StArch Sigmaringen, Wü 29/3, Acc. 33/1973, Nr. 1752: StA Tübingen, Anklage Otto Mauthe, 1 Js 85–87/47, 4 Jan. 1949, p. 9v.

26. GStA Frankfurt, Anklage Schumann, Js 18/67 (GStA), 12 Dec. 1969, pp. 78–79.

27. GStA Frankfurt, Sammlung Euthanasie: Württemberg Innenminister to Landrat Münsingen, 12 Oct. 1939.

28. StArch Sigmaringen, Wü 29/3, Acc. 33/1973, Nr. 1752: StA Tübingen, Anklage Mauthe, 1 Js 85–87/47, 4 Jan. 1949, p. 10.

29. Ibid., p. 12v; GStA Frankfurt, Anklage Schumann, Js 18/67 (GStA), 12 Dec. 1969, pp. 80–81. Apparently ninety-five patients were gassed at Grafeneck during January 1940 (NARA, RG 338, Microfilm Publication T-1021, roll 18, "Hartheim Statistics," p. 2), and the first victims on 20 January were about forty persons from Eglfing-Haar (Morlok, *Grafeneck*, p. 41).

30. GStA Frankfurt, Anklage Schumann, Js 18/67 (GStA), 12 Dec. 1969, pp. 79–80, 83; StArch Sigmaringen, Wü 29/3, Acc. 33/1973, Nr. 1752: StA Tübingen, Anklage Mauthe, 1 Js 85–87/47, 4 Jan. 1949, pp. 12v–13.

31. AMM, B/15/2: Auszug aus der Gemeindechronik Alkoven; AMM, B/15/38, B/15/54: reports on Hartheim by Hans Marsalek; GStA Frankfurt, Anklage Kaufmann, Js 16/63 (GStA), 27 June 1966, p. 25; DÖW, file 14900: StA Linz, Anklage Anna Griessenberger, 3 St 466/46, 28 July 1947, p. 3; DÖW, file E18370/1: Kreisgericht Wels, interrogation Stefan Schachermeyer, 11 Mar. 1964; DÖW, file E18370/3: Kriminalpolizei Linz, interrogation Vinzenz Nohel, 4 Sept. 1945 (partially published in *Widerstand und Verfolgung in Oberösterreich, 1939–1945*, ed. Dokumentationsarchiv des österreichischen Widerstandes [Vienna, 1982], vol. 2, chap. 14, doc. 16). During May 1940, apparently 633 patients were

gassed at Hartheim. NARA, RG 338, Microfilm Publication T-1021, roll 18, "Hartheim Statistics," p. 2.

32. AMM, B/15/3: Auszug aus der Pfarrerchronik Alkoven; Florian Zehethofer, "Das Euthanasieprogram im Dritten Reich am Beispiel Schloss Hartheim (1938–1945)," *Oberösterreichische Heimatblätter* 32 (1978): 46–62, esp. 53–55; DÖW, file E18370/3: Kriminalpolizei Linz, interrogation Vinzenz Nohel, 4 Sept. 1945; DÖW, file 11440: StA Linz, Anklage Franz Stangl, Karl Harrer, Leopold Lang und Franz Mayrhuber, 3 St 466/46, 24 Apr. 1948, p. 5.

33. LG Dresden, Urteil Nitsche, 1 Ks 58/47, 7 July 1947, p. 3. See also ZStL, Heidelberg Doc. 127,491: Paul Nitsche to Ernst Rüdin, 5 Dec. 1941.

34. GStA Frankfurt, Anklage Ullrich, Bunke, Borm und Endruweit, Js 15/61 (GStA), 15 Jan. 1965, p. 210.

35. GStA Frankfurt, Anklage Schumann, Js 18/67 (GStA), 12 Dec. 1969, pp. 85–86; GStA Frankfurt, Anklage Ullrich, Bunke, Borm und Endruweit, Js 15/61 (GStA), 15 Jan. 1965, p. 211. See also U.S. Military Tribunal, Transcript of the Proceedings in Case 1, p. 7767 (testimony Viktor Brack).

36. GStA Frankfurt, Anklage Schumann, Js 18/67 (GStA), 12 Dec. 1969, pp. 84, 86. Apparently only 10 patients were gassed at Sonnenstein in June 1940; in July the number was already 1,116. NARA, RG 338, Microfilm Publication T-1021, roll 18, "Hartheim Statistics," p. 2.

37. GStA Frankfurt, Anklage Kaufmann, Js 16/63 (GStA), 27 June 1966, p. 29; GStA Frankfurt, Anklage Ullrich, Bunke, Borm und Endruweit, Js 15/61 (GStA), 15 Jan. 1965, pp. 186, 188–89, 205–6.

38. GStA Frankfurt, Anklage Ullrich, Bunke, Borm und Endruweit, Js 15/61 (GStA), 15 Jan. 1965, pp. 186–89.

39. The first patients gassed at Hadamar were apparently killed in January 1941 (a total of 956 for that month). NARA, RG 338, Microfilm Publication T-1021, roll 18, "Hartheim Statistics," p. 3.

40. Roer and Henkel, *Psychiatrie im Faschismus*, pp. 82–83; Vanja and Vogt, *Euthanasie in Hadamar*, pp. 91–94; Winter et al., *Verlegt nach Hadamar*, pp. 92, 212–15 (drawings); GStA Frankfurt, Anklage Schumann, Js 18/67 (GStA), 12 Dec. 1969, p. 84; GStA Frankfurt, Anklage Kaufmann, Js 16/63 (GStA), 27 June 1966, pp. 25–28; GStA Frankfurt, Anklage Renno, Becker und Lorent, Js 18/61 (GStA), Js 7/63 (GStA), Js 5/65 (GStA), 7 Nov. 1967, p. 43; HHStA, 461/32061/1: contract between T4 and Bezirksverband Nassau; HHStA, 461/32061/6: interrogation Philipp Prinz von Hessen, 14 Jan. 1947; HHStA, 461/32061/7: LG Frankfurt, Verfahren Adolf Wahlmann, Bodo Gorgaß, Irmgard Huber, 4a KLs 7/47 (4a Js 3/46), Protokoll der öffentlichen Sitzung der 4. Strafkammer, 25 Feb. 1947, pp. 1–2 (testimony Irmgard Huber), pp. 6, 19 (testimony Hans-Bodo Gorgaß); HHStA, 461/32061/13: StA Frankfurt, Anklage Adolf Wahlmann, Irmgard Huber, 4a Js 3/46, 2 Aug. 1946, pp. 34–35.

41. GStA Frankfurt, Anklage Vorberg und Allers, Js 20/61 (GStA), 15 Feb. 1966, pp. 57–58. See also GStA Frankfurt, Eberl Akten, I/250/1–6, 1:150–55: "Organisation der Anstalt Bernburg," n.d., [1941].

42. See, for example, Nuremberg Doc. NO-665: NSDAP Kreisleiter Weissenburg to NSDAP Gauleitung Franken, "Beunruhigung der Bevölkerung von Absberg durch auffälliges Wegschaffen von Insassen des Ottilienheimes," 24 Feb. 1941, NSDAP Ortsgruppe Absberg to NSDAP Kreisleitung Weissenburg, 25 Feb. 1941 (with attached report), NSDAP Gaustabsamt Franken (sig. Sellmer) to Hans Hefelmann (KdF), 27 Feb. 1941, and Aktennotiz by Sellmer, 5 Mar. 1941.

43. See, for example, GStA Frankfurt, Anklage Vorberg und Allers, Js 20/61 (GStA), 15 Feb. 1966, pp. 92–93; GStA Frankfurt, Anklage Ullrich, Bunke, Borm und Endruweit, Js

15/61 (GStA), 15 Jan. 1965, p. 109; StArch Sigmaringen, Wü 29/3, Acc. 33/1973, Nr. 1752: StA Tübingen, Anklage Mauthe, 1 Js 85–87/47, 4 Jan. 1949, p. 46v.

44. See Friedlander, "Euthanasieprogramm."

45. HHStA, 461/32061/13: StA Frankfurt, Anklage Wahlmann, Huber, 4a Js 3/46, 2 Aug. 1946, p. 30; DÖW, file E18370/1: StA Frankfurt, Js 18/61 (GStA), interrogation Georg Renno, 3 Feb. 1965, pp. 24–25; DÖW, file E18370/2: VG bei dem LG Linz, Hauptverhandlung Karl Harrer, Leopold Lang und Franz Mayrhuber, Vg 6 Vr 2407/46 (186), 2–3 July 1948, p. 7.

46. DÖW, file E18370/3: Kriminalpolizei Linz, interrogation Vinzenz Nohel, 4 Sept. 1945; GStA Frankfurt, Anklage Ullrich, Bunke, Borm und Endruweit, Js 15/61 (GStA), 15 Jan. 1965, pp. 204–5 (testimony Erich Sporleder); GStA Frankfurt, Anklage Vorberg und Allers, Js 20/61 (GStA), 15 Feb. 1966, pp. 92–93; HHStA, 461/32061/7: LG Frankfurt, Verfahren Wahlmann, Gorgaß, Huber, 4a KLs 7/47 (4a Js 3/46), Protokoll der öffentlichen Sitzung der 4. Strafkammer, 24 Feb. 1947, pp. 16–17 (testimony Hans-Bodo Gorgaß), 25 Feb. 1947, p. 13 (testimony Lydia Thomas), p. 19 (testimony Paul Reuter).

47. DÖW, file E18370/3: Kriminalpolizei Linz, interrogation Vinzenz Nohel, 4 Sept. 1945; DÖW, file E18370/1: StA Frankfurt, Js 18/61 (GStA), interrogation Georg Renno, 1 Feb. 1965, pp. 3–4, 7, 17, and LG Frankfurt, Untersuchungsrichter, Verfahren Js 18/61 (GStA), interrogation Fritz Tauscher, Hamburg, 2 June 1964; GStA Frankfurt, Anklage Ullrich, Bunke, Borm und Endruweit, Js 15/61 (GStA), 15 Jan. 1965, pp. 109, 204–5 (testimony Erich Sporleder), p. 213; GStA Frankfurt, Anklage Vorberg und Allers, Js 20/61 (GStA), 15 Feb. 1966, pp. 92–93; HHStA, 461/32061/7: LG Frankfurt, Verfahren Wahlmann, Gorgaß, Huber, 4a KLs 7/47 (4a Js 3/46), Protokoll der öffentlichen Sitzung der 4. Strafkammer, 24 Feb. 1947, pp. 16–18 (testimony Hans-Bodo Gorgaß).

48. U.S. Military Tribunal, Transcript of the Proceedings in Case 1, pp. 2423–25 (testimony Karl Brandt), pp. 7572–73 (testimony Viktor Brack); HHStA, 461/32061/7: LG Frankfurt, Verfahren Wahlmann, Gorgaß, Huber, 4a KLs 7/47 (4a Js 3/46), Protokoll der öffentlichen Sitzung der 4. Strafkammer, 24 Feb. 1947, pp. 17, 31 (testimony Hans-Bodo Gorgaß); GStA Frankfurt, Anklage Ullrich, Bunke, Borm und Endruweit, Js 15/61 (GStA), 15 Jan. 1965, p. 109; GStA Frankfurt, Anklage Vorberg und Allers, Js 20/61 (GStA), 15 Feb. 1966, p. 93.

49. DÖW, file E18370/1: StA Frankfurt, Js 18/61 (GStA), interrogation Georg Renno, 1 Feb. 1965, p. 9; GStA Frankfurt, Anklage Ullrich, Bunke, Borm und Endruweit, Js 15/61 (GStA), 15 Jan. 1965, p. 109; GStA Frankfurt, Anklage Vorberg und Allers, Js 20/61 (GStA), 15 Feb. 1966, pp. 92–93.

50. GStA Frankfurt, Anklage Ullrich, Bunke, Borm und Endruweit, Js 15/61 (GStA), 15 Jan. 1965, p. 109; LG Frankfurt, Urteil Aquilin Ullrich, Heinrich Bunke und Klaus Endruweit, Ks 1/66 (GStA), 23 May 1967, p. 49; GStA Frankfurt, Anklage Vorberg und Allers, Js 20/61 (GStA), 15 Feb. 1966, p. 92; LG Frankfurt, Urteil Kurt Borm, Ks 1/66 (GStA), 6 June 1972, p. 40.

51. DÖW, file E18370/3: Kriminalpolizei Linz, interrogation Vinzenz Nohel, 4 Sept. 1945; DÖW, file 11440: StA Linz, Anklage Stangl, Harrer, Lang und Mayrhuber, 3 St 466/46, 24 Apr. 1948, p. 5.

52. HHStA, 461/32061/7: LG Frankfurt, Verfahren Wahlmann, Gorgaß, Huber, 4a KLs 7/47 (4a Js 3/46), Protokoll der öffentlichen Sitzung der 4. Strafkammer, 25 Feb. 1947, p. 13 (testimony Lydia Thomas); DÖW, file E18370/3: Kriminalpolizei Linz, interrogation Vinzenz Nohel, 4 Sept. 1945; DÖW, file E18370/1: Bundesministerium für Inneres, interrogation Bruno Bruckner, Vienna, 24 May 1962, and StA Frankfurt, Js 18/61 (GStA), interrogation Georg Renno, 2 Feb. 1965, p. 18; GStA Frankfurt, Anklage Ullrich, Bunke, Borm und Endruweit, Js 15/61 (GStA), 15 Jan. 1965, p. 109; U.S. Military Tribunal, Transcript of the Proceedings in Case 1, p. 7644 (testimony Viktor Brack).

53. See GStA Frankfurt, Anklage Kaufmann, Js 16/63 (GStA), 27 June 1966, p. 35, for filming at Sonnenstein.

54. StA München I, Verfahren Hermann Pfannmüller, 1 Ks 10/49 (1b Js 1791/47): Protokoll der öffentlichen Sitzung des Schwurgerichts bei dem LG München I, 21 Oct. 1949, p. 33.

55. GStA Frankfurt, Anklage Ullrich, Bunke, Borm und Endruweit, Js 15/61 (GStA), 15 Jan. 1965, p. 110; GStA Frankfurt, Anklage Vorberg und Allers, Js 20/61 (GStA), 15 Feb. 1966, p. 93.

56. DÖW, file E18370/3: Kriminalpolizei Linz, interrogation Vinzenz Nohel, 4 Sept. 1945; StA Linz, Anklage Stangl, Harrer, Lang und Mayrhuber, 3 St 466/46, 24 Apr. 1948, p. 5. See also U.S. Military Tribunal, Transcript of the Proceedings in Case 1, pp. 7654–55 (testimony Viktor Brack).

57. DÖW, file E18370/3: Bezirksgericht Ybbs, interrogation Hermine Gruber, 15 Mar. 1946.

58. Ibid.: Kriminalpolizei Linz, interrogation Vinzenz Nohel, 4 Sept. 1945.

59. GStA Frankfurt, Anklage Ullrich, Bunke, Borm und Endruweit, Js 15/61 (GStA), 15 Jan. 1965, pp. 204–5 (testimony Erich Sporleder).

60. LG Frankfurt, Untersuchungsrichter, Verfahren Js 18/61 (GStA), interrogation Fritz Tauscher, Hamburg, 2 June 1964.

61. StArch Sigmaringen, Wü 29/3, Acc. 33/1973, Nr. 1752: StA Tübingen, Anklage Mauthe, 1 Js 85–87/47, 4 Jan. 1949, p. 13v.

62. GStA Frankfurt, Anklage Ullrich, Bunke, Borm und Endruweit, Js 15/61 (GStA), 15 Jan. 1965, p. 110; GStA Frankfurt, Anklage Vorberg und Allers, Js 20/61 (GStA), 15 Feb. 1966, p. 93.

63. DÖW, file E18370/1: StA Frankfurt, Js 18/61 (GStA), interrogation Georg Renno, 1 Mar. 1965, p. 68.

64. DÖW, file E18370/3: Kriminalpolizei Linz, interrogation Vinzenz Nohel, 4 Sept. 1945; DÖW, file E18370/1: StA Frankfurt, Js 18/61 (GStA), interrogation Georg Renno, 2 Feb. 1965, p. 20.

65. DÖW, file E18370/3: Kriminalpolizei Linz, interrogation Vinzenz Nohel, 4 Sept. 1945; StArch Sigmaringen, Wü 29/3, Acc. 33/1973, Nr. 1752: StA Tübingen, Anklage Mauthe, 1 Js 85–87/47, 4 Jan. 1949, pp. 46v–47. For the delivery of gas canisters, see DÖW, file E18370/1, and BAK, R58/1059: correspondence between the KTI, the KdF, and I.G. Farbenindustrie; StA Stuttgart, Anklage Widmann und Becker, (19) 13 Js 328/60, 29 Aug. 1962, p. 41; and StA Stuttgart, Verfahren Widmann, Ks 19/62 (19 Js 328/60), interrogation August Becker, 16 May 1961.

66. Nuremberg Doc. PS-630. See also HHStA, 461/32061/7: LG Frankfurt, Verfahren Wahlmann, Gorgaß, Huber, 4a KLs 7/47 (4a Js 3/46), Protokoll der öffentlichen Sitzung der 4. Strafkammer, 24 Feb. 1947, pp. 18–19 (testimony Hans-Bodo Gorgaß).

67. LG Frankfurt, Urteil Ullrich, Bunke und Endruweit, Ks 1/66 (GStA), 23 May 1967, pp. 49–50.

68. DÖW, file E18370/1: StA Frankfurt, Js 18/61 (GStA), interrogation Georg Renno, 1 Feb. 1965, pp. 4, 18, 31–32.

69. Ibid., p. 18.

70. GStA Frankfurt, Anklage Ullrich, Bunke, Borm und Endruweit, Js 15/61 (GStA), 15 Jan. 1965, p. 214; HHStA, 461/32061/7: LG Frankfurt, Verfahren Wahlmann, Gorgaß, Huber, 4a KLs 7/47 (4a Js 3/46), Protokoll der öffentlichen Sitzung der 4. Strafkammer, 25 Feb. 1947, p. 19; DÖW, file E18370/1: LG Frankfurt, Untersuchungsrichter, Verfahren Js 18/61 (GStA), interrogation Fritz Tauscher, Hamburg, 2 June 1964.

71. DÖW, file E18370/3: Kriminalpolizei Linz, interrogation Vinzenz Nohel, 4 Sept. 1945. See also DÖW, file 14900: StA Linz, Anklage Griessenberger, 3 St 466/46, 28 July 1947, p. 6.

72. DÖW, file E18370/1: StA Frankfurt, Js 18/61 (GStA), interrogation Georg Renno, 2 Feb. 1965, p. 19; HHStA, 461/32061/7: LG Frankfurt, Verfahren Wahlmann, Gorgaß, Huber, 4a KLs 7/47 (4a Js 3/46), Protokoll der öffentlichen Sitzung der 4. Strafkammer, 24 Feb. 1947, p. 19 (testimony Hans-Bodo Gorgaß).

73. DÖW, file E18370/1: StA Frankfurt, Js 18/61 (GStA), interrogation Georg Renno, 1 Feb. 1965, p. 4; DÖW, file E18370/3: Kriminalpolizei Linz, interrogation Vinzenz Nohel, 4 Sept. 1945.

74. GStA Frankfurt, Anklage Ullrich, Bunke, Borm und Endruweit, Js 15/61 (GStA), 15 Jan. 1965, p. 183 (testimony Erich Sporleder).

75. HHStA, 461/32061/7: LG Frankfurt, Verfahren Wahlmann, Gorgaß, Huber, 4a KLs 7/47 (4a Js 3/46), Protokoll der öffentlichen Sitzung der 4. Strafkammer, 3 Mar. 1947, p. 9 (testimony Maximilian Friedrich Lindner).

76. U.S. Military Tribunal, Transcript of the Proceedings in Case 1, p. 7657 (testimony Viktor Brack). See also GStA Frankfurt, Anklage Heyde, Bohne und Hefelmann, Ks 2/63 (GStA), Js 17/59 (GStA), 22 May 1962, pp. 391–92.

77. DÖW, file E18370/3: Kriminalpolizei Linz, interrogation Vinzenz Nohel, 4 Sept. 1945; GStA Frankfurt, Anklage Ullrich, Bunke, Borm und Endruweit, Js 15/61 (GStA), 15 Jan. 1965, pp. 183, 204–5 (testimony Erich Sporleder).

78. GStA Frankfurt, Eberl Akten, II/210/1–3, 1:1–3: Irmfried Eberl to Paul Nitsche, 16 Apr. 1942; GStA Frankfurt, Anklage Ullrich, Bunke, Borm und Endruweit, Js 15/61 (GStA), 15 Jan. 1965, pp. 111, 187, 204–5.

79. DÖW, file E18370/3: Kriminalpolizei Linz, interrogation Vinzenz Nohel, 4 Sept. 1945; DÖW, file 11440: StA Linz, Anklage Stangl, Harrer, Lang und Mayrhuber, 3 St 466/46, 24 Apr. 1948, p. 5.

80. HHStA, 461/32061/7: LG Frankfurt, Verfahren Wahlmann, Gorgaß, Huber, 4a KLs 7/47 (4a Js 3/46), Protokoll der öffentlichen Sitzung der 4. Strafkammer, 3 Mar. 1947, p. 32 (testimony Ingeborg Seidel).

81. See StA Stuttgart, Verfahren Widmann, Ks 19/62 (19 Js 328/60), testimony Klara Mattmüller, 17 Feb. 1966; StA Düsseldorf, Verfahren Widmann, 8 Ks 1/61 (8 Js 7212/59), interrogation Albert Widmann, 15 Jan. 1960, p. 5.

82. DÖW, file E18370/3: Kriminalpolizei Linz, interrogation Vinzenz Nohel, 4 Sept. 1945. See also DÖW, file E18370/1: Bundesministerium für Inneres, Gruppe Staatspolizei, interrogation Matthias Buchberger, 24 Feb. 1964; and GStA Frankfurt, Anklage Ullrich, Bunke, Borm und Endruweit, Js 15/61 (GStA), 15 Jan. 1965, p. 205 (testimony Erich Sporleder).

83. DÖW, file E18370/3: Kriminalpolizei Linz, interrogation Vinzenz Nohel, 4 Sept. 1945; GStA Frankfurt, Anklage Ullrich, Bunke, Borm und Endruweit, Js 15/61 (GStA), 15 Jan. 1965, pp. 183–84 (testimony Erich Sporleder).

84. DÖW, file 11440: StA Linz, Anklage Stangl, Harrer, Lang und Mayrhuber, 3 St 466/46, 24 Apr. 1948, p. 5.

85. DÖW, file E18370/1: Bundesministerium für Inneres, Gruppe Staatspolizei, interrogation Matthias Buchberger, 24 Feb. 1964.

86. GStA Frankfurt, Anklage Ullrich, Bunke, Borm und Endruweit, Js 15/61 (GStA), 15 Jan. 1965, pp. 183–84 (testimony Erich Sporleder).

87. StA Düsseldorf, Verfahren Widmann, 8 Ks 1/61 (8 Js 7212/59): interrogation Albert Widmann, 11 Jan. 1960, p. 8.

88. See GStA Frankfurt, Eberl Akten, II/135n, 7:56–57: "Bernburg Personalaufstellung und Diensteinteilung."

89. DÖW, file E18370/1: LG Linz, interrogation Heinrich Barbl, 5 Oct. 1964; DÖW, file E18370/3: Kriminalpolizei Linz, interrogation Vinzenz Nohel, 4 Sept. 1945.

90. See interrogations of Hans Hefelmann in GStA Frankfurt, Verfahren Heyde, Bohne und Hefelmann, Ks 2/63 (GStA), Js 17/59 (GStA).

91. See, for example, DÖW, file 11440: StA Linz, Anklage Stangl, Harrer, Lang und Mayr-huber, 3 St 466/46, 24 Apr. 1948, p. 7; DÖW, file E18370/1: LG Frankfurt, Untersuchungs-richter, Verfahren Js 18/61 (GStA), interrogation Fritz Tauscher, Hamburg, 2 June 1964; DÖW, file E18370/3: Gendarmeriepostenkommando Gmunden, interrogation Gertraud Dirnberger, 13 Aug. 1946, and Gemeindeamt Alkoven to Anstalt Niedernhart, 24 May 1946; StArch Sigmaringen, Wü 29/3, Acc. 33/1973, Nr. 1752: StA Tübingen, Anklage Mauthe, 1 Js 85–87/47, 4 Jan. 1949, pp. 51–51v; GStA Frankfurt, Anklage Schumann, Js 18/67 (GStA), 12 Dec. 1969, pp. 80–81, 87; GStA Frankfurt, Anklage Ullrich, Bunke, Borm und Endru-weit, Js 15/61 (GStA), 15 Jan. 1965, pp. 181, 202–3, 212; LG Frankfurt, Urteil Ullrich, Bunke und Endruweit, Ks 1/66 (GStA), 23 May 1967, p. 64; HHStA, 461/32061/7: LG Frankfurt, Verfahren Wahlmann, Gorgaß, Huber, 4a KLs 7/47 (4a Js 3/46), Protokoll der öffentlichen Sitzung der 4. Strafkammer, 24 Feb. 1947, p. 16 (testimony Hans-Bodo Gorgaß). See also GStA Frankfurt, Sammlung Euthanasie: Standesbeamte Grafeneck to Landrat Münsingen, 11 Apr. 1940.

92. BDC, dossier Christian Wirth; GStA Frankfurt, Anklage Ullrich, Bunke, Borm und Endruweit, Js 15/61 (GStA), 15 Jan. 1965, pp. 181, 202–3; StArch Sigmaringen, Wü 29/3, Acc. 33/1973, Nr. 1752: StA Tübingen, Anklage Mauthe, 1 Js 85–87/47, 4 Jan. 1949, pp. 48v–51v, 53–54; DÖW, file E18370/1: LG Frankfurt, Untersuchungsrichter, Verfahren Js 18/61 (GStA), interrogation Fritz Tauscher, Hamburg, 2 June 1964, and Bundesministerium für Inneres, Gruppe Staatspolizei, interrogation Matthias Buchberger, 24 Feb. 1964; LG Düsseldorf, Urteil Franz Stangl, 8 Ks 1/69, 22 Dec. 1970, pp. 1–13.

93. HHStA, 461/32061/7: LG Frankfurt, Verfahren Wahlmann, Gorgaß, Huber, 4a KLs 7/47 (4a Js 3/46), Protokoll der öffentlichen Sitzung der 4. Strafkammer, 3 Mar. 1947, p. 32 (testimony Ingeborg Seidel); GStA Frankfurt, Anklage Renno, Becker und Lorent, Js 18/61 (GStA), Js 7/63 (GStA), Js 5/65 (GStA), 7 Nov. 1967, pp. 42–43.

94. See, for example, GStA Frankfurt, Anklage Ullrich, Bunke, Borm und Endruweit, Js 15/61 (GStA), 15 Jan. 1965, pp. 114–15; GStA Frankfurt, Anklage Vorberg und Allers, Js 20/61 (GStA), 15 Feb. 1966, pp. 96–99; HHStA, 461/32061/7: LG Frankfurt, Verfahren Wahlmann, Gorgaß, Huber, 4a KLs 7/47 (4a Js 3/46), Protokoll der öffentlichen Sitzung der 4. Straf-kammer, 3 Mar. 1947, p. 27 (testimony Elfriede Häfner).

95. StArch Sigmaringen, Wü 29/3, Acc. 33/1973, Nr. 1752: StA Tübingen, Anklage Mauthe, 1 Js 85–87/47, 4 Jan. 1949, p. 54; HHStA, 461/32061/7: LG Frankfurt, Verfahren Wahlmann, Gorgaß, Huber, 4a KLs 7/47 (4a Js 3/46), Protokoll der öffentlichen Sitzung der 4. Strafkammer, 3 Mar. 1947, p. 25 (testimony Hildegard Rützel).

96. HHStA, 461/32061/7: LG Frankfurt, Verfahren Wahlmann, Gorgaß, Huber, 4a KLs 7/47 (4a Js 3/46), Protokoll der öffentlichen Sitzung der 4. Strafkammer, 3 Mar. 1947, p. 6 (testimony Maximilian Friedrich Lindner), p. 30 (testimony Elisabeth Utry).

97. Ibid., p. 31 (testimony Ingeborg Seidel).

98. Ibid., p. 8 (testimony Maximilian Friedrich Lindner); LG Frankfurt, Urteil Ullrich, Bunke und Endruweit, Ks 1/66 (GStA), 23 May 1967, pp. 36, 114–15; DÖW, file E18370/3: interrogation Helene Hintersteiner, Linz, 18 Aug. 1945.

99. The papers of Paul Nitsche—correspondence, memos, and reports—were captured by the U.S. Army and partly used as evidence at Nuremberg; thereafter, the papers were stored until the late 1960s in U.S. Army facilities at Heidelberg. Copies made in Heidel-berg by OStA Johannes Warlo before the papers were shipped to the United States are now located at the ZStL and are known as the Heidelberg Documents. Less readable copies are also at BAK in record group R96I. Archivist Richard Boylan and I rediscovered the origi-nals in the late 1980s at NARA, Suitland (RG 338, Cases Tried, General Administration, Medical Experiments). These originals do not include everything available at the ZStL but do include material missing at the ZStL. Another portion of the Nitsche papers, mostly reports but also correspondence, is held at the BA-MA in record group H20, files 463 and

465. The statistical reports captured at Hartheim, now known as the "Hartheim Statistics," have been available on microfilm in NARA, RG 338, Microfilm Publication T-1021, roll 18. Boylan and I rediscovered the original bound volume of the "Hartheim Statistics" at Suitland during our search for the original Heidelberg Documents. The volume (in color) is located in NARA Suitland, RG 338, USAREUR 1942–, War Crimes Branch, Cases Not Tried, File Lot 600-12-463, but is currently on exhibit at the United States Holocaust Memorial Museum. For the story of how the reports were discovered, see the certification attached to the volume and also an eyewitness report in DÖW, file E18370/3: interrogation Helene Hintersteiner, Linz, 18 Aug. 1945. See also Henry Friedlander, "Fundstücke und Berichte: Nitsche-Dokumente," *Beiträge zur nationalsozialistischen Gesundheits- und Sozialpolitik* 4 (1987): 190.

100. The pocket diary is part of the files of GStA Frankfurt, Verfahren Heyde, Bohne und Hefelmann, Ks 2/63 (GStA), Js 17/59 (GStA).

101. See, for example, DÖW, file E18370/3: Bezirksgericht Eferding-Grieskirchen, interrogation Aneliese Gindl, 25 July 1947.

102. HHStA, 461/32061/7: LG Frankfurt, Verfahren Wahlmann, Gorgaß, Huber, 4a KLs 7/47 (4a Js 3/46), Protokoll der öffentlichen Sitzung der 4. Strafkammer, 27 Feb. 1947, pp. 24–25 (testimony Fritz Schirwing); DÖW, file E18370/1: LG Linz, interrogation Heinrich Barbl, 5 Oct. 1964, and Bundesministerium für Inneres, interrogation Bruno Bruckner, Vienna, 24 May 1962; GStA Frankfurt, Anklage Ullrich, Bunke, Borm und Endruweit, Js 15/61 (GStA), 15 Jan. 1965, p. 181; ZStL, interrogation Franz Suchomel, 21 Sept. 1962; DÖW, file E18370/2: Vg bei dem LG Linz, Hauptverhandlung Harrer, Lang und Mayrhuber, Vg 6 Vr 2407/46 (186), 2–3 July 1948, p. 7 (testimony Franz Mayrhuber); DÖW, file E18370/3: interrogation Franz Hödl, n.d.

103. DÖW, file E18370/2: Bezirksgericht Gmunden, interrogation Siegfriede Muckenhuber, 20 July 1946; DÖW, file E18370/3: Gendarmeriepostenkommando Gmunden, interrogation Siegfriede Muckenhuber, 19 July 1946, LG Linz, interrogation Karl Harrer, 6 Mar. 1947, Bezirksgericht Ybbs, interrogation Anna Griessenberger, 31 May 1946, Gendarmeriepostenkommando Gmunden, interrogation Gertraud Dirnberger, 13 Aug. 1946, and interrogation Helene Hintersteiner, Linz, 18 Aug. 1945.

104. DÖW, file E18370/3: Bezirksgericht Ybbs, interrogation Hermann Merta, 3 Dec. 1945.

105. HHStA, 461/32061/7: LG Frankfurt, Verfahren Wahlmann, Gorgaß, Huber, 4a KLs 7/47 (4a Js 3/46), Protokoll der öffentlichen Sitzung der 4. Strafkammer, 3 Mar. 1947, p. 12 (testimony Judith Thomas).

106. GStA Frankfurt, Eberl Akten, II/135n, 7:56–57: "Bernburg Personalaufstellung und Diensteinteilung"; DÖW, file E18370/3: Bundespolizeikommissariat, Kriminalbeamtenabteilung, interrogation Karoline Burner, Steyr, 23 Sept. 1946; HHStA, 461/32061/7: LG Frankfurt, Verfahren Wahlmann, Gorgaß, Huber, 4a KLs 7/47 (4a Js 3/46), Protokoll der öffentlichen Sitzung der 4. Strafkammer, 3 Mar. 1947, p. 12 (testimony Judith Thomas); DÖW, file E18370/3: interrogation Helene Hintersteiner, Linz, 18 Aug. 1945.

107. See, for example, HHStA 461/32061/18: Landesheilanstalt Eichberg to Wilhelm Schramm, 21 May 1941. See also DÖW, file E18229: letter from Anstalt Gallneukirchen, 22 Jan. 1941. For rules prohibiting precise notification, especially of those paying for upkeep, see GStA Frankfurt, Sammlung Euthanasie: Gemeinnützige Stiftung to Baden Ministerium des Innern, 4 Apr. 1941, and Gemeinnützige Stiftung to Anstalt Wiesloch, 13 Dec. 1941; and NARA, RG 338, Microfilm Publication T-1021, roll 17, frame 296: Gemeinnützige Stiftung (sig. Allers) to Direktor Dr. Möckel, Anstalt Wiesloch, 13 Feb. 1941. For the prohibition of any notification reaching foreign countries, see GStA Frankfurt, Sammlung Euthanasie, and NARA, RG 338, Microfilm Publication T-1021, roll 17, frame 452: RAG (sig. Heyde) to Anstalt Weinsberg, 14 Nov. 1941.

108. See, for example, DÖW, file E18370/2: twenty-one completed transfer forms from Oberösterreichische Landes- Heil- und Pflegeanstalt für Geisteskranke Niedernhart-Linz a.D.

109. Ibid.: Bezirksgericht Ybbs, interrogation Franz Sitter, 20 Mar. 1947; GStA Frankfurt, Anklage Renno, Becker und Lorent, Js 18/61 (GStA), Js 7/63 (GStA), Js 5/65 (GStA), 7 Nov. 1967, p. 46.

110. DÖW, file E18370/3: Gemeindeamt Alkoven to Anstalt Niedernhart, 24 May 1946. See also GStA Frankfurt, Sammlung Euthanasie: Standesbeamte Grafeneck to Landrat Münsingen, 11 Apr. 1940.

111. DÖW, file E18370/3: interrogation Maria Hirsch, Linz, 26 June 1946.

112. See GStA Frankfurt, Anklage Ullrich, Bunke, Borm und Endruweit, Js 15/61 (GStA), 15 Jan. 1965, p. 112; BA-MA, H20/463, 465: Anstalt Hadamar to Gemeinnützige Stiftung, 7 July 1942.

113. GStA Frankfurt, Eberl Akten, II/155, 7:66–67: Rudolf Lonauer to Irmfried Eberl, 29 Oct. 1941; LG Frankfurt, Urteil Ullrich, Bunke und Endruweit, Ks 1/66 (GStA), 23 May 1967, p. 62. For sample causes of death, see GStA Frankfurt, Anklage Heyde, Bohne und Hefelmann, Ks 2/63 (GStA), Js 17/59 (GStA), 22 May 1962, pp. 397–99.

114. ZStL, Bd. 513, and GStA Frankfurt, Eberl Akten, I/253/1–4, 1:157–60: Irmfried Eberl to Rudolf Lonauer, copy to Werner Heyde, 16 July 1940.

115. HHStA, 461/32061/7: LG Frankfurt, Verfahren Wahlmann, Gorgaß, Huber, 4a KLs 7/47 (4a Js 3/46), Protokoll der öffentlichen Sitzung der 4. Strafkammer, 3 Mar. 1947, p. 19 (testimony Hans-Bodo Gorgaß); LG Frankfurt, Urteil Ullrich, Bunke und Endruweit, Ks 1/66 (GStA), 23 May 1967, pp. 51, 59–60, 62; LG Frankfurt, Urteil Borm, Ks 1/66 (GStA), 6 June 1972, p. 40.

116. StArch Sigmaringen, Wü 29/3, Acc. 33/1973, Nr. 1752: StA Tübingen, Anklage Mauthe, 1 Js 85–87/47, 4 Jan. 1949, p. 51. See also the correspondence in HHStA, 461/32061/22.

117. ZStL, Bd. 513: Anstalt Sonnenstein to Adolf Wächtler, 2 Aug. 1940; DÖW, file 18229: postcard from Anstalt Sonnenstein concerning patient Anna Stroitz.

118. GStA Frankfurt, Anklage Renno, Becker und Lorent, Js 18/61 (GStA), Js 7/63 (GStA), Js 5/65 (GStA), 7 Nov. 1967, p. 36; GStA Frankfurt, Anklage Ullrich, Bunke, Borm und Endruweit, Js 15/61 (GStA), 15 Jan. 1965, p. 112; HHStA, 461/32061/7: LG Frankfurt, Verfahren Wahlmann, Gorgaß, Huber, 4a KLs 7/47 (4a Js 3/46), Protokoll der öffentlichen Sitzung der 4. Strafkammer, 3 Mar. 1947, p. 18 (testimony Paula Siegert), p. 2 (testimony Margot Schmidt). For typical letters, see the files on patients in HHStA, 461/32061/6.

119. Nuremberg Doc. NO-840, and BAK, R22/5021: Anstalt Grafeneck (sig. Dr. Keller) to Barbara Schmidt, 6 Aug. 1940.

120. Nuremberg Doc. PS-628: Anstalt Brandenburg (sig. Dr. Schmitt) to Frau Johanne M., 17 Apr. 1940; BAK, R22/5021: Anstalt Hartheim to Alfred Rothmann, 24 June 1940.

121. Nuremberg Doc. PS-628: Anstalt Brandenburg (sig. Dr. Schmitt) to Frau Johanne M., 17 Apr. 1940.

122. DÖW, file E18371: Anstalt Brandenburg (sig. Dr. Schmitt) to Valentin Resetschnig, 25 July 1940; ZStL, Bd. 513: Anstalt Brandenburg (sig. Dr. Schmitt) to Adolf Wächtler, 13 Aug. 1940.

123. Nuremberg Doc. NO-828: Anstalt Brandenburg letter (sig. Dr. Meyer), 20 Feb. 1940.

124. BAK, R22/5021: Anstalt Hadamar (sig. Dr. Moos) to Margarethe Weber, 6 Feb. 1941.

125. StA Frankfurt, Anklage Ullrich, Bunke, Borm und Endruweit, Js 15/61 (GStA), 15 Jan. 1965, p. 112.

126. ZStL, Bd. 513: Anstalt Brandenburg (sig. Dr. Schmitt) to Adolf Wächtler, 13 Aug. 1940.

127. Nuremberg Doc. NO-840, and BAK, R22/5021: Anstalt Grafeneck (sig. Dr. Keller) to Barbara Schmidt, 6 Aug. 1940.

128. HHStA, 461/32061/18: Anstalt Hadamar (sig. illegible) to Wilhelm Schramm, 1 June 1941. See similar phraseology in HHStA, 461/32061/19: Anstalt Bernburg (sig. Dr. Keller) to Jakob Heun, 16 Feb. 1941, and LG Frankfurt, Urteil Borm, Ks 1/66 (GStA), 6 June 1972, p. 28b: facsimile of letter from Anstalt Bernburg (sig. Dr. Strom), 3 Apr. 1941.

129. GStA Frankfurt, Sammlung Euthanasie: Gemeinnützige Stiftung für Anstaltspflege to Landessekretär Alfons Klein, Hadamar, 2 Mar. 1943; HHStA, 461/32061/7: LG Frankfurt, Verfahren Wahlmann, Gorgaß, Huber, 4a KLs 7/47 (4a Js 3/46), Protokoll der öffentlichen Sitzung der 4. Strafkammer, 3 Mar. 1947, p. 22 (testimony Johanna Schrettinger); DÖW, file E18229: Anstalt Sonnenstein to Evangelische Diakonissen-Anstalt Gallneukirchen, 10 Feb. 1941, and Ortspolizeibehörde, Abteilung Friedhofverwaltung, Sonnenstein, to Verwaltung des Evangelischen Friedhofes Gallneukirchen, 11 Feb. 1941; DÖW, file E18370/3: interrogation Elisabeth Lego, Linz, 29 June 1946.

130. StArch Sigmaringen, Wü 29/3, Acc. 33/1973, Nr. 1752: StA Tübingen, Anklage Mauthe, 1 Js 85–87/47, 4 Jan. 1949, p. 14.

131. GStA Frankfurt, Anklage Vorberg und Allers, Js 20/61 (GStA), 15 Feb. 1966, pp. 98–99.

132. DÖW, file E18370/3: LG Linz, interrogation Karl Harrer, 6 Mar. 1947, Bezirksgericht Ybbs, interrogation Anna Griessenberger, 31 May 1946, and Hermann Merta, 3 Dec. 1945.

133. Nuremberg Doc. NO-840, and BAK, R22/5021: Anstalt Grafeneck (sig. Dr. Keller) to Barbara Schmidt, 6 Aug. 1940.

134. HHStA, 461/32061/18: Hadamar death certificate of Maria Hedwig Schramm, 31 May 1941; HHStA, 461/32061/19: Bernburg death certificate (sig. Klein) of Günter Josef Heun, 16 Feb. 1941. See also HHStA, 461/32061/22, and GStA Frankfurt, Anklage Ullrich, Bunke, Borm und Endruweit, Js 15/61 (GStA), 15 Jan. 1965, p. 114.

135. ZStL, Sammlung Verschiedenes, Bd. 132: Landesversicherungsanstalt Thüringen to Thüringen Ministerium des Innern, 6 Aug. 1942, and Zentralverrechnungsstelle Heil- und Pflegeanstalten to Thüringen Ministerium des Innern, 23 Sept. 1943, concerning pension of patients killed 28 Sept. 1940; GStA Frankfurt, Anklage Vorberg und Allers, Js 20/61 (GStA), 15 Feb. 1966, pp. 98–99. See also NARA, RG 338, Microfilm Publication T-1021, roll 17, frame 349: "Anmerkung zur Nachweisung über die Kostenträger."

136. StArch Sigmaringen, Wü 29/3, Acc. 33/1973, Nr. 1752: StA Tübingen, Anklage Mauthe, 1 Js 85–87/47, 4 Jan. 1949, p. 14.

137. GStA Frankfurt, Anklage Renno, Becker und Lorent, Js 18/61 (GStA), Js 7/63 (GStA), Js 5/65 (GStA), 7 Nov. 1967, pp. 36–37.

138. ZStL, Bd. 513: Anstalt Sonnenstein to Adolf Wächtler, 2 Aug. 1940 (notice of arrival of Anna Frieda Lohse née Wächtler), Anstalt Sonnenstein to Adolf Wächtler, 7 Aug. 1940 (reply to inquiry by Adolf Wächtler with information that Anna Frieda Lohse née Wächtler had been transferred to an unknown destination), and Anstalt Brandenburg (sig. Dr. Schmitt) to Adolf Wächtler, 13 Aug. 1940 (notice that Anna Frieda Lohse née Wächtler had died there); HHStA, 461/32061/19: Anstalt Hadamar to Familie Heun, 4 Feb. 1941 (notice of arrival of Josef Heun), and Anstalt Bernburg (sig. Dr. Keller) to Jakob Heun, 16 Feb. 1941 (notice that Josef Heun had died there).

139. DÖW, file E18370/3: Bezirksgericht Eferding-Grieskirchen, interrogation Aneliese Gindl, 25 July 1947.

140. Klee, *"Euthanasie" im NS-Staat*, p. 291, argues that Grafeneck was not closed through Himmler's intervention but because both Brandenburg and Grafeneck had already fulfilled their function and were scheduled to close.

141. See, for example, GStA Frankfurt, Sammlung Euthanasie: Dr. Wilhelm Weskott, director, Anstalt Weissenau, to Dr. Eugen Stähle, Württemberg MdI, 12 July 1940.

142. Nuremberg Doc. NO-829: GStA Stuttgart to RJM, 1 Aug. 1940; BAK, R22/5021: Lagebericht des Oberlandesgerichtspräsidenten Stuttgart, 6 Nov. 1940.

143. BAK, R22/5021, and Nuremberg Doc. NO-830.

144. Nuremberg Doc. NO-001: Else von Löwis to Frau Buch, 25 Nov. 1940 (also in ZStL, Sammlung Schumacher, Bd. 121, Faszikel 401).

145. Nuremberg Doc. NO-002: Walter Buch to Heinrich Himmler, 7 Dec. 1940 (also in ZStL, Sammlung Schumacher, Bd. 121, Faszikel 401).

146. Ibid. NO-002: Heinrich Himmler to Walter Buch, 19 Dec. 1940 (also in ZStL, Sammlung Schumacher, Bd. 121, Faszikel 401).

147. Ibid. NO-018: Heinrich Himmler to Viktor Brack, 19 Dec. 1940 (also in ZStL, Sammlung Schumacher, Bd. 121, Faszikel 401).

148. See, for example, *JuNSV*, vol. 7, no. 225a: LG Koblenz, Urteil 9/5 KLs 41/48, 28 July 1950, and *JuNSV*, vol. 3, no. 088: LG Koblenz, Urteil 3 KLs 36/48, 4 Oct. 1948.

149. U.S. Military Tribunal, Transcript of the Proceedings in Case 1, p. 1879 (testimony Friedrich Mennecke). See also *JuNSV*, vol. 3, no. 088: LG Koblenz, Urteil 3 KLs 36/48, 4 Oct. 1948; *JuNSV*, vol. 7, no. 226: LG Hannover, Urteil 2 Ks 9/49, 29 July 1950; and *JuNSV*, vol. 11, no. 380: LG Dortmund, Urteil 12 Ks 2/53, 2 Dec. 1953.

150. DÖW, file E18370/3: interrogation Josef Falkner, Linz, 9 July 1945.

151. GStA Frankfurt, Sammlung Euthanasie: Gemeinnützige Stiftung für Anstaltspflege to Baden MdI, 4 Apr. 1941, with guidelines for notification.

152. GStA Frankfurt, Anklage Vorberg und Allers, Js 20/61 (GStA), 15 Feb. 1966, p. 91.

153. U.S. Military Tribunal, Transcript of the Proceedings in Case 1, pp. 2415–16 (testimony Karl Brandt), pp. 7572–73 (testimony Viktor Brack).

154. GStA Frankfurt, Anklage Heyde, Bohne und Hefelmann, Ks 2/63 (GStA), Js 17/59 (GStA), 22 May 1962, p. 575.

155. NARA, RG 338, Microfilm Publication T-1021, roll 17, frame 295: RAG to Anstalt Wiesloch, 12 Feb. 1941; GStA Frankfurt, Sammlung Euthanasie, and NARA, RG 338, Microfilm Publication T-1021, roll 17, frame 363: RAG to Baden MdI, 4 Apr. 1941. See also GStA Frankfurt, Sammlung Euthanasie: Württemberg MdI to RAG, 19 Apr. 1941.

156. DÖW, file E18370/1: StA Frankfurt, Js 18/61 (GStA), interrogation Georg Renno, 3 Feb. 1965, p. 25.

157. StArch Sigmaringen, Wü 29/3, Acc. 33/1973, Nr. 1752: StA Tübingen, Anklage Mauthe, 1 Js 85–87/47, 4 Jan. 1949, p. 12; U.S. Military Tribunal, Transcript of the Proceedings in Case 1, pp. 1833–36 (testimony Walter Schmidt), p. 1879 (testimony Friedrich Mennecke).

158. DÖW, file E18370/1: StA Frankfurt, Js 18/61 (GStA), interrogation Georg Renno, 2 Feb. 1965, p. 15.

159. DÖW, file E18370/2: Polizeidirektion Linz, Schlußbericht Hartheim, 29 July 1946.

160. DÖW, file E18370/1: StA Frankfurt, Js 18/61 (GStA), interrogation Georg Renno, 1 Feb. 1965, p. 3, and 3 Feb. 1965, p. 24; DÖW, file 11440: StA Konstanz, Einstellungsbericht Josef Vonbun, 2 Js 524/61, 21 June 1966, pp. 5–6, and VG bei dem LG Linz, Urteil Karl Harrer, Leopold Lang und Franz Mayrhuber, Vg 6 Vr 2407/46 (188), 3 July 1948; DÖW, file E18370/2: interrogation Johann Thorwartl, Linz, 21 July 1945, and LG Linz, interrogation Dr. Franz Wiesinger, 22 Sept. 1947; DÖW, file E18370/3: interrogation Johann Baumgartner, 10 July 1945, and interrogation Josef Falkner, Linz, 9 July 1945.

161. DÖW, file E18370/3: Kriminalpolizei Linz, interrogation Vinzenz Nohel, 4 Sept. 1945; DÖW, file E18370/1: StA Frankfurt, Js 18/61 (GStA), interrogation Georg Renno, 2 Feb. 1965, p. 20, and Bundesministerium für Inneres, interrogation Bruno Bruckner, Vienna, 24 May 1962.

162. HHStA, 461/32061/7: LG Frankfurt, Verfahren Wahlmann, Gorgaß, Huber, 4a KLs 7/47 (4a Js 3/46), Protokoll der öffentlichen Sitzung der 4. Strafkammer, 3 Mar. 1947, p. 25

(testimony Hildegard Rützel); DÖW, file E18370/1: StA Frankfurt, Js 18/61 (GStA), interrogation Georg Renno, 1 Feb. 1965, p. 6, and Bundesministerium für Inneres, interrogation Bruno Bruckner, Vienna, 24 May 1962.

163. DÖW, file E18370/1: Bundesministerium für Inneres, interrogation Bruno Bruckner, Vienna, 24 May 1962.

164. HHStA, 461/32061/7: LG Frankfurt, Verfahren Wahlmann, Gorgaß, Huber, 4a KLs 7/47 (4a Js 3/46), Protokoll der öffentlichen Sitzung der 4. Strafkammer, 25 Feb. 1947, p. 2 (testimony Irmgard Huber), p. 23 (testimonies Hubert Gomerski and Maximilian Friedrich Lindner). See also Winter et al., *Verlegt nach Hadamar*, p. 95.

165. NARA, RG 338, Microfilm Publication T-1021, roll 18, "Hartheim Statistics," p. 1.

166. See GStA Frankfurt, Anklage Ullrich, Bunke, Borm und Endruweit, Js 15/61 (GStA), 15 Jan. 1965, pp. 133–38; GStA Frankfurt, Anklage Heyde, Bohne und Hefelmann, Ks 2/63 (GStA), Js 17/59 (GStA), 22 May 1962, pp. 695–701.

167. NARA, RG 338, Microfilm Publication T-1021, roll 18, "Hartheim Statistics," p. 4.

168. Ibid., p. 9.

CHAPTER SIX

1. U.S. Military Tribunal, Transcript of the Proceedings in Case 1, pp. 2530–31 (testimony Karl Brandt), p. 7629 (testimony Viktor Brack). See also "Aktenvermerk" by Irmfried Eberl, cited in GStA Frankfurt, Anklage Werner Heyde, Gerhard Bohne und Hans Hefelmann, Ks 2/63 (GStA), Js 17/59 (GStA), 22 May 1962, p. 680.

2. For a similar interpretation, see Denzler and Fabricius, *Kirchen im Dritten Reich*, 1: 117ff.

3. The attitude and behavior of the churches in matters relating to eugenics, sterilization, and euthanasia have been treated in detail in Klee, *"Euthanasie" im NS-Staat*, esp. pp. 278–89; Schmuhl, *Rassenhygiene, Nationalsozialismus, Euthanasie*, pp. 305–54; and Nowak, *"Euthanasie" und Sterilisierung*, pp. 91–177.

4. See BAK, R22/5021: report on BBC broadcasts in English and German about the "euthanasia" killings, Jan. 1941. See also Klee, *"Euthanasie" im NS-Staat*, p. 334.

5. U.S. Military Tribunal, Transcript of the Proceedings in Case 1, p. 2531 (cross-examination of Karl Brandt).

6. For a discussion of these jurisdictional conflicts, see Schmuhl, *Rassenhygiene, Nationalsozialismus, Euthanasie*, pp. 211–13. On Leonardo Conti's position in the Nazi hierarchy, see Kater, "Conti and His Nemesis." On the support role of Reinhard Heydrich and the RSHA, see BAK, R22/5021: handwritten note by Dr. Günther Joël transmitting to Franz Gürtner comments by Heydrich concerning his relationship to the euthanasia program, 1 Nov. [1940], and BA-MA, H20/463, 465: Viktor Brack to Heinrich Müller, 5 July 1941, and Viktor Brack to RSHA, Abteilung IVb2, 9 Apr. 1942.

7. U.S. Military Tribunal, Transcript of the Proceedings in Case 1, p. 2413 (testimony Karl Brandt). See also Friedrich Mennecke's testimony at Nuremberg: "They wanted to avoid unrest among the people, which was very important during the war and for that reason the thing should not be discussed." Ibid., p. 1923.

8. See, for example, Nuremberg Docs. NO-665, NO-795, D-906.

9. Ibid. NO-018: Heinrich Himmler to Viktor Brack, 19 Dec. 1940.

10. U.S. Military Tribunal, Transcript of the Proceedings in Case 1, pp. 2401, 2482 (testimony Karl Brandt).

11. Nowak, *"Euthanasie" und Sterilisierung*, pp. 91–119; Schmuhl, *Rassenhygiene, Nationalsozialismus, Euthanasie*, pp. 305–12; Klee, *"Euthanasie" im NS-Staat*, pp. 48–53.

12. See ZStL, Heidelberg Docs. 127,381–82: report by Dr. Schneider, Berlin, 27 Aug. 1942; ibid. 127,389–90: RAG (Nitsche) to Herbert Linden, 21 Aug. 1942.

13. See BAK, R22/5021: Pastor L. Schlaich, director of the Heil- und Plegeanstalt für Schwachsinnige und Epileptische, Stetten i.R., to Reich minister of justice, Dr. Frank [*sic*], copy to Hans Heinrich Lammers, 6 Sept. 1940 (also in Nuremberg Doc. NO-520 and ZStL, Sammlung Schumacher, Bd. 121, Faszikel 401).

14. BAK, R22/5021: Theophil Wurm to Wilhelm Frick, copy to Franz Gürtner, 19 July 1940, and Wurm to Frick, 5 Sept. 1940; Nuremberg Doc. PS-623: Wurm to Gürtner, 6 Sept. 1940 (cover letter for copy of 5 Sept. letter to Frick).

15. For Braune's own postwar account, see HHStA, 461/32061/22: Paul Gerhard Braune to OStA Frankfurt, 12 Sept. 1946.

16. Nuremberg Doc. PS-631: Pastor Braune, "Planwirtschaftliche Verlegung von Insassen der Heil- und Pflegeanstalten," Lobetal, 9 July 1940 (published in Hase, *Evangelische Dokumente*, pp. 14–22).

17. BAK, R18/5586: Pastor F. v. Bodelschwingh to Hans Heinrich Lammers, 31 Oct. 1940.

18. Nuremberg Doc. PS-625: Adolf Bertram to Hans Heinrich Lammers, 11 Aug. 1940, and Bertram to Franz Gürtner, 16 Aug. 1940 (cover letter for copy of 11 Aug. letter to Lammers).

19. Schmuhl, *Rassenhygiene, Nationalsozialismus, Euthanasie*, pp. 348–49. See also, for example, HStA Düsseldorf, RW 36-22, p. 9: Paul Gutfleisch to Offices of the Bishop of Münster, 1 Oct. 1941.

20. Schmuhl, *Rassenhygiene, Nationalsozialismus, Euthanasie*, p. 349.

21. Nuremberg Docs. NO-846, PS-617: Michael Faulhaber to Franz Gürtner, 6 Nov. 1940.

22. See correspondence and memos in BAK, R22/5021.

23. Nowak, *"Euthanasie" und Sterilisierung*, p. 160; Schmuhl, *Rassenhygiene, Nationalsozialismus, Euthanasie*, pp. 349–50. Quote cited in Nuremberg Doc. PS-616.

24. Nuremberg Doc. PS-615: Antonius Hilfrich to RJM, 13 Aug. 1941, text also in Klee, *Dokumente*, pp. 231–32, and English translation in *TWC*, 1:845–47.

25. Nuremberg Doc. PS-616: Wilhelm Berning to RJM, 28 Aug. 1941.

26. Text in Denzler and Fabricius, *Kirchen im Dritten Reich*, 2:198–208. For a report on the sermon read in Catholic churches, see HStA Düsseldorf, RW 18-26I, pp. 173–75.

27. Schmuhl, *Rassenhygiene, Nationalsozialismus, Euthanasie*, pp. 351–52.

28. Ibid., p. 351, lists four members of the lower clergy, three Catholics, and one Protestant who were convicted by the People's Court (Volksgerichtshof) and executed, supposedly for distributing the pronouncements of Wurm and von Galen.

29. BAK, R22/5021: Bernhard Lichtenberg to Leonardo Conti, with cover letter to Reich minister of justice, 26 Aug. 1941.

30. Nowak, *"Euthanasie" und Sterilisierung*, pp. 164–65.

31. Eschwege, *Kennzeichen J*, p. 340.

32. On the role of the judiciary, see Gruchmann, *Justiz im Dritten Reich*, pp. 497–534, and "Euthanasie und Justiz"; and Kramer, "Selbstentlastung der Justiz."

33. See NARA Suitland, Heidelberg Docs. 125,339–66: 20. Sitzung der Strafrechtskommission, 16 Apr. 1934, pp. 1–29. At the start of the euthanasia program, the KdF had requested copies of the commission's meetings. Ibid. 125,338: RJM to KdF, 11 Aug. 1939.

34. For the view that Hitler's authorization had legalized the killings, see U.S. Military Tribunal, Transcript of the Proceedings in Case 1, p. 2426 (testimony Karl Brandt).

35. See Roth and Aly, "Diskussion über die Legalisierung der nationalsozialistischen Anstaltsmorde."

36. StGB §211, §212, §139, English translation in *Statutory Criminal Law of Germany*, pp. 97, 128; *Strafprozeßordnung* (StPO) §152. Postwar West German courts have rejected Hitler's authorization as legalizing the euthanasia killings and have thus ruled them murder under the German penal code. See summary and court decisions cited in GStA Frankfurt, Voruntersuchungsantrag Franz Schlegelberger, Js 20/63 (GStA), 22 Apr. 1965, pp. 23–

25. On the postwar German proceedings, see Rückerl, *NS-Verbrechen vor Gericht*; Jäger, *Verbrechen unter totalitärer Herrschaft*; Henkys, *Nationalsozialistischen Gewaltverbrechen*; and Friedlander, "Judiciary and Nazi Crimes."

37. GStA Frankfurt, Voruntersuchungsantrag Schlegelberger, Js 20/63 (GStA), 22 Apr. 1965, pp. 26–27. See also reports cited in Michelberger, *Berichte aus der Justiz*, pp. 482–94. For a good example of how the information was transmitted privately, see DÖW, file E18282: interrogation Johann Stich, Vienna, 12 Aug. 1946 (a physician told Stich, who was attorney general in Vienna).

38. GStA Frankfurt, Voruntersuchungsantrag Schlegelberger, Js 20/63 (GStA), 22 Apr. 1965, p. 28; HHStA, 461/32061/7: LG Frankfurt, Verfahren Adolf Wahlmann, Bodo Gorgaß, Irmgard Huber, 4a KLs 7/47 (4a Js 3/46), Protokoll der öffentlichen Sitzung der 4. Strafkammer, 11 Mar. 1947 (testimony Werner Heyde), 13 Mar. 1947 (testimony OStA Hans Quambusch); StA München I, Verfahren Hermann Pfannmüller, 1 Ks 10/49 (1b Js 1791/47): Protokoll der öffentlichen Sitzung des Schwurgerichts bei dem LG München I, 21 Oct. 1949, p. 31 (testimony Dr. Moritz Schnittmann); StA Hamburg, Anklage Friedrich Lensch und Kurt Struve, 147 Js 58/67, 24 Apr. 1973, pp. 622–23; BAK, R36/881: Ergebnis der Rundfrage des Deutschen Gemeindetages bei den Verwaltungen der Provinzial- bezw. Bezirksverbände vom 24. 6. 1938 betr. Sicherheitsverwahrte in Heil- und Pflegeanstalten, 26 Aug. 1938. See also Klee, *"Euthanasie" im NS-Staat*, p. 123, and Schmidt, *Selektion in der Heilanstalt*, p. 47. For StGB §42b, see English translation in *Statutory Criminal Law of Germany*, p. 27. For background on placement of persons committed under §42a and e, see BAK, R36/1847.

39. See BAK, R22/5021: GStA Breslau to RJM, 15 Apr. 1941, GStA Düsseldorf to RJM, 16 May 1941, GStA Jena to RJM, 17 July 1941, GStA Dresden to Roland Freisler, 24 Aug., 10 Oct. 1940, and GStA Naumburg (Saale) to Freisler, 13 Sept. 1940; Nuremberg Doc. PS-618: GStA Dresden to Reichsminister der Justiz, 20 Oct. 1940.

40. See BAK, R22/5021: GStA Dresden to Roland Freisler, two letters of 24 Aug. 1940 (ten cases), and OStA Chemnitz to GStA Dresden, 3 Dec. 1940 (six cases); and Nuremberg Doc. PS-622: GStA Naumburg (Saale) to Freisler, 13 Sept. 1940 (six cases).

41. StGB §42f, English translation in *Statutory Criminal Law of Germany*, p. 29.

42. See BAK, R22/5021: GStA Breslau to RJM, 15 Apr. 1941, with attached form letter to the GStA from the Bunzlau state hospital and nursing home.

43. See ibid.: GStA Dresden to Roland Freisler, first letter of 24 Aug. 1940 (case of Erich Strelow).

44. Ibid.: GStA Dresden to Roland Freisler, second letter of 24 Aug. 1940 (case of Arnold Koepke); ZStL, Bd. 513: Landes-Pflegeanstalt Brandenburg to GStA Dresden, 29 Feb. 1940.

45. See Nuremberg Doc. PS-624: Landes-Heil- und Pflegeanstalt Waldheim (Sachs.) to Saxony MdI, 2 Aug. 1940, transmitting inquiries from state attorneys in Chemnitz and Dresden.

46. NARA, RG 338, Microfilm Publication T-1021, roll 17, frame 237: OStA Heidelberg (Haas) to GStA Karlsruhe, 12 June 1940.

47. Ibid., frame 271: GStA Karlsruhe to OStA Heidelberg, 9 July 1940.

48. GStA Frankfurt, Sammlung Euthanasie: Amtsgerichtsrat Dr. Kreyssig to Reichsminister der Justiz, 8 July 1940.

49. See BAK, R22/5021: Amtsgerichtspräsident Vienna to Oberlandesgerichtspräsident Vienna, 22 Aug. 1940, with cover letter from Oberlandesgerichtspräsident Vienna to RJM, 26 Aug. 1940, Oberamtsrichter in Coesfeld to Landesgerichtspräsident Münster, 26 July 1941, with cover letter from Oberlandesgerichtspräsident Hamm to RJM, 29 July 1941, and Oberlandesgerichtspräsident Frankfurt to Reichsminister der Justiz, 29 Aug. 1941. See also Nuremberg Doc. PS-681: Franz Schlegelberger to Hans Heinrich Lammers, 4 Mar. 1941.

50. See BAK, R22/5021: handwritten letter to Oberreichsanwalt bei dem Reichsgericht, n.d., with cover letter from Oberreichsanwalt to Reichsminister der Justiz, 10 July 1941, and handwritten letter to Justizminister, District Loest, 1 Aug. 1941. See also Nuremberg Doc. NO-845: GStA Köln to RJM, 20 Oct. 1941.

51. Nuremberg Doc. PS-629: Oberregierungsrat N. to Reichsjustizminister, Ulm, 8 July 1940.

52. See Michelberger, *Berichte aus der Justiz*, pp. 482–94. See also Nuremberg Doc. PS-681: Franz Schlegelberger to Hans Heinrich Lammers, 4 Mar. 1941.

53. Nuremberg Docs. PS-626, NO-829: GStA Stuttgart to RJM, 1 Aug. 1940; ibid., PS-619, NO-836: GStA Stuttgart to RJM, 12 Oct. 1940; BAK, R22/5021: Oberlandesgerichtspräsident Stuttgart to RJM, 31 Aug. 1940.

54. Nuremberg Doc. NO-156: GStA Stuttgart to RJM, 15 July 1940.

55. BAK, R22/5021: Oberlandesgerichtspräsident Frankfurt to Reichsminister der Justiz, 16 May 1941.

56. Ibid.: GStA Graz to Reichsminister der Justiz, 29 Sept., 24 Nov. 1940 (emphasis in original).

57. See Nuremberg Doc. PS-681: Franz Schlegelberger to Hans Heinrich Lammers, 4 Mar. 1941.

58. BAK, R22/5021: GStA Linz to RJM, 17 Oct. 1940; DÖW, file 17845: OStA in Wels to GStA Linz, 3 July 1941; BAK, R22/5021: report on Günther Rottmann, 9 June 1940; DÖW, file 17845: StA in Wels to GStA Linz, 9 Oct. 1940, GStA Linz to StA in Wels, 22 Oct. 1940, OStA in Wels to GStA Linz, 20 Nov. 1940, and GStA Linz to RJM, 28 Nov. 1940.

59. BAK, R22/5021: Roland Freisler to GStA Stuttgart, 9 Aug. 1940 (also in Nuremberg Doc. NO-831). See also BAK, R22/5021: Vermerk from Freisler to Ministerialdirektor Wilhelm Crohne, 27 Nov. 1940.

60. HHStA, 461/32061/22: Paul Gerhard Braune to OStA Frankfurt, 12 Sept. 1946.

61. See Gruchmann, *Justiz im Dritten Reich*, p. 511.

62. Nuremberg Docs. PS-627, NO-832: Franz Gürtner to Hans Heinrich Lammers, 24 July 1940.

63. BAK, R22/5021: Franz Schlegelberger to Philipp Bouhler, 27 July 1940 (also in Nuremberg Doc. NO-833).

64. BAK, R22/4209: Philipp Bouhler to Franz Gürtner, 5 Sept. 1940 (also in Nuremberg Docs. NO-156, NO-834).

65. BAK, R22/5021: Franz Gürtner to Hans Heinrich Lammers, 25 Sept. 1940, with reference also to another communication of 26 Aug. 1940, Franz Gürtner to Hans Heinrich Lammers, 2 Oct. 1940, and Franz Schlegelberger to Hans Heinrich Lammers, 5 Oct. 1940.

66. BAK, R22/4209: Hans Heinrich Lammers to Franz Gürtner, 2, 9 Oct. 1940 (also in Nuremberg Doc. PS-621).

67. BAK, R22/5021: RJM to RMdI, 21 Sept. 1940.

68. Ibid.: Leonardo Conti to RJM, 8 Oct. 1940 (also in Nuremberg Doc. NO-835).

69. Nuremberg Doc. PS-630 (also in BAK, R22/4209).

70. Gruchmann, *Justiz im Dritten Reich*, pp. 512–13.

71. See Nuremberg Docs. PS-626, NO-829: GStA Stuttgart to RJM, 1 Aug. 1940.

72. See DÖW, file 17845: RJM to GStA Linz, 24 Sept. 1941, and BAK, R22/5021, Vermerk about 22 June 1941 meeting.

73. Gruchmann, *Justiz im Dritten Reich*, p. 511 (based on information supplied by Lothar Kreyssig).

74. GStA Frankfurt, Sammlung Euthanasie: Lothar Kreyssig to institutions in Brandenburg-Görden, Teupitz, Eberswalde, Sorau, Neuruppin, Göttingen, and Lansberg-Warthe, 27 Aug. 1941.

75. Ibid.: Lothar Kreyssig to RJM, 30 Aug. 1941.

76. Gruchmann, *Justiz im Dritten Reich*, p. 512 (based on information supplied by Lothar Kreyssig).

77. BAK, R22/5021: Viktor Brack to Franz Schlegelberger, 22 Apr. 1941, and Roland Freisler to Philipp Bouhler, 20 June 1941.

78. GStA Frankfurt, Sammlung Euthanasie: Viktor Brack to Franz Schlegelberger, 18 Apr. 1941 (also in Nuremberg Doc. NO-842; BAK, R22/5021; and ZStL, Bd. 513).

79. BAK, R22/5021: GStA Düsseldorf to RJM, 16 May 1941, and GStA Jena to RJM, 17 July 1941.

80. Ibid.: Viktor Brack to Franz Schlegelberger, 22 Apr. 1941, Viktor Brack to Roland Freisler, 4 Aug. 1941, Freisler note to Wilhelm Crohne, 9 Aug. 1941, and RJM to Viktor Brack, 10 Sept. 1941.

81. Ibid.: Vermerk about 22 June 1941 meeting and KdF to Ministerialdirektor Crohne, 24 Nov. 1941.

82. GStA Frankfurt, Voruntersuchungsantrag Schlegelberger, Js 20/63 (GStA), 22 Apr. 1965, p. 34.

83. Ibid., p. 35.

84. Ibid., pp. 39–42. See also U.S. Military Tribunal, Transcript of the Proceedings in Case 1, pp. 7590–91 (testimony Viktor Brack).

85. BAK, R22/5021: Schlegelberger memo, 22 Apr. 1941.

86. GStA Frankfurt, Voruntersuchungsantrag Schlegelberger, Js 20/63 (GStA), 22 Apr. 1965, p. 42.

87. See BAK, R22/5021: Oberlandesgerichtspräsident Köln to RJM, 30 Apr. 1941, and RJM to Oberlandesgerichtspräsident Köln, 7 May 1941.

88. U.S. Military Tribunal, Transcript of the Proceedings in Case 1, pp. 1819–22 (testimony Walter Schmidt).

89. GStA Frankfurt, Sammlung Euthanasie: RJM to Generalstaatsanwälte, 2 July 1943, and RMdI to Leiter der Heil- und Pflegeanstalten, 8 Aug. 1943; BAK, R18/3768: RMdI circular (sig. Linden), 17 Apr. 1944.

90. Weiss, "Race Hygiene Movement," p. 214; Bergmann, Czarnowski, and Ehmann, "Objekte humangenetischer Forschung," p. 126; Müller-Hill, "Selektion," pp. 142–43.

91. Müller-Hill, *Tödliche Wissenschaft*, p. 26. My translation is based in part on *Murderous Science*, p. 22, the English edition of Müller-Hill's study.

92. For a list of the *Ordinarien* in psychiatry or psychiatry-neurology at German universities, see Thom and Caregorodcev, *Medizin unterm Hakenkreuz*, p. 140, table 4.

93. Pross and Aly, *Wert des Menschen*, p. 191.

94. ZStL, Heidelberg Doc. 126,419: Paul Nitsche to Karl Brandt, 30 Aug. 1941.

95. See, for example, BAK, R73/14005 (research projects of Robert Ritter), and BAK, R73/14095 (research projects of Ernst Rüdin). On courses for SS physicians, see BAK, R73/15341: Otmar Freiherr von Verschuer to DFG, 31 Oct. 1936, and Pross and Aly, *Wert des Menschen*, p. 98.

96. Thom and Caregorodcev, *Medizin unterm Hakenkreuz*, p. 134. See also BAK, R36/1373: Kurt Pohlisch, "Das Rheinische Provinzial Institut für psychiatrisch-neurologische Erbforschung in Bonn," in *Der Erbarzt: Beilage zum Deutschen Ärzteblatt*, Nr. 4 (1936).

97. Thom and Caregorodcev, *Medizin unterm Hakenkreuz*, pp. 132, 136.

98. Müller-Hill, *Tödliche Wissenschaft*, pp. 86, 97.

99. BAK, R73/12781: Prof. Frhr. von Wettstein, Kaiser Wilhelm Institut für Biologie, to DFG, 14 Dec. 1937.

100. Ibid.: Konrad Lorenz to DFG, n.d. (registry date, 18 May 1937).

101. Ibid.: Prof. Frhr. von Wettstein, Kaiser Wilhelm Institut für Biologie, to DFG, 14 Dec. 1937.

102. Ibid.: DFG cover sheet.

103. Ibid.: Fritz Knoll to Prof. Frhr. von Wettstein, Kaiser Wilhelm Institut für Biologie, 17 Oct. 1937.

104. Ibid.: A. Pichler to Prof. Frhr. von Wettstein, Kaiser Wilhelm Institut für Biologie, 4 Aug. 1937.

105. Ibid.: Otto Antonius to Prof. Frhr. von Wettstein, Kaiser Wilhelm Institut für Biologie, 5 July 1937.

106. Ibid.: Ferdinand Hochstetter to Prof. Frhr. von Wettstein, Kaiser Wilhelm Institut für Biologie, 5 July 1937.

107. Ibid.: Konrad Lorenz, Personal-Fragebogen zu dem Gesuch um ein Forschungsstipendium, with attached "Nachweis der arischen Abstammung" from Konrad Lorenz and Mary Bertha Lorenz, 11 Jan. 1938.

108. BDC, dossier Konrad Lorenz: Nazi party membership file card, 1 May 1938; BAK, R73/12781: Lorenz to Reichsforschungsrat, 1 Dec. 1940.

109. See Müller-Hill, "Selektion," pp. 146–48; and DÖW, *Mitteilungen* 12 (Feb. 1974): Korrespondenz mit Nobelpreisträger Konrad Lorenz. For a more positive evaluation, see Weindling, *Health, Race, and German Politics*, p. 507.

110. See Aly, "Der saubere und der schmutzige Fortschritt," pp. 48–71.

111. GStA Frankfurt, Anklage Aquilin Ullrich, Heinrich Bunke, Kurt Borm und Klaus Endruweit, Js 15/61 (GStA), 15 Jan. 1965, p. 251.

112. ZStL, Heidelberg Docs. 127,878–85: Carl Schneider, Bericht über Stand, Möglichkeit und Ziele der Forschung an Idioten und Epileptikern im Rahmen der Aktion, 24 Jan., 2 Feb. 1944.

113. Ibid. 127,116–17: Heinze memo, 18 Mar. 1942; DÖW, file E19292.

114. BDC, dossier Ernst Illing: Reichsärztekammer file card.

115. BDC, dossier Friedrich Mennecke: Reichärztekammer file card; HHStA, 461/32442/2: interrogations Friedrich Mennecke, May 1945; HHStA, 461/32442/12: correspondence between Friedrich Mennecke, Fritz Bernotat, and Carl Schneider, July 1942; HHStA, 461/32442/14: Friedrich Mennecke to Paul Nitsche, 2 July 1942; Chroust, *Friedrich Mennecke*, pp. 343–44 (Mennecke to Hans Hefelmann, 7 June 1942).

116. GStA Frankfurt, Eberl Akten, II/210/1–210/3, 1:1–3: Irmfried Eberl to Paul Nitsche, 16 Apr. 1942.

117. See Müller-Hill, *Tödliche Wissenschaft*, pp. 68–70, and Pross and Aly, *Wert des Menschen*, pp. 248–49.

118. Rimpau, "Viktor von Weizsäcker," pp. 119–20.

119. Aly, "Mord an behinderten Kindern," p. 155.

120. GStA Frankfurt, Irmfried Eberl Taschenkalender 1940, 5 Oct. 1940 entry.

121. ZStL, Heidelberg Doc. 127,898: Julius Hallervorden to Paul Nitsche, 9 Mar. 1944; GStA Frankfurt, Anklage Ullrich, Bunke, Borm und Endruweit, Js 15/61 (GStA), 15 Jan. 1965, p. 228.

122. ZStL, Heidelberg Doc. 127,149: Paul Nitsche memo, 18 Sept. 1941.

123. Ibid. 127,149–50: Paul Nitsche memo, 20 Sept. 1941.

124. Ibid. 127,050–55: Hans Heinze, Bericht über die bisherige Tätigkeit der Beobachtungs- und Forschungsabteilung bei der Landesanstalt Görden, 9 Sept. 1942. Patients remained at Görden for several months, a few as long as ten months. Ibid. 127,075–77.

125. Ibid. 127,056–59: Aufstellung sämtlicher in der Forschungs- und Beobachtungs-Abteilung der Landesanstalt Görden untergebracht gewesenen Kranken für die Zeit vom 1. 4. 1942 bis 31. 3. 1943; ibid. 127,068–72: Krankenstand der Beobachtungs- und Forschungsabteilung Görden, Stand vom 28. 1. 43; ibid. 127,059A–65C: Hans Heinze, Bericht über die Arbeit der Beobachtungs- und Forschungsabteilung bei der Landesanstalt Görden bei Brandenburg/Havel im 3. Halbjahr ihres Bestehens.

126. Ibid. 127,120–22: Carl Schneider to Hans Heinze, 13 Mar. 1942, with attached Stellenplan der Forschungsabteilung; ibid. 127,134: Paul Nitsche to Jennerwein (Viktor Brack), 25 Feb. 1942; ibid. 127,132: Nitsche to Schmiedel, 4 Mar. 1942; ibid. 127,098: Nitsche to Schneider, 12 Sept. 1942.

127. Ibid. 127,973–74: Paul Nitsche to Carl Schneider, 3 Dec. 1943.

128. Ibid. 127,696–98: handwritten note on Schneider memo, 12 Mar. 1942.

129. See ibid. 127,443–44: Carl Schneider to Baden MdI, Karlsruhe, 5 June 1942; ibid. 127,436–38: Dietrich Allers, Vermerk über die Reise nach Heidelberg, 4 Nov. 1942.

130. Ibid. 128,048–50: Arnold Oels memo, T4 Personnel Office, 11 Mar. 1943.

131. NARA Suitland, Heidelberg Doc. 126,551; ZStL, Heidelberg Docs. 127,443–44.

132. ZStL, Heidelberg Docs. 127,434–35: Carl Schneider to Paul Nitsche, 15 Oct. 1942; ibid. 128,032: Baden MdI (Sprauer) to RAG, 26 July 1943.

133. GStA Frankfurt, Sammlung Euthanasie: Friedrich Mennecke to Fritz Bernotat, 19 July 1942, and Verwaltung des Bezirksverbandes Nassau to Friedrich Mennecke, 24 July 1942.

134. HHStA, 461/32442/12–13: Fritz Bernotat to Anstalt Eichberg, 25 May 1942, and Deussen to Anstalt Eichberg, 6 July, 13, 25 Nov. 1944.

135. BA-MA, H20/463, 465: Carl Schneider, Bericht über einen Besuch in der Heil- und Pflegeanstalt Eichberg, 11 Feb. 1943.

136. ZStL, Heidelberg Docs. 128,038–39: Carl Schneider to Paul Nitsche, 19 June 1943.

137. See, for example, ibid. 128,066–67: Carl Schneider to RAG, 21 Jan. 1943; ibid. 128,185: Schneider memo, 1 Oct. 1943.

138. Ibid. 128,189–91: Carl Schneider to Paul Nitsche, 26 Nov. 1942.

139. Ibid. 128,038–40: Carl Schneider to Paul Nitsche, 19 June 1943.

140. Ibid. 127,434–35: Carl Schneider to Paul Nitsche, 15 Oct. 1942 (handwritten addendum).

141. Ibid. 127,912–13: Carl Schneider to Werner Blankenburg, 28 Aug. 1944. See also ibid. 128,189–91: Schneider to Paul Nitsche, 26 Nov. 1942.

142. Ibid. 127,903–4: Carl Schneider to Paul Nitsche, 2 Sept. 1944.

143. Mitscherlich and Mielke, *Medizin ohne Menschlichkeit*, remains the best documentation of these experiments. For an analysis, see also Baader, "Humanexperiment," pp. 48–69.

144. For this categorization, see Hilberg, *Destruction* (1961), pp. 600–609.

145. Indictment in *TWC*, 1:11; Mitscherlich and Mielke, *Medizin ohne Menschlichkeit*, pp. 20–50.

146. Indictment in *TWC*, 1:11; Mitscherlich and Mielke, *Medizin ohne Menschlichkeit*, pp. 51–71.

147. Indictment in *TWC*, 1:13; Mitscherlich and Mielke, *Medizin ohne Menschlichkeit*, pp. 72–90.

148. Indictment in *TWC*, 1:13–14; Mitscherlich and Mielke, *Medizin ohne Menschlichkeit*, pp. 91–130.

149. Indictment in *TWC*, 1:12–13; Mitscherlich and Mielke, *Medizin ohne Menschlichkeit*, pp. 131–65.

150. Indictment in *TWC*, 1:12; Mitscherlich and Mielke, *Medizin ohne Menschlichkeit*, pp. 166–73.

151. *JuNSV*, vol. 17, no. 500: LG Münster, Urteil Johann Paul Kremer, 6 Ks 2/60, 29 Nov. 1960; Langbein, *Menschen in Auschwitz*, pp. 389–92; Friedlander, "Nazi Concentration Camps," pp. 52–54; Kater, *Doctors under Hitler*, p. 125.

152. On Rascher, see BDC, dossier Sigmund Rascher; Müller-Hill, *Tödliche Wissenschaft*, p. 98; Kater, *Doctors under Hitler*, pp. 125–26.

153. BDC, dossier Carl Clauberg; *TWC*, 1:724–32; Mitscherlich and Mielke, *Medizin ohne*

Menschlichkeit, pp. 246–47. See also Kaupen-Haas, "Experimental Obstetrics and National Socialism."

154. BDC, dossier Horst Schumann; *TWC*, 1:719–24; Mitscherlich and Mielke, *Medizin ohne Menschlichkeit*, pp. 240–45; GStA Frankfurt, Anklage Horst Schumann, Js 18/67 (GStA), 12 Dec. 1969.

155. See Lifton, *Nazi Doctors*, pp. 271–84.

156. Mitscherlich and Mielke, *Medizin ohne Menschlichkeit*, pp. 174–82.

157. See Müller-Hill, *Tödliche Wissenschaft*, pp. 72–75; Langbein, *Menschen in Auschwitz*, pp. 380–85; Kater, *Doctors under Hitler*, pp. 233–35; and Lifton, *Nazi Doctors*, pp. 337–83.

158. For biographical data on Mengele, see BDC, dossier Josef Mengele (including Reichsärztekammer file card, SS master file card, NSDAP master file card, and autobiography in RuSHA file).

159. See Weindling, *Health, Race, and German Politics*, pp. 560–61, chart.

160. BAK, R73/15342: Otmar von Verschuer to DFG, 30 Sept. 1938.

161. Langbein, *Menschen in Auschwitz*, pp. 381–85.

162. BAK, R73/15342: Verschuer to Reichsforschungsrat, 20 Mar. 1944.

163. ZStL, interrogation Hans Nachtsheim, 19 Aug. 1966. See also Müller-Hill, "Kollege Mengele," p. 672, and *Tödliche Wissenschaft*, pp. 72–74.

CHAPTER SEVEN

1. The following account is based on LG Hannover, Urteil Kurt Eimann, 2 Ks 2/67, 20 Dec. 1968, and Nuremberg Doc. NO-2275: Gruppenführer Richard Hildebrandt, Bericht über Aufstellung, Einsatz und Tätigkeit des SS-Wachsturmbann E., n.d.

2. Although Stutthof was operated like a concentration camp, it did not officially receive this name and status until 1942. See Friedlander, "Nazi Concentration Camps," p. 43.

3. LG Hannover, Urteil Eimann, 2 Ks 2/67, 20 Dec. 1968, p. 10.

4. See U.S. Military Tribunal, Transcript of the Proceedings in Case 1, pp. 7595, 7600–602 (testimony Viktor Brack).

5. On requests for the nationality of patients in questionnaires, see NARA, RG 238, Microfilm Publication M-1019, roll 46: interrogation Friedrich Mennecke, 11 Jan. 1947, p. 34. On the deportation of Polish patients, see BAK, R36/1842: city of Mark Trofaiach, Steiermark, to DGT, 21 Feb. 1940, and DGT reply, 5 Mar. 1940.

6. ZStL, Sammlung UdSSR, Bd. 245 Ad 1: German summary of information concerning the killing of mental patients presented at Nuremberg by the Hauptkommission zur Untersuchung deutscher Verbrechen in Polen. See also ZStL, Sammlung Verschiedenes, Bd. 17, pp. 276–313.

7. ZStL, Sammlung Polen, Bd. 340: Magistrate Court Chelm, testimony of Dr. Gizela Langer née Madziarska, 18 Sept. 1946 (German translation).

8. StA Hamburg, Verfahren Friedrich Lensch und Kurt Struve, 147 Js 58/67: Gutachten by Prof. Jozef Radzicki (German translation), p. 62. Only five to ten patients remained in order to perform janitorial services. See also ibid., p. 78, for a list of Polish institutions and the number of patients killed.

9. BDC, dossier Herbert Lange.

10. For a brief survey of the Lange Commando, see LG Bonn, Untersuchungsrichter II, Anlage zur Abschluss-Verfügung vom 30. September 1963 in der Voruntersuchung Wilhelm Koppe, 13 UR 1/61, 6/62, 7/62, 10/62, pp. 15–18.

11. On Tiegenhof, see StA Hamburg, Anklage Friedrich Lensch und Kurt Struve, 147 Js 58/67, 24 Apr. 1973, pp. 338–59.

12. StA Bonn, Anklage Wilhelm Koppe, 8 Js 52/60, 10 Sept. 1964, pp. 182–83. See also StA Hamburg, Verfahren Lensch und Struve, 147 Js 58/67: Gutachten Jozef Radzicki (Ger-

man translation), p. 63. For the development of the later gas vans and how they differed from the earlier ones, see Browning, *Fateful Months*, chap. 3. See also StA Düsseldorf, Verfahren Albert Widmann, 8 Ks 1/61 (8 Js 7212/59), interrogations Albert Widmann, 11 Jan. 1960, pp. 1–2, 7, 15 Jan. 1960, pp. 1–3, and StA Stuttgart, Verfahren Albert Widmann, Ks 19/62 (19 Js 328/60), interrogation Hans Schmidt, 6 Apr. 1961, p. 18. The Widmann interrogation in Düsseldorf, 11 January 1960, has been published in Friedlander and Milton, *Zentrale Stelle*, doc. 131.

13. *JuNSV*, vol. 7, no. 231.

14. Nuremberg Doc. NO-1073: statement by SS Brigadeführer Otto Rasch, 16 June 1943; ibid. NO-1074: statement by SS Hauptsturmführer Dr. Friedrich Horst Schlegel, 3 June 1943.

15. Ibid. NO-1076: Chef der Sipo und SD (Ernst Kaltenbrunner) to SS Richter bei dem RFSS, "Vorkommnisse im Durchgangslager Soldau," Feb. 1943, p. 3.

16. StA Bonn, Anklage Koppe, 8 Js 52/60, 10 Sept. 1964, pp. 184–87.

17. See U.S. Military Tribunal, Transcript of the Proceedings in Case 1, pp. 7721–23, and marginalia concerning Brack in Nuremberg Doc. NO-2911.

18. Nuremberg Doc. NO-2909: HSSPF Wilhelm Rediess to Gruppenführer Karl Wolff, 7 Nov. 1940; ibid. NO-2911: HSSPF Wilhelm Koppe to Gruppenführer Karl Wolff, 22 Feb. 1941.

19. Ibid. NO-2908: HSSPF Wilhelm Koppe to HSSPF Jakob Sporrenberg, 18 Oct. 1940; StA Bonn, Anklage Koppe, 8 Js 52/60, 10 Sept. 1964, pp. 184–87.

20. On the use of code words (*Tarnsprache*), see Friedlander, "Manipulation of Language."

21. Nuremberg Doc. NO-2908: HSSPF Wilhelm Koppe to HSSPF Jakob Sporrenberg, 18 Oct. 1940.

22. Ibid. NO-2909: HSSPF Wilhelm Rediess to Gruppenführer Karl Wolff, 7 Nov. 1940; GStA Frankfurt, Sammlung Euthanasie, and ZStL, Sammlung USA, Bd. 8: telegram from HSSPF Rediess to Gruppenführer Karl Wolff, 26 Nov. 1940.

23. Nuremberg Doc. NO-2911: HSSPF Wilhelm Koppe to Gruppenführer Karl Wolff, 22 Feb. 1941.

24. See Ebbinghaus and Preissler, "Ermordung psychisch kranker Menschen in der Sowjetunion." See also ZStL, Sammlung UdSSR, Bd. 245 Ac, p. 318, for the killing by the SS of 6,000 Jews, 280 Gypsies, and 485 handicapped patients in one Soviet town.

25. See Krausnick and Wilhelm, *Truppe des Weltanschauungskrieges*.

26. On the killing of the handicapped, see U.S. Military Tribunal, Transcript of the Proceedings in Case 1, pp. 2545–47. On the killing of Soviet POWs, see Streim, *Behandlung sowjetischer Kriegsgefangener*, and Streit, *Keine Kameraden*.

27. See, for example, Nuremberg Doc. L-180: Einsatzgruppe A Gesamtbericht bis zum 15. Oktober 1941 (Stahlecker report), p. 37; ibid. NO-2621: affidavit by Oskar Dansker (Latvian Generaldirektor des Innern under the German occupation), 31 Mar. 1947; ibid. NO-1758: excerpts from diary of Franz Halder (Generalstab des Heeres); StA Düsseldorf, Verfahren Widmann, 8 Ks 1/61 (8 Js 7212/59), interrogation Albert Widmann, 11 Jan. 1960, pp. 4–5 (also in Friedlander and Milton, *Zentrale Stelle*, doc. 131).

28. Nuremberg Doc. NOKW-604.

29. On Himmler's involvement, see Breitman, *Architect of Genocide*, p. 196, and Krausnick and Wilhelm, *Truppe des Weltanschauungskrieges*, p. 543.

30. StA Stuttgart, Anklage Albert Widmann und August Becker, (19) 13 Js 328/60, 29 Aug. 1962, p. 42.

31. StA Düsseldorf, Verfahren Widmann, 8 Ks 1/61 (8 Js 7212/59), interrogation Karl Schulz, 9 Mar. 1959, pp. 23, and interrogations Albert Widmann, 11 Jan. 1960, pp. 1–8, 12 Jan. 1960, pp. 1–2; StA Stuttgart, Verfahren Widmann, Ks 19/62 (19 Js 328/60), interro-

gation Albert Widmann, 18 Apr. 1962, pp. 2–3, and interrogations Hans Schmidt, 6 Apr. 1961, pp. 23–25, 4 May 1962, pp. 1–5, including pictures of car and hoses used in Mogilev; ibid., Protokoll der öffentlichen Sitzung des Schwurgerichts, 15 Aug. 1967, pp. 11–19 (testimony Albert Widmann), 22 Aug. 1967, pp. 77–88 (testimony Hans Schmidt).

32. On the killing of Turkmen, see Breitman, *Architect of Genocide*, pp. 178–81.

33. NARA Suitland, RG 153, Records of the Judge Advocate General (Army), entry 143, box 575, folder 21-11: interrogation Wilhelm Gustav Schueppe, 15 Apr. 1945. I am grateful to Richard Breitman for directing my attention to this document; his calculations led him to reduce the number of those killed to just above 80,000. See his *Architect of Genocide*, pp. 181, 293, n. 56.

34. See Friedlander, "Nazi Concentration Camps," esp. pp. 47–48, and Grode, "*Sonderbehandlung 14f13*," p. 82. See also Breitman, *Architect of Genocide*, pp. 87–88, for a discussion of the search by the SS late in 1939 for a killing method inside the concentration camps.

35. GStA Frankfurt, Anklage Georg Renno, Hans-Joachim Becker und Friedrich Robert Lorent, Js 18/61 (GStA), Js 7/63 (GStA), Js 5/65 (GStA), 7 Nov. 1967, p. 48; LG Frankfurt, Urteil Hans-Joachim Becker und Friedrich Robert Lorent, Ks 1/69 (GStA), 27 May 1970, p. 49.

36. GStA Frankfurt, Anklage Werner Heyde, Gerhard Bohne und Hans Hefelmann, Ks 2/63 (GStA), Js 17/59 (GStA), 22 May 1962, p. 603.

37. Ibid., p. 604. See also Friedlander, "Manipulation of Language," p. 110.

38. ZStL, Sammlung Arolsen, Bd. 311, S. 01104: circular from Inspekteur der Konzentrationslager, Oranienburg, 21 Oct. 1941. See also Dressen, "Euthanasie," p. 66, for a slightly different numbering system.

39. AMM, P16/48: circular from WVHA Amtsgruppe D, Oranienburg, 14 Nov. 1942 (also in BAK, NS3/425). The SS camp physicians earlier had been granted the status of institutional directors and during the 1930s could apply for authorization to the hereditary health courts. See LA Berlin, Rep. 142, 1-2-6 Akt. 1, Bd. 2: RMdI circular (sig. Gütt), "Durchführung des Gesetzes zur Verhütung erbkranken Nachwuchses bei Häftlingen in Konzentrationslagern," 2 May 1936.

40. U.S. Military Tribunal, Transcript of the Proceedings in Case 1, pp. 7534–37 (testimony Viktor Brack).

41. NARA, RG 238, Microfilm Publication M-1019, roll 46: interrogation Friedrich Mennecke, 11 Jan. 1947, pp. 12–13, 20–21.

42. Nuremberg Doc. PS-1151: circular from Inspekteur der Konzentrationslager, Oranienburg, 10 Dec. 1941.

43. Ibid.: sample Meldebogen. See also U.S. Military Tribunal, Transcript of the Proceedings in Case 1, p. 1914 (testimony Friedrich Mennecke), and GStA Frankfurt, Anklage Horst Schumann, 18/67 (GStA), 12 Dec. 1969, pp. 104–5, 120.

44. Nuremberg Doc. PS-1151: Arthur Liebehenschel to Arthur Rödl, Oranienburg, 10 Jan. 1942; ibid. NO-2799: affidavit Julius Muthig, 16 Apr. 1947.

45. Postwar affidavit of the Buchenwald SS physician Waldemar Hoven, cited in Mitscherlich and Mielke, *Medizin ohne Menschlichkeit*, p. 213.

46. See Nuremberg Doc. PS-1151: sample Meldebogen, and NARA, RG 238, Microfilm Publication M-1019, roll 46: interrogation Friedrich Mennecke, 11 Jan. 1947, pp. 20–21.

47. LG Frankfurt, Urteil Becker und Lorent, Ks 1/69 (GStA), 27 May 1970, pp. 54–56.

48. Nuremberg Doc. PS-1151: circular from WVHA Amtsgruppe D, Oranienburg, 26 Mar. 1942.

49. GStA Frankfurt, Anklage Schumann, 18/67 (GStA), 12 Dec. 1969, p. 116 (testimony of Auschwitz prisoner Stefan Boratynski); LG Frankfurt, Urteil Becker und Lorent, Ks 1/69 (GStA), 27 May 1970, pp. 53–54; AMM, B/15/6–7: lists of prisoners transferred to "Lagersanatorium Dachau," 12–13 Aug. 1941. See also Dressen, "Euthanasie," pp. 71–75.

50. For the way a T4 panel of physicians in 1940 combed through the Austrian mental hospital in Ybbs, see DÖW, file E18370/3: Bezirksgericht Ybbs, interrogations Theresia Helmreich, 21 Mar. 1946, Franz Stempfl, 22 Mar. 1946, and Aron Heindl, 20 Mar. 1946. See also Klee, *"Euthanasie" im NS-Staat*, pp. 244–46, for the work of such a panel at the Neuendettelsau hospital in Bavaria.

51. See HHStA, 461/32442/3: StA Frankfurt, Anklage Friedrich Mennecke, Walter Schmidt, 4a Js 13/46, 7 Oct. 1946, p. 22. See also Klee, *"Euthanasie" im NS-Staat*, pp. 323–26.

52. GStA Frankfurt, Anklage Schumann, 18/67 (GStA), 12 Dec. 1969, p. 100; LG Frankfurt, Urteil Becker und Lorent, Ks 1/69 (GStA), 27 May 1970, p. 56.

53. U.S. Military Tribunal, Transcript of the Proceedings in Case 1, pp. 7534–37 (testimony Viktor Brack).

54. Grode, *"Sonderbehandlung 14f13,"* pp. 83–85.

55. Although most criteria that supposedly had governed the selection of the handicapped were waved in the 14f13 selection process, the prohibition against the selection of wounded World War I veterans, imposed to protect T4 from criticism, was also applied in 14f13. Nuremberg Doc. PS-1151: sample Meldebogen.

56. Grode, *"Sonderbehandlung 14f13,"* p. 85. GStA Frankfurt, Anklage Heyde, Bohne und Hefelmann, Ks 2/63 (GStA), Js 17/59 (GStA), 22 May 1962, p. 670, provides the same list of physicians but omits Gorgaß, and that list is repeated in Klee, *"Euthanasie" im NS-Staat*, p. 343. On Gorgaß, who maintained after the war that he accompanied Schumann to Buchenwald only to observe and not to participate, see HHStA, 461/32061/7: LG Frankfurt, Verfahren Adolf Wahlmann, Bodo Gorgaß, Irmgard Huber, 4a KLs 7/47 (4a Js 3/46), Protokoll der öffentlichen Sitzung der 4. Strafkammer, 24 Feb. 1947, p. 15 (testimony Hans-Bodo Gorgaß), and Nuremberg Doc. NO-3010: affidavit Hans-Bodo Gorgaß, 23 Feb. 1947. Other physicians have been mentioned here and there, but their participation is not certain. See, for example, Mennecke's comment about the presence of Friedrich Berner at Buchenwald (Chroust, *Friedrich Mennecke*, p. 237) and his testimony that fifteen physicians were involved in 14f13 (U.S. Military Tribunal, Transcript of the Proceedings in Case 1, p. 1891).

57. See ZStL, Heidelberg Docs. 127,890–93.

58. On the use of a single T4 physician when no one else was available, see Mennecke letter, Fürstenberg, 19 Nov. 1941, in Chroust, *Friedrich Mennecke*, pp. 202–4.

59. See, for example, the sources cited in GStA Frankfurt, Anklage Schumann, 18/67 (GStA), 12 Dec. 1969, pp. 109–20, 129–31.

60. I consulted these handwritten letters at the office of Oberstaatsanwalt Johannes Warlo at the OLG Frankfurt but have cited them from Chroust, *Friedrich Mennecke*.

61. Mennecke letter, Oranienburg, 4 Apr. 1941, in Chroust, *Friedrich Mennecke*, pp. 184–85.

62. Ibid., p. 185.

63. Mennecke letters, Oranienburg, 4, 6 Apr. 1941, ibid., pp. 184–85, 192–94.

64. Mennecke letter, Oranienburg, 7 Apr. 1941, ibid., p. 195; Grode, *"Sonderbehandlung 14f13,"* p. 86.

65. Mennecke letters, Munich, 3 Sept. 1941, and Fürstenberg, 20 Nov. 1941, in Chroust, *Friedrich Mennecke*, pp. 198–200, 205–6; GStA Frankfurt, Anklage Renno, Becker und Lorent, Js 18/61 (GStA), Js 7/63 (GStA), Js 5/65 (GStA), 7 Nov. 1967, p. 48; GStA Frankfurt, Anklage Schumann, Js 18/67 (GStA), 12 Dec. 1969, pp. 99, 115–16; Nuremberg Doc. PS-1151: Arthur Liebehenschel to Arthur Rödl, Oranienburg, 10 Jan. 1942. See also ibid.: sample Meldebogen.

66. See, for example, Mennecke letter, Oranienburg, 7 Apr. 1941, in Chroust, *Friedrich Mennecke*, pp. 195–96.

67. See BDC dossiers of Werner Heyde, Rudolf Lonauer, Friedrich Mennecke, and Viktor Ratka.

68. GStA Frankfurt, Anklage Renno, Becker und Lorent, Js 18/61 (GStA), Js 7/63 (GStA), Js 5/65 (GStA), 7 Nov. 1967, pp. 48–49.

69. See Mennecke letter, Weimar, 30 Nov.–2 Dec. 1941, in Chroust, *Friedrich Mennecke*, pp. 258–70.

70. Mennecke letter, Weimar, 25–26 Nov. 1941, ibid., pp. 241–45; NARA, RG 238, Microfilm Publication M-1019, roll 46: interrogation Friedrich Mennecke, 11 Jan. 1947, p. 12. For Mennecke's visits to seven concentration camps, see ibid., p. 14, and for Wewelsburg as probably the eighth camp, see Mennecke letter, Eichberg, 4 Apr. 1942, in Chroust, *Friedrich Mennecke*, p. 338.

71. See Nuremberg Doc. PS-1151: sample Meldebogen.

72. Mennecke letter, Fürstenberg, 20 Nov. 1941, in Chroust, *Friedrich Mennecke*, p. 205.

73. Mennecke letter, Weimar, 25–26 Nov. 1941, ibid., pp. 143–44.

74. Cited in GStA Frankfurt, Anklage Heyde, Bohne und Hefelmann, Ks 2/63 (GStA), Js 17/59 (GStA), 22 May 1962, pp. 646–47.

75. Mennecke letters, Munich and Leoni am Starnberger See, 2–4 Sept. 1941, Fürstenberg, 19 Nov. 1941, Weimar, 27–28 Nov. 1941, and Berlin, 14–15 Jan. 1942, in Chroust, *Friedrich Mennecke*, pp. 196–200, 203, 246–51, 323–31. On their postwar denials, see, for example, GStA DDR (StA Dresden), Verfahren Paul Nitsche, (S) 1 Ks 58/47 (1/47), Bd. 1: interrogation Paul Nitsche, 26 Mar. 1946; NARA, RG 238, Microfilm Publication M-1019, roll 46: interrogation Friedrich Mennecke, 11 Jan. 1947, pp. 14–15; and DÖW, file E18370/1: StA Frankfurt, Js 18/61 (GStA), interrogation Georg Renno, 1 Feb. 1965, pp. 4–5, 31–32, 40–44.

76. On Schumann, see GStA Frankfurt, Anklage Schumann, Js 18/67 (GStA), 12 Dec. 1969, pp. ii, 126–27. On Lonauer, see DÖW, file E18370/3: report from Inspektor Haas for LG Linz, 25 July 1946.

77. See, for example, the evidence provided by a Hartheim staff member in DÖW, file E18370/3: Bezirksgericht Ybbs, interrogation Hermine Gruber, 15 Mar. 1946.

78. Ibid.: Bezirksgericht Eferding-Grieskirchen, interrogation Aneliese Gindl, 25 July 1947.

79. GStA Frankfurt, Anklage Schumann, Js 18/67 (GStA), 12 Dec. 1969, p. 108; DÖW, file E18370/3: affidavit Hans Marsalek, 9 Apr. 1946; AMM, B/15/6–7: KL Mauthausen, "Veränderungsmeldung für den 11. August 1941," 12 Aug. 1941, and "Veränderungsmeldung für den 12. August 1941," 13 Aug. 1941.

80. Grode, "*Sonderbehandlung 14f13*," p. 86.

81. HHStA, 461/32061/12: LG Frankfurt, Urteil Adolf Wahlmann, Bodo Gorgaß, Irmgard Huber, 4a KLs 7/47, 21 Mar. 1947, p. 13. See also Winter et al., *Verlegt nach Hadamar*, p. 117.

82. DÖW, file E18370/1: LG Linz, interrogation Heinrich Barbl, 16 Nov. 1964.

83. Nuremberg Doc. PS-1151: Heil- und Pflegeanstalt Bernburg to KL Gross-Rosen, 3 Mar. 1942, and KL Gross-Rosen to Heil- und Pflegeanstalt Bernburg, 6 Mar. 1942.

84. Ibid.: telegram from KL Gross-Rosen to WVHA Amtsgruppe D, 25 Mar. 1942. Actually, 127 prisoners were sent from Gross-Rosen to Bernburg. For lists of transferred Gross-Rosen prisoners, see ibid. PS-1151, NO-1873.

85. Ibid. PS-1151, NO-1992: circular from Arthur Liebehenschel, WVHA Amtsgruppe D, Oranienburg, 26 Mar. 1942.

86. Ibid. NO-1007: circular from Richard Glücks, WVHA Amtsgruppe D, Oranienburg, 27 Apr. 1943.

87. DÖW, file E18370/1: StA Frankfurt, Js 18/61 (GStA), interrogation Georg Renno, 1 Feb. 1965, pp. 4–5.

88. Hans Marsalek, *Die Geschichte des Konzentrationslagers Mauthausen*, 2d ed. (Vienna, 1980), pp. 212–24, and *Die Vergasungsaktionen im Konzentrationslager Mauthausen* (Vienna, 1988), pp. 20–32. For statistics of Mauthausen and Gusen prisoners killed at Hartheim, see AMM, B/15/23.

89. AMM, B/15/8, 13, 19.

90. GStA Frankfurt, Anklage Heyde, Bohne und Hefelmann, Ks 2/63 (GStA), Js 17/59 (GStA), 22 May 1962, p. 679; AMM, B/15/23. See also Grode, *"Sonderbehandlung 14f13,"* pp. 86–87, 116–18, and Dressen, "Euthanasie," pp. 78–80.

CHAPTER EIGHT

1. See U.S. Military Tribunal, Transcript of the Proceedings in Case 1, p. 2432 (testimony Karl Brandt); DÖW, file 18282: LG Wien, interrogation Ernst Illing, 22 Oct. 1945; and StA Hamburg, Anklage Friedrich Lensch und Kurt Struve, 147 Js 58/67, 24 Apr. 1973, pp. 324–25.

2. See Aly, "Medizin gegen Unbrauchbare," p. 29.

3. See Schmidt, *Selektion in der Heilanstalt*, pp. 18–21.

4. See Hilberg, *Destruction* (1961), pp. 190–219, 586–600; Friedlander, "Nazi Concentration Camps," pp. 57–59; and Broszat, "Konzentrationslager," pp. 108–20.

5. See, for example, U.S. Military Tribunal, Transcript of the Proceedings in Case 1, p. 2432 (testimony Karl Brandt); NARA, RG 238, Microfilm Publication M-1019, roll 46: interrogation Friedrich Mennecke, 12 Jan. 1947, p. 2; ZStL, Heidelberg Doc. 125,165: circular from Paul Nitsche, 21 Aug. 1943; ibid. 127,387–88: RMdI (Linden) to Verwaltung des Provinzialverbandes Rheinprovinz (vertraulich), 3 Nov. 1941; ibid. 127,959: list of medical experts, 8 Feb. 1944; NARA Suitland, Heidelberg Docs. 127,425–26: memo concerning 6 Oct. 1942 meeting; and BA-MA, H20/463, 465: Paul Nitsche to Hans Heinze, 8 July 1944.

6. See, for example, DÖW, file 18282: LG Wien, interrogation Ernst Illing, 22 Oct. 1945.

7. ZStL, Heidelberg Docs. 127,060–61: Nitsche notes for the files, 18, 20 Sept. 1941.

8. NARA, RG 238, Microfilm Publication M-1019, roll 46: interrogation Friedrich Mennecke, 11 Jan. 1947, p. 45; StA Hamburg, Anklage Lensch und Struve, 147 Js 58/67, 24 Apr. 1973, pp. 327–29.

9. HHStA, 461/32061/12: LG Frankfurt, Urteil Adolf Wahlmann, Bodo Gorgaß, Irmgard Huber, 4a KLs 7/47, 21 Mar. 1947, p. 13.

10. StA Hamburg, Anklage Lensch und Struve, 147 Js 58/67, 24 Apr. 1973, p. 330; U.S. Military Tribunal, Transcript of the Proceedings in Case 1, pp. 1819–22 (testimony Walter Schmidt).

11. StA Hamburg, Anklage Lensch und Struve, 147 Js 58/67, 24 Apr. 1973, pp. 338–88.

12. See, for example, the fate of patients in the Klagenfurt state hospital and nursing home in DÖW, file E18371: StA Graz, Anklage Franz Niedermoser, 10 St 2245/46, 21 Feb. 1946, and DÖW, file 19134: VG bei dem LG Graz, Senat Klagenfurt, Urteil Franz Niedermoser, Vg 18 Vr 907/45, 4 Apr. 1946.

13. The information on the euthanasia killings in the Hamburg city-state was collected during a thorough postwar investigation by the Hamburg state attorney. See StA Hamburg, Verfahren Friedrich Lensch und Kurt Struve, 147 Js 58/67.

14. StA Hamburg, Anklage Lensch und Struve, 147 Js 58/67, 24 Apr. 1973, pp. 516–22. On the children's wards, see ibid., pp. 157–62.

15. Ibid., pp. 524–34.

16. Ibid., pp. 730, 759.

17. Ibid., pp. 726–78. For the Eichberg killing of Inge Meyer, the last surviving Alsterdorfer child (listed ibid., p. 776), see HHStA, 461/32442/4: LG Frankfurt, Verfahren Friedrich Mennecke, Walter Schmidt, 4 KLs 15/46 (4a Js 13/46), Protokoll der öffentlichen Sitzung der 4. Strafkammer, 12 Dec. 1946, pp. 30–31.

18. StA Hamburg, Anklage Lensch und Struve, 147 Js 58/67, 24 Apr. 1973, pp. 690–725.

19. StA Hamburg, Verfahren Lensch und Struve, 147 Js 58/67: Gutachten Jozef Radzicki (German translation), pp. 70–71. See also StA Hamburg, Anklage Lensch und Struve, 147 Js 58/67, 24 Apr. 1973, pp. 592–607.

20. StA Hamburg, Verfahren Lensch und Struve, 147 Js 58/67: Gutachten Jozef Radzicki (German translation), pp. 57ff. See also StA Hamburg, Anklage Lensch und Struve, 147 Js 58/67, 24 Apr. 1973, pp. 608–90.

21. See, for example, HHStA, 461/32061/2: correspondence between Alfons Klein (Hadamar) and Gekrat, 7 Aug. 1942, Hadamar Abwicklungsstelle, 4, 18 Feb. 1943, Gemeinnützige Stiftung für Anstaltspflege, 2 Mar. 1943, and RAG, 25 Feb., 1 June 1944, and Nuremberg Doc. NO-892: Gekrat to Hadamar, 20 July 1943.

22. For a detailed discussion of this killing method, see StA Hamburg, Verfahren Lensch und Struve, 147 Js 58/67: Gutachten Jozef Radzicki (German translation), pp. 11–38.

23. Roth, *Erfassung zur Vernichtung*, pp. 138–39, doc. 5 (testimony Hans Hefelmann). See also HHStA, 461/32061/7: LG Frankfurt, Verfahren Adolf Wahlmann, Bodo Gorgaß, Irmgard Huber, 4a KLs 7/47 (4a Js 3/46), Protokoll der öffentlichen Sitzung der 4. Strafkammer, 11 Mar. 1947 (testimony Werner Heyde).

24. ZStL, Bd. 513: Irmfried Eberl to Reichsausschuß, 6 July 1940.

25. Roth, *Erfassung zur Vernichtung*, pp. 113–14.

26. ZStL, Heidelberger Docs. 126,659–90.

27. See, for example, U.S. Military Tribunal, Transcript of the Proceedings in Case 1, p. 7581 (testimony Viktor Brack); Nuremberg Doc. PS-627 (NO-832): RJM to Hans Heinrich Lammers, 24 July 1940.

28. Roth, *Erfassung zur Vernichtung*, p. 116.

29. Himmler to Gottlob Berger, 28 July 1942, in Heiber, *Reichsführer*, pp. 167–68.

30. BA-MA, H20/463, 465: Hans Heinze to Paul Nitsche, 20 Jan. 1944.

31. This correspondence is available as the so-called Heidelberg Documents at the ZStL, NARA Suitland, and the BA-MA. See above, chap. 5, n. 99. For a partial list of physicians belonging to the circle of т4 friends, see ZStL, Heidelberg Docs. 128,215, 128,223.

32. See, for example, BA-MA, H20/463, 465: Paul Nitsche and Ernst Rüdin correspondence, 1943–44, and Karl Thums to Paul Nitsche, 3 Jan. 1944, and book reviews in BAK, R18/5585.

33. See Thom and Caregorodcev, *Medizin unterm Hakenkreuz*, p. 139.

34. Ibid., pp. 130, 139; NARA Suitland, Heidelberg Doc. 124,977. See also Cocks, *Psychotherapy*, pp. 106–10.

35. ZStL, Heidelberg Doc. 128,173; NARA Suitland, Heidelberg Doc. 124,977.

36. ZStL, Heidelberg Doc. 125,019: Ernst Rüdin to Philipp Bouhler, 19 July 1941; ibid. 128,174: Rüdin to RAG, 17 July 1941; ibid. 124,922–22a: Paul Nitsche to Rüdin, 17 June 1941; NARA Suitland, Heidelberg Docs. 124,885–86: Nitsche to Rüdin, 26 Apr. 1941.

37. NARA Suitland, Heidelberg Docs. 124,903–4: Ernst Rüdin to Paul Schröder, 23 May 1941; ibid. 124,912–13: Schröder to Rüdin, 31 May 1941; ibid. 124,942–43: Paul Nitsche to Rüdin, 17 July 1941; ibid. 124,951–53: Nitsche to Rüdin, 25 July 1941; ibid. 124,968–69: Rüdin to Herbert Linden, copy to Nitsche, 24 July 1941; ZStL, Heidelberg Docs. 124,906–7: Rüdin to Hans Reiter, 28 June 1941; ibid. 124,908–11: Rüdin to Linden, copy to Nitsche, 28 June 1941; ibid. 124,934: Rüdin to Nitsche, 8 July 1941; ibid. 124,935: Werner Villinger to Rüdin, 4 July 1941; ibid. 124,936–37: Rüdin to Nitsche, 14 July 1941; ibid. 124,946–48: Rüdin to Werner Heyde, 19 July 1941. See also Cocks, *Psychotherapy*, pp. 107–8.

38. See, for example, NARA Suitland, Heidelberg Docs. 127,403–5: memo by Carl Schneider, 25 Mar. 1941.

39. ZStL, Heidelberg Docs. 124,894–96: Ernst Rüdin to Paul Nitsche, 6 Feb. 1941; NARA Suitland, Heidelberg Docs. 124,887–88: Nitsche to Herbert Linden, 9, 16 Apr. 1941; ibid. 124,889–93: Linden to Nitsche, 29 Mar., 5 Apr. 1941; ibid. 124,903–4: Rüdin to Paul Schröder, 23 May 1941; ibid. 124,968–69: Rüdin to Linden, copy to Nitsche, 24 July 1941; ibid. 124,905: Rüdin to Hans Reiter, copy to Schröder, 23 May 1941; ibid. 124,951–53: Nitsche to Rüdin, 25 July 1941.

40. See, for example, NARA Suitland, Heidelberg Docs. 124,968–69: Ernst Rüdin to Herbert Linden, copy to Paul Nitsche, 24 July 1941.

41. ZStL, Heidelberg Doc. 126,419: Paul Nitsche to Karl Brandt, 30 Aug. 1941.

42. Thom and Caregorodcev, *Medizin unterm Hakenkreuz*, p. 129. See also the discussion in Hohendorf and Magull-Seltenreich, *Von der Heilkunde zur Massentötung*, pp. 109–10.

43. ZStL, Heidelberg Docs. 126,418–27: policy paper, "Gedanken und Anregungen betr. die künftige Entwicklung der Psychiatrie," submitted to Karl Brandt by Ernst Rüdin, Max de Crinis, Carl Schneider, Hans Heinze, and Paul Nitsche, 26 June 1943.

44. Pross and Aly, *Wert des Menschen*, p. 24.

45. See, for example, BA-MA, H20/463, 465: W. Holzer (Vienna), "Vorschlag zur Gründung einer Forschungsanstalt für aktive Therapie der Nerven- und Geisteskrankheiten," and Paul Nitsche to Holzer, with acknowledgment of receipt of paper, 21 Sept. 1944. See also Thom and Caregorodcev, *Medizin unterm Hakenkreuz*, pp. 137–38.

46. BA-MA, H20/463, 465: memo for Paul Nitsche, "Lieferung von Siemens-Konvulsatoren," 2 Nov. 1943, Nitsche to Herbert Linden, 9 Oct. 1943, Linden to Nitsche, 18 Oct. 1943, Nitsche to Berthold Kihn, 19 Nov. 1943, and Nitsche to Kurt Borm, 25 Oct. 1943; NARA Suitland, Heidelberg Docs. 125,157–58: Friedrich Meggendorfer (Erlangen University Clinic) to Nitsche, 5 Jan. 1943.

47. NARA Suitland, Heidelberg Docs. 125,108–14: Carl Schneider to Herbert Linden, 2, 3 Feb. 1942; ibid. 125,157–58: Friedrich Meggendorfer (Erlangen University Clinic) to Paul Nitsche, 5 Jan. 1943; ZStL, Heidelberg Doc. 127,088: Nitsche to Hans Heinze, 30 Oct. 1942; ibid. 127,930–32: Schneider to Nitsche, 21 June 1944. See also Ulrich Knödler, "Das Insulinproblem: Eine Studie zum Zusammenbruch der Arzneimittelversorgung der Zivilbevölkerung im Zweiten Weltkrieg," in Pross and Aly, *Wert des Menschen*, pp. 250–60.

48. ZStL, Heidelberg Docs. 127,846–60: Herbert Linden to Viktor Brack, May 1942, Paul Nitsche to Linden, 15 Sept. 1942, and various applications to rename institutions.

49. Mennecke letters, Berlin, 14–15 Jan. 1942, in Chroust, *Friedrich Mennecke*, pp. 323–31.

50. BA-MA, H20/463, 465: report on July 1942 planning inspection of institutions in Baden (including Alsace), 15 Sept. 1942.

51. GStA Frankfurt, Sammlung Euthanasie: *Reichsgesetzblatt* 1941, 1:653, Verordnung über die Bestellung eines Reichsbeauftragten für die Heil- und Pflegeanstalten (sig. Wilhelm Frick), 23 Oct. 1941; BAK, R18/3768: RMdI announcement of appointment of Dr. Linden, 29 Oct. 1941.

52. For Brandt's original appointment of 28 July 1942, see BA-MA, H20/463, 465: *Reichsgesetzblatt* 1942, 1:515–16; for his enlarged powers, see BAK, R18/3810: Zweiter Erlaß des Führers über das Sanitäts- und Gesundheitswesen, 5 Sept. 1943. For correspondence, decrees, and reports about the allocation of hospital beds, see BAK, R18/3791. For the Brandt-Conti rivalry, see BAK, R18/3810: Karl Brandt to Leonardo Conti, 28 May 1943, Conti to Brandt, 1 June 1943, Conti to Martin Bormann, 23 June 1943, and draft of Brandt-Conti agreement, June 1943. See also Kater, "Conti and His Nemesis," pp. 314–20.

53. See ZStL, Heidelberg Docs. 127,967–68: Paul Nitsche to Carl Schneider, 14 Jan. 1944, and BA-MA, H20/463, 465: Nitsche to Max de Crinis, 30 Oct. 1943, 20 Apr., 17 May 1944, de Crinis to Nitsche, 31 Aug., 9 Nov. 1943, 26 May 1944, Nitsche to Karl Brandt, 10 July, 24 Aug. 1944, and Brandt to Nitsche, 26 July 1944.

54. BA-MA, H20/463, 465: list of handicapped patients by states and Prussian provinces for Feb., Sept., Oct., and Nov. 1943, list of institutions with location, ownership, and number of beds, n.d., list of institutions by German states and Prussian provinces with number of free beds for men, women, and children, 15 Sept., 15 Oct., 15 Nov. 1943, and summary of occupied and free beds in state, Catholic, Protestant, and private institutions, Jan. 1944; NARA Suitland, Heidelberg Docs. 126,528–34: "Freibettenaufstellung" by German states and Prussian provinces, 15 Apr. 1943.

55. BA-MA, H20/463, 465: "Zur Planung," report by Robert Müller, Berlin, 9 Feb. 1943.

56. Reports available in BA-MA, H20/463, 465, include those for the states of Baden (including Alsace), July 1942; Bavaria, Apr.–May 1941 (summary, Oct. 1942); Braunschweig, Sept. 1942; Bremen, Apr. 1942; Hamburg, Apr. 1942; Hessen, Feb. 1942; Lippe, July 1942 (summary, Sept. 1942); Saxony, Aug. 1941; Thuringia, Nov. 1941; and Württemberg, Nov. 1942 (summary, Feb. 1943). Reports are also available for the Prussian provinces of Brandenburg, Aug. 1941 (summary, Nov. 1942); Danzig–West Prussia, Sept. 1942 (summary, Feb. 1943); East Prussia, Oct. 1942; Hanover, June 1942 (summary, Nov. 1942); Hessen-Nassau, Mar. 1942 (summary, Dec. 1942); Mecklenburg, June 1941; Oldenburg, Apr. 1942; Pomerania, Oct. 1941 (summary, Dec. 1942); Rhineland, Oct. 1941 (summary, Sept. 1942); Saxony, Dec. 1942; Schleswig-Holstein, Sept. 1941 (summary, Sept. 1942); Lower Silesia, Sept. 1941; Upper Silesia, Sept. 1941; combined Lower and Upper Silesia, Oct. 1941; and Westphalia, May 1942; and also for the Protectorate, Sept. 1942; the Sudetenland, Aug. 1942; and the Wartheland, Sept. 1942. See also NARA Suitland, Heidelberg Docs. 125,171–86, 125,195–223, 125,236–42: reports on Saxony, various dates; ibid. 126,867–97, 126,898–928: reports on Bethel, 1942; ZStL, Heidelberg Docs. 125,226, 125,228, 125,230, 125,232, 125,234: report on Saxony, Feb. 1943; and ibid. 127,381–82: report on Baden, Aug. 1942.

57. See, for example, BA-MA, H20/463, 465: report by Ludwig Trieb on inspection of the Städtisches Arbeits- und Bewahrungshaus Rummelsburg, Berlin-Lichtenberg, 17 Dec. 1941.

58. See, for example, NARA Suitland, Heidelberg Docs. 125,171–86: analysis of institutions in Saxony, n.d.

59. See, for example, ibid. 126,867–97: Bericht über die Planungsbesichtigung der Anstalt für Epileptische Bethel, 24 June 1942.

60. BA-MA, H20/463, 465: report on July 1942 planning inspection of institutions in Baden (including Alsace), 15 Sept. 1942, and report on planning inspection of institutions in Saxony, n.d. [Aug. 1941].

61. Ibid.: summary by Robert Müller of report on Pomerania, 11 Dec. 1942.

62. Ibid.: report on planning inspection of institutions in Saxony, n.d. [Aug. 1941], and summary of report on Rhine province, 5 Sept. 1942. See also ibid.: "Zur Planung," report by Robert Müller, Berlin, 9 Feb. 1943.

63. Ibid.: report on the Protectorate, Sept. 1942. On Slovakia, see ZStL, Sammlung Verschiedenes, Bd. 168, pp. 14–16: Franz Karmasin (owner of Pressburg *Grenzbote*) to RFSS, 28 July 1942.

64. BA-MA, H20/463, 465: report on the Wartheland, Sept. 1942. In the Lodz ghetto, all Jewish hospital patients had been deported to the Chelmno killing center during the roundups of September 1942. See Dobroszycki, *Chronicle of the Lodz Ghetto*, pp. 248–49.

65. See, for example, BA-MA, H20/463, 465: report on Schleswig by Aquilin Ullrich, 2 Oct. 1941, p. 12, and report on Württemberg by August Becker, 25 Nov. 1942, pp. 9, 11. See also ZStL, Heidelberg Docs. 127,926–29: report from Kurt Runckel for Paul Nitsche, 30 June 1944.

66. BA-MA, H20/463, 465: report on Württemberg by August Becker, 25 Nov. 1942, pp. 20–22 (concerning the Ziegler'sche Taubstummenanstalt Wilhelmsdorf). See also Aly, "Medizin gegen Unbrauchbare," pp. 17–18.

67. BA-MA, H20/463, 465: Herbert Becker to Paul Nitsche, 18 Dec. 1943, 9, 19 Jan. 1944.

68. GStA DDR (StA Dresden), Verfahren Paul Nitsche, (S) 1 Ks 58/47 (1/47), Bd. 1: interrogation Paul Nitsche, 26 Mar. 1946. See also ZStL, Heidelberg Docs. 127,967–68: Paul Nitsche to Carl Schneider, 14 Jan. 1944.

69. BA-MA, H20/463, 465: Paul Nitsche to Dietrich Allers, 2 Dec. 1943. For the distribution of drugs to institutions, see also ZStL, Heidelberg Docs. 127,942–46: notes from Kurt Borm for Friedrich Robert Lorent and Paul Nitsche, 26 Apr., 15, 16 Aug. 1944.

70. For the delivery of drugs, see ZStL, Bd. 141; ibid., Heidelberg Docs. 127,942–46; BAK,

R58/1059; and GStA Frankfurt, Sammlung Euthanasie: Reichsausschuß to Anstalt Eichberg, 3 Jan. 1944.

71. See BA-MA, H20/463, 465: report on Württemberg by August Becker, 25 Nov. 1942.

72. Ibid.: Valentin Faltlhauser to Paul Nitsche, 27 Sept. 1944, and Nitsche to Hans-Joachim Becker, 30 Sept. 1944.

73. See ZStL, 439 AR-Z 340/59 Ord. Euthanasie: interrogation Hans Hefelmann, Munich, 14 Sept. 1960; ibid., Heidelberg Docs. 127,389–90: Paul Nitsche to Herbert Linden, 21 Aug. 1942; ibid. 127,947–50: Otto Hebold to Nitsche, 23 Mar. 1944, and Nitsche note, 29 Mar. 1944; DÖW, file E18371: report of Gendarmeriepostenkommando Spittal, 4 Apr. 1946; GStA Frankfurt, Sammlung Euthanasie: RJM to Generalstaatsanwälte, 2 July 1943; Nuremberg Doc. PS-3896: affidavit by Ministerialrat Dr. Ludwig Sprauer, Nuremberg, 23 Apr. 1946; and Thom and Caregorodcev, *Medizin unterm Hakenkreuz*, pp. 131, 136–37. In 1944 state hospitals were empowered to transfer patients committed under StGB §42 to the custody of the Kripo. See BAK, R18/3768: RMdI circular (sig. Linden), 17 Apr. 1944.

74. BA-MA, H20/463, 465: planning report for Baden, July 1942.

75. HHStA, 461/32442/3: letter of 22 Nov. 1946.

76. HHStA, 461/32442/2: StA Frankfurt, Verfahren 4 KLs 15/46, "Aufstellung über die in der Landesheilanstalt Eichberg, Gemeindebezirk Erbach/Rhg. einschl. des Altersheims Rheinhöhe in der Zeit vom 1. Januar 1941 bis 31. März 1945 verstorbenen Insassen." See also StA Hamburg, Anklage Lensch und Struve, 147 Js 58/67, 24 Apr. 1973, pp. 409–12.

77. BDC, dossier Emil Gelny.

78. DÖW, file E18281: report of Gendarmeriepostenkommando Amstetten, "Gelny Emil Dr. und Genossen," 30 Jan. 1946; StA Wien, Anklage Josef Mayer, 15 St 6271/45, 25 Sept. 1947; VG bei dem LG Wien, Urteil Josef Mayer, Vg 11h Vr 455/46 (Hv 42/48), 14 July 1948; DÖW, file 16209: VG bei dem LG Wien, Urteil Marie Gutmann und Auguste Kabelka, Vg 1d Vr 189/49 (Hv 124/49), 28 Feb. 1949; DÖW, file 18860: LG Wien, Hauptverhandlung Dr. Mayer, Vg 11h Vr 455/46 (Hv 42/48), 14–24 June 1948.

79. BA-MA, H20/463, 465: Emil Gelny to Paul Nitsche, 7 Feb. 1944, Dietrich Allers to Nitsche, 22 Feb. 1944, and Nitsche to Gelny, 29 Feb. 1944.

80. This discussion of Meseritz-Obrawalde is based on GStA Berlin, Anklage Hilde Wernicke und Helene Wieczorek, 11 Js 37/45, 5 Feb. 1946; LG Berlin, Urteil Hilde Wernicke und Helene Wieczorek, 11 Ks 8/46, 25 Mar. 1946; *JuNSV*, vol. 20, no. 587: LG München I, Urteil 112 Ks 2/64, 12 Mar. 1965; StA Hamburg, Anklage Lensch und Struve, 147 Js 58/67, 24 Apr. 1973, pp. 359–88; and StA Hamburg, Verfahren Lensch und Struve, 147 Js 58/67: Gutachten Jozef Radzicki (German translation).

81. StA Hamburg, Anklage Lensch und Struve, 147 Js 58/67, 24 Apr. 1973, pp. 378–79.

82. StA Hamburg, Verfahren Lensch und Struve, 147 Js 58/67: Gutachten Jozef Radzicki (German translation), p. 56.

83. StA Hamburg, Anklage Lensch und Struve, 147 Js 58/67, 24 Apr. 1973, p. 363; *JuNSV*, vol. 20, no. 587: LG München I, Urteil 112 Ks 2/64, 12 Mar. 1965.

84. On Hadamar as a killing center for German handicapped patients during the period of "wild" euthanasia, see StA Hamburg, Anklage Lensch und Struve, 147 Js 58/67, 24 Apr. 1973, pp. 388–95, and HHStA, 461/32061/2: Gekrat to Anstalt Hadamar, 7 Aug. 1942, Zentralverrechnungsstelle Heil- und Pflegeanstalten, Berlin, to Alfons Klein, Hadamar, 12 Aug. 1942, and RAG to Alfons Klein, 25 Feb., 1 June 1944. See also NARA Suitland, RG 338, Case File 12-449, United States v. Alfons Klein et al., box 1, file 3: interrogation Alfons Klein, 19 Sept. 1945.

85. See, for example, HHStA, 461/32061/12: LG Frankfurt, Urteil Wahlmann, Gorgaß, Huber, 4a KLs 7/47, 21 Mar. 1947, p. 13.

86. BAK, R96II/43.

87. BAK, R18/3768: RMdI circular, "Geisteskranke Ostarbeiter und Polen," 6 Sept. 1944.

88. See, for example, Nuremberg Docs. NO-1430, NO-1436.

89. HHStA, 461/32061/7: LG Frankfurt, Verfahren Wahlmann, Gorgaß, Huber, 4a KLs 7/47 (4a Js 3/46), Protokoll der öffentlichen Sitzung der 4. Strafkammer, 24 Feb. 1947, p. 28 (testimony Adolf Wahlmann); NARA Suitland, RG 338, Case File 12-449, United States v. Alfons Klein et al., box 1, file 6: interrogation Adolf Wahlmann, 11 Apr. 1945; Nuremberg Doc. NO-1427: sworn statement by Irmgard Huber, 4 Jan. 1947.

90. See the Trial Record (8–15 Oct. 1945), in NARA Suitland, RG 338, Case File 12-449, United States v. Alfons Klein et al., box 3, files 12–18. For a slightly abbreviated printed version, see Kintner, *Hadamar Trial*. See also Jaworski, *After Fifteen Years*.

91. NARA Suitland, RG 338, Case File 12-449, United States v. Alfons Klein et al., box 3, file 17: Trial Record (8–15 Oct. 1945), p. 305.

92. See StA Hamburg, Anklage Lensch und Struve, 147 Js 58/67, 24 Apr. 1973, pp. 395–404. See also Mader, *Das erzwungene Sterben*.

93. Nuremberg Doc. PS-1696: list of children killed between Dec. 1941 and early 1945.

94. Ibid.: report from Detachment F1F3, 2 July 1945.

95. Ibid., p. 4.

96. Ibid.: medical record of Richard Jenne.

CHAPTER NINE

1. For oral histories, see Delius, *Das Ende von Strecknitz*. For a collection of letters (which was published too late for use in this study), see Neuhauser and Pfaffenwimmer, *Hartheim —wohin unbekannt*. On the failure of the Federal Republic of Germany to recognize handicapped survivors as victims of Nazi crimes, see Ernst Klee in *Die Zeit*, 25 Apr. 1986.

2. See, for example, the pictures in *Hundert Jahre deutscher Rassismus*, pp. 131–49.

3. See, for example, the pictures in Winter et al., *Verlegt nach Hadamar*, pp. 62, 98–99, 102–4, 107, 128.

4. ZStL, Sammlung Verschiedenes, Bd. 132: Gemeinnützige Kranken-Transport G.m.b.H. to Thüringisches Ministerium des Innern, 8 Jan., 9 Feb. 1942.

5. Ibid.: Landesversicherungsanstalt Thüringen to Thüringisches Ministerium des Innern, 6 Aug. 1942, and Zentralverrechnungsstelle Heil- und Pflegeanstalten to Thüringisches Ministerium des Innern, 23 Sept. 1943.

6. DÖW, file E18370/2: LG Linz, interrogation Stadler Matthias, 2 Oct. 1947.

7. See Milton, "Spanish Republican Refugees and the Holocaust."

8. Cited in GStA Frankfurt, Anklage Reinhold Vorberg und Dietrich Allers, Js 20/61 (GStA), 15 Feb. 1966, pp. 313–14.

9. HHStA, 461/32442/3: letter, "An den Herrn Oberstaatsanwalt bei dem Landgericht Frankfurt a.M.," Frankfurt, 22 Nov. 1946.

10. Platen-Hallermund, *Die Tötung Geisteskranker*, p. 67.

11. Klee, *"Euthanasie" im NS-Staat*, p. 407.

12. Ibid., pp. 407–10.

13. Schmidt, *Selektion in der Heilanstalt*, p. 120.

14. StA München I, Verfahren Hermann Pfannmüller, 1 Ks 10/49 (1b Js 1791/47): Protokoll der öffentlichen Sitzung des Schwurgerichts bei dem LG München I, 28 Oct. 1949, pp. 101–2. For the Eglfing *Hungerhäuser*, see Schmidt, *Selektion in der Heilanstalt*, pp. 132–49, and Richarz, *Heilen, Pflegen, Töten*, pp. 174–77.

15. Schmidt, *Selektion in der Heilanstalt*, p. 114. See also Klee, *"Euthanasie" im NS-Staat*, p. 450.

16. See documents in Sick, *"Euthanasie" im Nationalsozialismus am Beispiel des Kalmenhofs*, pp. 42–51.

17. HHStA, 461/32442/4: LG Frankfurt, Verfahren Friedrich Mennecke, Walter Schmidt,

4 KLs 15/46 (4a Js 13/46), Protokoll der öffentlichen Sitzung der 4. Strafkammer, 12 Dec. 1946, p. 5. See also the account in Winter et al., *Verlegt nach Hadamar*, p. 93, which concluded that the pregnant woman was murdered with an injection at Eichberg after her return from Hadamar.

18. HHStA, 461/32442/4: LG Frankfurt, Verfahren Mennecke, Schmidt, 4 KLs 15/46 (4a Js 13/46), Protokoll der öffentlichen Sitzung der 4. Strafkammer, 12 Dec. 1946, p. 23 (testimony Friedrich Jäger).

19. HHStA, 461/32061/6: Ortspolizeibehörde-Gesundheitspolizei Wiesbaden to Karl Krämer, 31 Oct. 1944, 15 June 1945, and Landeheilanstalt Eichberg, Bescheinigung, 23 May 1945.

20. Klee, *"Euthanasie" im NS-Staat*, p. 184.

21. Cited in Platen-Hallermund, *Die Tötung Geisteskranker*, pp. 65–66, and Klee, *"Euthanasie" im NS-Staat*, p. 183.

22. Schmidt, *Selektion in der Heilanstalt*, pp. 112–13.

23. DÖW, file E18281: StA Wien I (Volksgerichtshof), Verfahren Vg 8a Vr 455/46, Bericht des Bezirksgendarmeriekommandos Amstetten, Niederösterreich, 1946; DÖW, file 18860/36: interrogation Dr. Michael Scharpf, 20, 21 Mar. 1946, published in Klamper, *Dokumentationsarchiv*, doc. 46.

24. HHStA, 461/32442/4: LG Frankfurt, Verfahren Mennecke, Schmidt, 4 KLs 15/46 (4a Js 13/46), Protokoll der öffentlichen Sitzung der 4. Strafkammer, 9 Dec. 1946, pp. 27–28 (testimony Dr. Otto Behringer).

25. See, for example, Krüger, "Kinderfachabteilung Wiesengrund," p. 160.

26. See Platen-Hallermund, *Die Tötung Geisteskranker*, p. 64, and Klee, *Was sie taten—Was sie wurden*, p. 49.

27. LG Frankfurt, Urteil Aquilin Ullrich, Heinrich Bunke und Klaus Endruweit, Ks 1/66 (GStA), 23 May 1967, pp. 76–77.

28. Schmidt, *Selektion in der Heilanstalt*, p. 59.

29. StArch Sigmaringen, Wü 29/3, Acc. 33/1973, Nr. 1752: StA Tübingen, Anklage Otto Mauthe, 1 Js 85–87/47, 4 Jan. 1949, p. 13v.

30. Schmidt, *Selektion in der Heilanstalt*, pp. 66–67.

31. Cited ibid., p. 60.

32. Cited in Platen-Hallermund, *Die Tötung Geisteskranker*, p. 55.

33. Cited in Klee, *"Euthanasie" im NS-Staat*, p. 186.

34. Cited in Richarz, *Heilen, Pflegen, Töten*, p. 159 (emphasis in original).

35. Cited in Platen-Hallermund, *Die Tötung Geisteskranker*, p. 54.

36. Cited in HHStA, 461/32442/4: LG Frankfurt, Verfahren Mennecke, Schmidt, 4 KLs 15/46 (4a Js 13/46), Protokoll der öffentlichen Sitzung der 4. Strafkammer, 9 Dec. 1946, p. 27 (testimony Dr. Otto Behringer).

37. Cited in Klee, *"Euthanasie" im NS-Staat*, p. 187.

38. Cited ibid., p. 245.

39. "Wir sterben ja, aber den Hitler holt der Teufel." Cited ibid., p. 187.

40. "Dieser Hitler, der mich morden und vergewaltigen will." Cited ibid., p. 264.

41. See Roth, "Filmpropaganda."

42. See, for example, BA-MA, H20/463, 465: Ernst Rüdin to Paul Nitsche, 21 Nov. 1941.

43. Schmidt, *Selektion in der Heilanstalt*, p. 94.

44. Götz Aly, "Der Mord an behinderten Kindern," in Ebbinghaus, Kaupen-Haas, and Roth, *Heilen und Vernichten im Mustergau Hamburg*, p. 151.

45. Schmidt, *Selektion in der Heilanstalt*, pp. 130–31.

46. Ibid., pp. 129–30.

47. Krüger, "Kinderfachabteilung Wiesengrund," p. 171.

48. ZStL, Sammlung USA, Bd. 12, p. 763: Erich Koch to Heinrich Himmler, 19 May 1944.

49. Nuremberg Docs. NO-886, NO-1101, PS-1969, D-906; Klee, *"Euthanasie" im NS-Staat*, pp. 313–14.

50. Klee, *"Euthanasie" im NS-Staat*, p. 307.

51. Ibid., p. 308.

52. See Friedlander, "Judiciary and Nazi Crimes," p. 32.

53. See Schmidt, *Selektion in der Heilanstalt*, p. 69.

54. Nuremberg Doc. PS-624: Landesheil- und Pflegeanstalt Waldheim (Sachsen) to Sächsisches Ministerium des Innern, 2 Aug. 1940.

55. Ibid.

56. BAK, R22/5021: GStA Dresden to StS Roland Freisler, 24 Aug. 1940.

57. Ibid.: GStA Naumburg (Saale) to StS Roland Freisler, 13 Sept. 1940.

58. Platen-Hallermund, *Die Tötung Geisteskranker*, p. 67.

59. Emmerich, "Forensische Psychiatrie," p. 113.

60. Schmidt, *Selektion in der Heilanstalt*, p. 70.

61. DÖW, file E19198: Dr. Alfred Hardix to Dr. Hermann Hans Vellguth, Reichsgau Wien, Hauptgesundheitsamt, 20 Feb. 1942, and Obermedizinalrat Dr. Dirschmid to Vellguth, 25 Mar. 1942.

62. *Die Ermordeten waren Schuldig?*, pp. 51–52.

63. BAK, R18/5585: memo, Munich, 10 June 1937.

64. ZStL, Bd. 513: memo from Dr. med. Irmfried Eberl, 10 Sept. 1940.

65. BA-MA, H20/463, 465: Nitsche Gutachten, 23 June 1942.

66. See, for example, Klee, *"Euthanasie" im NS-Staat*, pp. 316–17.

67. BAK, R22/5021: GStA Dresden to StS Roland Freisler, 24 Aug. 1940.

68. HHStA, 461/32442/4: LG Frankfurt, Verfahren Mennecke, Schmidt, 4 KLs 15/46 (4a Js 13/46), Protokoll der öffentlichen Sitzung der 4. Strafkammer, 12 Dec. 1946, pp. 1–2 (testimony Gretel Weckmann).

69. Nuremberg Doc. NO-890: Reichsausschuß (Blankenburg) to Walter Schmidt, 16 Nov. 1943.

70. GStA Frankfurt, Eberl Akten, I/152a, 1:123: Irmfried Eberl to Paul Nitsche, 4 Dec. 1942.

71. BA-MA, H20/463, 465: Reinhold Vorberg (Hintertal) to Paul Nitsche, 28 Sept. 1943, Nitsche to Vorberg, 7 Oct. 1943, Nitsche to Theo Steinmeyer, 7 Oct. 1943, Steinmeyer to Nitsche, 17 Nov. 1943, Nitsche to Steinmeyer, 24 Nov. 1943, Nitsche to Vorberg, 24 Nov. 1943, Nitsche to Steinmeyer, 3 Jan. 1944, telegram from Steinmeyer to Nitsche, 19 Jan. 1944, KdF to Steinmeyer, 22 Jan. 1944, Steinmeyer to Nitsche, 7 Feb. 1944, telegram from Steinmeyer to Nitsche, 12 Feb. 1944, Steinmeyer to Nitsche, 17 Feb. 1944, Nitsche to Steinmeyer, 23 Feb. 1944, and Vorberg to Nitsche, 28 Feb. 1944.

72. ZStL, Bd. 513: Landes- Heil- und Pflegeanstalt Sonnenstein to Adolf Wächtler, 2, 7 Aug. 1940, and Landes-Pflegeanstalt Brandenburg to Wächtler, 13 Aug. 1940 (copy in LG Frankfurt, Urteil Kurt Borm, Ks 1/66 [GStA], 6 June 1972, p. 28a).

73. HHStA, 461/32061/6: Landes- Heil- und Pflegeanstalt Hadamar to Daniel Riedesel, 10 Feb. 1941, and Heil- und Pflegeanstalt Bernburg to Riedesel, 19 Feb. 1941.

74. Ibid.: Heilerziehungsanstalt Kalmenhof to Hugo Seidler, 30 Apr. 1941, and Landes-Heil- und Pflegeanstalt Hadamar to Seidler, 5, 15 May 1941.

75. Ibid.: Landes-Heilanstalt Eichberg to Barbara Bauer, 10 Mar. 1941, and Landes- Heil- und Pflegeanstalt Hadamar to Bauer, 10 Mar. 1941.

76. DÖW, file 18869/87: Anstalt Wien-Gugging to Maria Wegscheider, 12 Apr. 1943.

77. HHStA, 461/32061/6: Landes-Heilanstalt Eichberg to Anna Krämer, 7 Feb. 1941, and Landes- Heil- und Pflegeanstalt Hadamar to Wilhelm Krämer, 23 Feb., 4 Mar. 1941.

78. Cited in Klee, *"Euthanasie" im NS-Staat*, p. 389.

79. Cited ibid., p. 310.

80. Letter published in Leipert, Styrnal, and Schwarzer, *Verlegt nach unbekannt*, p. 239, doc. 81.

81. Cited in Klee, *"Euthanasie" im NS-Staat*, p. 309.

82. DÖW, file E17845: R. Buddrich to StA Linz, n.d.

83. Letters cited in Platen-Hallermund, *Die Tötung Geisteskranker*, pp. 116–20.

84. HHStA, 461/32442/12: Johann Risch to Walter Schmidt, 29 Feb. 1944.

85. Exchange of letters in Winter et al., *Verlegt nach Hadamar*, pp. 162–64.

86. Cited in Platen-Hallermund, *Die Tötung Geisteskranker*, pp. 52–53.

87. ZStL, Sammlung Verschiedenes, Bd. 132 (doc. from Thuringian MdI): Thüringisches Landeskrankenhaus Stadtroda (sig. Kloos) to Thüringisches Ministerium des Innern, 5 Oct. 1944.

88. See, for example, Henry Friedlander and Sybil Milton, "Surviving," in Grobman, Landes, and Milton, *Genocide*, pp. 233–35.

89. Klamper, *Dokumentationsarchiv*, doc. 38 (testimony Anny Wödl, 1 Mar. 1945); Aly, "Medizin gegen Unbrauchbare," p. 12.

90. Klamper, *Dokumentationsarchiv*, doc. 40 (testimony Katharina Budin, 2 Mar. 1945).

91. DÖW, file E18282: testimony of Leopold Widerhofer, Vienna, 27 Feb. 1946.

92. HHStA, 461/32061/6: Irmgard Hörnecke to LG Frankfurt, 12 Dec. 1946.

93. Nuremberg Doc. NO-3357: memo, Eglfing-Haar, 23 Apr. 1941; ibid. NO-3358: Transport-Liste Nr. 23, Eglfing-Haar, 29 Apr. 1941 (Maria Mader's name added in handwriting as number 8).

94. Ibid. PS-618: GStA Dresden to RJM, 20 Oct. 1940.

95. Frau Helene S. to OStA Frankfurt, 16 Jan. 1947, published in Sick, *"Euthanasie" im Nationalsozialismus am Beispiel des Kalmenhofs*, pp. 70–71, doc. 29.

96. See Klee, *"Euthanasie" im NS-Staat*, pp. 184–85.

97. StA München I, Verfahren Pfannmüller, 1 Ks 10/49 (1b Js 1791/47): Protokoll der öffentlichen Sitzung des Schwurgerichts bei dem LG München I, 21 Oct. 1949, p. 26.

98. HHStA, 461/32442/3: StA Frankfurt, Anklage Friedrich Mennecke, Walter Schmidt, 4a Js 13/46, 7 Oct. 1946, pp. 39–40.

99. Ibid., p. 31.

100. Cited in Richarz, *Heilen, Pflegen, Töten*, p. 181.

101. DÖW, file E18371: report of Gendarmeriepostenkommando Spittal-Drau, Kärnten, 4 Apr. 1946.

102. Winter et al., *Verlegt nach Hadamar*, pp. 99–101.

103. HHStA, 461/32061/1: interrogation Frieda Nardoni, 25 June 1945. After the fall of Mussolini, Marshal Badoglio headed the Italian government that took Italy out of the war in 1943. In retaliation, the Germans incarcerated thousands of Italian soldiers and civilians. See Weinberg, *A World at Arms*, p. 485.

104. Cited in Kintner, *Hadamar Trial*, p. 201.

CHAPTER TEN

1. For the latest attempt to analyze the perpetrators, a study of one small group of common soldiers in the East, see Browning, *Ordinary Men*.

2. Arendt, *Eichmann in Jerusalem*.

3. See Müller-Hill, "Selektion," pp. 146–47.

4. Goldhagen, "Weltanschauung und Endlösung," pp. 397–400.

5. GStA Frankfurt, Sammlung Euthanasie: Wilhelm Weskott to Eugen Stähle, 12 July 1940.

6. See Gernot Jochheim, *Frauenprotest in der Rosenstrasse* (Berlin, 1993).

7. Lifton, in *Nazi Doctors*, p. 115, interviewed Speer, who told him that Brandt was a close friend.

8. GStA Frankfurt, Sammlung Euthanasie: Regierungspräsident, Minden (Westf.) to SS Gruppenführer Karl Wolff, 20 Nov. 1940.

9. On dealings with other agencies, see HHStA, 461/32061/6: interrogation of Philipp Prinz von Hessen, 14 Jan. 1947. On the budget, see NARA, RG 238, Microfilm Publication M-1019, roll 8: interrogation Viktor Brack, 4 Sept. 1946 P.M., pp. 16–17.

10. U.S. Military Tribunal, Transcript of the Proceedings in Case 1, pp. 1534–37; Nuremberg Doc. NO-426: affidavit Viktor Brack.

11. NARA, RG 238: interrogation Karl Brandt, 1 Oct. 1945 P.M., p. 4.

12. See, for example, Friedlander, "From Euthanasia to the Final Solution," pp. 91–113, and "Euthanasia and the Final Solution," pp. 51–61.

13. See Rückerl, *NS-Vernichtungslager*, and Scalpelli, *San Sabba*.

14. Using the designation "middle management" for the T4 bureaucrats does not mean that they fell into the middle of the bureaucratic hierarchy. It means that they operated below the policy-making level, that is, not only below Hitler, who made all major policy decisions, but also below the men — including Brandt and Bouhler — who advised Hitler and made decisions about how policy would be developed. At the same time, Brack and his associates managed the technical implementation of policy and directed the administration that carried out orders.

15. See the BDC dossiers of Allers, Becker, Blankenburg, Bohne, Brack, Hefelmann, von Hegener, Kaufmann, and Lorent. See also Nuremberg Docs. NO-426, NO-820 (affidavits Viktor Brack); NARA, RG 238, Microfilm Publication M-1019, roll 8: interrogations Viktor Brack; U.S. Military Tribunal, Transcript of the Proceedings in Case 1, pp. 7413–72 (testimony Viktor Brack); and Klee, *Was sie taten — Was sie wurden*, pp. 34–36, 75–76, 78–79, 81–82, 293–95. On von Hegener, see also correspondence in BAK, NL263, Nachlaß Rheindorf, no. 50; ibid., Landeskriminalpolizeiabteilung Mecklenburg, Anklage Richard von Hegener, 5-0/410/47/B1, 5-0/339/49/B1, Schwerin, 9 Sept. 1949; and ZStL, Sammlung Verschiedenes, Bd. 18: LG Magdeburg, Urteil Richard von Hegener, 11 KLs 139/51, 20 Feb. 1952. On Allers and Vorberg, see also GStA Frankfurt, Anklage Reinhold Vorberg und Dietrich Allers, Js 20/61 (GStA), 15 Feb. 1966, pp. 267–77; LG Frankfurt, Urteil Reinhold Vorberg und Dietrich Allers, Ks 2/66 (GStA), 20 Dec. 1968, pp. 2–9. On Becker and Lorent, see also GStA Frankfurt, Anklage Georg Renno, Hans-Joachim Becker und Friedrich Robert Lorent, Js 18/61 (GStA), Js 7/63 (GStA), Js 5/65 (GStA), 7 Nov. 1967, pp. 79–99; and LG Frankfurt, Urteil Hans-Joachim Becker und Friedrich Robert Lorent, Ks 1/69 (GStA), 27 May 1970, pp. 3–10. On Kaufmann, see also GStA Frankfurt, Anklage Adolf Gustav Kaufmann, Js 16/63 (GStA), 27 June 1966, pp. 3–8, 21–36. See also Friedlander and Milton, *Berlin Document Center*, pp. xvii, xix, docs. 14, 51, 58–61.

16. GStA Frankfurt, Anklage Vorberg und Allers, Js 20/61 (GStA), 15 Feb. 1966, pp. 284–85.

17. See tables 3.2, 4.2, and 4.3.

18. GStA Frankfurt, Anklage Kaufmann, Js 16/63 (GStA), 27 June 1966, pp. 21, 40–41.

19. GStA Frankfurt, Anklage Renno, Becker und Lorent, Js 18/61 (GStA), Js 7/63 (GStA), Js 5/65 (GStA), 7 Nov. 1967, p. 80.

20. Sereny, *Into That Darkness*, p. 79. See also GStA Frankfurt, Anklage Vorberg und Allers, Js 20/61 (GStA), 15 Feb. 1966, p. 273.

21. GStA Frankfurt, Anklage Renno, Becker und Lorent, Js 18/61 (GStA), Js 7/63 (GStA), Js 5/65 (GStA), 7 Nov. 1967, p. 88.

22. ZStL, interrogation Arnold Oels, Hanover, 24 Apr. 1961.

23. U.S. Military Tribunal, Transcript of the Proceedings in Case 1, p. 7508. One inconsis-

tency in Brack's testimony involves the date he left for the front. Brack testified at Nuremberg that he left for the front in April 1942 (ibid., p. 7447). Surviving documents show, however, that he was still completing work at the KdF in early July 1942 (GStA Frankfurt, Sammlung Euthanasie: Viktor Brack to Heinrich Himmler, 6 July 1942) but had departed by mid-August 1942 (Nuremberg Doc. NO-207: Werner Blankenburg to Heinrich Himmler, 14 Aug. 1942).

24. Cited in Klee, *Was sie taten — Was sie wurden*, p. 73.

25. Browning, *Ordinary Men*, p. 162.

26. GStA Frankfurt, Anklage Kaufmann, Js 16/63 (GStA), 27 June 1966, pp. 25–30.

27. Cited ibid., p. 38.

28. DÖW, file E18370/1: StA Frankfurt, Js 18/61 (GStA), interrogation Georg Renno, 1 Feb. 1965, p. 8.

29. LG Frankfurt, Urteil Vorberg und Allers, Ks 2/66 (GStA), 20 Dec. 1968, pp. 50–55; GStA Frankfurt, Anklage Vorberg und Allers, Js 20/61 (GStA), 15 Feb. 1966, p. 282.

30. GStA Frankfurt, Anklage Vorberg und Allers, Js 20/61 (GStA), 15 Feb. 1966, pp. 276, 297; LG Frankfurt, Urteil Vorberg und Allers, Ks 2/66 (GStA), 20 Dec. 1968, p. 61; Sereny, *Into That Darkness*, p. 80.

31. Klee, *Was sie taten — Was sie wurden*, p. 36.

32. GStA Frankfurt, Anklage Renno, Becker und Lorent, Js 18/61 (GStA), Js 7/63 (GStA), Js 5/65 (GStA), 7 Nov. 1967, p. 82. See also DÖW, file E18370/1: StA Frankfurt, Js 18/61 (GStA), interrogation Georg Renno, 3 Feb. 1965, pp. 27, 51.

33. GStA Frankfurt, Anklage Renno, Becker und Lorent, Js 18/61 (GStA), Js 7/63 (GStA), Js 5/65 (GStA), 7 Nov. 1967, pp. 89–91.

34. See, for example, BAK, R58/1059: memo, 8 Mar. 1944, concerning telephone conversation with Dietrich Allers, and DÖW, file E18370/1: correspondence of Friedrich Robert Lorent and Hans Hefelmann, 1944, concerning delivery of gas and poisons.

35. See, for example, Browning, *Ordinary Men*, pp. 169–75, 184–86.

36. For a discussion of duress as a defense in postwar trials, see Rückerl, *NS-Verbrechen vor Gericht*, pp. 281–88.

37. For specific examples of how duress has been used as a defense argument in postwar proceedings, see Friedlander, "Deportation of the German Jews." For conclusive evidence that duress had never applied during the war, see Jäger, *Verbrechen unter totalitärer Herrschaft*, pp. 94–122.

38. See, for example, Daniel Jonah Goldhagen in *New Republic*, 13, 20 July 1992, pp. 49–52.

39. See, for example, DÖW, file E18370/3: interrogation Theresia Strauss, 25 June 1946.

40. See testimonies cited in Platen-Hallermund, *Die Tötung Geisteskranker*, pp. 109–11.

41. GStA Frankfurt, Anklage Vorberg und Allers, Js 20/61 (GStA), 15 Feb. 1966, pp. 360–61.

42. U.S. Military Tribunal, Transcript of the Proceedings in Case 1, pp. 7532–33 (testimony Viktor Brack).

43. Nuremberg Doc. NO-205: Viktor Brack to Heinrich Himmler, 23 June 1942.

44. NARA, RG 238, Microfilm Publication M-1019, roll 8: interrogation Viktor Brack, 13 Sept. 1946. Brack's first name was misspelled as "Vicktor" in the interrogation record.

45. "Der war immer dabei bei diesen ganzen Sachen." NARA, RG 238, Microfilm Publication M-1019, roll 8: interrogation Viktor Brack, 4 Sept. 1946 A.M., p. 10.

46. See BDC, dossier Herbert Linden.

47. See Aly, "Medizin gegen Unbrauchbare," p. 12.

48. See BDC, dossier Werner Heyde. See also Friedlander and Milton, *Berlin Document Center*, p. xxiv, docs. 109–11, 168–75.

49. See Aly, "Der saubere und der schmutzige Fortschritt," pp. 9–13.

50. BDC, dossier Paul Nitsche; GStA DDR (StA Dresden), Verfahren Paul Nitsche, (S) 1 Ks 58/47 (1/47), Bd. 1: German translation of Soviet interrogation of Paul Nitsche, n.d., and interrogation Paul Nitsche, 25 Mar. 1946; ibid., Bd. 3: recommendation from Prof. Karl Bonhoeffer, 23 Nov. 1907; ibid., Bd. 5: interrogation Paul Nitsche, 2 May 1947.

51. See DÖW, file E19198: Reichsgau Vienna, Hauptgesundheitsamt records.

52. See BDC, dossiers Eugen Stähle, Otto Mauthe, and Ludwig Sprauer.

53. Klee, *"Euthanasie" im NS-Staat*, p. 163.

54. See StArch Sigmaringen, Wü 29/3, Acc. 33/1973, Nr. 1752: StA Tübingen, Anklage Otto Mauthe, 1 Js 85–87/47, 4 Jan. 1949, p. 9v. For Stähle's Nazi past and antisemitism, see also Kater, *Doctors under Hitler*, pp. 61, 185.

55. See StArch Sigmaringen, Wü 29/3, Acc. 33/1973, Nr. 1752: StA Tübingen, Anklage Mauthe, 1 Js 85–87/47, 4 Jan. 1949, p. 18, and LG Tübingen, Urteil Otto Mauthe, Ks 6/49, 5 July 1949, pp. 12–14.

56. See Nuremberg Doc. PS-3896: affidavit by Ministerialrat Dr. Ludwig Sprauer, Nuremberg, 23 Apr. 1946.

57. Hans Hefelmann in his interrogations (GStA Frankfurt, Sammlung Euthanasie) stressed this conflict repeatedly.

58. BDC, dossier Christian Wirth. See also Friedlander and Milton, *Berlin Document Center*, p. xxxv, docs. 419–41. Wirth was killed in Yugoslavia in 1944.

59. U.S. Military Tribunal, Transcript of the Proceedings in Case 1, pp. 7704, 7733 (testimony Viktor Brack); GStA Frankfurt, Eberl Akten II/151, 7:58–62: Aktenvermerk by Dr. Heinrich Bunke, 9 July 1941.

60. See, for example, DÖW, file E18370/1: StA Frankfurt, Js 18/61 (GStA), interrogation Georg Renno, 2 Feb. 1965, p. 20, and DÖW, file E18370/3: Bezirksgericht Ybbs, interrogation Hermann Merta, 3 Dec. 1945.

61. DÖW, file E18370/1: StA Frankfurt, Js 18/61 (GStA), interrogation Georg Renno, 2 Feb. 1965, p. 20.

62. Ibid.: Bundesministerium für Inneres, interrogation ("formlose Befragung") Bruno Bruckner, Vienna, 24 May 1962.

63. Rückerl, *NS-Vernichtungslager*, p. 46, n. 28.

64. On Reichleitner and Stangl, see LG Düsseldorf, Urteil Franz Stangl, 8 Ks 1/69, 22 Dec. 1970, pp. 1–13; on Gottlieb Hering, see ibid. and Winter et al., *Verlegt nach Hadamar*, pp. 109–14; on Jacob Wöger, see StArch Sigmaringen, Wü 29/3, Acc. 33/1973, Nr. 1752: StA Tübingen, Anklage Mauthe, 1 Js 85–87/47, 4 Jan. 1949, pp. 50–51; on Hermann Holzschuh, see ibid., pp. 53–54; on Fritz Tauscher, see DÖW, file E18370/1: LG Frankfurt, Untersuchungsrichter, Verfahren Js 18/61 (GStA), interrogation Fritz Tauscher, Hamburg, 2 June 1964; and on Fritz Hirsche, see GStA Frankfurt, Anklage Aquilin Ullrich, Heinrich Bunke, Kurt Borm und Klaus Endruweit, Js 15/61 (GStA), 15 Jan. 1965, p. 181.

65. Sereny, *Into That Darkness*, pp. 48, 53.

66. Ibid., pp. 48–53.

67. Werner denied that he had ever had anything to do with the transfer of police personnel. He also claimed that he had never even heard of the notorious Christian Wirth and that he knew nothing concrete about euthanasia or the work of the KTI. See StA Stuttgart, Verfahren Albert Widmann, Ks 19/62 (19 Js 328/60), interrogation Paul Werner, 18, 19 July 1962.

68. LG Düsseldorf, Urteil Stangl, 8 Ks 1/69, 22 Dec. 1970, pp. 1–13; Rückerl, *NS-Vernichtungslager*, p. 76.

69. StArch Sigmaringen, Wü 29/3, Acc. 33/1973, Nr. 1752: StA Tübingen, Anklage Mauthe, 1 Js 85–87/47, 4 Jan. 1949, pp. 50v–51.

70. Ibid., pp. 50–50v.

71. Ibid., pp. 53–54.

72. ZStL, Sammlung Verschiedenes, Bd. 1: list of Bernburg staff; GStA Frankfurt, Eberl Akten, II/153, 7:63: Irmfried Eberl to Fritz Hirsche, 26 Jan. 1943; GStA Frankfurt, Anklage Ullrich, Bunke, Borm und Endruweit, Js 15/61 (GStA), 15 Jan. 1965, pp. 181, 202–3.

73. GStA Frankfurt, Anklage Ullrich, Bunke, Borm und Endruweit, Js 15/61 (GStA), 15 Jan. 1965, p. 212.

74. DÖW, file E18370/1: LG Frankfurt, Untersuchungsrichter, Verfahren Js 18/61 (GStA), interrogation Fritz Tauscher, Hamburg, 2–3 June 1964.

75. Winter et al., *Verlegt nach Hadamar*, pp. 109–14; Rückerl, *NS-Vernichtungslager*, p. 76. Hering died in 1945.

76. Winter et al., *Verlegt nach Hadamar*, p. 152; NARA Suitland, RG 338, Case File 12-449, United States v. Alfons Klein et al., box 1, file 3: interrogation Alfons Klein, 19 Sept. 1945; StA Stuttgart, Verfahren Widmann, Ks 19/62 (19 Js 328/60), interrogation Erwin Lambert, 26 Apr. 1961, p. 13.

77. Quote in Sereny, *Into That Darkness*, p. 36.

78. Quote ibid., p. 39. Stangl used the word "Piefke," a derogatory term Austrians apply to Germans.

79. Cited in LG Hagen, Urteil Werner Dubois, 11 Ks 1/64, 20 Dec. 1966, pp. 302–4 (emphasis in original).

80. BDC, dossier Albert Widmann; StA Düsseldorf, Anklage Albert Widmann, 8 Js 7212/59, 13 Sept. 1960, pp. 10–11. See also Friedlander and Milton, *Berlin Document Center*, p. xxxv, docs. 413–16.

81. See BAK, R58/1059: Vermerk, 8 Mar. 1944, Herbert Linden to Albert Widmann, 17 May 1944, and correspondence between the KdF, the KTI (Widmann), and I. G. Farben, 1943–44; and DÖW, file E18370/1: Widmann correspondence, 1944.

82. StA Düsseldorf, Verfahren Albert Widmann, 8 Ks 1/61 (8 Js 7212/59), interrogation Albert Widmann, 11 Jan. 1960, p. 8.

83. See StA Düsseldorf, Anklage Widmann, 8 Js 7212/59, 13 Sept. 1960; LG Düsseldorf, Urteil Albert Widmann, 8 Ks 1/61, 16 May 1961; StA Stuttgart, Anklage Albert Widmann und August Becker, (19) 13 Js 328/60, 29 Aug. 1962; and StA Düsseldorf, Verfahren Widmann, 8 Ks 1/61 (8 Js 7212/59), interrogation Albert Widmann, 11–12, 15, 27 Jan. 1960.

84. StA Düsseldorf, Verfahren Widmann, 8 Ks 1/61 (8 Js 7212/59), interrogation Paul Werner, 17 Feb. 1959.

85. Ibid., interrogation Albert Widmann, 11 Jan. 1960, pp. 4–5.

86. BDC, dossier August Becker; StA Stuttgart, Anklage Widmann und Becker, (19) 13 Js 328/60, 29 Aug. 1962, pp. 12–13.

87. ZStL, interrogation August Becker, 26 Mar. 1960; StA Stuttgart, Verfahren Widmann, Ks 19/62 (19 Js 328/60), interrogation August Becker, 4 Apr. 1960.

88. StA Stuttgart, Verfahren Widmann, Ks 19/62 (19 Js 328/60), interrogation August Becker, 4 Apr. 1960, 16 May 1961; ZStL, interrogation August Becker, 20 June 1961.

89. StA Stuttgart, Verfahren Widmann, Ks 19/62 (19 Js 328/60), interrogation August Becker, 4 Apr. 1960; DÖW, file E18370/1: StA Frankfurt, Js 18/61 (GStA), interrogation Georg Renno, 3 Feb. 1965, p. 29.

90. StA Stuttgart, Verfahren Widmann, Ks 19/62 (19 Js 328/60), interrogation August Becker, 16 May 1961.

91. ZStL, interrogation August Becker, 26 Mar. 1960.

92. StA Stuttgart, Anklage Widmann und Becker, (19) 13 Js 328/60, 29 Aug. 1962, pp. 12–13; ZStL, interrogation August Becker, 10, 26 Mar. 1960, 8 Oct. 1963. See also Browning, *Fateful Months*, chap. 3.

93. StA Stuttgart, Verfahren Widmann, Ks 19/62 (19 Js 328/60), interrogation Helmut Kallmeyer, 20 July 1961 (StA Kiel, 2 Js 269/60).

94. Nuremberg Doc. NO-365: Alfred Wetzel to Heinrich Lohse, 25 Oct. 1941. See also ibid. NO-997: Reichsminister für die besetzten Ostgebiete to Lohse, draft, Oct. 1941.

95. Klee, *Was sie taten—Was sie wurden*, p. 302.

96. "Die halbe Zeit des Lebens wartet der Soldat vergebens." StA Stuttgart, Verfahren Widmann, Ks 19/62 (19 Js 328/60), interrogation Helmut Kallmeyer, 20 July 1961 (StA Kiel, 2 Js 269/60).

97. StA Düsseldorf, Verfahren Widmann, 8 Ks 1/61 (8 Js 7212/59), interrogation Irmgard Raabe, 14 Oct. 1959.

98. For Kallmeyer's admissions and additions, see ZStL, interrogation Helmut Kallmeyer, Hanover, 15 Sept. 1961.

99. ZStL, Bd. 141: correspondence, 1943–44.

100. ZStL, interrogation Gertrud Kallmeyer, 31 May 1960.

101. Ibid., 27 Feb. 1961.

102. ZStL, memo from Landeskriminalpolizeiamt Kiel, 19 Aug. 1961.

103. ZStL, interrogation Gertrud Kallmeyer, 5 Sept. 1961.

104. ZStL, Untersuchungsrichter comment attached to interrogation, 5 Sept. 1961.

105. ZStL, Gertrud Kallmeyer to Untersuchungsrichter, 7 Sept. 1961.

106. ZStL, interrogation Gertrud Kallmeyer, 10 Feb. 1966. See also Klee, *Was sie taten—Was sie wurden*, p. 105.

107. ZStL, Untersuchungsrichter to GStA Frankfurt, 15 Feb. 1966.

108. StA Stuttgart, Verfahren Widmann, Ks 19/62 (19 Js 328/60), interrogation Erwin Lambert, 26 Apr. 1961, and continuation, 4 May 1961, pp. 20–22. See also ZStL, interrogations Erwin Lambert, 3 Apr. 1962, 12 Feb. 1963.

109. StA Düsseldorf, Anklage Kurt Franz, 8 Js 10904/59, 29 Jan. 1963, pp. 50–51; LG Düsseldorf, Urteil Kurt Franz, 8 I Ks 2/64, 3 Sept. 1965, pp. 477–82; StA Stuttgart, Verfahren Widmann, Ks 19/62 (19 Js 328/60), interrogation Erwin Lambert, 26 Apr. 1961, and continuation, 4 May 1961.

110. See, for example, LG Hagen, Urteil Karl Frenzel, 11 Ks 1/64, 4 Oct. 1985, pp. 5–11, and DÖW, file E18370/1: Bundesministerium für Inneres, Gruppe Staatspolizei, interrogation Matthias Buchberger, 24 Feb. 1964.

111. HHStA, 461/32061/13: StA Frankfurt, Anklage Adolf Wahlmann, Irmgard Huber, 4a Js 3/46, 2 Aug. 1946, pp. 34–35; HHStA, 461/32061/7: LG Frankfurt, Verfahren Adolf Wahlmann, Bodo Gorgaß, Irmgard Huber, 4a KLs 7/47 (4a Js 3/46), Protokoll der öffentlichen Sitzung der 4. Strafkammer, 27 Feb. 1947, pp. 24–25 (testimony Fritz Schirwing).

112. StA Stuttgart, Verfahren Widmann, Ks 19/62 (19 Js 328/60), interrogations Herbert Kalisch, Mannheim, 25 Jan., 22 June 1960.

113. LG Hagen, Urteil Dubois, 11 Ks 1/64, 20 Dec. 1966, p. 275.

114. StA Stuttgart, Verfahren Widmann, Ks 19/62 (19 Js 328/60), interrogation Erwin Lambert, 26 Apr. 1961, and continuation, 4 May 1961.

115. LG Düsseldorf, Urteil Franz, 8 I Ks 2/64, 3 Sept. 1965, p. 478. For his work in Bernburg, see GStA Frankfurt, Anklage Ullrich, Bunke, Borm und Endruweit, Js 15/61 (GStA), 15 Jan. 1965, p. 186; for Hartheim, see DÖW, file E18370/1: StA Frankfurt, Js 18/61 (GStA), interrogation Georg Renno, 3 Feb. 1965, p. 26.

116. LG Hagen, Urteil Dubois, 11 Ks 1/64, 20 Dec. 1966, pp. 268–73.

117. LG Düsseldorf, Urteil Franz, 8 I Ks 2/64, 3 Sept. 1965, p. 480.

118. Arad, *Belzec, Sobibor, Treblinka*, p. 196.

119. LG Düsseldorf, Urteil Franz, 8 I Ks 2/64, 3 Sept. 1965, p. 481; LG Hagen, Urteil Dubois, 11 Ks 1/64, 20 Dec. 1966, pp. 268–73; Scalpelli, *San Sabba*, 1:15.

1. GStA DDR (StA Dresden), Verfahren Paul Nitsche, (S) 1 Ks 58/47 (1/47), Bd. 1: German translation of Soviet interrogation of Paul Nitsche, n.d., and interrogation Paul Nitsche, 25 Mar. 1946.

2. Ibid.: interrogation Paul Nitsche, 26 Mar. 1946; ibid., Bd. 5: interrogation Paul Nitsche, 2 May 1947.

3. See Klee, *Was sie taten—Was sie wurden*, for numerous examples from postwar public testimonies and court decisions.

4. Lifton, *Nazi Doctors*, pp. 17, 123.

5. Ibid., p. 15.

6. Ibid., pp. 114–19.

7. Müller-Hill, *Tödliche Wissenschaft*, p. 87. On the financial position of physicians and their students and on their adherence to the Nazi movement, see Kater, *Doctors under Hitler*, pp. 242–61, tables.

8. Müller-Hill, *Tödliche Wissenschaft*, esp. pp. 87–102.

9. DÖW, file E18370/1: StA Frankfurt, Js 18/61 (GStA), interrogation Georg Renno, 2 Feb. 1965, p. 18.

10. Nuremberg Doc. PS-1696 (emphasis in original).

11. DÖW, file E18370/1: StA Frankfurt, Js 18/61 (GStA), interrogation Georg Renno, 1 Feb. 1965, p. 10.

12. See LG Frankfurt, Urteil Reinhold Vorberg und Dietrich Allers, Ks 2/66 (GStA), 20 Dec. 1968, p. 33.

13. GStA DDR (StA Dresden), Verfahren Nitsche, (S) 1 Ks 58/47 (1/47), Bd. 5: interrogation Paul Nitsche, 2 May 1947.

14. ZStL, Heidelberg Docs. 127,890–93: list of T4 physicians. Only thirteen physicians are listed as serving in the killing centers because Schmalenbach is listed under those serving at T4 headquarters. See also table 5.1.

15. StArch Sigmaringen, Wü 29/3, Acc. 33/1973, Nr. 1752: StA Tübingen, Anklage Otto Mauthe, 1 Js 85–87/47, 4 Jan. 1949, pp. 13–13v; GStA Frankfurt, Anklage Horst Schumann, Js 18/67 (GStA), 12 Dec. 1969, p. 84; Klee, *Was sie taten—Was sie wurden*, p. 95. Postwar court records and secondary works have spelled Baumhard's name as "Baumhardt" with a "t," but his BDC records show "Baumhard" without a "t."

16. Rückerl, *NS-Vernichtungslager*, p. 76; Klee, *Was sie taten—Was sie wurden*, p. 97.

17. DÖW, file E18370/3: Krim. Rev. Inspektor Haas, Bericht an das LG Linz, 25 July 1946, and interrogation Zazilia Dickinger, 5 July 1946.

18. GStA Frankfurt, Anklage Schumann, Js 18/67 (GStA), 12 Dec. 1969, p. 4; Klee, *Was sie taten—Was sie wurden*, pp. 102–7.

19. BDC, dossiers Horst Schumann, Rudolf Lonauer, Irmfried Eberl, and Ernst Baumhard; GStA Frankfurt, Anklage Schumann, Js 18/67 (GStA), 12 Dec. 1969, p. 3. See also Friedlander and Milton, *Berlin Document Center*, pp. xxi, xxviii, xxxi, docs. 10, 12, 96–99. On the spelling of Baumhard's name, see n. 15.

20. GStA Frankfurt, Anklage Schumann, Js 18/67 (GStA), 12 Dec. 1969, pp. 1–3; U.S. Military Tribunal, Transcript of the Proceedings in Case 1, p. 7528 (testimony Viktor Brack); ZStL, interrogation Werner Heyde, Würzburg, 9 Dec. 1959.

21. DÖW, file E18370/3: Krim. Rev. Inspektor Haas, Bericht an das LG Linz, 25 July 1946; DÖW, file E18370/1: StA Frankfurt, interrogation Georg Renno, Js 18/61 (GStA), 1 Feb. 1965, p. 2.

22. GStA Frankfurt, Eberl Akten, II/611, 3:1–13: Eberl's handwritten Lebenslauf, Innsbruck, 4 Nov. 1934, Berlin, 29 Aug. 1937, Berlin, 7 Oct. 1937, and typed Lebenslauf, Dessau,

n.d. See also Eberl's completed Personal- und Fragebogen for the Rassenpolitisches Amt der NSDAP, Bernburg, 18 Mar. 1943 (ibid., II/149, 1:119–21).

23. Ibid., I/673, 2:153–58: Deutsche Arbeitsfront, Personal-Fragebogen, Berlin, 2 Mar. 1940.

24. Ibid., I/677, 2:159: Ruth Eberl to Befehlshaber der Sipo, Paris, 27 Mar. 1943.

25. The circle included, besides Karl Brandt, Herbert Linden, Werner Heyde, and SS Reich Physician Ernst Robert Grawitz, children's euthanasia specialists Hellmuth Unger and Ernst Wentzler, directors of university hospitals Werner Catel, Max de Crinis, and Carl Schneider, and hospital directors Valentin Faltlhauser, Hans Heinze, Berthold Kihn, Paul Nitsche, and Hermann Pfannmüller.

26. GStA Frankfurt, Anklage Schumann, Js 18/67 (GStA), 12 Dec. 1969, p. 120.

27. GStA Frankfurt, Eberl Akten, II/210/1–3, 1:1–3: Irmfried Eberl to Paul Nitsche, 16 Apr. 1942.

28. DÖW, file E18370/1: StA Frankfurt, Js 18/61 (GStA), interrogation Georg Renno, 1 Feb. 1965, pp. 4–5; Mennecke postcards, Munich, 2, 3 Sept. 1941, Leoni am Starnberger See, 3 Sept. 1941, and Mennecke letter, Munich, 3–4 Sept. 1941, in Chroust, *Friedrich Mennecke*, pp. 196–200. See also AMM, B/15/23: statistics on Mauthausen prisoners killed at Hartheim.

29. GStA Frankfurt, Anklage Schumann, Js 18/67 (GStA), 12 Dec. 1969, p. 3; GStA DDR (StA Dresden), Verfahren Nitsche, (S) 1 Ks 58/47 (1/47), Bd. 1: German translation of Soviet interrogation of Paul Nitsche, n.d.; ZStL, Heidelberg Docs. 125,690–92; Nuremberg Doc. NO-208: Werner Blankenburg to Heinrich Himmler, 29 Apr. 1944, with Schumann report.

30. Klee, *"Euthanasie" im NS-Staat*, p. 95. BDC records show that Berner received his medical license in 1931, joined the Nazi party in 1933, and became a member of the SS in 1934.

31. GStA Frankfurt, Anklage Aquilin Ullrich, Heinrich Bunke, Kurt Borm und Klaus Endruweit, Js 15/61 (GStA), 15 Jan. 1965, pp. 211–12; Mennecke letters, Weimar, 30 Nov.–2 Dec. 1941, in Chroust, *Friedrich Mennecke*, pp. 258–70.

32. BDC, dossiers Kurt Borm, Heinrich Bunke, Klaus Endruweit, Hans-Bodo Gorgaß, Georg Renno, Aquilin Ullrich, and Ewald Worthmann; GStA Frankfurt, Anklage Ullrich, Bunke, Borm und Endruweit, Js 15/61 (GStA), 15 Jan. 1965, pp. 1–2, 6–7, 9–10, 14–15; DÖW, file E18370/1: StA Frankfurt, Js 18/61 (GStA), interrogation Georg Renno, 1 Feb. 1965, pp. 1–2; Nuremberg Doc. NO-3010: affidavit Hans-Bodo Gorgaß, 23 Feb. 1947; HHStA, 461/32061/7: LG Frankfurt, Verfahren Adolf Wahlmann, Bodo Gorgaß, Irmgard Huber, 4a KLs 7/47 (4a Js 3/46), Protokoll der öffentlichen Sitzung der 4. Strafkammer, 24 Feb. 1947, pp. 2–3; Klee, *"Euthanasie" im NS-Staat*, p. 119.

There are some discrepancies among the sources. GStA Frankfurt, Anklage Ullrich, Bunke, Borm und Endruweit, Js 15/61 (GStA), 15 Jan. 1965, lists NSDStB and SA membership for Endruweit and SA and Hitler Youth membership for Ullrich, but their BDC records do not show these memberships. Based on a 1965 interrogation of Worthmann by German prosecutors, Klee, in *"Euthanasie" im NS-Staat*, p. 119, reports that Worthmann joined only the SA, but his BDC dossier includes an NSDAP membership file card indicating membership since 1937 and an Ärztekammer file card listing membership in NSDAP and SA.

33. GStA Frankfurt, Anklage Ullrich, Bunke, Borm und Endruweit, Js 15/61 (GStA), 15 Jan. 1965, pp. 9–10, 235.

34. Ibid., pp. 1–3.

35. Ibid., pp. 6–8.

36. Ibid., pp. 14–15.

37. Klee, *"Euthanasie" im NS-Staat*, pp. 119–20.

38. DÖW, file E18370/1: StA Frankfurt, interrogation Georg Renno, Js 18/61 (GStA), 1 Feb. 1965, pp. 1–2; GStA DDR (StA Dresden), Verfahren Nitsche, (S) 1 Ks 58/47 (1/47), Bd. 1: interrogation Paul Nitsche, 26 Mar. 1946; ibid., Bd. 2: interrogation Paul Nitsche, 20 June 1946; LG Dresden, Urteil Hermann Paul Nitsche, 1 Ks 58/47, 7 July 1947, p. 3.

39. HHStA, 461/32061/7: LG Frankfurt, Verfahren Wahlmann, Gorgaß, Huber, 4a KLs 7/47 (4a Js 3/46), Protokoll der öffentlichen Sitzung der 4. Strafkammer, 24 Feb. 1947, pp. 2–3; Winter et al., *Verlegt nach Hadamar*, pp. 109–10.

40. GStA Frankfurt, Anklage Ullrich, Bunke, Borm und Endruweit, Js 15/61 (GStA), 15 Jan. 1965, pp. 3–5, 7–8, 15–16, 218; Klee, *"Euthanasie" im NS-Staat*, p. 119.

41. See the letters and forms concerning Schmalenbach in BDC, Parteikorrespondenz. Schmalenbach's party membership file card at the BDC lists November 1940 as the date he applied for membership and 1 January 1941 as the date he was accepted.

42. GStA Frankfurt, Anklage Ullrich, Bunke, Borm und Endruweit, Js 15/61 (GStA), 15 Jan. 1965, pp. 3–5, 218–22.

43. Ibid., pp. 7–8.

44. Ibid., pp. 15–16, 241.

45. BDC, dossier Kurt Borm: SS Führungshauptamt, SS Sanitätsamt, to KdF, 11 July 1942.

46. DÖW, file E18370/1: StA Frankfurt, Js 18/61 (GStA), interrogation Georg Renno, 1 Feb. 1965, p. 2.

47. Ibid., pp. 56–59, 60–64.

48. HHStA, 461/32061/7: LG Frankfurt, Verfahren Wahlmann, Gorgaß, Huber, 4a KLs 7/47 (4a Js 3/46), Protokoll der öffentlichen Sitzung der 4. Strafkammer, 24 Feb. 1947, pp. 10–15.

49. See, for example, ibid., pp. 3–5 (testimony Hans-Bodo Gorgaß).

50. Ibid., pp. 10, 36.

51. Ibid., p. 12.

52. HHStA, 461/32061/43: Direktor Großmann to Frau Gorgaß, 14 Dec. 1942, 19, 25 Jan. 1943, and Direktor Großmann to Fritz Bernotat, 19 Jan. 1943.

53. HHStA, 461/32061/7: LG Frankfurt, Verfahren Wahlmann, Gorgaß, Huber, 4a KLs 7/47 (4a Js 3/46), Protokoll der öffentlichen Sitzung der 4. Strafkammer, 24 Feb. 1947, p. 12.

54. GStA Frankfurt, Anklage Ullrich, Bunke, Borm und Endruweit, Js 15/61 (GStA), 15 Jan. 1965, pp. 251–52.

55. Ibid., p. 229.

56. Ibid., p. 244.

57. ZStL, Heidelberg Docs. 127,890–93.

58. See table 3.4.

59. Cited in StA München I, Verfahren Hermann Pfannmüller, 1 Ks 10/49 (1b Js 1791/47): GStA München to StA München I, 11 Sept. 1947.

60. U.S. Military Tribunal, Transcript of the Proceedings in Case 1, pp. 7350, 7384. See also NARA, RG 238: interrogations Hermann Pfannmüller, 5 Sept. 1945, p. 8, 21 Sept. 1946, pp. 4–5, 9, and 4 Oct. 1946, pp. 1–6.

61. U.S. Military Tribunal, Transcript of the Proceedings in Case 1, pp. 7305–6. For the Lehner testimony, see ibid., pp. 1538–39, and Nuremberg Doc. NO-863.

62. StA München I, Verfahren Pfannmüller, 1 Ks 10/49 (1b Js 1791/47): Protokoll der öffentlichen Sitzung des Schwurgerichts bei dem LG München I, 20 Oct. 1949, pp. 23–24.

63. U.S. Military Tribunal, Transcript of the Proceedings in Case 1, p. 7348; Schmidt, *Selektion in der Heilanstalt*, p. 114.

64. StA München I, Verfahren Pfannmüller, 1 Ks 10/49 (1b Js 1791/47): Protokoll der öffentlichen Sitzung des Schwurgerichts bei dem LG München I, 19 Oct. 1949, pp. 4–7; NARA, RG 238: interrogation Hermann Pfannmüller, 5 Sept. 1945, pp. 1–2.

65. StA München I, Verfahren Pfannmüller, 1 Ks 10/49 (1b Js 1791/47): Protokoll der

öffentlichen Sitzung des Schwurgerichts bei dem LG München I, 19 Oct. 1949, p. 6.

66. Ibid., pp. 6–7.

67. NARA, RG 238: interrogation Hermann Pfannmüller, 5 Sept. 1945, pp. 1–2, 4.

68. On payment to experts, see ZStL, Heidelberg Doc. 128,217: memo from Werner Heyde and Viktor Brack (Jennerwein), n.d.

69. NARA, RG 238: interrogation Pfannmüller, 5 Sept. 1945, p. 8.

70. StA München I, Verfahren Pfannmüller, 1 Ks 10/49 (1b Js 1791/47): Protokoll der öffentlichen Sitzung des Schwurgerichts bei dem LG München I, 19 Oct. 1949, p. 7.

71. On the number of victims selected by Mennecke, see U.S. Military Tribunal, Transcript of the Proceedings in Case 1, p. 1880.

72. Ibid., p. 1945.

73. Chroust, *Friedrich Mennecke*, pp. 9–12.

74. Ibid., pp. 3–4; BDC, dossier Friedrich Mennecke: Mennecke Reichsärztekammerkarte and Approbationsurkunde (published in Friedlander and Milton, *Berlin Document Center*, docs. 296–97); U.S. Military Tribunal, Transcript of the Proceedings in Case 1, pp. 1866–68 (testimony Friedrich Mennecke); NARA, RG 238, Microfilm Publication M-1019, roll 46: interrogation Friedrich Mennecke, 11 Jan. 1947, pp. 1–3.

75. Chroust, *Friedrich Mennecke*, pp. 4–6; BDC, dossier Friedrich Mennecke: NSDAP master file card, SS-Stammrolle, RuSHA Fragebogen (published in Friedlander and Milton, *Berlin Document Center*, docs. 295, 298–99); U.S. Military Tribunal, Transcript of the Proceedings in Case 1, pp. 1866–68 (testimony Friedrich Mennecke).

76. HHStA, 461/32442/4: LG Frankfurt, Verfahren Friedrich Mennecke, Walter Schmidt, 4 KLs 15/46 (4a Js 13/46), Protokoll der öffentlichen Sitzung der 4. Strafkammer, 10 Dec. 1946, pp. 1–2 (testimony Wilhelm Hinsen); Chroust, *Friedrich Mennecke*, pp. 4–6; NARA, RG 238, Microfilm Publication M-1019, roll 46: interrogation Friedrich Mennecke, 11 Jan. 1947, pp. 3–4.

77. BDC, dossier Friedrich Mennecke: Friedrich Mennecke to RuSHA, 27 Apr. 1937 (published in Friedlander and Milton, *Berlin Document Center*, doc. 300).

78. U.S. Military Tribunal, Transcript of the Proceedings in Case 1, pp. 1868–70, 1916–17; NARA, RG 238, Microfilm Publication M-1019, roll 46: interrogation Friedrich Mennecke, 11 Jan. 1947, pp. 4–5; Chroust, *Friedrich Mennecke*, p. 13, n. 10.

79. NARA, RG 238, Microfilm Publication M-1019, roll 46: interrogation Friedrich Mennecke, 11 Jan. 1947, pp. 12, 14–15, 20–21, 31, 36–37; ZStL, Heidelberg Docs. 127,896–97, 127,903–4, 127,912–13, 128,060–61: Carl Schneider's correspondence concerning Eichberg research.

80. Chroust, *Friedrich Mennecke*. See also Platen-Hallermund, *Die Tötung Geisteskranker*, p. 80.

81. HHStA, 461/32442/4: LG Frankfurt, Verfahren Friedrich Mennecke, Walter Schmidt, 4 KLs 15/46 (4a Js 13/46), Protokoll der öffentlichen Sitzung der 4. Strafkammer, 10 Dec. 1946, pp. 1–2 (testimony Wilhelm Hinsen).

82. ZStL, Heidelberg Doc. 127,419: Friedrich Mennecke to RAG, 19 July 1942; NARA Suitland, Heidelberg Docs. 127,420–21: Bescheinigungen from Carl Schneider for Mennecke and Eva Wehlan, 18 July 1942; HHStA, 461/32442/14: Mennecke to Paul Nitsche, Heidelberg, 2 July 1942; HHStA, 461/32442/2: interrogations Friedrich Mennecke, May 1945.

83. See Platen-Hallermund, *Die Tötung Geisteskranker*, p. 58.

84. BA-MA, H20/463, 465: Bericht über Heil- u. Pflegeanstalt Loben O/S, 3 July 1942.

85. NARA, RG 238, Microfilm Publication M-1019, roll 46: interrogation Friedrich Mennecke, 11 Jan. 1947, pp. 22–25, 36; HHStA, 461/32442/2: interrogations Friedrich Mennecke, May 1945.

86. See BA-MA, H20/463, 465: Friedrich Mennecke to Paul Nitsche, 27 Oct. 1943, reply, 29 Nov. 1943, Mennecke to Nitsche, 3 Dec. 1943, Nitsche to Dietrich Allers, 2 Dec. 1943,

Nitsche to Mennecke, 15 Dec. 1943, Mennecke to Nitsche, 5 Jan. 1944, reply, 12 Jan. 1944, Mennecke to Nitsche, 11 Feb., 17 Apr. 1944, Nitsche to Allers, 20 Apr. 1944, Nitsche to Mennecke, 20 Apr. 1944, Mennecke to Nitsche, 14 Aug. 1944, and reply, 21 Sept. 1944.

87. Correspondence in BDC, Research Collection.

88. See also Platen-Hallermund, *Die Tötung Geisteskranker*, pp. 90–91.

89. Ibid., p. 106.

90. LG Frankfurt, Urteil Vorberg und Allers, Ks 2/66 (GStA), 20 Dec. 1968, p. 36. See also Friedlander, "Manipulation of Language."

91. DÖW, file E18370/1: StA Frankfurt, interrogation Georg Renno, Js 18/61 (GStA), 3 Feb. 1965, pp. 26, 39.

92. See, for example, statements by male and female nurses who collaborated at Hadamar during the period of "wild" euthanasia in NARA Suitland, RG 338, Case File 12-449, United States v. Alfons Klein et al., box 1, file 2: handwritten affidavits by Irmgard Huber, 5 Sept. 1945, and Adolf Merkle, 15 Sept. 1945; ibid., box 1, file 6: interrogation Irmgard Huber, 5 Apr. 1945.

93. See, for example, GStA Berlin, Anklage Hilde Wernicke und Helene Wieczorek, 11 Js 37/45, 5 Feb. 1946, and LG Berlin, Urteil Hilde Wernicke und Helene Wieczorek, 11 Ks 8/46, 25 Mar. 1946.

94. See StA München I, Verfahren Pfannmüller, 1 Ks 10/49 (1b Js 1791/47): Hermann Pfannmüller to StA Oechsner, 16 Sept. 1948; DÖW, file E18370/3: interrogation Anna Lindner, Linz, 11 July 1945.

95. See, for example, StA Hamburg, Anklage Friedrich Lensch und Kurt Struve, 147 Js 58/67, 24 Apr. 1973, pp. 353–56 (Tiegenhof), pp. 382–83 (Meseritz-Obrawalde).

96. On Katschenka, see DÖW, file 18282: VG bei dem LG Wien, Urteil Anna Katschenka, Vg 12g Vr 5442/46 (Hv 301/48), 9 Apr. 1948, LG Wien, interrogations Anna Katschenka, 27 Nov. 1945, 15 Apr., 24 July 1946, and Gutachten for LG Wien on Anna Katschenka by Hofrat Prof. Dr. Ernst Straimler, 12 Oct. 1946.

97. See, for example, DÖW, file E18370/3: Notdienstverpflichtung of Maria Draxler, 19 Dec. 1940.

98. GStA Frankfurt, Anklage Reinhold Vorberg und Dietrich Allers, Js 20/61 (GStA), 15 Feb. 1966, pp. 36–37.

99. LG Hagen, Urteil Werner Dubois, 11 Ks 1/64, 20 Dec. 1966, p. 120.

100. StA Düsseldorf, Anklage Kurt Franz, 8 Js 10904/59, 29 Jan. 1963, p. 47 (August Miete).

101. ZStL, interrogation Franz Suchomel, 5 Feb. 1963; LG Hagen, Urteil Dubois, 11 Ks 1/64, 20 Dec. 1966, pp. 210–13 (Franz Wolf).

102. DÖW, file E18370/3: interrogation Margit Troller, Linz, 25 June 1946.

103. DÖW, file E18370/1: Kreisgericht Wels, interrogation Stefan Schachermeyer, 11 Mar. 1964; DÖW, file E18370/2: VG bei dem LG Linz, Hauptverhandlung Karl Harrer, Leopold Lang und Franz Mayrhuber, Vg 6 Vr 2407/46 (186), 2–3 July 1948, p. 14 (testimony Stefan Schachermeyer).

104. StA Stuttgart, Verfahren Albert Widmann, Ks 19/62 (19 Js 328/60), interrogation Herbert Kalisch, Mannheim, 25 Jan. 1960.

105. DÖW, file E18370/1: StA Frankfurt, Js 18/61 (GStA), interrogations Georg Renno, 1 Feb. 1965, p. 4, 2 Feb. 1965, p. 18, 3 Feb. 1965, p. 29, and 4 Feb. 1965, pp. 31–32.

106. GStA Frankfurt, Anklage Ullrich, Bunke, Borm und Endruweit, Js 15/61 (GStA), 15 Jan. 1965, pp. 182–83, 203, 212.

107. DÖW, file E18370/3: Kriminalpolizei Linz, interrogation Vinzenz Nohel, 4 Sept. 1945 (published in Klamper, *Dokumentationsarchiv*, doc. 28).

108. DÖW, file E18370/1: LG Linz, interrogation Heinrich Barbl, 5 Oct. 1964.

109. Ibid.: StA Frankfurt, Js 18/61 (GStA), interrogation Georg Renno, 1 Feb. 1965, p. 5.

110. StArch Sigmaringen, Wü 29/3, Acc. 33/1973, Nr. 1752: StA Tübingen, Anklage Mauthe, 1 Js 85-87/47, 4 Jan. 1949, pp. 46-47; LG Hagen, Urteil Dubois, 11 Ks 1/64, 20 Dec. 1966, pp. 324-29.

111. DÖW, file E18370/3: Bezirksgericht Ybbs, interrogation Hermann Merta, 3 Dec. 1945.

112. Ibid.: LG Linz, interrogation Karl Harrer, 6 Mar. 1947.

113. StArch Sigmaringen, Wü 29/3, Acc. 33/1973, Nr. 1752: StA Tübingen, Anklage Mauthe, 1 Js 85-87/47, 4 Jan. 1949, pp. 48-49.

114. DÖW, file E18370/3: Bezirksgericht Ybbs, interrogation Maria Raab, 27 Mar. 1946, interrogation Anna Griessenberger, 31 May 1946, interrogation Maria Wittmann, 15 Mar. 1946, and interrogation Hermine Gruber, 15 Mar. 1946.

115. Jäger, *Verbrechen unter totalitärer Herrschaft*, pp. 94-122.

116. Ibid., pp. 155-57.

117. DÖW, file E18370/3: Bezirksgericht Ybbs, interrogation Hermann Merta, 3 Dec. 1945.

118. Ibid.: interrogation Theresa Strauss, Linz, 7 July 1945.

119. Platen-Hallermund, *Die Tötung Geisteskranker*, p. 107.

120. DÖW, file E18370/3: Bezirksgericht Eferding-Grieskirchen, interrogation Aneliese Gindl, 25 July 1947.

121. GStA Frankfurt, Anklage Adolf Gustav Kaufmann, Js 16/63 (GStA), 27 June 1966, p. 31.

122. DÖW, file E18370/2: Bezirksgericht Ybbs, interrogation Franz Sitter, 20 Mar. 1947.

123. DÖW, file E18370/3: Bundespolizeikommissariat, Kriminalbeamtenabteilung, interrogation Karoline Burner, Steyr, 23 Sept. 1946.

124. Ibid.: interrogation Margit Troller, Linz, 25 June 1946.

125. Ibid.: interrogation Emil Reisenberger, Linz, 8 Feb. 1946.

126. Ibid.: Bundesministerium für Inneres, Gruppe Staatspolizei, interrogation Matthias Buchberger, 24 Feb. 1964.

127. HHStA, 461/32061/7: LG Frankfurt, Verfahren Wahlmann, Gorgaß, Huber, 4a KLs 7/47 (4a Js 3/46), Protokoll der öffentlichen Sitzung der 4. Strafkammer, 3 Mar. 1947, p. 32 (testimony Ingeborg Seidel).

128. DÖW, file E18370/1: Bundesministerium für Inneres, interrogation Bruno Bruckner, Vienna, 24 May 1962.

129. See Platen-Hallermund, *Die Tötung Geisteskranker*, p. 61. See also DÖW, file E18370/1: Bundesministerium für Inneres, interrogation Bruno Bruckner, Vienna, 24 May 1962.

130. GStA DDR (StA Dresden), Verfahren Nitsche, (S) 1 Ks 58/47 (1/47), Bd. 5: interrogation Paul Nitsche, 2 May 1947.

131. DÖW, file E18370/3: summary evaluation of Franz Hödl, n.d. [postwar].

132. Sereny, *Into That Darkness*, pp. 188, 236.

133. StA Düsseldorf, Anklage Franz, 8 Js 10904/59, 29 Jan. 1963, pp. 46-47, 151-52; LG Düsseldorf, Urteil Kurt Franz, 8 I Ks 2/64, 3 Sept. 1965, pp. 292-94.

134. LG Hagen, Urteil Dubois, 11 Ks 1/64, 20 Dec. 1966, pp. 342-46.

135. StA Düsseldorf, Anklage Franz, 8 Js 10904/59, 29 Jan. 1963, pp. 49-50; LG Düsseldorf, Urteil Franz, 8 I Ks 2/64, 3 Sept. 1965, pp. 445-48.

136. Sereny, *Into That Darkness*, p. 221.

137. Rückerl, *NS-Vernichtungslager*, p. 230.

138. ZStL, interrogation Kurt Franz, Düsseldorf, 9 May, 5 Dec. 1962; StA Düsseldorf, Anklage Franz, 8 Js 10904/59, 29 Jan. 1963, pp. 41-43; LG Düsseldorf, Urteil Franz, 8 I Ks 2/64, 3 Sept. 1965, pp. 94-97.

139. StA Düsseldorf, Anklage Franz, 8 Js 10904/59, 29 Jan. 1963, pp. 54-55; LG Düsseldorf, Urteil Franz, 8 I Ks 2/64, 3 Sept. 1965, pp. 491-94.

140. LG Hagen, Urteil Dubois, 11 Ks 1/64, 20 Dec. 1966, pp. 210-13.

141. StA Düsseldorf, Anklage Franz, 8 Js 10904/59, 29 Jan. 1963, pp. 48–49; LG Düsseldorf, Urteil Franz, 8 I Ks 2/64, 3 Sept. 1965, pp. 395–98; ZStL, interrogations Franz Suchomel, 24, 25 Oct. 1960, 21 Sept. 1962, 5 Feb. 1963, 24 Apr. 1964, 14, 18 Sept. 1967.

142. DÖW, file E18370: LG Linz, interrogation Heinrich Barbl, 5 Oct. 1964.

143. LG Hagen, Urteil Dubois, 11 Ks 1/64, 20 Dec. 1966, pp. 119–23; LG Hagen, Urteil Karl Frenzel, 11 Ks 1/64, 4 Oct. 1985, pp. 5–11.

144. See Rückerl, NS-Vernichtungslager, p. 64.

145. LG Hagen, Urteil Dubois, 11 Ks 1/64, 20 Dec. 1966, pp. 253–57.

146. StA Düsseldorf, Anklage Franz, 8 Js 10904/59, 29 Jan. 1963, p. 47; LG Düsseldorf, Urteil Franz, 8 I Ks 2/64, 3 Sept. 1965, pp. 335–37.

147. Arad, Belzec, Sobibor, Treblinka, pp. 194–95.

148. LG Hagen, Urteil Dubois, 11 Ks 1/64, 20 Dec. 1966, pp. 346–48.

149. StA Düsseldorf, Anklage Franz, 8 Js 10904/59, 29 Jan. 1963, pp. 44–45; LG Düsseldorf, Urteil Franz, 8 I Ks 2/64, 3 Sept. 1965, pp. 260–62. See also Arad, Belzec, Sobibor, Treblinka, pp. 193–94.

150. StA Düsseldorf, Anklage Franz, 8 Js 10904/59, 29 Jan. 1963, pp. 43–44; LG Düsseldorf, Urteil Franz, 8 I Ks 2/64, 3 Sept. 1965, pp. 241–43. See also Sereny, Into That Darkness, p. 166.

151. StA Düsseldorf, Anklage Franz, 8 Js 10904/59, 29 Jan. 1963, pp. 51–52; LG Düsseldorf, Urteil Franz, 8 I Ks 2/64, 3 Sept. 1965, pp. 505–8. But see also Sereny, Into That Darkness, pp. 86–88.

152. StA Düsseldorf, Anklage Franz, 8 Js 10904/59, 29 Jan. 1963, pp. 53–54.

153. StArch Sigmaringen, Wü 29/3, Acc. 33/1973, Nr. 1752: StA Tübingen, Anklage Mauthe, 1 Js 85–87/47, 4 Jan. 1949, pp. 46–47; LG Hagen, Urteil Dubois, 11 Ks 1/64, 20 Dec. 1966, pp. 324–29.

154. U.S. Military Tribunal, Transcript of the Proceedings in Case 1, p. 2420 (testimony Karl Brandt); GStA DDR (StA Dresden), Verfahren Nitsche, (S) 1 Ks 58/47 (1/47), Bd. 1: interrogation Paul Nitsche, 12 Apr. 1946.

155. U.S. Military Tribunal, Transcript of the Proceedings in Case 1, pp. 7508, 7515–16 (testimony Viktor Brack).

156. Sereny, Into That Darkness, p. 102.

157. LG Hagen, Urteil Dubois, 11 Ks 1/64, 20 Dec. 1966, pp. 242–46.

158. GStA Frankfurt, Anklage Ullrich, Bunke, Borm und Endruweit, Js 15/61 (GStA), 15 Jan. 1965, pp. 253a–b.

159. LG Hagen, Urteil Dubois, 11 Ks 1/64, 20 Dec. 1966, pp. 242–46.

160. Ibid., pp. 300–305.

161. Ibid., pp. 281–84.

162. See, for example, Rückerl, NS-Vernichtungslager, p. 208.

163. For the use of the Milgram experiment as a limited explanation of Nazi behavior, see Browning, Ordinary Men, pp. 171–73.

CHAPTER TWELVE

1. See Pommerin, "Sterilisierung der Rheinlandbastarde." See also Kaupen-Haas, Griff nach der Bevölkerung, pp. 112–14.

2. Pommerin, "Sterilisierung der Rheinlandbastarde," pp. 7–22.

3. Ibid., p. 72.

4. Ibid., pp. 45–48.

5. Ibid., pp. 49–52. See also Bergmann, Czarnowski, and Ehmann, "Objekte humangenetischer Forschung," pp. 131–32.

6. Pommerin, *"Sterilisierung der Rheinlandbastarde,"* pp. 77–84.

7. See Adam, *Judenpolitik*, and Schleunes, *Twisted Road to Auschwitz*. See also Adler, *Der verwaltete Mensch*, pp. 3–57, 91–167, and Hilberg, *Destruction* (1961), pp. 18–174. For the laws, decrees, and regulations, see Walk, *Sonderrecht für die Juden*.

8. Hohmann, *Zigeunerverfolgung in Deutschland*, pp. 13–47.

9. Ibid., pp. 48–84.

10. Staatsministerium des Innern, Erlaß, Munich, 28 Mar. 1899, published in Eiber, *Verfolgung der Sinti und Roma in München*, pp. 14–15.

11. StA Hamburg, Verfahren Ruth Kellermann, 2200 Js 2/84: Preußisches Ministerium des Innern (sig. Bethmann-Hollweg), Verfügung, "Anweisungen zur Bekämpfung des Zigeunerwesens," 17 Feb. 1906.

12. On the anti-Gypsy decree, see Fings and Sparing, *"Z.Zt. Zigeunerlager,"* p. 110. On similar, later (15 June 1938) anti-Jewish decrees, see Walk, *Sonderrecht für die Juden*, p. 229, no. 488.

13. StA Hamburg, Verfahren Kellermann, 2200 Js 2/84: Preußisches MdI circular, "Fingerabdruckverfahren bei Zigeunern," 3 Nov. 1927.

14. For background, see August Fraser, *The Gypsies*, 2d ed. (Oxford: Blackwell, 1995).

15. See Eiber, *Verfolgung der Sinti und Roma in München*, pp. 21–45.

16. BDC, dossier Robert Ritter: Lebenslauf, n.d., and Ärztekammer file card; Hohmann, *Robert Ritter*, pp. 133–36.

17. The BDC holds no membership card for Ritter in the Nazi party or its formations. Letters of recommendation for Ritter from the RuSHA, 4, 8 Aug. 1941, mention his qualifications but no party connections. His Ärztekammer file card has the entry "no" under Nazi party membership and NS-Ärztebund and lists "Führungskorps der H.J." under party formations.

18. BAK, R73/14005: Robert Ritter to DFG, 2 Feb. 1938, 22 Feb. 1939.

19. Ibid.: Ernst Rüdin to DFG, 14 Mar. 1935, Hans Reiter to DFG, 16 June 1937, 2 Feb. 1938, 22 Feb. 1939, and Herbert Linden to DFG, 9, 15 Sept. 1937.

20. Ibid.: Ritter Arbeitsbericht, with cover letter from Robert Ritter to Sergius Breuer, 20 Jan. 1940.

21. BDC, dossier Robert Ritter: Lebenslauf, n.d.; Hohmann, *Robert Ritter*, pp. 136–37, 146–48.

22. For other members of Ritter's team, see Hohmann, *Robert Ritter*, pp. 232–329.

23. Gilsenbach, "Wie Lolitschai zur Doktorwürde kam," p. 103.

24. BAK, R73/14005: DFG Fragebogen for Eva Justin, 5 Jan. 1942, and Privat-Dienstvertrag between Dr. Ritter and Eva Justin, 4 Jan. 1942.

25. Gilsenbach, "Wie Lolitschai zur Doktorwürde kam," p. 113.

26. Ibid., p. 114. Her dissertation was entitled "Lebensschicksale artfremd erzogener Zigeunerkinder und ihrer Nachkommen," accepted at the University of Berlin on 5 November 1943, and published in 1944 (oral examination on 24 March 1943 by Eugen Fischer, Richard Thurnwald, Robert Ritter, and Wolfgang Abel).

27. Gilsenbach, "Wie Lolitschai zur Doktorwürde kam," pp. 112–15; Bergmann, Czarnowski, and Ehmann, "Objekte humangenetischer Forschung," p. 133. In her dissertation, all three sponsors are listed as equal "Berichterstatter."

28. ZStL, interrogation Adolf Würth, Stuttgart, 5 Dec. 1984 (published in Friedlander and Milton, *Zentrale Stelle*, doc. 116). See also Müller-Hill, *Tödliche Wissenschaft*, pp. 152–57 (interview with Adolf Würth).

29. Hohmann, *Robert Ritter*, pp. 323–24; ZStL, interrogation Sophie Ehrhardt, Tübingen, 6 May 1982 (published in Friedlander and Milton, *Zentrale Stelle*, doc. 117).

30. See Hohmann, *Robert Ritter*, pp. 185–217.

31. On Goddard and the Kallikak family, see Gould, *Mismeasure of Man*, pp. 168–74. On Ritter's evaluation of Goddard's research, see BAK, R73/14005: Ritter report, n.d., with cover letter from Hildegard Ritter, 2 Mar. 1935, pp. 14–20.

32. BAK, R73/14005: Robert Ritter to DFG, 25 June 1940. Some of these records are now deposited in BAK, R165. See also Regener, "Ausgegrenzt," pp. 23–38.

33. Allen, "Eugenics Record Office," p. 244.

34. BAK, R73/14005: Ritter report, n.d., with cover letter from Hildegard Ritter, 2 Mar. 1935.

35. Eiber, *Verfolgung der Sinti und Roma in München*, p. 59.

36. See BAK, R73/14005: Ritter Arbeitsbericht, with cover letter from Robert Ritter to Sergius Breuer, 20 Jan. 1940, p. 3.

37. See, for example, StA Hamburg, Verfahren Kellermann, 2200 Js 2/84: RFSS circular, "Bekämpfung der Zigeunerplage," 8 Dec. 1938.

38. BAK, R73/14005: Paul Werner to DFG, 6 Jan. 1940.

39. See Müller-Hill, *Tödliche Wissenschaft*, pp. 135–51.

40. StA Hamburg, Verfahren Kellermann, 2200 Js 2/84: RFSS circular, "Auswertung der rassenbiologischen Gutachten über zigeunerische Personen," 7 Aug. 1941. See also Eiber, *Verfolgung der Sinti und Roma in München*, p. 59.

41. Walk, *Sonderrecht für die Juden*, p. 12, no. 46.

42. Milton, "Nazi Policies toward Roma and Sinti," p. 2.

43. Bock, *Zwangssterilisation*, p. 362.

44. Milton, "Nazi Policies toward Roma and Sinti," pp. 4–5.

45. Kreisleitung NSDAP, Kreis Groß-Frankfurt, to Polizeipräsident Frankfurt, 16 Nov. 1936, cited in Wippermann, *Nationalsozialistische Zigeunerverfolgung*, p. 76. See also Hase-Mihalik and Kreuzkamp, *Du kriegst auch einen schönen Wohnwagen*, chap. 3.

46. Fings and Sparing, "Das Zigeunerlager in Köln-Bickendorf," pp. 15–28.

47. Fings and Sparing, "Z.Zt. Zigeunerlager," pp. 36–37.

48. Bruckner-Boroujerdi and Wippermann, "Das 'Zigeunerlager' Berlin-Marzahn."

49. See Klamper, *Dokumentationsarchiv*, doc. 55: letter from Bezirkshauptmannschaft, Zell am See, to Landeshauptmannschaft, Salzburg, 22 Aug. 1938, and ibid., doc. 60: letter from Gendarmeriestation, Weißbach bei Lofer, to Gendarmerieinspektion, Zell am See, 29 May 1939.

50. Thurner, *Zigeuner in Österreich*, pp. 36–49.

51. See Klamper, *Dokumentationsarchiv*, docs. 66–68: correspondence between Anton Böhmer, Sturmbannführer and Kriminalrat of the Salzburg Kripo, and the Salzburg Gaufürsorgeamt concerning Gypsies used by Riefenstahl-Film G.m.b.H. with name lists, 4, 19 Oct. 1940.

52. Thurner, *Zigeuner in Österreich*, pp. 60–167. See also Klamper, *Dokumentationsarchiv*, docs. 85–88.

53. For use of these terms, see BAK, R18/5644: Dr. Zindel to Hans Pfundtner, 4 Mar. 1936, and Leonardo Conti circular, 24 Jan. 1940.

54. Ibid.: Dr. Zindel to Hans Pfundtner, 4 Mar. 1936, with attached report, "Gedanken über den Aufbau des Reichszigeunergesetzes."

55. StA Hamburg, Verfahren Kellermann, 2200 Js 2/84: RMdI circular, "Bekämpfung der Zigeunerplage," 6 June 1936.

56. Ibid.: RFSS circular, "Bekämpfung der Zigeunerplage," 13 May 1938.

57. Ibid.: RKPA to Kripoleitstelle Wien, "Vorbeugende Maßnahmen zur Bekämpfung der Zigeunerplage im Burgenland," 5 June 1939.

58. See BAK, R36/1022: Gewährung öffentlicher Fürsorge an Juden und Zigeuner.

59. *Reichsgesetzblatt* 1939, 1:1097. See Walk, *Sonderrecht für die Juden*, p. 297, no. 211 (copy in BAK, R36/1022).

60. BAK, R36/1022: RMdI internal memo, 6 Oct. 1941.

61. See, for example, ibid.: Stadt Magdeburg, Fürsorge- und Jugendamt, to DGT, 9 Sept. 1942, and reply, 10 Nov. 1942.

62. See RMdI circular, 5 June 1936, published in Hase-Mihalik and Kreuzkamp, *Du kriegst auch einen schönen Wohnwagen*, pp. 43–44.

63. Milton, "Nazi Policies toward Roma and Sinti," p. 6.

64. BAK, R58/473: listing of structure of RKPA, n.d., including Reichszentrale with brief description of function. For the collaboration between the RKPA and Ritter, see StA Hamburg, Verfahren Kellermann, 2200 Js 2/84: RKPA, Ausführungsanweisungen, 1 Mar. 1939. For local Kripo Gypsy bureaus, see HHStA, 407/875: Kriminaldirektion Frankfurt, "Anweisungen zur Errichtung einer Zigeuner-Nachrichtenstelle," 25 Mar. 1939.

65. No complete collection of anti-Gypsy decrees has been published. The most important circulars and announcements were collected for postwar prosecutions. I have used the collection assembled by StA Hamburg as part of the Kellermann proceedings (2200 Js 2/84). A similar, but not identical, collection has recently become available at the United States Holocaust Memorial Museum as the Fojn-Felczer Collection.

66. StA Hamburg, Verfahren Kellermann, 2200 Js 2/84: RMdI circular, "Vorbeugende Verbrechensbekämpfung durch die Polizei," 14 Dec. 1937. See also ibid.: RKPA to Kripo-(leit)stellen, 1 June 1938. For the continued presence of Gypsies in the camps, see DÖW, file 1212: list of members of Zigeunertransport transferred from KL Buchenwald to KL Mauthausen, 28 June, 4 July 1941.

67. StA Hamburg, Verfahren Kellermann, 2200 Js 2/84: RKPA circular (sig. Heydrich), 4 Apr. 1938.

68. United States Holocaust Memorial Museum, Fojn-Felczer Collection: RSHA Amt V (RKPA) to all Kripo(leit)stellen, 20 Nov. 1939.

69. Gütt, Linden, and Maßfeller, *Blutschutz- und Ehegesundheitsgesetz* (2d rev. ed.), pp. 16, 21, 150, 226; Stuckart and Globke, *Reichsbürgergesetz*, p. 153.

70. Cited in Milton, "Nazi Policies toward Roma and Sinti," p. 2.

71. See StA Hamburg, Verfahren Kellermann, 2200 Js 2/84: RMdI circular, "Ehegenehmigungsanträge von Zigeunermischlingen auf Grund des §6 der ersten Ausführungsverordnung zum Blutschutzgesetz," 20 June 1941.

72. Klamper, *Dokumentationsarchiv*, doc. 1.

73. See StA Hamburg, Verfahren Kellermann, 2200 Js 2/84: RSHA circular, 21 Nov. 1941, transmitting circular of Reichsminister für Wissenschaft, Erziehung und Volksbildung, 22 Mar. 1941, Reichsarbeitsministerium circular (sig. Seldte), 13 Mar. 1942, and RFSS circular, "Arbeitseinsatz von Zigeunern und Zigeunermischlingen," 13 July 1942; and Klamper, *Dokumentationsarchiv*, doc. 73.

74. See, for example, Strauss, "Jewish Emigration from Germany."

75. Moser, "Nisko," pp. 1–30. See also Adler, *Der verwaltete Mensch*, pp. 126–40.

76. Adler, *Der verwaltete Mensch*, pp. 140–43.

77. Breitman, *Architect of Genocide*, p. 133.

78. Adler, *Der verwaltete Mensch*, pp. 155–60.

79. Ibid., pp. 147–52.

80. StA Hamburg, Verfahren Kellermann, 2200 Js 2/84: RSHA Schnellbrief to Kripo-(leit)stellen, 17 Oct. 1939.

81. Friedlander and Milton, *Zentrale Stelle*, doc. 33.

82. Ibid., doc. 34.

83. Ibid., doc. 37.

84. BAK, R58/473: Heydrich circular, "Umsiedlung von Zigeunern," 27 Apr. 1940.

85. StA Hamburg, Verfahren Kellermann, 2200 Js 2/84: RKPA circular, "Richtlinien für die Umsiedlung von Zigeunern," 27 Apr. 1940.

86. Zimmermann, *Verfolgt, Vertrieben, Vernichtet*, p. 45; Müller-Hill, *Murderous Science*, pp. 153–54. For details about the Hohenasperg deportations, see HHStA, 407/863.

87. For expected Austrian deportations, see Klamper, *Dokumentationsarchiv*, doc. 65. For the resistance of the General Government to deportations, see Präg and Jakobmeyer, *Diensttagebuch des deutschen Generalgouverneurs in Polen*, pp. 93, 146–47, 158, 262.

CHAPTER THIRTEEN

1. U.S. Military Tribunal, Transcript of the Proceedings in Case 1, pp. 7596–99, 7602, 7616–19, 7621; NARA, RG 238, Microfilm Publication M-1019, roll 8: interrogation Viktor Brack, 4 Sept. 1946 A.M., p. 7.

2. U.S. Military Tribunal, Transcript of the Proceedings in Case 1, p. 2413.

3. Ibid., pp. 7295–97, 7322, 7334–35, 7375–77; NARA, RG 238, Microfilm Publication M-1019, roll 52: interrogation Hermann Pfannmüller, 4 Oct. 1946, pp. 1–6.

4. See, for example, Hilberg, *Destruction* (1961), p. 292 (ibid. [1985], pp. 449–50).

5. See GStA Frankfurt, "Schlußvortrag der Staatsanwaltschaft bei dem Oberlandesgericht Frankfurt/Main in der Strafsache gegen Dietrich Allers und Reinhold Vorberg," p. 179b.

6. For background, see Hoss, "Die jüdischen Patienten," pp. 60–64, and Hühn, "Schicksal der jüdischen Patienten."

7. Schabow, *Juden in Bendorf*, pp. 13–16.

8. Founded in 1933, at first with the name of Reich Representation of the Jewish State Associations in Germany (Reichsvertretung der jüdischen Landesverbände Deutschlands), and soon thereafter renamed Reich Representation of German Jews (Reichsvertretung der deutschen Juden), the organization served as the federal umbrella established by Jewish organizations in Germany to represent the Jewish community vis-à-vis the German government. Reflecting the Nazi government's attitude that Jews were not a part of the German community regardless of citizenship, the name had to be changed after the Nuremberg racial laws of 1935 from "of German Jews" (der deutschen Juden) to "of Jews in Germany" (der Juden in Deutschland). On 4 July 1939, the Tenth Decree to the Reich Citizenship Law created the Reich Association of Jews in Germany (Reichsvereinigung der Juden in Deutschland) to replace the Reichsvertretung; it was to serve as the only group representing German Jews. On the creation of the Reich Association of Jews in Germany, see Walk, *Sonderrecht für die Juden*, p. 297, no. 211. For the full text, see BAK, R36/1022: Zehnte Verordnung zum Reichsbürgergesetz vom 4. Juli 1939.

9. On the Berlin Jewish hospital, see Leo Baeck Institute, New York, Memoir Collection: Herman O. Pineas, "Unser Schicksal seit dem 30. 1. 1933," p. 24. On the Jewish ward of the Heil- und Pflegeanstalt Lohr, which provided services for observant Jews, see BAK, R36/1842: Archiv für Wohlfahrtspflege to DGT, 25 Nov. 1938.

10. Verordnung über die öffentliche Fürsorge für Juden, 19 Nov. 1938, text in LA Berlin, Rep. 214, Acc. 794, Nr. 13. For veterans, see ibid.: *Dienstblatt* 1938, VII/373. See also Walk, *Sonderrecht für die Juden*, p. 257, no. 20.

11. Zehnte Verordnung zum Reichsbürgergesetz, 4 July 1939, text in BAK, R36/1022. See also Walk, *Sonderrecht für die Juden*, p. 297, no. 211.

12. See LA Berlin, Rep. 214, Acc. 794, Nr. 13: RMdI and Reichsarbeitsministerium circular, "Durchführung der Verordnung über die öffentliche Fürsorge für Juden," 25 May 1939, and BAK, R36/1022: DGT to Fürsorgeamt Frankfurt, 16 Feb. 1940, and RMdI to DGT, 20 July 1942.

13. See LA Berlin, Rep. 214, Acc. 794, Nr. 13: *Dienstblatt* 1938, VII/395.

14. For the agreement, see ibid. and BAK, R36/1022: Oberbürgermeister Berlin circular

to Bezirksbürgermeister, Wohlfahrts- und Jugendämter, "Betr.: Betreuung hilfsbedürftiger Juden vom 1. 5. 1939 ab."

15. BAK, R36/1022: Bezirksfürsorgeverband Reichshauptstadt Berlin, Wohlfahrts- und Jugendamt, Berlin-Weissensee, to DGT, 30 June 1939, Oberbürgermeister der Reichshauptstadt Berlin, Hauptwohlfahrtsamt, to DGT, 12 July 1939, 26 Feb. 1940, Oberbürgermeister der Kreisstadt Zwickau, Wohlfahrtsamt, to DGT, 28 Aug. 1939, and DGT to Hauptwohlfahrtsamt Berlin and Wohlfahrtsamt Zwickau, draft, Oct. 1940.

16. See, for example, Hoss, "Die jüdischen Patienten," p. 69.

17. BAK, R36/1022: Oberpräsident der Provinz Hannover, Verwaltung des Provinzialverbandes, to RMdI, 10 July 1939.

18. Ibid.: draft contract between Oberkantor Samuel Herskovits and Landesfürsorgeverband der Provinz Hannover, July 1939.

19. Ibid.: Landrat des Kreises Delitzsch, Bezirksfürsorgeverband, to DGT, 26 Sept. 1940.

20. Ibid.: Oberbürgermeister Heidelberg to Baden MdI, 9 Nov. 1940, Baden MdI to Wohlfahrts- und Jugendamt Heidelberg, 30 Nov. 1940, and DGT, Landesdienststelle Baden, to DGT, 9 Jan. 1941.

21. Ibid.: Wohlfahrtsamt, Kriegsfürsorge, Munich, to Staatsministerium des Innern, Munich, 23 Oct. 1940, and RMdI to Bayerisches Staatsministerium des Innern, 20 Mar. 1941.

22. Ibid.: DGT to Verwaltung des Provinzialverbandes, Provinz Hannover, 18 Mar. 1941, DGT to RMdI, 18 Mar. 1941, and RMdI to DGT, 20 July 1942.

23. StA Hamburg, Verfahren Friedrich Lensch und Kurt Struve, 147 Js 58/67, Sonderband Alsterdorfer Anstalten betr. Juden-Entlassungen: Abschrift aus *Wirtschaftsbriefe für die Anstaltsleitung*, Jg. 1938, Heft 1 (Jan.).

24. See BAK, R36/1842: Verwaltung des schlesischen Provinzialverbandes, Landeswohlfahrtsamt, Breslau, to DGT, 10 Jan. 1939, and HStA Stuttgart, Bestand J355, Büchel 259: Israelitisches Fürsorgeamt, Stuttgart, to Württemberg MdI, Stuttgart, 12 Apr. 1939.

25. StA Hamburg, Verfahren Lensch und Struve, 147 Js 58/67, Sonderband Alsterdorfer Anstalten betr. Juden-Entlassungen: Gesundheits- und Fürsorgebehörde, Fürsorgewesen, Ärztliche Abteilung, Hamburg, to Alsterdorfer Anstalten, Hamburg, 11 Aug. 1937.

26. Ibid.: Alsterdorfer Anstalten to Gesundheits- und Fürsorgebehörde, Fürsorgewesen, Ärztliche Abteilung, Hamburg, 21 Aug. 1937.

27. Ibid.: Psychiatrische und Nervenklinik der Hansischen Universität to Gesundheits- und Fürsorgebehörde, Fürsorgewesen, Ärztliche Abteilung, 13 Jan. 1938.

28. Ibid.: Gesundheits- und Fürsorgebehörde, Fürsorgewesen, Ärztliche Abteilung, to Ricklinger Anstalten, 25 Feb. 1938.

29. Ibid.: Landesverein für Innere Mission in Schleswig-Holstein, Kiel, to Pastor Friedrich Lensch, Hamburg-Alsterdorf, 7 Mar. 1938.

30. Ibid.: Friedrich Lensch to Dr. Epha, 9 Mar. 1938.

31. Ibid.: Alsterdorfer Anstalten to Gesundheits- und Fürsorgebehörde, Fürsorgewesen, Ärztliche Abteilung, Hamburg, 3 Sept. 1937, 30 Mar. 1938, Alsterdorfer Anstalten to Jugendamt, 30 Mar. 1938, Alsterdorfer Anstalten to Dr. Jahn, Sozialverwaltung, 24 Oct. 1938, and Alsterdorfer Anstalten to Versorgungsheim Oberaltenallee, 29 Oct. 1938.

32. BAK, R36/1842: DGT Vermerk, 20 Mar. 1939.

33. See Wunder and Jenner, "Alsterdorfer Anstalten," pp. 155–61.

34. BAK, R36/1842: RMdI circular (sig. Pfundtner), "Mißstände in Krankenanstalten," 22 June 1938.

35. Ibid.: Provinzialverband Schlesien to DGT, 10 Oct., 21 Dec. 1938, Provinzialverband Brandenburg to DGT, 5 Nov. 1938, Provinzialverband Hohenzollern-Sigmaringen to DGT, 9 Nov. 1938, Provinzialverband Schleswig-Holstein to DGT, 12 Nov. 1938, Provinzialver-

band Provinz Sachsen to DGT, 17 Nov. 1938, Provinzialverband Pommern to DGT, 25 Nov. 1938, Provinzialverband Ostpreußen to DGT, 29 Nov. 1938, and Provinzialverband Westfalen to DGT, 7 Dec. 1938.

36. Ibid.: Provinzialverband Nassau (sig. Bernotat) to DGT, 17 Nov. 1938.

37. Finzen, *Auf dem Dienstweg*, pp. 23–25.

38. HStA Stuttgart, Bestand J355, Büchel 259: Israelitisches Fürsorgeamt, Stuttgart, to Württemberg MdI, Stuttgart, 12 Apr. 1939. See also ibid., Büchel 252: Jüdische Nothilfe to Württemberg MdI, 4 Aug. 1939.

39. Ibid., Büchel 252: Heilanstalt Weinsberg to Württemberg MdI, 5 May 1939.

40. Ibid.: Mauthe memo, 20 May 1939, and Stähle draft letter, 15 May 1939.

41. See ibid.: Heilanstalt Rottenmünster to Württemberg MdI, 26 May 1939.

42. Ibid.: Württembergische Heilanstalt Zwiefalten to Württemberg MdI, 31 May 1939, and handwritten notes on Zwiefalten letter.

43. Ibid.: Heil- und Pflegeanstalt für Schwachsinnige und Epileptische, Stetten, to Württemberg MdI, 29 June 1939.

44. See ibid.: Württembergische Heilanstalt Zwiefalten to Württemberg MdI, 21 Aug. 1939, and Heil- und Pflegeanstalt für Schwachsinnige und Epileptische, Stetten, to Württemberg MdI, 29 June 1939.

45. Ibid., Büchel 259: Württemberg MdI to Heil- und Pflegeanstalt für Schwachsinnige und Epileptische, Stetten, 4 July 1939.

46. Ibid., Büchel 262: Zentralleitung für das Stiftungs- und Anstaltswesen in Württemberg, Stuttgart, to Württemberg MdI, 25 Oct. 1939, and handwritten answer. See also Sauer, *Dokumente*, 2:130.

47. HStA Stuttgart, Bestand J355, Büchel 252: Württemberg MdI to Jüdische Nothilfe, 18 Dec. 1939.

48. Ibid.: Hanne Leus to Württemberg MdI, 18 Apr. 1940. The handwritten German marginalia reads as follows: "Fort!: Und die Frauen u. Kinder der gefallenen deutschen Männer! Die Urheber des Krieges ist dieses Gesindel der kein Mitleid verdient! Siehe Polenfeldzug!!"

49. StA Hamburg, Verfahren Lensch und Struve, 147 Js 58/67, Sonderband Alsterdorfer Anstalten betr. Juden-Entlassungen: LG Hamburg, Entschädigungskammer 1, Beschluß in der Entschädigungssache Gerda B., 26 June 1964; GStA Frankfurt, Eberl Akten, I/472/2, 2:59: Protokoll über Willy Abramowicz, n.d. [postwar].

50. LA Berlin, Rep. 214, Acc. 794, Nr. 13: Oberbürgermeister Berlin circular (sig. Conti), 27 Apr. 1938, citing RMdI regulations, and *Dienstblatt* 1938, VII/395. See also Walk, *Sonderrecht für die Juden*, p. 367, no. 323, for the RMdI circular, 19 Mar. 1942, prohibiting further sterilization of Jews under the sterilization law.

51. Nuremberg Docs. NO-720, NO-1135.

52. For accounts that accept the deception, see Hilberg, *Destruction* (1961), p. 292 (ibid. [1985], pp. 449–50), and Lifton, *Nazi Doctors*, pp. 77–78. For accounts that do not accept the deception, see GStA Frankfurt, Anklage Werner Heyde, Gerhard Bohne und Hans Hefelmann, Ks 2/63 (GStA), Js 17/59 (GStA), 22 May 1962, pp. 448–71, and Klee, *"Euthanasie" im NS-Staat*, pp. 258–63. See also Friedlander, "Jüdische Anstaltspatienten," pp. 34–44.

53. BAK, R36/1022: Reichsvereinigung der Juden in Deutschland to Oberbürgermeister Königsberg, Wohlfahrtsamt, 24 May 1940. See also ZStL, 208 AR-Z 268/59, Bd. V, Bl. 20–21: interrogation Gerhard Simon, 5 Dec. 1962. Simon remembered handling about 3,000 to 4,000 files of murdered Jewish patients.

54. Published by the Archivdirektion Stuttgart in 1969. See also Sauer, *Schicksale*, pp. 263–65.

55. Archivdirektion Stuttgart, *Opfer der nationalsozialistischen Judenverfolgung*, p. 219.

56. Ibid., pp. 41, 160.

57. Ibid., p. 106; HStA Stuttgart, Bestand J355, Büchel 252: Moritz "Israel" Gundelfinger to Landes-Fürsorgeanstalt Markgröningen, 19 Dec. 1940.

58. Nuremberg Doc. NO-3356. For the first transport, see Klee, *"Euthanasie" im NS-Staat*, p. 136, and Richarz, *Heilen, Pflegen, Töten*, pp. 154–55, neither of whom, however, mentions the Jewish patient.

59. BAK, R36/1022: Jugend- und Fürsorgeamt Halle to DGT, 6 Jan. 1942.

60. See GStA Frankfurt, "Schlußvortrag der Staatsanwaltschaft bei dem Oberlandes-gericht Frankfurt/Main in der Strafsache gegen Dietrich Allers und Reinhold Vorberg," pp. 163–79b. See also Schmidt, *Selektion in der Heilanstalt*, p. 73.

61. GStA Frankfurt, Sammlung Euthanasie: Israelitische Kultusverwaltung, Aschaffen-burg, to Heil- und Pflegeanstalt Lohr, 8, 11 Apr. 1940 (for report to Stapo Würzburg).

62. For copies of the circular, see ibid.: RMdI (sig. Linden) to Württemberg MdI, 15 Apr. 1940, and StA Hamburg, Verfahren Lensch und Struve, 147 Js 58/67, Gesundheitsbehörde, Bd. 1: RMdI (sig. Linden) to Reichsstatthalter in Hamburg, 15 Apr. 1940.

63. StA Hamburg, Verfahren Lensch und Struve, 147 Js 58/67, Gesundheitsbehörde, Bd. 1: correspondence, pp. 17–29.

64. Ibid.: RMdI (sig. Linden) to Reichsstatthalter in Hamburg, 12 June 1940.

65. Ibid.: Staatsverwaltung der Hansestadt Hamburg to RMdI, 25 June 1940.

66. Ibid.: "Aufstellung," p. 32.

67. Staatsarchiv Potsdam (today Bundesarchiv-Potsdam), Provinz Brandenburg, Rep. 55c, Neuruppin, Akte 42: Regierungpräsident Potsdam to Brandenburgische Landesanstalt Neuruppin, 20 Apr. 1940, transmitting Linden circular.

68. Ibid.: Gekrat to Brandenburgische Landesanstalt Neuruppin, 7 June 1940. Copies kindly provided by Dr. Götz Aly, Berlin.

69. Dokumentationszentrum der Staatlichen Archivverwaltung der DDR, Dok./K891: Oberpräsident der Provinz Brandenburg, Verwaltung des Provinzialverbandes, to Bran-denburgische Landesanstalt Neuruppin, 12 July 1940.

70. Böhme and Meyer, "Schicksal jüdischer Anstaltspatienten," pp. 7–8.

71. Dokumentationszentrum der Staatlichen Archivverwaltung der DDR, Dok./K891: Städtische Heil- und Pflegeanstalt Buch to Brandenburgische Landesanstalt Neuruppin, 22 July 1940.

72. GStA Frankfurt, Sammlung Euthanasie: Verwaltung des Provinzialverbandes, Kiel, to Landesheilanstalt Neustadt in Holstein, 6 Sept. 1940, transmitting Oberpräsident der Provinz Schleswig-Holstein to Provinzialverband, Kiel, 3 Sept. 1940, including RMdI to Oberpräsident der Provinz Schleswig, 6 Sept. 1940.

73. Ibid.: Landesheilanstalt Neustadt in Holstein to Verwaltung des Provinzialverbandes, Kiel, 10 Sept. 1940.

74. Ibid.: Landesheilanstalt Neustadt in Holstein to Heil- und Pflegeanstalt Hamburg-Langenhorn, 14 Sept. 1940.

75. See also *Die jüdischen Opfer des Nationalsozialismus in Hamburg*, pp. 84–87.

76. GStA Frankfurt, Sammlung Euthanasie: Staatsministerium des Innern, Munich, to Heil- und Pflegeanstalt Lohr, 4 Sept. 1940.

77. Ibid.: Bahnhof Lohr to Plegeanstalt Lohr, 13 Sept. 1940, and list of Jewish patients transferred on 16 Sept. 1940.

78. Cited in Schmidt, *Selektion in der Heilanstalt*, p. 74.

79. Nuremberg Doc. NO-1135: transport list of Jewish patients from Eglfing-Haar, 20 Sept. 1940; ibid. NO-720: affidavit Moritz Schmidtmann, 8 Nov. 1946, and postwar compilation of total Jewish transport list from institutional files, 8 Nov. 1946.

80. Ibid. NO-1310: Hermann Pfannmüller to Bayerisches Staatsministerium, Abteilung Gesundheitswesen, 20 Sept. 1940.

81. DÖW, file E19198: Reichsgau Wien, Hauptgesundheitsamt, Hauptabteilung E to

Hauptgesundheitsamt, 26 Oct. 1942; Israelitische Kultusgemeinde Wien, "Monatsbericht August 1940," kindly provided by Dr. Jonny Moser, Vienna.

82. Finzen, *Auf dem Dienstweg*, pp. 24–25.

83. Ibid., p. 27, facsimile reproduction of Schnellbrief from RMdI to Oberpräsident Hannover, 10 Sept. 1940.

84. Ibid., p. 32. See also *JuNSV*, vol. 7, no. 226: LG Hannover, Urteil 2 Ks 9/49, 29 July 1950.

85. Klüppel, *Haina und Merxhausen*, pp. 33–34, and facsimile documents, pp. 35–37.

86. Nuremberg Doc. PS-3871: Gekrat to Dr. Herz'sche Privatklinik, Bonn, 15 Jan. 1941.

87. Ibid.: Gesundheitsamt des Stadtkreises Bonn to Dr. Hertz'sche Privatklinik Bonn, 29 Jan. 1941.

88. Ibid.: list of transferred patients, 10 Feb. 1941.

89. Ibid. PS-3883: Provinzial-Heil- und Pflegeanstalt Andernach to Office of U.S. Chief of Counsel, Nuremberg, 8 Apr. 1946. See also GStA Frankfurt, interrogation Johann Recktenwald (director Andernach), 17 May 1961, and Hoss, "Die jüdischen Patienten," p. 72.

90. Nuremberg Doc. NO-1143 contains numerous such letters from Eglfing-Haar to welfare offices, insurance companies, and state attorneys (copies in Boston University Library, Leo Alexander Collection, box 57).

91. The following Wunstorf information is based on the correspondence cited in Finzen, *Auf dem Dienstweg*, pp. 41–60.

92. The Reichsvereinigung correspondence is cited ibid., pp. 57–58.

93. GStA Frankfurt, Sammlung Euthanasie: Gekrat to Heil- und Pflegeanstalt Lohr, 21 Feb. 1941.

94. See, for example, StA München I, Verfahren Hermann Pfannmüller, 1 Ks 10/49 (1b Js 1791/47): Protokoll der öffentlichen Sitzung des Schwurgerichts bei dem LG München I, 19 Oct. 1949, p. 11 (testimony Hermann Pfannmüller); GStA DDR (StA Dresden), Verfahren Paul Nitsche, (S) 1 Ks 58/47 (1/47), Bd. 1: interrogation Paul Nitsche, 26 Mar. 1946.

95. For the Chelm spelling, see letter in DÖW, file 4608, and in ZStL, Sammlung Verschiedenes, Bd. 2. For the Cholm spelling, see facsimile letter in Finzen, *Auf dem Dienstweg*, p. 59.

96. See, for example, the following documents involving notices from Chelm: Nuremberg Doc. NO-3354: Frieda Kahn to Eglfing-Haar (concerning her sister Meta Frankenberg), 2 Mar. 1941; ibid. NO-1141: Franz Frühbeißer, Rechtsbeistand, to Eglfing-Haar (concerning Berta Wertheimer), 25 Apr. 1941; and BAK, R22/5021: Oberamtsrichter Coesfeld to Landgerichtspräsident Münster (concerning "Jüdin" Oppenheimer), 26 July 1941.

97. Copies of such "standesamtliche Eintragungen" as Chelm II and as Cholm II are available in GStA Frankfurt, Sammlung Euthanasie.

98. See, for example, Dressen, "Euthanasie," pp. 53–54.

99. ZStL, Sammlung Polen, Bd. 340: Amtsgericht Chelm, Zeugenvernehmung von Dr. Gizela Langer geb. Madziarska (German translation), 18 Sept. 1946.

100. LA Berlin, Rep. 214, Acc. 794, Nr. 13: Oberbürgermeister Berlin, Hauptwohlfahrtsamt, to Bezirksbürgermeister, Wohlfahrts- und Jugendämter, "Geisteskranke Juden in öffentlichen Anstalten," 7 Nov. 1940.

101. StA Stuttgart, Verfahren Albert Widmann, Ks 19/62 (19 Js 328/60), interrogation Herbert Kalisch, Mannheim, 25 Jan., 4 Mar. 1960, 22 June 1961.

102. Ibid., 25 Jan. 1960.

103. Ibid., 4 Mar. 1960.

104. GStA Frankfurt, Irmfried Eberl Taschenkalender 1940. On the front is stamped: "Dr. med. Irmfried Eberl, Berlin-Schöneberg, Innsbrucker Str. 34/1. Aufg./II, Fernruf 716279."

105. GStA Frankfurt, Eberl Akten, I/250/1–6, 1:150–55: "Organisation der Anstalt Bernburg," n.d.

106. Ibid., I/472/3, 2:60: Bericht, Berlin, 11 Feb. 1946 (testimony Rebeca Adler).

107. GStA Frankfurt, list of transferred patients, 14 Sept. 1940, with handwritten entries about Chelm notices, with dates, by postwar prosecutors.

108. ZStL, Sammlung Verschiedenes, Bd. 2.

109. DÖW, file 4608.

110. Schmidt, *Selektion in der Heilanstalt*, p. 75.

111. ZStL, 208 AR-Z 268/59, Bd. V: interrogation Gerhard Simon, 10 May 1962 (Bl. 14–15), 5 Dec. 1962 (Bl. 20–21), and interrogation Arnold Behrens, 28 May 1963 (Bl. 45), 12 July 1965 (Bl. 52).

112. LG Frankfurt, Urteil Reinhold Vorberg und Dietrich Allers, Ks 2/66 (GStA), 20 Dec. 1968, p. 47. See also ZStL, 208 AR-Z 268/59, Bd. V: interrogation Arnold Behrens, 12 July 1965 (Bl. 52), and ZStL, interrogation Erich Fettke, 2 Sept. 1965.

113. LG Berlin, Akten 2 P Aufh. 2/81.

114. ZStL, Heidelberg Docs. 127,398–401: "Entscheidungen der beiden Euthanasie-Beauftragten hinsichtlich der Begutachtung, Berlin, 30. Januar 1941," and "Entscheidungen der beiden Euthanasie-Beauftragten hinsichtlich der Begutachtung (unter Einbeziehung der Ergebnisse der Besprechung in Berchtesgaden am 10. 3. 1941)."

115. RMdI circular, "Aufnahme jüdischer Geisteskranker in Heil- und Pflegeanstalten," 12 Dec. 1940, copies in BAK, R18/3768, R36/1842; GStA Frankfurt, Sammlung Euthanasie; and HStA Stuttgart, Bestand J355, Büchel 252.

116. See, for example, BAK, R36/1842, for the correspondence concerning the failed attempt to move Uszer Bender from a hospital in the Wartheland to Bendorf-Sayn.

117. See, for example, StA Hamburg, Verfahren Lensch und Struve, 147 Js 58/67, Gesundheitsbehörde, Bd. 1: Gesundheitsverwaltung Hamburg, circular, "Behandlung jüdischer Patienten," 28 Aug. 1941, and HStA Stuttgart, Bestand J355, Büchel 252: RAG to Württemberg MdI, 20 May 1942, Heilanstalt Zwiefalten to Württemberg MdI, 26 May 1942, Pflegeanstalt Heggbach to Württemberg MdI, 26 May 1942, Württemberg MdI to RAG, 1 June 1942, and Jüdische Kultusvereinigung Württemberg to Württemberg MdI, 8 July 1942, with handwritten note by ministry official.

118. See, for example, BAK, R36/1842: DGT to Verwaltung des Bezirkverbandes Wiesbaden, 28 Oct. 1941.

119. RJM circular, "Unterbringung jüdischer Geisteskranker in Heil- und Pflegeanstalten," 6 Feb. 1942, copies in GStA Frankfurt, Sammlung Euthanasie, and HStA Stuttgart, Bestand J355, Büchel 252.

120. See Adler, *Der verwaltete Mensch*, pp. 168–204, and Friedlander, "Deportation of the German Jews," pp. 209–18.

121. For Jewish handicapped patients from institutions in Württemberg and Baden killed after deportation to Riga, Izbica, Lublin, and Auschwitz, see Archivdirektion Stuttgart, *Opfer der nationalsozialistischen Judenverfolgung*, pp. 7, 26, 34, 58–59, 75, 84, 95, 105, 108, 178, 216, 250, 279, 298, 312–13, 343, 418, 435.

122. See Schabow, *Juden in Bendorf*, pp. 18–27. The original deportation transport lists are in the possession of the Koblenz Jewish community. Dietrich Schabow kindly supplied me with copies of these lists (Stapostelle Koblenz, Transportlisten). The deportation transport lists have also been published, but with names rearranged alphabetically, in Landesarchivverwaltung Rheinland Pfalz in Verbindung mit dem Landesarchiv Saarbrücken, ed., *Dokumentation zur Geschichte der jüdischen Bevölkerung in Rheinland-Pfalz und im Saarland von 1800 bis 1945* (Koblenz, 1974), 7:264–82.

123. I am grateful to Dietrich Schabow for information and documentation about the

history of the Bendorf-Sayn hospital and for taking me on a visit to the former Jewish hospital grounds.

124. See Landeshauptarchiv Koblenz, Bestand 700,208/1, Nachlaß Dr. Rosenau: postcard from Bendorf-Sayn staff member Tana Sternau, Arbeitslager Trawniki, to Dr. Wilhelm Rosenau, mid-June 1943.

125. Yivo, Berlin Collection, Occ E 2-2: Hauptabteilung Propaganda, "Wochenberichte der Distrikte im Monat April 1942," Lublin, 18 Apr. 1942.

126. Hilberg, *Destruction* (1961), p. 292 (ibid. [1985], pp. 449–50).

127. RMdI circular, "Aufnahme jüdischer Geisteskranker in Heil- und Pflegeanstalten," 10 Nov. 1942, copies in BAK, R18/3768, R36/1842; GStA Frankfurt, Sammlung Euthanasie; and HStA Stuttgart, J355, Büchel 252.

128. Leo Baeck Institute, Memoir Collection: Herman O. Pineas, "Unser Schicksal seit dem 30. 1. 1933," p. 24, and author's interview with Dr. Herman O. Pineas, New York, 1985.

CHAPTER FOURTEEN

1. Krausnick and Wilhelm, *Truppe des Weltanschauungskrieges*, pp. 173–205; Krausnick, "Judenverfolgung," 2:297–313.

2. See Alfred Streim, "The Tasks of the SS Einsatzgruppen," *Simon Wiesenthal Center Annual* 4 (1987): 309–28, and "Correspondence (Krausnick and Streim)," ibid. 6 (1989): 311–47.

3. On Gypsies, see Headland, *Messages of Murder*, pp. 53–54, 63–64, 71, 114, 142, 157, 169; *JuNSV*, vol. 20, no. 588: LG Essen, 29 Ks 1/64, 29 Mar. 1965; and ZStL, Sammlung UdSSR, Bd. 245Ac, p. 318 (from 1945 Soviet report). On the handicapped, see U.S. Military Tribunal, Transcript of the Proceedings in Case 1, pp. 2545–47; Nuremberg Doc. L-180: Einsatzgruppe A Gesamtbericht bis zum 15. Oktober 1941 (Stahlecker report), p. 37; and Klee, *"Euthanasie" im NS-Staat*, pp. 367–69.

4. Nuremberg Doc. NO-1758.

5. Ibid. NG-2586: Besprechungsprotokoll, Am Grossen Wannsee Nr. 56–58, 20 Jan. 1942.

6. Ibid. PS-710, NG-2586: Hermann Göring to Reinhard Heydrich, 31 July 1941.

7. See, for example, Fleming, *Hitler and the Final Solution*; Breitman, *Architect of Genocide*; and Browning, *Fateful Months* and *Path to Genocide*.

8. See Rückerl, *NS-Vernichtungslager*, pp. 256–57, for one such proposal from the Wartheland.

9. U.S. Military Tribunal, Transcript of the Proceedings in Case 1, pp. 2369, 2402 (testimony Karl Brandt). Accounts differ about the origin of the language used in this authorization; some claimed Hitler dictated it, others that Max de Crinis wrote it, and still others that it was prepared for the KdF by a committee that included leading psychiatrists. See GStA Frankfurt, Anklage Werner Heyde, Gerhard Bohne und Hans Hefelmann, Ks 2/63 (GStA), Js 17/59 (GStA), 22 May 1962, pp. 201–3. Text available as Nuremberg Doc. PS-630.

10. See, for example, Breitman, *Architect of Genocide*, and Fleming, *Hitler and the Final Solution*, chap. 5.

11. Nuremberg Docs. PS-710, NG-2586: Hermann Göring to Reinhard Heydrich, 31 July 1941.

12. Hilberg, *Destruction* (1985), p. 401.

13. BAK, NS neu 19/180: Martin Bormann to Heinrich Himmler, 3 Dec. 1942. The handwritten notation reads: "Führer. Aufstellung. Wer sind Zigeuner."

14. See also Scheffler, "Entstehungsgeschichte."

15. See Reitlinger, *Final Solution*, chaps. 8–9, and Hilberg, *Destruction* (1961), chap. 7.

16. See Beer, "Entwicklung der Gaswagen," and Browning, *Fateful Months*, chap. 3.

17. *JuNSV*, vol. 21, no. 594: LG Bonn, 8 Ks 3/62, 30 Mar. 1963 (Chelmno trial); Rückerl, *NS-Vernichtungslager*, pp. 243–94.

18. Rückerl, *NS-Vernichtungslager*, pp. 87–242.

19. *JuNSV*, vol. 21, no. 595: LG Frankfurt, Urteil Robert Mulka, 4 Ks 2/63, 19–20 Aug. 1965; LG Düsseldorf, Urteil Hermann Hackmann, 8 Ks 1/75, 30 June 1981.

20. Nuremberg Doc. NG-2586; Adam, *Judenpolitik*, pp. 310–11; Adler, *Der verwaltete Mensch*, p. 173; Scheffler, "Entstehungsgeschichte," p. 5.

21. See Dobroszycki, "Jewish Elites under German Rule."

22. The following account of the deportation of German Jews and of their fate relies on Adler, *Der verwaltete Mensch*, pp. 168–204, based partly on the Würzburg Gestapo files, and Friedlander, "Deportation of the German Jews," pp. 209–18, based partly on GStA Berlin (Kammergericht), 1 Js 1/65 (RSHA), Vermerk über das Ergebnis der staatsanwaltschaftlichen Ermittlungen nach dem Stande vom 30. April 1969 in dem Ermittlungsverfahren gegen Friedrich Bosshammer, Richard Hartmann, Otto Hunsche, Fritz Wörn wegen des Verdachtes der Teilnahme am Mord im Rahmen der "Endlösung der Judenfrage," 3 vols. (parts A–C).

23. See Friedlander, "Deportation of the German Jews," p. 212.

24. Walk, *Sonderrecht für die Juden*, p. 357, no. 272.

25. Cited in Adler, *Der verwaltete Mensch*, p. 173.

26. See Rückerl, *NS-Vernichtungslager*, pp. 257–59.

27. Facsimile in Adalbert Rückerl, ed., *NS-Prozesse* (Karlsruhe, 1972).

28. Reitlinger, *Final Solution*, pp. 92, 218.

29. See sample contract in Krausnick, "Judenverfolgung," pp. 329–30.

30. GStA Berlin, 1 Js 1/65 (RSHA), Vermerk, part B, pp. 257–59.

31. See John Mendelsohn, ed., *The Holocaust: Selected Documents* (New York: Garland, 1982), vol. 11.

32. See Kenrick and Puxon, *Sinti und Roma*, p. 135; Necas, "Die tschechischen und slowakischen Roma," pp. 62–64; Sijes et al., *Vervolging van Zigeuners*; and Gotovitch, "L'extermination des tsiganes de Belgique."

33. StA Hamburg, Verfahren Ruth Kellermann, 2200 Js 2/84: RSHA to Kripoleitstelle Königsberg, 22 July 1941.

34. Zimmermann, *Verfolgt, Vertrieben, Vernichtet*, pp. 48–50; Thurner, *Zigeuner in Österreich*, pp. 174–79.

35. See Dobroszycki, *Chronicle of the Lodz Ghetto*, pp. 82, 85, 96, 101, 107, and Milton, "Nazi Policies toward Roma and Sinti," p. 7.

36. Rückerl, *NS-Vernichtungslager*, p. 289.

37. Klamper, *Dokumentationsarchiv*, doc. 75.

38. Hilberg, Staron, and Kermisz, *Warsaw Diary of Adam Czerniakow*, pp. 346–47, 351, 364–68, 375; Zülch, *In Auschwitz vergast*, pp. 102–3; Rückerl, *NS-Vernichtungslager*, p. 197.

39. StA Hamburg, Verfahren Kellermann, 2200 Js 2/84: RMdI circular, 23 Apr. 1941.

40. Ibid.: RMdI circular, 20 June 1941.

41. Ibid.: RFSS circular, 3 Oct. 1941.

42. Ibid.: RSHA circular, 21 Nov. 1941.

43. Ibid.: RSHA circular, 27 Feb. 1942.

44. Ibid.: Reichsarbeitsminister decree (sig. Franz Seldte), 13 Mar. 1942. For the parallel laws for Jews, see "Verordnung über die Beschäftigung von Juden," 3 Oct. 1941, *Reichsgesetzblatt* 1:675, and "Verordnung zur Durchführung der Verordnung über die Beschäftigung von Juden," 31 Oct. 1941, ibid. 1:681.

45. StA Hamburg, Verfahren Kellermann, 2200 Js 2/84: RSHA circular, 28 Aug. 1942, transmitting OKW Verfügung of 27 July 1942.

46. No copy of the Himmler directive (Tgb. Nr. I 2652/42 Ad./RF/V) has been found, but the text is available, ibid.: RSHA circular, 29 Jan. 1943.

47. Czech, *Kalendarium der Ereignisse im Konzentrationslager Auschwitz-Birkenau*, pp. 423, 434.

48. See HHStA, 407/863: Richtlinien für die Umsiedlung von Zigeunern, Berlin, 27 Apr. 1940, and Klamper, *Dokumentationsarchiv*, docs. 79–80.

49. Czech, *Kalendarium der Ereignisse im Konzentrationslager Auschwitz-Birkenau*, pp. 837–38. See also State Museum of Auschwitz-Birkenau and Documentary and Cultural Center of German Sinti and Roma, *Memorial Book: The Gypsies in Auschwitz-Birkenau*, and Zimmermann, " 'Familienlager' Auschwitz."

50. See Fings and Sparing, "Z.Zt. Zigeunerlager," pp. 77–80.

51. BAK, R18/5644: RMdI circular (sig. Conti), 24 Jan. 1940.

52. Nuremberg Doc. NO-205: Viktor Brack to Heinrich Himmler, 23 June 1942.

53. Ibid. NO-203: Viktor Brack to Heinrich Himmler, 28 Mar. 1941, with attached report (sig. Brack), "Bericht über die Versuche betr. Röntgenkastration"; ibid. NO-204: RFSS Persönlicher Stab to Brack, 12 May 1941, copy to Reinhard Heydrich; ibid. NO-206: Himmler to Brack, 11 Aug. 1942, copies to Oswald Pohl and Ernst Robert Grawitz; ibid. NO-207: Werner Blankenburg to Himmler, 14 Aug. 1942; ibid. NO-208: Blankenburg to Himmler, 29 Apr. 1944; U.S. Military Tribunal, Transcript of the Proceedings in Case 1, pp. 7520–21 (testimony Viktor Brack).

54. See BAK, R165/45: list of Lalleri incarcerated at Marzahn, 5 Dec. 1939; compare with State Museum of Auschwitz-Birkenau and Documentary and Cultural Center of German Sinti and Roma, *Memorial Book: The Gypsies in Auschwitz-Birkenau*, list of Gypsies deported to Auschwitz.

55. StA Hamburg, Verfahren Kellermann, 2200 Js 2/84: RSHA circular, 13 Oct. 1942.

56. See Zimmermann, " 'Familienlager' Auschwitz," pp. 107–8.

57. See StA Hamburg, Verfahren Kellermann, 2200 Js 2/84: RFSS circular, "Auswertung der rassenbiologischen Gutachten über zigeunerische Personen," 7 Aug. 1941.

58. This interpretation was first advanced by Zimmermann, *Verfolgt, Vertrieben, Vernichtet*, pp. 64–65.

59. StA Hamburg, Verfahren Kellermann, 2200 Js 2/84: RSHA circular, 11 Jan. 1943.

60. See, for example, BAK, R36/1442: DGT Vermerk, 17 Jan. 1945.

61. The following account of the Mulfingen children is based on Meister, "Schicksale," and "Zigeunerkinder"; and Fings and Sparing, "Zigeunerkinder und -jugendliche."

62. StArch Sigmaringen, Wü 29/3, Acc. 33/1973, Nr. 1752: StA Tübingen, Anklage Otto Mauthe, 1 Js 85–87/47, 4 Jan. 1949, pp. 11–11v.

63. On the deportation of pregnant Gypsy girls, see StA Köln, Verfahren Hans Maly, 24 Ks 1/64 (24 Js 429/61): Anklage Hans Maly, 20 Feb. 1964.

64. Czech, *Kalendarium der Ereignisse im Konzentrationslager Auschwitz-Birkenau*, p. 772.

65. HHStA, 461/32061/7: Frau L. Dietzel, Gießen, to LG Frankfurt, 1 Mar. 1947.

66. HHStA, 461/32061/12: LG Frankfurt, Urteil Adolf Wahlmann, Bodo Gorgaß, Irmgard Huber, 4a KLs 7/47, 21 Mar. 1947, p. 13. See also Platen-Hallermund, *Die Tötung Geisteskranker*, pp. 56–58, and Winter et al., *Verlegt nach Hadamar*, pp. 136–43.

67. RMdI to Verwaltung des Bezirksverbandes Nassau in Wiesbaden, 15 Apr. 1943, facsimile reproduction in Scholz and Singer, "Die Kinder von Hadamar," p. 231. See also Nuremberg Doc. NO-896: affidavit Otto Schellmann, 23 Jan. 1947.

68. See, for example, HHStA, 461/32442/4: interrogations Anneliese Panhuysen and Werner Fischer-Defoy, 22 Jan. 1947.

69. HHStA, 461/32442/13: Fritz Bernotat to Eichberg hospital, 15 May 1943, and Walter Schmidt to Bernotat, 19 May 1943.

70. Reichsvereinigung to Neuerkeröder Anstalt, 15 Feb. 1943, reply, 18 Feb. 1943, Reichs-vereinigung to Neuerkeröder Anstalt, 23 Feb. 1943, reply, 26 Feb. 1943, Braunschweig MdI to Neuerkeröder Anstalt, 25 May, 16 June 1943, Neuerkeröder Anstalt to Erziehungsheim Hadamar, 19 June 1943, and Hadamar receipt for two patients, 21 June 1943, copies of all of which were kindly provided to me by Annegret Ehmann, Berlin.

71. See Nuremberg Doc. NO-1527: affidavit Irmgard Huber, 4 Jan. 1947.

72. This was first pointed out by Dörner, "Nationalsozialismus und Lebensvernichtung," p. 121.

73. See BAK, R22/5021: handwritten note by Dr. Günther Joël to Franz Gürtner, 1 Nov. [1940], transmitting comments by Reinhard Heydrich concerning his relationship to the euthanasia program.

74. DÖW, file E19198: Reichsgau Wien, Hauptgesundheitsamt, SD Leitabschnitt Wien to Medizinalrat Dr. Hermann Hans Vellguth, Gesundheitsamt, n.d. [1940].

75. See Breitman, *Architect of Genocide*, p. 190, for the dating of Himmler's assignment to Globocnik.

76. Nuremberg Doc. NO-426: affidavit Viktor Brack, 14 Oct. 1946; U.S. Military Tri-bunal, Transcript of the Proceedings in Case 1, pp. 1534–37 (testimony Viktor Brack).

77. See LG Hagen, Urteil Werner Dubois, 11 Ks 1/64, 20 Dec. 1966, p. 39.

78. For the recruitment of volunteers, particularly among the women, see HHStA, 461/32061/7: LG Frankfurt, Verfahren Adolf Wahlmann, Bodo Gorgaß, Irmgard Huber, 4a KLs 7/47 (4a Js 3/46), Protokoll der öffentlichen Sitzung der 4. Strafkammer, 25 Feb. 1947, p. 13 (testimony Lydia Thomas).

79. U.S. Military Tribunal, Transcript of the Proceedings in Case 1, pp. 7504–5 (testimony Viktor Brack); Mennecke letter, Berlin, 14–15 Jan. 1942, in Chroust, *Friedrich Mennecke*, pp. 323–31 (account of Brack unit on p. 329).

80. GStA Frankfurt, Eberl Akten, II/691/1, 7:98–100: Irmfried Eberl to Werner Blanken-burg, 4 Feb. 1942; ibid., II/691/3–5, 7:103–8: Eberl Aktenvermerke, 14, 15 Feb. 1942. See also U.S. Military Tribunal, Transcript of the Proceedings in Case 1, p. 2528 (testimony Viktor Brack).

81. GStA Frankfurt, Eberl Akten, II/691/8, 7:116–17: Eberl Tätigkeitsbericht, 7 Mar. 1942.

82. Klee, *"Euthanasie" im NS-Staat*, pp. 372–73.

83. GStA Frankfurt, Eberl Akten, III/656, 7:125–28: Irmfried Eberl to Ruth Eberl, Minsk, 15 Feb. 1942; ibid., II/691/6, 7:109–10: Eberl to Kameradschaft Bernburg, 19 Feb. 1942; ibid., II/691/7, 7:111–15: Eberl to Werner Blankenburg, 3 Mar. 1942.

84. Nuremberg Doc. NO-860: affidavit Fritz Bleich, registrar in Brandt's office, 27 Nov. 1946.

85. U.S. Military Tribunal, Transcript of the Proceedings in Case 1, p. 7514 (testimony Viktor Brack).

86. See ibid. for Brack's denial. See also Browning, *Fateful Months*, pp. 24, 30–31, for an attempt to date the construction of Belzec.

87. LG Hagen, Urteil Dubois, 11 Ks 1/64, 20 Dec. 1966, pp. 35–36. See also Browning, *Fateful Months*, pp. 30–31.

88. U.S. Military Tribunal, Transcript of the Proceedings in Case 1, pp. 7509–10 (testi-mony Viktor Brack).

89. Nuremberg Doc. NO-205: Viktor Brack to Heinrich Himmler, 23 June 1942.

90. Globocnik report, 27 Oct. 1943, cited in Rückerl, *NS-Vernichtungslager*, pp. 117–18.

91. StA Düsseldorf, Anklage Kurt Franz, 8 Js 10904/59, 29 Jan. 1963, pp. 98–99.

92. Copies in Yivo, Occ E 2-131, and ZStL, Sammlung Polen, Bd. 217, 362.

93. *Fedorenko v. United States*, 449 U.S. 490, 493 (1981).

94. U.S. Military Tribunal, Transcript of the Proceedings in Case 1, p. 7516 (testimony Viktor Brack).

95. ZStL, interrogation of T4 courier Erich Fettke, 2 Sept. 1965. See also GStA Frankfurt, Eberl Akten, II/166, 7:86–87: Irmfried Eberl in Sobibor to Fräulein Dittmann in Bernburg, 26 Apr. 1942.

96. GStA Frankfurt, Eberl Akten, III/683/5, 7:147–48: Irmfried Eberl to Ruth Eberl, 29 June 1942.

97. Rückerl, *NS-Vernichtungslager*, p. 73; DÖW, file E18370/1: LG Linz, interrogation Heinrich Barbl, 16 Nov. 1964.

98. LG Hagen, Urteil Dubois, 11 Ks 1/64, 20 Dec. 1966, pp. 35–36.

99. The best account is Scalpelli, *San Sabba*.

100. See Rückerl, *NS-Vernichtungslager*, pp. 208–9; StA Düsseldorf, Anklage Franz, 8 Js 10904/59, 29 Jan. 1963, p. 132; and ZStL, interrogation Josef Oberhauser, Munich, 18 Nov. 1968.

101. GStA Frankfurt, Eberl Akten, III/683/6, 7:149–50: Irmfried Eberl to Ruth Eberl, 30 July 1942.

102. ZStL, interrogation Josef Oberhauser, Munich, 18 Nov. 1968.

103. See Nuremberg Doc. NO-064 and ZStL, Sammlung Polen, Bd. 216, 217, 362.

104. See LG Frankfurt, Urteil Hans-Joachim Becker und Friedrich Robert Lorent, Ks 1/69 (GStA), 27 May 1970, p. 115; StA Stuttgart, Verfahren Albert Widmann, Ks 19/62 (19 Js 328/60): interrogation Klara Mattmüller, Freiburg, 17 Feb. 1966 (StA Frankfurt, Js 7/63, Js 15/63 [GStA]); and Klee, *"Euthanasie" im NS-Staat*, p. 375.

105. ZStL, interrogation Josef Oberhauser, Munich, 18 Nov. 1968.

106. For the technique in the euthanasia killing centers in Germany, see DÖW, file E18370/3: Kriminalpolizei Linz, interrogation Vinzenz Nohel, 4 Sept. 1945. For the technique in the camps of Operation Reinhard, see LG Hagen, Urteil Karl Frenzel, 11 Ks 1/64, 4 Oct. 1985, pp. 98–104.

107. See *JuNSV*, vol. 21, no. 595: LG Frankfurt, 4 Ks 2/63, 19–20 Aug. 1965.

108. See, for example, U.S. Military Tribunal, Transcript of the Proceedings in Case 1, pp. 2506, 2510, 2515–16 (testimony Karl Brandt), pp. 7571–72 (testimony Viktor Brack), p. 1906 (testimony Friedrich Mennecke).

109. Lifton, *Nazi Doctors*, p. 4.

110. See, for example, Langbein, *Menschen in Auschwitz*, pp. 37–40, 376–77.

111. Müller-Hill, "Selektion," pp. 151–52.

BIBLIOGRAPHY

ARCHIVAL DOCUMENTS

Allgemeines Verwaltungsarchiv, Vienna
  Akte Josef Bürckel
Archiv und Museum Mauthausen, Vienna
Berlin Document Center
Boston University Library
  Leo Alexander Collection, box 57, Folder Euthanasia
Bundesarchiv Koblenz
  R18 Reichsministerium des Innern
  R22 Reichsjustizministerium
  R36 Deutscher Gemeindetag
  R58 Reichssicherheitshauptamt
  R73 Deutsche Forschungsgemeinschaft
  R96 II Reichstuberkolosenausschuß
  NL263 Nachlaß Rheindorf
  Reichsgesetzblatt (1933–45)
Bundesarchiv-Militärarchiv, Freiburg im Breisgau
  H20/463, 465
Dokumentationsarchiv des österreichischen Widerstandes, Vienna
Generalstaatsanwalt der Deutschen Demokratischen Republik, Berlin
  Staatsanwaltschaft Dresden, Akten des Verfahrens gg. Dr. Paul Nitsche u.A., (S) 1 Ks
    58/47 (1/47)
Generalstaatsanwalt Frankfurt (Staatsanwaltschaft bei dem Oberlandesgericht)
  Akten des Verfahrens gg. Werner Heyde, Gerhard Bohne und Hans Hefelmann, Ks
    2/63 (GStA), Js 17/59 (GStA)
  Eberl Akten
  Mennecke Letters
  Sammlung Euthanasie
Hauptstaatsarchiv Düsseldorf
Hauptstaatsarchiv Stuttgart
  Bestand J355, Büchel 249
  Bestand J355, Büchel 252
  Bestand J355, Büchel 259
  Bestand J355, Büchel 262
Hessisches Hauptstaatsarchiv, Wiesbaden
  407/863, 407/875: Kripo files on Gypsies
  461/32061: Landgericht Frankfurt, Akten des Verfahrens gg. Adolf Wahlmann, Bodo
    Gorgaß, Irmgard Huber u.A., 4a KLs 7/47 (4a Js 3/46)
  461/32442: Landgericht Frankfurt, Akten des Verfahrens gg. Friedrich Mennecke,
    Walter Schmidt u.A., 4 KLs 15/46 (4a Js 13/46)
Landesarchiv Berlin
  Rep. 142, 1-2-3 Akt 1, Bd. 2
  Rep. 214, Acc. 794, Nr. 13

Rep. 214, Acc. 2740, Nr. 154–55
Landeshauptarchiv Koblenz
Leo Baeck Institute, New York
    Memoir Collection: Herman O. Pineas, "Unser Schicksal seit dem 30. 1. 1933"
National Archives and Records Administration, National Archives Building, Washington,
    D.C.
    RG 238, International Military Tribunal Interrogations
        Karl Brandt
        Hermann Pfannmüller
    RG 238, Microfilm Publication M-1019, Records of the U.S. Nuernberg War Crimes
        Trials, Interrogations, 1946–49
        Roll 8: Viktor Brack
        Roll 46: Friedrich Mennecke
        Roll 52: Hermann Pfannmüller
        Roll 52: Walter Schmidt
    RG 238, Nuremberg Documents
    RG 338, Microfilm Publication T-1021, German Documents among the War Crimes
        Records of the Judge Advocate Division Headquarters, U.S. Army, Europe
National Archives and Records Administration, Suitland (Maryland) Records Branch
    RG 153, Records of the Judge Advocate General (Army)
    RG 338, Cases Tried, General Administration, Medical Experiments
        Heidelberg Documents
    RG 338, Records of U.S. Army Commands, 1942–
        Case File 12-449, United States v. Alfons Klein et al., 8–15 October 1945
Politisches Archiv des Auswärtigen Amtes, Bonn
Staatsanwaltschaft bei dem Landgericht Düsseldorf
    Akten des Verfahrens gg. Dr. Albert Widmann, 8 Ks 1/61 (8 Js 7212/59)
Staatsanwaltschaft bei dem Landgericht Hamburg
    Akten des Verfahrens gg. Dr. Ruth Kellermann u.A., 2200 Js 2/84
    Akten des Verfahrens gg. Friedrich Lensch und Dr. Kurt Struve, 147 Js 58/67
        Gesundheitsbehörde, Bd. 1
        Gutachten by Prof. Dr. Jozef Radzicki, Poznan
        Sonderband Alsterdorfer Anstalten Betr. Juden-Entlassungen
        Sonderbände Langenhorn: Allgemeines Krankenhaus Ochsenzoll, Bd. 1, Teil 1–2,
            Bd. 2
Staatsanwaltschaft bei dem Landgericht Köln
    Akten des Verfahrens gg. Dr. Alfred Leu, 24 Ks 1/51 (24 Js 527/50, 24 Js 642/51)
    Akten des Verfahrens gg. Dr. Hans Maly, 24 Ks 1/64 (24 Js 429/61)
Staatsanwaltschaft bei dem Landgericht München I
    Akten des Verfahrens gg. Dr. Hermann Pfannmüller, 1 Ks 10/49 (1b Js 1791/47)
Staatsanwaltschaft bei dem Landgericht Stuttgart
    Akten des Verfahrens gg. Dr. Albert Widmann, Ks 19/62 (19 Js 328/60)
Staatsarchiv Sigmaringen
    Wü 29/3, Acc. 33/1973, Nr. 1752: Akten des Verfahrens gg. Otto Mauthe u.A., Ks 6/49
        (Js 85–87/47)
United States Holocaust Memorial Museum, Washington, D.C.
    Fojn-Felczer Collection
Yivo Institute for Jewish Research, New York
    Berlin Collection, Occ E 2-74, Occ E 3-60, Occ E 3-61, Occ E 3a-11
Zentrale Stelle der Landesjustizverwaltungen, Ludwigsburg
    Heidelberger Dokumente

Interrogations
Sammlung Arolsen
Sammlung Polen
Sammlung Schumacher
Sammlung UdSSR
Sammlung USA
Sammlung Verschiedenes

COURT RECORDS: INDICTMENTS, DECISIONS, AND REPORTS

Buck v. Bell, 274 U.S. 200 (1927).

Fedorenko v. United States, 449 U.S. 490 (1981).

Generalstaatsanwalt Berlin (Staatsanwaltschaft bei dem Kammergericht). 1 Js 1/65 (RSHA). Vermerk über das Ergebnis der staatsanwaltschaftlichen Ermittlungen nach dem Stande vom 30. April 1969 in dem Ermittlungsverfahren gg. Friedrich Bosshammer, Richard Hartmann, Otto Hunsche, Fritz Wörn wegen des Verdachtes der Teilnahme am Mord im Rahmen der "Endlösung der Judenfrage." 3 vols. (A–C).

Generalstaatsanwalt Berlin (Staatsanwaltschaft bei dem Landgericht). Anklageschrift gg. Hilde Wernicke und Helene Wieczorek. 11 Js 37/45. 5 February 1946.

Generalstaatsanwalt Frankfurt (Staatsanwaltschaft bei dem Oberlandesgericht). Anklageschrift gg. Werner Heyde, Gerhard Bohne und Hans Hefelmann. Ks 2/63 (GStA), Js 17/59 (GStA). 22 May 1962.

———. Anklageschrift gg. Adolf Gustav Kaufmann. Js 16/63 (GStA). 27 June 1966.

———. Anklageschrift gg. Georg Renno, Hans-Joachim Becker und Friedrich Robert Lorent. Js 18/61 (GStA), Js 7/63 (GStA), Js 5/65 (GStA). 7 November 1967.

———. Anklageschrift gg. Horst Schumann. Js 18/67 (GStA). 12 December 1969.

———. Anklageschrift gg. Aquilin Ullrich, Heinrich Bunke, Kurt Borm und Klaus Endruweit. Js 15/61 (GStA). 15 January 1965.

———. Anklageschrift gg. Reinhold Vorberg und Dietrich Allers. Js 20/61 (GStA). 15 February 1966.

———. Voruntersuchungsantrag gg. Franz Schlegelberger u.A. Js 20/63 (GStA). 22 April 1965.

Landeskriminalpolizeiabteilung Mecklenburg. Anklageschrift gg. Richard von Hegener. 5-0/410/47/B1, 5-0/339/49/B1. Schwerin, 9 September 1949.

Landgericht Berlin. Urteil gg. Hilde Wernicke und Helene Wieczorek. 11 Ks 8/46. 25 March 1946.

Landgericht Bonn. Untersuchungsrichter II. Anlage zur Abschluss-Verfügung vom 30. September 1963 in der Voruntersuchung gg. Wilhelm Koppe. 13 UR 1/61, 6/62, 7/62, 10/62.

Landgericht Dresden. Urteil gg. Hermann Paul Nitsche u.A. 1 Ks 58/47. 7 July 1947.

Landgericht Düsseldorf. Urteil gg. Walter Creutz u.A. 8 KLs 8/48. 24 November 1948.

———. Urteil gg. Walter Creutz u.A. 8 KLs 8/48. 27 January 1950.

———. Urteil gg. Kurt Franz u.A. 8 I Ks 2/64. 3 September 1965.

———. Urteil gg. Hermann Hackmann u.A. 8 Ks 1/75. 30 June 1981.

———. Urteil gg. Franz Stangl. 8 Ks 1/69. 22 December 1970.

———. Urteil gg. Albert Widmann. 8 Ks 1/61. 16 May 1961.

Landgericht Frankfurt. Urteil gg. Hans-Joachim Becker und Friedrich Robert Lorent. Ks 1/69 (GStA). 27 May 1970.

———. Urteil gg. Kurt Borm. Ks 1/66 (GStA). 6 June 1972.

———. Urteil gg. Friedrich Mennecke, Walter Schmidt u.A. 4 KLs 15/46. 21 December 1946.

———. Urteil gg. Aquilin Ullrich, Heinrich Bunke und Klaus Endruweit. Ks 1/66 (GStA). 23 May 1967.

———. Urteil gg. Reinhold Vorberg und Dietrich Allers. Ks 2/66 (GStA). 20 December 1968.

———. Urteil gg. Adolf Wahlmann, Bodo Gorgaß, Irmgard Huber u.A. 4a KLs 7/47. 21 March 1947.

Landgericht Hagen. Urteil gg. Werner Dubois u.A. 11 Ks 1/64. 20 December 1966.

———. Urteil gg. Karl Frenzel. 11 Ks 1/64. 4 October 1985.

Landgericht Hamburg. Urteil gg. Viktor Arajs. (37) 5/76. 21 December 1979.

Landgericht Hannover. Urteil gg. Kurt Eimann. 2 Ks 2/67. 20 December 1968.

Landgericht Köln. Urteil gg. Alfred Leu. 24 Ks 1/51. 24 October 1951.

———. Urteil gg. Alfred Leu. 24 Ks 1/51. 4 December 1953.

Landgericht Magdeburg. Urteil gg. Richard von Hegener u.A. 11 KLs 139/51. 20 February 1952.

Landgericht München I. Urteil gg. Hermann Pfannmüller. 1 Ks 10/49. 5 November 1949.

Landgericht Schwerin. Urteil gg. Hans-Heinrich Braunroth u.A. 1 KLs 3/46. 16 August 1946.

Landgericht Tübingen. Urteil gg. Otto Mauthe u.A. Ks 6/49. 5 July 1949.

Staatsanwaltschaft Bonn. Anklageschrift gg. Wilhelm Koppe. 8 Js 52/60. 10 September 1964.

Staatsanwaltschaft Düsseldorf. Anklageschrift gg. Walter Creutz u.A. 8 Js 116/47. 23 January 1948.

———. Anklageschrift gg. Kurt Franz u.A. 8 Js 10904/59. 29 January 1963.

———. Anklageschrift gg. Franz Stangl. 8 Js 1045/69. 29 September 1969.

———. Anklageschrift gg. Albert Widmann u.A. 8 Js 7212/59. 13 September 1960.

Staatsanwaltschaft Frankfurt. Anklageschrift gg. Friedrich Mennecke und Walter Schmidt. 4a Js 13/46. 7 October 1946.

———. Anklageschrift gg. Adolf Wahlmann, Irmgard Huber u.A. 4a Js 3/46. 2 August 1946.

Staatsanwaltschaft Graz. Anklageschrift gg. Franz Niedermoser. 10 St 2245/46, 21 February 1946.

Staatsanwaltschaft Hamburg. Anklageschrift gg. Wilhelm Bayer, Werner Catel u.A. 14 Js 265/48. 7 February 1949.

———. Anklageschrift gg. Friedrich Lensch und Kurt Struve. 147 Js 58/67. 24 April 1973.

———. Sachstandsvermerk. 147 Js 58/67. 25 February 1970.

Staatsanwaltschaft Innsbruck. Anklageschrift gg. Hans Czermak. St 3782/48. 26 July 1949.

Staatsanwaltschaft Köln. Anklageschrift gg. Hermann Hackmann u.A. 130 (24) Js 200/62 (Z). 15 November 1974.

———. Anklageschrift gg. Alfred Leu. 24 Js 527/50. 10 July 1951.

———. Anklageschrift gg. Hans Maly. 24 Js 429/61. 20 February 1964.

Staatsanwaltschaft Konstanz. Einstellungsbericht gg. Josef Vonbun. 2 Js 524/61. 21 June 1966.

Staatsanwaltschaft Linz. Anklageschrift gg. Anna Griessenberger u.A. 3 St 466/46. 28 July 1947.

———. Anklageschrift gg. Franz Stangl, Karl Harrer, Leopold Lang und Franz Mayrhuber. 3 St 466/46. 27 April 1948.

Staatsanwaltschaft München I. Anklageschrift gg. Hermann Pfannmüller. 1b Js 1791/47. 16 June 1948.

Staatsanwaltschaft Stuttgart. Anklageschrift gg. Albert Widmann und August Becker. (19) 13 Js 328/60. 29 August 1962.

Staatsanwaltschaft Tübingen. Anklageschrift gg. Otto Mauthe u.A. 1 Js 85–87/47.
  4 January 1949.
Staatsanwaltschaft Wien. Anklageschrift gg. Ernst Illing, Marianne Türk und Margarete
  Hübsch. 15 St 9103/45. 18 June 1946.
———. Anklageschrift gg. Josef Mayer u.A. 15 St 6271/45. 25 September 1947.
United States Military Tribunal. Official Transcript of the Proceedings in Case 1, United
  States v. Karl Brandt et al. (Medical Case).
Volksgericht bei dem Landesgericht Graz. Senat Klagenfurt. Urteil gg. Franz
  Niedermoser u.A. Vg 18 Vr 907/45. 4 April 1946.
Volksgericht bei dem Landesgericht Innsbruck. Urteil gg. Hans Czermak. Vg 10 Vr
  4740/47. 1 December 1949.
Volksgericht bei dem Landesgericht Linz. Urteil gg. Karl Harrer, Leopold Lang und Franz
  Mayrhuber. Vg 6 Vr 2407/46 (188). 3 July 1948.
Volksgericht bei dem Landesgericht Wien. Urteil gg. Marie Gutmann und Auguste
  Kabelka. Vg 1d Vr 189/49 (Hv 124/49). 28 February 1949.
———. Urteil gg. Ernst Illing, Marianne Türk und Margarete Hübsch. Vg 1a Vr 2365/45
  (Hv 1208/46). 18 July 1946.
———. Urteil gg. Anna Katschenka. Vg 12g Vr 5442/46 (Hv 301/48). 9 April 1948.
———. Urteil gg. Josef Mayer u.A. Vg 11h Vr 455/46 (Hv 42/48). 14 July 1948.
———. Urteil gg. Maximilian Thaller. Vg 11e Vr 5502/46 (Hv 328/48). 25 October 1948.

PUBLISHED DOCUMENTS

Archivdirektion Stuttgart, comp. *Die Opfer der nationalsozialistischen Judenverfolgung
  in Baden-Württemberg, 1933–1945: Ein Gedenkbuch.* Stuttgart: W. Kohlhammer
  Verlag, 1969.
Chroust, Peter, ed. *Friedrich Mennecke, Innenansichten eines medizinischen Täters im
  Nationalsozialismus: Eine Edition seiner Briefe, 1935–1947.* 2 vols. Hamburg: Hamburger
  Institut für Sozialforschung, 1987.
Control Commission for Germany (British Element). Legal Division. British Special Legal
  Research Unit. "Translations of Nazi Health Laws Concerned with Hereditary Diseases,
  Matrimonial Health, Sterilization, and Castration (8 Nov. 1945)." Mimeograph.
Czech, Danuta, ed. *Kalendarium der Ereignisse im Konzentrationslager Auschwitz-
  Birkenau, 1939–1945.* Reinbek bei Hamburg: Rowohlt, 1989.
Dobroszycki, Lucjan, ed. *The Chronicle of the Lodz Ghetto, 1941–1944.* New Haven: Yale
  University Press, 1984.
Ebbinghaus, Angelika, and Gerd Preissler, eds. and trans. "Die Ermordung psychisch
  kranker Menschen in der Sowjetunion: Dokumentation." *Beiträge zur natio-
  nalsozialistischen Gesundheits- und Sozialpolitik* 1 (1985): 75–107.
*Die Ermordeten waren Schuldig?: Amtliche Dokumente der Direction de la Santé Publique
  der französischen Militärregierung.* 2d ed. Baden-Baden: Schröder-Verlag, n.d.
Friedlander, Henry, and Sybil Milton, eds. *Berlin Document Center.* 2 vols. Archives of
  the Holocaust Series, vol. 11. New York: Garland Publishing, 1991.
———. *Bundesarchiv of the Federal Republic of Germany, Koblenz and Freiburg.* Archives
  of the Holocaust Series, vol. 20. New York: Garland Publishing, 1992.
———. *Zentrale Stelle der Landesjustizverwaltungen, Ludwigsburg.* Archives of the
  Holocaust Series, vol. 22. New York: Garland Publishing, 1992.
Gütt, Arthur, Herbert Linden, and Franz Maßfeller. *Blutschutz- und Ehegesundheitsgesetz:
  Gesetz zum Schutze des deutschen Blutes und der deutschen Ehre und Gesetz zum
  Schutze der Erbgesundheit des deutschen Volkes nebst Durchführungsverordnungen sowie*

einschlägigen Bestimmungen, dargestellt, medizinisch und juristisch erläutert. Munich: J. F. Lehmanns Verlag, 1st ed., 1936; 2d rev. ed., 1937.

Gütt, Arthur, Ernst Rüdin, and Falk Ruttke. *Gesetz zur Verhütung erbkranken Nachwuchses vom 14. Juli 1933 nebst Ausführungsverordnungen, bearbeitet und erläutert.* Munich: J. F. Lehmanns Verlag, 1st ed., 1934; 2d rev. ed., 1936.

Hase, Hans Christoph von, ed. *Evangelische Dokumente zur Ermordung der "unheilbar Kranken" unter der nationalsozialistischen Herrschaft in den Jahren 1939–1945.* Innere Mission und Hilfswerk der Evangelischen Kirche in Deutschland. Stuttgart: Evangelisches Verlagswerk, 1964.

Heiber, Helmut, ed. *Reichsführer: Briefe an und von Himmler.* Munich: Deutscher Taschenbuch Verlag, 1970.

Hilberg, Raul, Stanislaw Staron, and Josef Kermisz, eds. *The Warsaw Diary of Adam Czerniakow: Prelude to Doom.* New York: Stein and Day, 1979.

Hohmann, Joachim S. *Zigeuner und Zigeunerwissenschaft: Ein Beitrag zur Grundlagenforschung und Dokumentation des Völkermordes im "Dritten Reich."* Marburg-Lahn: Verlag Guttandin und Hoppe, 1980.

Die jüdischen Opfer des Nationalsozialismus in Hamburg. Hamburg: Staatsarchiv, 1965.

Kintner, Earl W., ed. *The Hadamar Trial: Trial of Alfons Klein, Adolf Wahlmann, Heinrich Ruoff, Karl Willig, Adolf Merkle, Irmgard Huber, and Philipp Blum.* London: William Hodge, 1949.

Klamper, Elisabeth, ed. *Dokumentationsarchiv des österreichischen Widerstandes, Vienna.* Archives of the Holocaust Series, vol. 19, edited by Henry Friedlander and Sybil Milton. New York: Garland Publishing, 1992.

Klee, Ernst, ed. *Dokumente zur "Euthanasie."* Frankfurt: Fischer Taschenbuch Verlag, 1985.

Mendelsohn, John, ed. *The Holocaust: Selected Documents.* 18 vols. New York: Garland Publishing, 1982.

Michelberger, Hans. *Berichte aus der Justiz des Dritten Reiches: Die Lageberichte der Oberlandesgerichtspräsidenten von 1940–1945 unter vergleichender Heranziehung der Lageberichte der Generalstaatsanwälte.* Pfaffenweiler: Centaurus Verlagsgesellschaft, 1989.

Mitscherlich, Alexander, and Fred Mielke, eds. *Medizin ohne Menschlichkeit: Dokumente des Nürnberger Ärzteprozesses.* Frankfurt: Fischer Taschenbuch Verlag, 1960.

Neuhauser, Johannes, and Michaela Pfaffenwimmer, eds. *Hartheim—wohin unbekannt: Briefe und Dokumente.* Weitra, Austria: Bibliothek der Provinz, 1992.

Präg, Werner, and Wolfgang Jakobmeyer, eds. *Das Diensttagebuch des deutschen Generalgouverneurs in Polen, 1939–1945.* Stuttgart: Deutsche Verlagsanstalt, 1975.

Reichsausschuß für Volksgesundheitsdienst. *The Law for the Prevention of Hereditarily Diseased Offspring.* Berlin: Reichsdruckerei, 1935.

Roth, Karl Heinz, and Götz Aly. "Die Diskussion über die Legalisierung der nationalsozialistischen Anstaltsmorde in den Jahren 1938–1941." *Recht & Psychiatrie* 1 (1983): 51–64, 2 (1984): 36–47.

————. "Das 'Gesetz über die Sterbehilfe bei unheilbar Kranken': Protokolle der Diskussion über die Legalisierung der nationalsozialistischen Anstaltsmorde in den Jahren 1938–1941." In *Erfassung zur Vernichtung: Von der Sozialhygiene zum "Gesetz über Sterbehilfe,"* edited by Karl Heinz Roth, pp. 101–79. Berlin: Verlagsgesellschaft Gesundheit, 1984.

Rückerl, Adalbert. *NS-Vernichtungslager im Spiegel deutscher Strafprozesse.* Munich: Deutscher Taschenbuch Verlag, 1977.

Rüter-Ehlermann, Adelheid L., and C. F. Rüter, eds. *Justiz und NS-Verbrechen: Sammlung deutscher Strafurteile wegen nationalsozialistischer Tötungsverbrechen.* 22 vols. Amsterdam: University Press Amsterdam, 1968–81.

Sauer, Paul. *Dokumente über die Verfolgung der jüdischen Bürger in Baden-Württemberg durch das nationalsozialistische Regime, 1933–1945.* 2 vols. Stuttgart: W. Kohlhammer Verlag, 1966.

Sick, Dorothea. *"Euthanasie" im Nationalsozialismus am Beispiel des Kalmenhofs in Idstein im Taunus.* 2d ed. Frankfurt: Fachhochschule Frankfurt am Main, FB Sozialarbeit, FB Sozialpädagogik, 1983.

State Museum of Auschwitz-Birkenau and Documentary and Cultural Center of German Sinti and Roma, eds. *Memorial Book: The Gypsies in Auschwitz-Birkenau.* 2 vols. Munich: K. G. Saur, 1993.

The Statutory Criminal Law of Germany. Edited by Eldon R. James; prepared by Vladimir Gsovski. Washington, D.C.: Library of Congress, 1947.

Stuckart, Wilhelm, and Hans Globke. *Reichsbürgergesetz vom 15. September 1935, Gesetz zum Schutze des deutschen Blutes und der deutschen Ehre vom 15. September 1935, Gesetz zum Schutze der Erbgesundheit des deutschen Volkes (Ehegesundheitsgesetz) vom 18. Oktober 1935 nebst allen Ausführungsvorschriften und den einschlägigen Gesetzen und Verordnungen, erläutert.* Munich: C. H. Beck'sche Verlagsbuchhandlung, 1936.

Trials of War Criminals before the Nuremberg Military Tribunals under Control Council Law No. 10 (Green Series), 14 vols. Washington, D.C.: Government Printing Office, 1950–52.

Tuchel, Johannes, ed. *"Kein Recht auf Leben": Beiträge und Dokumente zur Entrechtung und Vernichtung "lebensunwerten Lebens" im Nationalsozialismus.* Berlin: Wissenschaftlicher Autoren-Verlag, 1984.

Walk, Joseph, ed. *Das Sonderrecht für die Juden im NS-Staat: Eine Sammlung der gesetzlichen Massnahmen und Richtlinien—Inhalt und Bedeutung.* Heidelberg: C. F. Müller Juristischer Verlag, 1981.

SECONDARY WORKS

Works only tangentially connected to the topic of this book and rarely cited are omitted from the following list; the first citation to such works in the notes provides all essential bibliographical information.

Adam, Uwe Dietrich. *Judenpolitik im Dritten Reich.* Düsseldorf: Droste Verlag, 1979.

Adler, H. G. *Der verwaltete Mensch: Studien zur Deportation der Juden aus Deutschland.* Tübingen: J. C. B. Mohr (Paul Siebeck), 1974.

Alexander, Leo. "Medical Science under Dictatorship." *New England Journal of Medicine* 241, no. 2 (1949): 39–47.

Allen, Garland E. "The Eugenics Record Office at Cold Spring Harbor, 1910–1940: An Essay in Institutional History." *Osiris,* 2d ser., 2 (1986): 225–64.

———. "The Misuse of Biological Hierarchies: The American Eugenics Movement, 1900–1940." *History and Philosophy of the Life Sciences,* Publicazioni della Stazione Zoologica di Napoli, Section II, 5, no. 2 (1983): 105–28.

Aly, Götz. "Medizin gegen Unbrauchbare." *Beiträge zur nationalsozialistischen Gesundheits- und Sozialpolitik* 1 (1985): 9–74.

———. "Der Mord an behinderten Kindern." In *Heilen und Vernichten im Mustergau Hamburg: Bevölkerungs- und Gesundheitspolitik im Dritten Reich,* edited by Angelika Ebbinghaus, Heidrun Kaupen-Haas, and Karl Heinz Roth, pp. 147–55. Hamburg: Konkret Literatur Verlag, 1984.

———. "Der saubere und der schmutzige Fortschritt." *Beiträge zur nationalsozialistischen Gesundheits- und Sozialpolitik* 2 (1985): 9–78.

Aly, Götz, and Karl Heinz Roth. *Die restlose Erfassung: Volkszählen, Identifizieren, Aussondern im Nationalsozialismus.* Berlin: Rotbuch Verlag, 1984.

Arad, Yitzhak. *Belzec, Sobibor, Treblinka: The Operation Reinhard Death Camps*. Bloomington: Indiana University Press, 1987.

Arbeitsgruppe zur Erforschung der Karl-Bonhoeffer-Nervenklinik, ed. *Totgeschwiegen, 1933–1945: Die Geschichte der Karl-Bonhoeffer-Nervenklinik*. Berlin: Edition Hentrich, 1988.

Arendt, Hannah. *Eichmann in Jerusalem*. New York: Viking, 1963.

Arndt, Ino, and Wolfgang Scheffler. "Organisierter Massenmord an Juden in nationalsozialistischen Vernichtungslagern." *Vierteljahrshefte für Zeitgeschichte* 24 (1976): 105–35.

Baader, Gerhard. "Das Humanexperiment in den Konzentrationslagern: Konzeption und Durchführung." In *Menschenversuche: Wahnsinn und Wirklichkeit*, pp. 48–69. Cologne: Kölner Volksblatt Verlag, 1988.

Baader, Gerhard, and Ulrich Schultz, eds. *Medizin und Nationalsozialismus: Tabuisierte Vergangenheit—Ungebrochene Tradition?* 2d rev. ed. Berlin: Verlagsgesellschaft Gesundheit, 1983.

Becker–von Rose, Peta. "Carl Schneider: Wissenschaftlicher Schrittmacher der Euthanasieaktion und Universitätspsychiater in Heidelberg, 1933–1945." In *Von der Heilkunde zur Massentötung: Medizin im Nationalsozialismus*, edited by Gerrit Hohendorf and Achim Magull-Seltenreich, pp. 91–108. Heidelberg: Wunderhorn, 1990.

Beer, Mathias. "Die Entwicklung der Gaswagen beim Mord an den Juden." *Vierteljahrshefte für Zeitgeschichte* 35 (1987): 403–17.

Bergmann, Anna, Gabriele Czarnowski, and Annegret Ehmann. "Menschen als Objekte humangenetischer Forschung: Zur Geschichte des Kaiser Wilhelm-Instituts für Anthropologie, menschliche Erblehre und Eugenik in Berlin-Dahlem, 1927–1945." In *Der Wert des Menschen: Medizin in Deutschland, 1918–1945*, edited by Christian Pross and Götz Aly, pp. 121–42. Berlin: Edition Hentrich, 1989.

Beyerchen, Alan. *Scientists under Hitler: Politics and the Physics Community in the Third Reich*. New Haven: Yale University Press, 1977.

Binding, Karl, and Alfred Hoche. *Die Freigabe der Vernichtung lebensunwerten Lebens: Ihr Maß und Ihre Form*. Leipzig: Verlag von Felix Meiner, 1920.

Blasius, Dirk. *Der verwaltete Wahnsinn: Eine Sozialgeschichte des Irrenhauses*. Frankfurt: Fischer Taschenbuch Verlag, 1980.

Bock, Gisela. *Zwangssterilisation im Nationalsozialismus: Studien zur Rassenpolitik und Frauenpolitik*. Opladen: Westdeutscher Verlag, 1986.

Böhme, Heidi, and Kerstin Meyer. "Zum Schicksal jüdischer Anstaltspatienten in der Provinz Brandenburg ab 1938." *Nachrichtenblatt des Verbandes der Jüdischen Gemeinden in der Deutschen Demokratischen Republik* (June 1988): 7–8.

Brecht, Karen, et al., eds. *"Hier geht das Leben auf eine sehr merkwürdige Weise weiter…": Zur Geschichte der Psychoanalyse in Deutschland*. Hamburg: Verlag Michael Kellner, 1985.

Breitman, Richard. *The Architect of Genocide: Himmler and the Final Solution*. New York: Alfred A. Knopf, 1991.

Bridgman, Jon M. *The Revolt of the Hereros*. Berkeley: University of California Press, 1981.

Broszat, Martin. "Nationalsozialistische Konzentrationslager, 1933–1945." In Hans Buchheim et al., *Anatomie des SS-Staates*, 2:11–133. Munich: Deutscher Taschenbuchverlag, 1967.

Browning, Christopher R. *Fateful Months: Essays on the Emergence of the Final Solution*. New York: Holmes and Meier, 1985.

———. *Ordinary Men: Reserve Police Battalion 101 and the Final Solution in Poland*. New York: Harper-Collins, 1991.

————. *The Path to Genocide: Essays on the Launching of the Final Solution*. New York: Cambridge University Press, 1992.

Brucker-Boroujerdi, Ute, and Wolfgang Wippermann. "Das 'Zigeunerlager' Berlin-Marzahn, 1936–1945." *Pogrom: Zeitschrift für bedrohte Völker* 18, no. 130 (1987): 77–80.

Bundesminister der Justiz, ed. *Im Namen des deutschen Volkes—Justiz und Nationalsozialismus: Katalog zur Ausstellung des Bundesministers der Justiz*. Cologne: Verlag Wissenschaft und Politik, 1989.

Büttner, Ursula, Werner Johe, and Angelika Voß, eds. *Das Unrechtsregime*. 2 vols. Hamburg: Hans Christians Verlag, 1986.

Calvelli-Adorno, Franz. "Die rassische Verfolgung der Zigeuner vor dem 1. März 1943." *Rechtssprechung zum Widergutmachungsrecht* 12, no. 12 (December 1961): 529–37.

Cesarani, David, ed. *The Final Solution: Origins and Implementation*. London: Routledge, 1994.

Chorover, Stephan L. *From Genesis to Genocide: The Meaning of Human Nature and the Power of Behavior Control*. Cambridge: MIT Press, 1980.

Cocks, Geoffrey. *Psychotherapy in the Third Reich: The Göring Institute*. New York: Oxford University Press, 1985.

Delius, Peter. *Das Ende von Strecknitz: Die Lübecker Heilanstalt und ihre Auflösung 1941*. Kiel: Neuer Malik Verlag, 1988.

Denzler, Georg, and Volker Fabricius. *Die Kirchen im Dritten Reich*. 2 vols. Frankfurt: Fischer Taschenbuch Verlag, 1984.

Dobroszycki, Lucjan. "Jewish Elites under German Rule." In *The Holocaust: Ideology, Bureaucracy, and Genocide*, edited by Henry Friedlander and Sybil Milton, pp. 221–30. Millwood, N.Y.: Kraus International, 1980.

Dörner, Klaus. "Nationalsozialismus und Lebensvernichtung." *Vierteljahrshefte für Zeitgeschichte* 15 (1967): 121–52.

Dörner, Klaus, et al. *Der Krieg gegen die psychischen Kranken*. Rehburg-Loccum: Psychiatrie Verlag, 1980.

Dressen, Willi. "Euthanasie." In *Nationalsozialistische Massentötungen durch Giftgas: Eine Dokumentation*, edited by Eugen Kogon, Hermann Langbein, and Adalbert Rückerl, pp. 27–80, 303–10. Frankfurt: S. Fischer Verlag, 1983.

Drobisch, Klaus, and Günther Wieland. *System der NS-Konzentrationslager, 1933–1939*. Berlin: Akademie Verlag, 1993.

Ebbinghaus, Angelika, ed. *Opfer und Täterinnen: Frauenbiographien des Nationalsozialismus*. Schriften der Hamburger Stiftung für Sozialgeschichte des 20. Jahrhunderts, vol. 2. Nördlingen: Franz Greno, 1987.

Ebbinghaus, Angelika, Heidrun Kaupen-Haas, and Karl Heinz Roth, eds. *Heilen und Vernichten im Mustergau Hamburg: Bevölkerungs- und Gesundheitspolitik im Dritten Reich*. Hamburg: Konkret Literatur Verlag, 1984.

Eiber, Ludwig. *"Ich wußte, es wird schlimm": Die Verfolgung der Sinti und Roma in München, 1933–1945*. Munich: Buchendorfer Verlag, 1993.

Emmerich, Norbert. "Die Forensische Psychiatrie, 1933–1945." In *Totgeschwiegen, 1933–1945: Die Geschichte der Karl-Bonhoeffer-Nervenklinik*, edited by Arbeitsgruppe zur Erforschung der Karl-Bonhoeffer-Nervenklinik, pp. 105–23. Berlin: Edition Hentrich, 1988.

Eschwege, Helmut, ed. *Kennzeichen J: Bilder, Dokumente, Berichte zur Geschichte der Verbrechen des Hitlerfaschismus an den deutschen Juden, 1933–1945*. Berlin: VEB Deutscher Verlag der Wissenschaften, 1981.

Fings, Karola, and Frank Sparing. " 'Tunlichst als erziehungsunfähig hinzustellen' —

Zigeunerkinder und -jugendliche: Aus der Fürsorge in die Vernichtung." *Dachauer Hefte* 9 (1993): 159–80.

———. "Das Zigeunerlager in Köln-Bickendorf, 1935–1958." *1999: Zeitschrift für Sozialgeschichte des 20. und 21. Jahrhunderts* 6, no. 3 (July 1991): 11–40.

———. "Z.Zt. Zigeunerlager": Die Verfolgung der Düsseldorfer Sinti und Roma im Nationalsozialismus. Cologne: Volksblatt Verlag, 1992.

Finzen, Asmus. *Auf dem Dienstweg: Die Verstrickung einer Anstalt in die Tötung psychischer Kranker.* Rehburg-Loccum: Psychiatrie Verlag, 1984.

Fleming, Gerald. *Hitler and the Final Solution.* Berkeley: University of California Press, 1984.

Frei, Norbert, ed. *Medizin und Gesundheitspolitik in der NS-Zeit.* Munich: R. Oldenbourg Verlag, 1991.

Friedlander, Henry. "The Deportation of the German Jews: Postwar Trials of Nazi Criminals." *Leo Baeck Institute Yearbook* 29 (1984): 201–26.

———. "Euthanasia and the Final Solution." In *The Final Solution: Origins and Implementation,* edited by David Cesarani, pp. 51–61. London: Routledge, 1994.

———. "From Euthanasia to the Final Solution." In *Medical Science without Compassion, Past and Present: Fall Meeting, Cologne, September 28–30, 1988,* Arbeitspapiere-Atti-Proceedings, no. 11, edited by Charles Roland, Henry Friedlander, and Benno Müller-Hill, pp. 91–113. Hamburg: Hamburger Stiftung für Sozialgeschichte des 20. Jahrhunderts, 1992.

———. "The Judiciary and Nazi Crimes in Postwar Germany." *Simon Wiesenthal Center Annual* 1 (1984): 27–44.

———. "Jüdische Anstaltspatienten im NS-Deutschland." In *Aktion T4, 1939–1945: Die "Euthanasie"-Zentrale in der Tiergartenstraße 4,* edited by Götz Aly, pp. 34–44. Berlin: Edition Hentrich, 1987.

———. "The Manipulation of Language." In *The Holocaust: Ideology, Bureaucracy, and Genocide,* edited by Henry Friedlander and Sybil Milton, pp. 103–13. Millwood, N.Y.: Kraus International, 1980.

———. "Das nationalsozialistische Euthanasieprogramm." In *Geschichte und Verant-wortung,* edited by Aurelius Freytag, Boris Marte, and Thomas Stern, pp. 277–97. Vienna: Wiener Universitätsverlag, 1988.

———. "The Nazi Concentration Camps." In *Human Responses to the Holocaust,* edited by Michael Ryan, pp. 33–69. New York: Edwin Mellon Press, 1981.

Gilsenbach, Reimar. "Erwin Baur: Eine deutsche Chronik." *Beiträge zur national-sozialistischen Gesundheits- und Sozialpolitik* 8 (1990): 184–97.

———. "Wie Lolitschai zur Doktorwürde kam: Ein akademisches Kapitel aus dem Völkermord an den Sinti." *Beiträge zur nationalsozialistischen Gesundheits- und Sozialpolitik* 6 (1988): 101–34.

Goldhagen, Erich. "Weltanschauung und Endlösung." *Vierteljahrshefte für Zeitgeschichte* 24 (1976): 379–405.

Gotovitch, José. "Quelques donnes relatives l'extermination des tsiganes de Belgique." *Cahiers d'Histoire de la Seconde Guerre Mondiale* 4 (1976): 161–80.

Gould, Stephen Jay. *The Mismeasure of Man.* New York: W. W. Norton, 1981.

Graham, Loren R. "Science and Values: The Eugenics Movement in Germany and Russia in the 1920s." *American Historical Review* 82 (1977): 1133–64.

Graml, Hermann. "Zur Genesis der 'Endlösung.'" In *Das Unrechtsregime,* edited by Ursula Büttner, Werner Johe, and Angelika Voß, 2:2–28. Hamburg: Hans Christians Verlag, 1986.

Graumann, Carl F. "Die Sprache der NS-Propaganda und ihre Wirkung." In *Von* der Heilkunde zur Massentötung: Medizin im Nationalsozialismus, edited by Gerrit Hohendorf and Achim Magull-Seltenreich, pp. 185–99. Heidelberg: Wunderhorn, 1990.

Grenville, John A. S. "Die 'Endlösung' und die 'Judenmischlinge' im Dritten Reich." In *Das Unrechtsregime*, edited by Ursula Büttner, Werner Johe, and Angelika Voß, 2:91–121. Hamburg: Hans Christians Verlag, 1986.

Grobman, Alex, Daniel Landes, and Sybil Milton, eds. *Genocide: Critical Issues of the Holocaust*. New York: Rossel Books and Simon Wiesenthal Center, 1983.

Grode, Walter. *Die "Sonderbehandlung 14f13" in den Konzentrationslagern des Dritten Reiches: Ein Beitrag zur Dynamik faschistischer Vernichtungspolitik*. Frankfurt: Peter Lang, 1987.

Gruchmann, Lothar. "Euthanasie und Justiz im Dritten Reich." *Vierteljahrshefte für Zeitgeschichte* 20 (1972): 235–79.

———. *Justiz im Dritten Reich, 1933–1940: Anpassung und Unterwerfung in der Ära Gürtner*. Munich: R. Oldenbourg Verlag, 1988.

Hafner, Karl Heinz, and Rolf Winau. "'Die Freigabe der Vernichtung lebensunwerten Lebens': Eine Untersuchung zu der Schrift von Karl Binding und Alfred Hoche." *Medizinhistorisches Journal* 9 (1974): 227–54.

Hamann, Matthias. "Die Morde an polnischen und sowjetischen Zwangsarbeitern in deutschen Anstalten." *Beiträge zur nationalsozialistischen Gesundheits- und Sozialpolitik* 1 (1985): 121–87.

Härtel, Christine, Marianne Hühn, and Norbert Emmerich. "Krankenmorde in den Wittenauer Heilstätten." In *Totgeschwiegen, 1933–1945: Die Geschichte der Karl-Bonhoeffer-Nervenklinik*, edited by Arbeitsgruppe zur Erforschung der Karl-Bonhoeffer-Nervenklinik, pp. 185–89. Berlin: Edition Hentrich, 1988.

Hase-Mihalik, Eva von, and Doris Kreuzkamp. *Du kriegst auch einen schönen Wohnwagen: Zwangslager für Sinti und Roma während des Nationalsozialismus in Frankfurt am Main*. Frankfurt: Brandes und Apsel, 1990.

Headland, Ronald. *Messages of Murder: A Study of the Reports of the Einsatzgruppen of the Security Police and the Security Service, 1941–1943*. Rutherford, N.J.: Fairleigh Dickinson University Press, 1992.

Henke, Josef. "Quellenschicksale und Bewertungsfragen: Archivische Probleme bei der Sicherung von Quellen zur Verfolgung der Sinti und Roma im Dritten Reich." *Vierteljahrshefte für Zeitgeschichte* 41 (1993): 61–77.

Henkys, Reinhard. *Die nationalsozialistischen Gewaltverbrechen*. Berlin: Kreuz Verlag, 1964.

Hilberg, Raul. *The Destruction of the European Jews*. Chicago: Quadrangle Books, 1961. Rev. ed., 3 vols., New York: Holmes and Meier, 1985.

Hohendorf, Gerrit, and Achim Magull-Seltenreich, eds. *Von der Heilkunde zur Massentötung: Medizin im Nationalsozialismus*. Heidelberg: Wunderhorn, 1990.

Hohmann, Joachim S. *Geschichte der Zigeunerverfolgung in Deutschland*. 2d rev. ed. Frankfurt: Campus Verlag, 1988.

———. *Robert Ritter und die Erben der Kriminalbiologie: "Zigeunerforschung" im Nationalsozialismus und in Westdeutschland im Zeichen des Rassismus*. Studien zur Tsiganologie und Folkloristik, vol. 4. Frankfurt: Peter Lang, 1991.

Hoss, Christiane. "Die jüdischen Patienten in den rheinischen Anstalten zur Zeit des Nationalsozialismus." In *Verlegt nach unbekannt: Sterilisation und Euthanasie in Galkhausen, 1933–1945*, edited by Matthias Leipert, Rudolf Styrnal, and Winfried Schwarzer, pp. 60–76. Cologne: Rheinland-Verlag, 1987.

Hühn, Marrianne. "Das Schicksal der jüdischen Patienten im Nationalsozialismus." In *Totgeschwiegen, 1933–1945: Die Geschichte der Karl-Bonhoeffer-Nervenklinik*, edited by

Arbeitsgruppe zur Erforschung der Karl-Bonhoeffer-Nervenklinik, pp. 125–35. Berlin: Edition Hentrich, 1988.

Hundert Jahre deutscher Rassismus: Katalog und Arbeitsbuch. Cologne: Kölnische Gesellschaft für Christlich-Jüdische Zusammenarbeit, 1988.

Jäckel, Eberhard, and Jürgen Rohwer, eds. *Der Mord an den Juden im Zweiten Weltkrieg.* Stuttgart: Deutsche Verlagsanstalt, 1985.

Jaeckel, Gerhard. *Die Charité: Die Geschichte eines Weltzentrums der Medizin.* Bayreuth: Hestia, 1963.

Jäger, Herbert. *Verbrechen unter totalitärer Herrschaft: Studien zur nationalsozialistischen Gewaltkriminalität.* 2d ed. Frankfurt: Suhrkamp Taschenbuch, 1982.

Jaworski, Leon. *After Fifteen Years.* Houston: Gulf Publishing, 1961.

Kater, Michael H. "Doctor Leonardo Conti and His Nemesis: The Failure of Centralized Medicine in the Third Reich." *Central European History* 18 (1985): 299–325.

———. *Doctors under Hitler.* Chapel Hill: University of North Carolina Press, 1989.

———. "Die 'Gesundheitsführung' des Deutschen Volkes." *Medizinhistorisches Journal* 18 (1983): 349–75.

Kaul, Friedrich Karl. *Ärzte in Auschwitz.* Berlin: VEB Verlag Volk und Gesundheit, 1968.

———. *Nazimordaktion T4: Ein Bericht über die erste industriemäßig durchgeführte Mordaktion des Naziregimes.* Berlin: VEB Verlag Volk und Gesundheit, 1973.

Kaupen-Haas, Heidrun. "Experimental Obstetrics and National Socialism: The Conceptual Basis of Reproductive Technology Today." *Reproductive and Genetic Engineering: Journal of International Feminist Analysis* 1 (1988): 127–32.

———, ed. *Der Griff nach der Bevölkerung: Aktualität und Kontinuität nazistischer Bevölkerungspolitik.* Nördlingen: Greno Verlag, 1986.

Kenrick, Donald, and Grattan Puxon. *The Destiny of Europe's Gypsies.* New York: Basic Books, 1972. German edition, *Sinti und Roma: Die Vernichtung eines Volkes im NS-Staat*, translated by Astrid Stegelmann. Göttingen: Gesellschaft für bedrohte Völker, 1981.

Klee, Ernst. *"Euthanasie" im NS-Staat: Die "Vernichtung lebensunwerten Lebens."* Frankfurt: S. Fischer Verlag, 1983.

———. *Was sie taten—Was sie wurden: Ärzte, Juristen und andere Beteiligten am Kranken- oder Judenmord.* Frankfurt: Fischer Taschenbuch Verlag, 1986.

Klemperer, Victor. *LTI: Aus dem Notizbuch eines Philologen.* Berlin: Aufbau Verlag, 1946.

Klüppel, Manfred. *"Euthanasie" und Lebensvernichtung am Beispiel der Landesheilanstalten Haina und Merxhausen: Eine Chronik der Ereignisse, 1933–1945.* Kassel: Gesamthochschule Kassel, 1984.

Knödler, Ulrich. "Das Insulinproblem: Eine Studie zum Zusammenbruch der Arzneimittelversorgung der Zivilbevölkerung im Zweiten Weltkrieg." In *Der Wert des Menschen: Medizin in Deutschland, 1918–1945*, edited by Christian Pross and Götz Aly, pp. 250–60. Berlin: Edition Hentrich, 1989.

Kogon, Eugen, Hermann Langbein, and Adalbert Rückerl, eds. *Nationalsozialistische Massentötungen durch Giftgas: Eine Dokumentation.* Frankfurt: S. Fischer Verlag, 1983.

Kramer, Helmut. "Oberlandesgerichtspräsidenten und Generalstaatsanwälte als Gehilfen der NS-'Euthanasie': Selbstentlastung der Justiz für die Teilnahme am Anstaltsmord." *Kritische Justiz* 17 (1984): 25–43.

Krausnick, Helmut. "Judenverfolgung." In Hans Buchheim et al., *Anatomie des SS-Staates*, 2:235–366. Munich: Deutscher Taschenbuchverlag, 1967.

Krausnick, Helmut, and Hans-Heinrich Wilhelm. *Die Truppe des Weltanschauungskrieges: Die Einsatzgruppen der Sicherheitspolizei und des SD, 1938–1942.* Stuttgart: Deutsche Verlagsanstalt, 1981.

Krausnick, Michail. *Abfahrt Karlsruhe: Die Deportation der Karlsruher Sinti und Roma.* Karlsruhe: Verband der Sinti und Roma, 1990.

Krüger, Martina. "Kinderfachabteilung Wiesengrund: Die Tötung behinderter Kinder in Wittenau." In *Totgeschwiegen, 1933–1945: Die Geschichte der Karl-Bonhoeffer-Nervenklinik*, edited by Arbeitsgruppe zur Erforschung der Karl-Bonhoeffer-Nervenklinik, pp. 151–76. Berlin: Edition Hentrich, 1988.

Kudlien, Fridolf, et al. *Ärzte im Nationalsozialismus.* Cologne: Kiepenheuer und Witsch, 1985.

Kühl, Stefan. *The Nazi Connection: Eugenics, American Racism, and German National Socialism.* New York: Oxford University Press, 1994.

Langbein, Hermann. *Menschen in Auschwitz.* Frankfurt: Ullstein, 1980.

Leipert, Matthias, Rudolf Styrnal, and Winfried Schwarzer, eds. *Verlegt nach unbekannt: Sterilisation und Euthanasie in Galkhausen, 1933–1945.* Cologne: Rheinland-Verlag, 1987.

Lifton, Robert Jay. *The Nazi Doctors: Medical Killing and the Psychology of Genocide.* New York: Basic Books, 1986.

Lockot, Regine. *Erinnern und Durcharbeiten: Zur Geschichte der Psychoanalyse und Psychotherapie im Nationalsozialismus.* Frankfurt: Fischer Taschenbuch Verlag, 1985.

Macrakis, Kristie. *Surviving the Swastika: Scientific Research in Nazi Germany.* New York: Oxford University Press, 1993.

Mader, Ernst T. *Das erzwungene Sterben von Patienten der Heil- und Pflegeanstalt Kaufbeuren-Irsee zwischen 1940 und 1945 nach Dokumenten und Berichten von Augenzeugen.* 2d ed. Blöcktach: Verlag an der Säge, 1985.

Marsalek, Hans. *Die Geschichte des Konzentrationslagers Mauthausen.* 2d ed. Vienna: Österreichische Lagergemeinschaft Mauthausen, 1980.

———. *Die Vergasungsaktionen im Konzentrationslager Mauthausen.* Vienna: Österreichische Lagergemeinschaft Mauthausen, 1988.

Medizin im Nationalsozialismus. Kolloquien des Instituts für Zeitgeschichte. Munich: R. Oldenbourg Verlag, 1988.

Mehrtens, Herbert, and Steffen Richter, eds. *Naturwissenschaft, Technik und NS-Ideologie.* Frankfurt: Suhrkamp Verlag, 1980.

Meister, Johannes. "Schicksale der 'Zigeunerkinder' aus der St. Josefspflege in Mulfingen." *Württembergisch Franken Jahrbuch* (1984): 197–229.

———. "Die 'Zigeunerkinder' von der St. Josefspflege in Mulfingen." *1999: Zeitschrift für Sozialgeschichte des 20. und 21. Jahrhunderts* 2, no. 2 (1987): 14–51.

Milton, Sybil. "The Context of the Holocaust." *German Studies Review* 13 (1990): 269–83.

———. "Gypsies and the Holocaust." *History Teacher* 24 (1991): 375–87, and correspondence (Milton and Bauer), 25 (1992): 515–21.

———. "Nazi Policies toward Roma and Sinti, 1933–1945." *Journal of the Gypsy Lore Society*, ser. 5, 2, no. 1 (1992): 1–18.

———. "Spanish Republican Refugees and the Holocaust, 1939–1945." In *German and International Perspectives on the Spanish Civil War: The Aesthetics of Partisanship*, edited by Luis Costa et al., pp. 408–25. Columbia, S.C.: Camden House, 1992.

Mommsen, Hans. "Die Realisierung des Utopischen: Die 'Endlösung der Judenfrage' im Dritten Reich." *Geschichte und Gesellschaft* 9 (1983): 381–420.

Morlok, Karl. *Wo bringt ihr uns hin?: "Geheime Reichssache" Grafeneck.* Stuttgart: Quell Verlag, 1985.

Moser, Jonny. *Die Judenverfolgung in Österreich, 1938–1945.* Vienna: Europa Verlag, 1966.

———. "Nisko: The First Experiment in Deportation." *Simon Wiesenthal Center Annual* 2 (1985): 1–30.

Mosse, George L. *The Crisis of German Ideology: Intellectual Origins of the Third Reich.* Reprint, New York: Grosset and Dunlap, 1964.

————. *Toward the Final Solution: A History of European Racism*. New York: Howard Fertig, 1978.

Müller-Hill, Benno. "Kollege Mengele—nicht Bruder Eichmann." In *Sinn und Form: Beiträge zur Literatur*, vol. 37, no. 3, pp. 671–76. Berlin: Akademie der Künste der Deutschen Demokratischen Republik, 1985.

————. "Selektion: Die Wissenschaft von der biologischen Auslese des Menschen durch Menschen." In *Medizin und Gesundheitspolitik in der NS-Zeit*, edited by Norbert Frei, pp. 137–55. Munich: R. Oldenbourg Verlag, 1991.

————. *Tödliche Wissenschaft: Die Aussonderung von Juden, Zigeunern und Geisteskranken, 1933–1945*. Reinbek bei Hamburg: Rowohlt Taschenbuch Verlag, 1984. English edition, *Murderous Science: Elimination by Scientific Selection of Jews, Gypsies, and Others, Germany, 1933–1945*, translated by George R. Fraser. Oxford: Oxford University Press, 1988.

Necas, Ctibor. "Die tschechischen und slowakischen Roma im Dritten Reich." *Pogrom: Zeitschrift für bedrohte Völker* 12, no. 80/81 (1981): 62–64.

Noakes, Jeremy. "Wohin gehören die 'Judenmischlinge'?: Die Entstehung der ersten Durchführungsverordnung zu den Nürnberger Gesetzen." In *Das Unrechtsregime*, edited by Ursula Büttner, Werner Johe, and Angelika Voß, 2:69–89. Hamburg: Hans Christians Verlag, 1986.

Nowak, Kurt. *"Euthanasie" und Sterilisierung im "Dritten Reich."* 2d ed. Weimar: Hermann Böhlaus Nachfolger, 1980.

Pingel, Falk. *Häftlinge unter SS-Herrschaft: Widerstand, Selbstbehauptung und Vernichtung im Konzentrationslager*. Hamburg: Hoffmann und Campe, 1978.

Platen-Hallermund, Alice. *Die Tötung Geisteskranker in Deutschland: Aus der deutschen Ärztekommission beim amerikanischen Militärgericht*. Frankfurt: Verlag der Frankfurter Hefte, 1948.

Pommerin, Reiner. *"Sterilisierung der Rheinlandbastarde": Das Schicksal einer farbigen deutschen Minderheit, 1918–1937*. Düsseldorf: Droste Verlag, 1979.

Proctor, Robert. *Racial Hygiene: Medicine under the Nazis*. Cambridge: Harvard University Press, 1988.

Projektgruppe für die vergessenen Opfer des NS-Regimes, ed. *Verachtet, Verfolgt, Vernichtet: Zu den "vergessenen" Opfern des NS-Regimes*. Hamburg: VSA-Verlag, 1986.

Projektgruppe Volk und Gesundheit, ed. *Volk und Gesundheit: Heilen und Vernichten im Nationalsozialismus*. Tübingen: Tübinger Vereinigung für Volkskunde, 1982.

Pross, Christian, and Götz Aly, eds. *Der Wert des Menschen: Medizin in Deutschland, 1918–1945*. Berlin: Edition Hentrich, 1989.

Pross, Christian, and Rolf Winau, eds. *Nicht Mißhandeln: Das Krankenhaus Moabit*. Berlin: Frölich und Kaufmann, 1984.

Regener, Susanne. "Ausgegrenzt: Die optische Inventarisierung der Menschen im Polizeiwesen und in der Psychiatrie." *Fotogeschichte* 10, no. 38 (1990): 23–38.

Reitlinger, Gerald. *The Final Solution: The Attempt to Exterminate the Jews of Europe, 1939–1945*. Reprint, New York: Perpetua Books, 1961.

Richarz, Bernhard. *Heilen, Pflegen, Töten: Zur Alltagsgeschichte einer Heil- und Pflegeanstalt bis zum Ende des Nationalsozialismus*. Göttingen: Verlag für Medizinische Psychologie im Verlag Vandenhoeck und Ruprecht, 1987.

Rimpau, Wilhelm. "Viktor von Weizsäcker im Nationalsozialismus." In *Von der Heilkunde zur Massentötung: Medizin im Nationalsozialismus*, edited by Gerrit Hohendorf and Achim Magull-Seltenreich, pp. 113–30. Heidelberg: Wunderhorn, 1990.

Roer, Dorothee, and Dieter Henkel, eds. *Psychiatrie im Faschismus: Die Anstalt Hadamar, 1933–1945*. Bonn: Psychiatrie-Verlag, 1986.

Roland, Charles, Henry Friedlander, and Benno Müller-Hill, eds. *Medical Science*

without Compassion, Past and Present: Fall Meeting, Cologne, September 28–30,
1988. Arbeitspapiere-Atti-Proceedings, no. 11. Hamburg: Hamburger Stiftung für
Sozialgeschichte des 20. Jahrhunderts, 1992.

Roth, Karl Heinz. " 'Erbbiologische Bestandsaufnahme': Ein Aspekt 'ausmerzender'
Erfassung vor der Entfesselung des zweiten Weltkrieges." In *Erfassung zur Vernichtung:*
Von der Sozialhygiene zum "Gesetz über Sterbehilfe," edited by Karl Heinz Roth, pp.
57–100. Berlin: Verlagsgesellschaft Gesundheit, 1984.

———. "Filmpropaganda für die Vernichtung der Geisteskranken und Behinderten im
'Dritten Reich.' " *Beiträge zur nationalsozialistischen Gesundheits- und Sozialpolitik* 2
(1985): 125–93.

———. "Schein-Alternativen im Gesundheitswesen: Alfred Grotjahn (1869–1931) — Inte-
grationsfigur etablierter Sozialmedizin und nationalsozialistischer 'Rassenhygiene.' " In
Erfassung zur Vernichtung: Von der Sozialhygiene zum "Gesetz über Sterbehilfe," edited
by Karl Heinz Roth, pp. 31–56. Berlin: Verlagsgesellschaft Gesundheit, 1984.

Rückerl, Adalbert. *NS-Verbrechen vor Gericht.* Heidelberg: C. F. Müller Juristischer
Verlag, 1982.

Rückleben, Hermann. *Deportation und Tötung von Geisteskranken aus den badischen*
Anstalten der Inneren Mission Kork und Mosbach. Karlsruhe: Verlag Evangelischer
Presseverband für Baden, 1981.

Rudnick, Martin. *Aussondern — Sterilisieren — Liquidieren: Die Verfolgung Behinderter im*
Nationalsozialismus. Berlin: Edition Marhold, 1990.

———. *Behinderte im Nationalsozialismus: Von der Ausgrenzung und der Zwangssteri-*
lisation zur "Euthanasie." Weinheim: Beltz Verlag, 1985.

Sauer, Paul. *Die Schicksale der jüdischen Bürger Baden-Württembergs während der*
nationalsozialistischen Verfolgungszeit, 1933–1945. Stuttgart: W. Kohlhammer
Verlag, 1968.

Scalpelli, Adolfo, ed. *San Sabba: Istruttoria e processo per il Lager della Risiera.* 2 vols.
Milan: ANED — Arnoldo Mondadori Editore, 1988.

Schabow, Dietrich. *Zur Geschichte der Juden in Bendorf.* Bendorf: Hedwig-Dransfeld-Haus
in Verbindung mit dem ökumenischen Arbeitskreis, 1979.

Scheffler, Wolfgang. "Gedanken zur Rassenpolitik des Nationalsozialismus." In *Macht-*
verfall und Machtergreifung: Aufstieg und Herrschaft des Nationalsozialismus, edited by
Rudolf Lill and Heinrich Oberreuter, pp. 275–86. Munich: Bayerische Landeszentrale
für politische Bildungsarbeit, 1983.

———. "Probleme der Holocaustforschung." In *Deutsche, Polen, Juden,* edited by Stefi
Jersch-Wenzel, pp. 259–81. Berlin: Colloquium Verlag, 1987.

———. "Rassenfanatismus und Judenverfolgung." In *Deutschland 1933: Machtzerfall der*
Demokratie und nationalsozialistische "Machtergreifung," edited by Wolfgang Treue and
Jürgen Schmädeke, pp. 16–44. Berlin: Colloquium Verlag, 1984.

———. "Zur Entstehungsgeschichte der 'Endlösung.' " *Aus Politik und Zeitgeschichte:*
Beilage zur Wochenzeitung das Parlament, B43/82, 30 October 1982, pp. 3–10.

Schleunes, Karl. *The Twisted Road to Auschwitz.* Urbana: University of Illinois Press,
1970.

Schmidt, Gerhard. *Selektion in der Heilanstalt, 1939–1945.* 2d ed. Frankfurt: Edition
Suhrkamp, 1983.

Schmuhl, Hans-Walter. *Rassenhygiene, Nationalsozialismus, Euthanasie: Von der Ver-*
hütung zur Vernichtung "lebensunwerten Lebens," 1890–1945. Göttingen: Vandenhoeck
und Ruprecht, 1987.

Scholz, Susanne, and Reinhard Singer. "Die Kinder von Hadamar." In *Psychiatrie im*
Faschismus: Die Anstalt Hadamar, 1933–1945, edited by Dorothee Roer and Dieter
Henkel, pp. 214–36. Bonn: Psychiatrie Verlag, 1986.

Schultz, Ulrich. "Dichtkunst, Heilkunst, Forschung: Der Kinderarzt Werner Catel." *Beiträge zur nationalsozialistischen Gesundheits- und Sozialpolitik* 2 (1985): 107–24.

Seidler, Horst, and Andreas Rett. *Rassenhygiene: Ein Weg in den Nationalsozialismus.* Vienna: Jugend und Volk, 1988.

———. *Das Reichssippenamt entscheidet: Rassenbiologie im Nationalsozialismus.* Vienna: Jugend und Volk, 1982.

Sereny, Gitta. *Into That Darkness: From Mercy Killing to Mass Murder.* New York: McGraw-Hill, 1974.

Sijes, B. A., et al. *Vervolging van Zigeuners in Nederland, 1940–1945.* The Hague: Nijhoff, 1979.

Steinmetz, Selma. *Österreichs Zigeuner im NS-Staat.* Vienna: Europa Verlag, 1966.

Stern, Fritz. *The Politics of Cultural Despair: A Study of the Rise of the Germanic Ideology.* Garden City, N.Y.: Doubleday Anchor Books, 1965.

Strauss, Herbert A. "Jewish Emigration from Germany: Nazi Policies and Jewish Responses." *Leo Baeck Institute Yearbook* 25 (1980): 313–61, 26 (1981): 343–409.

Streim, Alfred. *Die Behandlung sowjetischer Kriegsgefangener im "Fall Barbarossa": Eine Dokumentation.* Heidelberg: C. F. Müller Juristischer Verlag, 1981.

Streit, Christian. *Keine Kameraden: Die Wehrmacht und die sowjetischen Kriegsgefangenen.* Stuttgart: Deutsche Verlagsanstalt, 1978.

Sydnor, Charles W. *Soldiers of Destruction: The SS Death's Head Division, 1933–1945.* Princeton: Princeton University Press, 1977.

Thom, Achim, and Genadij Ivanovic Caregorodcev, eds. *Medizin unterm Hakenkreuz.* Berlin: VEB Verlag Volk und Gesundheit, 1989.

Thom, Achim, and Horst Spaar, eds. *Medizin im Faschismus.* Berlin: VEB Verlag Volk und Gesundheit, 1989.

Thurner, Erika. *Nationalsozialismus und Zigeuner in Österreich.* Vienna: Geyer Edition, 1983.

Tuchel, Johannes. *Konzentrationslager: Organisationsgeschichte und Funktion der "Inspektion der Konzentrationslager," 1934–1938.* Schriften des Bundesarchivs, no. 39. Boppard on the Rhine: Harald Boldt Verlag, 1991.

Vanja, Christina, and Martin Vogt, eds. *Euthanasie in Hadamar: Die nationalsozialistische Vernichtungspolitik in hessischen Anstalten.* Kassel: Landeswohlfahrtsverband Hessen, 1991.

Waite, Robert G. L. *Vanguard of Nazism: The Free Corps Movement in Postwar Germany, 1918–1923.* Cambridge: Harvard University Press, 1952.

Weinberg, Gerhard L. *A World at Arms: A Global History of World War II.* Cambridge: Cambridge University Press, 1994.

Weindling, Paul. *Health, Race, and German Politics between National Unification and Nazism, 1870–1945.* Cambridge: Cambridge University Press, 1989.

Weinreich, Max. *Hitler's Professors: The Part of Scholarship in Germany's Crimes against the Jewish People.* New York: Yivo, 1946.

Weiss, Sheila Faith. "The Race Hygiene Movement in Germany." *Osiris,* 2d ser., 3 (1987): 193–236.

———. "Die rassenhygienische Bewegung in Deutschland, 1904–1933." In *Der Wert des Menschen: Medizin in Deutschland, 1918–1945,* edited by Christian Pross and Götz Aly, pp. 153–73. Berlin: Edition Hentrich, 1989.

Winter, Bettina, et al., eds. *Verlegt nach Hadamar: Die Geschichte einer NS-"Euthanasie"-Anstalt.* Kassel: Landeswohlfahrtsverband Hessen, 1991.

Wippermann, Wolfgang. *Die nationalsozialistische Zigeunerverfolgung.* Leben in Frankfurt zur NS-Zeit, vol. 2. Frankfurt: Amt für Volksbildung-Volkshochschule, 1986.

Wunder, Michael. "'Ausgesuchte, abgelaufene sekundäre Demenzen...': Die Durchführung des 'Euthanasie'-Programms in Hamburg am Beispiel der Alsterdorfer Anstalten." In *Verachtet, Verfolgt, Vernichtet: Zu den "vergessenen" Opfern des NS-Regimes*, edited by Projektgruppe für die vergessenen Opfer des NS-Regimes, pp. 85–101. Hamburg: VSA-Verlag, 1986.

Wunder, Michael, and Harald Jenner. "Das Schicksal der jüdischen Bewohner der Alsterdorfer Anstalten." In *Auf dieser schiefen Ebene gibt es kein Halten mehr: Die Alsterdorfer Anstalten im Nationalsozialismus*, edited by Michael Wunder, Ingrid Genkel, and Harald Jenner, pp. 155–67. Hamburg: Vorstand der Alsterdorfer Anstalten, 1987.

Wunder, Michael, and Udo Sierck, eds. *Sie nennen es Fürsorge: Behinderte zwischen Vernichtung und Widerstand*. Berlin: Verlagsgesellschaft Gesundheit, 1982.

Wunder, Michael, Ingrid Genkel, and Harald Jenner, eds. *Auf dieser schiefen Ebene gibt es kein Halten mehr: Die Alsterdorfer Anstalten im Nationalsozialismus*. Hamburg: Vorstand der Alsterdorfer Anstalten, 1987.

Wuttke-Groneberg, Walter. *Medizin im Nationalsozialismus: Ein Arbeitsbuch*. Wurmlingen: Schwäbischer Verlagsgesellschaft, 1980.

Zimmermann, Michael. *Verfolgt, Vertrieben, Vernichtet: Die nationalsozialistische Vernichtungspolitik gegen Sinti und Roma*. Essen: Klartext Verlag, 1989.

———. "Von der Diskriminierung zum 'Familienlager' Auschwitz: Die nationalsozialistische Zigeunerverfolgung." *Dachauer Hefte* 5 (1989): 87–114.

Zülch, Tilman, ed. *In Auschwitz vergast, bis heute verfolgt: Zur Situation der Roma (Zigeuner) in Deutschland und Europa*. Reinbek bei Hamburg: Rowohlt Taschenbuch Verlag, 1979.

execution of, 200; and Kallmeyer, 211, 212–13, 214; conflict with Heyde, 219; relations with employees, 231, 236; and killing handicapped Jews, 263, 270, 276

Brain research, 1–2, 129, 130

Brandenburg (province): compulsory sterilization in, 36

Brandenburg-Görden state hospital: children's killing ward, 46–47, 49; research station, 127, 129–30

Brandenburg killing center, 93, 118; establishment of, 87, 88–89, 328 (n. 19); experimental gassing demonstration at, 87–88, 194, 210; closed and replaced by Bernburg, 88, 92, 106–7, 108, 188; physical configuration, 89, 90, 95; gas chamber, 89–90, 96; crematorium, 90, 98, 106; numbers killed at, 109–10; handicapped Jews killed at, 277–78

Brandt, Karl: and killing of Knauer baby, 39, 40, 44, 312 (n. 2); as Hitler's accompanying physician, 39, 189; appointed plenipotentiary for children's euthanasia, 39–40, 44; appointed plenipotentiary for adult euthanasia, 63–64; and establishment of euthanasia killing program, 67, 68, 81; and selection of victims, 81, 82, 144, 176; and Hitler's "stop" order, 85, 111; and development of gassing technique, 86, 87–88, 194, 327 (n. 6); Nuremberg trial testimony, 86, 263; and "wild" euthanasia, 157, 158–59; as plenipotentiary for medicine and health, 157, 189; role as administrator of euthanasia killing program, 189, 197, 297; evaluation of, 217–18; denial of knowledge of killings, 243, 263; and killing of handicapped Jews, 263, 282

Braune, Pastor Paul Gerhard, 113–14, 115, 120

Breisacher, Korin, 271

Brenner. See Blankenburg, Werner

Brigham, Carl C., 5, 6

Broca, Paul, 1

Buch, Walter, 107

Buchberger, Matthias, 237

Buchenwald concentration camp, 144, 146–47

Büchner, Herbert, 33

Buddrich, Walter, 179

Budin, Katharina, 183

Bünger (supervisor), 110

Bunke, Heinrich, 127, 129, 222, 223, 224, 225–26

Bürckel, Josef, 65

"Burdensome lives" (Ballastexistenzen), 15, 81, 112

"Bureaucratic killers" (Schreibtischtäter), 194, 216

Burt, Sir Cyril, 4, 5, 7

Cancer: terminal patients, 14–15

Carbon monoxide gas, 86, 300

Castration, 24, 31

Catel, Werner, 230; and killing of Knauer baby, 39, 312 (nn. 2, 5); as expert for children's euthanasia, 44, 46, 53, 124

Catholic Charity Association (Caritasverband), 113, 266

Central Accounting Office for State Hospitals and Nursing Homes, 73–74, 164

Central Office for Economy and Administration (WVHA), 287, 301

Central Office for Reich Security (RSHA): administrative structure, 55; collaboration with T4, 55, 202, 210; implementation of gassing techniques, 210, 218, 286; and Gypsies, 252, 291, 294; implementation of final solution, 285, 286, 288, 289–90

Central Office of the Reich Detective Forces (RKPA), 55; collaboration with T4, 55, 205, 207; and Gypsy research, 251, 258, 293; arrest and deportation of Gypsies, 258, 261, 291, 292. See also Technical Institute for the Detection of Crime

Central Office to Combat the Gypsy Pest, 258

Chancellery of the Führer (KdF), 176, 230; and killing of Knauer baby, 39; assigned responsibility for killing programs, 40, 63–64, 111–12, 116, 145; administrative structure, 40–41, 42; Central Office II, 40–41, 42, 64, 69; collaboration of Reich Ministry of Interior with, 42–43, 45–46, 47–48, 64, 153, 157, 295; creation of Reich Committee front for children's euthanasia, 44; recruitment of physicians and staff, 46–47, 48, 64–65, 66, 77, 192, 193, 196, 226; and implementation of children's euthanasia, 46–47, 53; procurement of medications and poisons,

54–55, 56; and implementation of adult euthanasia, 64–65, 66, 68, 69, 98–99, 121, 136, 285; and Hitler's authorization of euthanasia, 67, 121, 285; creation of front organizations for adult euthanasia, 68, 72–73; Reich Ministry of Justice complaints to, 121; cooperation of Reich Ministry of Justice with, 122–24; collaboration in Operation 14f13, 142, 145; proposal of euthanasia law, 154; collaboration in final solution, 190, 296, 297, 298; cooperation of hospitals and government agencies with, 200; deceptions to maintain secrecy, 281

Charitable Foundation for Institutional Care, 73

Charitable Foundation for the Transport of Patients, Inc. (Gekrat), 164; created as T4 front, 73; transfer of handicapped patients by, 83–84, 85, 94, 152–53; transfer of handicapped Jews by, 272, 274, 277, 279, 283; public suspicion of, 112; evasiveness to questions about victims, 117–18, 275–76; patients' fear of, 170–71; administration of, 194

Chelmno (Kulmhof) extermination camp, 286, 287–89, 291, 301, 353 (n. 64)

Chemists, 208–9, 214, 296

Children: eugenic theories of heredity and, 7–8; illegitimate, 19; sterilization of "Rhineland bastards," 246–47

Children's euthanasia, 39, 62, 232; assignment of responsibility for, 39–41, 69; organization and staffing of, 41–42, 44, 48; physicians in, 44, 48, 53, 54, 57–58, 60, 166; registration of children for, 44–46; selection of victims, 46, 57–58, 169; killing wards, 46–47, 48–53, 152, 169; financing of, 48; methods of killing, 50, 53–54, 152; continuation after end of war, 51–52, 162–63; procurement of medication for, 54–56; transfer of children to killing wards, 56–57, 170; medical research on victims of, 58–59, 131, 152, 156–57; deception of parents of victims, 59–61, 166–68, 183–84; number of victims of, 61; continuation after "stop" order, 61, 111, 151; killing of Jewish hybrids, 161, 294–95; Allied troops' discovery of, 162, 218–19; parental opposition to killing of children, 166–68, 179–

84; parental requests for killing of children, 171–72. *See also* Reich Committee for the Scientific Registration of Severe Hereditary Ailments; T4, Operation

Children's killing wards, 46–54, 56–57, 59–60, 131, 152, 156–57, 162–63, 169, 176, 183, 216, 218–19, 225, 229; for Jewish hybrid children, 161, 295. *See also* T4, Operation

Churches, 111, 112, 116

Citizenship, 24, 25, 288

Civil service: exclusion of Jews from, 24; implementation of sterilization law, 26, 37; Nazi party power struggle with, 36–37; ranks, 192

Clauberg, Carl, 132–33, 134

Clergy, 114–16, 339 (n. 28)

Cologne Gypsy camp, 254

Columbus House, 68, 71, 73, 78, 235, 241, 281

Concentration camps, 327 (n. 1); transfer of psychiatric patients to, 18, 166; medical experiments on prisoners in, 131–32, 134–35; sterilization of prisoners in, 143; physicians in, 143–48, 301; and Operation 14f13, 143–50; forced labor in, 151; used as threat, 235, 236; as killing centers, 286–87

Concordat with the Vatican (1933), 27, 113

Condolence letter (*Trostbrief*), 104–5

Conti, Leonardo: as Reich physician leader, 37–38, 62; as state secretary for health, 37–38, 62, 64; power struggle for control of killing program, 63–64, 145, 157, 196; involvement in T4, 64, 66, 78, 111–12, 189, 190; order for registration of handicapped institutions, 75; and development of gassing technique, 86, 87, 194; giving deadly injections, 88; and protests from churches and judiciary, 115, 121; advocacy of sterilization of Gypsies, 292

Cope, E. D., 2

Craniometry, 1–2, 3–4

Crematoria, 98, 300

Creutz, Walter, 52–53, 155

Criminal Biological Institute, 258

Criminality, 3, 6, 17, 23–24, 249, 252

Crinis, Max de, 66, 155, 230, 321 (n. 39), 380 (n. 9)

Croatia, 290

Crohne, Wilhelm, 122
Cropp, Fritz, 64, 190
Czechoslovakia. *See* Bohemia and Moravia, Protectorate of

Dachau concentration camp, 65–66, 131–32
Damzog, Ernst, 137, 140
Danzig–West Prussia, 136
Darwin, Charles R., 1, 9
Davenport, Charles Benedict, 4, 7, 252
Deafness, xi, 26, 28–29, 81
Death certificates, 101–2, 277
Decontaminators (*Desinfektoren*), 97, 233
"Degeneration" (*Entartung*), 9, 125
Deportation: of Jews, 260–61, 282–83, 288–90, 291, 379 (n. 122); of Gypsies, 261–62, 288, 290–91, 292; of handicapped Jews, 282, 283
Deussen (physician), 130
DFG. *See* German Research Foundation
DGT. *See* German Association of Cities
Disabilities. *See* Handicapped, the
Diseases, hereditary, 26, 29, 33–34, 36, 37
Dreer, Karen, 176
Dubois, Werner, 241–42
Düsseldorf Gypsy camp, 254–55

East European Jews, 253
Eastern workers (*Ostarbeiter*), 161–62
Eberl, Irmfried: at Brandenburg gassing demonstration, 87, 88, 210; as physician-in-charge at Brandenburg and Bernburg, 89, 92, 96, 99, 176, 203, 219; documentation left by, 100, 102, 154, 278–79, 296; on cause-of-death assignments, 102; medical research on victims, 129, 222; suicide of, 219; background, 220–21; in Operation Reinhard, 296–97, 298, 299–300
Eglfing-Haar state hospital, 95; children's killing ward, 49, 50–51; starvation houses, 167; handicapped Jewish patients, 273–74
Ehrhardt, Sophie, 134, 250, 251
Eichberg state hospital, 318 (n. 118); children's killing ward, 51, 156–57; as transit institution, 109; research station, 130–31
Eichmann, Adolf, 260, 261, 288, 290
Eicke, Theodor, 65–66, 143, 228
Eigruber, August, 194, 233
Eimann, Kurt, 136, 137

Eimann Battalion, 136, 137, 141, 158
Einsatzgruppen of the Sipo and SD, 141, 211, 284, 286, 289, 290, 296
Electroshock therapy, 156, 160, 169
Endruweit, Klaus, 222, 223, 224, 226, 365 (n. 32)
Enke, Willi, 92
Epilepsy, xi, 3, 26, 28–29, 81
Erler, Willy, 173
Eugenics: in United States, 4–8, 9, 16; in Germany, 9–14; and euthanasia, 15–16; Nazi regime and, 16–20, 23, 123–26, 175; and the handicapped, 18, 23; German churches and, 113; and Gypsies, 249, 250, 251–52, 253, 258, 293, 294; and Jews, 251
Eugenics Record Office (ERO), 4–5, 6–7
Euphemisms, xi, xxi, 50, 57, 129, 158, 188, 231, 233
Euthanasia, xxi, 14–16, 21–22. *See also* Children's euthanasia; T4, Operation
Evolution, 2–3, 9
Ewald, Gottfried, 78, 217, 324 (n. 108)
Exclusionary policies: race science as basis of, 1, 17, 18, 19, 20; killing as logical extension of, 1, 17, 21, 39, 62; applied to the handicapped, 17, 18, 21, 23, 25–26, 112, 252–53; applied to Gypsies, 17, 18, 21, 25, 252, 253–54, 259–60, 291–92, 293; applied to Jews, 17, 18–19, 21, 24, 247, 253, 259, 260, 263–64, 266; Nazi codification of, 17–19, 23–26, 187–88, 259; applied to blacks, 18, 246–47; role of physicians in implementation of, 216
Extermination camps, 111–12, 286–88, 297–301; T4 managers' visit to, 72, 194, 224, 297–98; T4 staff at, 205–6, 237–45, 297–99; construction work at, 215; number of victims, 287; removal of valuables from victims, 299; killing procedure in, 300–301; functions of physicians at, 301–2. *See also* Operation Reinhard
Eyrich, Max, 294

Faltlhauser, Valentin, 51–52, 66, 159, 162–63, 216, 219
Faulhaber, Cardinal Michael (archbishop of Munich), 114–15
"Feeblemindedness" (*Schwachsinn*): eugenic studies of, 4, 6, 7–8, 305 (n. 25); compulsory sterilization for, 8, 26, 28, 29, 31–33, 37; euthanasia theorists and,

Katschenka, Anna, 231–32
Katz, Flora, 271
Kaufbeuren-Irsee children's killing ward, 51–52, 162–63, 218–19
Kaufmann, Adolf Gustav: background, 72, 191, 192, 193; as chief of T4 Inspector's Office, 72, 194; at Brandenburg killing center, 89; establishment of T4 killing centers, 91, 92, 93, 194; recruitment of T4 personnel, 234, 236
Kautsky, Karl, 10
KdF. See Chancellery of the Führer
Kehr, Marie, 172
Keller, Helen, 58
Kerrl, Hanns, 115
Kiev Pathological Institute, 142
Kihn, Berthold, 66
"Killers on the scene" (tatnahe Täter), 202, 216
Killing centers of euthanasia. See T4 killing centers
Killing centers of final solution. See Extermination camps
Killing hospitals of "wild" euthanasia, 152–53, 160–61, 162–63, 185–86, 207, 218–19; numbers killed in, 161; compared to concentration camps, 166; chances for survival of the handicapped in, 182
Kirchert, Werner, 221
Klee, Ernst, xii
Klein, Alfons, 161, 181, 207
Kloos, Gerhard, 182
Knauer baby, 39, 312 (n. 2)
Knoll, Ernst, 176
Knoll, Fritz, 126
Koch, Erich, 139, 140, 172
Kochan, Richard, 281
Königslutter transit institution, 152–53
Koppe, Wilhelm, 137, 139–40
Kovno, 289
Krämer, Anna, 178
Krämer, Karl, 168
Krämer, Ludwig, 178
Krause, Hans, 139
Kremer, Johann Paul, 132
Kreyssig, Lothar, 119, 121
Kripo (Kriminalpolizei), 54–55, 354 (n. 73); and Gypsies, 258, 262, 291, 293
KTI. See Technical Institute for the Detection of Crime
Kühnke (physician), 52

Kulmhof extermination camp. See Chelmno extermination camp
Kuntschik, Ludwig, 174

Lachmann, Erich, 244
Lackenbach Gypsy camp, 255–56
Lalleri. See Gypsies
Lamarck, Jean-Baptiste, 2
Lambert, Erwin, 214–15, 232
Lammers, Hans Heinrich, 37, 40, 63, 67, 114, 120–21, 285
Lange, Herbert, 137–39, 286, 288
Lange Commando, 137, 139–40, 296
Langenhorn state hospital, 152, 153
Lanzman, Claude, 240
Laughlin, Harry Hamilton, 4, 6
Lavenberger, Johann, 166–67
Law against Dangerous Habitual Criminals (1933), 23
Law for the Prevention of Offspring with Hereditary Diseases (sterilization law, 1933), 23, 25–27, 30, 310 (n. 31); illegal applications of, 18, 247, 253–54; opposition of churches to, 113. See also Sterilization
Law for the Protection of German Blood and German Honor (1935), 24, 25, 31
Law for the Protection of the Hereditary Health of the German Nation (Marriage Health Law, 1935), 23, 31
Law for the Restoration of the Professional Civil Service (1933), 24, 253
Law on Measures of Security and Reform (1933), 23
Le Bon, Gustave, 1–2
Ledermann, Max, 264–65
Legal security (Rechtssicherheit), 20, 188, 252
Lehmann, Julius Friedrich, 13
Lehner, Ludwig, 50, 227, 315 (n. 57)
Lensch, Pastor Friedrich, 267, 268
Lenz, Fritz, 12, 13, 19, 123, 175, 247
Leu, Alfred, 53
Leus, Hanne, 269
Ley, Robert, 175
Lichtenberg, Bernhard, 115–16
Lichtenstein née Graff, Eva "Sara," 280
"Life unworthy of life" (lebensunwerten Lebens), 14–15, 21–22, 62–63, 64, 78, 81, 208
Lifton, Robert Jay, 217–18, 301

Linden, Herbert, 114, 155; as Reich Ministry of Interior health official, 42, 43, 64, 313 (n. 16); medical background, 43; Nazi party membership, 43, 200–201, 313 (n. 18); suicide of, 43–44; in children's euthanasia, 44, 48, 52; recruitment of physicians for killings, 48, 66, 193; responsibility for killing program, 64, 152, 157, 190, 200; as plenipotentiary for state hospitals and nursing homes, 64, 157; as expert for selection of patients to be killed, 79, 83, 165, 172, 182–83; at Brandenburg gassing demonstration, 87; establishment of Grafeneck killing center, 90, 201; medical research on victims, 130–31, 156; on problem of "Rhineland bastards," 247; and Gypsy research, 250; and murder of handicapped Jews, 272, 274, 282, 283; and murder of Jewish hybrid children, 295

Lippmann, Toni Louise, 279

Lodz (Litzmannstadt) ghetto, 288–89, 291, 353 (n. 64)

Lohse, Heinrich, 211

Lohse née Wächtler, Anna Frieda, 177

Lombroso, Cesare, 3

Lonauer, Rudolf: as physician-in- charge at Hartheim killing center, 91, 109, 165, 183, 203, 219, 225, 299; and cause-of-death assignments, 102; as director of Niedernhart state hospital, 109, 165; and Operation 14f13, 145, 148, 149, 222; background, 208, 220, 221; suicide of, 219, 220; relations with staff, 236, 237

Lorent, Friedrich Robert, 71, 72, 191, 192–93, 195, 244

Lorenz, Konrad, 126–27

Lowara. See Gypsies

Löwe, Alfred "Israel," 271

Madagascar, 260

Mader, Anna, 183

Mader, Maria, 183

Magnussen, Karin, 135

Majdanek concentration and extermination camp, 287

Mändle, Berta, 271

Mann, Thomas, 274

Marriage: race hygiene movement and, 11, 12; Nazi regulations on, 23, 24, 25, 31, 189, 266

Marriage Health Law. See Law for the Protection of the Hereditary Health of the German Nation

Martin, Otto, 164

Matthes, Heinrich Arthur, 242

Mauthausen concentration camp, 149–50

Mauthe, Otto, 52, 201, 268, 269

Mayer, Josef, 160

"Medical experts" (Gutachter), 77–79, 80, 81, 83

Medication, 54–56

Mein Kampf (Hitler), 13

Meissner, Otto, 40

Memmel, Karl, 166–67

Mendel, Gregor, 2

Mengele, Josef, 134–35, 216–17

Mennecke, Eva Wehlan, 146, 229

Mennecke, Friedrich: as director of Eichberg state hospital, 51, 168, 227, 228, 229, 230; background, 58, 228–29; as expert for selection of patients to be killed, 78, 79, 80, 168, 228, 229, 325 (n. 124); Nuremberg trial testimony, 78, 228, 325 (n. 124), 338 (n. 7); medical research on victims, 127–29, 130–31; and Operation 14f13, 145–46, 147–48, 149, 166, 229–30; letters to wife, 146, 147, 228, 230; Nazi party membership, 229; drafted and sent to the front, 230

Mentally disabled. See Handicapped, the

Mentz, Willi, 238

Merta, Hermann, 234–35, 236

Meseritz-Obrawalde state hospital, 152, 160–61, 166

Metzger, Erna, 185

Miete, August, 232, 242

Milgram, Stanley, 245

Minsk, 141, 235, 289, 297

Mirkolo, Boris, 165

Möckel (physician), 130

Mogilev, 141

Mollison, Theodor, 134, 251

Moses, Julius, 17

Muckermann, Hermann, 10, 13, 19

Müller, Robert, 145, 157

Müller-Hill, Benno, xii, 123–24, 217, 302

Münzberger, Gustav, 238–39

Murder: in German penal code, 66–67, 115, 116–17, 339 (n. 36)

Rothenburgsort children's hospital, 152
RSHA. *See* Central Office for Reich
  Security
Rüdin, Ernst, 10, 12, 13, 19, 155, 247, 250
Rueff, Karl, 174
Rum, Franz, 239–40

SA (Sturmabteilung), 245
Sachsenberg children's killing ward, 53
Sachsenhausen concentration camp, 146
Salzburg Gypsy camp, 255
San Sabba. *See* Risiera di San Sabba
Sauckel, Fritz, 194
Sauerbruch, Ferdinand, 114
Schachermeyer, Stefan, 233
Schallmayer, Wilhelm, 9, 10
Schemel (police officer), 206
Schirwing, Fritz, 214
Schizophrenia, 28
Schlegelberger, Franz, 120, 121–22, 123
Schmalenbach, Kurt, 145, 222, 224, 226,
  296, 366 (n. 41)
Schmidt, Franziska, 104
Schmidt, Hans, 141
Schmidt, Johanna Karoline, 183
Schmidt, Johannes, 33, 175
Schmidt, Margarethe, 170
Schmidt, Walter Eugen: supervision of
  Eichberg children's killing ward, 51, 57,
  176, 229, 295; medical background, 58;
  mistreatment and killings of patients,
  165, 168, 184–85; medical procedures
  performed on children, 169; disinforma-
  tion and threats to victims' relatives,
  179–81
Schmiedel, Ernst, 173
Schmiedel, Fritz, 71, 191, 192, 193, 244
Schmieder (physician), 130
Schmorl (physician), 130
Schneider, Carl, 155, 169, 225, 230; on T4
  physicians, 58; as Heidelberg University
  clinic director, 59, 127, 229; in planning
  of adult euthanasia, 66; medical research
  on victims, 129, 130, 131
Schneider, Willy, 71, 191, 192, 193
Schreck, Josef Artur, 52
Schueppe, Wilhelm Gustav, 142
Schulheimer, Charlotte, 269
Schumacher (physician), 130
Schumann, Horst: at Brandenburg gassing
  demonstration, 87; as physician-in-

charge of Grafeneck killing center, 90,
  213, 220, 221; as physician-in-charge of
  Sonnenstein killing center, 92, 172; mass
  sterilization experiments, 133, 134, 198,
  222, 292, 299; and Operation 14f13, 145,
  148, 222, 225; in Ghana after war, 213, 219;
  medical background, 220, 221
Schütt, Hans-Heinz, 208, 244
Schwede-Coburg, Franz, 136, 160
Scientists: human inequality theories, 1–2;
  eugenic research, 4–7, 9–12, 13; status of,
  9; synchronization of, 19–20; participa-
  tion in Nazi crimes, 123–26, 175, 216;
  medical research on victims, 127–35
SD (Sicherheitsdienst), 55, 141, 284
Seidler, Heinz, 177–78
Seidler, Hugo, 177–78
Sendung und Gewissen (Unger), 44
Senility, 81
Sereny, Gitta, 243–44
Sexual offenders, 24, 31
Shoah (film), 240
Siebert, Gerhard, 72, 191, 193
Simon, Gerhard, 281
Sinti. *See* Gypsies
Sipo (Sicherheitspolizei), 54–55, 139, 141,
  154, 258, 284
Sitter, Franz, 236
Slovakia, 158
Sobibor extermination camp, 190, 237,
  286–87, 298, 301. *See also* Operation
  Reinhard
Social Darwinism, 4, 9
Soldau camp, 139
Sonnenstein killing center, 93; establish-
  ment of, 88, 91, 214, 329 (n. 36); physical
  configuration, 91–92, 95; crematorium,
  98; numbers killed at, 109–10; and Oper-
  ation 14f13, 148–49
Sonntag (physician), 147
Soviet Union: German invasion of, 140,
  284; murder of prisoners of war from,
  141; murder of the handicapped in, 141–
  42, 151; liberation of Meseritz-Obrawalde
  state hospital, 160; murder of forced
  laborers from, 161; murder of Jews and
  Gypsies in, 284, 286, 287–88
Spearman, Charles, 4
Speer, Albert, 189
Sporrenberg, Jakob, 140
Sprauer, Ludwig, 52, 130, 201, 202

SS (Schutzstaffel): collaboration with
T4, 54–55, 108, 142–43, 295–96; concentration camp physicians, 81, 143–44,
145, 146, 225, 301–2, 347 (n. 39); killing
squads, 88, 136–37, 141, 151, 211, 284, 286,
290; chain of command, 138; and Operation 14f13, 142–44, 149–50; Berlin factory
roundups, 189; recruitment of T4 staff
from, 209, 233, 245; implementation of
final solution, 285, 286, 290, 294, 296,
299–302; Gypsy research, 293
Stadie, Otto, 242–43
Stähle, Eugen: and children's euthanasia,
52, 56; collaboration with adult euthanasia, 90, 201; and killing of handicapped
Jews, 268, 269, 270
Stahlecker, Franz, 289
Stangl, Franz, 243–44, 362 (n. 78); as
Hartheim killing center officer, 99–100,
204, 205; Nazi background, 204–5;
recruitment to T4, 205, 207–8; as commandant of Sobibor and Treblinka, 206,
244, 299
State hospitals and nursing homes (Heil-
und Pflegeanstalten), xxii–xxiii, 311
(n. 57), 354 (n. 73); compulsory sterilization of patients in, 33–34, 35, 36, 39; registration of patients in, 75–76; killing of
patients in, 137; exclusion of Jews from,
268–69, 273–74
States (Länder), 248, 312–13 (n. 13)
Steinmeyer, Theodor, 145, 146, 148, 176
Sterilization: eugenicists and, 7–8; U.S.
Supreme Court and, 8–9; and the handicapped, 8–9, 18, 23, 26–31, 32–36, 39, 62;
passage of compulsory law for, 18, 23,
25–27, 30, 310 (n. 31); and blacks, 18, 247;
as means of eliminating hereditary diseases, 26, 29, 142; hereditary health court
enforcement of, 26–27, 32–33, 34, 37;
methods of, 30–31; and institutionalized
patients, 33–36; medical establishment
and, 125; medical experimentation on
methods of, 132–33; and concentration
camp prisoners, 143; and Jews, 198–99,
270; and Gypsies, 253–54, 292. See also
Law for the Prevention of Offspring
with Hereditary Diseases
Stern, Heinz "Israel," 275
Stokers (Heizer, Brenner), 97, 98, 233, 234,
240–41

Streicher, Julius, 227
Strelow, Erich, 173
Stuckart, Wilhelm, 45
Stuttgart children's killing ward, 52
Stutthof concentration camp, 136–37, 345
(n. 2)
Suchomel, Franz, 233, 239, 240
Suckow (physician), 130
Suicide, xxii, 14–15
Survivors, 164, 168–69, 176–77, 182–83

Tauber, Alfred Israel, 280
Tauber, Flora, 280
Tauscher, Fritz, 99, 204, 206–7
Technical Institute for the Detection of
Crime (KTI), 55–56; procurement of
poisons for killing, 55, 56, 139, 159;
extraction of gold from victims' teeth,
209–10, 299
Terman, Lewis M., 4, 6, 7
Terminal illness, 14–15
T4, Operation, 68; as logical extension of
exclusionary policies, 1, 17, 21, 39, 62;
Hitler's authorization of, 17, 21, 39, 62,
67–68, 116, 121, 122, 189, 285, 321 (n. 39),
339 (n. 36), 380 (n. 9); ideological justifications for, 21–22, 64, 123, 196–98, 225;
final solution as logical extension of, 22,
39, 281–82; number of victims, 48, 61, 85,
110, 112, 151, 270–71; euphemisms used
in, 57, 231; Hitler's "stop" order, 61, 85,
110, 111, 136, 148, 151, 153–54, 177; assignment of administrative responsibility
for, 62–64; recruitment of physicians
for, 64–65, 77–78, 216, 221, 225–26; organization and staffing of, 64–66, 68–69;
physicians in planning of, 66, 124; illegality under German penal code, 66–67,
115, 116–17, 339 (n. 36); Hitler's refusal
to legalize euthanasia, 67, 112, 116, 120,
154, 188, 257; use of pseudonyms in, 69,
102–3; administrative structure, 69–72;
financing of, 71–72, 73, 106, 276, 277,
279–80; front organizations, 73–74,
112; registration of patients for, 74–77,
152; selection of victims by "medical
experts," 77–79, 80, 81, 82–83; psychiatrists in, 79, 155–57; criteria for selection
of victims, 80–81, 82–83, 172–73; exemptions for war veterans, 81–82, 174, 348
(n. 55); transfer of patients to killing

centers, 83–84, 85, 94, 108–9, 152–53, 272, 274, 277, 279; victims' awareness of their fate, 84, 93–94, 96, 170–71; deception of relatives of victims, 84–85, 103–4, 105–6, 166–67, 177–82; notification of relatives of victims' deaths, 85, 103–6, 177–78, 280–81; killing centers of, 86, 87, 88–93, 95, 148–49, 152, 214–15, 232; killing of handicapped patients by physicians, 86, 96, 97, 99, 186, 216, 218, 263; killing methods, 86–88, 96–97, 141–42, 158–59, 160; "processing" of victims in killing centers, 93–98; functions of physicians in killing centers, 94–95, 97, 98, 99, 101–3, 200, 202–3, 219; removal of valuables from victims, 95, 97–98, 209–10; propaganda efforts, 95, 112, 164, 171, 188; cremation and disposal of victims' remains, 98, 105; supervisors of killing operations, 99–100, 202–8, 218; record keeping, 100, 101, 110, 148, 195, 279; rank-and-file staff, 100–101, 109–10, 232–33, 236, 237–45; nurses, 100–101, 231–32, 234–35, 236, 242–43; cause-of-death assignments, 101–2; public awareness of, 106–8, 111, 112, 151, 188–89, 295; accounting of costs saved by, 110; objections by churches to, 111, 112, 113–16; judicial inquiries about, 117–21; judicial cooperation with, 122–23, 173; complicity of scientists in, 123–25, 175; medical research on victims of, 127, 129–31; killings in Poland, 136–37, 139, 140, 158; killings in the Soviet Union, 141–42, 151; concentration camp prisoners killed in, 142–50; Eastern workers (*Ostarbeiter*) killed in, 161–62; survivors of, 164, 168–69, 176–77, 182–83; dearth of surviving information on victims, 164–65; brutality of treatment of victims, 165–68, 169; used as model for final solution, 166, 284, 300–301; killing of Nazi party members, 174–76; perpetrators of, 187, 189–90; T4 personnel employed in final solution, 190, 237, 243–45, 296–300; bureaucratic managers of, 190–95, 196, 197, 359 (n. 14); recruitment of T4 personnel, 192, 193, 196, 205, 214, 232–33, 235–36; killers' denials of culpability, 198, 200, 211–14, 243, 263, 270; backgrounds and motivations of physicians, 200, 201–2, 216–18, 219–31;

procurement of poison supplies, 208–9; employees' oaths of silence, 236. *See also* Children's euthanasia; Jews, handicapped; "Wild" euthanasia

T4 Administrative Office, 71, 99, 104

T4 Central Finance Office, 71, 72

T4 Central Office, 70, 98, 153, 158, 159, 161, 279

T4 Inspector's Office, 72

T4 killing centers, 327 (n. 1); physicians as "medical experts" for selection of victims, 77–79, 80, 81, 82–83; establishment of, 86, 87, 88–93, 194; killing by physicians, 86, 96, 97, 99, 216, 218; gas chambers, 87, 88, 93, 95, 96–97; "processing" of patients in, 93–96, 300; transport of patients to, 94, 108–9, 170–71; functions of physicians in, 94–95, 97, 98, 99, 101–3, 203, 219; removal of valuables from victims, 95, 97–98; killing procedure in, 95–97; cremation of victims, 98, 105; as administrative units, 99; supervisors of killings, 99–100, 202–8; record keeping, 100, 101; rank-and-file staff, 100–101, 109–10, 232–33, 236, 237–45; employment in, 101; cause-of-death assignments, 101–2; notification of relatives of victims' deaths, 103–6, 177–78; public awareness of activities at, 106–8, 111, 112, 188; numbers killed at, 109–10; pause in operations after "stop" order, 111, 151; investigation by judiciary of, 117–20; medical research on victims in, 127, 129–31; and Operation 14f13, 142, 148–50, 152; extermination camps modeled on, 166, 298, 300; backgrounds and motivations of physicians in, 216–18, 219–31; construction work at, 214–15; murder of handicapped Jews in, 271, 272, 274–75. *See also* Children's killing wards

T4 Medical Office, 70–71, 73, 77, 83, 99, 101, 127

T4 Personnel Office, 72

T4 Transport Office, 72, 73, 83

Theresienstadt (Terezin) ghetto, 289–90, 292

Thierack, Georg, 123

Thurnwald, Richard, 251

Tiefland (film), 255

Tiegenhof (Dziekanka) state hospital, 137, 152, 153

Wiesloch children's killing ward, 52
"Wild" euthanasia, 152–54, 160–61, 188;
    attempts at centralization of, 154, 157–59;
    killing of Eastern forced laborers, 161–
    62; letters to relatives, 178; survivors of,
    182; nurses in, 231. *See also* Killing hospi-
    tals of "wild" euthanasia
Wirsting, Hermann, 173
Wirth, Christian, 297; at Brandenburg
    gassing demonstration, 87, 203; as
    supervisor of killing centers, 96, 99, 203,
    204, 206; killings of patients, 96, 203;
    brutality of, 109, 203–4, 207; back-
    ground, 203; treatment of subordinates,
    203, 235, 236, 237, 299; recruitment of
    killing personnel, 234; as inspector of
    camps of Operation Reinhard, 298
Wischer, Gerhard, 145, 148
Wlach, Marie, 296
Wödl, Anny, 182–83
Wöger, Jacob, 99, 204, 206, 208
Wolf, Franz, 233, 239, 240
Wolf, Josef, 240
Wolff, Karl, 140
Women, 10; intelligence studies on, 1–2, 6;
    forced sterilization of, 29, 30–31, 132–33;
    Gypsy, 248, 258
World War I: German veterans of, 81–82,
    174, 264, 348 (n. 55); psychiatric treat-
    ment during, 156; Allied occupation of
    Rhineland after, 246
World War II, 21, 39, 67, 259
Worthmann, Ewald, 222, 223, 224, 365
    (n. 32)
Wunstorf state hospital, 274, 275–76
Wurm, Theophil (bishop of Württem-
    berg), 113
Würth, Adolf, 134, 250, 251, 262
Württemberg: killing of children in, 52, 56,
    113; Ministry of Interior, 52, 56, 268–69;
    segregation of handicapped Jewish
    patients in, 268–70; killing handicapped
    Jewish patients in, 271; deportation of
    Gypsy children from, 294
WVHA. *See* Central Office for Economy
    and Administration

Yerkes, Robert M., 4, 5, 6

Zey, Karl-Heinz, 167–68
Zey, Maria, 168
Ziereis, Franz, 149
Zierke, Ernst, 242
Zindel (senior councillor), 256–57
Zucker, Konrad, 130
Zwickau welfare agency, 264–65
Zwiefalten state hospital, 269
Zyklon B gas, 287, 300–301